DATE DUE

11:51	

DEMCO, INC. 38-2971

General Viticulture

GENERAL VITICULTURE

by A. J. Winkler
J. A. Cook
W. M. Kliewer
L. A. Lider

UNIVERSITY OF CALIFORNIA PRESS
Berkeley · *Los Angeles* · *London*

University of California Press
Berkeley and Los Angeles, California

University of California Press, Ltd.
London, England

Revised and enlarged edition,
copyright © 1962, 1974 by
The Regents of the University of California
(Originally published 1962)

ISBN: 0-520-02591-1
Library of Congress Catalog Card Number: 73–87507
Printed in the United States of America

Contents

Contents

Contents

Contents

ix

Contents

Illustrations

The figures not acknowledged in the legends are from the files of the authors or from those of the Department of Viticulture and Enology, University of California, Davis.

Illustrations

Illustrations

Tables

Tables

Preface to the Second Edition

Research in many countries has added to our knowledge of viticulture since the first edition was published. This has been especially true of the composition of the fruit and the factors influencing the development of the various components of the mature grapes, improving and preserving the quality of table fruit; raisins, including on-the-vine-drying; production; propagation, training, supports; vineyard operations, including weed control; sprinkler irrigation and frost and heat control; and mechanical harvesting of raisin and wine grapes.

Many new references have been added and some that are no longer relevant have been deleted.

We have corrected errors and clarified the meaning in a number of instances.

To insure a more complete coverage of the various topics included, Professors J. A. Cook, W. M. Kliewer, and L. A. Lider, members of the Department of Viticulture and Enology, have been added as editors. Each of these men is a specialist in the phase of the discipline he covers, both in research and teaching.

We are indebted to a number of our colleagues of the University of California at Davis for the reading and criticizing various chapters; particular acknowledgment is due the following: Professors K. E. Nelson and Curtis J. Alley, of the Department of Viticulture and Enology; Martin W. Miller, of the Department of Food Science and Technology; W. B. Hewitt, of the Department of Plant Pathology; E. M. Stafford and H. Kido, of the Department of Entomology and Parasitology; and Messrs. Rene Guillow, Emeritus Specialist in Agricultural Engineering; and H. B. Richardson, Emeritus Extension Specialist in Viticulture, University of California.

1

History

The grape comes to us out of the abyss of antiquity. Its great age is attested by fossil leaves and seed discovered in North America and Europe in deposits of the Tertiary period of geologic time (Bassermann-Jordan, 1923, and Kirchheimer, 1938).* Seeds found in the refuse mounds of the pile dwellers of the lakes in south-central Europe reveal that man used the grape during the Bronze Age. It is evident that the grape has been a food of man from earliest times.

The tradition of the grape is as old as that of man and is intermingled with it. Details of grape growing figure in mosaics of the Fourth Dynasty of Egypt (2440 B.C.) and later. Noah, says the Bible, planted a vineyard. Early written accounts of grapes and wine production, by Vergil, Cato, the Plinys, and Columella, describe numerous varieties, listed many types of wine, and gave directions for training and pruning vines and making wine.

Grape culture began in Asia Minor, in the region between and to the south of the Black and Caspian seas. That region, most botanists agree, is the home of *Vitis vinifera*, the species from which all cultivated varieties of grapes were derived before the discovery of North America. From there, culture of the grape spread both west and east. Before 600 B.C. the Phoenicians probably carried wine varieties to Greece, thence to Rome, and on to southern France. No later than the second century A.D. the Romans took the vine to Germany. Probably at even an earlier date, raisin and table grapes were moving around the eastern end of the Mediterranean Sea to the countries of North Africa. The lines of spread of wine varieties

* References are listed at the end of the chapters.

differed from those of raisin and table varieties because of differences in custom and religion between the peoples on the northern and southern shores of the Mediterranean. Grapes spread to the Far East by way of Persia and India. Many years later, when Europeans colonized new lands, the grape was always among the plants taken along. At present, world plantings of grapes total about twenty-five million acres.

VITICULTURE IN CALIFORNIA

Viticulture was brought to the western shores of the Americas by the conquistadors. As the unexplored frontiers were pushed back, grape culture advanced. In fact, the industry so flourished that the court in Madrid feared the loss of its wine sales to the colonies. Only seventy years after Cortez, as governor of Mexico, had ordered the planting of grapes and other fruits, the King of Spain forbade, in 1595, new plantings or replacements of vineyards (Bancroft, 1833). During the next century and a half, the viceroys were repeatedly instructed to permit no new plantings. The Spanish rulers and their hirelings thus checked commercial plantings generally, and this action tended to discourage the making of records or reports on the industry, but it gave impetus to continued plantings within the missions, for the Church was strong enough to resist the civil decrees. Thus, in western North America during the seventeenth and eighteenth centuries the spread of grape and wine production was, as in Europe, largely associated with the Church.

The mission period.—Vines were first planted on California soil, now Baja California, by Father Juan Ugarte at Mission San Francisco Xavier about the year 1697. From there, vines were taken to the other missions. Even so, at the peak of development of the missions in that area only five or six possessed vineyards and made wine. The soil was too poor and thin to permit the development of vines at some missions, and to allow viticulture to attain the status of an industry at the others (Clavigero, 1937).

The expeditions that led to the establishment of Mission San Diego, the first in what is now the state of California, took place between 1769 and 1773 (Bancroft, 1883). These expeditions brought many fruits from Lower California, including the grape. According to the records of Vallejo (1874), Father Serra brought the vine to San Diego in 1769. As the mission chain was extended northward, vine cuttings were taken along. The vineyard at San Gabriel (established 1771), because of its large size, favorable soil and moisture conditions, and central location among the missions in the south, was recognized as the "viña madre"—the mother vineyard.

By the end of the century wine was made at five of the missions in the south—San Diego, San Juan Capistrano, San Buenaventura, San Gabriel, and Santa Barbara—and vineyards were established in the north at San Carlos, Soledad, San Antonio, San Luis Obispo, and Santa Clara. Although wine was a necessity of the Church, not much more than a beginning was made in its production for several years. The padres were beset with limitations and difficulties. Fermentation vats and containers for aging and storage were most difficult to procure or construct, although substitutes for winery machinery could be improvised. For the crushing, a shallow, open, boxlike structure was built and lined with clean hides. Grapes were dumped into this container, and "some well-washed Indians, having on only a zapeta, the hair carefully tied up and hands covered with cloth to wipe away perspiration, each having a stock to steady himself withal, were put to treading out the grape juice, which was caught in coras or leathern bags" (Bancroft, 1888). After the fermentation (or before, with white wines) the wine or juice that did not flow off was removed in wooden presses operated with long beams and weights.

Early in the nineteenth century the missions had more and more contact with the rest of the world, especially as ships began to stop frequently at California ports. The facilities for wine production were thereby augmented greatly. The second thirty-year period of the mission era showed tremendous progress in viticulture. By the end of that period Mission San Gabriel was producing annually up to six hundred barrels of wine and two hundred barrels of brandy, San Fernando was producing two thousand gallons each of wine and brandy, and, in the north, San Francisco Solano had extensive plantings of vines.

The Mexican revolt against Spain checked agricultural pursuits within the missions, and after independence, secularization marked the beginning of the end of those enterprises. The period from 1834 to 1846 witnessed a gradual abandonment of orchards, vineyards, and presses. Some of the padres were so angered by the secularization act that they destroyed mission property, sometimes to the extent of uprooting most of the vines (Ballard, 1880). In other instances the irrigation canals were neglected, so that the plantings deteriorated rapidly, and broken-down fences permitted cattle to forage in the fields. Other mission properties, however, passed into private hands while still in good condition.

Grapes of the mission period.—The first missionaries who arrived at San Diego found wild vines in the interior. According to Humboldt (1822), these vines produced large grapes that were very sour. Despite the large berries this must have been *Vitis girdiana*, the native species of the area. The wild vine was itself of no value, but it definitely indicated the possibilities for grapes in the new land. The padres brought cuttings of the variety they had been growing in Lower California. This variety is still grown, under the name of Mission, and is very vigorous, productive, and hardy. It is of the species *vinifera*, which indicates that it came originally from Europe, although to date no identical Old World representative of this variety has been found. F. T. Bioletti, the second professor of viticulture at the University of California, thought it to be a seedling of Monica, a variety common in Spain. Perhaps at some future date its direct ties will be traced to a source in Europe, but it will still be the Mission grape. This variety or a very similar one is common in the vine-growing countries of South America, where it is called Criolla de vino. It was carried there by mission fathers belonging to the same order as those who brought it to California.

The fruit of the Mission attains a high sugar content, but is deficient in acid and color. This condition, together with the warm climate of southern California, accounts for some of the difficulty that the padres, as well as settlers after them, had in producing acceptable dry wines. The Mission was adapted for, and still ranks among, our good sweet, or dessert, wine varieties. Its vigor and hardiness have been displayed in many specimens of enormous size. The vine at San Gabriel Mission was the best known and the last to give way to urban expansion. One vine in Santa Barbara County covered twelve thousand square feet when sixty-five years old and produced crops of more than ten thousand pounds. Another, at Carpinteria, planted in 1842, bore eight tons in 1893, U.S. Dept. Agric. (1904); its trunk circumference was reported to be nine feet (fig. 1).

Beginnings of the industry.—The earliest commercial or private plant-

FIGURE 1: The Carpinteria vine in its prime. It produced eight tons of fruit in 1893, when it was 51 years old. (*From U.S.D.A. Yearbook, 1904*)

ings of vines in California were on the Los Angeles pueblo lands. In 1824 Joseph Chapman, an easterner who had worked for several years at the Santa Ynez and San Gabriel missions, bought a house in Los Angeles and planted several acres of vines. During the 1830's a number of men arrived in Los Angeles who gave impetus to vine and wine production. Newmark (1926) reported that Louis Vignes, from the Bordeaux region of France, planted a vineyard of about one hundred acres. He was joined a few years later by a nephew, Pierre Sansevaine, and in 1855 Pierre's brother, Jean Louis Sansevaine, bought the uncle's holding. Davis (1929) states that Vignes imported cuttings of different varieties of grapes in small lots from France, yet no record has been preserved of either the success of this venture or the names of the varieties. In 1857 the Sansvaine brothers produced the first champagne for California (Newmark, 1926). Their product was not very good.

William Wolfskill, a Kentucky trapper, planted a forty-acre vineyard at Los Angeles in 1838. He was the first to ship fresh grapes to the northern towns. In 1849 grapes were selling at 12.5 cents a pound on the vine, and thousands of boxes were shipped to San Francisco. During most of the 1850's, the Los Angeles producers received good returns for the grapes they shipped north. Warner *et al.* (1876) stated that 21,000 boxes of grapes were sent to San Francisco in 1857.

Viticulture in private hands developed more rapidly in the south than the north, but the discovery of gold led to a marked increase in the consumption of both grapes and wines in the north and an unprecedented expansion of viticulture in that area. Strong competitors for the high prices obtained in San Francisco were M. G. Vallejo, G. C. Yount, and A. Haraszthy, of the central coast area, and John Wolfskill and John Sutter, of the Sacramento area. Expansion of the industry was further augmented by the coming to California of many experienced European producers, fleeing the political upheavals and oppressions of the time. Then, too, the great distances between the marketing areas fostered planting in the different regions, so that, in addition to the Los Angeles and the central coastal regions, many new plantings were made adjacent to the gold diggings in the central Sierra foothills. Expansion was great in all these regions, but greatest around Los Angeles. Nearly everyone who could acquire land and vines did so, and when this was impossible many persons combined small holdings to form cooperatives, such as the Los Angeles Vineyard Society, which established large plantings at Anaheim, or the Buena Vista Vinicultural Society, which took over a part of the Vallejo ranch at Sonoma. Not only were individual producers stampeding to grape and wine production—but the State Agricultural Society reported that "Capital put into vineyards would bring greater returns than when outlayed in fluming rivers for golden treasures" (Bancroft, 1890).

History

From the earliest plantings until near the middle of the nineteenth century, the basis of grape production both at the missions and in commerce was a single variety, the Mission. With the development of the industry, especially the production of grapes for fresh consumption and for raisins, the need for different and better varieties became apparent. About 1850, action was taken. Nurserymen imported many varieties: for instance, Warren and Son, of Sacramento, listed 4 varieties in their 1853 catalogue; A. P. Smith, of Sacramento, listed 19 varieties in 1856, including Black Hamburg, Black Morocco, Black Prince, Chasselas doré, and Muscat of Alexandria; A. Delmas, of San Jose, listed 108 varieties in 1858; B. S. Fox, of San Jose, listed 86 varieties in 1858 and 122 in 1860; and S. Thompson, of Suscol Ferry, listed 35 varieties in 1861, including Tokay, Palomino, Blue Portugal, Traminer, and White Riesling. Growers were also importing varieties. Butterfield (1938) reported that L. Mel, of Livermore, introduced the Semillon and Sauvignon blanc; H. M. Naglee, of San Jose, introduced the Trousseau and Charbono; and G. West, of Stockton, introduced French Colombard (West's White Prolific), Malaga, and Feher Szagos. Colonel Agoston Haraszthy (1862) was commissioned by Governor Downey in 1861 to go abroad to select and bring back to California the best varieties of Europe. He introduced about three hundred varieties, but, owing to difficulties in handling the cuttings, some varieties were lost before they could be tested.

Haraszthy and Wetmore did more than introduce better varieties and European knowledge of grape and wine production. Not only did Haraszthy's enormous and contagious optimism stimulate planting and increase production per unit of area—he was determined from the beginning that the new industry should be built on a sound foundation. In talks before growers and in extensive writings he advocated planting only the best varieties, concentrating vineyards in areas of the most favorable environment, and using the latest procedures of vinification and aging. During his time in California (1849–1868), the first real advance toward a commercial industry was made. Wetmore also went to Europe. He collected the best varieties and information, and returned no less an optimist than Haraszthy. He lacked the fire of Haraszthy, but his enthusiasm was so infectious that another boom in planting resulted (1880–1886). His profound interest in and production of good grapes and fine wines aided greatly in setting new standards. His example and his many articles in the press led other persons of means to produce fine wines, thereby initiating another advance in the industry—a trend toward stability, to offset the highly speculative interest then generally prevalent.

Table and raisin grapes.—Although grapes were eaten fresh from the time they first came into fruiting in California, there was no table grape industry, as we consider it today, until the necessary varieties were introduced in the 1850's. R. B. Blowers, of Woodland, and G. G. Briggs, of Davisville (now Davis), were among the first to plant table varieties. This phase of viticulture continued to expand with the demand, but its outlet was confined largely to California until the turn of the century.

Blowers, besides introducing a number of varieties, including the Emperor, pioneered the movement of table grapes to the eastern markets. His first car, according to Chopin (1896), was shipped to Chicago in 1869. The separate clusters were placed in paper bags, and these were packed in 22-lb. boxes. A number of varieties were included in the shipment, which was sent by ordinary freight. The venture produced no profit, but it stimulated an interest that led to development of the refrigerator car. The Hutchins car, in 1879, was the first with sufficient ice capacity and insulation to carry fruit successfully on transcontinental hauls. It made possible the real beginning of the shipment of California table grapes to eastern markets. At about this time 200 tons were moved to Philadelphia in one season. The trend was gradually upward until 1907, when the 50,000-ton market was reached. Thereafter the increase was more rapid, so that by 1916 more than 150,000 tons was sold beyond the borders of California, mainly in the eastern states. According to Henderson and Kitterman (1971), sales outside of California during 1969–1971 averaged 346,000 tons.

The earliest settlers dried grapes to preserve them for out-of-season use, but true raisins were produced only after suitable varieties were available. The Muscat of Alexandria was introduced by Smith in 1856 and the Muscat Gordo Blanco, a strain of Muscat of Alexandria, by Haraszthy in 1861. Blowers obtained cuttings of the latter variety in 1863, and in 1867 produced one of the first crops of commercial raisins. Briggs grafted over an

FIGURE 2: A very productive seventy-seven-year-old Tokay vineyard.

old Mission vineyard near Davis to Muscat of Alexandria in 1869 and produced about one thousand boxes of raisins in 1873. He and Blowers were operating dehydrators earlier than 1880. The Thompson Seedless did not appear until 1878, when it was planted by W. Thompson in Sutter County.

The Muscat of Alexandria was not planted in the Fresno area until 1873, when G. Eisen (1890) planted twenty-five acres. In the period from 1876 to 1878 the Raisina vineyard, the Hedgerow vineyard, and other plantings of this variety were made. About this time a large acreage of raisin varieties was also planted in southern California. The first planting of Thompson Seedless in the San Joaquin Valley came later. The production of raisins in California rose as follows: 110 tons in 1875; 750 tons in 1880; 4,700 tons in 1885; and 10,000 tons in 1890. According to Henderson and Kitterman (1971), the production in 1970 was near 200,000 tons.

Ups and downs of the industry.—Carosso (1951) states that the state legislature encouraged grape growing because it attracted industrious immigrants, and the press advocated more vineyards because grapes and grape products commanded higher prices than other agricultural produce, required less labor, and yielded greater profits. In other words, by 1870 there was a general belief that the future of the wine industry was assured. Grape growing was a new industry, and probably no one considered what the production would be when all the vines then being planted were in full bearing. Planting did not cease until the depression of the middle seventies.

The increase in acreage, however, was but one of the factors that caused the crash. Equally to blame were inferior quality, resulting from ignorance and inexperience, and the desire of growers and dealers to get rich quick. Because interest rates were high, wine was frequently placed on the market too soon after the fermentation, and it suffered from competition with properly matured European products.

Eastern dealers, too, were open to severe criticism. Many complaints were heard regarding "unscrupulous traders who sell strange compounds labeled in imitation of the best brands of California wines" (Carmany, 1867). By 1876 adulteration had spread to include European wines, and the profits of this nefarious business were so great that the practice was taken up in the California markets (Leggett 1940).

Compounding the difficulties of the viticulturist was the general business depression of 1875, which had its beginning in the panic in the East in 1873. In 1876 grape prices ranged from $2 to $10 per ton. Only the premium-quality varieties brought the higher figure, and wines were moving at 10 cents or less per gallon. Large stocks for which there was little or no demand brought fear to many growers, and, as recorded by Haraszthy (1879), for the first time, some privately owned commercial vineyards were uprooted.

The older, well-financed vintners with experienced personnel emerged from the depression with only little damage, whereas the inexperienced and poorly financed producers went out of business. The depression emphasized the great need for more skill in harvesting the crop, in vinification, and in aging the wines. It served also as an incentive for the establishments of larger wineries.

Hilgard (1879), the first Professor of Viticulture and Enology at the University of California, later wrote:

As the depression was, beyond doubt, attributable chiefly to the hasty putting upon the market of immature and indifferently made wines, so the return of prosperity has been, in a great measure, the result of steady improvement in the quality of the wines marketed—such improvement being partly due to the introduction of grape varieties better adapted than the Mission grape to the production of wines suited to the taste of wine-drinking nations; partly to a real improvement in methods of treatment, and their better adaptation to the peculiarities of California-grown grapes.

Recovery was further aided when the plant louse, Phylloxera, removed a considerable acreage of vines from production. This insect was introduced into California on planting material brought in the late 1850's from either the eastern United States or Europe. At first it went unnoticed, and even after it had destroyed sizable areas in some vineyards its presence was still disrgarded because the growers did not want to admit that they were in trouble. As a result, nothing was done to check the spread until large areas were infested and the insects were advancing into adjacent clean vineyards. By 1878 the original plantings in Sonoma were wiped out and other sections were infested.

However, by 1879 the youth industry was rebounding from the disasters with new ambitions and reckless abandon. According to Bundschu (1937), the desire to get rich quick ran rampant again from 1880 to 1886. In that period, plantings increased by more than 100,000 acres. Overproduction resulted again. This period was long remembered by growers, not merely for the recurrence of economic difficulties, but also because thousands of acres of vines in southern California, especially around Anaheim, were destroyed by the "California vine disease"—a malady mysterious at that time, but now known to be Pierce's disease, caused by a rickettsia-like pathogen.

The industry survived again, and another period of prosperity began in the early 1890's. Progress toward high-quality wines by numerous producers was fortunately continued.

The 1890's found the California grape industry—still predominantly wine—well on its way to becoming business-like in organization and attaining greater stability. Yet, with fluctuations in economic conditions, with the growers at liberty to plant as they saw fit, and with, in general, only individual effort to control the quality of the products, prosperous periods were again bound to be followed by recessions. The period from 1904 to 1909 was quite difficult. This time the raisin industry suffered too, although shipments of table grapes continued to increase. With only slight recessions in 1912 and 1921, prices remained high until well into the 1920's.

From 1912 to 1919 wine production dropped almost one half in anticipation of Prohibition, which to most wine producers presaged disaster. Instead, it only shifted wine production to the basements and bathrooms of private houses and the suppliers of bootleggers. According to Carosso (1951), fresh grape shipments expanded phenomenally because of the return of prosperity, confusion over interpretation of various legal requirements relating to home production of nonalcoholic fruit juices, and the increased production of wine. Throughout the country, prices of all grapes rose to unheard-of levels—and an unprecedented planting spree followed. As in earlier periods, great expansion attracted the unscrupulous and the inexperienced. The exclusively profit-minded growers planted without considering the suitability of the variety; or to mature vines of good varieties they grafted varieties that shipped well, but made only mediocre wine. The largest acreage in the history of the state (648,000 acres) was reached in 1927. This overexpansion, largely by inexperienced growers, brought confusion, disorganization, and demoralization that kept the entire industry unstable throughout the Prohibition era. The latter years of this era were, without doubt, the most trying that the industry has experienced.

At the repeal of National Prohibition in 1933 the industry faced such difficulties as dilapidated wineries, unsound cooperage, lack of capital, lack of experienced personnel, and, possibly worst of all, thousands of acres of

TABLE 1

CALIFORNIA'S LEADING FRUIT CROPS FOR THE YEARS 1969–1971
(Averages of annual figures)

Crop	Bearing acreage	Production (tons)	Farm value (in dollars)
Apples	21,763	240,000	16,774,000
Apricots	32,600	206,000	21,010,000
Grapes	449,682	3,300,665	259,508,000
Citrus fruits	218,500	2,189,090	159,044,333
Peaches	80,773	967,330	82,239,000
Pears	38,193	315,666	34,021,000
Prunes	94,000	162,266	38,408,000
Plums	21,330	97,000	19,562,600

SOURCE OF DATA: Henderson and Kitterman, 1969–1971.

unsuited varieties. For years the industry was burdened with an oversupply of table and raisin variety grapes and an undersupply of wine grape varieties. There also was a lack of appreciation of the value of wine varieties for wine production. Even at present, with relatively stable outlets for table fruit and raisins, the continued planting, especially of Thompson Seedless, is out of proportion to foreseeable demands. The table grape acreage has been reduced by 16 percent since 1962. Then, too, some table grape varieties have found a favorable place in the wine industry. For example, the Tokay for brandy production.

The Thompson Seedless is utilized in the industry for sherry, wine, and spirits, yet there is no question but what better sherries and wines can be made of recognized wine varieties. Nevertheless, the acreage of this raisin and table variety constitutes 47 percent of the total acreage of the state. It is a heavy producer, easy to grow, and until recently many wineries made no meaningful differential in the price they paid for its fruit as compared to that of real wine grapes. At best, its wines, even when harvested early, possess very little character.

In the 1950's proportionately more wine grapes, particularly of the premium quality varieties, were planted. The better products of these varieties along with education on the value of wine in the diet lead to a renewed interest in wines. Rapid expansion of the market for table wine in the late 1960's and early 1970's has created a pressing need for the planting of more wine grapes. In fact, the industry is in the midst of another planting boom. Capital for new vineyards of wine grapes is easy to obtain. Individuals from outside the industry, who know little or nothing of grape production, are planting vineyards. Unless caution with restraint is exercised, the industry may again, in the not too distant future, find itself with an oversupply of grapes, even wine grapes.

It is of vital interest to the entire industry that only desirable varieties be planted, and these only in the climatic region or regions to which they are adapted. Virus-free varieties with the potential of producing superior wines in regions I, II, and III are available. However, varieties for the production of above average quality table wines in the warm to hot interior valleys are limited. Only those that are best adapted to interior valley regions should be planted. Better varieties for these areas are now in the final stage of testing at Davis. With the rapid methods of propagation (see p. 202) now in use, they should constitute a sizeable portion of the new plantings. To wait for these varieties with high potential for better table wines in the interior valleys will place the grower in an advantageous position in years to come.

The grape industry ranks first among the fruit crops of California. The position of this crop is shown in table 1. The divisions of the industry by principal types in table 2.

TABLE 2

CALIFORNIA'S TABLE, RAISIN, AND WINE GRAPES FOR THE PERIOD 1969–1971
(Averages of annual figures)

Class	Bearing acreage	Non-bearing acreage	Production (tons)	Farm value (in dollars)
Table Grapes	71,396	1,920	486,333	38,978,000
Raisin Grapes	246,063	5,245	2,120,666	142,982,000
Wine Grapes	132,223	47,448	693,666	77,548,000
Average 1969–1971	449,682	54,613	3,300,665	259,508,000

SOURCE OF DATA: Henderson *et al.*, 1971.

VITICULTURE IN THE EASTERN UNITED STATES

Colonists landed on the eastern shore of North America a hundred and fifty years before Mission San Diego was established. The profusion of wild grapes roused enthusiasm, although the settlers found displeasing the unaccustomed odor and flavors of the most readily available of these native species. The abundance of vines, however, encouraged them to introduce varieties of V*itis vinifera*, the grape of their former homelands. From the beginning these led a precarious existence in the new environment.

The history of the trials with *vinifera* varieties in the eastern part of the United States is summarized by Bailey (1912) and Hedrick (1907). An early introduction of these grapes, with French growers to tend them, was instigated by Lord Delaware in 1619. Some historians attribute their failure principally to the Indian massacre of 1622. In 1623 the assembly of Virginia passed a law enforcing the planting of grapes, and in 1693 it tried to encourage grape growing by offering a premium to successful growers. Even so, the ventures did not succeed. Again, in 1769, an attempt was made to establish wine making in Virginia. In 1793 P. Legaux imported grapes from France and planted them at Spring Mill, near Philadelphia. This planting was abandoned after several years. Seven years later, J. J. Dufour, an experienced Swiss grower who had visited most vineyards in the states, made an extensive planting of *vinifera* varieties in Kentucky. Help was skilled and financial backing was ample, but the vines became sick in three years, and the project was a failure. In 1821 thousands of vines were planted on the Tombigbee River in Alabama by former Napoleonic officers—again, costs were not a limiting factor, yet the history of the vineyard is a record of misfortune; probably owing to Pierce's disease which, as reported by Hewitt (1958), is indigenous there.

Attempts to grow *vinifera* grapes continue in the eastern part of the United States. There are a few small collections of *vinifera* varieties, such as that at the New York Agricultural Experiment Station, at Geneva, and a few small private plantings. The limitation in plantings there is largely attributed to occasional very low winter temperatures in the north; and to the ravages of Pierce's disease in the Gulf States and north in the Mississippi Valley.

The grapes now grown successfully in the eastern United States are (a) varieties selected from the native species, (b) hybrids of native species, and (c) hybrids of native species with varieties of vinifera. Representative varieties of these groups, according to Hedrick (1907), are respectively, (a) Concord, Moore Early, Scuppernong, and Worden, (b) Beacon, Clinton, and Elvira, and (c) Catawba, Delaware, Dutchess, and Niagara.

These hybrids developed in the United States with or without the aid of man. They have been standard varieties for many years. More recently other hybrids are finding a place in the viticulture of the eastern and midwestern United States and Canada. These, too, are *vinifera* x Native American species hybrids which were produced by directed breeding programs in France, hence the name "French hybrids." Until recently most of these were identified by the name of the hybridizer and a number. However, now that they are finding a definite place in industry names are being adopted (Anon, 1972). Some of these, according to Wagner (1917) Kimball *et al.* (1970) and Einset and Robinson (1972), with the original number (in parentheses) followed by adopted name are: (Baco No. 1) Baco noir, (Seyve Villard 5276) Seyval, (Seyve Villard 12375) Villard blanc, (Seibel 5279) Aurora, (Seibel 7053) Chancellor, (Seibel 9549) De Chaunac, (Seibel 13053) Cascade, Foch (Kuhlmann 1882) and two Geneva N.Y. hybrids GR3 and (GW3) Cayuga white. Because of their resistance to fungus diseases, some of these and other hybrids are grown extensively in many parts of Europe.

BIBLIOGRAPHY

Anon. 1972. Seibel 9549 becomes De Chaunac. Wines & Vines, 53(10):6.

Bailey, L. H. 1912. Sketches of the evolution of our native fruits. New York, Macmillan.

Ballard, Helen M. 1880. San Luis Obispo County in Spanish and Mexican times. California Historical Society Quarterly. I(2):152–172.

Bancroft, H. H. 1883. History of Mexico. San Francisco, The History Company, Vol. III. (*See* p. 613.)

———. 1888. California Pastoral. San Francisco, The History Company, Vol. 34. (*See* p. 371–372.)

———. 1890. History of California. San Francisco, The History Company, Vol. 7. (*See* p. 46.)

Bassermann-Jordan, F. 1923. Geschichte des Weinbaus. Frankfurt am Main, Frankfurter Verlags-Anstalt A. G. Vol. I. (*See* p. 1.)

Bundschu, C. 1937. California Weinbau. California Staats-Zeitung (Los Angeles), Albert Ebert.

Butterfield, H. M. 1938. The builders of California's grape and raisin industry. Blue Anchor, 15:2–4, 23–25.

Carmany, J. H. 1867. A review of the year 1866. Mercantile Gazette, San Francisco, H. H. Bancroft. (*See* p. 64.)

Carosso, V. P. 1951. The California wine industry, 1830–1895. Berkeley and Los Angeles, University of California Press.

Chopin, F. S. 1896. The pioneer in the raisin industry—lessons from the life of a California fruit grower. Irrigation Age, 9:234–239.

Clavigero, F. X. 1937. The history of (Lower) California. Trans. and ed. by Sarah E. Lake and A. A. Gray. Stanford, Calif., Stanford University Press.

Davis, W. H. 1929. Seventy-five years in California. San Francisco, J. Howell. (*See* p. 120.)

Einset, J., and W. B. Robinson. 1972. Cayuga white, the first of a Finger Lakes series of wine grapes for New York. New York's food and life sciences bulletin. No. 22.

Eisen, G. 1890. The raisin industry. San Francisco, H. S. Crocker (*See* pp. 38–40.)

Haraszthy, A. 1862. Grape culture, wines and wine-making. New York, Harper and Brothers.

———. 1879. Report of the annual meeting of the California State Viticultural Society. San Francisco Merchant. Sept. 12, p. 5.

Hedrick, U. P. 1907. The grapes of New York. (Fifteenth annual report. Dept. of Agriculture, State of New York.) Albany, J. B. Lyon, State Printer. Part II:1–564.

Henderson, W. W., and J. M. Kitterman, 1969 and 1971. California fruit and nut statistics. Sacramento, California State Department of Agriculture.

Henderson, W. W., J. Kitterman, J. Swedberg, G. Boeger, G. Nelson, D. Johnson, and C. Weems. 1971. California fruit and nut statistics. Sacramento, California State Department of Agriculture.

Hewitt, W. B. 1958. The probable home of Pierce's disease virus. Amer. Jour. Enol., 9:94–98.

Hilgard, E. W. 1879. Supplement to biennial report of the College of Agriculture, University of California. Sacramento, State Printing Office, p. 61.

Humboldt, von, A. 1822. Political essay on the kingdom of New Spain. Vol. II. London, Longman, Hurst, Rees, Orme, and Brown. (*See* p. 294.)

Kimball, K., N. J. Shaulis, and J. Einset. 1970. Wine grape variety trials in New York. Proc. N. Y. Hort. Soc., 115:280–282.

Kirchheimer, F. 1938. Aus der Geschichte der Rebengewächse. Wein u. Rebe., 20:188–192.

Leggett, H. B. 1940. Early history of wine production in California. Unpublished Master's thesis. University of California, Berkeley.

Newmark, W. H. 1926. Sixty years in southern California. New York, The Knickerbocker Press. (*See* p. 199.)

United States Department of Agriculture. 1904. Yearbook. Washington, Government printing office (*See* p. 366.)

Vallejo, M. G. 1874. Documentos para la historia de California. Bancroft Library Photostat Vol. XXXVI, *Document* 288:606–610.

Wagner, J., and P. 1971. Boody Vineyard grape book. Riderwood, Maryland.

Warner, J. J., B. Hayes, and J. P. Widney. 1876. Historical sketches of Los Angeles County. Los Angeles, Louis Lewin & Co. (*See* p. 8.)

2

Classification of Grapes

The botanical genus *Vitis* includes two sub-genera: *Euvitis*—true grapes—and *Muscadinia*.

The shoots of the species of *Euvitis*—true grapes—have bark that is longitudinally striate-fibrose, shedding at maturity; pith interrupted in the nodes by a diaphragm; forked tendrils, with mostly elongated flower clusters; berries adhering to the stems at maturity; and seeds pyriform, with long or short beak. In contrast, the shoots of the species of *Muscadinia* have tight, non-shedding bark with prominent lenticels; nodes without diaphragm; simple tendrils; short, small clusters; berries that detach one by one as they mature; and seeds oblong, without beak.

SPECIES

There are fewer than 60 known *Vitis* species, many of them indistinctly separated from others. Their origin is chiefly, if not entirely, limited to the Northern Hemisphere, and they are particularly abundant in North America.

The following list, after Bailey (1934), gives the names of the species used for fruit or as rootstocks in pure or hybrid form, the names of the authors who first described them, and their native habitats. Descriptions and further information on these and other species may be found in Bailey (1917), Galet (1921), Levadoux *et al.* (1962), Manaresi (1947), and Munson (1909).

The principal Old World species of *Euvitis* is:

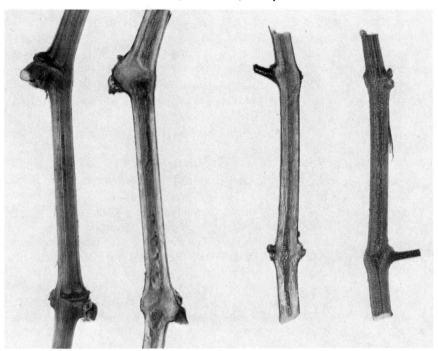

FIGURE 3: Single cane segments with two nodes. Segment at left Euvitis showing diaphragms across the pith at the node and striated bark which is shed in long strips. Segment at right Muscadinia showing continuous pith (no diaphragms at nodes) and bark with lenticels which is not shed.

Vitis vinifera, Linnaeus. It is native south of the Caucasus Mountains and Caspian Sea and into Asia Minor.

The American species of *Euvitis* which have contributed to viticulture, with their habitats are as follows:

Vitis aestivalis, Michaux. Massachusetts and southern New Hampshire to Michigan, southward to central Missouri and Georgia.

Vitis berlandieri, Planchon. Limestone soils of southwestern Arkansas and through Texas into northeastern Mexico.

Vitis california, Bentham. Along streams in central and northern California and southern Oregon (only of local interest).

Vitis candicans, Englemann. Western Arkansas and Louisiana, Oklahoma, central and eastern Texas, and northern Mexico, mostly on limestone soils.

Vitis champini, Planchon. Central and southern Texas, in limy soils.

Vitis cinerea, Engelmann. Central states, Louisiana to Wisconsin, on river banks, bottom land, and pond margins.

Vitis cordifolia, Michaux. In thickets and along streams in the area from Pennsylvania to eastern Kansas and south to Texas and Florida.

Vitis doaniana, Munson. Chiefly northwestern Texas, Oklahoma and New Mexico. (Native habitat about the same as that of *V. solonis*.)

Vitis girdiana, Munson. Along streams in southern California (only of local interest).

Vitis labrusca, Linnaeus. Central New England to Georgia, chiefly east of the Appalachian Mountains.

Vitis lincecumii (Linsecomii), Buckley. High post-oak lands of southwestern Missouri, northern and eastern Texas, and western Louisiana.

Vitis Longii, Prince (*V. solonis*, Hort. Berol). Western Oklahoma, northern Texas, eastern New Mexico, and southeastern Colorado.

Vitis monticola, Buckley. Limestone hills of southwestern Texas.

Vitis riparia, Michaux (*V. vulpina*, Linnaeus). Nova Scotia and New Brunswick to Manitoba, west to the Rocky Mountains, south into Texas, and east to Arkansas, Tennessee, and Virginia.

Vitis rufotomentosa, Small. Sandy soils, Florida to Louisiana.

Vitis rupestris, Scheele. Sandy stream banks, low hills, and mountains, southern Missouri, Illinois, Kentucky, and western Tennessee to southwest Texas.

There are a number of species of *Vitis* native to Asia. These are omitted since they have contributed little to grape growing. Varieties of *Vitas cognetiae* and *Vitis thumbergi* are grown on a very limited scale in Japan.

There are two American species of *Muscadinia*:

Vitis rotundifolia, Michaux. Southern United States.
Vitis Munsoniana, Simpson. Central and southern Florida.

The distribution of the important native species of *Vitis* in the United States is shown in figure 4.

Species Used for Fruiting

Many species, especially of the American vines, produce fruit that may be regarded as palatable. Yet, varieties belonging to a single species produce more than 90 per cent of the world's grapes. This species, *Vitis vinifera*, is commonly referred to as the Old World grape, the European grape, and, more recently, in the United States, the California grape. The grapes grown extensively in Europe and other important grape-growing regions outside the United States are either pure *vinifera* or *vinifera* hybridized with one or more American species. Even in the United States about 90

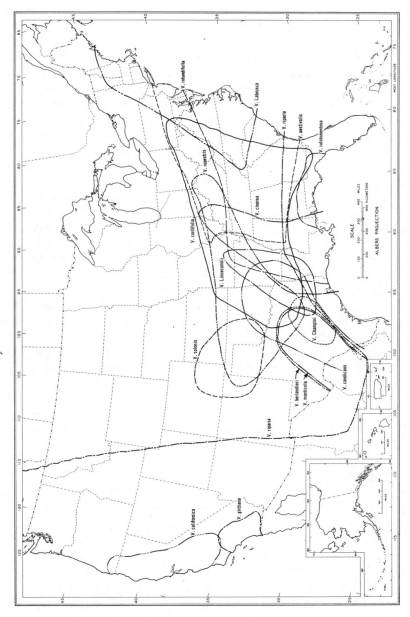

FIGURE 4: The distribution of the important and interesting native species of *Vitis* in the United States.

per cent of total production is of pure *vinifera* varieties. These are grown mostly in California, with a limited acreage in Arizona, Oregon and Washington.

The *vinifera* varieties are difficult to grow east of the Rocky Mountains because they are susceptible to freezing in the north and to Pierce's disease in the south. In that region the successful varieties are derived from native species, with *Vitis labrusca* predominating. About 80 per cent of total production is of a single variety, Concord, which is generally considered to be a pure *labrusca*. Hedrick (1907) lists some 1,400 varieties of American grapes. Analysis of the parentage of these varieties shows that 27 per cent are pure species, 53 per cent are hybrids of known parentage, and the remaining 20 per cent are of unknown origin.

Pure species.—The varieties representing *pure species* have been derived from 13 species as follows in the order of their contribution: *labrusca, aestivalis, riparia, rotundifolia, lincecumii, champini, longii* (Solonis), *doaniana, rupestris, candicans monticola,* and *berlandieri.* Of these 68 per cent are of *labrusca,* 10 per cent *aestivalis* and so on until only 0.3 per cent are of *candicans, monticola,* or *berlandieri.*

Hybrids.—The hybrid varieties have been obtained by crossing a variety of one species with a variety of another species or with a hybrid previously produced. In some instances two hybrid varieties have been crossed with each other. Of the many hybrids, 42 per cent are crosses involving only *labrusca* and *vinifera.* Only 8 per cent do not contain *labrusca* in their ancestry, and only 6 per cent contain neither *labrusca* nor *vinifera.*

SPECIES USED FOR ROOTSTOCKS

Two soil pests of the grape—phylloxera and nematodes—are largely controlled by the use of species or hybrids that are resistant.

Rootstocks resistant to phylloxera.—So far, the only practical means of controlling phylloxera, the grape root louse (*Daclylosphaera vitifoliae,* Shimer), is to use rootstocks that resist its attack. The phylloxera is native to the Mississippi Valley, and all grape species native to that region of the United States resist its attacks to some degree. The first varieties used for rootstocks were selections from the wild vines. These were mostly pure species or natural hybrids. All have since been discarded except a few *riparia* and *rupestris* varieties, such as Riparia Gloire and Rupestris St. George (du Lot). Most rootstock varieties used today are hybrids of two or more species. The principal American species used in producing the hybrid rootstocks resistant to phylloxera are: *aestivalis, berlandieri, cordifolia, monticola, riparia* and *rupestris.* Of much the greatest importance are *riparia, rupestris,* and *berlandieri.*

The species V. *rotundifolia* and V. *munsoniana* are immune, or nearly so (but are useless as rootstocks because they have insufficient affinity with fruiting varieties and are difficult to propagate. Progress in the hybridization of V. *vinifera* and V. *rotundifolia* reported by Patel and Olmo (1955) supports the hope that the immunity of these muscadines may someday become available in hybrid rootstocks resistent to both phylloxera and nematodes. V. *labrusca*, V. *californica*, and V. *girdiana* are not sufficiently resistant. V. *berlandieri*, besides being very resistant to the attacks of phylloxera, is also resistant to lime-induced chlorosis. In pure form its cuttings root very poorly, but when hybridized with *ripara, rupestris,* or *vinifera* this difficulty is partially overcome. Certain of its hybrids are of special value as rootstocks for *vinifera* varieties in calcareous soils.

Rootstocks resistant to nematodes.—Present fumigants show more promise of practical effectiveness against nematodes than against phylloxera. It still seems, however, that long-time control of nematodes will depend on the use of resistant rootstocks. The principal species showing resistance, either in pure form or as hybrid rootstocks, are V. *candicans*, V. *champini*, V. *solonis*, V. *rufotomentosa*, and V. *rotundifolia*.

Kunde *et al.* (1968) have also shown that V. *candicans*, V. *rufotomentosa*, and V. *solonis* have a very high degree of resistance to the nematode species, *Xiphinema index*, the primary vector of the fanleaf virus complex (see p. 471). Although considered to by synonymous by Bailey (1934), the above authors found the genotype of V. *solonis* they tested to have a very high resistance to X. *index*, while that of V. *Longii* had none.

COMMERCIAL CLASSES OF GRAPES

The grapes of commerce are divided by use into four major groups and one minor group. These are: table grapes, raisin grapes, wine grapes, sweet juice grapes, and—the minor group—canning grapes. The mature fruit of all grape varieties that have been named—some 8,000 or more—will ferment into a kind of wine when crushed, and most of them can be dried or eaten fresh. Only a limited number of the varieties, however, produce wines of standard quality or better. Similarly, the raisins of commerce are produced mainly from three varieties, and fewer than a dozen varieties are grown extensively as table grapes. Most of the sweet juice produced in America is from one variety. Only one or two varieties are used for canning.

Table grapes.—Grapes intended for use as fresh fruit, either for food or decorative purposes, are commonly designated table grapes. They must be attractive in both appearance and eating quality, must have good shipping and keeping qualities, and must be produced and sold at a reasonable cost.

The most important single factor governing the sale of table grapes on display in retail markets is appearance. Many grapes are purchased for decorative purposes, to which they are admirably suited. Even when purchased solely as food, their appearance is important. From the fruit vendor's standpoint, the eye and not the mouth holds the key to the stomach, though of course the grapes must be palatable. Appearance is influenced by: size of berry; shape of berry; shape, size, and compactness of cluster; color of berry; and physical condition. In general, the demand is for berries of uniform and large size, and most of the well-known table grape varieties are characterized by large berries. Only a very few table grape varieties have small or medium-sized berries, and these are popular only because they possess some other unusual and outstanding property, such as seedlessness or striking flavor, that appeals to the buyer, but even with these varieties the grower constantly strives to produce berries as large as possible. The berries must be not only large, but of uniform size. Few things detract more from the appearance of an otherwise fine cluster than numerous small grapes interspersed among large ones. The actual geometric shape of the berries, though it has been emphasized in selection over the years, seems to be of small importance. The most popular varieties of table grapes include some that are spherical, some that are oval, and some that are much elongated. It is probably correct to say that differences in shapes between varieties are more appealing than a single shape for all varieties, regardless of what the shape might be. All of the berries on a single cluster, however, should be uniform in shape, as should all of the clusters in a given package.

The most frequent shape is conical, but globular (when berry-thinned) and cylindroidal clusters are common, and there seems to be no discrimination among them. Size of cluster is more important than shape. Very small clusters (weighing a quarter of a pound or less) and very large clusters (2 lbs. or more) are undesirable. No one likes a very small cluster, and most buyers do not like clusters that have been mutilated by cutting. The average retail purchase of grapes in the United States is between 1 and 3 pounds, and if the clusters are all very large, some must be cut up and divided among purchasers. Very large clusters are also subject to considerable damage in standard packing. Medium-sized clusters (from three quarters of a pound to 1.5 lbs.) pack best and are preferred by most vendors and consumers. For special decorative or display purposes, very large clusters are occasionally useful, whereas very small clusters are always objectionable.

The clusters should be well filled out but not so compact as to be inflexible. When the cluster is suspended by the main stem there should be enough berries on it to cover up most of the stems and leave no obvious gaps in the general shape of the cluster. Very compact clusters are hard and rigid, and usually damaged in packing. Some of the berries may be crushed and others loosened from the pedicels (cap stems). Not only do these broken berries deteriorate in transit, but the juice they leak may spoil the entire cluster as well as adjacent clusters.

The color of the berries is very important. Grapes are usually classed in three color groups—white, red, and black—and the more nearly the color of a variety approaches the class color, the more attractive it is to the consumer. Intermediate shades—pink, brown, or greenish-black—are less desirable. The uniformity and brilliance of the color are more important than its intensity. Clusters or berries are unattractive when red or black on one side and white or green on the other. Dull colors are less attractive than brilliant colors. Color in grapes is more or less a varietal characteristic, but the color's shade, uniformity, and brilliance are much influenced by climate and cultural practices. Cool regions or cool seasons produce grapes of more intense color than hot regions or seasons—yet this darker color is not necessarily more brilliant. Heavy and very fertile soils tend to produce grapes that are less well colored than grapes produced in sandy soils or soils relatively low in nitrogen. Cultural practices that produce very vigorous vegetative growth usually tend to produce grapes of light and irregular coloration.

Good physical condition is imperative. Table grapes must be free of scars, bruises, insect and disease injuries, dust, dirt, and the like. They must be handled in harvesting and packing so that the bloom on the berries is kept intact as much as possible. Crushed and broken berries, and berries loosened from the pedicels, are of special concern because they provide excellent opportunities for the development of molds and other decay-causing organisms.

Eating quality (palatability) is affected by aroma, taste, texture of skin and pulp, and the presence or absence of seeds. If seeds are present, their texture and taste are also involved. Aroma is determined by the kinds and quantities of volatile substances that are present and perceived in the nose. Tastes detected in the mouth are sweet, sour, saline, bitter, and astringent. The flavors of grapes are many, but are usually grouped into three classes—neutral or vinous, muscat, and foxy. Aside from flavor characteristics, grapes may be sweet or sour according to the relative amounts of sugars and acids present, and may or may not be astringent or puckery in varying degree, according to tannin content. Since individuals vary greatly in likes and dislikes with respect to flavors and tastes, no particular combination of flavors and tastes is equally pleasing to all people. Some prefer strong flavors and others do not. Likewise, individuals differ in taste preferences. Some people like very sweet grapes, and others prefer a tart taste. Most individuals, however, prefer a firm but juicy pulp texture, and relative freedom from astringency.

The fruit must be attractive not only when harvested, but when it reaches the consumer. Since a large proportion of California's table grapes are sold in the eastern half of the United States, 2000 to 3000 miles from the vineyards, they must have good shipping and keeping qualities. Characters contributing to good shipping quality are: firm texture of the pulp; tough and fairly thick skin, not easily broken or bruised; strong attachment of the berries and pedicels; and tough stems. Almost any kind of grape can be harvested and marketed locally, because use is not long delayed. With long-distance shipment, however, six to ten or more days often elapse between harvest and use; bruises become discolored, broken and crushed berries deteriorate, stems dry, and some berries become loosened. Good keeping quality requires, besides the characters that contribute to good shipping quality, berries and stems that lose water slowly.

Cost of production is considered after meeting the requirements of attractiveness and good shipping and keeping quality. To enjoy wide general use in competition with other fruits, table grapes must be grown and marketed as a reasonable cost. Factors contributing to reasonable production costs are: moderately large, regular crops; low susceptibility to damage from insects, diseases, frost, wind, and other unfavorable climatic conditions; and adaptability to simple methods of production and handling, such as pruning, thinning, and trimming.

Light or irregular bearing of most varieties can be largely overcome through suitable pruning to ensure ample buds, and thinning to control crop size. Occasionally, however, some variety cannot be made to produce good crops with certainty in some regions. Such a variety is the Dizmar (Bismark or Crystal) in California. Varieties differ widely in their susceptibility to damage by unfavorable climate. Some start growth very early in the spring, for example, Monukka, and for that reason are often damaged by late spring frosts that later-starting varieties escape. Other varieties, such as Muscat of Alexandria and Emperor, set poorly and produce straggly clusters if the weather during bloom is cold and wet. Very hot, windy weather during the growing season, and especially just before ripening, will cause some varieties to sunburn very badly, while others may be damaged only lightly or not at all. The Flame Tokay and Muscat of Alexandria are particularly susceptible to sunburn; the Perlette and Emperor are not. Varieties that require elaborate supports, such as arbors (Almeria), or much expensive handywork, such as berry thinning (Perlette), should be grown only if they possess properties that are valuable enough to offset these extra costs.

The varieties that are grown as table grapes in a given region are determined by climate and the distances to preferred markets. Many of the choicest eating varieties are too soft or delicate to be shipped long distances. Tough skin, firm texture, and tough stems are usually associated with table grape varieties—not for good eating quality, but for reaching consumers in distant markets in an attractive condition. The principal table grape varieties grown in California for distant markets are Almeria (Ohanez), Calmeria, Cardinal, Emperor, Italia, Muscat of Alexandria, Perlette, Red Malaga (Molinera), Ribier (Alfonse Lavalée), Thompson Seedless, (Sultanina), and Tokay. Less important varieties, grown principally for local markets, are Black Hamburg, Black Rose, Muscat Hamburg, Rish Baba, Pierce (California Concord), and Concord.

East of the Rocky Mountains and north of the Gulf states the Concord is of outstanding importance in United States production. Commercial varieties of less importance are Moore's Early, Champion, Worden, Delaware, Niagara, and Catawba. Many others are grown for home use or for limited local markets.

In Europe the table grape industry and the varieties grown may be divided into three parts: outdoor culture in the warm Mediterranean region, outdoor culture in central Europe, and hothouse culture in north-central Europe. The varieties grown in the Mediterranean region, especially Spain, southern France, and Italy, are not greatly different from those grown in California. Because of differences in production practices, local adaptations, and local demand, a few varieties not grown in California may be added to the list and others may be dropped. Because of the short distances to market, the Mediterranean countries can place more emphasis on eating quality than on shipping and keeping quality. Climate in central Europe—central France, Germany, Austria, and Hungary—is such that only early-ripening varieties are successful outdoors. Varieties of the hothouses are the same as, or similar to, the large-berried sorts of California (see the Low Countries, in chap. 3).

Raisin grapes.—These are grapes that produce an acceptable dried product. Thus, raisins are actually dried grapes, but the product varies greatly with different varieties and different methods of drying. Hence raisins are distinguished from "dried grapes" in most grape-growing regions. To be a good raisin variety, the dried product must possess: soft texture; seedlessness, a marked, pleasing flavor; large or very small size; and little tendency to become sticky in storage.

Soft texture of the dried product is perhaps the most important single factor governing the quality of raisins. It is influenced by variety, sugar content of the fresh grapes, method of drying, and the amount of moisture in the raisins. The last can be varied within only narrow limits: the maximum for safe keeping is usually 17 per cent moisture. Within this limit, the higher the moisture content, the softer the raisins are. Likewise, very high sugar content produces soft raisins of high weight per unit volume. Certain varieties normally attain a high sugar content in average seasons and, partly on that account, are well suited to the production of raisins.

Seedlessness is a varietal characteristic. Only a very few varieties containing seeds are used for raisins, and these varieties have only few or soft, tasteless seeds and possess other characters that make them suitable for raisins despite the seeds.

Marked flavor in raisins, like strong flavor in fruit, is wanted by many individuals and is objectionable to others. Strong flavor is the chief asset of the raisins of the Muscat of Alexandria. Most grapes, when dried, do not retain their delicate distinctive flavor, and furthermore the flavor of the raisins is influenced by the method of drying.

The trade prefers either a large or a very small raisin. Bakers prefer the very small raisins, because a better distribution can be obtained through the dough or on the surface of the product. For eating out of hand and most purposes other than baking, large raisins seem to be preferred. Seed-lessness is, however, of so much greater importance than large size that the medium-sized seedless raisins dominate the markets. There is no demand for a small or medium-sized raisin with seeds.

It is also desirable that raisin varieties should ripen early and dry easily. Earliness of ripening is important because most raisins are dried without artificial heat, and varieties that mature early can be dried when weather is more favorable to drying. Later in the season, the days are shorter, the temperature lower, and rains more frequent. Ease of drying depends upon the rate of water loss through the skin, the berry size, and the size and density of the clusters. The easiest and fastest to dry are small, loose clusters of small berries that lose water rapidly.

The tendency of raisins to be dry or sticky is influenced by variety, method of drying, and moisture content. Stickiness results chiefly from sugars on the surface of the berries that absorb water from the air. Sticky raisins "set," forming a tough, solid mass that is often difficult to break up. Stickiness is therefore very objectionable.

Many varieties satisfy some of the requirements to a fair degree, but only a very few satisfy the requirements to an unusual degree. Such varieties are used almost exclusively in commercial production. They are (a) Thompson Seedless (Sultanina and Sultanieh in Near East, Oval Kishmish in Asia; Sultana in South Africa and Australia; Chekirdeksiz in Turkey; and Ak-Kishmish in Russia); (b) Black Corinth, Zante Currant, or Panariti; and (c) Muscat of Alexandria (Gordo blanco in Australia). Varieties of minor importance are Seedless Sultana, Red Corinth, Cape Currant (South Africa and Australia), Black Monukka, and Dattier. Other varieties are dried occasionally, but the product should logically be called dried grapes rather than raisins.

Wine grapes.—By far the most extensive use of grapes is in producing wine. The production of wine grapes occupies most of the vineyards of Europe, North Africa, South Africa, and South America, about two-fifths of those of Australia, and one third of those of the United States. A wine grape may be defined as a variety known to be capable of producing an acceptable wine in some locality. Wines are roughly classified in two groups: table wines and desert wines. Table wines contain less than 14 per cent alcohol; these are also referred to as "light," "natural," or "dinner" wines. They contain little or no unfermented sugar, and therefore are said to be "dry." Yet it is not uncommon for some of them to have a residue of natural grape sugar. Historically, the French Sauternes are always sweet; all other table wines are produced from grapes of only moderately high sugar content and of moderate or higher acidity. Champagne is a table wine.

Dessert wines contain more than 14 per cent alcohol, usually 17 to 20 per cent. Some of these, such as sherry, are also called aperitif or appetizer wines. Some of these may be quite dry; most, however, contain moderate to considerable amounts of unfermented grape sugars. Grape spirits are added, at the desired level of sugar, to arrest the fermentation. These wines are produced from grapes high in sugar content and low in acid.

Besides the constituent balances indicated, wines of high quality, outstanding in bouquet, flavor, and general balance, are the product of grapes possessing special characteristics—such as White Riesling, Chardonnay, Cabernet Sauvignon, Tinta Madeira, and Muscat blanc (Muscat Canelli) varieties—and grown in a favorable climate. That is, the variety, when processed by proper vinification and aging, determines through inherent characteristics—such as its particular aroma and flavoring constituents—the type of wine that may be produced; and the regional conditions, by influencing the sugar-acid ratio, total acidity, and tannin content, etc., determine the quality within the type.

It is beyond the scope of this book to discuss wine production, yet the growing of the varieties used is an integral part of grape production. The varieties used in wine production are numerous. For information on the more important ones see the variety discussions in chapter 24.

Sweet juice grapes.—The varieties known as sweet juice grapes are those whose juice produces an acceptable beverage when it is preserved by pasteurization, germ-proof filteration, or other means. For the making of sweet juice it is necessary, or at least desirable, for the juice to retain the natural-fresh-grape flavor throughout clarification and preservation. In the United States, only pasteurization has been used to preserve grape juice. Most *vinifera* varieties, including the strong-flavored Muscats, lose their fresh flavor and acquire an unpleasant "cooked" taste when pasteurized by the usual methods. The strong-flavored American varieties, particularly the Concord, are affected less by pasteurization. This fact largely accounts for the general use of the Concord for juice in the United States —and, of course, many people like the flavor of this variety. Concord juice is also used in quantity for making jelly, either commercially or in the home. In recent years, large quantities have been used as a blend in the production of a sparkling red wine—Cold Duck.

In central Europe before World War II a thriving industry was developed by the use of close filtration for sterilization. *Vinifera* varieties such as the White Riesling and Chasselas doré are used for juice there. In southern France, according to Flanzy and André (1959), sweet juice is preserved by sulfiting the must for storage and then desulfiting at a moderate temperature under vacuum, in special apparatus, at bottling. The varieties grown there for ordinary wines—Aramon, Carignane, etc.—are employed for sweet juice.

Canning grapes.—Grapes are generally canned in combination with other fruits, in fruit salad and fruit cocktail. Only seedless varieties are used, usually Thompson Seedless and Canner.

BIBLIOGRAPHY

Bailey, L. H. 1934. The species of grape peculiar to North America. Gentes Herbarum, 3:151–244.
————. 1917. Standard cyclopedia of horticulture. Vol. VI. New York, Macmillan Co. (*See* pp. 3481–3492.)
Flanzy, M., and P. André. 1959. Desulfitation des jus de raisin. Ann. Inst. Nat. Res. Agron., Ser. E, Ann. Tech. Agr., 8:171–192.
Galet, Pierre. 1921. Cepages et vignobles de France. Montpellier, France, Imprimerie P. Déhan.
Hedrick, U. P. 1907. The grapes of New York. (Fifteenth annual report. Dept. of Agr., State of New York) Albany, State Printers. Part II:1–564.
Kunde, R. M., L. A. Lider, and R. V. Schmidt. 1968. A test of *Vitis* resistance to *Xiphinema index*. Amer. Jour. Enol. and Vitic. 19:30–36.
Levadoux, L., D. Boubals, and M. Rives. 1962. Le genre vitis et ses espèces. Ann. Amélíor. Plantes, 12:19–44.
Manaresi, A. 1947. Trattato di viticoltura. Bologna, Edizioni Agricole.
Munson, T. V. 1909. Foundations of American grape culture. New York, Orange Judd Co.
Patel, G. I., and H. P. Olmo. 1955. Cytogenetics of Vitis. I. The hybrid V. *vinifera* x V. *rotundifolia*. Amer. Jour. Bot., 42(2): 141–159.

3

Geographical Distribution
of Grape Growing

Grapes are grown everywhere that the environment is reasonably favorable.* The extent of this industry and the relative importance of its several products in the various countries are discussed in this chapter.

NORTH AMERICA

North America is the native habitat of more than 70 per cent of the grape species of the world. Every section of the United States, except the lofty peaks and high plateaus of the western mountain ranges, have their native grapes. Even in the desert regions of the southwest, native species— *Vitis arizonica*, *V. berlandieri*, and *V. californica*—grow wild along the streams. The great valley of the Mississippi River and its tributaries is especially rich in its variety and abundance of native grapes. Some of the grapes of the mid-western and eastern sections of the United States overlap into Canada and Mexico. These regions are the source of the fruiting varieties that make grape growing possible in the area east of the Rocky Mountains, where *vinifera* grapes do not thrive. It is also the source of

* The acreage, production, and export figures reported in this chapter, except those for the United States, are average (rounded) for the years 1968 through 1970 as reported by Protin (1968–1970). The figures for California acreage, production, and use for the years 1969 through 1971 are by Henderson and Kitterman (1969–1971) and those for Arizona, Oregon, and Washington by personal correspondence.

Geographical Distribution of Grape Growing

some of the source of some of the world's most destructive grape diseases—powdery mildew (Oïdium), downy mildew (Peronospora), black rot, and the worst insect pest of the grape, phylloxera. After these diseases and pests were carried to Europe, where they destroyed most of the vineyards, North America contributed much to the control of them. Since the native grapes flourished despite the diseases and phylloxera, the European viticulturists reasoned that they must be at least resistant to attack. American species taken to Europe were tested, propagated, and hybridized there, and from these investigations came most of the rootstocks now used in the vineyards of nearly every part of the world. From these stocks, also, have been developed the direct-producing hybrids that possess resistance to some of the cryptogamic diseases. More recently, the western south-central section of the United States has been the source of species resistant to nematodes (see p. 21).

Canada.—In Canada, grapes are grown mainly in the province of Ontario around the western end of Lake Ontario, and in the southern part of British Columbia, particularly in the Okanagan Valley. The grapes of eastern Canada are primarily American varieties and hybrids between these and *vinifera* varieties; in British Columbia the grapes are hybrids and a few *vinifera* varieties. The vineyards cover about 21,000 acres. Average annual wine production is about 6,500,000 gallons. Some table grapes are produced for local consumption.

Mexico.—This republic, the oldest grape-producing country in the Americas (since 1518), has about 40,000 acres in grapes and produces about 3,000,000 gallons of wine annually. A large part of the crop is used as table grapes. Wine production is increasing. No commercial raisins are produced. Much of the wine is distilled to produce beverage brandy.

The principal grape areas are in the northern part of Baja California, and in southern Coahuila and limited areas in adjacent Durango. There are other limited areas in central Chihuahua, central Aguascalientes, and southern Querétaro. Except in Baja California, some or much rains falls during the development and ripening of the fruit.

United States.—Grapes are grown in every state except Alaska. The percentage of farms having vineyards, except for California, is lowest in the western north-central states and highest in New York, Ohio, and Pennsylvania. Next to the apple, the grape is the most widely grown fruit. Unfortunately, the Bureau of the Census does not report the area devoted to grape culture, and instead reports the number of vines. Except in the western states, the acreage can only be estimated. Average annual production is about 300,000 tons (not including California, Arizona, Oregon, and Washington). Although a portion of this crop is consumed on the farms and in the production of sweet juice, an ever increasing major portion goes into wine.

Geographical Distribution of Grape Growing

The following non-western states, listed in the order of their production, are responsible for most of the grapes of American varieties: New York, Michigan, Pennsylvania, Ohio, Arkansas, Missouri, Iowa, Illinois, and North Carolina. No other states produce more than 2,000 tons annually.

Arizona, which lies to the east of Southern California, and Oregon and Washington, which border on the Pacific Ocean to the north of California, are the other states that have substantial plantings of *vinifera* grapes. Arizona has about 4000 acres and the 1971 crop was 14,500 tons, all of early table varieties—Perlette, Thompson Seedless, and Cardinal. The vineyards are in the vicinity of Glendale and Phoenix, with smaller areas near Yuma. These desert areas are sometimes subject to summer rains.

The vineyards of Oregon are near Grants Pass and Roseburg, with several plantings in the Willamette Valley. According to Professor R. Garren of Oregon State University, the state has a quarantine against importation of rooted vines; only cuttings certified to be free of known viruses and phylloxera may be brought in. The state has about 300 acres of mostly non-bearing vines. At the moment, interest in *vinifera* is very high.

In Washington the vineyards are located in the Yakima and Columbia River Valleys. Other than California, it ranks second among the states in grape production, about 80,000 tons in 1971. The plantings are principally for sweet juice and wine production. The acreage, currently about 18,100, has increased 70 per cent since 1968 (Folwell and Dailey, 1972). The production is mostly Concord, although some other American varieties and French hybrids are grown. A small acreage of *vinifera* varieties, mostly in trial stage, has been planted in recent years and interest in these is increasing in spite of danger of winter freezing.

CALIFORNIA.—Few countries or even provinces have the advantages for grape growing found in California. In general the grape areas of California have mild to moderate winters, with rainfall varying from 3 to 4 inches in the southern deserts to 40 inches in parts of northern Sonoma and Mendocino counties. The growing season is long, with few unseasonable frosts, and the summers are warm to hot and practically rainless. The ripening season is usually rainless except in the dry-wine areas of the coastal valleys, where occasional rains may occur after September 1. Damaging hailstorms almost never occur. The hot, dry summers all but eliminate the natural, winged spread of phylloxera. Downy mildew (Peronospora), black rot, and anthracnose are unknown in cultivated vineyards. Similarly, the grape moths *Eudemis*, *Cochylis*, and the berry moth are absent.

Geographical Distribution of Grape Growing

Grapes can be grown in California wherever soil and water conditions are favorable, except at high elevations or near the northern coast, where the temperatures and/or heat summations are too low. As the industry developed, however, certain sections were found better adapted than others for certain kinds of grape growing. Professor F. T. Bioletti (of the University of California from 1890 to 1935) recognized these differences as arising primarily from variations in climate brought about by the topography of the state and its proximity to the ocean. He designated six geographic regions that still guide growers in selecting locations for planting table and raisin grapes. The five climatic regions (see chap. 4)

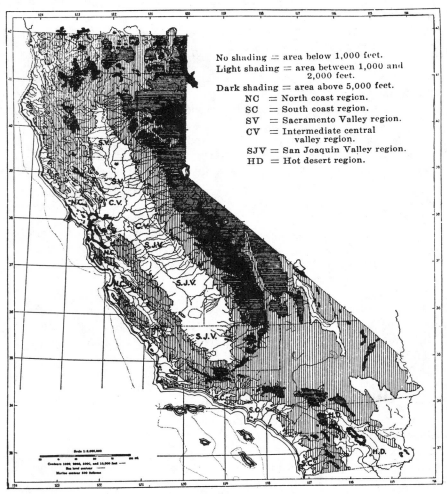

FIGURE 5: Geographic grape-growing regions of California. (From Ext. Cir. 30)

are a more accurate guide in selecting locations for wine grapes. The geographic regions are known as the North Coast, South Coast, Intermediate Central Valley, Sacramento Valley, San Joaquin Valley, and Hot Desert.

Since the North Coast and South Coast regions (the counties adjacent to the Pacific Ocean or San Francisco Bay) produce mostly wine grapes, the reader is referred to the discussion of climatic regions I, II, and III, on page 66.

In the North Coast region the rainfall diminishes from 40 inches in Mendocino County to 13 inches in San Benito County. Some vineyards are dry-farmed, but irrigation is becoming more general in the areas of low rainfall or shallow soils. The sprinkler irrigation systems are also used for protection against unseasonal frosts and occasional high temperatures.

In the South Coast region the rainfall varies from 18 inches at Santa Barbara to 9 inches at San Diego. Irrigation is generally necessary except at the higher elevations. Besides wine grapes, some table grapes are grown for local markets.

The Intermediate Central Valley (climatic region IV, with limited areas in III) extends roughly from Sacramento to Livingston, in the great interior valley. It is air conditioned by ocean breezes that pass inland through Carquinez Strait and over Altamont Pass, in the coastal range of mountains adjacent to San Francisco Bay. The rainfall varies from 18 inches in the north to 11 inches in the south, so irrigation is necessary. Here the brilliant (Flame) Tokay table grape comes nearest to perfection. There are also large acreages of heavily bearing table- and dessert-wine varieties. Recent plantings include varieties of greater potential for table wines of better quality. The region is too cool for the production of natural raisins, but "golden bleached" raisins are produced in quantity around Modesto.

Northward through the Sacramento Valley (climatic region V), the influence of the ocean breeze diminishes, and the seasonal rainfall increases from 18 inches at Sacramento to about 24 inches at Chico and 37 inches at Redding. The temperature, which is high, *increases* from south to north. Irrigation is beneficial except on the deep soils at the northern end of the region. Here the autumn rains come early, making the sun-drying of raisins hazardous. Wine grapes adapted to the heat of region V, however, do very well; as the market for California wines expands and new varieties are introduced, the acreage in this valley may be extended. The occasional severe north winds in early summer make most of the valley unsuited for table grapes, but some of the good quality are grown in sheltered locations along the eastern side.

South of the Central Valley, and likewise deprived of the ocean breeze, is the San Joaquin Valley (climatic region V). The temperature, which

Geographical Distribution of Grape Growing

increases from north to south, is high enough for the varieties that require abundant heat. The annual rainfall decreases gradually from 11 inches at Merced to about 5 inches at Arvin. Irrigation is necessary. This region produces a large part of the world's raisins. The table grape varieties Cardinal, Emperor, Ribier, Red Malaga, and Thompson Seedless, among others, thrive along the eastern side of the valley from east of Fresno to Arvin. Common table and dessert-wine varieties are grown extensively. This area is adapted for the production of good dessert wine varieties.

The Hot Desert consists of certain areas in the Coachella and Imperial valleys, in the southeastern corner of the state. This, the hottest and driest grape-growing region of California, produces the earliest grapes. Yields are low and production costs high, but their earliness gives the table grapes of the desert a prominent place in the grape industry. Owing to the intense heat and high costs, raisins and wine grapes are not produced.

California, with about 2 per cent of the world's grape acreage, produces about 3 per cent of the grapes crushed, 11 per cent of the table fruit, and 30 per cent of the raisins.

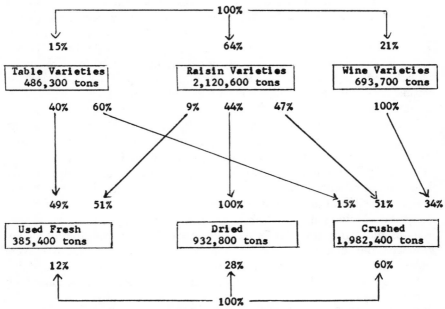

PRODUCTION, ALL VARIETIES. 3,300,600 TONS

FIGURE 6: The production and utilization of table, raisin, and wine grapes in California: 1969–1971. (*Source of Data: Henderson et al., 1969–1971*)

SOUTH AMERICA

Grape growing on a large scale in South America is limited to the republics of Argentina and Chile, lying respectively on the eastern and western sides of the lofty Andes Mountains. Bolivia, Brazil, Peru, and Uruguay also produce grapes that are important as wine or table grapes in their domestic markets.

Argentina.—Grapes were brought to Argentina by the Jesuit fathers in 1560. Development was slow at first and the industry did not expand substantially until the nineteenth century. The vineyards are found primarily on the high plateau (2,000 to 2,500 feet) bordering the Andes in the states of Mendoza and San Juan, with less extensive areas in Rio Negro. These are semiarid areas that usually have ample gravity water for irrigation, from numerous streams arising in the Andes. The climate is temperate and characterized by cool winters, and warm to hot, relatively dry summers. The rainfall varies, but it is generally light, with occasional storms, accompanied by hail, during the growing season. Irrigation is necessary. The area in vineyards is about 750,000 acres, with usual production amounting to about 490,000,000 gallons of wine, 91,000 tons of table grapes, and 9,000 tons of raisins.

Most of the Argentine wine is consumed within the country. Yields are good. In recent years phylloxera has been taking a damaging toll, and in some years downy mildew becomes a serious problem; hence, costs of production are increasing. Owing to the abundance of heat, most of the wines are deficient in natural acid. Moderate quantities of good wine, of some of the premium-quality varieties, are produced. The best of the dry wines are produced in the state of Rio Negro. All varieties are of European origin. The leading premium-quality variety is the Malbec.

In recent years the export of table grapes to the United States has assumed importance. These arrive mostly between February 15 and June 1. The bulk of the shipments are of Almeria, Emperor, Alphonose Lavallée (Riber), Tokay, and Thompson Seedless. These have sold well, but greater attention to proper maturity would make for wider consumer acceptance.

Local outlets take all of the raisins that are produced.

Brazil.—Most of Brazil has a tropical climate. Vines have been most successful in the states of Rio Grande do Sul, São Paulo, and Minas Gerais. Some table grapes are grown in São Paulo. The total area in grapes is about 177,000 acres, the yearly wine production approaches 78,000,000 gallons and that of table grapes 165,000 tons. Hybrid varieties are the basis of the industry, with Isabella ranking first in acreage. The planting of *vinifera* varieties is increasing.

Bolivia.—The principal center of grape production in Bolivia is in the region around Sucre (Chuquisaca). Some grapes are grown near La Paz, however, at elevations of 5,000 to nearly 9,000 feet above sea level, at a latitude of 16° south. There are about 4,700 acres in vineyards. Wine is the principal product, with the annual yield running around 157,000 gallons.

Chile.—The vineyards of Chile are located mostly between 33° and 38° south latitude, in the valleys between the coastal hills and the Andes. The climate is very favorable, markedly resembling that of California. The soils are alluvial in origin. Irrigation, with gravity water from streams fed by the snow fields of the Andes, is common. Diseases are easily controlled because the climate is so dry. The entire country is said to be free of phylloxera. The total area in vineyards approximates 294,100 acres, with an annual production of about 118,000,000 gallons of wine, 72,000 tons of table grapes, and 840 tons of raisins.

The northern districts produce fortified wines, brandies, and raisins. The white and red dry wines are produced around and to the south of Santiago. Some of the dry wines are of very good quality. Except for exports of a few million gallons, Chile's wines are consumed within the country.

Because of its favorable geographic position, Chile enjoys an increasing export market for table grapes in the United States. The varieties are the same as those grown in Argentina.

Peru.—Grape growing in Peru dates back to the latter part of the sixteenth century. The most favorable regions are the provinces of Ica and and Moquegua. The total vineyard area is about 23,800 acres, and the annual production of wine about 2,200,000 gallons.

Uruguay.—Although Uruguay has about 46,000 acres planted to grapes, the annual production of about 22,060,000 gallons of wine does not equal the demand. The vineyards are located principally in the provinces of Montevideo, Canelones, Colonia, San José, and Soriano. Table grapes are produced for domestic markets, and there is a limited production of sweet juice.

AUSTRALASIA

In the tropical islands of the Pacific Ocean grapes are rarely found, but farther south there is important production in Australia and a modest acreage in New Zealand.

Australia.—Grape growing in the Commonwealth of Australia is largely centered in the southeastern part of the continent, in the states of South Australia, Victoria, and New South Wales. A few grapes are grown in Western Australia. Climatically, Australia has much in common with California, except that more of its annual rainfall comes in summer.

Grapes were first planted in 1813 or 1814. There are now 145,300 acres, with an annual production of about 36,000,000 gallons of wine, 30,000 tons

Geographical Distribution of Grape Growing

of table grapes, and 85,000 tons of raisins and currants. South Australia produces two thirds of the wine (fig. 7), and Victoria produces nearly three-fourths of the raisins and half of the currants. Table grape production is fairly equally divided among Victoria, New South Wales, and Western Australia, with some early table grape production in Queensland. All of the raisins and table grapes, and some of the wine grapes, are irrigated. Most of the new plantings of wine grape varieties are being made in the heavily producing irrigated areas and the cooler area south of Adelaide.

The wines and table grapes are largely consumed within the commonwealth. Some wine (1,900,000 gals.), principally sherry and dessert types, is exported to England and Canada. Table grapes are exported in small quantities, mainly to countries in southeastern Asia. Normally, more than two thirds of the raisins and currants are exported.

The principal table grape varieties are Almeria (Ohanez), Bicane, Black Prince, Cornichon, Muscat Gordo blanco (Muscat of Alexandria),

FIGURE 7: A vineyard in South Australia. (*Courtesy of Gramp and Sons, South Australia*)

and Waltham Cross (Dattier). The wine grapes are of European origin; Doradillo ranks first in acreage. The raisins are made primarily of Sultana (Thompson Seedless) and the currants of Black Corinth.

New Zealand.—Some 1,200 miles to the southeast of Australia, New Zealand, another nation in the British Commonwealth, has about 2,500 acres of grapes. The vineyards are near Auckland and Hawke's Bay. Some 3,500,000 gallons of wine, 25,000 gallons of juice, and 400 tons of table grapes are produced.

AFRICA

In Africa, grapes are grown only in the extreme north and extreme south. The chief producing countries are Algeria, Morocco, and Tunis in the north and the Union of South Africa in the south. Some grapes are grown for local consumption in Libya, Egypt, and Ethiopia.

Algeria.—Wine grapes constitute the bulk of production in Algeria. Table grapes are grown in moderate quantities for local use and export for the early table grape markets of Europe. These—principally Chasselas doré—are grown along the coast west of Algiers and to a lesser extent in the Atlas Mountains. The vineyard area is about 760,000 acres. The production of wine averages about 258,131,770 gallons. Since Algeria won independence from France in 1962, its acreage has dropped over 200,000 acres and its wine production by 175,418,200 gallons. Formerly, France took 90 per cent of the production. Now new markets are being developed in the east.

Grape growing in Algeria came into prominence between 1860 and 1890, when phylloxera was destroying the vineyards of France. During this period, there was a sixfold increase in Algerian acreage. French vineyardists moved into Algeria, bringing with them the varieties of southern France—Alicante Bouschet, Aramon, Carignane, Grenache, Mataro, and others. The principal producing districts are in the vicinities of Algiers, Bône, Bougie, Philippeville Oran, Mascara, Mostagenem, Sidi bel Abbès, and Tlemcen.

Egypt.—About 127,000 tons of table grapes are produced for local markets and include such varieties as Bashansi, Red and White Rourmi, and Ghariby. The climate is not well suited to usual grape growing, being too nearly tropical. Nevertheless, there are about 26,000 acres in grapes. Wine production amounts to about 107,000 gallons.

Libya.—Libya produces grapes in the Cyrenaica region, near the capital city of Bengasi. The total grape area covers 74,000 acres, of which a large part is in wine grapes. Data on the production of wine are unavailable. Some early table grapes are exported.

Morocco.—The climate of Morocco is similar to that of Algeria. The

Geographical Distribution of Grape Growing

grape industry is not fully developed, and cultural methods are somewhat primitive. Table grapes are important for the home markets. There are more than 150,000 acres in grapes, producing about 32,000,000 gallons of wine and 6,000 tons of table grapes. Some grapes are dried for raisins.

Tunisia.—The very hot desert wind (sirocco) limits grape growing in Tunisia to a few places, principally near Grombalia and Sousse. There are about 108,000 acres, with a wine production of 21,000,000 gallons. About half of the wine is exported. Some 2,000 tons of early table grapes of such varieties as Chasselas doré, Madeleine Royale, Madeleine Angevine, and Madeleine Celine are grown for export. Later-maturing sorts are grown for domestic use.

Union of South Africa.—Grapes were introduced to South Africa in 1655. Most of the vineyards are in the southwest, where the temperature is favorable and most rainfall is in the winter. The vineyards on the Cape peninsula are the oldest and smallest, but their wines are among the best. Constantia, the greatest of South African wines, was developed in the base of the Cape. Next in importance is an area extending inland somewhat beyond False Bay and then north to Wellington and the first range of

FIGURE 8: A table grape vineyard area in the Hex Valley of South Africa. (*Courtesy of K. E. Nelson*)

mountains. Here are produced most of the table wines, as well as other wines. Beyond, to the east and north, is the Little Karroo, with scattered vineyards that produce dessert wines and brandy. The extensively grown varieties are Stein (similar to Sauvignon blanc), Greengrape (similar to Sémillon), Pontac (Teinturier mâle), White French (similar to Palomino), Hermitage (Black Malvoisie), and the white and red Hannepoot (White and Red Muscat of Alexandria). The total grape area of the Union is about 239,000 acres, with an annual production of about 120,000,000 gallons of wine, 40,000 tons of table grapes, and 10,000 tons of raisins. About 4,000,000 gallons of wine are exported.

The table grapes are grown in the Graaff Reinet, Paarl, Stellenbosch, and Worcester areas, which are irrigated. The varieties are Almeria (Ohanez), Alphonse Lavallée (Ribier), Barlinka, Muscat (Red and White), Tokay, and Waltham Cross (Dattier). About 80 per cent of production is exported, primarily to England.

Raisins are produced along the Orange River and in the Worcester area, where irrigation is practiced. The varieties are Muscat of Alexandria, Sultana (Thompson Seedless), and Black Corinth.

EUROPE

The wine production of Europe far overshadows that of all the rest of the world. About five-sixths of the world's wine is produced in Europe and consumed there. Southern Europeans use wine as Americans use milk—as an essential part of their diet. Except for the raisin varieties and a few table grape varieties, Europe has supplied almost all the grape varieties that are now grown extensively. The countries of heaviest production are France, Italy, Portugal, and Spain, but also important are Austria, Bulgaria, Germany, Greece, Hungary, Romania, Switzerland, the Soviet Union, and Yugoslavia. Important in raisin production are Greece, the island of Crete, and Spain. Table grape production is an important industry in Bulgaria, France, Greece, Italy, Romania, Spain, the Soviet Union, and Yugoslavia. In some parts of Europe large quantities of the grapes that are consumed fresh are selected clusters of wine grapes.

Albania.—A small country on the east coast of the Adriatic Sea, Albania has about 31,000 acres of grapes, a part of which is planted to table grape varieties. Mean annual production of wine is 1,100,000 gallons.

Austria.—Grape growing in Austria dates back to the time of the Roman Empire. The principal regions of production are Burgenland and Lower Austria. The climate of northern Burgenland is tempered by Lake Neusiedler, but spring frosts and hail storms occur at times; that of Lower Austria is mid-continental European, with cold winters, warm summers, and occasional late frosts.

Geographical Distribution of Grape Growing

The wines of Austria are produced primarily for consumption within the country. This fact, together with the somewhat unfavorable climate, may account in part for their different character, even though the varieties grown are mainly from Germany and France. The best wines are produced in the communities of Gumpoldskirchen and Wachaw. Some of the more interesting of these are the products of Gewürztraminer, Walschriesling, Pinot blanc, Müller-Thurgau, Spät-Rotgipler, Greenburger, and Pinot noir.

There are about 118,000 acres of grapes, with an annual production of about 68,000,000 gallons of wine. Production of table grapes is for local markets mainly from locally known varieties.

Bulgaria.—Climatically, Bulgaria is well suited to grape growing. The vineyards are scattered over the whole country, except for the higher parts of the Balkan Mountains. Cultural and vinification practices are improving. Wines of the districts of Pleven, Ruse, Svishtov, Sukhindol, and Varna, in the north, are rated good. The plantings are of both European and Asian varieties. The vineyard area of about 409,000 acres is expanding, and so is the annual wine production of 115,000,000 gallons. Export amounts to 2,400,000 gallons.

Table grapes are grown for domestic markets and for export. The table grape crop averages about 190,000 tons, 30 per cent of which is exported. This acreage is expanding very rapidly. Both European and Near Eastern varieties are grown. The principal variety is Bolgar (Dattier).

Czechoslovakia.—The vineyard area of Czechoslovakia totals about 80,000 acres, with a yearly production of about 22,000,000 gallons of wine. The wine ranges in quality from ordinary to superior.

The better areas of production are: the southern part of Slovakia, near Bratislava; the area south of Moravia; the Carpatho-Ruthenian district; and the vineyards of Bohemia, concentrated chiefly around Melnik and Litomerice, north of Prague, on the Elbe River. The best red wines are produced of Pinot noir and Klevener, at Melnik; Traminer and Sylvaner are the source of much of the white wines.

France.—The Phoenicians are credited with bringing the grape to the south of France in about 600 B.C. In 1870 the vineyards covered some 5,750,000 acres. Then, during the next two decades, the scourge of phylloxera ravaged the country, killing more than nine-tenths of the vines. Many vineyards were replanted on American rootstocks, but the total area has never regained its former magnitude. The present vineyards cover about 3,333,000 acres, with an annual production of about 1,650,000,000 gallons of wine, 360,000 tons of table grapes, and 10,000,000 gallons of sweet grape juice. About one-seventh of the population of France is employed directly or indirectly by this industry.

Despite the enormous wine production, France imports more wine than is exported. The annual imports amount to about 89,100,000 gallons, compared to exports of about 50,000,000 gallons. Some of these exports reach nearly every country of the world.

During the course of centuries French viticulture has become highly localized, so that certain varieties are grown in certain districts for the production of wines characteristic of the variety or varieties in those particular environments. In the case of a number of these wines the region of origin has acquired world-wide recognition as a wine type. Everyone acquainted with wines knows that the wines of France that are labeled Burgundy, Champagne, or Sauternes are the products of certain varieties grown in the regions of those names. For generations the same varieties of grapes have been grown on the same soils and used to make the same types of wine. The production of these wines is now protected by the law of appellation of origin, which names the varieties that may be planted, the tonnage that may be produced, and the processes of vinification. Wines so protected account for about 12 per cent of the total production of France.

Although grapes are grown in all but the northernmost tiers of provinces in France, of most general interest are the following regions, because of the nature of their products: Champagne, Burgundy, Bordeaux, the Midi, and Cognac.

The CHAMPAGNE region is in the rolling country northeast of Paris, principally in the department of Marne, but reaching into Aisne and Aube. It includes famous vineyard areas in the valley of the Marne around Épernay and in the Vesle Valley, near Reims. The varieties grown are Pinot noir, Chardonnay, and, to a much lesser extent, Meunier. This is the only region permitted, by French law, to label its effervescent product "Champagne," and then only when it is made from the above varieties. Large quantities of mousseux (sparkling) wines are made in other parts of France, particularly in the Anjou region in the Loire Valley, but these cannot be labeled Champagne.

The BURGUNDY area is small, extending about forty miles, from Dijon on the north to Chagny, on the south. The vineyards lie on the Côte-d'Or—the slope of hills on the west side of the broad Saône Valley. There are the famous vineyards of Clos de Nuits, Le Chambertin, Clos de Vougeot, Romanée Conti, Beaune, and Pommard. Both red and white wines are produced. The reds derive their character and quality from the Pinot noir, and the whites from Chardonnay.

To the northwest of Burgundy is the Chablis region, where white varieties predominate. To the south along the Saône is the Beaujolais region, where a number of Gamay varieties set the type of wine.

All BORDEAUX wines must, to bear this name on the label, be produced from acceptable grape varieties grown in the department of Gironde. The vineyards are in the valleys of the Garonne, Gironde, and Dordogne rivers. The districts of this region famous for red wines are Médoc, Saint-Emilion, and Pomerol; for red and white wines, Graves; and for white wines, Barsac and Sauternes.

The red wines are made almost entirely from Cabernet Sauvignon, Cabernet franc, Merlot, Malbec, and Petite Verdot, and the white wines from Sémillon, Sauvignon blanc, and a little Muscadelle. The Médoc is the most northernly of the districts, lying north of the city of Bordeaux and on the west side of the Gironde and Garonne rivers; Saint-Emilion and Pomerol are east of the city, in the valley of the Dordogne River; Graves extends south from Bordeaux for about twenty miles along the west bank of the Garonne, to just beyond Pondensac. The Barsac and Sauterne districts occupy a small area immediately southeast of the Graves district. There are many renowned Chateaux (wine-producing estates) in this region.

The MIDI is the mass-production region of France. The regions already discussed are largely responsible for France's reputation for fine wines—wines of appellation of origin—yet the Midi (the south of France) produces more wine than all the other regions put together. It stretches across southern France from the delta of the Rhone Valley to the Spanish border, including all or parts of the departments of Var, Vaucluse, Bouches-du-Rhône, Gard, Hérault, Aude, and Pyrénées-Orientales. Heavy-yielding red varieties such as Aramon, Alicante Bouschet, Carignane. Grand noir, Grenache, Mataro, and Picpoule noir, and white varieties such as Chenin blanc, Clairette, Picpule blanc, Terret Bourret, and Terret blanc, are grown for the production of common wines destined largely for domestic consumption. Coöperative wineries use a large proportion of the grapes of this region.

FIGURE 9: A typical vineyard scene in the Champagne region of France. (*Courtesy of French Government Tourist Office, Paris*)

The departments of Avignon and Vaucluse grow quantities of table grapes. The varieties are Chasselas doré (40 per cent of the total), Dattier, Gross vert, Italia, Muscat Hamburg, Ribier, and Servant.

The Midi also produces large quantities of sweet grape juice (André, 1958). This industry has become important in recent years and is expanding. The principal varieties used are Aramon and Carignane.

The COGNAC region is foremost in brandy production in France. It lies in the department of Charente, surrounding the city of Cognac. The region is divided into zones according to the quality of the product. The zone of highest repute extends southeast from Cognac, with its center near the village of Segonzac. The varieties grown are: Saint-Emilion, with limited and decreasing acreages of French Colombard, and Folle blanche.

Another brandy-producing region—Armagnac—lies to the southeast of Bordeaux, in the department of Gers.

Germany.—The most northernly vineyards of the world are in Germany. Grape growing is an important industry only in the warmer locations, principally along the Rhine River and its tributaries. Most of the vineyards are planted on steep southerly or westerly slopes of the river valleys. There are more than 240,000 acres of vines, with an annual production of about 192,000,000 gallons of wine.

Despite the coolness of the climate, the yields are high for the varieties, testifying to the skill and ingenuity of the growers. The quality of certain German white wines, such as the so-called *spätlese* ("late harvest") and *Trockenbeeren-auslese* ("dry-berry selection"), has received world-wide recognition. These are among the world's most highly prized wines. Although the vineyard industry of Germany occupies only a small fraction of the total agricultural land, it is of national importance since it chiefly uses steep, stony slopes that are unsuitable for other crops (fig. 10).

The principal regions are the Moselle, which includes the Moselle, Saar, and Ruwer valleys; the Rheingau, the slope on the north side of the Rhine River extending from Rüdesheim to Hochheim; Hesse, the undulating area south and west of the Rhine River, extending from Bingen to Mainz, on the north, and south to Worms; Franconia, which lies along the Main River between Gemünden and Schweinfurt; the Palatinate, which lies between the Rhine River and the Vosges Mountains and extends from Bad Dürkheim on the north to the French border on the south; and scattered vineyard areas in the states of Württemberg and Baden. The wines of the Rheingau and Moselle are the most famous, yet some wines of very good quality are produced in all regions. Those of the Palatinate may be very heavy; they also may have an overpowering, flowery bouquet. The leading varieties, in order of importance, are: White Riesling, Sylvaner, Müller-Thurgau, and Gewürztraminer; lesser sorts include Elbling, Gutedel, and the Veltliners.

Only limited quantities of red wines are produced. The best, made of a selection of Pinot noir, is grown at Assmannshausen. Other red wines are produced in Württemberg, of the Klevener, Limberger, Trollinger, and Meunier varieties.

Small quantities of the fine wines of Germany, and also some wines of ordinary quality, are exported. The exports amount to about 5,800,000 gallons.

Table grape production is unimportant. Germany imports large quantities of table grapes, particularly from the countries of southeastern Europe, and to a lesser extent from Spain, Italy, and France, and also from hothouses in the Low Countries.

The production of sweet grape juice has acquired some magnitude. Much of this juice is preserved by very careful, close filtration, or storage under carbon dioxide at several atmospheres of pressure, which preserves the aroma and quality of the fine wine grapes used in its production.

Greece.—History does not record the earliest date that grapes were grown in Greece. It is believed to be the oldest producing region of

FIGURE 10: A vineyard area in the Moselle Valley of Germany. (*Courtesy Presse- und informalionsamt der Bundesregierung, Bonn*)

Europe and, after Asia Minor, the oldest in the world. There are about 540,000 acres planted to grapes. In ancient times Greek wines held an enviable reputation for quality.

Today Greece is much better known abroad for its raisins than its wines, being the world's third largest producer, exceeded only by California and Turkey. Approximately 185,000 tons of raisins are produced; 66 per cent of which are currants, made from the Black Corinth grape, and the remainder from Sultanina (Thompson Seedless). The Greek currant crop is produced mainly on the northern coast of the Peloponnesus from Corinth to Patras and down the west coast, and on the Ionian islands of Ithaca, Leucas, Zante, and Cephalonia. Nearly half of the raisins other than currants are produced on the island of Crete. Exports take about half of the currants and an even greater proportion of the raisins.

Greece produces about 225,000 tons of table grapes annually. These are largely of local varieties, grown primarily for consumption within the country.

Many of the wines of Greece are flavored with such substances as herbs, spices, and resin. For this reason a liking for them is usually an acquired taste. It is said that, once one becomes accustomed to the flavors, these wines are satisfying. Also produced, besides the flavored wines, are dry table, blending and sweet wines. Total production is some 130,000,000 gallons, of which about 22,000,000 gallons are exported.

Hungary.—The history of grape growing in Hungary dates back at least to the second century A.D. About half of the vineyards are on sandy soil, which is unsuitable to phylloxera. Large contiguous areas of sandy soil lie between the Danube and Tisza rivers and on the left side of the Tisza in the so-called Nyirseg. Cultural costs on this soil are low, but fertilization is required. There are about 572,000 acres of vineyards. The yearly production of wine, which is predominantly white, is about 132,000,000 gallons.

Tokaj, produced from the Harslevelii, Leanka, Furmint, and Muscat grapes, is the world-renowned wine of Hungary. It is grown in a number of small settlements surrounding the towns of Egger and Tokaj, in the foothills of the Carpathian Mountains. In Mor, a small community not far from Budapest, a good natural sweet wine is produced from the Ezerjo grape. The adjoining area of Neszmely has won recognition for its Riesling wine. Shand (1929) states that somyló, a white wine of premium quality, is produced of the Furmint grape in the counties of Veszprem and Vas. The Alföld region lies on the great sandy plain in southeastern Hungary. Large-scale production is the rule there, where a large part of the country's wines are produced from many varieties with local names.

Table grapes, mostly for domestic markets, are grown in nearly every grape-producing district. Production amounts to about 34,000 tons. Early ripening varieties, such as Pearl of Csaba and Chasselas doré, are most common, but various muscats, Othello, and Delaware are grown.

Italy.—The vineyard industry in Italy was already flourishing at least a century before the birth of Christ. The climates of Italy are varied, since the country stretches over eleven degrees of latitude, yet grapes are grown in nearly every province. Annual rainfall ranges from 55 inches on some of the slopes of the Alps to 16.5 inches at Cagliari, Sardinia, and 23.6 inches at Palermo, Sicily. The diversity in climate, soil, exposure, and grape varieties is responsible in part for a great variety of wines—but only a very small proportion are superior.

Next to France, Italy is the world's largest producer and consumer of wine. Table grapes are also important for domestic use; considerable quantities are exported to other European countries. Some grapes are dried for local consumption as raisins, but a commercial raisin industry hardly exists.

The total area on which grapes are grown in Italy far exceeds even that of France. Much of the area, however, is interplanted with other crops. The vines are spaced wide apart and trained on trees, fences, or other supports. Yet, if all the vines were in a solid stand there would be approximately 3,800,000 acres. Total wine production is about 1,822,000,000 gallons annually.

The better-known wines of Italy are produced in the regions of Piedmont, Venetia, and Tuscany. The best red varietal wine of Italy is produced of the Nebbiolo grape from the vineyards of Barolo, in Piedmont. Other varietal wines of the region are Barbaresco, Barbera, Grignolino, and Fresia. It is also the home of the Italian vermouths and the widely known Asti *spumante*—a sparkling wine—made of Muscat blanc (Muscat Canelli). The best wine of Venetia is Soave, a white wine produced in the area between Verona and Vicenza. Chianti, a product of a small area in Tuscany, is the best known of all the red wines of Italy. It derives its character and quality from the Sangioveto grape and the area in which it is grown. It is really a blend, mostly Sangioveto, with minor amounts of Canaiolo nero, Trebbiano, and Malvasia. Of the many, many other wines produced in Italy, a fair number deserve a rating of good, but none is distinguished.

Italy produces about 1,100,000 tons of table grapes, making it, along with Turkey, the top producer of grapes for table use. About half of this tonnage, especially that consumed at home, is selected clusters of wine varieties. The area of table grape production, which is expanding, lies to the south of Rome but centers in Bari. The leading variety is Regina (Dattier). Italy exports table grapes to Germany, France, and Switzerland.

A large quantity of sweet (unfermented) grape juice is produced in Italy.

Luxembourg.—The Grand Duchy of Luxembourg, where the boundaries of Germany, France, and Belgium meet, has some 3,000 acres of vineyards and produces annually about 430,000 gallons of wine. The vineyards are mostly along the upper Moselle and Sauer rivers, and the wines resemble those of Germany. They are not, however, equal in quality to the wines of the middle Moselle Valley.

The Low Countries (Belgium and Holland).—The grape industry, covering about 500 acres, is principally under glass. The climate is not favorable for outdoor culture to be entirely successful. There are, however, a few vineyards in southern Belgium.

The industry in the hothouses is concerned entirely with table grapes. Production amounts to about 3,800 tons, 900 tons of which are exported. By judicious regulation of the temperature of the houses, grapes can be placed on the market at any season of the year. Cluster and berry sizes

FIGURE 11: A wide sloping-top trellis used in northern Italy. (*Courtesy of Professor I. Cosmo*)

are controlled by careful thinning. The more extensively grown varieties are Black Alicante, Black Hamburg, Gros Colman, Muscat of Alexandria, Prince of Wales, Ribier, and Royal.

Portugal.—As early as 1367, Portugal exported wine to England. Grapes are grown in all the provinces of the country. The total vineyard area is about 840,000 acres, with an annual production of about 284,800,000 gallons of wine. In general, the wines are quite variable in type and quality. Port, however, the prime product of the country, is renowned the world over.

The principal producing districts are as follows:

The PORT region includes the upper valley of the Douro River, together with the valleys of some of its tributaries in the northern part of the country. The wines at the higher elevations are better than those grown at lower levels. This is the region of origin of port. Production is expanding. The port wines are produced principally from Alvarelhão, Bastardo, Mourisco preto, Souzão, Touriga, and a few other minor varieties.

The PLAINS OF MINHO region lies north of the Douro River. Its wines appear in commerce as *vinhos verdas*, the beverage wines of northern Portugal; the quality is not comparable to that of the wines of the upper Douro Valley, east from Villa Real. The vinhos verdas are usually consumed young, hence the name "green wines."

The TAGUS PLAINS region lies mostly in the area between Coimbra and Setubal and comprises the coastal plain north and south of Lisbon, together with the lower valley of the Tagus River. Mostly light, common wines are produced. They are produced of such varieties as Arinto, Castello, and Donna branca.

The southern region between Portalegre and Faro, to the east and south of Lisbon, also produces common wines, except around Faro, where some estimable red and white wines are produced.

Some 60,000,000 gallons of wine are exported; about one-eighth of the total is port wine. England is still the principal outlet.

The production of table grapes in Portugal is of only local interest.

The MADEIRA Islands are part of Portugal and are situated to the southwest of it, in the Atlantic Ocean. Grapes have been grown on the main island of the group, Madeira, since 1421. The important districts are on the south coast, near Funchal and Câmarâ de Lôbos. The best known wine is malmsey, which is the true Madeira wine. The wines are made from Boal, Malvasia, Verdelho, and Sercial grapes. The grape industry is no longer so important as it was before the advent of phylloxera in 1873.

Romania.—The climate of Romania is mostly typical mid-continental European, with cold winters and hot summers. In some sections the vines must be covered in winter to prevent freezing. The wine varies in quality from some very good, of Central European varieties, to common wine,

Geographical Distribution of Grape Growing

made from certain direct-bearing hybrids. Romania has some 840,000 acres in grapes and produces about 158,000,000 gallons of wine.

Table grapes, such as Afus Ali (Dattier), Chasselas doré and Muscat Hamburg, are produced both for domestic markets and export. About 30 per cent is exported to Russia, Czechoslovakia, and Central Europe. Production is about 360,000 tons.

Russia (U.S.S.R.).—Grape growing in Russia is largely limited to the areas adjacent to the Black and Caspian seas, the area between these seas, and parts of Turkestan (in Asia). Acreage declined during the Russian Revolution and the phylloxera attack on the vineyards. Early reconstruction was largely with direct-producing hybrids. More recently, under government control, the vineyards in the better locations have been replanted with European varieties. At this time there are about 2,600,000 acres of grapes, producing about 623,000,000 gallons of wine, many thousands of gallons of sweet juice, about 700,000 tons of table grapes, and 23,000 tons of raisins. The acreage is being expanded very rapidly. In many of the vineyards not protected by the tempering influence of the Black and Caspian seas the vines are covered to guard against freezing in winter. Although done by machine, covering with soil is costly in the loss of buds. According to Gerasimova (1965), a fungus, *Rhacodiella vitis*, which causes spotted necrosis, destroys many buds. Other types of protection—mats, rushes, or tarpaulin—overcome the necrosis, but are limited in their application. Chemical controls also are effective but hardly applicable in soil covering.

Moldavia, which lies next to Romania, is the most important grape-producing territory. Many of its vineyards are planted to such varieties as Riesling, Traminer, Aligote, and Cabernet. According to Gerasimov (1956), the Traminer yields the best white table wine and the Cabernet the best red. These wines are known throughout Russia. The Ukraine grows the same European varieties just listed for Moldavia, plus the Sémillon and Chenin blanc and a somewhat higher proportion of non-European varieties. The southern part of the Crimea is regarded very highly by the Russians because of the high degree of sweetness attained by the grapes there. Tokaj-type wine is produced from the Furmint and other varieties used in Hungary, and from local varieties. Other European varieties grown there include Pedro Ximenes, Sémillon, Zante (Black Corinth), Mataro, and Carignane. The Crimea also produces dessert wines. Around Sevastopol, in this area, and in the region surrounding the towns of Anapa-Novorossisk, Krasnodar, and Stravropol, both dry table and sparkling wines are made. This is the champagne region of Russia. One of the cellars has been producing sparkling wine of Pinot noir and Chardonnay for 140 years. To the north, along the lower reaches of the Don River, the primary product is light table wines. In the northern Caucasus and Dagestan, ordinary table wines are produced. To the south, in Georgia, Armenia, and Azerbaijan, and to the east, in southern Turkestan, large quantities of dessert and ordinary table wines are produced, mostly from Russian and mid-Asian varieties. For further information see Dalmasso and Tyndalo (1957).

Table grapes are grown around the northern end of the Caspian Sea—in Dagestan, Georgia, Armenia, and Azerbaijan—and in the central Asian states of Turkmenistan, Uzbekistan, and Tadzhikistan. Some of these are European varieties, but most are such varieties as Hussaine, Maska, Narma, Nimrang, Obak, Tcheljagi, Sultoni, and Vasergua from Asia. Some of these varieties are said to ship well and be marketed widely in Russia.

According to Egoroff, 1940), raisin production is largely limited to the states of Turkmenistan, Uzbekistan, and Tadzhikistan. The monthly mean temparture and rainfall records for Samarkand, in Uzbekistan, are similar to those for Fresno, California. The leading varieties are Ak-Kish-mish (Thompson Seedless) and Kara-Kishmish (monukka). Three types of raisins are produced: natural, dried on packed earth slabs or on roofs, without pretreatment; lye-dipped, dried on earth slabs; and sulfur-bleached, dried in well-ventilated houses.

Spain.—The Spanish vineyards cover much of the slopes and valleys of every province. The total vineyard area approximates 3,900,000 acres, with an annual production of about 615,000,000 gallons of wine, 6,500 tons of raisins, and 340,000 tons of table grapes. The vineyard area is large, but yields are very low in some districts.

The climate is favorable for grape growing, especially in the eastern and southern parts of the country, and less so in the central and northern parts. Annual rainfall on the Mediterranean coast varies from 12 to 24 inches, falling mostly during winter and spring. The dryness of the summers assists disease control. The south coast, from Jerez to Alicante, and the region around Córdoba have the highest annual mean temperatures. Maximum summer temperatures, however, are higher in the province of Valencia than in the southern provinces. Much of the interior country is semiarid. Many of the vineyards have the vines planted wide apart so that they will have sufficient moisture to endure the long, dry summers.

The most important wine-producing regions are as follows:

The RIOJA region is in the upper Ebro Valley, in the provinces of Logroño and Álava. This region, in north-central Spain, produces mostly red wine—*Rioja*—made principally from Grenache, Tempranillo, Graciano, Mazuela, Malvasia, and Viura grapes. These are the best red table wines of Spain. This region profited materially during the years when grapes were short in France because of the ravages of phylloxera. French vintners came and supervised the making of wines, which were then shipped to France and sold as clarets and burgundies. In consequence, the vineyards were expanded and the quality of the wines was improved.

Probably the richest wine-producing region of Spain, is CATALONIA, in the northeastern corner of the country. Both red and white vines of various types are produced there.

In the southeastern quadrant of the country, from VALENCIA to around SEVILLE, many kinds of wine—red and white dry wines, fortified sweet wines, muscatel, etc.—are produced. The vines are grown on both level and rolling land, and in some cases far back in the mountains.

At the southern point of Spain, JEREZ DE LA FRONTERA, in the province of Cádiz, produces the fortified white wine known in commerce as sherry. The characteristic flavor and bouquet of this wine is obtained by holding it at favorable temperatures in partly filled casks for extended periods. Often the casks are exposed to the direct rays of the sun. A film-forming yeast grows on the surface and imparts the special bouquet and flavor to the wine. When the desired character is obtained, the types are standardized by passing the wines through a series of casks—the solera process. Wine is withdrawn from the oldest cask and replaced with wine from the next-oldest cask, and so on down the line to the youngest cask, to which is added wine of the last season. Only a fraction of the wine in the oldest cask is withdrawn each year. Sherry is produced of Palomino, Albillo, Mantuo Pilas, Mantuo Castellano, and Pedro Ximenes grapes. It is Spain's most distinguished wine.

The table grapes are grown in the southern and southeastern parts of the country. Probably every country of western Europe and nearly every country of North and South America has received Spanish Almeria (Ohanez) grapes, which are packed in granulated cork. Another important variety is the Molinera gordo (Red Malaga in California).

The raisin industry of Spain dates back to ancient times; according to Eisen (1890), raisins are known to have been exported from Málaga since 1295 A.D. and were produced in Spain many centuries before that. There are two main producing districts, both bordering on the Mediterranean coast. The southern district is in the province of Málaga, and the northern district is in the provinces of Valencia and Alicante. Practically all of the Spanish raisins are made from the Muscat of Alexandria, which are dried on the clusters without pretreatment and are marketed unstemmed as "cluster raisins" or "layers." They are particularly in demand in European markets during the holiday season. To shorten the drying period, the Valencia raisins are dipped in hot water or in a hot solution of soda or lye before being dried. The dried product, stemmed, enters the market as loose raisins. A high proportion of all raisins is exported.

Switzerland.—Grape growing is of great importance in districts of western, northern, and southern Switzerland. The largest areas of contiguous vineyards are in the Rhone Valley, on the north shore of Lake Geneva

Geographical Distribution of Grape Growing

from Rolle to Montreux, and in Neuchâtel. There the principal variety is Chasselas doré. In other parts of the country—the upper Rhine Valley and Ticino—are numerous small areas on the warmer southern slopes.

The number of vineyards and volume of wine production were once much greater that at present. At present there is a shift in the Rhine basin from white to red grapes, for which there is greater demand. The change is from the white varieties—Elbling, Chasselas doré, Riesling—to selections of Pinot noir. Currently the acreage amounts to about 29,000 acres. Wine production amounts to about 26,000,000 gallons. No table grapes are grown. Sweet juice production, however, is important, with an annual output of over 1,000,000 gallons.

Yugoslavia.—Vineyards are found in all parts of Yugoslavia, but about 85 per cent of production is in the states of Croatia and Serbia. Most of the wines are of ordinary quality. Mostly white wines are produced in Croatia, in the inland area along the Sava and Drava rivers; red wines predominate along the coast of the Adriatic Sea. The best wines of the latter area are made of local varieties, grown on the hillsides. The islands along the coast produce wines that have merit for blending.

The most important Serbian vineyards are widely scattered over the hills throughout the northern and eastern parts of the state. Both white and red wines are produced. The better white wines are found in the northern part, mostly north of the Sava and Danube rivers, where white varieties of central Europe are grown.

In Slovenia, in the northwestern part of the country, some wines are of superior quality. The principal vineyard districts lie on the Adriatic slope, and in the Sava and Drava valleys. The best wines of this state and of the country are those of the Drava Valley. Again, these are the product of central European varieties: Walschriesling, Sylvaner, Sauvignon blanc, and Traminer.

The other regions produce only moderate quantities and their wines are less well known.

The vineyards cover some 650,000 acres, producing annually about 163,000,000 gallons of wine and 190,000 tons of table grapes. The principal table grape areas are in Croatia and Serbia. The varieties grown are Italia, Regina (Dattier), Servant, and a number of local sorts.

ASIA

Grape culture had its beginnings in Asia. Grapes are mentioned in Biblical history. Hesiod, who wrote during the 8th century b.c., is credited with giving very pratical directions for the care of the vine.

Grape production is now centered largely in Cyprus, Turkey, Israel, Syria, Iran, and Afghanistan. Elsewhere in Asia, aside from the Russian territories mentioned earlier, grape growing is relatively unimportant and is limited almost entirely to the production of table grapes, raisins, or wine for home and local consumption.

Cyprus.—This island in the eastern Mediterranean, just off the coast in Asia Minor, has hot, dry summers in which grapes thrive. The vineyard area is about 93,000 acres. Wine production amounts to about 20,422,000 gallons, of which a large part is exported. Raisin production, mostly for export, amounts to 8,000 tons and table grapes 25,400 tons annually.

Turkey.—Turkey has a favorable climate and, according to Oraman and Agaolia (1969), has had a grape industry since 3500 B.C. It ranks equally with Italy as one of the two most important producers of table grapes, second in raisin production, and fifth in acreage among the grape growing countries with 1,975,000 acres. Because of their light color and good quality, the raisins, particularly the Sultana type, have acquired an enviable reputation in European markets. Present production is about 199,080 tons annually. The most important provinces in raisin production are Izmir (Smyrna) and Manisa. The authors mentioned above indicate that 37 per cent of the crop goes for raisins, 23 per cent (1,014,000 tons) for fresh consumption, 35 per cent for sweet juice, and 5 per cent (12,400,000 gallons) for wine.

Israel.—Grape growing and wine production flourished here in Biblical times. The industry has ebbed and flourished depending on who ruled the land. At present there are 22,500 acres producing 9,251,380 gallons of wine, 30,200 tons of table grapes, and 500 tons of raisins. Both wines and table grapes are exported in limited amounts. For a discussion of the viticulture of Israel see de Leon (1960).

Syria.—Syria has been producing grapes for centuries. Like its neighbors, Syria produces grapes primarily for home markets. At present there are about 210,000 acres producing 179,000 gallons of wine, 135,000 tons of table grapes and 10,000 tons of raisins. Some 25,000 tons of table grapes are exported.

Iran.—Some authors designate Iran as the place of origin of commercial grape growing. Grapes, either in the wild or cultivated state, grow almost everywhere in the mountains between the Persian Gulf and the Caspian Sea. There are numerous varieties of Persian (Iranian) origin. Now, there are about 185,000 acres in vineyards which produce 51,000 tons of raisins, 33,000 tons of table grapes and 95,000 gallons of wine. Iran ranks fifth in raisin production. About one-third of its raisins are exported, while the table grapes and wines are consumed locally.

Afghanistan.—Grncarevic (1969) estimates the grape area of Afghanistan at 148,260 acres. The production of table grapes amounts to about 190,000 tons, half of which is exported. The bulk of the crop, or 130,000 tons, is dried to produce some 34,000 tons of raisins. Of this tonnage, 60 per cent is exported.

Japan.—The wet climate of Japan is not favorable for *vinifera* grapes. A few are grown on the island of Hokkaido. Native grapes are *Vitis cognetiae* and *V. thumbergi* produce edible fruit, but most plantings are selections of *V. labrusca* or its hybrids. According to Yokotsuka (1955), the varieties Delaware, Koshu (supposedly *vinifera*), and Campbell Early account for almost half of the 57,000 acres of vines. Some 262,460 tons are used as table fruit. Wine production amounts to about 6,700,000 gallons annually.

China.—The grapes of China are mostly in Chinese Turkestan and in the provinces of Shansi and Kansu. No accurate estimate of acreage or production is available. The industry is, however, not extensive. Wine is made, grapes are used as table fruit, and grapes are dried for raisins.

GRAPES IN THE TROPICS

In tropical climates the grapevine is evergreen and in nature produces very poorly. It has been found, however, that by forcing the vine into two growth cycles, one in the wet and the other in the dry season, it produces profitably. By pruning at the beginning of the wet season a growth cycle is initiated in which a small crop of little value is produced. Following this, the vine is pruned again to induce another cycle of growth. During this cycle, in the dry season, the main crop of quality fruit is produced. Under dry tropical conditions, irrigation is used in conjunction with pruning to manage the growth cycles.

India.—This country has pioneered in the production of grapes under wet tropical conditions. Scattered vineyards have existed in the northern (temperate zone) states in India for many years; however, the primary industry, which is of relatively recent origin, is developing in the peninsula states, particularly Maharashta, Mysore, Andhra Pardesh, and Tamil Nadu. Table grapes predominate. According to Olmo (1970), there were 19,826 acres of grapes in 1968, which was an increase of 130 per cent over 1963. The vines are supported on overhead arbors. Yields are high. The principal varieties are Anab-e Shahi, Bangalore blue. Thompson Seedless, Bhakri, Cheeria-7, Perlette, and Muscat Hamburg. The acreage of wine grapes is expanding.

Thailand.—The grape industry in Thailand, like that in India, is of relatively recent origin. L. A. Lider (personal communication, 1972), who places the acreage at 9,000, indicates the principal districts of production as Nakru Pathom, Rajburi, Samut Sakorn, and Samut Songkram. The industry is developing in the "rice paddies." Raised beds, 10 feet wide and 3 to 4 feet high, alternate with open ditches about 4 feet wide. The ditches function as drains during the wet season and as a source of irrigation water

Geographical Distribution of Grape Growing

in the dry period. The vine rows are in the middle of the raised bed. The vines are trained to two to four cordons and supported on 4-foot high, flat top trellises, with 6 wires. The fruit produced in the dry season is of very good quality.

Vine management in the tropics is a problem and the vines are short lived. There is a very strong tendency for few or only the apical buds on the fruiting units to grow. Thus many units are required to produce the large crops; as a result, the vines tend to become brushy.

Pansoit and Libert (1971) and Vega (1971) list a number of other tropical countries that are growing grapes. Among these with their approximate acreage are Taiwan 2,500, Columbia 850, Ethiopia 400, Equador 380, the Phillippines 250, and Venezuela 250.

BIBLIOGRAPHY

André, P. 1958. Le jus de raisin. Vignes et Vins, 6(72):16–18.

Dalmasso, G., and V. Tyndalo. 1957. Viticoltura e ampelografia dell' U.R.S.S. Atti. Accad. Ital. Vite e Vino, 9:446–548.

Egoroff, P. 1940. The raisin industry in the U.S.S.R. Unpublished report, Dept. of Viticulture, University of California.

Eisen, G. 1890. The raisin industry. San Francisco, H. S. Crocker Co.

Folwell, R. J., and R. T. Dailey. 1972. Washington grape acreage. Washington Agric. Exp. Sta. Circular 558:1–7.

Geraimov, Z. 1965. Spotted necrosis in Kirgizia and its control (trans. title). Vinodelie i Vinogradarstvo, 25:35–37. (See also Hort. Abs. 36:2768.)

Gerasimova, M. A. 1956. Viticulture et viniculture en Union Sovetique. Vignes et Vins, 6(48):14–16, (49):12.

Grncarevic, M. 1969. Drying and processing grapes in Afghanistan. Amer. J. Enol. Vitic., 20:198–202.

Henderson, W. W., and J. M. Kitterman. 1969 and 1971. California fruit and nut statistics. Sacramento, California State Department of Agriculture.

Henderson, W. W., J. Kitterman, J. Swedberg, G. Boeger, G. Nelson, D. Johnson, and C. Weems. 1971. California fruit and nut statistics. Sacramento, California State Department of Agriculture.

Leon, de J. 1960. La viticolura in Palestina. Atti Accad. Ital. Vite e Vino., 11:231–306.

Olmo, H. P. 1970. F.A.O. report to the government of India on grape culture, Rome. United Nations Development Programme. No. TA 2825.

Oraman, M. N., and Y. S. Agaolia. 1969. Some characteristics of Turkey's viticulture and the comparison of its districts in viticulture. Yr. Book, Faculty Univ. Ankara.

Pansoit, F. P., and J. R. Libert. 1971. Culture de la vigne en pays tropicaux. Bull. Off. Int. Vin, 44:596–661.

Protin, R. 1968, 1969, and 1970. Situation de la viticulture dans le monde. Vols. 42, 43, and 44.

Shand, P. M. 1929. A book of other wines than French. New York, Knopf.

Vega, J. 1971. Culture de la vigne en pays tropicaux. Bull. Off. Int. Vigne et du Vin, 44:775–786.

Yokotsuka, S. 1955. The grape growing and wine industry of Japan. Amer. Jour. Enol., 6(3):16–22.

4

Climate and Soils

Grapes are native to the warm temperate zone and their culture is most successful between 34° and 49° north and south latitude. Using mean temperature, the principal limiting factor, Prescot (1965) further circumscribed the areas suitable for grape production as follows: "The mean temperature of the warmest monthly period must be in excess of 66° F. and that of the coldest monthly period must be in excess of 30° F." Grapes are grown beyond both of these demarcations in both hemispheres, but only in special areas.

The most northerly distribution of vineyards is in Germany, in the Rhine Valley, where grapes are grown between 50° and 51° north latitude. Only the warmest locations at low altitudes are suitable, and the vines are planted on steep south and west slopes. There the shortening length of day beginning in August is an important factor in production, since, as Alleweldt (1963) has shown, the shorter days retard cane growth, accelerate fruit maturing, and stimulate cane ripening, which increases winter hardiness.

At the other extreme, in tropical climates, the vine is evergreen, produces poorly, and tends to be short lived. In the past, grapes grown in the tropical zones were planted at higher and higher elevations as the equator was approached. For example, some plantings in Bolivia at 16° south latitude are above 9,000 feet. These grapes in reality are still in or near temperate zone conditions. In recent years, however, by control of the growth cycles of the vine, grape production has become an expanding industry in a number of tropical countries (see p. 55).

In California, because of the long growing season and the almost continuous favorable conditions of light and temperature, grapes are grown in numerous locations near the coast (in region I) where the mean monthly temperature for the warmest monthly period never reaches 66° F. In this State grapes are grown at elevations from 200 feet below sea level, in the Coachella Valley, to above 4,000 feet, in the Owens Valley. Most commercial vineyards, however, are above sea level and below 1,000 feet. In general, the upper limit of grape growing is 5,000 to 6,500 feet below the timber line.

Vineyards are usually highly localized areas within the limits outlined above. It is common knowledge that different localities at the same latitude and altitude differ greatly in climates. Local variations are very important, not only in their general influence on the cost and returns of the industry, but also because they affect greatly the choice of varieties, the training and pruning, the cultural practices, and the quality of the product.

For best development the *vinifera* grape requires long, warm-to-hot, dry summers and cool winters. It is not suited to humid summers, owing to its susceptibility to certain fungus diseases and insect pests that flourish under humid conditions. Neither will it withstand intense winter cold. A long growing season is required to mature the fruit, and, since the green parts of growing vines are likely to be frozen at temperatures below 30° F., areas regularly subject to late spring and early fall frosts must be avoided. Rain is desirable during the winter, but deficiencies in rainfall can be made up by irrigation. Rains early in the growing season make disease and pest control difficult, but are otherwise not deterimental to the growth of the vine. Rains or cloudy weather during the blooming period may result in a poor set of the berries, especially in some varieties, and rains during ripening and harvest cause damage through fruit rot. Where raisins are to be produced by sun-drying between the vine rows, as in California, a month of clear, warm, rainless weather is essential after the grapes are mature. Higher humidity can be tolerated in cool regions than in warm regions.

American grapes—mostly *labrusca* varieties and hybrids containing *labrusca*—and European direct producers that are hybrids of *vinifera* with one or more American species will withstand humid summers and cold winters better than pure *vinifera* varieties. The *labrusca* and *labrusca*-hybrid varieties do best in moderate summer humidity and are not suited to semi-arid climates, such as those in the interior valleys of California and parts of the southwestern United States. Varieties of *Vitis rotundifolia* thrive in very warm, humid areas of the southeastern states.

Broadly, climate limits grape production to the Temperate Zone and further limits the highest development of individual varieties to localized areas within this zone. For example, the table-grape variety Tokay (Flame Tokay) attains its best development in the warm, dry area within a radius of five miles surrounding the city of Lodi, California. Similarly, the table-grape variety Emperor is restricted to a hot, dry district in eastern Fresno, Tulare, and Kern counties. Comparable examples for given varieties, though seldom so restricted, are to be found in most countries that produce table grapes.

The centuries of experience and research of European growers and enologists have definitely established the effect of climate on wine grapes. Climate influences the rates of change in the constituents of the fruit during development and the composition at maturity. Moderately cool weather, under which ripening proceeds slowly, is favorable for the production of dry table wines of quality. Cool weather fosters a high degree of acidity, a low pH, and a good color, and in most table wine varieties it brings to the mature fruit optimum development of the aroma and flavoring constituents and the precursors of the bouquet and flavoring substances of the wines. The combination of specific environmental conditions with the qualities of a given variety has made possible the Rieslings of Germany, the Clarets and Burgundies of France, the Chiantis of Italy, the Constantias of South Africa, and other renowned wines. If, however, varieties lack special character, even the most favorable climate will not endow the resulting wines with good quality. Table wines from such varieties will be improved—because of a better balance of the sugar, acid, tannin, and flavor of the grapes at maturity—but they will still lack such special qualities as the bouquet and freshness that are characteristic of premium-quality wines.

In warm climates the aromatic qualities of the grapes lose delicacy and richness, and the other constituents of the fruit are less well balanced; hence the resulting table wines, even from the best grape varieties, cannot compare with the best wines of cooler regions. In very hot regions, where growth and ripening changes proceed with great rapidity, the taste of most dry wines is harsh and coarse, and the other components are so poorly balanced that usually only common dry table wines can be made.

The abundance of heat in some regions, which makes them poorly suited for dry wines, makes them ideal for such dessert wines as port, muscatel, and sherry. With abundant heat the varieties especially suited to the production of such wines attain their most nearly perfect development. Large summations of heat, especially just before and during ripening, favor a high ratio of sugar to acid in the fruit, and the ill effect of the heat on aroma and flavor is less than in the case of table wines.

CLIMATIC REGIONS

In the investigations of factors affecting wine quality, begun in 1935, it was found that the geographic regions of California (chap. 3) that had served well for locating table and raisin grapes did not delineate the effects of climate sharply enough to serve similarly for wine grapes (Amerine and Winkler, 1944). In some instances the geographic regions showed widely varying climatic factors, especially in heat summation, and in other instances there were no differences, in certain factors, between one region and another. For example, the range of heat summation in the Sacramento Valley is almost identical with that in the San Joaquin Valley, whereas there is a wide diversity of heat summations within the North Coast region.

Therefore, available climatological data of United States Weather Bureau stations and the stations of the Department of Viticulture and Enology, University of California, were summarized for the areas where grapes are produced successfully for wine making. Then the principal climatic factors of the areas were correlated with the analytical data and quality scores of the matured wines of the areas. The only factor of climate that proved to be of predominant importance was temperature.

Other factors, such as rainfall, fog, humidity, and duration of sunshine, may have effects, but these are much more limited than the effect of heat summation. Amount and time of rainfull definitely restrict the production of natural raisins to certain areas. Rainfall, fog, and humidity also influence the development of organisms that may have a marked effect on production costs and, as in the case of *Botrytis cineria* (noble rot), may, in certain varieties, be beneficial. Further, these factors of climate influence temperature, but no data show that they have a direct effect on the balance of the composition of the fruit at maturity, except when the noble rot intervenes. This finding, together with the very marked effect of temperature when expressed as heat summation above 50° F. from April through October, led Professors Amerine and Winkler (1944) to use heat summation as a basis for segregating the grape-producing areas of the state into five climatic regions.

Heat summation, as used here, means the sum of the mean monthly temperature above 50° F. for the period concerned. The base line is set at 50° F., because there is almost no shoot growth below this temperature. The summation is expressed as degree-days. For example, if the mean for a day is 70° F., the summation is 20 degree-days, and, if the mean for June is 65° F., the summation is 450 degree-days (15 degrees times 30 days). The importance of heat summation above 50° F. (10° C.) as a factor in grape quality has also been indicated by Koblet and Zwïcky (1965). They found that degree Brix was more closely correlated with heat summation above 50° F. than with total heat summation or hours of sunshine, under the cool condition of Wädenswil.

The heat summations for the climatic regions are: I, less than 2,500 degree-days; II, 2,501 to 3,000 degree-days; III, 3,001 to 3,500 degree-days;

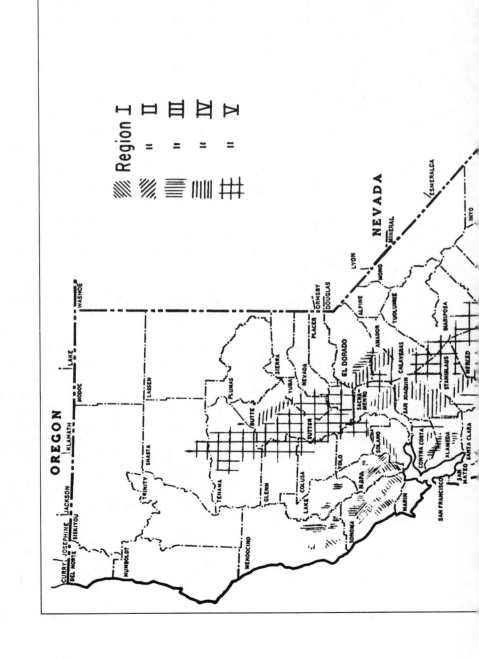

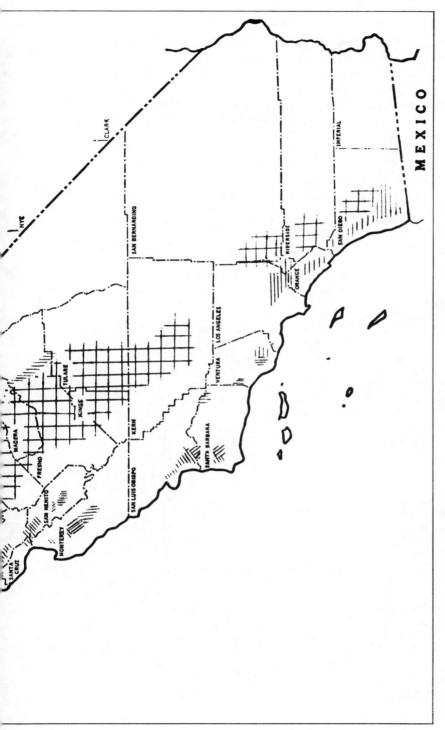

FIGURE 12: The climatic regions of California, based on heat summation above 50°F.

Climate and Soils

IV, 3,501 to 4,000 degree-days; and V, 4,001 or more degree-days. Some characteristics of the climatic regions in California and their adaptation to important wine-producing localities follow. For further information on the location of the different climatic regions in California see figure 12. Typical and potential wine producing locations and their heat summation as degree-days for California along with a few well-known foreign areas are shown in table 3.

TABLE 3

HEAT SUMMATION AS DEGREE-DAYS ABOVE 50° F. FOR THE PERIOD
APRIL 1 TO OCTOBER 31 AT VARIOUS COUNTY LOCATIONS
IN CALIFORNIA AND A FEW FOREIGN LOCATIONS

Station and county or country	Heat summation	Station and county or country	Heat summation
Climatic Region I locations			
Trier, Germany	1700 *	Woodside, San Mateo	2320
Geisenheim, Germany	1790 *	Nevada City, Nevada	2320
Branscomb, Humboldt	1810	Santa Cruz, Santa Cruz	2320
Reims, France	1820 *	Gonzales, Monterey	2350
Lompoc, Santa Barbara	1970	Hegglalya, Hungary	2360 †
Salem, Oregon	2030	Hayward, Alameda	2370
Weitchpec, Trinity	2080	Betteravia, Santa Barbara	2370
Watsonville, Santa Cruz	2090	Peachland, Sonoma	2380
Bonny Doon, Santa Cruz	2140	Ben Lomond, Santa Cruz	2390
Campbell, Santa Clara	2160	Bordeaux, France	2390 *
Coonawarra, Australia	2170 W	Geneva, New York	2400
Aptos, Santa Cruz	2190	Cuyamaca, San Diego	2410
Wrights, Santa Clara	2220	Anderson Valley High	
Roseburg, Oregon	2220	School, Mendocino	2400
Blocksburg, Humboldt	2230	Erie, Pennsylvania	2450
Idlewilde, Riverside	2240	Santa Maria, Santa Barbara	2490
Geneva, Switzerland	2260 N	El Gavlin Vd., San Benito	2480
Beaune, France	2300 *		
Climatic Region II locations			
Willits, Mendocino	2520	Grass Valley, Nevada	2830
Aukland, New Zealand	2540 N	Crocket, Contra Costa	2840
Santa Clara, Santa Clara	2550	Ankara, Turkey	2840 N
Weaverville, Trinity	2550	Atascadero,	
Sunnyside, Washington	2570	San Luis Obispo	2870
Odessa, Russia	2580 *	Redwood City, San Mateo	2870
Budapest, Hungary	2570 N	Soledad, Monterey	2880 ‡
Palo Alto, San Mateo	2590	Napa, Napa	2880

TABLE 3 (*Continued*)

Station and county or country	Heat summation	Station and county or country	Heat summation
Yakima, Washington	2600	Santa Barbara, Santa Barbara	2820
San Luis Obispo, San Luis Obispo	2620	Los Gatos, Santa Clara	2880
Gilroy, Santa Clara	2630	San Mateo, San Mateo	2880
Sebastapol, Sonoma	2630	Hollister, San Benito	2890
Grants Pass, Oregon	2680	Monte Rosso Vd., Sonoma	2900
Covelo, Mendocino	2710	Asti, Italy	2930 †
Santiago, Chile	2710 N	Kelseyville, Lake	2930
Hulville, Sonoma	2720	Santa Rosa, Sonoma	2950
Petaluma, Sonoma	2740	Sonoma, Sonoma	2950
Dyerville, Humboldt	2750	Bucharest, Romania	2960 N
Melbourne, Australia	2750 N	Placerville, El Dorado	2980
San Jose, Santa Clara	2760	Novorossisk, Russia	2990 *

Climatic Region III locations

Station and county or country	Heat summation	Station and county or country	Heat summation
Oakville, Napa	3100 ‡	Milan, Italy	3310 N
Ukiah, Mendocino	3100	Pinnacles, San Benito	3330
Upper Lake, Lake	3100	Cuyama, Santa Barbara	3340
Paso Robles, San Luis Obispo	3100	Santa Ana, Orange	3360
Calistoga, Napa	3150	Tibilis, Russia	3370 *
King City, Monterey	3150	Jamestown, Tuolumne	3400
Hopland, Mendocino	3150 ‡	Camino, El Dorado	3400
Astrakhan, Russia	3160 *	Queretaro, Mexico	3400 ++
St. Helena, Napa	3170	Mokelumne Hill, Calaveras	3400
Santa Margarita, San Luis Obispo	3180	Livermore, Alameda	3400
Healdsburg, Sonoma	3190	Potter Valley, Mendocino	3420
Poway, San Diego	3220	Cloverdale, Sonoma	3430
Clear Lake Park, Lake	3260	Ramona, San Diego	3470
North Fork, Madera	3260	Mandeville Island, San Joaquin	3480
Hamadan, Iran	3280 D		

Climatic Region IV locations

Station and county or country	Heat summation	Station and county or country	Heat summation
Martinez, Contra Costa	3500	Gallo Vd., Merced	3740
Escondido, San Diego	3510	Nacimento, San Luis Obispo	3740
Upland, San Bernardino	3520	Davis, Yolo	3780
Suisun, Solano	3530	Vacaville, Solano	3780
Florence, Italy	3530 N		

TABLE 3 (*Continued*)

Station and county or country	Heat summation	Station and county or country	Heat summation
Colfax, Placer	3530	Sidney, Australia	3780 [N]
Venice, Italy	3530	Sacramento, Sacramento	3830
Sao Paulo, Brazil	3540 [N]	Delta, Shasta	3850
Turlock, Stanislaus	3600	Clarksburg, Yolo	3860
Linden, San Joaquin	3620	Sonora, Tuolumne	3880
Mendosa, Argentina	3640 [**]	San Miguel,	
Vista, San Diego	3660	San Luis Obispo	3890
Beck, Stanislaus	3676 [G]	Aguascalentas, Mexico	3900 [++]
Pomona, Los Angeles	3680	Fontana, San Bernardino	3900
Lodi, San Joaquin	3720	Auburn, Placer	3990
Capetown, South Africa	3720 [N]		

Climatic Region V locations

Ojai, Ventura	4010	Shiraz, Iran	4390 [D]
Modesto, Stanislaus	4010	Reedley, Tulare	4410 [‡]
Perth, Australia	4020 [N]	Merced, Merced	4430
Oakdale, Stanislaus	4030	Chico, Butte	4450
Split, Yugoslavia	4090 [N]	Fresno, Fresno	4680
Brentwood, Contra Costa	4100	Red Bluff, Tehama	4930
Palermo, Italy	4100	Bakersfield, Kern	5080
Stockton, San Joaquin	4160	Algeria, Algers	5200 [†]
Antioch, Contra Costa	4200	Tehran, Iran	5210 [N]
Woodland, Yolo	4210	Terreon, Mexico	5900 [++]
Peking, China	4290 [N]		

SOURCE OF DATA: Climatological Data Reports, U.S. Weather Bureau;
    * Prescott (1965); **, Eggenberger (1971); †, U.S. Trade Consuls; ++, Mr. M. Ibarra; ‡, Department of Viticulture and Enology Stations; [N], Nelson (1968); [W], Wynn (1968); [D], Development and Resources Corp. Sacramento, California; [G], Grape Improvement Association.

Region I.—This region contains restricted areas of fertile soils. As a rule, hillside slopes and valley areas of moderate productivity are available for vines. The early maturing premium-quality dry table wine varieties attain their best development here. Heavy-bearing varieties should not be planted, since their production cannot compete with that of warmer districts with more fertile soils.

Region II.—An area of great importance. The valleys can produce most of the premium-quality and good standard white and red table wines of

Climate and Soils

California. The less productive slopes and hillsides vineyards cannot compete in growing grapes for standard wines, because of lower yield, but, nevertheless, can produce favorable yields of fine wines. Irrigation is beneficial in the areas of low rainfall.

Region III.—Another important region. The lands are generally level or slightly sloping and fertile, except for some that are gravelly or stony and of only moderate depth. The moderately warm climate favors the production of grapes of favorable sugar content—sometimes with low acid, as may occur in warm years. Excellent red wines of later maturing premium quality varieties are the rule here. White wines of fine quality may be produced in limited areas on the lighter soils and on slopes with exacting vineyard management. Excellent natural sweet wines and good white and red wines can be produced on the more fertile soils. The best of the port varieties of moderate productivity will produce excellent port-type wines. Irrigation is beneficial in the areas of low rainfall.

Region IV.—The soils in region IV are generally fertile. Most vineyards

FIGURE 13: A wine grape vineyard in region I of the North Coastal area of California in spring. (*Courtesy of Wine Institute*)

are irrigated and are capable of producing large crops. Some of the soils on the slopes of the east side of the Intermediate Central Valley region and in San Diego County are less fertile and less productive, but their grapes may be of better quality. Natural sweet wines are possible here, but in warm years the fruit of the most acceptable varieties tends to be low in acid. The white and red dessert wines produced here are of good quality. The white and red table wines are satisfactory if produced from the better, high-acid varieties.

Region V.—This region embraces the Sacramento Valley from Sacramento to Redding and the San Joaquin Valley from Merced to Arvin. The soils are the most uniformly fertile in California. Except for a few vineyards near Redding and some in the lower foothills, the region is entirely in the highly productive irrigated interior valleys. Of the regions that can produce wine grapes, this has the hottest climate. Standard red and white table wines of varying qualities can be made from the better high-acid varieties. The white and red dessert wines produced can be very good.

Table 4 shows typical effect of heat summation on the color content and total acidity of several varieties of wine grapes in California.

The climatic regions into which the grape-producing areas of California have been divided is a basic advance in the development of variety-climatic relationships. The climatic conditions of the present regions merge from one into the other, so the boundaries are not definite. Neither are conditions uniform within a given region. Nevertheless, the figures for heat summation in regions I, II and III provide a valuable indicator of the quality level of the wines of the premium varieties produced in the coastal areas of California. Similarly, heat summation provides a basis for differentiating the interior valleys into regions; some limited areas there have the same heat summation as the warmer coastal regions, but quality levels of the interior valley wines of the same varieties and same climatic regions are not comparable. As reported by Alley *et al.* (1971), the wines of the interior areas tend to be flat, unbalanced, lacking in varietal aroma and finish. These deficiencies are likely owing to factors of climate, such as the heat summation above a given temperature, say 70° F., differences in heat summation during the ripening period, and lower relative humidity. For instance, three region III locations, each with a heat summation of 3,400° day above 50° F., have the following degree-days above 70° F.: Livermore (coastal area) 15, Jamestown and Mokelume Hill (both interior areas) 295 and 353, respectively. The average yearly degree-days above 70° F. for four well known locations—namely, Bakersfield with 1,168, Fresno with 913, Lodi with 311. and St. Helena with 72—when related to the scores of table wines from those areas further indicate the injurious effects of higher and higher temperatures on wine quality. Working with Tokay over a period of 13 years, Winkler and Williams (1939),

TABLE 4

INFLUENCE OF REGIONAL CONDITIONS ON THE COLOR AND PER CENT
ACIDITY OF GRAPES, CALIFORNIA

Variety	Region				
	I	II	III	IV	V
	Color value by vino-colorimeter				
Carignane	100	83	57	49	45
Mataro	65	55	20	15	8
Petite Sirah	200	140	89	80	64
Zinfandel	200	110	65	40	20
	Total acid, per cent of grapes (as tartaric)				
Burger	0.90	0.69	0.49	0.42	0.41
Petite Sirah	.93	.74	.66	.60	.51
Zinfandel	.88	.67	.56	.57	.44

SOURCE OF DATA: Winkler and Amerine (1938) and Winkler (1938).

found that the heat summation during the ripening period had a marked
influence on table grape quality. In years with near 700 degree-days during
ripening the fruit was very good, while in years when the heat summation
above 50° F. was near 600 degree-days the fruit scored very poor.

These divisions into climatic regions should be considered as general
demarcations. Normal year-to-year fluctuations in heat summation may
in some years show a borderline area, as shown in table 3, to be in a lower
region one year or a higher region of heat summation the next, as the case
may be. It is to be hoped that refinements will be developed so as to
delimit subregions within the present regions, thereby ensuring the greatest potential for quality when the most favorable climatic subregion for
a given variety is planted to that variety. Such refinements will largely be
the responsibility of local information agencies and alert grower-wine producers. This is being done by the agricultural extension service with numerous temperature stations in Sonoma County (Mr. R. L. Sission, personal
communication), and in Stanislaus County (P. D. La Vine, 1971), as well
as by a number of growers in various parts of the state. Valuable climatic
information can be obtained in several years by comparing the readings of
a calibrated weather unit with those of a nearby Standard Weather
Bureau Station. The importance of a more restricted climatic area is
stressed by the above work, by the well-known relations of area of production to quality in Germany, France, and Italy, and by the work of
Vagulans (1954) in Russia.

Seasonal conditions.—In addition to the general effect of climate there

FIGURE 14: A vineyard in the San Joaquin Valley district, with grapes on trays for raisin production (region V). (*Courtesy of California Raisin Advisory Board*)

is a seasonal influence that is more or less marked according to the position of the producing region in the Temperate Zone. Wines of best quality are usually produced in the hot years of the coolest regions, whereas in the warm regions the cool years produce the higher-quality wines. Deviations from optimum conditions for maturing of the fruit are greater and most frequent in the coolest regions. Because California's present grape acreage is primarily in the warm part of the zone adapted for grape production, the belief is prevalent that every year is a "vintage year" in California. If this term simply designates years in which the grapes attain full maturity, such a belief is correct. By general as well as historical usage, however, the term "vintage year" properly designates a year of outstanding

Climate and Soils

quality. To say that California wines of all years are of outstanding or superior quality, or even to say that the wines of all years are of equal quality, is not in keeping with the facts. Data on the effects of seasonal conditions on palatability are presented in the discussion of table-grape maturity standards (p. 556).

SOILS FOR GRAPES

Grapes are adapted to a wide range of soil types. True, one finds a decided preference for certain soil types in nearly every grape-growing district. Nevertheless, when all soils used for growing the various kinds of grapes in the many different grape-producing regions of the world are compared, one finds that they range from gravelly sands to heavy clays, from shallow to very deep, and from low to high fertility. One should avoid heavy clays, very shallow soils, poorly drained soils, and those that contain high concentrations of salts of the alkali metals, boron, or other toxic substances.

Soils for Vinifera *grapes.*—Varieties of *Vitis vinifera* are deep-rooted plants that fully explore the soil to 6 to 10 feet or more if root penetration is not obstructed by hardpan, impervious clay substratum, toxic concentration of salts, or a free water table. The largest vines and the heaviest crops are produced on deep, fertile soils. The quality of the fruit is better, although yields are usually lower, on soils of lower fertility or soils limited in depth by hardpan, rocks, or clay substrata. In regions of heavy rainfall, good drainage is essential. Where rainfall is scanty and irrigation is practiced, sub-drainage must allow enough water to escape to prevent the accumulation of injurious concentrations of salts; otherwise, the vines will be short-lived.

Since *vinifera* grapes grow best in regions that have few or no summer rains, enough of the winter rains must be stored in the soil to carry the vines through the summer, or irrigation must be supplied. The first condition—dry farming—requires that the soil be deep and retain moisture. For example, in climatic region I of California, about 16 inches of water is required by the average vineyard of wine grapes each year. Each foot in depth of a loam soil will hold about 3 inches of available water. Thus, such a soil must be 5 feet or more in depth, or the vines will lack water before the crop is mature. Sandy soils hold less water, and must be correspondingly deeper. Where good irrigation water is available and carefully managed, grapes are being grown successfully on soils less than 2 feet deep.

High soil fertility, it is generally agreed, is not so important as soils of such structures that favor extensive root development. On such soils vine growth is less rank, and the ripening changes start earlier and proceed more slowly. At maturity, therefore, the fruit is firmer, of better balance, and has a rich, more pleasing aroma and flavor. Similar results may be obtained in shallow soils of somewhat higher fertility by using a summer cover crop to check vine growth early and by keeping the vines in good condition with judicious irrigation. The crop will, of course, be larger on very fertile soils, but the fruit will be of coarse texture, with composition poorly balanced, and its general character will be less pleasing. The less fertile soils are especially adapted for fine table grapes and premium-quality dry table-wine varieties. Returns on deep, fertile soils will generally be best from heavy-bearing varieties grown for raisins or for bulk-produced common wines.

When grown on their own roots, most *vinifera* varieties tolerate high concentrations of lime in the soil—50 to 70 per cent calcium carbonate. However, when rootstocks that resist phylloxera must be used, it is much easier to secure a suitable stock for soils of low or moderate lime content than for soils that are very high in lime. Grafted vines, such as the American grapes and hybrids, will also do better on somewhat deeper and more fertile soils.

Soils for American grapes.—The American grape varieties—Concord, Niagara, Catawba, etc.—and the direct producers—are, in general, more particular in their soil requirements. Compared to the *vinifera* varieties, they are not so deeply rooted, require a higher degree of fertility, cannot tolerate such high concentrations of lime, and are even more sensitive to the alkali salts. When water is adequate, either as summer rainfall or irrigation, and when a good supply of plant food is maintained, the American varieties can be grown on fairly shallow soils.

Soils of various grape-growing regions.—In most of the famous grape-growing and wine-producing regions of Europe and elsewhere, the belief is firm that a particular soil has much to do with the local success. Perhaps it does in some instances, but in others it is largely irrelevant. If the soil were so important a factor as is often claimed, there should be some uniformity in one or more characteristics between the soils of the various good districts. That there is little uniformity is revealed by a comparison of the soils of some of the best-known areas in a number of the older grape-producing countries.

In old vineyard areas of Europe, variety, soil, and climate are found in a most harmonious relationship. The soils of some of these areas, such as Burgundy, Champagne, and the upper Moselle Valley are very high in lime. Others, such as the Médoc, Graves, and some of the better vineyards in the Palatinate, are on light-to-heavy gravelly soils, with little lime. In Italy, the better areas vary from very light volcanic soils to heavy clays. In the Rheingau of Germany, Schloss Johannisberg has a red shale soil, yet the grapes of Steinberg, not far away, grow on loam to clay-loam soils.

This rather wide variation, or lack of uniformity, of soils in the areas generally recognized as among the best indicates the wide adaptability of *vinifera* varieties.

The French viticulturists, nevertheless, attribute great importance to the lime fraction of their soil. In the cool areas their opinion may be valid. The Italian viticulturists, in contrast, attach no special virtue to lime content. In Germany, much benefit is attributed to the slate-stone and shale soils, even though many of their excellent wines are made from grapes grown on soils of other types. Possibly the stony soils are of particular value in cool areas because, being low in moisture-holding capacity, they warm up more quickly, thereby fostering the earlier development of both the vines and the fruit. The slate stones also conserve fertility and soil by checking erosion on steep slopes.

In Australia Rankine *et al.* (1971) found that the quality of table wines is most closely related to grape variety, followed by climatic region, and, least of all, by soil type. They also state that soil type influenced the level of certain constituents of the grapes and wines, but had no significant effect on wine quality.

Turning to California, we find that the raisin grapes of the state are grown on irrigated, fertile alluvial valley soils varying in texture from sands to loams. Generally, the Thompson Seedless is grown on light to medium soils, and the Muscat on heavier soils. The soils range in age from old to very young, and are derived various kinds of rocks, with granitic and basaltic predominating. Vineyard soils in California rarely contain as much as 10 per cent free lime. Certain soil series, such as Hanford and Foster, are preferred because of high productivity, but Madera, Fresno, and Oakley soils are used extensively. The soils of the Hanford, Foster, and Oakley series are free of hardpan or compact clay strata to 6 feet or more, are easily worked, and are well drained. The coarse sands, particularly in the Hanford and Oakley series, may be low in fertility, whereas the sandy loams, when free of alkali, are ideal for raisin grapes. The Fresno and Madera soil series are respectively characterized by heavy clay and hardpan substrata at less than 6 feet. The deeper soils of the Madera, and the loam phases of the Fresno series of soils, are also extensively used for raisin production. They are not so desirable as the deep Hanford and Foster soils, but are used because they occur in great expanses in the climatic region that is almost ideal for raisin production.

Although the shallow soils of the San Joaquin series and the poorly drained alkali soils of the light-colored phase of the Fresno series occur in the raisin-producing area, they should generally be avoided.

California table grapes are produced on a number of soil types. The very early varieties, Perlette, Thompson Seedless, and Cardinal in the Hot Desert District— The Coachella and Imperial valleys—should be, and principally are, grown only on sandy or sandy-loam soils. Earliness is the essence of success in these areas, and grapes ripen earliest on sandy soils, which are the warmest. In the San Joaquin Valley the early grapes of Cardinal, Red Malaga, Ribier, and Thompson Seedless are also produced on sandy soils. Midseason and later grapes of these same varieties are grown on sandy loam or loam soils, where the berries grow larger and are of somewhat better over-all quality. Used extensively are soils of the Madera series, which are characterized by a hardpan at 3 to 6 feet. About 60 per cent of the Tokay acreage of the state is on Hanford fine sandy-loam soil, which occur extensively near Lodi, in the Intermediate Central Valley region. A smaller percentage is on sandy loam and on loams of the San Joaquin soil series that do not exceed 2 feet in depth. Over 90 per cent of the Emperor table grapes are grown on Madera sandy loam soil in a narrow belt along the eastern side of the San Joaquin Valley, from Fresno to Arvin, in climatic region V.

California wine grapes are grown on all the soil types and textures used for raisin and table grapes. as well as on the following soils: Akin, Bale, Esparto, Los Gatos, Pinole, Pleasanton, Rincon, Ryde, and other series. The Ryde soils differ from the mineral soils in their high organic content (10 to 20 per cent) and low pH (3.4 to 4.5) in the subsoil. As shown by Kissler and Carlton (1969), these differences in soil composition have little to no effect on vine growth, production, or wine quality when grown under similar climatic conditions. That roots tolerate low pH conditions was demonstrated in late 1920 (see p. 83). This is also supported by the work of Hiroyasu (1961). Grapes of good to excellent quality are produced by numerous varieties on practically all of the soil types, except those of the very heaviest texture. Premium-quality wines are produced on most of the soils when the climate is favorable.

The many soils on which vines are grown in the different grape-producing countries emphasizes the wide adaptation of the varieties of V. *vinifera* for soil. It is also a matter of record that a number of the varieties of highest quality produce excellent wines when grown on a number of quite different soil types. Also, there is no correlation between the level of mineral elements of an adapted soil and that of the musts or wines of grape grown on it (Siegel and Tartter, 1961). Thus, the differences in the character of wines can hardly be attributed to specific soil types. For an explanation of these it is necessary to consider the organic constituents, such as alcohol, acids, esters, color, tannins, and aldehydes, which have a direct bearing on the bouquet, taste and other qualities of individual wines. The levels and balance of these constituents in the musts or wines in turn are largely determined by climate (heat summation). This fact is pointed up in particular by the marked differences in the quality of wine of the same variety or varieties grown on similar soil types and texture but under different conditions of heat summation.

Climate and Soils

Climate is further emphasized by the highly localized production of certain table grapes, Tokay and Emperor, in California. As indicated, these grapes are grown primarily on single soil types covering large expanses in the San Joaquin Valley; yet it is only in the limited area of favorable heat summation that the fruit attains near perfection.

Even in the renowned wine-producing areas of Europe, with their varied soils, heat summation must be accepted as the principal factor in the control of quality: their vintage years always coincide with abundance of heat, and such years occur uniformly across all the soil types. The variety, with proper vinification and aging and through such inherent characteristics as aroma and flavoring constituents, determines the type of wine to be produced; but climate (primarily heat summation), by influencing the sugar-acid ratio, total acidity, tannin content, and minor constituents, determines the quality within the type.

BIBLIOGRAPHY

Alleweldt, G. 1963. Die Bedentung der Tageslänge für Rebenzüchtung und Weinbau. (The importance of day length for vine breeding and growing.) Gartenbauwissenschaft, 28:59–74.

Alley, C. J., C. S. Ough, and M. A. Amerine. 1971. Grapes for table wines in California's regions IV and V. Wines and Vines, 52(3):20–22.

Amerine, M. A. and A. J. Winkler. 1944. Composition and quality of musts and wines of California grapes. Hilgardia, 15:493–675.

Eggenberger, W. 1971. Weinbau und Traubenverwartung in Argentinien. Schweiz. Zeits., Obst. un Weinbau, 107:264–272.

Hiroyasu, T. 1961. Nutritional and physiological studies on grapevine. IV. Growth of vines as affected by the hydrogenion concentration of cultural solution. J. Jap. Soc. Hort. Sci., 30:357–360.

Kissler, J. J., and A. B. Carlton. 1969. The potential of wine grape production in the San Joaquin Delta Area of California. Amer. Jour. Enol. and Vitic., 20:40–47.

Koblet, W., and P. Zwicky. 1965. Der einfluss von Ertrag, Temperatur und Sonnenstunden auf die Qualität der Trauben. Wein-Wissen., 20:237–244.

La Vine, P. D. 1971. Grape Improvement Association weather study. Mimo. Farm Advisors Office, Modesto, California.

Nelson, H. L. 1968. Climatic data, for representative stations of the world. Lincoln, Nebraska, Univ. of Nebraska Press.

Prescott, J. A. 1965. The climatology of the vine (Vitis vinifera L.) the cool limits of cultivation. Trans. Roy. Soc. S. Aust., 89:5–23.

Rankine, B. C., J. C. M. Farnachon (deceased), E. W. Boehm, and K. M. Celler. 1971. Influence of grape variety, climate, and soil on grape composition and quality of table wines. Vitis, 10:33–50.

Siegel, O., and I. Tartter. 1961. Spektralanalytische Untersuchung von Traubenmost und Boden. Vitis, 2:283–287.

Vagulans, J. 1954. Sugar content and yield of grapes in relation to the active temperature sum during vegetation. [Trans. title.] Latvijas P. S. R. Zindatnu Akad. Vestis, 12(89):55–66. (*See also:* Chem. Abs., 49:8394a.)

Winkler, A. J., and M. A. Amerine. 1938. Color in California wines. II. Preliminary comparisons of certain factors influencing color. Food Res., 3: 439–447.

Winkler, A. J. 1938. The effect of climatic regions. Wine Review, 6:14–16, 32.

———, and W. O. Williams. 1939. The heat required to bring Tokay grapes to maturity. Proc. Amer. Soc. Hort. Sci., 37:650–652.

Wynn, Allan, 1968. The fortunes of Samuel Wynn. Melbourne, Australia, Wilke and Company.

5

Structure of the Vine

The grower usually thinks of the vine as the unit in grape production. The vine is a multicellular organism, however, and as such is influenced in functions and responses by the sum of the activities of the individual cells and by the coördination of the reactions arising between individual cells or between groups of cells. Pertinent to understanding efficient vine functioning, therefore, is an appreciation of the relation of the cells, tissues, and parts of the vine to the performance of the plant as a whole.

THE CELL

Microscopic examination of any part of the vine reveals that it is made up of many small units, or compartments, each called a cell. The cell is both the unit of structure and the functional unit. Cells support the vine, and the complex physical and chemical transformations of the living plant take place in the cells.

Structure of the cell.—The basic structure of the cell is the same, regardless of its ultimate shape or function. Its principal parts are the cell wall, the protoplasm, and the vacuole containing the cell sap. The wall consists almost entirely of cellulose, with some hemicellulose. Protoplasm, a fine granular liquid or jelly-like material, is the living substance within the cell cavity. This complex and highly coördinated material, including the cytoplasm and nucleus, is also called the protoplast. It includes carbohydrates, protein, and fatty substances, as well as compounds of mineral elements such as calcium, magnesium, phosphorus, and potassium. A certain viscosity characterizes the protoplasm as a whole, but it is divided into more or less definite areas, such as the cytoplasm, the nucleus, and that of the plastids.

The cytoplasm includes all of the protoplasm of the cell outside of the nucleus. Young cells may be largely occupied by cytoplasm, whereas in a typical mature cell it is present as a thin layer lining the cell wall, with or without cross strands. The layer of cytoplasm immediately inside the cell wall is less granular than the rest; it is called the cytoplasmic membrane. Similar membranes surround the vacuoles of the cell. These membranes function in governing the movement of substances into and out of the cell. In absorption they permit water and certain other substances in solution to pass freely, whereas they prevent or greatly retard the passage of other substances.

The nucleus is a round or roundish body, somewhat less translucent than the remainder of the cytoplasm, composed of much the same material, but holding a more definite shape. It is enclosed in a membrane and is embedded in the cytoplasm. By means of enzymes, the nucleus governs the form and character of the vine and controls the physiological processes. Bodies within the nucleus are responsible for the inheritance by organisms of the characteristics of their progenitors.

Other specialized cytoplasmic bodies are the plastids. The chloroplasts —green plastids—are the site of the process of photosynthesis, by which carbon dioxide from the air and water from the soil are combined by light energy to form sugar. Other plastids are the leucoplasts, which function in the formation of starch grains, and the chromoplasts, which are responsible for the color of the fruits.

Another function of the protoplasm is to govern metabolism. This consists of two reactions, both aided by enzymes. One forms new constituents of protoplasm, for growth or to replace used substances. The other breaks down compounds to release energy. Metabolism is most active in the areas where new cells are being produced and where cell expansion is rapid.

In the new cells the clear liquid inclusions of the cytoplasm appear as droplets, but an increase in the volume of this material is accompanied by the formation of small vacuoles—a watery solution of various substances imbedded in the cytoplasm. With further cell growth and increases in the liquid inclusions, the vacuoles fuse, reducing their number, but the volume of the cell occupied becomes larger and larger. The liquid of the vacuole is the *cell sap*. It contains many substances dissolved in water: gases, salts, organic acids, compounds of acids and metals, sugars, soluble proteins, and other substances. When this fluid of the epidermal cell of mature grape berries contains dissolved anthocyanin pigments, the fruit will be colored.

TISSUES

The cells of the vine vary in form, wall thickness, protoplasm life-span, and function. Cells of similar structure, which together perform a particular function, constitute a tissue. The principal tissues of the vine are tissues of growth, manufacturing and storage, protection, support, and conduction.

The growth (meristematic) tissue is composed of thin-walled, compact, actively growing cells that form new cells by division. The very rapid elongation of shoots in the spring results from division and subsequent enlargement of the cells of this tissue. This tissue is also active in root extension. The greatest continuous mass of growth tissue is the cambium layer—the region where the bark and wood meet. Cell division in this layer adds one or more layers of both wood and bark to the vine each year. These additions cause the vine parts to increase in diameter. The added wood is permanent, but the older layers of bark are shed. Field budding and grafting require that the cambium layers of the scion and stock be in contact. The cambium layer alone has the ability to produce the cells that make the union.

The manufacturing and storage tissue (parenchyma) is composed of large cells that are isodiametric (having equal diameter), with thin walls and large intercellular spaces. These cells are very long-lived and may undergo change and again divide, as in the formation of the cork cambium. This tissue makes up a large volume of various parts of the vine, such as the leaf, bark, wood, and pith, and also the pulp of the fruit. It forms the greater part of the internal tissue of the leaves, in which case the cells contain chloroplasts. In the stem and roots this tissue functions in storing nutrients as reserves. Crystals of calcium oxalate are often found as inclusions in these cells, in both wood and bark.

A protective tissue, the epidermis, is composed of one to several layers of flattened cells. It forms the surface covering of the leaves, fruit, shoots, and young roots. The outer walls of the surface cells are thickened and covered with a layer of cutin, a waxy, waterproof substance secreted by the protoplasm of these cells. On canes, arms, trunk, and older roots the epidermal layer is replaced by layers of a tissue called cork. It forms the outer bark. This tissue arises from the division of cells of the cork cambium, a layer of cells formed by transformation of certain parenchyma cells in the outer portion of the living bark. As the cells formed on the outside of the cork cambium mature, their walls become impregnated with suberin, a fatty substance impermeable to water, and become corky. These cells then die for lack of water. As the stem increases in circumference, the dead outer layers of bark split and then slough off in strips or segments. The bark lost by shedding is successively replaced, by cell division, with a new

Structure of the Vine

cork cambium, formed in deeper layers of the living bark. The epidermis and the cork cambium protect against the entrance of parasites, mechanical injury, and excessive evaporation from the delicate inner tissues.

The support and conducting tissue is made up of a number of different kinds of cells. These cells have greatly thickened walls, entirely or in part, and those of the stems and roots are much elongated. The thick walls give mechanical strength and rigidity to the vine parts. The cells of the support tissues die when their walls attain maximum thickness, yet they continue to function. This tissue provides avenues for conduction of materials from one part of the vine to another. The xylem—conducting tissue of the wood—conducts water, dissolved mineral elements, and, at certain times, foods, such as amino acids. The phloem—conducting tissue of the bark—mainly carries elaborated organic materials, such as sugar, amino acids, and organic acids.

Conduction in the xylem occurs in the tracheid cells and trachea. These cells are dead. The tracheid cells are tubelike, with tapered, overlapping ends and reinforced walls. The thickening of the walls is of various types, such as rings, spirals, and, over all, pits. The trachea are formed by end-to-end union of cells, the end walls disappearing. These tubes are very large and long in the vine. They, like the tracheids, have parts of the area of

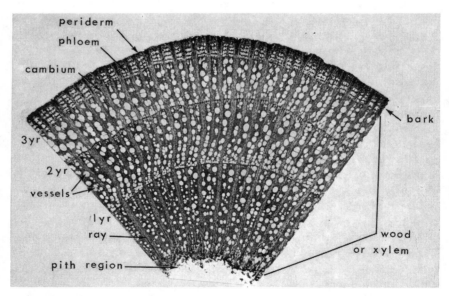

FIGURE 15: A cross section of a three-year-old grape stem (trunk): showing the periderm and phloem of the bark, the cambium at the juncture of bark and wood, and the wood or xylem, with vascular rays. x8. (*From Hilgardia, vol. 18, No. 5, 1948*)

their walls thickened. Both of these structures are well adapted for the movement of water and dissolved substances (fig. 15).

In the phloem the sieve tubes, elongated thin-walled cells, form the path of conduction (fig. 15). These cells contain cytoplasm, but no nucleus. The cytoplasm is united between cells through the pores of the sieve-like plates of the overlapping ends of abutting or overlapping cells. This structure lets materials pass that have difficulty in penetrating the cell walls. The sieve tubes are accompanied by slender companion cells, also living. These have nuclei. Their position and structural relation with the sieve tube indicates that they may exercise a certain control over the cytoplasm of the latter. In the dormant season the sieve plates are plugged with callus, which stops the movement of foods or food material during dormancy (Esau, 1948). Sugars and starch in the canes cannot be conducted to the stem and roots after the callus pads are formed in the sieve tubes, in autumn. With the beginning of growth in spring the callus is dissolved and the sieve tubes function again. Phloem and xylem differentiations begins in the spring and is usually completed by the end of July.

THE PARTS OF THE VINE

Each vine is capable of carrying on all the life processes necessary to its life. To retain their true characters varieties must be propagated by cuttings. To carry on the different processes to maintain its life and to produce offspring, the vine, like other higher plants, has developed separate parts, each with a special function. These parts may be classified into two groups by the work they perform: those that carry on vegetative activity, and those that produce seeds or fruit. The roots, trunk, shoots, and leaves are largely concerned with keeping the vine alive—that is, with absorption of water and minerals from the soil, manufacture of carbohydrate and other foods in the leaves, respiration, translocation, growth, and the like. The flowers, on the other hand, produce seeds and fruit—in the wild preserving the life of the species, and under cultivation supplying man with grapes, raisins, and wine.

THE ROOT SYSTEM

The root system of the vine is the entire collection of roots, the below-ground part of the vine. Unlike the shoots, roots are not divided into nodes and internodes. Branch roots arise at irregular intervals from the interior of the root, from cells of the pericycle that become meristematic, whereas branch shoots arise at regular intervals on the surface, from buds at the nodes.

The root system of the cultivated vine is both spreading and descend-

Structure of the Vine

ing. Under conditions that favor growth, the roots spread over a wide area, permeating the soil mass to a considerable depth. Although the bulk of the roots will usually be in the upper 2 to 5 feet of the soil, penetration to depths from 6 to 12 feet is common in soils of favorable texture, composition, and aeration. Roots have been followed as deep as 40 feet. Root penetration may be greatly limited by: shallow soils; hardpan—a substratum of soil that is impervious to root growth; a water table—free water in the soil, limiting aeration; or a chemical composition of the soil that is toxic to root growth. In any of these conditions, root growth is restricted to the soil above the obstruction. Shallow rooting limits the supply of both the water and the mineral elements that are available to the vine. The lateral growth of roots is rarely restricted by natural conditions.

Under conditions favorable for growth, cuttings—the usual means by which vines are propagated—generally produced numerous roots. Woodham and Alexander (1966) reported that the root temperature of Thompson Seedless most favorable for maximum growth was about 86° F. These are the main roots of the vine. As the vine attains maturity in the vineyard, several of the main roots will develop rapidly, others will grow very little, and still others may even disintegrate. In growth, the main roots not only increase in diameter and length, but divide to form new roots. These additional roots, together with their subdivisions that persist from year to year, are branch roots. The finest roots, the growth of a single season, are called rootlets (feeder roots). Most of these are short-lived; some are being formed at all times during the growing season. Those that survive a single season become branch roots, which in turn produce additional rootlets. Tens of thousands of rootlets are produced by a vine of moderate size; the daily increase in the absorption surface of the root system is enormous.

During active growth, each rootlet has at its end a cream-colored region varying in length from practically nothing to 1 inch or more. This region contains the abosrption zone, the zone of elongation, the growing point, and the root cap. The apical meristem of the root is protected by the root cap as it grows into new soil. The *absorption zone* is the region through which most of the water and mineral nutrients pass in entering the vine. Back of this zone the roots are covered with a corky layer which greatly retards or prevents the entry of water. The parts of the rootlet younger than the absorption zone are not developed enough to absorb water or solutes. To facilitate the intake of water and mineral nutrients, the absorption zone of the rootlets of most plants is provided with root hairs. The *root hair* is a slender protuberance of an epidermal cell. These slender, hairlike structures penetrate between the soil particles and are frequently distorted as they force their way among the bits of clay, silt, or sand. The root hairs not only make contact with the soil particles more intimate; they also greatly increase the absorptive area as well as the volume of soil with which the root system comes in contact. Root hairs live only a short time: the ones farthest back on the root deteriorate while new ones are formed near the tip as the root grows into unexplored soil.

In many California soils the vine produces only a small number of root hairs. This condition is contrary to statements in viticultural textbooks, but it is not unlikely that a similar condition exists in other arid regions where the soils are almost neutral to slightly alkaline. It has been demonstrated experimentally that the production of root hairs was abundant—476 to a centimeter of root—under slightly acid conditions (pH 5.7) and was reduced to only 180 in slightly alkaline conditions (pH 7.5). At intervening, higher, and lower pH values, the production of root hairs was proportional to the two levels indicated here (Winkler, A. J. unpublished data). This restricted production of root hairs in many California soils has not interfered with either the growth or the production of the vines.

The primary functions of roots are (*a*) absorption of water and mineral nutrients, (*b*) storage of reserves, and (*c*) anchorage.

All substances that enter the roots from the soil must be dissolved in water and pass through the cytoplasmic membrane of the cells of the absorption zone of the root, either of the root hairs or of the epidermal cells. The cellulose cell walls permit all substances in solution to pass unhindered, but the cytoplasmic membrane may exercise some control over the intake of substances in solution (see chap. 6).

Once water and dissolved substances are inside the root hairs they move inward in the root by diffusion to the next layer of cells, from this layer to the next, and so on to the xylem. In the region of the root where absorption occurs, the xylem and phloem tissues are opposite one another; thus the water and dissolved elements may reach the xylem without traversing the phloem. After reaching the xylem, the substances in solution are conducted upward to the shoot system of the vine.

Under favorable conditions the tissues of the vine roots accumulate high concentrations of starch, amino acids, especially arginine, and citric acid, in the late summer and autumn. These materials serve as foods and food material in the next year, and possibly over into the year after or until they are again being produced in excess of total use in the shoot system of the vine.

Once the vine is planted in its position in the vineyard, it is held permanently in place by the roots. Also, by the time the desired form of the vine is obtained, which requires five to eight years, vines trained to a head are largely self-supporting. The roots have become strong enough to hold the stem upright, and the stem is rigid enough not to bend under the weight of the shoots, leaves, and fruit. When training develops a trunk that is very much elongated, as in cordon training, or when canes of considerable length are retained to produce fruit, as in cane pruning, some sort of support is necessary for the elongated parts during the entire life of the vine.

THE SHOOT SYSTEM

The shoot system consists of the above-ground parts of the vine. These parts are the trunk, the arms, the shoots (canes, when mature), and the leaves.

The shoot.—The succulent growth arising from a bud is called a *shoot*. In autumn, when the shoot becomes woody, matures, and drops its leaves, it is called a *cane*. The shoot of the vine is divided into several distinct parts: the growing tip, the nodes, the internodes, the buds, the tendrils, and the laterals. These parts are not equally concerned in the production of fruit, yet conditions that favor normal development of each part of the shoot also favor high yields of good fruit.

The growing tip.—At the end of the shoot is the growing tip, 4 to 8 inches long, in which new cells are being formed by division of older cells and in which elongation is taking place through an increase in size of the newly formed cells. Once a shoot has made its annual growth, it does not increase in length. Thus, a cane brought up to form the trunk of a vine must be cut back at the height desired for the head. The internodes of a cane do not increase in length; hence laterals must be permitted to grow only at the desired height for the formation of the head of the vine. It is erroneous to suppose that the arms of a vine will be elevated as the vine becomes older. The trunk of the vine grows only in diameter. The fruiting surface gradually rises higher, but only from the slight annual increase in the length of the arms. A short segment of the two-year-old wood of the spur, renewal spur, or fruit cane is usually retained at the annual pruning.

At more or less regular intervals along the shoot there are slight enlargements from which the leaves arise and at which the buds develop. These are the *nodes*. In all vines except *Vitis rotundifolia* and *Vitis Munsoniana* the pith of the shoot is interrupted at each node by a woody layer called the *diaphragm*. The part of the shoot between two nodes is an *internode*. In the internode the center of the shoot is occupied by the *pith*.

The buds.—Normally a bud develops at each node just above the leaf; that is, in the leaf axil. A *bud* of the vine usually consists of three partially developed shoots, with rudimentary leaves or with both rudimentary leaves and flower clusters. These are compound buds, often called "eyes." Under normal conditions only the middle one of the three partially developed shoots—the primary growing point—of the bud grows when the vine leafs out in the following spring. If it is destroyed, the more advanced of the lateral growing points will grow. Under abnormal conditions—such as over-severe pruning, destruction of part of a vine, or a boron deficiency—two or even all three of the growing points may burst into growth. Some of the rudimentary leaves of the bud are large enough to enfold the other parts; covering these are bud scales. The bud scales are impregnated with suberin and lined with hairs that protect the tender inner parts against drying out; the rigid scales ward against mechanical injury. This bud usually remains dormant on the growing shoot. In addition to the three growing points just indicated there is another growing point that regularly develops into a lateral shoot in the axil of the leaves of most grape shoots (see fig. 16 right and laterals p. 85) and is called a lateral bud. This bud begins to grow in the same season in which it is formed; it may cease growth early and grow only a few millimeters or it may develop into a lateral branch (Pratt, 1959).

The buds of the vine may be classified as to (*a*) the nature of the structures they contain, or (*b*) their position on the shoot or arm.

As to the nature of the structures they contain, buds may be leaf buds or fruit buds. The *leaf bud* in the grape is a rudimentary *sterile* shoot; that is, it elongates into a shoot that bears only leaves and tendrils. Thus, a shoot arising from a leaf bud cannot bear fruit. A *fruit bud* contains a shoot having both rudimentary leaves and flower clusters. When a bud of

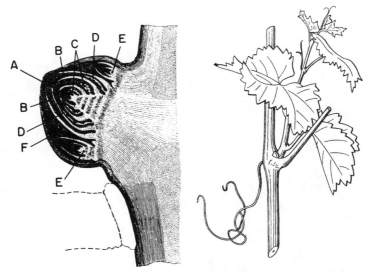

FIGURE 16: The grape bud. At left a longitudinal section of the compound bud with three shoot primordia: A, main growing point; E, lateral growing points; B, leaf primordia; C, flower clusters primordia; D, tendril primordia; and F, hair for protection against water loss. At right the fourth growing point of the bud complex in the leaf axil (*after Babo and Mach, 1923*).

this type unfolds, it produces a leafy shoot that bears one to four (usually two) flower clusters opposite the leaves at the third and fourth, fourth and fifth, or fifth and sixth nodes from the base, depending on the variety (fig. 17). Alleweldt (1959) showed that the position of the clusters, as well as the number per shoot, is a varietal characteristic. The number of clusters may be influenced by the rootstock. It is impossible to distinguish leaf from fruit buds by their outer appearance. Experience and microscopic examinations have shown, however, that the fruitful buds of most *vinifera* varieties are the buds beginning with the first—with a one-fourth internode below it—and extending out as far as the cane is well ripened. In a few varieties, such as Thompson Seedless, the buds toward the base of the cane tend to be sterile. The fruitfulness of the basal buds of some other varieties, such as Emperor, Malaga, and Palomino, is intermediate between Thompson Seedless and the great majority of the commercial varieties. Temperature, light intensity, and other conditions, especially during the critical period of fruit primordia initiation (3- to 6-week period following bloom), influence the fruitfulness of the buds of all varieties. Similarly, it is known that all three of the rudimentary shoots (growing point) of the buds are fruitful in some varieties; only the central (primary) growing point and the more advanced of the laterals are fruitful in other varieties; and only the primary growing points are usually fruitful in still other varieties.

The leaf and fruit buds of the vine arise in the leaf axils; hence they are

FIGURE 17: A shoot showing the relative position of the leaves, flower clusters, and tendrils.

called *axillary buds*. An axillary bud that for some reason has remained undeveloped for a season or longer is called a *latent bud*. Such buds may remain domant indefinitely, elongating only enough to keep from being overgrown by woody tissue as the vine part grows. At any time, however, when conditions favor their growth—as a result of too severe pruning, an injury to the vine, or the like—they may become active and produce shoots. The shoots, water sprouts on the arms and older parts of the vine, and suckers from below the ground, arise from these latent buds. On varieties that have fruitful buds at the base of the canes, shoots arising from such buds will bear fruit.

The leaf.—The leaf is an expanded, lateral outgrowth of a shoot, arising at a node, and having a bud in its axil. It develops at the growing tip as the shoot elongates. The leaf arrangement on the shoot is distichous (disposed in two vertical rows). Each leaf has three distinct parts: the petiole (stalk), the bracts, and the blade. The *petiole* (leaf stalk) attaches the blade to the shoot. It is generally cylindrical, with a flattened or slightly grooved segment extending along the upper side. In structure the petiole is especially fitted for conducting food material to and from the leaf blade and for maintaining the blade in the position most favorable for the performance of its functions. The leaf *bracts* are broad, short scales arising from the enlarged base of the petiole. They drop off early in the growing season.

The *blade* or *lamina* is the expanded or broad, flat part of the leaf. As commonly used in English, the term "leaf" refers to the blade only. At the point of attachment to the leaf, the petiole divides into five large veins or ribs, one of these going to each of the (usually) five lobes of the leaf. Arising from the large veins are side branches, which themselves branch. These latter branches again divide, until the entire blade is traversed with a network of veins, all interconnected. Many of the finest veins, however, have free ends in the mesophyll—the soft inner tissues of the leaf. The structure of the veins (conducting tissue), together with their intimate connection with all parts of the leaf blade, indicates their chief function— to conduct water, mineral nutrients, and foods to and from the leaf. They also give mechanical support to the mesophyll tissue, which is the principal tissue of the leaf. The cells of this tissue are especially adapted for the manufacture of carbohydrates, having numerous chloroplasts to absorb light (energy), the large intercellular spaces to supply air, and the network of veins to supply water. Stomata, the small pores through which carbon dioxide, oxygen, and water vapor enter or leave the leaf, are located primarily on the underside of the blade in grapes.

Leaves undergoing rapid expansion have tightly packed palisade and mesophyll tissues with little intercellular spaces (Kriedemann *et al.*, 1970). In fully expanded leaves, transverse sections indicate a less compressed assemblage of cells, with readily discernible cellular outlines and greater incidence of intercellular spaces.

The tendrils.—From the point of view of structure, the tendrils of the vine are clusters. The two have a common origin. The tendrils give physical support to the primary shoots by coiling themselves about anything that comes within their grasp. The support of the tendrils helps protect the shoot from wind damage, keep it in position to provide shade, and keep the fruit off the ground. *Vitis labrusca* has a tendril opposite every leaf. All other species have discontinuous tendrils; that is, tendrils opposite two adjacent leaves, but with no tendril opposite each third leaf.

Lateral shoots.—In the vine the fourth growing point in the axillary buds do not remain inactive until the following season, but develop immediately into *lateral shoots*. If the shoot is injured or pinched early in the season, the axillary buds develop into laterals, which become woody and develop buds and secondary laterals in their leaf axils. A horizontal or drooping direction of growth of the shoot also fosters the development of these strong laterals. Laterals of this type serve the grower in the same capacity as canes, provided their position is such that they can be retained in part for the production of fruit. The second crop of fruit produced by some varieties is borne on these laterals. The primary laterals may even produce laterals, bearing a third crop. This third crop may set normally, but it matures only rarely.

Other laterals remain fairly short and never become woody; hence they are called temporary laterals. They may drop off at the end of the growing season. The function of the temporary lateral seems to be that of increasing the leaf surface of the vine. Still others, may make practically no growth but they do grow.

The arms.—The permanent divisions of the vine, arising from or along the top of the trunk, are called arms. The arms bear the spurs and canes retained at pruning for the production of the next year's crop of wood and fruit. Their structure is the same as that of a shoot except that they are retained and become thicker from year to year. The length of the arms increases a little each year, since it is usually necessary to retain segments of the spurs, renewal spurs, or fruit canes of the previous season in order to obtain suitable, well-placed bearing units for the coming year.

The trunk.—The permanent stem of the vine is the trunk. It is an upward continuation of the underground stem; thus, it forms a connecting link and pipeline between the roots and the arms. By virtue of its position we might say that the trunk is the body of the vine. On its continued healthy state depends the vegetative vigor, fruiting, and long life of the entire vine.

The structure of the trunk, like that of the arms, is the same as that of a shoot. It grows in diameter each year by adding a new layer of wood—

Structure of the Vine

an annual ring of growth—just beneath the bark. This growth results from the formation of new cells by the division of already existing cells of the cambium layer.

The trunk has the functions of (a) supporting the bearing wood of the vine at the desired height from the ground, (b) supplying the vessels through which water and mineral nutrients absorbed by the roots are conducted to the above-ground parts of the vine, (c) supplying channels for translocation to the roots of elaborated foods from the above-ground parts, and (d) storage of food reserves.

BIBLIOGRAPHY

Alleweldt, G. 1959. Untersuchung über die Gescheinzahl der Reben. Wein Wissenschaft, 14:61–69.

Babo, A. W., and E. Mach. 1923. Handbuch des Weinbaues und der Kellerwirtschaft. Berlin, Paul Parley. pp. 276 and 277.

Esau, K. 1948. Phloem structure in the grapevine and its seasonal changes. Hilgardia, 18:217–296. Plate 6B.

Kriedemann, P. E., W. M. Kliewer, and J. M. Harris. 1970. Leaf age and photosynthesis in Vitis vinifera L. Vitis, 9:97–104.

Pratt, C. 1959. Radiation damage in shoot apices of Concord grapes. Amer. J. Bot., 46:103–109.

Woodham, R. C., and D. M. Alexander. 1966. The effect of root temperature on development of small fruiting Sultana vines. Vitis, 5:345–350.

6

The Physiology
of the Vine

Many separate physical, chemical, and vital activities of the vine and its parts are involved in the intake of materials, the synthesis of needed substances, the processes of growth, and the development of flowers and fruit. The activities discussed in this chapter are limited to those most essential to an understanding of these physiological functions of the vine.

TRANSPIRATION

Very large amounts of water are lost from the green parts of the vine especially from the leaves. The quantity of water required for normal growth and fruiting of mature vines varies from about 15 to 50 acre-inches of water annually, depending upon the climate. This water loss is often referred to as evaporation, but the process is not entirely physical, since it is partly controlled by the plant.

Of the external conditions that affect the rate of water loss, the more important are light intensity, temperature, humidity, and wind. Light has a twofold influence, principally in its effect upon the opening and closing of the stomata. These microscopic structures in grapevines are found in greatest abundance on the lower surface of the leaf. They are opened in the light and closed in darkness. The second influence of light is upon leaf temperature. In sunlight the temperature of the leaves is usually 5° to 20° F higher than that of the surrounding air; hence the vapor pressure inside the leaves may be distinctly greater than that of the air. A rise in temperature is invariably accompanied, other conditions being equal, by an increase in water loss. This greater loss results from an increase in the steepness of the diffusion gradient between the water vapor of the outside air and that within the leaf. At any temperature, a rise in humidity reduces the steepness of the diffusion gradient of water vapor through the stomata, and transpiration is slowed. An increase in wind velocity usually increases the rate of water loss by removing the moisture-laden air adjacent to the surface of the leaf and by flexing large leaves (Wooly, 1961).

The rate of water loss through the leaves has a direct effect on the upward movement of the transpiration stream in the xylem. Koblet (1969) in Switzerland found this movement to be approximately 30 centimeters per hour. It would be accelerated by the high temperatures and very low relative humidity of desert regions.

Not all plants lose water at the same rate under the same environmental conditions. The factors responsible are probably differences in stomatal behavior, volume of intercellular space of the leaves, sap concentration, etc. With the same expanse of roots to supply water, the leaves of the vine with the smaller leaf surface are supplied more abundantly. A similar condition may arise with two vines of the same leaf surface when one is carrying a normal crop and the other an overcrop. The vine with the normal crop will have enough carbohydrates to nourish both the fruit and vine; hence root growth will be active and enough water will be absorbed to offset all losses. In the other vine, the demands for the developing of the overcrop of fruit will take enough additional carbohydrates to cause root growth to suffer, with a water deficit resulting. Vines with overcrops are especially sensitive to rapid increases in temperature; their fruit sunburns more readily.

During a protracted cool period in early summer, when water loss is slow and soil moisture is ample, vines may make rapid shoot growth at the expense of root development. A sudden hot spell following such a period may lead to burning, especially of the fruit, and under very severe conditions the shoot tips may dry out: the rapidly growing vines are not prepared to meet conditions of stress. A gradual change from the cool of spring to the intense heat of midsummer, in contrast, brings on a steady increase in transpiration, greatly lessening the likelihood of burn. Shoot and root growth under this gradual change is conditioned for the demand for more and more water as the weather becomes warmer.

In the unirrigated vineyards of the coastal valleys of California, except on shallow soils, the vines go through the season without showing much distress. Shoot growth slows early, and continued root growth seems to enable these vines to absorb enough water to mature a normal crop of fruit. Few new leaves develop after midseason, and the vines obtain enough moisture from the roots to function more or less normally until the end of the season sufficiently so to properly ripen the fruit and to mature the wood for the next year's crop.

Water Intake by the Roots

Most of the water that enters the roots of the vine is sucked in from the soil. The loss of water by the cells of the leaf in transpiration increases their absorptive power by concentrating the substances dissolved in their sap and by partially drying the solid and semisolid materials. These partially dried cells, which now have a greater tendency to absorb water, take water from the xylem, the water-conducting tissue. The absorptive force thus applied to the water in the xylem, which extends as a continuous system from the leaves to the roots, is passed down to the roots. The high cohesive force of water keep the system from breaking. So long as the vine is transpiring actively, the absorptive pull, or the diffusion pressure deficit produced, is sufficient to overcome the resisting forces on the plant and the surface tension by which water is held in by the particles of a soil containing available moisture; water is pulled into the root, from cell to cell across the absorption zone, and up the conducting systems to the leaves.

In the absence of the pull of transpiration, and when it is low (at night, or during period of very high relative humidity), water is absorbed by osmosis. This is called active absorption. Energy supplied by the living cell is utilized. When the osmotic pressure (diffusion pressure deficit) of the sap of the epidermal cells of the absorption zone of the roots is greater than that of the soil solution surrounding the roots, water moves into the roots freely. This method of absorption is but slightly different from that resulting from the pull of transpiration, since the osmotic pressure required for its functioning results primarily from the removal of water from the local epidermal root cells by the movement of water inward and up in the vine in response to the transpiration pull exerted by the leaves. The pull occurs in large volume only during transpiration.

The above description of water intake slights the role played by the cells of the roots. These physical processes assist us in understanding how the vine's great need for water is largely met. A process that is not fully understood, however, is the removal of water from the soil by the epidermal cells of the root and its movement into the xylem under sufficient pressure to produce "bleeding," as often occurs when the vine is pruned late.

Losses of as much as 5 to 7 gallons of exudate have been recorded for individual vines when new cuts were made every other day (unpublished data). Nitsch and Nitsch (1965) and Skene (1967) found that the root exudate of grapevines contain the plant hormones, cytokinin and gibberellin. The level of sugars, mineral nutrients and other compounds in root exudate are usually very low. However Moreau and Vinet (1922) showed that under relatively low temperatures sugars may be present in the bleeding liquid in larger amounts. The physiological significance of hormones and other compounds in root exudate is not known, but they may regulate budbreak and growth of aerial parts of the vine (Galston and Davies, 1969). It would seem that, under conditions of active root growth and with an ample supply of reserve foods, the root cells are, as a result of vital activity, capable of absorbing water against pressure. This condition usually develops about the time that the vine leafs out—before the vine has developed a leaf surface and when root growth is very active. Bleeding may occur at any time during active growth if a large part or most of the top growth is removed. It occurs in mid-dormancy, also, if irrigation with warm water activates root growth. Similarly, vigorously growing vines in spring may exhibit guttation—the exudation of water at the tips of the serration of the lobes of the leaves—in the early morning. Guttation is simply a means of pressure release. The state of the nutrition of the plant, through its relation to cell activity, affects guttation (Raleigh 1946).

The rate of absorption and amount of water taken from the soil are influenced, within limits, primarily by the factors that affect transpiration and by the rate at which the root system is being extended. Even if soil moisture is between field capacity and the wilting range, appreciable water intake over a prolonged period can occur only if the roots of the vine are growing. Because the movement of moisture in the soil is very slow or lacking, the root soon removes all of the water directly available to it and can obtain more only by growing into soil that still has available water (Kramer and Coile, 1940). The absorption zone moves forward progressively with root growth. Thus, conditions that influence root growth will affect the rate of water absorption. Once the soil moisture in contact with the roots is reduced to the wilting percentage, water intake stops. When the intake of water is checked by the reduction of the moisture content to the wilting point in much or most of the soil mass occupied by its roots, the vine stops growing, the older leaves yellow and then drop, and the fruit sunburns. Actual wilting of vines is, however, rare under field conditions because of the deep and wide ramification of grapevine roots.

Water intake by vines in free water or in soils of fairly high water content may be slowed because of inadequate soil aeration resulting in oxygen deficiency. This condition slows the respiration of the roots, thereby slowing growth; if the condition unfavorable to respiration persists, the roots disintegrate. We have, however, observed vines that were entirely covered with water for over a month in the dormant season without ill effects.

ABSORPTION OF MINERAL NUTRIENTS

All substances that enter the vine roots from the soil must be in solution in water. Entry is primarily through the epidermal cells and root hairs of the absorption zone of the roots. There are two mechanisms whereby ions enter the vine roots. One of these is by diffusion and absorption; that is, ions in the "outer" space of the root cells diffuse out, and others from the soil solution diffuse in, until equilibrium is attained. Such entry is non-linear with time, for when equilibrium is approached the process slows down. This mode of entry does not require expenditure of energy by the roots. Also, since the entry is passive, it is not highly selective with respect to various ions. Hylmo (1953) reported that the passive movement of ions into the roots, and in turn into the shoots, is dependent upon the rates of water absorption and of transpiration. However, according to Wright and Barton (1955), who worked with radioactive phosphorus, high rates of transpiration were directly associated with greater ion intake and accumulation in the leaves.

The other mechanism by which ions enter the vine roots is the active transport of ions, which involves the operation of carriers (Epstein, 1956). The essential features of this mode of entry are the attachment of the ions to carrier molecules, the movement of the resulting carrier-ion complexes through the root cell barriers (cytoplasm), and the subsequent discharge of the ions into the xylem cells of the root. This mechanism of entry may be likened to a constantly rotating belt conveyer. Absorption is linear with time, since no equilibrium is reached. Expenditure of energy being involved, the rate depends on respiration (Hoagland, 1948). In fact absorption depends on the cellular respiration process and occurs only under aerobic conditions, and then only when sugars or other readily utilizable carbohydrates are available in the roots. It is selective with respect to various ions and groups of ions.

More often than not, salts and their ions are moved into the plant against a concentration gradient; that is, the concentration of the ion being absorbed is higher in the root cells than in the soil solution. Intake under such conditions again involves expenditure of energy by the root cells: they work. Hoagland (1948) demonstrated that the rate of accumulation of ions by plant cells is closely correlated with their respiration rate.

Within the plant the ions of the mineral nutrients must be moved to the point of use. This movement—translocation—may also be against a concentration gradient. The relation of the nourishment of the roots to the upward movement of salts has been shown by Broyer and Hoagland (1943) and by Lundegärdh (1950). The importance of both absorption and movement of ions of minerals is further supported by selectivity of intake; the cells have the ability to absorb some ions in much greater quantity than others. Potassium and nitrates are absorbed several times as rapidly as calcium, magnesium, or sulfate. Thus, the presence of a dissolved ion in the soil solution does not necessarily mean its intake by the roots.

PHOTOSYNTHESIS

Photosynthesis is without question the most important physiological process of plants. It is the process of food manufacture in the leaves. The primary product is sugar, the basic food from which all other foods in nature, for both plants and animals, are synthesized. Sugar, of course, is also used directly. In the process the green plastids use light energy to split water and release oxygen, while the hydrogen from the water is combined with carbon dioxide to produce carbohydrates. This process is often represented by the reaction 6 CO_2 + 6 H_2O + light energy = $C_6H_{12}O_6$ + 6 O_2. It is not that simple, however, for a number of steps are involved. The seat of activity is in the lamellae of the chloroplasts of the cytoplasm of green plants. Chloroplasts contain, in addition to chlorophyll, carotenoids and minerals, among which phosphorus and iron are very important and copper may have significance. The chloroplast and each of its numerous laminated grana are surrounded by protein-lipid membranes with an outer lipoid covering.

Almost all plant physiologists agree that the release of oxygen in photosynthesis is from water. This is the first step in the process. It is termed the "Hill reaction." This reaction has been demonstrated with isolated chloroplasts and is carried on in the lamellae within the grana. In the second step, carbon dioxide and two atoms of hydrogen from the water are combined to form the products of photosynthesis and these reactions can occur in the dark. The dark reactions occur in the stroma of the chloroplast. The exact role of chlorophyll in this step is not completely understood. The absorption of light, an important function of chlorophyll, is apparent since neither water nor carbon dioxide absorbs the visible rays of the spectrum. The energy obtained from sunlight drives four types of reactions in the chloroplast; the photolysis of water (the Hill reaction), photosynthetic phosphorylations, the fixation of carbon dioxide, and the synthesis of starch. The photolysis of water and photosynthetic phosphorylations are carried out within the lamellae of the chloroplast, while carbon dioxide fixation and starch synthesis are reactions of the soluble enzyme systems in the stroma of the chloroplast.

Sugars were formerly considered to be the first product of photosynthesis. Now, with refinements in experimental techniques, including the use of radioactive isotopes, evidence shows the first compound to be phosphoglyceric acid—a 3-carbon acid, formed by the carboxylation of ribulose 1, 5 diphosphate. Almost immediately after the appearance of this product, sugars, amino acids, lipids, and other large-molecular substances are produced.

The water used in photosynthesis is absorbed from the soil by the vine roots. It is then moved to the mesophyll cells of the leaves through the xylem ducts of the roots, trunk, arms, shoots, and petioles. The carbon dioxide is obtained directly from the air. It enters the leaves through the stomata by diffusion. This is simple gaseous diffusion from the higher concentration of carbon dioxide in the atmosphere to the lower concentration in the air in the intercellular spaces inside the leaf. The carbon dioxide goes into solution when it makes contact with the walls of the mesophyll cells; it then moves into the cells and reaches the chloroplasts, where it is used.

Although sugar is the primary plant food, the plant produces other carbohydrates and also proteins and fats. The sugar, mainly sucrose, manufactured in the green cells undergoes many transformations. Some of it is used directly as food in the process of respiration. The energy stored in the sugar is thereby released to carry on the work of the plant. Sugar that is not used immediately is, for the most part, transported to storage tissues in the fruit, roots, trunk, etc., and then transformed into other carbohydrates. Among these carbohydrates are: glucose and fructose, the sugars of the mature grape; starch, the principal storage food of the vine; and hemicellulose and cellulose, the building materials of which the cells of the various parts of the vine are constructed. Hemicellulose is not a storage material in the vine. Its level is not reduced by acute carbohydrate restriction resulting from defoliation (Winkler and Williams, 1938).

The sugar not used for food reserves or for manufacture of other carbohydrates may be synthesized into proteins, fats, or other compounds. Light is not directly necessary for these transformation; the needed energy is obtained from the chemical energy of the sugar. The manufacture of proteins requires not only carbon dioxide and water, but also substances obtained from the soil, such as nitrogen, phosphorus, sulfur, and, in some cases, iron and possibly other elements. These enter the roots as ions of nitrates, phosphates, and other compounds, and are transported to all parts of the plant. Some of these mineral elements are necessary for photosynthesis, some are used as components of certain plant foods, and some function in other phases of plant development and growth.

Proteins are compounds essential to life and growth. They occur in plants as protoplasmic proteins, storage proteins, and nulceoproteins. Proteins are normally produced by the combining of simpler compounds, the amino acids. Amino acids are mainly formed from organic acids and nitrogen. A few of these also contain sulfur. In the construction of proteins the amino acids are linked together to form the large, complex protein molecules. The linking of the amino acids to form proteins is brought

The Physiology of the Vine

about by enzymatic activities. That many different proteins occur in plants is not surprising. More than 30 amino acids have been found in the vine and its fruit (Nassar and Kliewer, 1966), and any combination of these acids may form a protein. A few proteins contain substances other than amino acids. The synthesis of amino acids can take place in many parts of the plant. Once formed, the amino acids may be stored free as such or used to produce proteins immediately or they may be translocated to other parts of the plant to be linked into proteins and stored.

Fats are synthesized from sugar. They contain the same elements, but the ratio of oxygen to carbon is lower. Fats serve more or less the same purpose in the plant as do carbohydrates. The supplying of energy seems to be their chief function. Fats are of limited importance in the vine, except as a food in the seeds and as a constituent of cuticular wax on the surface of berries and leaves. The seeds contain, as oil, 10 to 20 per cent of fats.

Basic to our understanding the principles of vine training, pruning, and trellising is how environmental factors, especially light intensity, temperature, moisture, and inherent factors, such as age, species and variety, influence the rate of photosynthesis in grapevines.

The light intensity required for maximum photosynthesis of grapevines

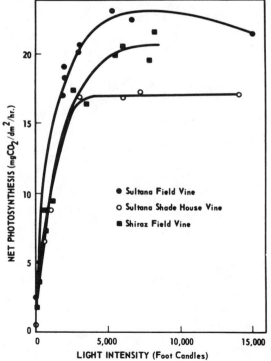

FIGURE 18: Graphs showing effect of light intensity on leaf photosynthesis of Sultana (Thompson Seedless) and Shiraz field vines. (*From Kriedemann and Smart, 1971*)

where environmental conditions are optimal; i.e., 77° F., adequate moisture, and nutrients, ranges from 2,500 to 5,000 foot candles (a unit of illumination) (fig. 18). This is known as the light saturation point and is strongly influenced by the previous exposure of a vine to light, being considerably lower for a vine grown under shaded conditions than for a vine grown in full sunlight, as shown in figure 18. In California the light intensity generally reaches about 12,000 foot candles at noon during the spring and summer months. Light intensities above the light saturation point and up to 12,000 foot candles are not usually detrimental to photosynthesis and vine growth, provided the temperature does not become excessively high. Kriedemann (1968) found that the light compensation point of mature Thompson Seedless leaves from field vines was reached at about 125 foot candles. At this light intensity the rate of photosynthesis just equals the rate of respiration and a vine neither gains nor loses weight. A single grape leaf of average thickness will absorb about 90 per cent of the solar radiation in the visible range of the spectrum, therefore the level of light intensity reaching leaves beneath the outer layer of the vine canopy is less than that required for maximum photosynthesis. Sometimes light intensities in the interior parts of vines are even below the light compensation point. This is especially true in vigorous vines or vines improperly trellised (Shaulis *et al.*, 1966). Consequently, in trellising grapevines one of the primary considerations should be to maximize the leaf surface exposed to direct sunlight.

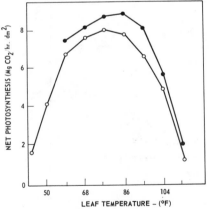

FIGURE 19: Graph showing effect of leaf temperature of Thompson Seedless vines on net photosynthesis. Light intensity was constant at about 4,000 foot-candles. Absolute magnitude of net photosynthesis values can change according to seasonal influences. Solid circles on graph are for vines grown under full sunlight and open circles are for vines grown in the greenhouse. (*From Kriedemann, 1968*)

Kriedemann (1968), who measured changes in the concentration of CO_2, found that the optimum temperature for photosynthesis by grape leaves is about 77° F. (figure 19). Buttrose (1968) and Kliewer *et al.* (1972), using controlled temperature growth rooms in which potted vines were grown, showed that the maximum increase in plant dry weight occurs at temperatures of 77° to 86° F. Photosynthesis declines rapidly above 86° F. and falls to zero between 113 and 122° F. Figure 19 also shows that the rate of CO_2 assimilation decreases very fast in grapevines at temperatures below 59° F. and net assimilation of CO_2 is near zero at 41° F.

Water is of considerable importance in photosynthesis, not only as a major reaction constituent, but also through its control of stomatal opening and its effect on wilting of leaves. Kriedemann and Smart (1971) showed that as long as leaf water potentials of field vines are less than 13 to 15 atmospheres, photosynthesis is not reduced (see p. 365); however, tensions above these values result in a rapid decline in photosynthesis. The reduction in photosynthesis at high leaf-water deficiency is attributed to stomatal closure. Vines that are allowed to wilt generally require considerable time to recover their normal photosynthetic rates, indicating that wilting probably results in some structural damage to the leaf cells.

The rate of photosynthesis of a vine leaf increases greatly during the period of rapid expansion and reaches maximum activity when the leaf attains full size—30 to 40 days after unfolding (figure 20). Thereafter photosynthesis declines gradually until the leaf becomes senescent. When a grape leaf reaches one-third full size, more food is exported from the leaf than imported, and a net contribution in growth occurs. Quantitatively, some of the products of CO_2 fixation also change with age. Sucrose is always the major sugar formed; but oligosaccharides, such as stachyose and raffinose, account for a higher proportion of the total CO_2 fixation products in older leaves. Synthesis of tartaric acid in grapevines is restricted to the rapidly expanding foliage; however, the other main organic acids in vines are formed regardless of leaf age (Saito and Kasai, 1968; Kriedemann *et al.*, 1970).

In addition to the environmental factors that effect rates of photosynthesis in grapevines there are inherent differences in photosynthetic capacities between *Vitis* species and among varieties within a species. Geisler (1963) reported that the CO_2 assimilation rate of V. *rupestris* and V. *vinifera* was about twice that of V. *labrusca*. Furthermore, he indicated that the light compensation point of V. *rupestris* was reached at about 30 foot candles, while nearly 150 foot candles was needed for V. *labrusca*; and the former species required nearly twice the amount of light to reach saturation than the latter species.

The demand or the need for photosynthate can also influence the rate of photosynthesis in grapevines as well as in other plants. For example,

The Physiology of the Vine

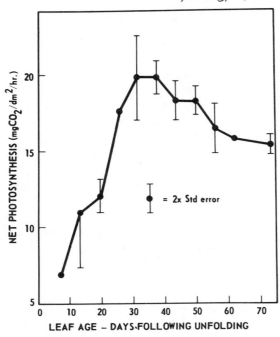

FIGURE 20: Graph showing the relationship between leaf age and net photosynthesis of Thompson Seedless vines. (*From Kriedemann, Kliewer, and Harris, 1970*)

vines which have a large amount of fruit in relation to total leaf area are able to photosynthesize at a higher rate than vines with few fruits and large leaf area (P. E. Kriedemann, personal communication). However, the amount that a vine can compensate for increased rate of photosynthesis due to a heavy crop load has a definite limit, beyond which growth, fruit maturity, and carbohydrate reserves are reduced (see p. 113, red cane).

RESPIRATION

The syntheses of foods that we have just discussed represent but a few of the processes that are occurring continuously in the cells of the vine. These are constructive changes; through them simple substances are combined to form complex foods or food materials. Other changes in the same cells are destructive, in that complex foods are broken down into simpler compounds. These changes are as necessary for vine growth and fruiting as the constructive processes. The constructive and destructive changes occur at the same time and are interdependent. Of the latter, respiration is the most important. Digestion, the bringing of the plant foods into solution so that they may be used or translocated, is an adjunct to respiration.

The Physiology of the Vine

Respiration releases the energy that is required to activate the chemical changes, other than photosynthesis, that occur in the vine. In this process sugar and other compounds are transformed into simpler substances. This may be indicated by the equation

$$C_6H_{12}O_6 + 6\,O_2 \longrightarrow 6\,CO_2 + 6\,H_2O + \text{energy}$$

$$\text{sugar} \qquad \text{oxygen} \qquad \underset{\text{dioxide}}{\text{carbon}} \qquad \text{water}$$

This reaction is the reverse of that used in indicating the reaction in photosynthesis. In photosynthesis, energy is stored; in respiration, energy is released. Thus respiration is an oxidation process in which oxygen reacts with the hydrogen and carbon of the sugar to form water and carbon dioxide, releasing energy. As in the synthesis of foods, there are successive steps in respiration, and the process is activated by enzymes.

In addition to sugar, starch, fats, amino acids, organic acids and other substances may be broken down to carbon dioxide and water through the process of respiration. Of particular importance to enologists is the rapid decrease in malic and tartaric acids in grapes during the period following véraison—i.e., when the fruit first begins to change color and soften—until fruit maturity. The loss of these acids is largely attributed to respiration. Geisler and Radler (1963) demonstrated that the increased respiratory quotient of grapes following véraison could account quantitatively for the entire loss in total acidity in fruits during the period of berry ripening.

Temperature, age of tissue, and the physiological stage of the plant are among the most important factors affecting the rate of respiration in grapevines. It is well known that an increase in temperature results in an increased rate of respiration of living organisms, and that for every 10° C (18° F.) rise in temperature the rate of respiration approximately doubles. Harris et al. (1971) showed that the rate of respiration of young, immature berries was 5 to 10 times greater than in mature fruit. They also found that the respiratory quotient suddenly changes from a value of less than 1 before véraison to a value greater than 1 just after véraison, suggesting a possible shift in respiratory substrate. Several investigators (Hardy, 1968; Kriedemann, 1968; Kliewer, 1971) have shown that malic acid and, to a lessor extent, tartaric acid, are readily respired in grapes after the berries begin to change color and soften. Prior to that time these acids are not readily available for respiration. There is relatively little change in the activity of enzymes responsible for the breakdown of malic acid in grapes before or after véraison (Hawker, 1969). However, increase in the availability of organic acids, located in the cell vacuoles, to enzymatic degradation, facilitated by an increase in membrane permeability, may explain why malic and tartaric acids are rapidly lost in ripening grapes but not in green, immature grapes. Kliewer (1971) showed that the rate of decrease of malic and tartaric acids during fruit ripening is directly related to temperature, but relatively independent of light intensity.

It is readily understood that energy is used in work, as in a man's handling of boxes of grapes, yet it is difficult for some persons to visualize how energy is expended in the immobile vine. Growth and the production of flowers, seeds, and fruit are external evidence of the utilization of energy by the vine. In vines, as in other plants, energy is used in the absorption of food materials, their synthesis into foods, and the conversion of food into structural parts—such as roots, leaves, shoots, and fruit—and into the living substance of the plant, protoplasm. The energy released by respiration is also used to synthesize substances which are necessary for the normal functioning of the vine, but which are neither living substance, structural material, nor plant foods. Some of these are: enzymes, colors, aromas and flavors, tartaric and malic acids, tannins, glucosides, and vitamins. Some of these substances add materially to the appearance and palatability of grapes and are important for the food value and quality of the fruit.

Grapes do not cease to live when they are harvested. Their respiration continues. The changes accompanying respiration after harvest detract from quality. The grape berries contain no additional food materials that can be brought into soluble form during storage, nor are there reserves for color or flavor. Therefore it is evident that measures are needed to reduce or control respiration. To date, rapid and thorough precooling, appropriate cold storage, and the judicious application of sulfur dioxide have been the most successful means of slowing respiration and thereby preserving the quality of the harvest grapes (see chap. 22).

TRANSLOCATION

It is obvious that materials are translocated in the vine. For example, water is applied to the soil to remove a moisture deficiency apparent in the leaves. It is generally recognized that the sugar of the ripe grapes is manufactured in the leaves. The application of fertilizers to the soil in order to stimulate vine growth again implies that the added elements or food materials of which they are constituents will be moved to the parts of the vine where growth occurs.

The movement of water is primarily in the xylem, the wood of the vine. Translocation is most active in the young woody tissue just beneath the bark. The older wood of the vine remains alive and active for years, however, and some water may be moved through wood that is several years old. Proper girdling of a cane or trunk probably does not affect the upward movement of water. Girdling that penetrates the wood, in contrast, must impede movement. (The forces that move water in the vine are indicated above, in the section on transpiration.)

Translocation of foods and mineral elements.—It has been shown that foods are stored in all parts of the vine. In order to be used, the sugar and the amino acids—the base materials for the stored starch, proteins, and fats—must be translocated. The carbohydrate materials are moved in the phloem of the vine in the form of sucrose (Swanson and El-shishiny, 1958; Stoev *et al.*, 1959); however, small amounts of higher sugars of the oligosaccharide series, especially raffinose and stachyose, are also translocated in the phloem of most woody plants including grapevines (Zimmermann, 1960; Trip *et al.*, 1965; Kliewer, 1965). Nitrogenous materials and organic acids are lessor constituents of the phloem sap of plants (Kursanov, 1962). The amino acids, alanine, serine, α-aminobutyric, glutamic, aspartic, and glutamine, and the carboxylic acids, malic, tartaric, and citric have been detected in the phloem exudate of grapevines (W. M. Kliewer, unpublished data). Other substances, including inorganic nutrients, plant hormones, and alkaloids are transported in the phloem sap of plants (Kursanov, 1962). In the xylem fluid, in contrast to the phloem sap, relatively large amounts of amino acids, especially glutamine, organic acids (mainly malic), and inorganic nutrients and small amounts of sugars are transported in grapevines (Hardy, 1969; Hardy and Possingham, 1969).

Many environmental factors affect the translocation and distribution of organic and inorganic substances in plants. These include temperature, light, carbon dioxide, water, nutrients, photoperiod, and diurnal and seasonal variations. The effect of these factors on movement and distribution of assimilates may be indirect and may be mediated through changes in the rate of growth of developing organs. These changes may, in turn, be influenced by hormone levels, through alterations in the rate of photosynthesis and outflow of assimilates from leaves, or they may have direct effects on assimilate translocation. Hormones have been shown to play an increasingly important role in regulating the amount and distribution of assimilates in plants (Galston and Davies, 1969); however, the factors affecting their production and the mechanism of their action are not well understood.

The stored foods used in respiration and growth must be moved to the areas of the vine where needed. These materials also move in the sieve tubes of the phloem. The practice of girdling is based on that movement: the purpose is to interrupt the downward flow of foods and for growth regulating hormones. However, when the girdle is too deep or too wide to heal over normally the vines suffer and some may die.

The principal movement of foods and food materials in the phloem is downward, yet some upward translocation occurs during most of the growing season. Thus, foods and food materials are moved toward such points of need as the shoot tips, flowers, new roots, and the like; then, as the supply exceeds demand, the movement is toward the spurs, arms, trunk, and roots, where these materials accumulate as reserves.

The elements taken in solution from the soil are moved upward in the vine, primarily in the wood. Some of these materials may, however, be moved in the phloem.

The cross movement of both foods and water occurs in the vascular rays, the tissue for radial translocation. The rays are also storage tissue. Foods moving down the phloem enter the ray cells and are carried to the xylem tissue or are stored. Water and food materials moving upward in the xylem enter the ray cells and move across the stem to the phloem.

GROWTH

To the grape grower, growth usually means elongation of the shoots. This growth results from the formation of new cells and their enlargement. The formation of new cells for length growth, as indicated on p. 84, is localized in the tip of the shoot, where meristematic tissue predominates. Just back of the meristematic zone the newly formed cells enlarge rapidly; this is the zone of elongation. The increase in size arises both from the intake of water and from cell enlargement. Some cells grow primarily in length, whereas others increase in all directions. The difference in type of growth among the cells of the zone of elongation is the beginning of differentiation. The cells of the zone of differentiation, just back of the zone of elongation, mature into the tissues of the shoot, such as support, conduction, storage, and protection.

The elongation of the roots is similar to that just indicated for the shoots. The same three zones of activity are present. To protect the root as, by growing, it pushes forward between the soil particles, the root tip is covered by a mass of loosely attached cells, the root cap.

The canes, arms, and trunk, as well as the permanent roots of the vine, continue to grow, but their growth is radial, increasing the diameter. The cambium divides. The cells on the inner side enlarge and differentiate into xylem and wood tissue; those on the outer side enlarge and differentiate into phloem and bark tissue.

ANNUAL CYCLE OF THE VINE

The vine is a conservative plant. It does not rush into growth in early spring, as do most deciduous fruit trees, but remains dormant until the mean daily temperature reaches about 50° F. (10° C.). Poenaru and Lazarescu (1959) reported that in the northern areas of grape production vines begin growth at 8° C. This may be owing to thorough chilling. Growth is slow at first, when the cells of the young shoot are actively dividing. Then, as the mean temperature rises, growth and shoot elongation accelerate from day to day. After three or four weeks, the season's period of most rapid growth—*the grand period of growth*—is under way. For a time the shoots of vigorous varieties may elongate as much as an inch or more a day. Weak-growing varieties evidence a similar period of rapid growth, but the daily increase is less. About the time of bloom, possibly as a result of momentary competition for foods, but probably owing to hormone and enzyme activity, the rapid shoot elongation slackens. The rise in the level of the carbohydrates for a brief period indicates hormone-enzyme activity as the more likely cause (Winkler, 1929). At first the decrease in the rate of growth is quite rapid; then it trails on at an ever slower rate to the end of the season (Winkler and Williams, 1936) (see graph A of fig. 21). Growth in diameter of the vine's permanent parts, as a result of rapid cell division in the cambium, follows a similar pattern, but it begins several weeks later.

The vine does not cease growth entirely, as trees do, by forming terminal buds. On the contrary, vine shoots never form *terminal buds*. The shoots may increase in rate of growth at any time if there is sufficient heat and an abundance of moisture in the soil, as after an irrigation or rain, and when there is ample available nitrogen. It is for this reason that young vines, with little or no crop to compete with vegetative growth for the products of the leaves, often continue growth into autumn and are killed by an early frost. The same is true for varieties that are harvested early. Under the favorable conditions for growth in most of California, the only means at the grower's disposal to slow the growth of such vines is to control the available nitrogen and irrigation water rigidly after midsummer.

About the time that length growth begins to slacken, the flowers, which develop simultaneously with the shoots, are ready to bloom. At the beginning of shoot growth the flower clusters on these shoots have developed only to the receptacle of the individual flowers. The flower clusters come out with the shoots, and during the next six to eight weeks, according to the season, the flower parts are formed. Blooming ordinarily occurs when the mean daily temperature reaches about 68° F. In areas where the mean temperature does not normally reach 68° F. at this season, blooming seems to be governed by some other factor, possibly a hormone activated by the increased hours of daylight.

The rapid shoot elongation, diameter increase of the older vine parts, and development of the flower parts are made possible by the reserves of foods stored in the dormant vine. These stored foods, no doubt, support most of the development indicated above, as well as the great expansion of the root system. Of course, by the time of blooming some of the leaves on the middle and basal parts of the shoots will be fully grown and producing more food materials than they utilize. Graph B of figure 21 shows the yearly utilization of the total available carbohydrates (sugar and starch), as indicated by the drop in the percentage of these materials in the basal segments of the one-year-old wood and their accumulation after midseason in the basal part of the shoots. Life processes are taking place in the vine while it is dormant, but the changes are small. For example, the utilization of carbohydrates amounts to about 0.5 per cent per month in California. This is indeed minor in comparison to the rate of use during the period of rapid growth in spring, when the level of these materials drops from about 17 to 8 per cent during the month of May.

After shoot elongation has slowed down, carbohydrates begin to accumulate in the shoots. The accumulation starts in the then midsection of the new shoot and progresses downward and upward during the remainder of the season (Winkler and Williams, 1945). The accumulation is slow at first, while there is still much shoot growth and the berries are rapidly increasing in size. Then the rate accelerates, except for a possible slowdown during the rapid movement of sugar into the berries at ripening, so that by late autumn the level of total stored reserve carbohydrates is essentially the same as it was in the previous autumn. The accumulation is principally starch. Except in the dormant period, when sugar accumulation offers protection against low temperature, the level of the sugars in the vine remains nearly constant (Winkler and Williams, 1945). If more sugar is produced, it is converted to starch, an insoluble storage material. The rate of accumu-

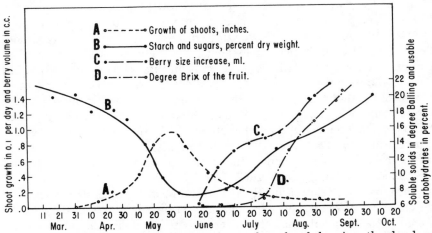

FIGURE 21: Graphs showing the annual growth cycle of the vine, the development of its fruit, and the seasonal levels of usable carbohydrates.

The Physiology of the Vine

lation will be affected by such factors as the amount of the crop, the time the fruit ripens, the health of the vines, the status of shoot growth, amount of leaves exposed to adequate light, and the climatic conditions. It is common knowledge that overcropping and continued rapid shoot growth delay the accumulation of carbohydrates in the vine reserve.

Radioactive labeling experiments using $^{14}CO_2$ showed that the sugar manufactured in the leaves in the fall (after harvest) and converted to starch in the wood tissues and roots is the first carbohydrate used by new shoots the following spring (W. M. Kliewer and R. Leach, unpublished data). The new shoots are dependent on these reserves until the first few leaves on the shoot are approximately half their full size, at which time they then start exporting more photosynthate than they import (Hale and Weaver, 1962; Koblet, 1969). Therefore, it is important that leaves remain active after harvest in order to build up carbohydrate reserves in storage tissues for growth and fruit cluster development the following spring.

In addition to the annual cyclic changes of starch and sugars in vines, other constituents, including many amino acids and carboxylic acids follow similar patterns (Kliewer, 1967a, b). The level of all these substances in canes and other woody tissues are high during dormancy up until budbreak, followed by a period of rapid decrease, which continues until August or September, and then gradually increases until dormancy sets in again.

Immediately after the shatter of impotent flowers following bloom, berry size increases rapidly. In berries with seeds the rate of increase continues for a time, then slows, and then accelerates again before berry maturation (see graph C, fig. 21). The growth of seedless berries is similar, except that the period of slower growth is shorter and the slowdown is less pronounced.

The accumulation of soluble solids in the berries, as measured by degrees Brix, changes little between the time of set and the beginning of ripening (see graph D, fig 21). Of course, total soluble solids—principally sugars—increase, because degrees Brix measures concentration, and the berries are growing. At the beginning of ripening there is an abrupt increase in degrees Brix (Balling, Oeschle, Baumé, etc.). The increase continues until full maturity and then slows (Winkler and Williams, 1936). The rate of this increase in degrees Brix differs widely between a variety that matures very early and one that matures its fruit very late. Seasonal conditions, particularly those of temperature, also affect the rate of the changes. Thus, during one season, the increase in degrees Brix and the other ripening processes may proceed very slowly, so that no varieties are ripe enough to harvest until after the average dates for picking are past; in another season, because of higher temperatures, the ripening changes may proceed very rapidly, resulting in any early harvest. For example, the average date for starting the

Tokay harvest in Lodi, California, is August 28, yet there have been years in which it was started on August 13 and others in which is was delayed until September 11. The other varieties of the same area were affected similarly.

BIBLIOGRAPHY

Broyer, T. C., and D. R. Hoagland. 1943. Metabolic activities of roots and their bearing on the relation of upward movement of salts in plants. Amer. Jour. Bot., 30:261–273.

Buttrose, M. S. 1968. Some effects of light intensity and temperature on dry weight and shoot growth of grapevines. Ann. Bot., 32:97–117.

Epstein, E. 1956. Mineral nutrition of plants: mechanisms of uptake and transport. Ann. Rev. Plant Physiol., 7:1–24.

Galston, A. W., and P. J. Davies. 1969. Hormonal regulation in higher plants. Science, 163:1288–1297.

Geisler, G. 1963. Art-und sortenspezifische CO_2-assimilutions raten von Reben unter Berücksichtigung wechselnder Beleuchtungsstärken. Mitt. (Kloster-neuburg), 13A:301–305.

———, and F. Radler. 1963. Entwicklungs-und Reifevorgänge an Trauben von *Vitis*. Ber. Deut. Botan. Ges., 76:112–119.

Hale, C. R., and R. V. Weaver. 1962. The effect of developmental stage on direction of translocation of photosynthate in *Vitis vinifera*. Hilgardia, 33:89–131.

Hardy, P. J. 1968. Metabolism of sugars and organic acids in immature grape berries. Plant Physiol., 43:224–228.

———. 1969. Selective diffusion of basic and acidic products of CO_2 fixation into the transpiration stream in grapevines. J. Expt. Bot., 20:856–862.

———, and J. V. Possingham. 1969. Studies on translocation of metabolites in the xylem of grapevine shoots. J. Expt. Bot., 20:325–335.

Harris, J. M., P. E. Kriedemann, and J. V. Possingham. 1971. Grape berry respiration: Effect of metabolic inhibitors. Vitis, 9:291–298.

Hawker, J. S. 1969. Changes in the activities of malic enzyme, malate dehy-drogenase, phosphopyruvate carboxylase, and pyruvate decarboxylase during the development of a non-climacteric fruit (the grape). Phytochem., 8: 19–23.

Hoagland, D. R. 1948. Lectures on the inorganic nutrition of plants. Waltham, Mass., Chronica Botanica.

Hylmo, B. 1953. Transpiration and ion absorption. Physiol. Plantarum, 6:333–405.

Kliewer, W. M. 1965. The sugars of grapevines. II. Identification and seasonal changes in the concentration of several trace sugars in *Vitis vinifera*. Amer. J. Enol. Vitic., 16:168–178.

————. 1967a. Annual cyclic changes in the concentration of free amino acids in grapevines. Amer. J. Enol. Vitic., 18:126–137.

————. 1967b. Annual cyclic changes in the concentration of sugars and organic acids in 'Thompson Seedless' grapevines. Proc. Amer. Soc. Hort. Sci., 91:205–212.

————. 1971. Effect of day temperature and light intensity on concentration of malic and tartaric acids in *Vitis vinifera* L. grapes. J. Amer. Soc. Hort. Sci., 96:372–377.

————, L. A. Lider, and N. Ferrari. 1972. Effects of controlled temperature and light intensity on growth and carbohydrate levels of 'Thompson Seedless' grapevines. J. Amer. Soc. Hort. Sci., 97:185–188.

Koblet, W. 1969. Wanderungen von Assimilaten in Rebrieben und Einfluss der Blattfäche auf Ertrag und Qualitat der Trauben. Wein Wissenschaft., 24:277–319.

Kramer, P. J., and T. S. Coile. 1940. An estimate of the volume of water made available by root extension. Plant Physiol., 15:743–747.

Kriedmann, P. E. 1968. Photosynthesis in vine leaves as a function of light intensity, temperature, and leaf age. Vitis, 7:213–220.

————, W. M. Kliewer, and J. M. Harris. 1970. Leaf age and photosynthesis in *Vitis vinifera* L. Vitis, 9:97–104.

————, and R. E. Smart. 1971. Effect of irradiance, temperature, and leaf water potential on photosynthesis of vine leaves. Photosynthetica, 5:6–15.

Kursanov, A. L. 1962. Metabolism and the transport of organic substances in the phloem. Advances in Bot. Res., 1:209–278.

Lundegärdh, H. 1950. The translocation of salt and water through wheat roots. Physiol. Plantarum, 3:103–151.

Moreau, L., and E. Vinet. 1922. Pleurer de la vigne. Compt. Rend. Acad. Agri. de France, 9:554–557.

Nassar, A. R., and W. M. Kliewer. 1966. Free amino acids in various parts of *Vitis vinifera* at different stages of development. Proc. Amer. Soc. Hort. Sci., 89:281–294.

Nitsch, J. V., and C. Nitsch. 1965. Présence de phytokinines et autres substances de croissance dans la sève d'Acer saccharum et de *Vitis vinifera*. Bull. Soc. Bot. France, 112:11–18.

Poenaru, I., and V. Lazarescu. 1959. The practical importance of an understanding of the leafing out of grape varieties. [Trans. title] (English, French and German summary). Grăchina Via Si Livada, 8:23–28.

Raleigh, G. J. 1946. Effect of various ions in gluttation of the tomatoes. Plant Physiol., 21:194–200.

Saito, K., and Z. Kasai. 1968. Accumulation of tartaric acid in the ripening process of grapes. Plant and Cell Physiol., 9:529–537.

Shaulis, N. J., H. Amberg, and D. Crowe. 1966. Response of Concord grapes to light, exposure, and Geneva Double Curtain training. Proc. Amer. Soc. Hort. Sci., 89:268–280.

Skene, K. G. M. 1967. Gibberellin-Like substances in root exudate of *Vitis vinifera*. Planta, 74:250–262.

Stoev, K. D., P. T. Mamarov, and I. B. Benčov. 1959. Chromatographic analysis of sugars and free amino acids in the sap of vines. (Trans. title) Fiziol. Rast., 6:408–414. (See also Hort. Abs., 30:1858, 1960).

Swanson, C. A., and E. D. H. El-shishiny. 1958. Translocation of sugars in the Concord grape. Plant Physiol., 33:33–37.

Trip, P., C. D. Nelson, and G. Krotkov, 1965. Selective and preferential translocation of C[14]-labeled sugars in White Ash and Lilac. Plant Physiol., 40: 740–747.

Winkler, A. J. 1929. The effect of dormant pruning on the carbohydrate metabolism of *Vitis vinifera*. Hilgardia, 4:153–173.

———, W. O. Williams. 1936. Effect of seed development on the growth of grapes. Proc. Amer. Soc. Hort, Sci., 33:430–434.

———, ———. 1938. Carbohydrate metabolism of *Vitis vinifera*: Hemicellulose. Plant Physiol., 13:381–390.

———, ———. 1945. Starch and sugars in *Vitis vinifera*. Plant Physiol., 20: 412–432.

Wooly, T. T. 1961. Mechanisms by which wind influences transpiration. Plant Physiol., 36:112–114.

Wright, K. E., and N. L. Barton. 1955. Transpiration and the absorption and distribution of radioactive phosphorus in plants. Plant Physiol., 30:386–388.

Zimmermann, M. H. 1960. Transport in the phloem. Ann. Rev. Plant Physiol., 11:167–190.

7

The Grape Flower
and Berry Set

FRUIT-BUD FORMATION

In discussing the structure of the vine we pointed out that there are two kinds of functional buds: leaf buds and fruit buds. When initiated in the axil of the leaf of the rapidly growing shoot, these buds are identical—simple leaf buds. They remain so until the vine is well along in its seasonal development; that is, until shoot growth slows, with the production of food material thereby becoming greater than is used.

Most grape varieties form enough fruit buds for a crop by the time the vines are large enough to bear, even though a large part of the annual growth is removed by pruning. A few varieties, notably Dizmar and Red Malaga, are erratic in both the number and the form of the clusters that are produced. These and other varieties that behave somewhat similarly make the problem of fruit-bud formation and the conditions that influence it of interest. The physiology of fruit-bud differentiation is not understood sufficiently to explain all the differences in fruitfulness between varieties. Nevertheless, observations supported by much analytical data indicate how the formation of fruit buds is influenced by different types of growth and certain food materials and mineral elements (Huglin, 1960).

Growth and fruit-bud formation.—Newly planted and young vines grow throughout the season and produce few or no fruitful buds. Older vines that are in good health and carrying normal crops grow rapidly in the spring, their shoots are very succulent, and more carbohydrate material is used than the leaves produce. Soon the reserve foods in the spurs, canes, and arms are reduced to the point where growth is checked. Water stresses arising from increasing transpirational losses may also be a factor in retarding shoot growth at this time and on into the summer. As shoot growth slows, organic reserve materials begin to accumulate and, accompanying this development, the lower mid- and basal parts of the shoots become woody. Following the marked slackening in growth, shoot elongation slows even more as the season advances, and the shoots mature over more and more of their length. This cycle of growth, with the further accumulation of reserve foods, fosters fruit-bud differentiation. Circumstances that upset the normal cycle of seasonal vine development—such as continued rapid growth, very weak growth owing to overcropping, extensive cloudiness, and the like—retard the initiation of fruit-bud formation and also reduce the number of clusters per shoot, their size, and the perfection of form of the clusters that are produced.

The relation of total shoot growth to yield, although important as a guide in pruning, varies with other conditions. In any investigation at Davis, California, it was found that, within the limits of good commercal practice, methods that excessively increase the vigor of shoot growth will diminish the fruitfulness of the buds, and methods that promote normal vigor will favor fruitfulness (Winkler, 1929). Working with Sultana (Thompson Seedless) in Australia, Thomas and Barnard (1937) found a similar correlation between total growth and fruiting. With vines making below-average to weak growth, the production of fruitful buds decreased in both Australia and California. The decrease in the number of fruitful buds formed by vines of above-normal vigor is usually compensated by the large size of clusters. Excessively vigorous shoots on strong vines are not only less fruitful, but the fruitful buds that are formed are farther up on the shoots (see fig 17).

Carbohydrate accumulation.—According to Thomas and Barnard (1937) the percentage of starch in the annual wood is closely associated with fruit-bud formation. Microscopic studies on the initiation of bud differentiation at Davis (Winkler and Shemsettin, 1937) show that this begins during early June, and analyses of shoots indicate that the accumulation of carbohydrates starts late in May (Winkler and Williams, 1945). The accumlation is most rapid in the mid-section of the shoot. Fruit-bud differentiation also occurs first in this section and is most rapid there (from the fourth to the eighth node).

The role of carbohydrates in the initiation of fruit-bud formation is not entirely clear. Their accumulation may be the means of increasing respiration or of stimulating the synthesis of nitrogenous substances that influence differentiation. The direct influence of carbohydrates on fruit-bud formation is further emphasized by the reduced crop in a year that follows severe pruning, defoliation by diseases or insects, or overcropping. The drain on the vine created by any of these conditions prevents or delays bud differentiation. Similarly, the distal ends of the shoots accumulate little or no starch, they rarely mature, and the number of fruitful buds is reduced toward this section of the shoot. Red canes (see p. 487) are a manifestation of the failure of a large part of or all of the individual shoots to mature; such canes are devoid of starch and also of fruitful buds.

Nitrogen supply.—In a four year-trial with Thompson Seedless vines grown in a mixture of Perlite and Vermiculite irrigated with Hoagland nutrient solutions containing various levels of nitrogen, Kliewer and Cook (1971) found that vine growth and bud-fruitfulness of vines irrigated with 0.5 millimoles of NO_3 or less were greatly reduced compared to vines irrigated with 1 to 4 millimoles of NO_3 solutions. The nitrogen deficient vines had less than 0.12 per cent NO_3 in the petioles at bloomtime and less than 300 ppm arginine in the juice of the grapes at harvest (Kliewer, 1971).

A nitrogen supply that induces normal growth and a good foliage color no doubt fosters fruit-bud formation. It will usually bring about a most favorable balance between growth and fruitfulness in regions having abundant sunshine. In regions with much cloudy weather, a smaller supply of nitrogen may be desirable.

An excess of nitrogen can also be detrimental to fruit-bud formation or to fruit set. Cook (1956) found that one in five vineyards in California is being fertilized so heavily with nitrogen that crop production is being reduced. Rank growth occurs only with an abundant supply of nitrogen, which when excessive reduces the formation of fruitful buds.

Carbohydrate-nitrogen ratio.—Because of the importance just shown for carbohydrates and nitrogen in the formation of fruit buds, an attempt has been made to formulate ratios of these substances that would serve as indicators of growth and fruiting response in the plant. If water and the various essential mineral elements are assumed to be adequate, a number of conditions may be indicated that are directly related to fruiting and vegetative growth:

(a) Moderate carbohydrates and very high nitrogen: strong vegetative growth, little or no fruit-bud formation or fruit production. This is typical of young vines on very fertile or heavily nitrogen-fertile soil with high moisture. Large leaves, long internodes, late growth, and poor wood maturity.

(b) High carbohydrates and moderate nitrogen: moderate vegetative growth, with abundant fruit-bud formation and fruit production. This is typical of mature vines on a moderately fertile soil, with adequate moisture. Leaves normal in size, average-length internodes, and early wood maturity.

(c) Very high carbohydrates and low nitrogen: poor vegetative growth, with very limited fruit-bud formation and fruit production. This is typical of plants growing in a poor soil that is very deficient in nitrogen. Leaves small, yellow-green; shoot growth retarded, internodes short, and small but mature wood.

These conditions, resulting from different ratios of the carbohydrates and nitrogen, help to explain failures in fruit-bud formation. Even more important, they indicate a need to modify cultural practices to bring vegetative growth and fruiting more nearly in balance.

Minerals.—Too little is known of the relation of the other elements to fruit-bud differentiation. We can only state that the supply seems to be ample if it is adequate for normal vine growth. A significant increase in the number of clusters produced by the Carman grape following the application of phosphorus has been reported in Texas (Randolph, 1944). Growth of the vine, however, was increased markedly. The proportion of fruitful buds has also been increased by applications of zinc in some areas where "little leaf" was very severe. Here, again, the improvement in vine condit on was great and preceded improved fruitfulness.

Water-supply.—Even with a good supply of soil moisture it is not unusual for the vine to lose more water through its leaves that the roots can supply in the middle part of the day, beginning in early summer. Deficits of this sort disappear in the late afternoon. After a time they doubtless check growth to an extent that favors the accumulation of carbohydrates. With an adequate supply of nitrogen, such a condition will stimulate fruitbud formation. Normal irrigation during midsummer may cause some increase in growth, but it will not check the accumulation of carbohydrates, once this is under way. When the soil moisture is depleted to the wilting point, however, with the vines under continuous stress, the number of fruitful buds that develop is reduced.

Temperature and light intensity.—The influence of temperature on fruit-bud formation is very closely associated with that of water, since it materially affects the water requirements of the vine. Antcliff and Webster (1955) found that weather conditions, especially in the spring, directly influenced the fruitfulness of the buds produced that year. During thirteen years in which microscopic examinations were made in Australia, the correlation between hours of sunshine from bud burst to bud differentiation (September 1 to November 15) and the per cent of fruitful buds at the end of the summer was 0.531, which was hardly significant. Yet, when the effect of the previous year's crop was eliminated the partial correlation was 0.636, which is statistically significant (5-per-cent level). A multiple correlation of per cent fruitful buds with both yield and sunshine gave a correlation of 0.809, which is highly significant (1-per-cent level). More recently, Baldwin (1964) showed that over an eighteen-year period in Australia, 74 per cent of the seasonal variation in the number of fruitful buds can be explained by the number of hours of bright sunshine and the mean daily temperatures during the time that fruit primordia are initiated in the late spring and

The Grape Flower and Berry Set

early summer. This correlation of fruitfulness of buds with sunshine in spring may be responsible in part for the high percentage of fruitful buds in the Thompson Seedless in California.

In very hot regions—severe desert conditions—fruitfulness is reduced. This is thought to result from a more active and continued growth of the vine, with accompanying changes in nutrition. The deduction is supported by the almost complete sterility of the vine in regions where the vine grows the year round. It has been shown conclusively that in very hot regions the accumulation of carbohydrates is both retarded and of lesser amount (Kliewer et al., 1972).

The role of temperature, light intensity, and daylength in fruit bud formation in grapes has been further explored by Buttrose (1969a, 1969b, 1969c) who used environmental control cabinets. He found that the fruitfulness of a bud was directly related to the temperature surrounding the bud during the period of about three weeks, during which time the node subtending it changed in position, as a result of shoot growth, from the shoot apex to ten nodes back on the shoot. The effect of temperature on the fruitfulness of the buds back of the shoot apex fell proportionately, reaching zero for buds at node ten from the shoot tip.

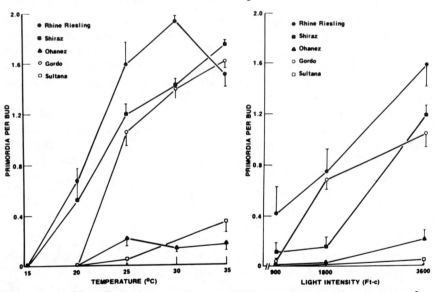

FIGURE 22: The effect of temperature and light intensity on the mean number of bunch primordia per bud for the basal 12 buds on shoots of five grape varieties grown in controlled environmental cabinets. In left side of figure light intensity was 3600 foot candles for 16-hour days. In right side of figure temperature was 25° C. (77° F.) for 16-hour days. The vertical bars equal 1 x standard error of the mean. (*Source of Data: Buttrose, 1970*)

Buttrose (1970a, 1970b) also showed that Muscat of Alexandria, Thompson Seedless and Almeria produced no fruitful buds when grown at 68° F. and 3,600 foot candles of light and in 16-hour days for 13 weeks, while White Riesling and Shiraz produced some fruitful buds at this temperature but none at 60° F. under the same condition of light and time of exposure. Maximum bud fruitfulness was obtained in all varieties when grown at 86° to 95° F. Furthermore, he found that bud fruitfulness was related to the maximum temperature experienced each day, rather than to heat summation, provided that the maximum temperature was maintained for at least a four-hour period at some time during the 24-hour day.

He also found that the number of bunch primordia per bud increased with increasing light intensity over the range of 900 to 3,600 foot candles (fig. 22), White Riesling formed some fruitful buds at the low light intensity (900 foot candles), while Muscat of Alexandria, Thompson Seedless, Almeria, and Shiraz remained barren. Buttrose (1969c) reported that fruitfulness of new buds depends on the daily duration of high light intensity (2,400 foot candles or more) but not on the length of the uninterrupted dark period. Thus, grapevines do not depend on daylength for fruit bud formation, yet the dry weight accumulation of the vine is related to total light energy rather than to hours of illumination. These findings indicate that the mechanism leading to induction of bud fruitfulness is not identical to that leading to dry weight accumulation. Thus, according to May (1965) and Sartorius (1968), it is the light actually falling on the bud itself that influences fruitfulness, rather than the whole plant illumination and total photosynthesis. The mode of action of temperature and light intensity for fruit bud formation is not yet known.

Cultural practices.—The type of vine support may have a marked effect on the fruitfulness of grape buds. Shaulis *et al.* (1966) and Shaulis and May (1971) found that bud fruitfulness and cluster size in Concord and Thompson Seedless vines were increased considerably when the exposure of the vine's leaf surface to light was improved. This was accomplished by tying the fruit cane on the two wires, four feet apart, of a wide-top trellis, thus producing two curtains of the current shoots, similar to the Geneva double curtain support designed by Shaulis and now used extensively in New York.

Rootstocks may also influence the fruitfulness of grapevines. In field trials with Chardonnay and Gamay Beaujolais grafted onto A x R #1 were found to be considerably more fruitful than when grafted onto the St. George rootstock (Lider *et al.*, 1973). Yet to be determined is the question as to whether or not the scions on St. George could be induced to be more fruitful on a high wide-topped trellis which provides a better leaf exposure than the present vertical trellis.

Proper pruning exerts a minor influence on fruit-bud formation. With most varieties it improves conditions for fruit-bud formation by preventing overcropping. Under California conditions too little as well as too much pruning is likely to reduce vine fruitfulness. Pruning, when accompanied by the appropriate method of thinning, very markedly improves flower development and set. It must be remembered, however, that excessive pruning may throw the vine into over-rank growth, thereby reducing the number of fruitful buds formed.

Other factors doubtless influence the formation of fruit buds. Defoliation, shading, and girdling are such factors. They act largely through their effect upon the accumulation of carbohydrates and the synthesis of other organic substances. The nitrogen supply of a vine on which the girdle is kept open for some time may be reduced sufficiently to be a factor; in this case root growth would be checked.

Other substances.—Of late, substances other than those named so far have received attention as agents that may have a role in the initiation of fruit-bud formation. For example, Kessler *et al.* (1959a, b) showed that spraying the basal part of shoots of the grapevine with 50 ppm of uracil or caffeine in May significantly increased the number of clusters per shoot in the following year. They produced figures to show that the increase in cluster formation paralleled increases in protein-nitrogen and in the ratio of ribonucleic to desoxyribonucleic acids. It might well be that the effect of these fruitful-bud-promoting substances results from their catalytic action on the synthesis of ribonucleic acid and protein.

More recently Stuart (1961) found that vegetative terminals of azalea plants of varying ages initiated flower buds promptly after application of the chemical growth retardants as soil drenches.

Although these substances were applied externally, they gave evidence of influence on normal changes or synthesis in the vine. Thus it may be assumed that within the vine there are substances—enzymes or growth regulators—that control these changes. Harada and Nitsch (1959) isolated a substance that seems to affect flower induction. However, no known compound has yet been found that can directly cause flower bud initiation to occur in grapevines. If and when such substances that are active in initiating fruit-bud formation are discovered, they will probably be found to have their origin in the leaves (Sartorius, 1968) or other green organs of the vine, and probably the conditions favoring their formation will be similar to those favoring the other conditions surrounding fruit-bud formation discussed above. Lavee *et al.* (1967) showed that a certain amount of leaf area is needed for induction of fruit primordia in grape buds. In Alphonse Lavallee and Thompson Seedless 18 to 21 leaves above a given bud were needed to bring about the induction of fruit primordia. Until more is learned of the function of these substances it will be well to give every consideration to the fact that the problem of

The Grape Flower and Berry Set

fruit-bud formation emphasizes the paramount importance of a large, well exposed leaf surface that is functioning normally.

THE CLUSTER AND FLOWERS

In the vine the flowers are borne in a cluster (or bunch). In position and origin, the cluster very closely resembles the tendril. The individual flower of the cluster is really a branch shoot bearing leaves specially modified to carry on reproduction.

The main axis of the cluster is called the *rachis*. Branches arise from the rachis at irregular intervals and divide to form the *pedicels* (cap stems) which bear the individual flowers. With varieties that develop large clusters, the main branches of the rachis may divide again, forming secondary or even tertiary branches. The pedicels are, of course, in all cases borne on the smallest division of the rachis. The region of the rachis extending from the shoot to its first branch is called the *peduncle*, or *stem*.

Flower-cluster development.—The rudiments of the flower cluster are formed during the season preceding the year in which the flowers bloom. The differentiation that results in the formation of fruit buds begins in early June at Davis, involving the buds that are farthest along in their development (on the lower part of the shoot) (Winkler and Shemsettin, 1937). At the end of June the percentages of buds of Thompson Seedless that were fruitful at the fifth, ninth, twelfth, fifteenth, and sixteenth nodes were, respectively, 80, 53, 26, 12, and 0. Five weeks later, more than 80 per cent of the buds of nodes four to sixteen, inclusive, were fruitful.

FIGURE 23: Photomicrographs of longitudinal sections through buds of Thompson Seedless (x 26).
1. Bud from node 10 on cane, June 19 collection; C, early stage in bud development; L, leaf initial.
2. Bud from node 10, July 11 collection; C, cluster primordium; B, bract subtending a branch of clusters primordium.
3. Bud from node 6, July 22 collection; C_1, upper-cluster primordium; C, lower-cluster primordium; C_b, branch of cluster; B, bract subtending branch of cluster primordium. (*From Hilgardia 10, No. 15*)

These figures indicate that differentiation proceeds rapidly, once it has started (see fig. 23). Differentiation is somewhat retarded in the buds at the base of the shoot. They mature early, but the accumulation of carbohydrates starts later than in the area between nodes four to eight. By late summer, however, all the buds that will develop into fruitful shoots next year have undergone differentiation. Both in California and in Australia the most fruitful part of the cane is between the fourth and twelfth nodes (Antcliff and Webster, 1955 A, B; Winkler and Shemsettin, 1937). The change to fruit buds occurs while the buds are still soft, at about the time they show a very rapid increase in size or plumpness.

Barnard (1932) and Barnard and Thomas (1933), who studied the fruiting of Sultana (Thompson Seedless), indicate an earlier initiation of fruit-bud differentiation in Australia than that just noted for California. According to Perold (1927), differentiation occurs at about the same time in South Africa as in Australia, mid-November to early December. In central Europe differentiation begins about mid-June and is complete by mid-August (Huglin, 1958).

Breviglieri (1956), working in the Tuscany region of Italy, found that Sangioveto buds showed definite differentiation on May 16, Malvasia on May 22, Canaiolo on May 28, and Trebbiano on June 1. These and other results indicate that the beginning of differentiation is influenced by region, season, and variety.

The rudimentary clusters formed at the time of differentiation continue to develop until late in the summer, when they enter into a winter rest that

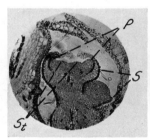 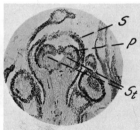 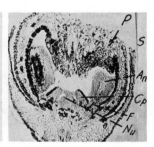

FIGURE 24: Photomicrographs showing initiation and development of the individual parts of Thompson Seedless flowers (x 100).

1. A flower two weeks after vines leafed out: S, calyx; lower line points to early stage of development; P, early stage of corolla development; St, initiation of stamen.
2. A flower three weeks after leafing out: S, calyx, sepals still appear coalesced; P, corolla, the petals are coming together above to form the calyptra; St, stame development.
3. A flower four weeks after leafing out: S, calyx; P, corolla; An, anther; Cp, carpel; F, filament; Nu, nucellus. (*From Hilgardia 10, No. 15*)

extends into early spring. The clusters in the buds on those parts of the shoot that become well matured usually develop to the stage of the rudiments (primordia) of the individual flowers by the beginning of this rest period. The shoots that develop from these buds in the following spring will, therefore, bear clusters that are typical in shape for the variety. In contrast, the rudimentary clusters in the buds on the upper parts of the shoot that are late in maturing do not advance so far in their development before the normal rest period begins. Clusters on shoots arising from these buds, if they grow, may undergo limited development in the spring, but they are usually smaller and imperfect in shape.

Branas (1957) showed that the number of individual flower primordia that develop on a cluster following differentiation is influenced in some varieties by the number of lateral shoots that are permitted to grow and by the flowers they produce.

The current crop would be expected to have a similar effect. This it does, but disbunching trials by Antcliff (1955) indicate that the current season's crop is but one of the factors affecting fruit-bud formation.

Development of the flowers.—As indicated above, by the time of the dormant season clusters have developed to the stage of being the receptacles of the individual flowers. Little change occurs during dormancy. In spring the flower clusters emerge with the leaves as shoot growth starts. With leafing out, the development of the several parts of the individual flowers is initiated.

The calyx, corolla, stamens, and pistil are differentiated in the order named. About one week after leafing out, the calyx is discernible on the side of the mass of meristematic tissue of the primordia of the flower (fig. 24). About a week later, initiation of the corolla is evident. The petals push up rapidly, the tips curving inward. When the tips come together, the projecting cells of one intermesh with those of the others, thus interlocking the petals to form a unit, the calyptra, which is shed in blooming. Even before the calyptra is competely formed, two-and-one-half to three weeks after leafing out, the beginning of stamen development is visible. A week or so later, the primordia of the carpels appear (fig. 25). With further development, the stamens differentiate to form the filaments and anthers, and the carpels unite to form the pistil and its parts—the ovules, stile, and stigma. The number of carpels in the grape flower is two, sometimes three. Two ovules arise in each carpel. As soon as the anthers have attained full development, pollen development gets under way. Paralleling this, egg cells are formed in the ovules. Six to eight weeks after leafing out, the development of the parts is complete and the pollen grains and egg cells are mature; the flowers are then ready to bloom.

Factors influencing flower development after growth begins.—The stage of development of the fruit bud at the time shoot growth begins influences

The Grape Flower and Berry Set

the rate of its continuing development. If there are two flower clusters on a shoot, the lower cluster is often more advanced when growth begins. The clusters of shoots on strong, well-ripened spurs will be more advanced in development than those on spurs that are weak. These differences in development, resulting from the more favorable position of the young shoot or the condition of the bearing wood of the vine, are seldom overcome by the weaker clusters. Possibly, the parts of the flower of clusters that have developed farthest in the bud will be formed more rapidly when growth begins; their conducting tissues will have developed ahead of those of clusters in less favorable positions and they will be getting more food. As a result, they continue to develop faster.

The importance of nutrition on the development of flowers after growth begins has been shown experimentally. When the number of flower clusters on a vine is restricted by the removal of some entire clusters just after growth starts, the remaining clusters will develop more rapidly than clusters on similar vines with none removed. When flower clusters are thus retained in reduced numbers they achieve a greater length before blooming and the pollen has greater viability. Similarly, clusters are larger on a vine carrying a normal crop than on a vine with an excessive crop. Winkler (1929) showed that the dropping of flowers at or shortly after blooming and, in certain varieties, the setting of shot berries are, in the absence of zinc deficiency, the result of unbalanced carbohydrate nutrition before and during blooming.

The influence of temperature on the rate of flower development up to

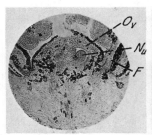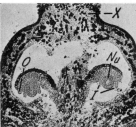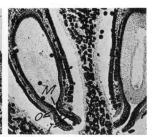

FIGURE 25: Photomicrographs showing the development of the individual parts of Thompson Seedless flowers (x 100).

1. A flower four to five weeks after leafing out: Ov, ovary; Nu, nucleus; F, filament.
2. A flower about one week to 10 days later than 1. The ovule is pointing downward and its parts have advanced in development; X, style; O, outer integument; Nu, nucellus; I, inner integument.
3. The mature megasporangium. The inner integuments elongate abnormally so that the micropile may be contorted; M, micropile; O, outer integument; I, inner integument. (*From Hilgardia 10, No. 15*)

The Grape Flower and Berry Set

blooming is readily observed. Vines in certain areas of a vineyard often bloom earlier than the others because they are on soil that warms up more rapidly in spring. When a vine is trained against a wall and the heat of the sun is intensified by reflection, the clusters that receive the benefit of the additional warmth may bloom several days to a week ahead of clusters on the same vine that do not receive additional heat. Continued cold weather in late spring tends to delay blooming. This is well illustrated by conditions in Germany in 1923, when the temperature remained very low during the first twenty-four days of June, delaying bloom for almost four weeks (Sartorius, 1926). Bloom in the Bonny Doon area of Santa Cruz County, California, was delayed three weeks in 1945 by temperatures considerably lower than normal.

Christiansen (1969) reported that the period from budbreak to blooming for Thompson Seedless in the Fresno area varied from 47 days in an early warm spring to 70 days in a late cool spring. However, the heat summation above 50° F. from budbreak to bloom was about the same in both seasons, i.e. 740 degree-days. In controlled growth cabinets using potted vines of several grape varieties (Buttrose and Hale, 1973) found the number of days between budbreak and blooming was reduced from 70 for vines grown at day/night temperatures of 57°/48° F. to 20 for plants held at 100°/91° F. They found that variations in day and night temperatures used to attain a mean daily temperature of approximately 65° F. had no effect on time to bloom, which was about 36 days under their conditions.

Perfect flowers.—Individual flowers are small, greenish, and usually perfect in the varieties of *Vitis vinifera* (fig. 26). A perfect vine flower has the following parts:

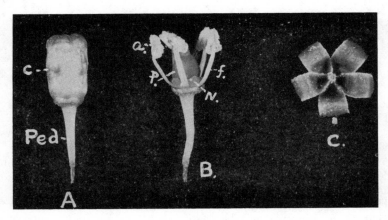

Figure 26: The grape flower: A, unopened; c, corolla, and Ped., pedicel; B, after blooming; a, anther; p, pistil; f, filament; and n, nectary; C, corolla petals shed at blooming, the calyptra (approx. x 10).

The Grape Flower and Berry Set

The *calyx* is usually made up five sepals, green in color, which enclose the other flower parts during their earliest development. Soon after the bunches appear, the sepals stop growth and dry up.

The *calyptra* (corolla) is usually made up of five (abnormally, three to nine) greenish petals. These petals are firmly united at the tip; hence the vine flower does not open from the tip, as is the rule with most flowers. Instead the calyptra becomes detached at the base and is shed as a little cap at the time of blooming (C of fig. 26).

The *stamens* are the pollen-bearing organs of the flower. Since the stamens are opposite the petals in the arrangement of the floral parts, they are usually present in equal numbers. Each stamen is made up of a stalk or *filament* (*f* of fig. 26), at the tip of which is the *anther* (*a* of fig. 26). The filament serves merely to support the anther, which performs the essential function of the stamen—pollen production. An anther consists of two lobes running lengthwise, and each lobe is divided into two longitudinal cavities, the *pollen sacs*.

At the base and between the filaments of the stamens there are small pads, the *nectaries*. In most species their function is the production of nectar, a sweet and odorous substance that may or may not attract insects. In most *vinifera* varieties these do not function, or their product is not very attractive, for few if any insects visit the flowers.

The *pistil* is the female part of the flower (*P* in fig. 26). The basal portion of the pistil, the *ovary*, is enlarged. In each half of the ovary there are two ovules. Each ovule has one *embryo sac*, containing the egg that, after fertilization, may develop into a seed. A column of tissue extending upward from the ovary is called the *style*. The extended part at the upper end of the style is the *stigma* (*s* in fig. 27). Immediately after a flower opens, its stigma is coated with a sweet and sticky solution secreted from within.

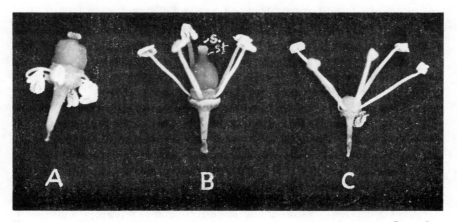

FIGURE 27: Type of grape flowers: A, pistillate; B, perfect; S, stigma; St, style; and C, staminate (approx. x 10).

This holds the pollen grains that fall on the stigma, and it may also serve as food for the growing pollen tubes.

Surrounding the ovary is the *pericarp*, a fleshy layer. The importance of this part of the flower is apparent, since the cells of the pericarp divide and expand to form the edible portion of the mature berry.

Imperfect flowers.—Although the flowers of the commercially important varieties of *Vitis vinifera* are mostly perfect—that is, they have well-developed male and female organs in the same flower—almost purely female or male flowers do occur (A and C in fig. 27). In grapes of American origin, in contrast, imperfect flowers are common and, therefore, of greater importance. This difference in the proportion of the varieties possessing imperfect flowers is doubtless the result of selection. Owing to the long time that V. *vinifera* has been cultivated, together with the very large number of varieties of this species, it has been possible to discard most of the varieties that have flowers so defective that fruiting is seriously limited. The American sorts, however, are of comparatively recent origin, and that elimination has not yet been possible.

Stout (1921) found that in the American sorts there are all degrees of intersexes, ranging from complete loss of femaleness at one extreme to almost complete loss of maleness, at the other. In flowers where the femaleness is completely lost, no pistil is in evidence, or it is a mere button-like structure within the cup formed by the nectaries (C of fig. 27). The stamens are well developed, and the pollen produced shows a very high percentage of germination. Several of the varieties used for rootstocks have such flowers; fruit is not produced. On the other hand, the flowers that have lost much of their maleness have well-devolped pistils and weakly developed stamens, the filaments of which are usually much re-curved (A of fig. 27). The pollen of these flowers is poorly nourished and usually fails to germinate on sugar-agar media. Between these two extremes of flower development, flowers of increasing degrees of perfection may be found until both the male and female parts of the flowers approach perfection in their development.

The range of intersexes in the *vinifera* varieties has not been researched so thorougly, but intensive studies have been made of various individual varieties. Among the more extensive of these is the work of Kozma (1954, 1955) on the variety Kadarka. He describes both the structural and fruiting defects and the differences in a wide range of flower types. There are generally well-known degrees of maleness and femaleness is certain commercial varieties of *vinifera* species. For example, Black Corinth has flowers in which the female parts are almost nonfunctional; the flowers have well-developed anthers that produce pollen of good germinability, but seeds are rarely produced; the setting of berries in this variety is by stimulative parthenocarpy, i.e., without fertilization. Others with flowers that are defective in femaleness are Thompson Seedless, Monukka, and Perlette. Ohanez is a variety showing well-developed female parts and very weak male parts; this variety always produces seeds in its fruit, but the stamens are strongly recurved and the pollen is very weak. The pollen of Ohanez regularly fails to germinate on sugar-agar media. Such flowers may show a high percentage of shatter (Avramov, 1954).

Of the commercially important varieties of grapes, only those of the species *rotundifolia* are dioecious—having male flowers on one plant and female flowers on another plant. In growing such varieties, male and female vines must be interplanted. Through breeding, however, varieties of this species have now been developed that have near-perfect flowers.

Blooming.—The time between leafing out and bloom is usually about eight weeks, varying from six to nine or more weeks according to weather conditions, especially temperature. Once flower development is complete, California grapes in the interior valleys and in the desert normally bloom when the mean daily temperature reaches 68° F. In areas where a mean of 68° F. is not reached, factors such as length of day seem to influence the time of blooming. For example, certain plants require long days and short nights for flower induction. It has been observed that when only a part of such a plant was given extra light for a number of days the effect of the extra exposure moved into the normally exposed part of the plant and caused flower development. Flower development is similarly induced in a plant that has had normal exposure (short days and long nights) when it is approach-grafted to one that has been exposed for a time to short nights and long days.

Harada and Nitsch (1959) have isolated a substance that appears in the plant one or two weeks before flower induction. Its time of appearance, together with its rapid increase, strongly indicates that it is the cause rather than a consequence of flower induction.

The number of days during which the vines are in bloom also depends on the weather. Eight or ten days may be taken as normal when conditions for blooming are favorable. The flowers at the base of the cluster bloom first. Those of a single cluster may open in the course of one or two days. The clusters of a vine do not all attain the proper development for blooming at the same time, however, and hence, with the most favorable conditions, blooming extends over a week or more.

To the casual observer the opening of a grape flower may seem to be very different from that of most other flowers, but the difference is not great. The calyptra becomes detached at the base instead of separating at the tip. It is shed entirely, as a cap (C of fig. 26), whereas the corolla petals of most flowers separate at the tip and remain attached to their base for a short time at least.

The grape calyptra becomes detached from the base without internal stress; the abscission is a normal function. A series of small cells in the region of detachment disintegrates to release it. Thus, the old opinion, that the calyptra is pushed off by the growth of the stamens, does not hold. The stamens may be involved in throwing it off, but they do not break it loose from the base.

Experience and experimental tests indicate that after the flower reaches the proper stage for blooming, temperature alone controls the time of opening. Below 60° F. few flowers open. With a rise in temperature to 65° or 70° F., blooming increases very rapidly. At temperatures of 95° to 100° F. the opening of the flowers is retarded, yet such severe temperatures do not seem to damage the flowers seriously.

Sunlight, rain, and the humidity of the air do not in themselves influence blooming. Their influence on temperature, however, may affect blooming indirectly.

Abnormal opening of flowers.—During cold or rainy weather it often happens that the calyptra comes only part way off, or not at all. Toward the end of the blooming season this condition may be observed with some varieties even when the weather favors detachment. It seems to result from a weakened condition of the flower, caused in some cases by unfavorable weather conditions and in others by too keen competition from flowers of more advanced development. This condition often occurs in such varieties as Malbec and Dizmar. During unfavorable weather it may occur in any variety. A persisting calyptra greatly reduces fruit setting, but does not appear to prevent it.

POLLINATION

The pollen.—The pollen grains of V*itis vinifera* are very small, being less than 0.001 inch in diameter. When shed from the anthers the grains are slightly oval. On soaking, however, they become round. Two membranes make up the wall of the mature grain—an outer thick wall and an inner thin one. The outer wall of the well-matured pollen grain has three bands or strips extending from pole to pole, perforated and much thinner than the rest of the wall. The grains contain a mass of protoplasm and stored food. The essential part of the contents is the three nuclei. One of these, the tube nucleus, enters into the growth of the pollen tube, whereas the two sperm nuclei fertilize the nuclei in the ovule.

Opening of the anthers.—As soon as the calyptra is thrown off in blooming, the stamens move away from the pistil (B of figs. 26 and 27). The anthers usually open immediately after blooming. It often happens that they open very rapidly and a veritable cloud of pollen can be seen to envelop the entire flower. In opening, the two pollen sacs of one of the lobes of an anther break loose along their common, median attachment. Thus,

The Grape Flower and Berry Set

there are two openings on each anther. They occur on the side toward the stigma.

The opening of the anthers is influenced by temperature in the same way as blooming. When temperatures are below 60° F., few if any of the anthers open. A rise above 60° F. is accompanied by an acceleration in the opening of the anthers, especially when the air is dry. Temperatures of 104° F. or above greatly reduce or completely inhibit pollination and fertilization of the ovaries.

Rain or high air-humidity tends to delay the opening of anthers. The reason is that the opening depends on stress arising from the drying of the outer surface of the anther. Drying pulls the walls of the pollen sacs loose at their medium connection, forming the slit through which the pollen is liberated. Cloudy days and fog will delay opening because of their similar tendency to increase air humidity and lower the temperature.

Is the vine flower self- or cross-pollinated?—The transfer of pollen from the anthers to the stigma is called *pollination*. There is difference of opinion among the viticulturists as to how pollination is brought about in the vine. It might be accomplished by insects, wind, or self-pollination. No doubt, each of these agencies comes into play in every vineyard. But which is the principal agency in pollination? It is on this point that opinions differ.

Insects visit grape flowers to a limited extent, so some pollen is transferred by them. The grape flower, however, owing to its inconspicuousness and its limited nectar, attracts only casual visits by insects. This fact, together with the total lack of any positive evidence that insects aid pollination materially, has brought most observers to the belief that insects rarely assist the pollination of *vinifera* grapes. There is evidence that insects may aid pollination in the *rotundifolia* varieties (Detjen, 1917).

Wind as an agency in vine pollination has many ardent supporters, yet its value is questionable. Naturally, as in the case of insect pollination, it is not impossible for pollen to be carried from the anthers of one flower to the stigma of another flower by wind. But does this happen in the vineyard, and, if so, to what extent? Available experimental evidence indicates that wind is not important in pollination. Here, again, the structure of the flower does not place the vine in the class of plants that are wind pollinated, such as the walnut, oaks, corn, etc. Bagged flowers usually set perfectly. Sartorius (1926) and others have shown that flower clusters whose stamens are removed will set only a few, straggling berries, if any, unless they are within 3 or 4 inches of other clusters still possessing stamens. Even in this case, the pollination might easily result from the throwing of the pollen onto the stigmas of the emasculated flowers by the rapid opening of the anthers on the adjacent unemasculated flowers. By hanging clusters with viable pollen among the clusters of a variety that usually sets only a few berries, we have found that clusters that are very near set a much larger number of berries. Clusters removed as much as 2 feet from the suspended clusters, however, showed no improvement in set. In the experimental vineyard at Davis a row of Hunisa, which usually sets clusters of mostly shot berries, was planted between rows of Cipro Nero and Emperor, both of which produce an abundance of good pollen. When hand-pollinated with pollen of either of these two varieties, the Hunisa set perfect clusters, but with the other varieties only 12 feet away it set shot berries. The blooming dates of the three varieties coincided almost perfectly, and the prevailing winds were crosswise to the rows.

Thus, it seems that self-pollination is the rule with *vinifera* grapes. It must be remembered, however, that cross-pollination is not only possible, but under certain conditions desirable, and that under still other conditions it is necessary. If and when cross-pollination is desirable or necessary, it will usually be necessary to do the pollinating by hand or machine. In Spain, detached clusters of other varieties are brushed over the blooming clusters of Almeria (Ohanez). In Australia the collected pollen is sprayed or dusted on (Boehm, 1961; Marriott, 1959). Cejtlin (1956) reports improvement in the set of some varieties by simply blowing a current of air or air and sulfur dust across the vine rows during bloom. Either of these procedures increases the amount of pollen that falls on each stigma which improves set and berry development (Tkačenko, 1960).

Formation of the pollen tube.—When the pollen grain reaches the stigma, pollination is complete. The pollen grain adheres to the stigma, whose surface is made up of short outgrowths (papillae) covered with a sticky secretion, the stigmatic fluid. The protoplasm of the pollen grain absorbs water from the stigmatic fluid and swells. With further development the inner wall is pushed out through one of the perforations of the outer wall to form a pollen tube. The pollen tube penetrates the tissue of the stigma and grows down through the style toward one of the ovules.

Factors influencing pollen germination and tube growth.—Temperature is the most common limiting factor of germination and pollen tube growth. In tests it has been found that percentage of germination is very low at 60° F. Tube growth is slow at that temperature, too—so slow that five to seven days elapse before the tube is long enough to penetrate the ovule. A rise in temperature above 60° F. raises both the percentage of grains that germinate and the rate of tube growth. Percentage of germination is usually highest at 80° to 90° F. At these temperatures the pollen tube also elongates rapidly, reaching the ovule in several hours.

Rain may reduce the percentage of germination by diluting the stigmatic fluid or completely washing it from the stigmas. Germination never occurs in pure water; the grains swell up and burst. Only one-third as many grains germinate in a 5-per-cent sugar solution as in a 15-per-cent solution.

The Grape Flower and Berry Set

The lower germination in the 5-per-cent solution is the result of the bursting of the grains. It seems quite probable that, where abundant rain falls while the flowers are opening, the stigmatic fluid may become so diluted that the number of pollen grains that germinate will be greatly reduced. However, in field trials at Davis with several grape varieties, sprinkling several hours each day during bloom resulted in little or no reduction in fruit set (Kliewer and Schultz, 1973).

SETTING OF THE BERRIES

Fruit set generally results from pollination that achieves fertilization and seed development. In most grape varieties the setting of berries is determined by this mechanism. Through the centuries, however, selection for special fruit characters has provided varieties in which there are different mechanisms of set. These function in the setting of completely and partially seedless and empty-seeded berries. Some varieties exhibit all these types of set in the same clusters, producing shot, seedless, and seeded berries. A more important fact is that, within this range of fruit setting, the behavior of certain varieties is relatively constant for a given type of berry set. For example, in some varieties, such as Black Corinth, there is hardly a trace of seed development; in others, such as Thompson Seedless, seed development is terminated by early embryo abortion and the berries are considered to be seedless; in still others, such as Chaouch, seed development proceeds until hard seed-coats of about normal size are formed, and then the embryo aborts and the seeds are empty. In most varieties, seed development is normal and viable seeds are produced. The mechanism involved in each of these types of set, and the special importance of the resulting fruit, are discussed here.

Stimulative parthenocarpy.—In Black Corinth, according to Pearson (1932), there is no ovule development beyond the time of bloom. Parthenocarpy, accordingly, was attributed to defective embryo sac formation with some or all of the nuclei degenerating. The pollen, in contrast, is of high germinability. Proceeding from these facts, Olmo (1936) showed that both the stimulus of pollination and the nutritional stimulus resulting from girdling were necessary to a satisfactory set of fruit. Thus, setting in this and similar varieties is by stimulative parthenocarpy. Later, Weaver and Williams (1950), Coombe (1950) and Weaver (1952) found that girdling can be completely replaced by spraying the open flowers with one of the synthetic auxin-like materials, such as 4-Chlorophenoxyacetic acid, or with gibberellin. It thus seems evident that girdling increases the auxin and gibberellin content of the flowers or clusters. Biological assay by Coombe (1960) suggests that the amount of these substances in berries is higher in girdled than in ungirdled vines.

Since it is recognized (Muir, 1942) that pollination causes a burst of production of growth hormone, the need for pollination to induce set in this and similar varieties indicates a deficiency of auxin. As pointed out by Nitsch (1950), auxin may arise from the pollen tube growth or from interaction between the pollen and the ovary. These sources of auxin ensure the continuity of berry development through anthesis, and the possible movement of auxin down through the pedicel prevents abscission. Auxin is probably also involved in development of the conducting elements through which food material moves into the growing ovary (Muir, 1942).

In most years some berries set without pollination; they may in some instances persist, but, not having sufficient auxin, they grow hardly at all. Even the berries that set by stimulative parthenocarpy remain small, because of limited auxin or gibberellin supply in the total absence of seed development.

The complete seedlessness and small size of Black Corinth fruit are characteristics that have made it one of the world's important varieties. The currants of commerce are made from it. The Cape Currant, Red Corinth, and White Corinth set their fruit similarly, but currents made from them are less popular because of differences in flavor and other characteristics.

Stenospermocarpy.—Typical fruit of the Thompson Seedless does not set without fertilization. The flowers of this and similar varieties—Sultana, Perlette, Monukka, etc.—have normal appearance and produce very good pollen. The abnormally long inner integument and the large micropyle of the ovules of Thompson Seedless seem to have little or no significance. The larger number of abnormal embryo sacs than in normal seeded varieties is of questionable importance. Even so, there are a number of normal-appearing embryo sacs in nearly all flowers that are entered by pollen tubes. According to Pearson (1932), in practically every one of the embryo sacs that have been entered by pollen the endosperm nucleus starts a series of divisions, the nucellar cells enlarge markedly, and may divide, but the zygote does not divide for probably two to four weeks, and then abortion occurs. Similar development is reported by Barritt (1970) for seedless varieties in New York. In these varieties the auxin content is ample for an abundant set of fruit. It is not sufficient to sustain embryo development, however, even with what seems to be an almost normal fertilization. In fact, in a number of varieties there is only a trace of seed development. That auxin is a limiting factor is shown by the marked increase in berry size that results from properly timed girdling or from spraying the newly set berries with synthetic auxin-like materials (Weaver and Winkler, 1952; Weaver, 1958). Since there has been pollination and fertilization followed by embryo abortion, the fruit set in these varieties is by *stenospermocarpy*. Berries so set are much larger than those resulting from stimulative parthenocarpy. Occasionally a few berries of these varieties may and do set by stimulative parthenocarpy. These remain small, like those of Black Corinth.

This type of fruit set—with its fairly large, yet seedless berries—is responsible for the prominence of Thompson Seedless. Most of the raisins of the world are produced from its fruit. In California it is also a leading table grape. When so used, it is either girdled or sprayed with gibberellin to increase berry size further (Weaver and Williams, 1950; Weaver, 1958). Raisins made of Monukka are, in the opinion of many people, superior in flavor to those of Thompson Seedless; however, the variety has the faults of developing more, harder, and large seed forms, and its raisins always become sticky in storage. In some years its seedlike structures are especially large and objectionable. As a table grape, the Perlette variety is handled similarly to Thompson Seedless, but, owing to the greater compactness of its cluster, thinning must be more extensive.

Empty-seededness.—Another condition, typified by the empty-seededness of the variety Chaouch, concerns seed development more than fruit set, since the character of the berries is changed little, if at all (Olmo, 1934). Nevertheless, the factors influencing fruit setting are involved, at least to a considerable degree. The empty seeds have the appearance of having contained embryos that aborted and endosperm that shriveled and degenerated, leaving them more or less hollow. Such seeds float in water, whereas normal seeds sink. According to Olmo (1936), who has worked with Chaouch at Davis, 99.5 per cent of the seeds are empty. In the development of such seeds, pollination and fertilization proceed normally, and the zygotes, before abortion, grow sufficiently to result in the formation of a seed coat of almost normal size and texture. This type of development follows that indicated for fruit set in Thompson Seedless, but proceeds much further before disintegration occurs. That the auxin level is higher here is seemingly indicated by the greater development of nucellus and endosperm, and the much larger berry. It has been suggested that this is a genetic factor, since the formation of empty seeds is largely controlled by the maternal parent. Yet, year-to-year variation in empty-seededness in certain varieties strongly indicates nutritional causes.

Normal set.—In the set of seeded varieties, such as Cardinal, Emperor, Muscat of Alexandria, Carignane, and Cabernet Sauvignon, the normal sequence of pollination, fertilization, and seed development takes place. The pollen grains are usually thrown on the stigma when the anthers open, and there they germinate. The tubes then grow down through the style into the ovary, the two sperm cells entering the embryo sac. One of these unites with the egg cell to form the zygote. The zygote develops into the embryo of the seed. The other sperm cell unites with the two polar nuclei of the embryo sac to give rise to the endosperm food storage in the seed with the embryo. Cell division to form the endosperm proceeds almost immediately, whereas that of the zygote is delayed.

Under favorable conditions of production this type of fruit setting results in maximum berry size for the variety. This desirable result may follow the threefold stimulus of pollination, fertilization, and seed development. Support is found in the direct correlation between berry size and the number of seeds per berry (Gartel, 1954; Müller-Thurgau, 1898. In view of work by Nitsch (1950) with strawberries, however, it seems likely that the threefold stimulus has a direct effect on the level of auxin and that this substance, at least to a degree, is the important factor in determining berry size within a variety. In the strawberry, the fruit develops from the large receptacle, and the achenes (seeds) develop on its surface. These achenes are rich in auxin, and berry size is in proportion to their number. When achenes were removed from an area of a berry while the berries were still small, that area made little further growth. When all the achenes were removed there was no growth. Yet, when all the achenes were removed and the berry was coated with a lanolin paste containing 100 ppm of beta-naphthoxyacetic acid, the berry enlarged almost normally. In other words, the strawberry receptacle requires auxin or an auxin-like material for growth (Nitsch, 1953). Other fruits regardless of the inflorescence from which they develop, are probably affected similarly.

This finding helps explain the relation of the type of fruit setting to berry size. It is known that auxin content is low in flowers that set by stimulative parthenocarpy, and the resulting berries remain very small. In stenospermocarpy there is a higher level of auxin, as evidenced by complete fertilization with slight seed development, and the berries are much larger. With the still higher auxin level accompanying the development of a full complement of normal seeds, berry size is maximum for the variety.

Two schools of thought exist as to what regulates fruit set in grapevines. One group maintains that fruit set is regulated by specific fruit setting factors (growth regulators) that originate at sites other than the cluster itself (Weaver, *et al.*, 1962; Sartorius, 1968). The other group maintains that fruit set is regulated by the supply of organic nutrients, such as carbohydrates, rather than by specific hormonal stimuli originating from organs external to the developing cluster. Strong evidence that fruit set is solely regulated by the supply of organic nutrients has been provided by Mullins (1967), who demonstrated that fruit set can occur in cuttings in which leaves, apices, and roots are removed as they appear and by inflorescences, which were cultured *in vitro* on a medium containing only sucrose, mineral salts, glycine, and vitamins. In other experiments comparing the effect of the growth retardant, cycocel (2-chloroethyltrimethylammonium chloride) and shoot tipping on fruit set, Skene (1969) and Coombe (1970) both showed that cycocel and shoot tipping increase fruit set slightly by reducing shoot growth and competition between the developing leaves and berries for organic nutrients (see p. 354). The practical value of the treatment remains to be proven under conditions in California.

High temperature and berry set.—High temperatures during and immediately following bloom may reduce fruit set in grapes. Using controlled temperature growth room for studies with Delaware grapevines Kobayashi *et al.* (1960) reported a progressive decrease in per cent of flowers which set berries with a rise in night temperature between 66° F. and 95° F. Buttrose and Hale (1973) also showed a marked reduction in fruit set in Cabernet-Sauvignon vines grown in growth cabinets with increasing day/night temperatures between 68°/59° F. and 100°/91° F. On the other hand, Alexander (1965), working with Thompson Seedless vines, found that poor fruit set associated with high temperatures at and after flowering in the field was due mainly to water stress and not to temperature in itself. Moisture stress was most critical during the first four weeks following bloom; thereafter berry drop is considerably more resistant to moisture stress.

Berry drop owing to high temperatures during and immediately following bloom, according to R. L. Sission (personal communication), accounts for considerable crop loss in the coastal counties of California in some years. This can be mitigated by using sprinkler irrigation as in frost control (see chap. 14, 366 and chap. 16, p. 406).

BIBLIOGRAPHY

Antcliff, A. J. 1955. A disbunching experiment on the Sultana. Austral. Jour. Sci. & Ind. Res., 21:106–107.

———, and W. J. Webster. 1955A. Studies on the Sultana vine. I. Fruit bud distribution and bud burst with reference to forecasting potential crop. Austral. Jour. Agr. Res., 6:565–588.

———, ———. 1955B. Studies on the Sultana vine. II. The course of bud burst. Austral. Jour. Agr. Res., 6:713–724.

Alexander, D. McE. 1965. The effect of high temperature regimes or short period of water stress on development of small fruiting Sultana vines. Austral. Jour. Agr. Res., 16:817–823.

Avramov, L. 1954. Flower drop in the more important indigenous and some foreign vine varieties in Serbia. Trans. title. Ark, poljopr. Nauk. 7(15): 67–84 (Hort. Abs. 25: 2541).

Baldwin, J. G. 1964. The relation between weather and fruitfulness of the Sultana vine. Aust. Jour. Agr. Res., 15:920–928.

Barnard, C. 1932. Fruit bud studies. I. The Sultana: an analysis of the distribution and behavior of the buds of the Sultana vine, together with an account of the differentiation and development of the fruit buds. Jour. Coun. Sci. & Ind. Res., 5:47–52.

———, and J. E. Thomas. 1933. Fruit bud studies. II. The Sultana: differentiation and development of the fruit buds. Jour. Coun. Sci. & Ind. Res., 6:285–294.

Barritt, B. H. 1970. Ovule development in Seeded and Seedless grapes. Vitis, 9:7–14.

Boehm, S. W. 1961. Should you pollen-Spray Ohanez grapes? Jour. Agr. So. Australia, 64(5):202–203.

Branas, J. 1957. Sur l'initiation florale. Prog. Agricol. et Viticol., 148:245–252.

Breviglieri, N. 1956. Richerche sulla differenziazione delle gemme e sulla micro e macrosporogenesi nel "Sangiovese," nel "Canaiolo," nel "Trebbiano," e nella "Malavasia" del Chianti. Atti. Accad. Ital. Vite e Vino, 8:98–129.

Buttrose, M. S. 1969a. Fruitfulness in grapevines: Effects of light intensity and temperature. Bot. Gaz., 130:166–173.

———. 1969b. Fruitfulness in grapevines: Effects of changes in temperature and light regimes. Bot. Gaz., 130:173–179.

———. 1969c. Fruitfulness in grapevines: Effects of daylength. Vitis, 8:188–190

———. 1970a. Fruitfulness in grapevines: The response of different cultivars to light, temperature, and daylength. Vitis, 9:121–125.

———. 1970b. Fruitfulness in grapevines: Development of leaf primordia in buds in relation to bud fruitfulness. Bot. Gaz., 131:78–83.

———, and C. R. Hale. 1973. Effect of temperature on development of the grapevine inflorescence after budburst. Amer. Jour. Enol. Vitic., 24:14–16.

Cejtlin, M. G. 1956. A method of obtaining more complete fertilization of flowers and better development of berries in bisexual varieties of vine. Trans. title Nauč. Tr. Uzb. s-h Insti., 90:197–215. (*See also:* Hort. Abs., 29:3363, 1959.)

Christiansen, P. 1969. Seasonal changes and distribution of nutritional elements in Thompson Seedless grapevines. Amer. Jour. Enol. Vitic. 20:176–190.

Cook, J. A. 1956. Petiole nitrate analysis as a criterion of nitrogen needs in California vineyards. Proc. Amer. Soc. Hort. Sci., 68:131–140.

Coombe, B. G. 1950. Artificial parthenocarpy in grape vines. Jour. Austral. Inst. Agr. Sci., 16:69–70.

———. 1960. Relationship of growth and development to changes in sugar, auxin, and gibberellins in fruit of seeded and seedless varieties of *Vitis vinifera*. Plant Physiol., 35:241–250.

———. 1970. Fruit set in grapevines: the mechanism of the CCC effect. Jour. Hort. Sci., 45:415–425.

Detjin, L. R. 1917. Pollination of the rotundifolia grapes. Jour. El. Mitchell Sci. Soc., 33:121–127.

Gartel, W. 1954. Beerengrösse, Kernzahl, und Mostgewicht beim Riesling. Weinberg u. Keller, 1:51–58.

Harada, H., and J. P. Nitsch. 1959. Changes in endogenous growth substances during flower development. Plant Physiol., 34:409–415.

The Grape Flower and Berry Set

Huglin, P. 1958. Recherches sur les bourgeons de la vigne; initiation florale et développement végtative. Ann. Amil. et Plantes, 8:113–272.

———. 1960. Untersuchungen über die Knospenfruchtbarkeit der Reben mit besonderer Berücksichtung ihrer Beziehungen zu den Unterlagen. Weinbau u. Keller, 7:127–137.

Kessler, B., R. Bak., and A. Cohen. 1959a. Flowering in fruit trees and annual plants as affected by purines, pyrimidines and triiodobenzoic acid. Plant Physiol., 34:605–608.

Kessler, B., and S. Lavee. 1959b. Effect of purines, pyrimidines, and metals upon the flowering of olive trees and grape vines. Ktavim, 9:261–263.

Kliewer, W. M. 1971. Effect of nitrogen on growth and composition of fruit from Thompson Seedless grapevines. Jour. Amer. Soc. Hort. Sci. 96:816–819.

———, and J. A. Cook. 1971. Arginine and total free amino acids as indicators of nitrogen status of grapevines. Jour. Amer. Soc. Hort. Sci., 96:581–587.

———, L. A. Lider, and N. Ferrari. 1972. Effect of controlled temperature and light intensity on growth and carbohydrate levels of Thompson Seedless grapevines. J. Amer. Soc. Hort. Sci., 97:185–188.

———, and H. B. Schultz. 1973. Effect of sprinkler cooling of grapevines on fruit growth and composition. Amer. Jour. Enol. Vitic., 24:17–26.

Kobayashi, A., H. Yukenoya, T. Fukushima, and H. Wada. 1960. Studies on the thermal conditions of grapes. II. Effects of night temperatures on the growth, yield and quality of Delaware grapes. Bull. Res. Inst. Food Science, Kyoto Univ., 24:29–42.

Kozma, P. 1954. The flower types of the variety Kadarka; the variety of flower types and their fertility. Trans. title. Acad. Hort. and Vitic. (Hungaricae), 2:31–111.

———. 1955. The variability and fruitlessness of the flower types of the variety Kadarka. Trans. title. Acta Agron. Acad. Sci. Hungaricae, 5:301–391.

Lavee, S., U. Regev and R. M. Samish. 1967. The determination of induction and differentiation in grape vines. Vitis 6:1–13.

Lider, L. A., A. N. Kasimatis, and W. M. Kliewer. 1973. The effect of pruning severity and rootstock on growth and yield of two grafted, caned, pruned wine grape cultivars. Jour. Amer. Soc. Hort. Sci. 98:8–12.

Marriott, P. F. 1959. Pollination of table grapes. Jour. Dept. Agric. Victoria, 48(9):391–394.

May, P. 1965. Reducing inflorescence formation by shading individual Sultana buds. Austral. Jour. Biol. Sci. 18:463–473.

Muir, R. M. 1942. Growth hormones as related to the setting and development of fruit in nicotiana tabacum. Amer. Jour. Bot., 29:716–720.

Muller-Thurgau, H. 1898. Abhangigkeit der Ausbildung der Traubenbeeren und einiger anderer Fruchte von der Entwicklung der Samen. Landw. Jahrb. Schweiz, 12:135–205.

Mullins, M. G. 1967. Regulation of fruit-set in the grape-vine. Aust. J. Biol. Sci., 20:1141–1147.

Nitsch, J. P. 1950. Plant hormones in the development of fruits. Quart. Rev. Biol., 27:33–57.

———. 1950. Growth and morphogenesis of the strawberry as related to auxin. Amer. Jour. Bot., 37:211–215.

———. 1953. The physiology of fruit growth. Ann. Rev. Plant Physiol., 4:199–236.

Olmo, H. P. 1934. Empty-seededness in varieties of *Vitis vinifera*. Proc. Amer. Soc. Hort. Sci., 32:376–385.

———. 1936. Pollination and the setting of fruit in the Black Corinth grape. Proc. Amer. Soc. Hort. Sci., 34:402–404.

Pearson, H. M. 1932. Parthenocarpy and seed abortion in *Vitis vinifera*. Proc. Amer. Soc. Hort. Sci., 29:169–175.

Perold, A. I. 1927. A treatise on viticulture. London, Macmillan and Co. (*See* p. 38.)

Randolph, U. A. 1944. Effects of phosphate fertilizer upon the growth and yield of the Carman grape in north Texas. Proc. Amer. Soc. Hort, Sci., 44:303–308.

Sartorius, O. 1926. Zur Entwicklung und Physiologie der Rebblüte. Angew Botanik, 8: 29–89.

———. 1968. Die Blütenknospen der Rebe. Wein. Wissenschaft, 23:309–338.

Shaulis, N. J., H. Amberg, and D. Crowe. 1966. Response of Concord grapes to light, exposure and Geneva Double Curtain training. Proc. Amer. Soc. Hort. Sci. 89:268–280.

———, and P. May. 1971. Response of Sultana vines to training on a divided canopy and to shoot crowding. Amer. Jour. Enol. Vitic. 22:215–222.

Skene, K. G. M. 1969. A comparison of the effects of "Cycocel" and tipping on fruit set in *Vitis vinifera* L. Austral. Jour. Biol. Sci. 22:1305–1311.

Stout, A. B. 1921. Types of flowers, and intersexes in grapes with special reference to fruit development. New York Agr. Exp. Sta. Bul., 82:1–16.

Stuart, N. W. 1961. Initiation of flower buds in Rhododendron after application of growth retardants. Science 134, No. 3471:50–52.

Thomas, J. E., and C. Barnard. 1937. Fruit bud studies. III. The Sultana (Thompson Seedless); some relations between shoot growth, chemical composition, fruit bud formation, and yield. Jour. Council Sci. Ind. Res., 10:143–157.

Tkačenko, G. V. 1960. The influence of the quantity of pollen on fruit setting in vines. Trans. title. Agrobiologija, No. 3, pp. 459–461. (Hort. Abs. 31: 4144).

Weaver, R. J., and W. O. Williams. 1950. Response of flowers of Black Corinth and fruit of Thompson Seedless grapes to applications of plant growth-regulators. Bot. Gaz., 111:477–485.

———, and A. J. Winkler. 1952. Increasing the size of Thompson Seedless grapes by means of 4-chlorophenoxyacetic acid, berry thinning, and girdling. Plant Physiol., 27:626–630.

———. 1952. Response of Black Corinth grapes to applications of 4-chlorophenoxyacetic acid. Bot. Gaz., 114:107–113.

————. 1958. Effect of gibberellic acid on fruit set and berry enlargement in seedless grapes of *Vitis vinifera*. Nature, 181:851–852.

————, S. B. McCune, and C. R. Hale. 1962. Effect of plant regulators on set and berry development in certain seeded and seedless varieties of *Vitis vinifera* L. Vitis 3:84–96.

Winkler, A. J. 1929. The effect of dormant pruning on the carbohydrate metabolism of the vine. Hilgardia, 4:153–173.

————, and E. M. Shemsettin. 1937. Fruit-bud flower formation in the Sultanina (Thompson Seedless). Hilgardia, 10:589–611.

————. 1945. Pruning *vinifera* grapevines. Calif. Ext. Ser. Cir., 89:1–68.

————, and W. O. Williams. 1945. Starch and sugars of *Vitis vinifera*. Plant Physiol., 20:412–432.

8

Development and Composition of Grapes

Once they set, the berries of grapes enlarge very rapidly. The extent and character of the growth is determined by the mechanism by which the berries set. In all grapes, berry enlargement proceeds through three distinct periods and follows a double sigmoid growth curve (fig. 28). For most grapes this type of growth can be described as follows:

Period I. During this initial period of rapid growth the pericarp and seed increase in size and weight while the embryos remain small. In the pericarp there is a period of rapid cell division lasting 3 to 4 weeks after anthesis, which is followed by rapid cell enlargement (Harris *et al.*, 1968). The berries remain green and firm and are characterized by rapid acid accumulation, a high rate of respiration and a respiratory quotient value of 1 or less. This period usually last 5 to 7 weeks in most grape varieties.

Period II. In the second period, in which the overall growth rate has slowed down markedly, there is initially rapid hardening of the endocarp and the embryo develops rapidly and generally reaches maximum size during this period. The berries reach their highest level of acidity and begin to accumulate sugar during this period. During the lag phase the berries lose chlorophyll and begin to undergo a color change. This period generally last 2 to 4 weeks.

Period III. This is the period of "final swell" in which growth in size and weight resumes a rate equal to or exceeding that of period I. Growth in berry size during this period is by cell enlargement. During this period the berry acquires a softer texture, accumulates sugar, decreases in acidity, the

Development and Composition of Grapes

skin becomes colored (in red and black varieties), and the characteristic aroma develops. The respiration rate continues to decrease during ripening and the respiratory quotient value is greater than 1. This period generally last 5 to 8 weeks.

This sequence of berry growth would seem to involve a certain competition between seed and fruit development. This hypothesis is supported by Nitsch (1953) and others, and by the correlation found between embryo abortion and earliness in stone fruits (Tukey, 1936). That is, materials that would have been used in embryo development accumulate in the fruit of such varieties to advance ripening. It has also been reported that the berries on a cluster that mature earliest contain few or no seeds (Müller-Thurgau, 1898). Even so, it is highly improbable that competition could account for the lag in the growth curve of the berries of Thompson Seedless, since the embryos abort weeks before the beginning of period II. Varieties that set by stimulative parthenocarpy also evidence a similar period of slower growth, followed by marked acceleration during ripening (Winkler, 1932); however, the lag phase is less marked with seedless varieties.

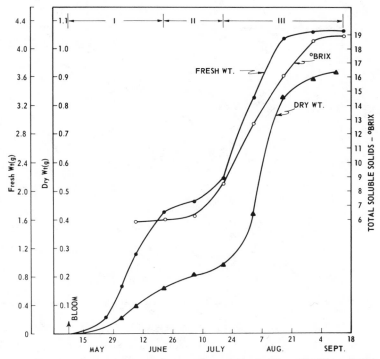

FIGURE 28: Relationship of growth periods I, II, and III and the accumulation of total soluble solids in Tokay berries.

Development and Composition of Grapes

Although the competition explanation of the double-sigmoid curve for fruit growth has been generally accepted, it can hardly be expected to apply in seedless varieties. Furthermore, data have been reported that tend to show that competition for carbohydrate material between vine and fruit or between seed and pericarp is unlikely to be the cause of the periodicity in berry growth. Moreau and Vinet (1932) and Marteau (1956) have found large accumulations of carbohydrate reserves in several parts of the vine, especially the permanent wood of the trunk and arms, before the beginning of period II of berry growth and well in advance of the beginning of ripening. These reserves may be available for rapid movement to the fruit at the beginning of ripening. Bouard (1966), however, found that carbohydrate translocation from reserves within the vine to fruit will only take place under abnormal conditions, such as those involved in defoliation. The rate of movement to the fruit—a sevenfold increase in one week in Gamay (Moreau and Vinet, 1932)—is too rapid to result simply from a change in competition for carbohydrates. A similar rapid accumulation of sugars in the fruit was reported for a number of varieties in California by Bioletti, *et al.* (1918) and by Coombe (1960). Coombe found that the sugar concentration in a number of *vinifera* varieties at Davis rises suddenly,

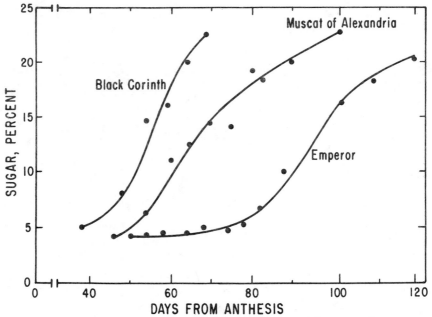

FIGURE 29: Showing very rapid accumulation of sugars in the fruit, once ripening begins: (a) Black Corinth, (b) Muscat of Alexandria, and (c) Emperor. (*Redrawn after Coombe, 1960*)

Development and Composition of Grapes

almost on a certain day, and that the increase reaches its maximum in the course of ten days (fig. 29). The change in concentration is remarkable, rising from 4 to 20 per cent in thirty to forty days, depending on the variety. These studies reveal a striking coincidence of the increase in sugar and the beginning of period III of berry growth. The sugaring and growth rate curves increased sharply in each variety, the maximum rate of sugaring being reached a few days earlier than the maximum growth rate. This suggests that the upturn in the growth curve could result from the influx of sugar into the berry. As the sugar moves into the flesh of the berries, water also moves in, to adjust osmotic potential.

Auxins are possibly a factor in these phenomena. It has been shown that the application of an auxin—2, 4, 5-trichlorophenoxyacetic acid—at the beginning of period II can restore the full growth rate in apricot fruits, which otherwise have a long period of retarded growth (Crane and Brooks, 1952). Such treatment also leads to a marked increase in earliness, even though the mature fruit is larger than normal. Analyses of the fruit indicated that the weight increases were principally water increase, for the dry weight, less the sugars, of the fruit treated with auxin was not much different from that of the controls (Crane et al., 1956). There was an increase in the amount of sugar per fruit, suggesting that the auxin caused a mobilization of soluble carbohydrates in the fruit (Leopold, 1958). Both the triggering of the rapid movement of sugar into the berries at the beginning of ripening and the accelerated berry growth during ripening are typical of hormone activity. Coombe (1960) has shown in berries of *vinifera* varieties a rise in the auxins that coincides with the beginning of sugaring. According to Nitsch et al. (1960), however, the increase in berry size in the Concord grape at the beginning of period III did not seem to coincide with a detectable increase in auxin concentration. Several investigators (Hale, 1968; Singh and Campbell, 1964; Weaver, 1955) have shown that the ripening of both seeded and seedless grapes is delayed by auxin, in direct contrast to other fruits. However, Hale et al. (1970) found that ethylene applied to clusters midway in the slow growth phase (period II) hastens the ripening of grapes, but if applied prior to this time it delayed ripening. They also showed that ethylene partially reverses the delayed maturation effects of auxins. These findings suggest that an auxin-ethylene relationship is involved in the regulation of grape ripening; however, further research will be required to confirm the roles of auxin and ethylene in berry growth and in the accumulation of sugars in grapes.

STAGES OF BERRY DEVELOPMENT

Aside from the increase in size, the berries pass through several stages or periods of development from the time of setting until they are fully ripe.

The changes in the fruit, although continuous, proceed at different rates during certain of these stages. As a result of these differences, such as the increase in sugars and the changes in texture, it is convenient to recognize the following stages of development:

The *green stage* extends from the setting of the berries up to the beginning of ripening. During this stage the main change is a rapid increase in berry size. Changes in the framework of the cluster are negligible after the berries have set. The level of sugars remains almost constant, the acidity is high and remains so, and the berries are hard. Glucose is present in larger amounts than fructose, and malic and tartaric acids increase to their maximum levels.

The *ripening stage* extends from the beginning of ripening until the grapes are ripe. The beginning of ripening may be called the turning point in the development of the berries. At this time the green color of the white varieties begins to fade and the white or yellow colors come into view. In red and black varieties the development of color begins. The berries, which up to this time have remained hard, begin to soften. This sudden change in color and berry softening is termed véraison by the French viticulturists. At this time the metabolism of the berry changes drastically and the fruit changes from an acid accumulating organ to a sugar accumulating organ. During ripening the red color becomes more intense, the green color fades, and the texture continues to soften. The changes in sweetness, acidity, and other constituents go forward much more rapidly. Berries enlarge rapidly during this stage. As ripeness is approached, these various changes decelerate.

The *ripe stage* in a grape comes when the fruit has reached the state best suited for the use to which it is to be put. The ripe stage is the condition that results when the changes in the several components of the fruit have proceeded to a point where their combined effect on the quality of a given variety is the nearest possible approach to an ideal for a given purpose. The ripe stage is not absolute, nor does it represent the end product in the changes that are proceeding in the berries. For example, a grape high in acid and low in sugar may be required for one purpose, and the reverse for another purpose. Thus, the condition of ripeness in a grape varies according to the use planned for it, as well as with the state of development of the fruit. The glucose fructose ratio is usually about 1 during the ripening stage.

The *overripe stage* in a grape is reached when the continuing changes subtract from rather than add to its quality. There is no further accumulation of sugars, and the acidity continues to decrease. The berries also rapidly lose their resistance to handling injuries, to the attack of decay-causing organisms, and to water loss, which results in shriveling. The tendency to shatter increases rapidly in some varieties. During the overripe stage the level of fructose often increases while glucose usually decreases or remains about the same.

FACTORS AFFECTING RIPENING

The time of ripening is determined primarily by variety and heat summation. From the time of setting until their removal at harvest, the berries are continually changing in composition. Some substances, such as sugar, are increasing as the grapes approach maturity, while others, such as acid, are decreasing. The rate of change in the various substances differs with the variety; the differences are large between a variety that matures very early and one whose fruit matures very late. Early-maturing varieties require 1,600 to 2,000 degree-days to bring their fruit from full bloom to palatable maturity, whereas late-maturing ones require 3,000 or more degree-days. All early varieties will attain full maturity every year, except possibly in cool regions (region I and colder), whereas late varieties will ripen normally only in warm and hot regions (IV and V).

Seasonal conditions, particularly temperature—heat summation—markedly influence the rates of the development changes. During a cool season, when heat summation is slow, the accumulation of sugar, as well as the other ripening processes, will proceed slowly. Then the grapes of no varieties are ripe enough for harvest until after the average dates for picking are past. In a hot year the ripening changes will proceed more rapidly than is normal, and harvest will be early. This seasonal influence is identical with that of cool and hot regions. A given summation of heat is required to bring a variety from full bloom to a given degree Brix*: when the season is cool and the heat summation is slow, the grapes matures slowly; when it is hot and the heat summation is rapid, the grapes ripen faster (Winkler and Williams, 1936). For example, in 1936, a hot year, the Tokay was ripe at Lodi on August 19; in 1938, a cool year, the first picking was on September 7. The average date of the first picking for this variety at Lodi is about August 28.

The time of ripening may also be influenced by vineyard management. Of the factors that influence ripening, level of crop is the most important one over which the vineyardist has control. Any crop above that which is normal for the vines will delay maturation of the fruit (Winkler and Williams, 1939). As the crop is increased above the normal for the vineyard, the ratio of leaves to fruit becomes less and less, so that more time is required for the sugar content of the fruit to reach a given degree Brix.

The type of trellising and training system may also influence the time of ripening as well as crop yields (Shaulis *et al.*, 1966; Shaulis and May, 1971). Trellising systems that increase the amount of leaves exposed to full sunlight will generally enhance fruit maturation and increase bud fruitfulness and vine yields.

Viruses, particularly leaf-roll virus, will generally reduce the rate of fruit ripening and the final maturity of the fruit (Alley *et al.*, 1963).

* See footnote on p. 556.

Therefore, in planting new vineyards it is extremely important to obtain certified material that is free of all known viruses.

Operations (girdling, limiting the water, etc.) that cause the vines to slow down or cease growing will, once the fruit reaches the ripening stage, tend to hasten ripening. Girdling for this purpose is a common practice on seeded varieties in the very early areas. Similarly, a limited supply of nitrogen will cause the vines to cease linear growth early, tending to advance ripening. (When girdling is done to advance maturation, its effect should not be offset by applications of nitrogen.) Likewise, grapes ripen earlier on sandy soils than on heavy soils, unless the sandy soils are abundantly supplied with nitrogen. These influences on ripening, though small in terms of total days to harvest, can be of great value in the areas of earliest maturation, where only a few days difference may have a marked effect on price. In contrast, applications of nitrogen or irrigation that cause vine growth to continue actively will delay fruit ripening. Depth of soil may also be a factor in maturing the crop. Some of the best Malaga grapes produced in California are grown on soils 2.5 to 3.5 feet deep. The same is largely true of Emperor. It is a simple matter to regulate growth on such soils through the judicious use of cover crops or moisture control, or both, and thereby hasten ripening. Such means of control, together with continued normal functioning of the vine, particularly its leaves, can bring the fruit to its best possible quality and maturity.

PHYSICAL COMPOSITION OF THE FRUIT

The fruit of the grape is a cluster consisting of stems and berries. Because of the great differences between varieties (Flanzy, 1959), only the range of variation of the physical components of the fruit is indicated here.

The *stems* (rachis, branches, and pedicels), on which the berries are borne, constitute 2 to 6 per cent of the total weight at maturity, differing with the variety. In stem structure there is much variation in length of parts, toughness, and adherence to the berries. These characteristics are of particular importance in table grapes, which are packed and shipped long distances, and in ease of mechanical harvest. Varieties differ greatly in the rate at which the drying and browning of the stems occurs in transit and in the market. Browning lessens the eye appeal of the fruit and increases berry shatter. The constituents of the stems are of little interest, with the exception that their tannin content is a factor in wine production.

The *seeds* constitute up to 10 per cent of the weight of the fruit. They are rich in tannin (5 to 8 per cent) and oil (10 to 20 per cent), with lesser amounts of resinous materials. The seeds are generally objectionable in table and raisin grapes. This fact accounts in part for the popularity of Thompson Seedless and several other seedless varieties for table use and raisin production. For composition of the oil see Morand and Silvestre (1960).

The grape berry normally contains four seeds, originating from the four ovules of the ovary. However, the number of seeds may be less than four, because of the absence or abortion of one or several ovules. The development of the seeds influences the size and composition of the grapes. Seeds are generally a rich source of hormones, and Iwahori *et al.* (1968) have demonstrated that seeded Tokay grapes contain considerably greater amounts of gibberellin than seedless Tokay grapes. Generally, the greater the number of seeds, the heavier the weight of the berry, the lower the sugar concentration and the higher the level of acidity (Ribéreau-Gayon and Peynaud, 1960).

The *skin* of the berries accounts for 5 to 12 per cent of the total weight. The skin consists of an epidermis and is composed of 6–10 layers of small, thick-walled cells. The firmness of the berry depends on the coherence of this epicarp. The skin is covered with a thin waxlike layer known as cutin and is sometimes referred to as the bloom. The cutin normally constitutes from 1 to 2 per cent of the total weight of the skin and consist mainly of oleanolic acid (79 per cent) and long chain alcohols with traces of esters, fatty acids, aldehydes, and paraffins (Radler, 1965a, b). The cutin protects the berries against water loss and the attack of organisms and, therefore, enhances the attractiveness of table grapes. The skin and the layers of cells immediately beneath the cutin contain most of the color, aroma, and flavor contituents of the berries and are richer in vitamin C than the pulp. In red grapes the skin also contains large amounts (3 to 6 per cent) of tannin. The skin to pulp ratio decreases as berry size increases. Thus, with equal concentrations of color and flavors in the skin, the juice or wine of a small-berried variety would have a greater proportion of these constituents. That is one reason why the large-berried table grape varieties, such as Emperor, Malaga, Ribier, and Tokay, which are only vinous to begin with, do not produce distinctive wines.

The thickness and toughness of the skin differ among varieties and are factors in the degree of resistance of table grapes to handling injury in packing, transport, and storage. These characteristics of the skin also influence the rate of water loss in raisin making and the sugaring of natural raisins in storage. The delicate skin of Monukka raisins renders them prone to sugar, whereas the tough skin of Black Corinth and Thompson Seedless usually prevents sugaring.

The *yield of juice* depends primarily on the variety's lack of pulpiness. There are, of course, other factors, such as stage of ripeness, size of berries, seediness, thoroughness of fermentation, and the efficiency of crushing, pressing, and other operations. Present available information indicates a range from 160 to 195 gallons of juice per ton of grapes, depending on the variety.

The characteristic *texture* of a variety at maturity is a physical property. The berries of some varieties are firm or hard; those of others are soft. Until the beginning of ripening there is practically no change in the texture of the berries: they are hard and remain so. During ripening, changes in the cell walls of the berries affect the texture, causing the berries to become soft. This softening is brought about by changes in the pectic substances of the cell walls. Variations in the character and degree of the softening process account in part for differences in the shipping and storing quality of different varieties. After maturity, the softening of the berries continues, with the fruit becoming more susceptible to mechanical injury and attack by decay-causing organisms.

CHEMICAL COMPOSITION OF THE FRUIT

The available figures on composition are for freshly expressed juice. Ranges in percentage of the more important organic and inorganic components of the fresh juice are shown in table 5.

Sugars.—During the early stages of fruit growth (period I) the developing ovules are nurtured in part at least by the ovary and its axillary parts, sepals, bracts and the receptacle. These are normally green and capable of photosynthesis. While the fruit is small these organs play an important part in its nutrition, but as the fruit grows, although the outer layer of cells may photosynthesize until almost fruit maturity, the main source of nutrition is the leaf. The main sugar translocated from the leaves to the fruits is sucrose (Swanson and El-Shishiny, 1958), but small amounts of other sugars, especially raffinose and stachyose may also be involved in carbohydrate movements (Kliewer, 1965c). Once sucrose reaches the fruit it is hydrolyzed into glucose and fructose by invertase (Hawker, 1969b).

During the first period of rapid growth of the berries the percentage of sugars present is low, usually less than 2 per cent of the berry fresh weight. Increases are little more than enough to maintain the percentage concentration during the rapid growth of the berries. During ripening, however, the sugars increase rapidly. In the ripe fruit they constitute a very large proportion of the total soluble solids. In fact, in the latter stage of ripening a curve showing the increase in sugars will parallel the curve showing the increase in total soluble solids (Bioletti *et al.*, 1918). After the fruit is ripe the percentage of sugars may continue to increase. It should not be forgotten, however, that this increase refers to the percentage composition of the juice of the grape. If the berries continue to in-

Development and Composition of Grapes

TABLE 5

COMPOSITION OF GRAPES

Ranges in percentages of the more important organic and inorganic
components of freshly expressed juice, by volume

	Per cent
Water	70–80
Carbohydrates	15–25
Dextrose (glucose)	8–13
Levulose (fructose)	7–12
Pentoses	0.01–0.05
Pectin	0.01–0.10
Inositol	0.02–0.08
Organic acids	0.3–1.5
Tartaric	0.2–1.0
Malic	0.1–0.8
Citric	0.01–0.05
Tannins	0.01–0.10
Nitrogenous compounds	0.03–0.17
Protein	0.001–0.01
Amino	0.017–0.11
Humin	0.001–0.002
Amide	0.001–0.004
Ammonia	0.001–0.012
Residual	0.01–0.02
Mineral compounds	0.3–0.6
Aluminum	T–0.003
Boron	T–0.007
Calcium	0.004–0.025
Chloride	0.001–0.010
Copper	T–0.0003
Iron	T–0.003
Magnesium	0.01–0.025
Manganese	T–0.0051
Potassium	0.15–0.25
Phosphate	0.02–0.05
Rubidium	T–0.001
Silicic acid	0.0002–0.005
Sodium	T–0.020
Sulfate	0.003–0.035

SOURCE OF DATA: Amerine *et al.* and Cruess (1972). T indicates trace.

crease in size, as is usual with a light crop, the increase in total soluble solids as sugars per berry or per acre may be large. When, however, mature fruit is permitted to hang on the vine without further irrigation and if the weather is very hot, the increase in soluble solids as indicated by degrees Brix results, more often than not, from loss of water and an actual shrinking of the berries. Such an increase is thus offset by a loss in tonnage of fruit per acre.

Most of the sugars in the berries are manufactured in the leaves (Koblet, 1969; Ribéreau-Gayon and Peynaud, 1971). Winkler (1930) showed that reduction of the leaf area per cluster below a critical value—3,244 cm.^{2} for Malaga and 2,280 cm.^{2} for Muscat of Alexandria—decreased berry growth. In defoliation experiments with Thompson Seedless in Australia (May *et al.*, 1969; Kliewer and Antcliff, 1970) as well as in Davis (Kliewer, 1970b; Kliewer and Ough, 1970; Kliewer and Weaver, 1971), reduction in leaf area below a critical value—10 cm.^{2} per gram of fruit or 4,540 cm.^{2} per pound of fruit, equivalent to about 22 to 26 leaves per average size cluster, decreased fruit maturity, berry weight, fruit coloration, total nitrogen, and other constituents in the fruit. Along with leaf reduction there is also a lowering of the total sugar and acid content and of the quality of the fruit (Novak, 1958). The sugars produced in the leaves are moved through the phloem to where they are used in growth or in the production of other food materials, or to where they accumulate as reserve foods. During early summer the vines are growing rapidly; most of the sugars are then being used in the growth of shoots, leaves, and roots, and in the increase of berry size. This rapid consumption of sugars for the production of new tissues in the vegetative parts of the vine, as well as in the rapidly growing fruit, precludes any large accumulation or increase of the sugars in the berries. By the time the fruit has reached one half to three fourths of full size, the vines have stopped active growth. The leaves, nevertheless, continue to function normally and according to Marteau (1956), the carbohydrate materials (sugars and starch) that begin to accumulate in the leaves and woody parts of the vine are translocated to the fruit, where there is a rapid build up of sugars. At the beginning of ripening the higher degrees Brix of the juice of the leaves (Amerine and Winkler, 1958) than that of the berries also favors translocation of these materials to the fruit. Moreau and Vinet (1932) reported that a large part of the sugars that are moved into the fruit comes from reserves mobilized from all parts of the vine, although mainly from the trunk and arms. Kliewer and Antcliff (1970) also found under some conditions as much as 40 per cent of the total sugar supplied to the fruit may come from parts of the vine other than the leaves. Such movements results in the often very rapid accumulation of sugars in the fruit at the beginning of ripening. In the latter stages of maturing the movement of sugars into the fruit is against an increasing concentration gradient. This is not an unusual phenomenon, since it has been shown that in several plants sugars may move out of leaves against a diffusion gradient (Loomis, 1945). Similarly, the vine expends energy in moving sugars into the berries.

Another possible source of the sugars in grape berries is from transformation of organic acids. Ribéreau-Gayon (1966) has shown that immature and mature grapes are capable of synthesizing carbohydrates from malic acid; however, the percentage of the total sugars in grapes formed in this manner is undoubtedly quite small. Drawert and Steffan (1966) reported that glucose and fructose can also be formed from tartaric acid in grape berries, however, sugar formed in this manner is believed to be very minor.

The sugars of the *vinifera* grape are primarily glucose and fructose, generally accounting for 99 per cent or more of the carbohydrates in the must and from 12 to 27 per cent or more of the weight of the mature berry. The ratio of glucose to fructose in grapes changes considerably between fruit set until fruit maturity. Generally, glucose predominates

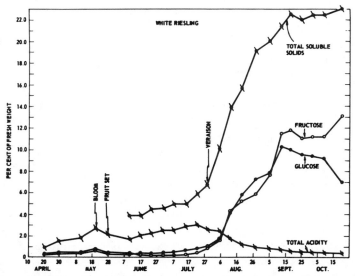

FIGURE 30: Season changes in the concentration of glucose, fructose, total soluble solids, and total acidity in White Riesling berries grown at Davis.

during the green berry and early ripening stages of berry growth; during the latter part of berry ripening and the ripe stage of berry growth glucose and fructose are present in about equal amounts, and in overripe grapes fructose generally exceeds glucose (fig. 30). The glucose-fructose ratio of 78 grape varieties grown at Davis ranged from 0.74 to 1.05 in mature fruits (Kliewer, 1967). Chardonnay, Pinot blanc, and Green Hungarian were among the cultivars classed as high-fructose varieties, while Chenin blanc, Emerald Riesling, and Zinfandel, among others, were classed as high-glucose varieties. The glucose to fructose ratio tended to be lower in warm seasons than in cool seasons. Genevois and Ribéreau-Gayon (1947) stated that glucose and fructose are present in equimolar amounts at maturity. According to Peynaud (1947), the glucose-fructose ratio for five Bordeaux varieties varied from 0.93 to 0.96 in 1937 and from 0.91 to 0.94 in 1938. Colagrande (1960), who analyzed several varieties, reports a variation from 1.14 to 0.79. Amerine and Thoukis (1958) found that the ratio for seven table grape varieties, in the degrees Brix range of 20.0 to 22.3, varied from 1.12 to 0.80 and for ten wine grape varieties, in the Brix range of 18.3 to 22.3, from 1.07 to 0.83; they also presented further data supporting the conclusion that the ratio continues to decrease as the fruit becomes overripe.

Fructose is much the sweeter: 15 per cent of fructose is about equal in sweetness to 22.8 per cent of glucose or 17.8 per cent of sucrose. Among early table grapes in the early-maturing regions, those high in fructose, such as Perlette and Early Muscat should taste sweeter at the same or lower degrees Brix. On the other hand, varieties higher in glucose, such as Blackrose or Malaga, might have greater acceptance for midseason and late marketing, since they should be less cloying when fully mature or even overripe. A similar situation might arise in the production of grape juice—varieties high in fructose would be best adapted to cool regions and those high in glucose to warm regions. In both table grapes and grape juice, consumer acceptance is markedly influenced by the sweetness-to-acid balance in the taste.

In addition to glucose and fructose several other sugars are present in small amounts in grapes. Kliewer (1965c, 1966) found sucrose, raffinose, stachyose, melibiose, maltose and galactose in the berries of eight varieties of V. *vinifera*; however, no pentoses could be detected. The level of sucrose and raffinose in mature grapes ranged from 0.019 to 0.18 per cent and 0.015 to 0.034 per cent, respectively. Astegiano and Graziano (1959) reported 0.35 to 0.40 per cent sucrose in grapes from fourteen V. *vinifera* varieties containing 15 to 22 per cent sugar and Lott and Barritt (1967) found 0.17 to 0.60 per cent sucrose in six V. *vinifera* varieties. *Vitis labrusca* and V. *rotundifolia* species contain sucrose in their fruit that range between 0.2 and 5 per cent of fresh berry weight (Caldwell, 1925).

Lott and Barrett (1967) confirmed that significant amounts of sucrose are found only in clones derived from V. *labrusca*. Pentoses, mainly arabinose and traces of xylose, have been reported to be present in small amounts in ripe grapes (Wali and Hassan, 1965; Guichard, 1954).

Carbohydrate content of cluster parts.—Amerine and Root (1960) reported on the carbohydrate content of various parts of grape clusters of three varieties. A summary of their findings is given in table 6.

As these varieties mature, the sucrose nearly disappears from the brush; its place is taken by an increase in reducing sugars. There is a rise in sucrose in the pedicels during ripening, and a decrease in the main and lateral stems. Starch increased in the pedicel and stem parts in Thompson Seedless and Grenache, but decreased slightly in Sémillon. These changes are, however, too small to have economic significance.

Acids.—The principal acids of the grape are d-tartaric and l-malic, constituting 90 percent or more of the total acidity. Citric acid is the third most adundant acid in grapes, but mature fruit usually contains only 0.02 to 0.03 per cent of this acid. In addition to these acids, there are more than 20 other non-nitrogenous organic acids in grapes—all present in small amounts (Colagrande, 1959; Kliewer, 1966; Peynaud and Ribéreau-Gayon, 1970). Included in these acids are members of the glycolytic pathway, Krebs cycle, glyoxylic acid cycle, and shikimic pathway, suggesting that all these metabolic cycles are operative in grapes.

In California, the titratable acidity of the juice of mature grapes varies from about 0.30 to 1.20 percent (calculated as tartaric acid) depending

TABLE 6

CARBOHYDRATE CONTENT OF DIFFERENT PARTS OF
THE GRAPE CLUSTER
Averages of Sémillon, Grenache, and
Thompson Seedless

Cluster part	Carbohydrate content as pounds per ton
Berries	440.66
Brush	1.32
Pedicels	0.76
Lateral stems	0.62
Main stem	0.66
Total	444.04

SOURCE OF DATA: Amerine and Root (1960).
NOTE: The data indicate the usable carbohydrate (starch and sugars) at maturity (22.2° to 25.9° Balling).

on the variety, season, and climatic region. The amount of malate and tartrate in ripe California grapes varies considerably, ranging from 0.15 to 0.85 per cent for the former acid to 0.38 to 1.08 per cent for the latter acid in 78 different varieties grown at Davis (Kliewer *et al.*, 1967a). Similarly, the ratio of tartrate to malate varies widely between varieties and generally ranges between 0.6 and 3.4 in mature grapes at Davis (Amerine, 1956; Kliewer *et al.*, 1967a). High malate varieties include Carignane, Chenin blanc, Malbec, Pinot noir, Pinot St. George, and Zinfandel. High tartrate varieties include Chasselas dore, Emerald Riesling, Palomino, Sémillon, Thompson Seedless, and White Riesling. At Davis it was found that the titratable acidity due to tartrates was 25 to 40 per cent of the total early in the season and 45 to 81 per cent late in the season (Amerine, 1951). Thus, the proportion of the titratable acidity that is due to tartaric acid and acid tartrate increase with fruit maturity.

In the warm, interior valleys of California (regions IV and V) grapes with low pH and high acidity at maturity are generally desired for table wines. Tartaric acid and acid tartrate are not as rapidly lost at high temperatures as are malic acid and acid malate (Gerber, 1897; Kliewer, 1971). Furthermore, tartaric acid is a stronger acid than malic acid (pK 2.98 vs. 3.40). Therefore, at the same total concentration of tartrate and malate, varieties with a higher percentage of their titratable acidity due to tartrates rather than to malates would have a lower pH. In selection of table wine varieties for warm growing regions those with high tartrate-malate ratios are generally preferable.

Grapevines are one of the few plants in which tartaric acid is synthesized in large amounts, however, it is found in small amounts in a relatively large number of angiosperm species (Stafford, 1959). Malate, on the other hand, is almost universally found in plants. Tartaric acid is found in all parts of the grapevine with the largest amounts in the photosynthesizing organs (Kliewer, 1966). Tartaric acid production appears to be associated with the processes of cell division and cell elongation as its synthesis in leaves occurs mainly during the period of leaf expansion and in berries during the initial period of berry growth (Kliewer and Nasser, 1966; Ribéreau-Gayon, 1968; Kriedemann *et al.*, 1970; Saito and Kasai, 1969). In leaves tartaric acid reaches a maximum about 40 days after unfolding, i.e. about the time the laminae is fully expanded, while malic acid continues to increase for 120 days or more after unfolding (Peynaud and Maurie, 1958; Kliewer and Nasser, 1966). Kliewer (1966) showed that between September 28 and November 1, there were approximately 3- and 7-fold decreases in tartrate and malate, respectively in the leaves of Thompson Seedless vines. During this same period the tartrate content of the wood doubled and the malate concentration increased nearly tenfold, suggesting that tartrate and malate are translocated to the woody tissue just prior to leaf fall.

Development and Composition of Grapes

In the growing berries, there is a progressive increase in malic and tartaric acids and total acidity following fruit set until about midway between the lag phase of berry growth, shortly before ripening begins (fig. 31). Both tartrate and malate, on a concentration or on a per berry basis, decrease during ripening. Malic acid usually decreases much more rapidly than tartaric acid, probably because it is more readily respired and there are several enzymes in grapes capable of metabolizing malic acid. The decrease in concentration of malic and tartaric acids during berry ripening is generally attributed to: (1) increase in membrane permeabilities allowing acids stored in cell vacuoles to be respired (Hardy, 1968; Kliewer, 1971); (2) reduction in the amount of acids translocated from leaves (Amerine, 1956; Hardy, 1969); (3) formation of salts of malic and tartaric acids due mainly to the movement of potassium into the fruit (Saito and Kasai, 1968; Kliewer, 1971); (4) reduced ability of berries to synthesize organic acid with fruit maturity (Hardy, 1968); (5) transformation of organic acids to sugars (Drawert and Steffan, 1966; Ribéreau-Gayon, 1968); and (6) dilution effect due to increased volume of the fruit.

The amount of *free* tartaric and malic acids in berries decreases markedly during ripening, and the mono and dibasic salts of these acids generally increase, with potassium usually present as the main cation. The dibasic salt of malic acid is present in very small amounts in grapes (Amerine, 1951; Kliewer *et al.*, 1967a). The increase in ratio of acid salts to free acids during fruit maturation is reflected by the steady increase

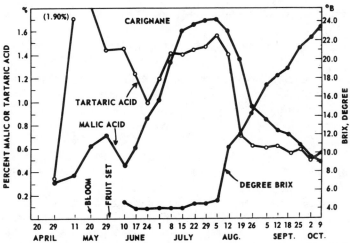

FIGURE 31: Seasonal changes in the concentration of malic and tartaric acids and total soluble solids (° Brix) in Carignane berries grown at Davis.

in pH and the decrease in titratable acidity. The amount of free acid present in mature fruits varies widely between varieties, with tartaric acid generally present in amounts between 5 and 40 per cent of the total tartrate, and malic acid usually present between 30 and 70 per cent of the total malate (Kliewer *et al.*, 1967a). At fruit maturity all varieties have a lower percentage of total tartrate as free acid than of total malate as free acid.

The acids are not evenly distributed throughout the flesh of the grape. At maturity, the zone near the skin has the lowest titratable acidity, the intermediate zone (pulp) has more, and that around the seeds has the highest (Amerine, 1956). This is nearly opposite of the distribution of the sugars. In green grapes, however, the distributon of acids may be different, for the peripheral zone sometimes has the higher titratable acidity. Within the fruit cells themselves most acids are believed to be located in the vacuoles.

The distribution of potassium acid tartrate (cream of tartar) and the other acid salts in the berries differs from the titratable acidity in that the quantity is greater near the skin than the center of the berry (von der Heide and Schmitthenner, 1922). In mature grapes, crystalline deposits of cream of tartar sometimes occur near the skin, indicating saturation of these cells.

Both leaves and fruits are capable of synthesizing malic and tartaric acids (Stafford and Loewus, 1958; Hale, 1962). It is not known what proportion of the acids in grapes is manufactured in the fruits themselves and what proportion is transported to the fruits from leaves or other organs such as the roots. Leaves are known to export organic acids in the phloem tissues to other parts of plants (Kursanov, 1962). Hardy (1969) demonstrated that ^{14}C-labeled malic acid and glutamine are transported from leaves administered $C^{14}O_2$ in grapevines, and Genevois *et al.* (1954) and Gatet (1939) also indicated that tartaric and malic acids are transported from leaves to fruits. W. M. Kliewer and A. R. Nasser (unpublished information) identified tartaric and malic acids in the phloem exudate of grapevines during the green berry stage of berry development, but not during the ripening stage. Giesler and Radler (1963) calculated that photosynthesis by the clusters themselves during the green stage of berry development could only account for about 50 per cent of the acids accumulated in the fruit, assuming that all assimilated CO_2 was converted to organic acids. Therefore, at least half or more of the acids in grapes are derived from sources outside the fruit cluster. Still unanswered, however, is the question of whether malic and tartaric acids are transported as such from leaves or other storage tissues to fruits, or whether sugar is translocated from leaves and then synthesized into organic acids in the fruit. More than likely both processes occur in grapevines.

Development and Composition of Grapes

The pathways for biosynthesis of tartaric and malic acids are different and not directly related. Tartaric acid is produced from sugar while malic acid is believed to be mainly synthesized by carboxylation of pyruvic or phosphoenolpyruvic acids (Peynaud and Ribéreau-Gayon, 1970). Ribéreau-Gayon (1968) showed that the carbon atom 1 of glucose is more rapidly introduced into tartaric acid than carbon atom 6. He also found that carbon 1 of glucose gives rise to tartaric acid mostly labelled in the carboxyl group. Saito and Kasai (1969) found that 70 per cent of label from ascorbic acid 1-C^{14} was incorporated into tartaric acid. Their data indicates that C_1–C_4 moiety of l-ascorbic acid is converted directly into tartaric acid. Ascorbic acid is synthesized from glucose via the uronic acid cycle (Loewus, 1963). Tartaric acid synthesis generally occurs only in the light while malic acid is synthesized in the light or dark.

The evidence for malic acid synthesis in grapes suggest several pathways. Drawert and Steffan (1966) were able to label malic acid from both labeled glucose and acetate, indicating that malic acid may be formed from the Krebs Cycle. Similarly, Hardy (1968) reported production of malic acid from labeled sucrose, glucose, and fructose fed to immature berries. However, the main biosynthetic pathway of malic acid is now believed to be by the β-carboxylation of pyruvate or phosphoenolpyruvate (Hawker, 1969c; Meynhardt, 1963, 1965; Ribéreau-Gayon and Peynaud, 1971). Malic enzyme and phosphoenopyruvate carboxylase, responsible for the fixation of CO_2 into malic acid, have been found in the leaves and fruits of grapevines (Hawker, 1969c; Meynhardt, 1965). Ribéreau-Gayon (1968) reported that malic acid can also be formed from citric acid that is stored in the roots.

Malic acid is readily respired or broken down in grapes to CO_2 and H_2O via the Krebs Cycle. Malic enzyme and malic dehydrogenase are found in grape berries (Hawker, 1969c), and both enzymes are able to break down malic acid. Hawker found that the activity of these two enzymes generally increase during fruit ripening.

Tartrate is considerably more stable in grapes than is malate. The mechanism for tartaric acid breakdown in grapes is unknown, and no enzymes capable of degradating tartaric acid have been identified. Saito and Kasai (1968) showed that free tartaric acid is readily broken down to CO_2 at all stages of berry development, but not the salt forms of tartaric acid. They suggested that the salts of tartaric acid are either not subject to enzymatic breakdown or are compartmentized in the cell vacuoles in such a manner that they do not come in contact with degradative enzyme.

Temperature is the most important environmental factor affecting the total acidity and the amount of malate and tartrate in grapes. Generally a variety will be higher in acid at the same degree Brix in a cool region or

Development and Composition of Grapes

TABLE 7

EFFECT OF THE MAXIMUM TEMPERATURE DURING RIPENING
ON THE TOTAL ACIDITY OF THOMPSON SEEDLESS GRAPES

Year	Mean maximum temperature	Per cent acidity
1929	109.0° F.	0.67
1931	98.0° F.	1.03

SOURCE OF DATA: Winkler (1932).

season than in a warm region or season (see table 7). It has been established that under controlled environmental conditions grapes ripened at cool day or night temperatures (59 to 68° F.) will be considerably higher in total acidity, particularly in malic acid, than fruit ripened at temperatures of 77 to 95° F. (Kliewer, 1968b, 1971, 1973; Kliewer and Lider, 1970; Buttrose et al., 1971). The per cent malate and the percentage of the titratable acidity due to malate is greater under cool temperatures than under warm temperatures. Kliewer (1971) showed that the amount of malic and tartaric acid in grapes is closely correlated negatively with temperature during the ripening period but relatively independent of light intensity.

Gerber (1897) studied the influence of temperature on the metabolism of organic acids in grapes and showed that the respiratory quotient changed with temperature, indicating a change in respiratory substrate. The respiratory quotient (R. Q. $= CO_2$ produced/O_2 absorption) approaches 1 when sugars are consumed, is approximately 1.33 when malic or citric acid is completely oxidized, and near 1.6 for the oxidation of tartaric acid. Gerber found R. Q. values in seedless grapes 0.70 at 32° F., 1.00 at 68° F., 1.33 at 86° F., and 1.44 at 99° F. These data suggest that tartaric acid is decarboxylated only at temperatures exceeding 86° F., while malic acid is respired at temperatures of 86° F. or less. Accordingly, one would expect and indeed find that the malate content of grapes from a hot region to be low (Amerine, 1956). This expectation is further supported in Genevois' (1938) review of the literature on the respiration of malic acid during the ripening of grapes, and by Bobadillo and Navarro (1949), when grapes were exposed to sunlight for a day after harvesting. Hennig and Burkhardt (1951) found that malic acid in grapes was lower in warm than in cool seasons. On the other hand, Peynaud (1947) did not find a constant relationship between the amount of malic acid retained in the hot year of 1937 and that retained in the cool year of 1938. Amerine's (1951) data also failed to indicate a uniform difference between cool and hot years. This failure to find a consistent low

Development and Composition of Grapes

malate content in warm years may be owing to the earlier harvest in such years. Another important factor is the rate and time of heat summation during the ripening period.

With regard to acid synthesis, Kliewer (1964) found that the optimum temperature for formation of acids from CO_2 in green Thompson Seedless berries was 68 to 77° F. and in ripe berries 59° F. Bremond (1937) noted that low temperatures at night stimulate the formation of acids, and temperatures higher than 86° F. cause the acid level to decline sharply. Reduced solar radiation received by either whole vines or individual fruit clusters has been shown to increase total acidity and malate in mature grape berries (Kliewer and Schultz, 1964; Kliewer et al., 1967b; Kliewer and Lider, 1968). These studies did not reveal whether the increases were due directly to low light intensity, to reduced tissue temperatures, or to a combination of both.

The physiological role of tartaric acid in grapevines is not known. Several possibilities exist and some of those that have been mentioned include regulation of metabolism through various pathways, balancing excess cations

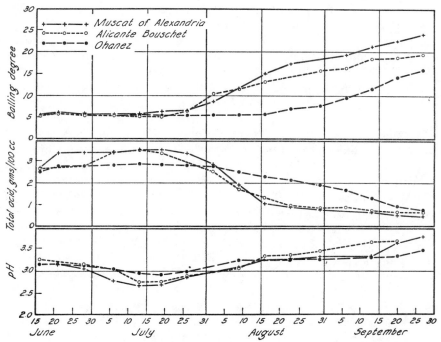

FIGURE 32: Ripening changes in three varieties of grapes. (From Amerine & Joslyn, 1951)

left when phosphate and nitrate ions are assimilated during rapid growth, and a detoxification mechanism during rapid growth.

pH.—The gradual rise in pH during ripening reflects the rise in acid salts at the expense of free acid (fig. 32). This ratio of acid salts to free acid is, of course, influenced by the temperature summation during ripening. The color and taste of grapes are influenced by pH. Crisci (1930) showed that pH and acid taste were more closely related than pH and total acidity. Since the grape is highly buffered, its pH increases very gradually during ripening. This change is so gradual that pH, though closely related to taste, is impractical as a measure of eating quality.

The pigment of colored grapes is affected by the acidity and pH of the grapes. The color is reddish and brilliant in fruit of moderate to high acidity and low pH, and tends to be bluish and dull in fruit of low acidity and high pH.

The pH is a factor in fermentation. At a low pH, other conditions being equal, the fermentation will be cleaner and the wine less liable to attack by spoilage organisms. La Rosa (1955) suggested pH as a standard for harvesting. This, however, is hardly tenable, since pH is only one factor in quality—and not a primary one.

Color.—The green coloring matter of the skin of grapes is chlorophyll. As this fades during ripening, other colors, previously masked, become discernible. White grapes that ripen gradually over a long period usually lose the chlorophyll almost completely and take on a translucent straw color. An example is the Malaga grown on shallow soil with a summer cover crop to check vine growth and initiate an early yet gradual ripening. The brilliance of the red color of the Tokay and Emperor is similarly enhanced.

Generally, the pigments of grapes is found only in the skin, where it is confined to the outer 3 or 4 layers of cells, but at times extends into the soft tissue below the skin. This is true of both white and colored varieties. The pigments occur mostly in the cell vacuole, although they may occur as amorphous masses or coarse or fine granules, and may impregnate the cell walls or occur in the cytoplasm. Ordinarily, however, the cytoplasm and cell walls show no pigments in the living cell but as cells die these tissues are stained as pigments diffuse from the vacuoles (Singleton and Esau, 1969). The pulp or flesh of the berry remains a pale green or takes on a light yellow-green color. Yet there are a few varieties of red or black grapes, such as Alicante Bouschet, whose juice is colored in both the skin and the pulp. As other red or black varieties, such as Salvador, become ripe to overripe, the inner cells of the skin rupture or exude color, so that the pulp—especially the pulp near the skin—becomes colored. The intensity of the color varies markedly with the variety (table 8), maturity, seasonal conditions, and level of crop.

Development and Composition of Grapes

Some varieties, especially when grown under cool conditions, retain the green color at maturity. Other varieties become yellow or orange owing to the presence of carotene and xanthophyll in the outer layers of the skin. This yellow pigment, of both white and red grapes, is quercetin—a flavone —and its glycoside, quercitrin—a flavonal. The oxidation of these pigments produces brownish-colored compounds that give the berries of some varieties an amber blush. Genevois and Ribéreau-Gayon (1947) suggest that the browning of freshly pressed grape juice is characteristic of a polyphenol of this type. The red color of the red, blue, purple, and black grapes is owing to pigments known as anthocyanins.

The pigments of grapes are anthocyanidins modified by attachment of a molecule of glucose. There are five anthocyanidins (cyanidin, delphinidin, petunidin, peonidin, and malvidin) that make up the basic part of grape pigments. Acylated forms of these pigments are also found in grapes. These result from esterification of the glucose hydroxyls with the organic acids, p-coumaric, caffeic, and acetic (Webb, 1970). The main anthocyanin in most V. *vinifera* varieties is malvidin-3-monoglucoside (oenin), which was first identified by Willstätter and Zollinger (1915, 1916). However, there are several *vinifera* varieties in which other anthocyanins predominate, for example, cyanidin 3-monoglucoside in Tokay and Red Malaga. The pigments of the red and black varieties of V. *vinifera* consist almost exclusively of monoglucoside anthocyanins while most other Vitis species, especially V. *rupestris* and V. *riparia*, contain both mono- and di-glucosides, with the latter pigments predominant (Ribéreau-Gayon et al., 1955; Ribéreau-Gayon, 1958, 1959, 1963).

The pigment pattern of over 167 V. *vinifera* varieties, using paper chromatography techniques, showed 2 to 9 anthocyans, with a similar pattern of 7 or 8 pigments being most prevalent; however, there were distinctly different color patterns in some varieties that are recognized as pure *viniferas* (Rankine et al., 1958; Albach et al., 1959; Ribéreau-Gayon, 1959). The variation in a number of these are given in table 8.

The figures of table 8 clearly show a marked qualitative and quantitative difference in pigment compositions within the general pattern of the varieties listed. In most varieties the greatest concentration of pigment was in band No. 5, which has been identified as malvidin-3-monoglucoside, except in Tokay, Emperor, and Red Malaga, in which band 5 consist mainly of cyanidin 3-monoglucoside (Akiyoshi et al., 1963). Rankine et al. (1958) found Pinot noir and a few closely related but obscure varieties to be completely free of the acylated pigments (band 1, 2, and 3, table 8). Gamay Beaujolais is now considered a clone of Pinot noir (Olmo, personal communication) and also contains no acylated pigments. Thus, the pigment patterns are of value in indicating varietal differences as well as similarities. A knowledge of the pigment patterns of varieties should be of great interest

TABLE 8

COMPARISON OF SKIN PIGMENTS OF VINIFERA VARIETIES

Band number [a]	1	2	3	4	5	6	7	8
Color	Blue	Mauve	Mauve-purple	Salmon pink	Mauve-purple	Bluish pink	Blue	Blue
Variety | Rf [b]	0.61	0.40	0.34	0.28	0.23	0.19	0.14	0.10
Aleatico	2	3	2	2	6	1	2	...
Aramon	1	...	2	3	4	1	1	...
Fresia	2	...	2	19	19	4	4	...
Cabernet-Sauvignon	1	2	8	1	10	1	1	1
Charbono	10	40	25	3	45	6	6	...
Gamay Beaujolais	...	...	...	5	12	2	2	1
Pinot noir	...	...	...	5	10	2	2	...
Pinot St. George	2	5	7	4	20	3	3	...
Tinta Madeira	2	4	4	5	9	1	1	2
Touriga	2	4	4	1	10	2	2	...
Emperor	...	...	...	...	1 [c]	0.5	...	...
Red Malaga	...	...	...	2	3 [c]	...	0.5	0.5
Ribier	2	3	1	2	8	1	1	0.5
Tokay	...	...	...	...	0.4 [c]	...	0.1	...

SOURCE OF DATA: Rankine et al. (1958).

[a] The position in the developed chromatogram of the pigment. Bands number 1, correspond respectively to one acylated pigments of several anthocyanidins; 2, malvidin and peonidin-3-monoglucoside acelated with ρ-coumaric acid; 3, same as (2) but acelated with caffeic acid; 4, peonidin-3-monoglucoside; 5, malvidin-3-monoglucoside or cyanidin-3-monoglucoside; 6, petunidin-3-monoglucoside; 7, delphinidin-3-monoglucoside; and 8, unknown.

[b] Relation of the flow of pigment to front of solvent.

[c] Orange pigment.

in breeding for given colors or color intensities. That the most attractive colors in table grapes need not be the most intense is definitely indicated by the figures for Emperor and Tokay. Albach et al. (1963, 1965a, b) and Akiyoshi (1963) have identified the pigments separated on paper chromatograms and these are listed in footnote a of table 8.

The pigment patterns of hybrids of vinifera, generally have a greater number of anthocyans than pure vinifera varieties. The pigments of Rubired and Royalty, both of which have some American species in their parentage, have been studied by Smith and Luh (1965) and Chen and Luh (1967).

They found as many as 18 anthocyans in these varieties with both mono- and di-glucosides being present.

The anthocyanin content ranges from zero, in a variety devoid of skin pigment to a maximum of about 2,500 to 3,000 mg/kg in a teinturier variety, such as Alicante Bouschet (Singleton and Esau, 1969). Puissant and Leon (1967) reported anthocyanin contents as high as 2,000 mg/kg for Baco noir, a dark colored hybrid; 890 mg/kg for Cabernet-Sauvignon and 450 mg/kg for Pinot noir. Most varieties suitable for red wine production have an average pigment content of about 800 mg/kg, while red or black table varieties generally have less than 500 mg/kg or anthocyanins. Anthocyanins account for about half the total phenol in the skin of grapes (Singleton and Esau, 1969). Ribéreau-Gayon (1964) found that anthocyanin per berry of Merlot grapes increased linearly from about 0.2 mg in early September to 1.6 mg/berry in late October, when the berries were mature and weighed 1.3 grams. Anthocyanin content decreased in berries warmed to simulate overmature conditions. Several investigators have shown that anthocyanin content of grapes may decrease in ripe or overripe grapes (Singleton and Esau, 1969).

In higher plants two mechanisms are responsible for the synthesis of the benzene ring found in anthocyanin: 1) the condensation of three molecules of acetyl co-enzyme A, and 2) the direct formation from sugar via shikimic acid (Ribéreau-Gayon, 1958). Shikimic acid synthesis is much greater in grape leaves than in berries, and most likely this acid is transported to the fruit where synthesis of anthocyanin is very rapid. In cluster transfers by approach-grafting experiments it was shown that the synthesis of pigments is entirely independent of the leaves of the particular variety. This is shown in figure 34, p.170, in which clusters of Muscat Albardiens colored normally even though they had developed on an Olivette blanche vine from the set of the berries. In general conditions that promote high carbohydrate accumulation in grapevines also favor the synthesis of pigments.

The tint of grape juice or wine is influenced by acidity and pH (see p. 158), tannin, flavones, and other co-pigments (e.g. alkaloids) and by iron and other metals. Blueness of tint is deepened by tannin. The presence of minute amounts of iron gives a violet tint. Other metals that form complex combinations also influence its color. The anthocyanins are amphoteric: acids increase the red tint and alkalies the blue tint.

Several environmental factors, especially light, temperature, soil moisture, and nutrition, markedly affect the level of pigments in grapes. Physiological factors, such as leaf area and crop levels, may also influence color development in grapes. In addition to these factors certain chemicals and plant growth substances affect grape coloration.

The requirement of light for color development has not been investigated thoroughly. According to Weaver and McCune (1960), there are distinct differences between varieties in their need for light. They found that such varieties as Mataro, Red Malaga, Ribier, and Zinfandel colored approximately as completely in black bags as in the open, whereas Emperor, Sultanina rose, and Tokay did not color without light. Not all of the varieties used responded equally. In some of those that colored in the dark, the development of one or more of the pigments may have been slowed, even though coloration was complete at full maturity. Similar results were reported from South Africa by Le Roux (1953). In the variety Tokay the placing of a strip of tin foil around the berry prevented the covered portion from developing any red color. Results in Tulare County with Emperor (Jensen, 1953) indicate that exposing the fruit to light by leaf removals, beginning at any time between July 15 and September 1, resulted in equally effective coloring. Naito (1964, 1966) and Naito et al. (1965) studied the effect of light intensity on the coloration of Delaware and Muscat Bailey A grapes in Japan. They found that light intensity had little effect on berry coloration in black grapes, but the maximum coloration in red grapes was considerably reduced under low light intensity. Although Naito and co-workers found that dark colored grapes showed no visible color difference when the clusters are matured in the dark, Kliewer (1970c) showed that low light intensity (500 to 1,000 foot candles) greatly reduced the coloration of Pinot noir grapes compared to fruit ripened at high light intensity (2,500 to 5,000 foot candles) when the pigment concentration was quantitatively measured. Torres (1971) and Jensen (1953) found that covering clusters with blue, red, green, yellow, or clear cellulose acetate plastic or cellophane had relatively little effect on the color of Tokay and Emperor grapes. These findings on requirements for color development may be the first steps toward an understanding of the effect of vineyard practices on coloring that may eventually lead to means of attaining more nearly the desired color for each variety.

Temperature has distinct influence on the development of color. In very hot regions, pigment formation is inhibited in many varieties of red and black grapes. Some of the delicately colored red table grapes become too dark in color when grown in the cooler regions. The Emperor, one of the most important shipping grapes of California, develops a brilliant red color when grown near the foothills of Fresno and Tulare Counties in the San Joaquin Valley; in the cooler area around Lodi it matures to a purplish black, and in the Hot Desert region of the Imperial Valley it is almost without color. Practically all of the other red and black varieties respond to temperature in the same manner (see table 4). Golodriga and Suyatinov (1966) showed that the average anthocyanin content of grapes from 22 varieties was 169 mg/kg in 1963 with a mean August–September temperature of 70° F., 286 mg/kg in 1962 with 66° F., and 358 mg/kg in 1964 with 63° F. There is, however, a difference in response among different varieties at the same temperature. At a given temperature one variety may remain light pink, another may develop a brilliant red, and still another may develop a jet black. The failure of certain varieties to color well in the coolest districts is a result of failure to ripen properly. In the hot years, when they attain full maturity, they may have an exceptionally brilliant color in such districts.

Both Kliewer (1970c) and Buttrose *et al.* (1971), using temperature controlled growth rooms or cabinets found that 68° F. day temperature (night temperature constant at 59° F.) greatly increased the level of pigments in the skins of Cardinal, Pinot noir, and Cabernet-Sauvignon grapes compared to fruits ripened at 86° F. day temperature. In a later study on the effect of day (7 A.M. to 7 P.M.) and night time (7 P.M. to 7 A.M.) temperatures on coloration of grapes Kliewer and Torres (1972) found that mature Cardinal, Pinot noir, and Tokay fruits ripened at cool-day (59° F.) and cool-night (59° F.) temperatures had much greater coloration than fruits ripened at hot-day (95° F.) and cool-night, hot-day and warm-nights (77° F.), or cool-day and warm-night temperatures. However, fruits grown at cool-day warm-night temperatures had significantly greater levels of anthocyanins than fruits ripened at hot-day temperatures, regardless of the night temperature. A day temperature of 95° F. completely inhibited anthocyanin synthesis in Tokay berries, regardless of night temperature. Cardinal and Pinot noir grapes, on the other hand, showed visible coloration, even though the level of anthocyanin was greatly reduced at 95° F. day temperature. The importance of night temperature on grape coloration is indicated in figure 33, which shows that 86° F. from 7 P.M. to 7 A.M. (day tempera-

FIGURE 33: This figure shows the effect of night temperature on the coloration of Tokay grapes grown in a phytotron. Day temperature was constant at 25° C (77° F). 15, 20, 25, and 30° C were equivalent to 59, 68, 77, and 86° F, respectively. (*Source of data: Kliewer and Torres, 1972*)

ture 77° F.) during the ripening period completely prevented pigment formation in Tokay grapes compared with fruits ripened at 59° and 68° F. night temperatures. A night temperature of 86° F. also greatly reduced the coloration of Cabernet-Sauvignon; however, 77° F. night temperature had relative little effect on pigmentation of Cabernet grapes but markedly reduced the color of Tokay fruit.

It should be emphasized that it is the brightness, not the density, of color that gives attractiveness to table grapes. Clusters of brilliant red Tokay or Emperor grapes are much more attractive than dull purple or black clusters. An ample, but not excessive, supply of water at ripening seems to favor a brilliant color in most fruits. With inadequate water the color tends to develop more abundantly, but it is dull and less attractive. The same dullness is usually obtained on clusters that hang in direct sunlight. In vineyard areas where vines are normally not irrigated Webster and Cross (1942) and Rankine (1964) reported that irrigation reduces color level of grapes.

Owing to a delay in the beginning of ripening and a slower accumulation of sugars, even the varieties that do not require direct light for coloring may not color well when nitrogen supply is overly abundant. Even when shallowness or some other soil deficiency prevents the growth of leafy shoots to shade the clusters, the fruit of all varieties is apt to be less well colored when the nitrogen supply in summer is abundant. Williams (1946) found that adding nitrogen fertilizer to a Tokay vineyard reduced the anthocyanin content of the berries by 23 per cent. Artyunayan *et al.* (1964) decreased grape pigmentation with nitrogen fertilization but increased tannin and pigments by adding potassium, phosphorus, or all three nutrients.

Leaf area and crop level have long been known to have a strong influence on fruit coloration. Winkler (1930) showed that thinning clusters just after fruit set produced earlier, more uniform, and better colored Tokay and Malaga fruit. Overcropping is generally associated with fruit of poor color (Winkler, 1954; Shaulis and Robinson, 1953; Weaver *et al.*, 1957; Koblet, 1967). Loomis and Lutz (1937) found that Concord grapes had very good color with 5 square meters of leaf surface per vine, while with 2 square meters or less of leaf area per vine the fruit was always rated poor in color. Kliewer and Weaver (1971) found a very close relationship (correlation coefficient of 0.91) between leaf area per unit weight of fruit and fruit coloration at harvest. They found that 11 to 14 square centimeters of leaf surface per gram of fruit was required to produce well colored Tokay fruit. This was equivalent to about 22 to 26 leaves per average size cluster with a weight of 1.4 pounds.

The relation of plant hormones to the development of pigment in grapes has received little attention. Recent experiments with ethephon, a chemical that slowly releases ethylene gas, showed that berry coloration was markedly

Development and Composition of Grapes

increased when this chemical was applied to fruit about two weeks after the initiation of coloring (Hale *et al.*, 1970; Weaver and Pool, 1971). Further work is needed to determine the effect of growth regulators on fruit coloration in grapes.

Tannin.—Tannins are complex esters of phenolic acids and sugars and occur primarily in the skins, stems, and seeds of grapes. Singleton (1966) found the total phenol content in mature berries of twelve wine varieties averaged 3770 mg/kg as gallic acid. The distribution of the phenols in the berries included about 1 per cent in the solid pressed pulp, 5 per cent in the juice, 50 per cent in the skins for red varieties and 25 per cent for white varieties, and the remaining 46–69 per cent was in the seeds. The distribution of total phenols in red and white wine grapes is shown in table 9. Generally, the fresh juice of red grapes contains 0.05 to 0.2 per cent tannin, and that of white grapes 0.01 to 0.03 per cent. During ripening, the tannin content of the skins increases at about the same rate as the color.

The tannins of grapes are classified as hydrolyzable (those which are like esters in character and can be broken down by hydrolysis) and condensed (phenolic polymers which are insoluble in water but soluble in neutral organic solvents). The hydrolyzable tannins occur mainly as galloyl esters of glucose (gallotannins), as galloyl esters of other sugars, or as galloyl esters of quinic acid (Haslam, 1966, 1967). The condensed tannins are not too well defined. They may be polymers of catechin, polymers of flavan-3, 4-diols, or compounds of catechin with leucoanthocyanins (Harborne, 1967). Most of the tannins of grapes are included in the condensed tannins. The catechin tannins constitute up to 73 per cent of the total tannins and l-epigallocatechin may make up as much as 54 per cent of the total (Hennig and Burkhardt, 1957, 1958). Durmishidze (1955, 1959) indicates that the basic path in the formation of tannins is sugars → mesoinositol → phloroglucin → tannins.

Hermann (1963) reported that grapes contain the following poly-

TABLE 9
Total Phenol Distribution in Vitis Vinifera Wine Grapes [a]

Portion	Red varieties	White varieties
Skins	1859	904
Pressed pulp	41	35
Juice	206	176
Seeds	3525	2778
Total	5631	3893

SOURCE OF DATA: Singleton and Essau, 1969.
[a] In gallic or tannic acid equivalents, mg/kg berries.

Development and Composition of Grapes

phenolic compounds (other than the anthocyan pigments): chlorogenic acid, isochlorogenic acid, neochlorogenic acid, p-coumaric acid ester; flavandiols and proanthocyanins: $(+)$-catechin, $(-)$-epicatechin, $(+)$-gallocatechin, $(-)$-epigallocatechin, epicatechin gallate; flavonols and flavons: isoquercitrin, quercitrin, myrictrin camphoryl glycoside; and other phenolic compounds: gallic acid, ellagic acid, and procatechuic acid.

Tannin influences the palatability of grapes and their products. In small quantities it adds to the acceptability of the flavor of table grapes, sweet grape juice, and wine. In wines it also improves the body, stabilizes color, and aids in fining. When grapes are canned or preserved with chemicals the tannin of seeds is objectionable, since it may be leached out to give the product a high astringency. This accounts in part for the use of seedless varieties almost exclusively for canning. In some varieties tannin is more perceptible in the very mature or overripe fruit.

Pectin.—Pectin substances are derivatives of polygalacturonic acid. They occur in three general types: protopectin, pectin, and pectic acid. Pectic compounds are a normal constituent of the vine and its fruit. Protopectin is found most abundantly in the primary cell wall. The middle lamella of the cell walls consists largely of pectic compounds that are mixtures of calcium and magnesium pectates. The calcium and magnesium salts of pectic acid are the important cementing substances of the middle lamella.

During ripening, the protopectin is transformed to pectin and the berries soften as a result of the removal of middle-lamella pectate (Bonner, 1950). This process is, in large measure, responsible for the characteristic texture of the fruit. The effect of the change in pectates on texture has an important influence on the keeping and shipping qualities of different varieties of table grapes; some varieties remain relatively firm in storage or

TABLE 10
RANGE IN PECTIN IN DIFFERENT LOCATIONS

Species and locality	Pectin content, per cent	Source of data
Vitis vinifera:		
Germany	0.11–0.33	von der Heide and Schmitthenner (1922)
France	0.14–0.39	Ventre (1930)
Italy	0.08–0.39	Garina-Canina (1928)
Switzerland	0.056–0.355	Solms, *et al.* (1952)
California	0.03–0.17	Marsh and Pitman (1930)
Vitis labrusca:		
New York	0.60	Willaman and Kertez (1931)
California	0.11–0.29	J. Besone (Unpublished data)

shipment, whereas others become very soft. The change in the pectic substances, like other ripening changes, is continuous, with the fruit becoming too soft as it approaches overripeness. The figures in table 10 show the level and range of variation in the pectin content of typical varieties in a number of locations.

Vinifera grapes contain only small amounts of pectin, as compared to American grapes, such as the Concord, which are rich in pectin. This difference in pectin content largely accounts for the greater suitability of the latter for making jelly.

Odorous constituents.—During ripening the grape develops various substances that give each variety its special aroma. It is these substances that distinguish the Muscats and give the Concord its foxiness. The kinds and intensities of these substances differ among varieties. In some they are very strong, and in others mild or neutral.

The foxy aroma of Vitis labrusca is among the most pronounced odors of grapes, and probably this fact attracted the investigators who some years ago isolated and identified the aroma substance as methyl anthranilate (Power and Chestnut, 1921). A well-matured Concord grape, grown under favorable conditions, may contain as much as 3.8 mg. of this aroma substance per liter of juice.

Unlike varieties of labrusca and rotundifolia, those of vinifera have an aroma that is delicate and subdued; only the aroma of the Muscat group is marked. Again, because of the great antiquity of vinifera grape culture, many varieties have been developed with widely differing aromas. Those of the Muscat group have an aroma or odor almost as pronounced as that of the labrusca selections and hybrids, whereas such a variety as Thompson Seedless is only mildly vinous. The aroma of many other viniferas is intermediate, although in a number of both the white and the red varieties it is quite distinct and readily distinguishable.

The minuteness of the amounts of the aroma or odor substances in vinifera varieties delayed their isolation and identification until recently, when sufficiently sensitive methods of analysis became available. Haagen-Smit, et al. (1949) reported the volatile (odorous) constituents of the Zinfandel shown in table 11.

Webb and Kepner (1957) isolated and identified the odorous (aroma) constituents of Muscat of Alexandria. Their findings are shown in table 12.

In a later investigation linaloöl and geraniol were isolated; they are believed to be the compounds of greatest importance to the "muscat" aroma (Webb et al., 1966; Webb, 1967). Cordonnier (1956), Stevens et al. (1966), and Usseglio-Tomasset et al. (1966) have identified linaloöl as the compound responsible for the muscaty odor in Muscat blanc. Linaloöl has also been identified in White Riesling.

Development and Composition of Grapes

TABLE 11

SUMMARY OF COMPONENTS OF THE VOLATILE OIL OF
ZINFANDEL GRAPES

Component	Amount, gm. per 1,000 kg. of grapes
Acetaldehyde	1.800
Leaf aldehyde	0.327
Ethyl alcohol	244.000
Acetylmethylcarbinol	0.013
Acetic acid	0.0053
N-butyric acid	0.003
N-caproic acid	0.0015
Glyoxylic acid	0.118
N-butyl phthalate	2.250
Waxy substances	0.024
Carbonyl compound	0.025
Sulfur	0.004

SOURCE OF DATA: Haagen-Smit, et al. (1949).

Drawert and Rapp (1966) and Van Wyk et al. (1967) reported on the volatile components of White Riesling grapes grown in Germany and California. They found 15 alcohols, 16 volatile organic acids, and only two esters, ethyl acetate and isoamylacetate, both present in trace amounts. Drawert and Rapp (1966) reported that most of the volatile components of White Riesling grapes remained remarkably constant during ripening.

TABLE 12

VOLATILE ESSENCE COMPONENTS OF MUSCAT OF ALEXANDRIA

Component	Amount, mg per kg of grapes	Component	Amount, mg per kg of grapes
Methanol	3.7	Methyl acetate	0.08
Ethanol	111.0	Ethyl caproate	0.04
N-butanol	0.03		
3-Methylbutanol	0.01	Butyrate ester	
N-hexanol	0.49	Valerate ester	
cis-3-Hexanol	0.26	Caproate ester	
Acetaldehyde	0.85	Caprylate ester	0.16
N-hexanal	0.03	Caprate ester	
2-Hexanal	0.05	Laurate ester	
2-Butanone	0.01	Ethyl esters	
2-Pentanone	0.01		

SOURCE OF DATA: Webb and Kepner (1957).

Among the compounds showing increases during ripening were n-amyl acetate, 1-butanol, ethyl caproate, n-butyl butyrate, and 1-hexanol. Van Wyk *et al.* (1967) attributed the green odor of freshly crushed Riesling grapes to linolenic acid and trans-hex-2-en-ol and possibly also to 1-hexanol, 3-methyl-1-butanol, and 2-methyl-1-butanol. The fruity note they attributed to 2-phenethyl alcohol, linaloöl, ethyl acetate, and isoamyl acetate. However, no single compound had the typical White Riesling odor.

Chaudhary *et al.* (1964) found 36 volatile compounds in Sauvignon blanc grapes and estimated their relative amounts. In 1968 they isolated and analyzed the essence from wines prepared from normal Sauvignon blanc grapes and those from similar grapes treated with Botrytis cinerea. No significant difference in either the acidic or neutral components of the volatile essence was found. Prillinger *et al.* (1968) reported that oxidized grape juice contained hexanol, isovaleraldehyde, and 1-propanol. Muller *et al.* (1971) isolated methionol, a compound that has a raw potato-like odor, in Cabernet Sauvignon and Ruby Cabernet wines. Another aroma compound (4-ethoxy-4-hydroxybutyric acid and γ-lactone) has been isolated and identified in Ruby Cabernet wine (Muller *et al.*, 1972). This compound has not been identified in any other wine or must.

The volatile essence compounds of mixed varieties of V. *rotundifolia* grapes have been determined to include methyl alcohol, ethyl alcohol, N-butyl alcohol, isoamyl alcohol, N-hexyl alcohol, β-phenyl-ethyl alcohol, acetaldehyde, isobutyraldehyde, biacetyl, N-hexanol, 2-hexanol, ethyl acetate, caproate ester, caprylate ester, caprate ester, laurate ester, and probably methylethyl ketone and acetal (Webb and Kepner, 1956).

These analyses, together with similar results on wine, indicate the complex nature of the aroma and bouquet (the aroma of wine) substances; they also point up the limitations of the analytical approach to variety and wine evaluation (Hennig and Villforth, 1942; Webb, 1967). Webb and Muller (1972) have documented more than 300 volatile aroma compounds found in wines. The limitations of analysis arise not only from the large number and minuteness of the quantities of the aroma and bouquet substance present, but also from the susceptibility of these substances to oxidation during isolation and to changes during aging. Until more efficient methods are perfected, the quality of both grapes and wines, as influenced by the odorous constituents, must continue to be evaluated by sensory means (taste).

On the basis of organoleptic analyses it has become recognized that: (*a*) Muscat aroma has the most pronounced aroma of *vinifera* grapes, and also one that carries over into the wine; (*b*) grapes of certain varieties that have distinct aromas, such as Cabernet Sauvignon, Sauvignon blanc, Sémillon, and White Riesling, also produce wines with very distinct bouquets; and (*c*) grapes of certain varieties that have very mild to neutral

Development and Composition of Grapes

aromas, such as Pinot noir and Zinfandel, produce wines of strikingly distinct bouquets. Although it is recognized that, in the case of fine wines, the grapes themselves contribute markedly to the aroma and bouquet it must be conceded that important aroma constituents in these arise through the action of the yeast on sugar and other compounds of the must. The above varieties, along with a few others, produce wines of distinct varietal character. Beyond these there is the great mass of varieties that are neutral in aroma or odor and produce wines with only a vinous odor. Most of the table grapes grown in California, except the Muscats, are neutral in aroma; most of them, however, possess a mild to pleasingly distinct flavor.

The aroma or odor substances are largely, but not entirely, confined to the skin of the berries. Although the precursor materials of these substances are produced in the leaves, the aroma is synthesized in the berries. Support for this view is indicated through cluster-transfer trials in which,

Figure 34: Cluster transfers by approach-grafting; A and B, clusters in natural position; C, Olivette blanche cluster on Muscat Albardiens shoot; and D, Muscat Albardiens cluster on Olivette blanche shoot.

by approach-grafting, clusters of one variety were placed on shoots of another (A. J. Winkler, unpublished information). Clusters of Muscat Albardiens were grafted on shoots of Olivette blanche, and vice versa. The attachment of the grafted cluster to its parent vine was severed immediately after the fruit set (fig. 34). At maturity the fruit of Muscat Albardiens on the Olivette blanche vines had a characteristic and pronounced Muscat Albardiens aroma and flavor. Likewise, the fruit of the Olivette blanche on the Muscat Albardiens vines had the typically neutral Olivette blanche aroma and flavor. Similar results were obtained in cluster transfers between Dattier and Danuque.

It has been *known for many years that the aroma accumulates in the berries only during the last stages of maturity* (Girard and Lindet, 1898). For example, the Muscat of Alexandria may be almost fully developed and still have hardly any detectable muscat aroma. The cause of the delay is not understood; it may be necessary for other constituents of the fruit—amino acids, sugars, etc.—to reach certain levels before the aroma is synthesized. Robinson, *et al.* (1949) followed the formation of methyl anthranilate in the Concord grape during one season and found a large increase between September 16 and October 20, while degrees Brix increased from 12.8 to 17.4. Their results suggest that the aroma substance is formed during the latter stages of ripening (fig. 35). Drawert and Rapp (1966) found that *vinifera* varietal flavor and aroma components develop fully only in ripe grapes.

Flavor.—Flavor is the complex reaction of taste and olfactory receptors. Many substances contribute to the flavor of grapes. The primary tastes of sugars (sweet) and acids (sour) are dominant. The relation of sugars to the palatability of grapes was the basis for the first standardization law, in 1915. To meet the requirement of this law the sugar was determined in degrees Brix of the expressed juice. More recently, the role of the sweet-to-acid taste in determination of the eating quality of grapes is being recognized (Winkler, 1932).

To a lesser extent, tannin influences the astringency of the fruit and, thereby, its flavor. A small amount of tannin gives grapes or their juice a sprightly zestfulness, too much renders the fruit astringent (puckery), and too little results in a "tired" flavor.

Flavor is determined not by the actual amounts of sugar, acid, or tannin present, but by the amounts of these in relation to one another: a given amount of acid or astringency may produce a very unpleasant flavor in grapes that are low in sugar, a pleasant flavor in grapes high in sugar.

The satisfaction one gets from eating different varieties of grapes is owing mainly to the aroma and flavor of the combined odorous constituents. Many persons rate the Muscats highly because of their pronounced aroma. Others prefer the mild formic-acid-like flavor of the Cardinal. Still

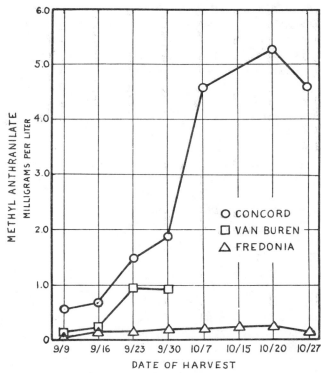

FIGURE 35: Methyl anthranilate development during ripening. (*From Fruit Prod. Jour.*, 29(2):36–37, 54, 62)

others like the mild vinous flavor of the Thompson Seedless. It might be argued, however, that the preference for the latter is influenced by its seedlessness. To those who grew up in the northern middle-west and easter states, the Concord type of flavor is often most appealing. The odorous substances named earlier, and some others, have been isolated and identified by chemists, but, because they occur in such minute quantities, indicating their function or importance in imparting flavors has been possible for only a few varieties. That they are important in consumer preferences is generally recognized.

Preferences in the eating of grapes are also influenced by the texture of the berries. Following bloom, rapid cell division lasts for only a short time, so that the principal growth of berries is by cell enlargement of the pericarp. As the cells enlarge, their walls become thinner. This type of cell wall in varieties that have a firm texture at maturity gives the fruit a crispness when eaten. The ease with which the cells are crushed together, with the rapid release of the cell contents, adds to the flavor and to the pleasure of eating. Varieties with thick-walled cells and a softer texture may be considered less desirable even though they contain essentially the same flavor and odor substances. The composition of the cell walls has much to do with their firmness or tenderness. In immature grapes the walls are composed of hemicellulose, cellulose, and pectic substances. As the grapes ripen, the pectic substances are hydrolized. The extent of this hydrolysis largely determines the tenderness of the fruit of a variety. The degree of softening may also be influenced by the proportions of the materials that constitute the cell walls. With a high proportion of cellulose the wall would remain firmer and tougher.

Enzymes.—Information concerning the enzymes of the grape is limited. Bayer *et al.* (1957) studied the polyphenoloxidase of grapes. Ivanov (1967) found that polyphenoloxidase is the main oxidizing system of grapes, with the greatest activity in the skins. He showed that varieties differed in the total amount of enzyme activity. Cassignard (1966) found the skins, seeds, and stems to contain the most enzyme. Pallavicini (1967) also reported that the enzymes of grapes (phenolase, phosphatase, proteinase, and sucrase) are found primarily in the skins and to a lesser extent in the pulp. Pool and Weaver (1970) found a direct relationship between total soluble solids and percentage of berries which developed internal browning. Fruits susceptible to internal browning had high levels of polypenoloxidase activity and low levels of dihydroxyphenolic substrate.

Hussein and Cruess (1940) reported peroxidase in California grapes. Golodriga and Pu-Chao (1963) determined the amounts of peroxidase, polypenoloxidase, and catalase in early and late ripening varieties. Catalase was particularly high in early-ripening varieties and polyphenoloxidase was present in largest amounts in late-ripening varieties. Garina-Canina (1946) also found catalase in grapes. Harel and Mayer (1971) found a high level of catechol oxidase in two white grape varieties.

Pantanelli (1910) found a protein-splitting enzyme in must but not in wine. Baglioni *et al.* (1937) found the juice of fresh grapes to have proteolytic activity. Bolcato *et al.* (1965) separated two proteases, a peroxidase, a phenolase, an acid phosphatase, and invertase from musts and wines. An enzyme that demethoxylates pectins was reported by Follenberg (1914) and Semichon and Flanzy (1926) found three types of pectic enzymes in grapes.

Invertase, an enzyme that hydrolyzes sucrose into glucose and fructose, has been found in grapes by several investigators (Casale and Garina-Canina, 1937; Arnold, 1965; Hawker, 1969b). Hawker (1969a) found both soluble and insoluble invertase in grapes, but indicated that insoluble invertase is probably an artifact of extraction caused by the formation of a tannin-protein complex or a protein-tannin-cell wall complex. Invertase reached maximum activity in the berries about six weeks after flowering.

Hawker (1969b) followed changes in the activity of enzymes concerned with sugar metabolism at weekly intervals during the development of Thompson Seedless grapes. These enzymes included invertase, hexokinase, glucose 6-phosphate dehydrogenase, sucrose synthetase, sucrose phosphate synthetase and sucrose phosphatase.

Hawker (1969c) also investigated enzymes that are concerned primarily with the synthesis and breakdown of malic acid in grapes. He followed changes in the activity of malic enzyme, pyruvate carboxylase, phospho-pyruvate carboxylase, and malate dehydrogenase in Thompson Seedless grapes, at weekly intervals, throughout their development. Phosphopyruvate carboxylase activity, which was high in young berries, decreased to a low value at about the time that net synthesis of malic acid ceased, i.e. immediately following veraison. However, malic enzyme and pyruvate decarboxylase did not show large increases in activities during the period in which malic acid decreases rapidly, as might be expected. Meynhardt (1965) found that mature Barlinka grapes contain phosphopyruvate car-boxylase and malic enzyme and both enzymes were active in the dark fixation of carbon dioxide in fruit, forming principally malic acid.

Vitamins.—Fresh grapes contain a number of vitamins. Morgan *et al.* (1935) found 1 international unit of vitamin A per gram of Thompson Seedless grapes, and Watt and Merrill (1950) reported 80 units per 100 grams of the edible portion of *vinifera* grapes. Muradov (1966) reported 0.37 to 1.30 mg per liter of vitamin A in 20 grape musts. Pasteurization resulted in the loss of 16 to 17 per cent of vitamin A. Dehydrated grapes, both sulfured and unsulfured, retain this factor in full. Natural raisins, however, contain no vitamin A, and grapes preserved by freezing storage, even after air evacuation, lose vitamin A rapidly.

The B-complex vitamins of grapes and musts have been studied by Burger *et al.* (1956), Castor (1953), Hall *et al.* (1956), Peynaud and Lafourcade (1955, 1956, 1957), Perlman and Morgan (1945), and Radler (1957). The amounts they report are shown in table 13. The variations in the content of the vitamins found by the different workers is, no doubt, owing to varietal and environmental influences. The highest figures reported by Radler are for *Vitis* species and species hybrids.

Compared with other fruits, grapes, together with blackcurrants, have the highest content of thiamine and mesoinositol (Peynaud and Lafourcade, 1958). They have fair amounts of nicotinic and pantothenic acids. Grapes are normal in pyridoxine and biotin but very poor in riboflavin. The thiamine content of grapes, both on a concentration and a per berry basis, increases during maturation, especially during the final stages of ripening (Ournac and Flanzy, 1957). About 75 per cent is found in the expressed juice and the remainder in the solid part of the skin and pulp. Most other vitamins also increase during ripening.

Development and Composition of Grapes

TABLE 13

VITAMIN-B LEVELS OF GRAPES AND MUSTS

(In micrograms per 100 grams or per 100 milliliters)

Vitamin	Amount in grapes	Amount in musts	Source of data
Thiamine	35–58	17–25	1
"	. . .	25–65	2,3,4
Riboflavin	20–25	20–35	1
"	. . .	6–40	2,3,5
Pyrodoxine	84–135	14–16	1
"	. . .	60–180	2,3,5
"	. . .	30–290	6
Pantothenic acid	78	25–50	1
"	. . .	50–150	2,3,5
"	. . .	30–340	6
Nicotinic acid	170–330	140–260	1
"	. . .	80–370	2,5
"	. . .	180–880	6
Inositol	. . .	22–73	4,5
Biotin	. . .	0.01–0.6	4,5,6
Folic acid	4.2–10.2	2–5	1,2

SOURCES OF DATA: 1, Burger et al. (1956); 2, Hall et al. (1956); 3, Perlman and Morgan (1945); 4, Peynaud and Lafourcade (1955); 5, Castor (1953); 6, Radler (1957).

Ough and Kunkee (1968) found 1.35 to 6.8 micrograms per liter of biotin in 33 red grape varieties and 0.6 to 2.55 micrograms in 34 white varieties. Biotin increased markedly in Cabernet-Sauvignon during maturation. The biotin content was positively correlated with rate of fermentation but normally is not directly a significant factor in determining the fermentation rate of grape juice.

In sound fresh grapes the B vitamins are reasonably stable in cold storage, whereas in cool storage their amount may decrease by as much as 10 to 30 per cent in a month (Di Castro, 1953). Thiamine is destroyed by sulfur dioxide in proportion to the amount of free sulfur dioxide present. Riboflavin and folic acid disappear rapidly during extraction of the juice. The light lability of these vitamins may largely account for this reduction. In dark containers a larger per cent is retained. Filtration with bentonite removes much of both thiamine and riboflavin. On the other hand, retained pyridoxine, pantothenic acid, nicotinic acid, and inositol are much more stable. They are not affected by light, and only mildly or not at all by sulfur dioxide. Biotin is much reduced by fermentation, and heating destroys inositol.

Development and Composition of Grapes

Ascorbic acid (vitamin C) is present in minute though measurable amounts. The quantities found by investigators in various countries indicate that fresh grapes contain 1 to 12.5 micrograms of ascorbic acid per 100 grams of grapes (see table 14). More recently, using improved techniques, Ournac (1965) reported 20 to 60 micrograms per liter of ascorbic acid in musts. Ournac and Poux (1966) found an early increase in the total amount of ascorbic acid in grape berries during the first few weeks after fruit set, followed by a decrease which lasted until the fruit started to ripen (veraison) and then increased during ripening followed by another decline during the latter stages of fruit maturation. The skin area contains a greater concentration of ascorbic acid than the juice, but the total amount in the juice is greater than that of the skin. In the crushing of grapes, much of this vitamin is lost. Treatment of the fresh juice with pectin-splitting enzymes for clarification reduced the ascorbic acid by about one third, and filtration reduces it by about two thirds (Zimmerman et al., 1940). Most of it is lost in natural sun-drying of raisins (Morgan et al., 1935).

Compounds possessing the chemical and physiological properties of

TABLE 14
Vitamin-C Content of Various Grapes

Variety	Ascorbic acid, micrograms per 100 grams of grapes	Source of data
Madeleine Celine	3.4–4.9	
Mission	4.7	
Folle blanche	7.1–7.8	1
Muscat of Alexandria	3.3–3.8	
Burger	8.4–9.3	
Pearl of Csaba	5.6	
22 varieties, Uruguay	1.3–4.7	2
Wild grapes, Russia	7.0–12.5	3
44 standard varieties, Russia	0.6–9.6	
2 hybrids of wild grapes, Russia	1.5–12.4	4
Eden	4.0–5.7	
James	2.0–5.5	
Labama	4.8–6.3	
Mish	0.8–1.8	
Scuppernong	4.6–8.2	5
Thomas	2.9–5.9	
Hopkins	10.2	

sources of data: 1, Amerine and Joslyn (1951), Table Wines (University of California Press, Berkeley and Los Angeles); 2, Ibarra (1941); 3, Anokhova (1937); 4, Berg (1940); 5, Bell et al. (1942).

rutin and similar compounds that are considered to be provitamins of the so-called vitamin P occur in grapes. According to Scarborough (1945) and Lavollay and Sevestre (1944), the grape is the richest natural source of vitamin P. Bukin and Eropeeva (1954) also reported that the tannin constituents of grapes have properties similar to those ascribed to vitamin P.

As usually reported, the vitamin content of Concord grapes is not as high as that for *vinifera* varieties. It has been suggested by Daniel and Munsell (1932), however, that the reportedly greater content of vitamins A, B, and C in the edible parts of Malaga and Thompson Seedless grapes than in those of Concord may be accounted for by a greater concentration of vitamins in the skins, which were retained in the Malaga and Thompson Seedless and were discarded in the determinations on Concord. Bell *et al.* (1942) reported that the skin of Scuppernong grapes contained three times more vitamins than the flesh.

Nitrogenous compounds.—In grapes, nitrogen compounds are found as ammonium cations and as organic compounds—amino acids, hexose amines, peptides, nucleic acids, and proteins. Only trace amounts of nitrate nitrogen are found in grape berries. Total nitrogen in must generally ranges from 10 to 200 mg per 100 ml (Hennig, 1955). The distribution of nitrogenous compounds in the grape berry is described by Ribéreau-Gayon and Peynaud (1961). The juice contains only about one-fifth of the total nitrogen, the remaining four-fifths being in the skin and seeds. These authors also report that there is some release of nitrogenous compounds from the seeds into the pulp of the mature grape and that about half the nitrogen content of the juice of ripe grapes is due to free amino acids. Kliewer (1969, 1970a) found that the amino acid fraction (amino acids and low molecular weight peptides) accounted for 50 to 90 per cent of the total nitrogen in the juice of 78 varieties investigated and the non-amino acid fraction accounted for 10 to 56 per cent.

During maturation the organic nitrogen in the fruit steadily increases, including total amino acids and protein, while ammonia decreases (Peynaud, 1939; Peynaud and Maurie, 1953; Ferenczi, 1966). In immature fruit ammonium ions account for more than half the total nitrogen. Peynaud (1939) found 19 to 144 milligrams of ammonia per liter and 156 to 879 mg. of total nitrogen in Bordeaux grapes. Casale (1937) reported 5 to 120 mg. of ammonia and 56 to 670 mg. of total nitrogen in the Piedmont grapes of Spain. Synthesis of amino acids, peptides, and protein occur mainly during the last six to eight weeks of berry ripening, and during this period ammonia decreases sharply. Kliewer (1968a) found that total free amino acids in the juice of eighteen grape varieties increased two- to five-fold during ripening and ranged from 200–800 mg. per 100 ml. juice (as leucine equivalents).

Development and Composition of Grapes

The findings of Hennig (1943), who determined seven nitrogen fractions in must of Germany, are summarized in table 15. These figures confirm earlier findings of the low level of protein nitrogen. The most important organic fractions are those of phosphotungstic and amino acid nitrogens. The phospho-tungstic nitrogen includes the tri- and tetra-peptides, diamino acids, such as arginine and lysine, and heterocyclic acids, such as histidine and proline, as well as any purines present. The amino acid nitrogen includes the dipeptides; the humin nitrogen fraction includes tyrosine and trytophane; the amide fraction contains asparagine and glutamine.

Koch (1963) and Koch *et al.* (1959) found several soluble proteins in the juice of grapes, which differed somewhat between varieties. The amounts increased during ripening and reached maximum quantities before full maturity, then decreased up to harvest. Whether grapes for wine are harvested at the peak of protein content or later may affect the clouding of wine. Greater amounts of soluble protein were formed during warm seasons than during cool seasons. The water soluble high molecular weight nitrogenous substances are believed to be low molecular weight polypeptides and proteins. The complete list of amino acids involved and their peptide linkage is unknown. Bayly and Berg (1967) reported 20 to 260 mg per liter of protein (average 121) in the juice of eleven California grown grape varieties.

The free amino acids in the juice of grapes have been extensively investigated and the amounts vary considerably, depending on the variety, location, maturity, cultural conditions, and method of determination. Using microbiological assays Castor (1953a, b) determined the free amino acids in the juice of seven varieties of grapes. Glutamic acid was the most

TABLE 15
LEVELS OF VARIOUS NITROGEN FRACTIONS IN
GRAPE MUSTS, GERMANY
(In milligrams per liter)

Nitrogen fractions	Year 1941	Year 1942
Total nitrogen	1,075	748
Protein nitrogen	40	18
Ammonia nitrogen	112	15
Phospho-tungstic nitrogen	349	231
Amino-acid nitrogen	408	319
Humin nitrogen	20	17
Amide nitrogen	34	16

SOURCE OF DATA: Hennig (1943).

Development and Composition of Grapes

prominent (mean 69 mg/100 ml; range 27–107) followed by arginine (mean 40; range 7–113; histidine, leucine, isoleucine, valine, aspartic acid, phenylalanine and tryptophane each averaged 5–10 mg/100 ml juice. The importance of proline, serine, and threonine was shown later (Castor and Archer, 1956), when the main amino acids of the French Colombard juice were given as proline 349 mg/100 ml, arginine 103, serine 48, glutamic acid 27, and threonine 21. It was also shown that, unlike most other amino acids, proline was not readily assimilated by yeast during fermentation. However, C. S. Ough (personal communication) has shown that proline can be utilized by yeast if the total supply of nitrogen is low. A similar range of amino acids in grape juice has been amply confirmed by many workers (Hennig and Venter, 1958; Lafon-Lafourcade and Peynaud, 1959; Lafon-Lafourcade and Guimberteau, 1962; Nassar and Kliewer, 1966; and Kliewer, 1968a, 1969, 1970a). However, there are some notable differences in the amino acid composition of grapes from that cited in the above literature. Terčelj (1965) found much more arginine than proline in the juice of the variety Servanti. Kliewer (1969, 1970a) showed that arginine was the predominant amino acid in 33 grape varieties, proline was predominant in 40 varieties, and α-alanine was the major amino acid in 4 varieties. The varieties in which alanine was predominant had some American species in their parentage. The amino acids that have been reported in the juice of grapes and their concentrations are given in table 16. In an investigation of 78 grape varieties grown at Davis, Kliewer (1969, 1970a) found that eight free amino acids (alanine, γ-aminobutyric acid, arginine, aspartic acid, glutamic acid, proline, serine, and threonine accounted for 29 to 85 per cent of the total nitrogen in the juice of grapes and for 50 to 95 per cent of the total free amino acids present. The variety and the degree of maturity of the fruits greatly affect the level of free amino acids in grape berries. This is especially true for arginine and proline, in which concentrations differ by as much as ten- to twelve-fold among varieties and from two- to six-fold between early- and late-harvested fruits of the same variety. Ough (1968) reported that the level of proline in grapes ranged from 304 to 4,600 mg per liter and that the Cabernet group of varieties (Cabernet-Sauvignon and Merlot) are particularly high in proline. Several investigators have shown that the level of proline in grapes is very closely related to fruit maturity (Lafon-Lafourcade and Guimberteau, 1962; Ough, 1968; Kliewer and Ough, 1970). Proline is usually present in larger amounts in grapes during warm years than in cool years (Flanzy and Poux, 1965). This relationship has been confirmed in grapes grown in temperature controlled growth rooms (Kliewer and Lider, 1970; Buttrose *et al.*, 1971). Generally other amino acids are largely unaffected by temperature.

In addition to the scion, degree of fruit maturity, and temperature, other

TABLE 16

LEVEL OF AMINO-ACIDS (mg/liter) IN GRAPE MUSTS, CALIFORNIA AND FRANCE

Amino Acids	Castor and Archer (1956) California — Five wine grape varieties [a]	Lafon-Lafourcade and Peynaud (1959) France — Merlot and Cabernet-Sauvignon	Kliewer (1968a), and Nassar and Kliewer (1966) California — 18 Grape varieties [c]	Thompson Seedless
α-Alanine			350	47
β-Alanine				<1
α-Aminobutyric acid				<1
α-Aminobutyric acid			220	97
Arginine	293	327	1080	905
Asparagine				24
Aspartic acid	46	2	130	44
Citrulline				<1
Cysteine				11
Cystine	3	0		5
Glutamic acid	548	173	510	51
Glutamine				18
Glycine	6	22		11
Histidine	92	11		29
Homoserine				<1
Hydroxyproline				<1
Isoleucine	64	7		29
Leucine	61	20		17
Lysine	15	16		28
Methionine	16	1		<1
Norvaline				<1
Phenylalanine	57	5		122
Pipecolic acid				<1
Proline	3490 [b]	266	1250	270
Serine	490 [b]	69	180	25
Threonine	210 [b]	258	240	86
Tyrosine	24	0		58
Tryptophan	48	1		51
Valine	64	6		39

[a] Aglianico, Cabernet-Sauvignon, French Colombard, Sauvignon blanc, and Tannat.
[b] French Colombard only.
[c] The 18 varieties included Alicante Bouschet, Black Corinth, Cardinal, Cabernet-Sauvignon, Carignane, Chardonnay, Chenin blanc, Flora, Gewurztraminer, Malbec, Muscat Hamberg, Palomino, Perlette, Pinot noir, Thompson Seedless, and Tokay.

Development and Composition of Grapes

factors such as rootstock, climate, mineral nutrition, crop level, trellising system, and diseases may influence the concentration of amino acids in grapes. Ough *et al.* (1968) showed that the nitrogen content of fruits from scions grown on St. George rootstock was considerably greater than when 99R was used as the rootstock. Fruits from vines with light crop loads generally have higher levels of nitrogen, arginine, proline, and total free amino acids than vines with heavy crops (Kliewer and Ough, 1970). The amount of arginine in Thompson Seedless fruits was positively correlated with total leaf area per vine.

Ammonia and the amine nitrogen of must, especially arginine, phenylalanine, histidine, valine, and glutamic acid, are largely assimilated by yeast during fermentation. Lysine, proline, and glycine are much less easily assimilated. Although present in very small amounts as compared to human daily requirements, isoleucine, leucine, lysine, methionine, phenylalanine, threonine, trytophane, and valine are required by man (Leverton *et al.*, 1956; Rose and Wixom, 1955).

Minerals.—The mineral constituents of grapes are the substances that the vine takes from the soil and moves into the plant and fruit. When the fruit is ashed, these substances remain in the ash, which amounts to 0.2 to 0.6 per cent of fresh fruit weight. Amerine *et al.* (1972) reported the range in amount of the various elements of the ash in fresh grape must. Their findings are shown in table 5. For further information on the role of the mineral constituents see chapter 17, on fertilizer elements.

Potassium, sodium, calcium, and iron—as carbonates or oxides—and phosphates, sulfates, and chlorides constitute almost all of the ash. In addition to the elements shown in table 5, traces of bromide, iodine, and fluoride are normally found in grapes. The level of all the mineral constituents may be influenced by soil conditions, that of some by the atmospheric environment, and that of others by the materials used in disease and insect control.

During maturation of grapes, the cation content (K, Ca, Mg, Na) increases 2 to 3 times in the skin, 1.2 to 1.9 times in the pulp, and 1.5 to 2.5 times in the peduncle (Peynaud and Ribéreau-Gayon, 1970). These authors also state that during the ripening period, heavy metals increase by about 50 per cent in grapes. The anions also increase, particularly phosphate, which is mostly concentrated in the seeds. Puissant (1960) reported that the potassium concentration, as mg per liter, changes very little during ripening. However, the calcium level decreased by about 50 per cent and magnesium by somewhat less during ripening. Potassium accounted for 50 to 70 per cent of the cations in the juice of grapes.

Iron is of little consequence in California grape production, since the problem of iron chlorosis is practically unknown in the state. It is of interest, however, as a factor in the clouding of wines induced by excess iron. Because of the role of iron in clouding, there has been much research to determine its source in grapes. Flanzy and Deibner (1956) found the dust on the harvested grapes to be an important source. The iron level in grapes is influenced directly by the iron content of the vineyard soil (Nègre and Cordonnier, 1953).

The lead content of California grapes is very low, since sprays containing lead are rarely used. In other areas and countries, however, where lead-containing sprays are employed, it is found in appreciable amounts in musts, wines, and other grape products. Another source of much of the lead in grape products is the lead containing equipment with which the must or wine comes in contact during processing (Greenblau and van der Westhuyzen, 1956). Larkin *et al.* (1954) reported less than 0.5 mg per liter in American grape jelly, and only 0.2 in a grape concentrate. It is not unusual, however, for the lead content of musts or juices to be higher. For example, of 55 lots of grape juice of the 1954 vintage imported into Germany, only one-third contained less than 1.6 mg of lead per liter; the others ranged up to 13.0 mg per liter (Koch and Breker, 1955). It is generally agreed that 1.6 mg per liter is much too high, but as yet no common maximum tolerance has been established. Figures from 1.6 down to 0.02 have been proposed as maximum tolerances by various researchers and governments.

Copper in trace amounts is a natural constituent of grapes. Small additional amounts may be present when sprays containing copper are used. Françot and Geoffroy (1956) found as much as 7 mg of copper per liter in the fresh must of grapes that had been sprayed four to five times with Bordeaux mixture.

Arsenical sprays are rarely used on grapes in California, except as a dormant spray for the control of black measles or esca; thus, arsenic is neither a health nor a residue problem in the vineyards of the state.

Rootstocks may influence the mineral composition of grapes (Bérnard *et al.*, 1963). Ough *et al.* (1968) found that fruit from scions grown on St. George rootstock generally had higher levels of potassium, phosphorus, nitrogen, and ammonia than when 99R was the rootstock. However, there is no conclusive evidence to indicate that differences in fruit composition are due directly to the rootstock itself, i.e. to the inherent capacity of the rootstock to take up plant nutrients, or whether rootstocks indirectly influence fruit composition through difference in leaf area—fruit weight ratio or perhaps total root growth.

BIBLIOGRAPHY

Akiyoshi, M., A. D. Webb, and R. E. Kepner. 1963. Major anthocyanin pigments of *Vitis vinifera* varieties Flame Tokay, Emperor, and Red Malaga. J. Food Sci., 28:177–181.

Albach, R. F., R. E. Kepner, and A. D. Webb. 1959. Comparison of anthocyan pigments of red *vinifera* grapes. II. Amer. J. Enol. Vitic., 10:164–172.

———, ———, ———. 1963. Peonidin-3-monoglucoside in *vinifera* grapes. J. Food Sci., 28:55–58.

———, ———, ———. 1965a. Structures of acylated athocyan pigments in *Vitis vinifera* variety Tinta Pinheira. Identification of anthocyanidin, sugar, and acid moieties. J. Food Sci., 30:69–76.

———, A. D. Webb, and R. E. Kepner. 1965b. Structures of acylated anthocyan pigments in *Vitis vinifera* variety Tinta Pinheira. II. Position of acylation. J. Food Sci., 30:620–626.

Alley, C. J., A. C. Goheen, H. P. Olmo, and A. T. Koyama. 1963. The effect of virus infections on vines, fruits, and wines of Ruby Cabernet. Amer. J. Enol. Vitic., 14:164–170.

Amerine, M. A. 1951. The acids of California grapes and wines. II. Malic acid. Food Tech., 5:13–16.

———. 1956. The maturation of wine grapes. Wines & Vines, 37(10):27–32, (11):53–55.

———, H. W. Berg, and W. V. Cruess. 1972. The technology of wine making. 3rd ed. Westport, Conn., Avi Publishing Co.

———, and G. A. Root, 1960. Carbohydrate content of various parts of the grape cluster, II. J. Amer. Soc. Enol. Vitic., 11:137–139.

———, and G. Thoukis. 1958. The glucose-frutose ratio of California grapes. Vitis, 1:224–229.

———, and A. J. Winkler. 1942. Maturity tests with California grapes. II. The titratable acidity, pH, and organic acid content. Proc. Amer. Soc. Hort. Sci., 40:313–324.

———, ———. 1958. Maturity studies of California grapes. III. The acid content of grapes, leaves, and stems. Proc. Amer. Soc. Hort. Sci., 71:199–206.

Arnold, W. N. 1965. β-fructofuranosidase from grape berries. Biochem. et Biophys. Acta, 110:134–147.

Artyunayan, A. S., L. M. Dzhanpoladyan, A. M. Samvelyan, and A. L. Khachatryan. 1964. The effect of fertilizers on the increase of the content of anthocyanins and aromatic compounds in grapes and wines. Tr. Armyansk. Nauchn. -Issled. Inst. Vinogradarstva Vinodeliya i Plodovodstva (6–7): 455–469; Chem. Abstr. 64:20575 (1966).

Astegiano, V., and M. T. Graziano. 1959. Sulla presenza di saccarosio nell'uva. Atti Acad. Ital. Della Vite. E. Del Vino, 10:614–620.

Baglioni, S. L., L. Casale, and C. Tarantola. 1937. L'attività proteolitia succo d'uva. R. Staz. Enol. Sper. di Asti, (II), 2:204–219.

Bayer, E., F. Born, and K. H. Reuther. 1957. Über die Polyphenoloxydase der Trauben. Z. Lebensm.-Untersuch. u-Forsch., 105:77–81.

Bayly, F. C., and H. W. Berg. 1967. Grape and wine proteins of white wine varietals. Amer. J. Enol. Vitic. 17:18–32.

Bell, T. A., M. Yarrbough, R. E. Clegg, and G. H. Scatterfield. 1942. Ascorbic acid content of seven varieties of muscadine grapes. Food Res., 7:144–147.

Bénard, P., C. Jouret, and M. Flanzy. 1963. Influence des porte-greffes sur la composition minérale des vins. Ann. Technol. Agr., 12:277–285.

Berg, V. A. 1940. Composition of grapes. [Trans. title.] Bioklaim. Kultur. Rastenii, 7:107–119. (*See also:* Chem. Abs., 35:25625.)

Besone, J. Pectin constituents in certain varieties of grapes. Unpublished data, Dept. of Vitic. and Enol., University of California, Davis.

Bioletti, F. T., W. V. Cruess, and H. Davi. 1918. Changes in the chemical composition of grapes during ripening. Univ. Calif. Pubs. Agr. Sci., 3:103–130.

Bobadillo, G. F. de, and E. Navarro. 1949. Vinos de Jerez. Estudios de sus ácidos desde el periódico de madurez de la uva hasta el envejecimiento del vino. Bol. Inst. Nacl. Invest. Agron. (Madrid), 9:473–486.

Bolcato, V., E. Pallavicini, and F. Lamparelli. 1965. Separazione con Sephadex degli enzimi dai mosti d'uva e dai vin. Rev. Viticolt. Enol., 18:42–48.

Bonner, J. 1950. Plant biochemistry. New York, Academic Press.

Bouard, J. 1966. Recherches physiologiques sur la vigne et en particulier sur l'aoûtement des sarments. Thèse Sciences Naturelles, Bordeaux.

Brémond, E. 1937. Contribution a l'étude analytique et physico-chemique de l'acidité des vins. Algiers, Imprimeries La Typo-Litho et Jules Carbonel Réunies.

Bukin, V. N., and N. N. Eropeeva. 1954. Comparative vitamin P content of tea catechins, tannin substances of grapes, and buckwheat rutin. [Trans. title.] Daklady Akad. Nauk. SSSR, 98(6):1011–1013. (*See* Abs. 28047, Zhur. Biol. 1956.)

Burger, M., L. W. Hein, L. J. Teply, P. H. Derse, and C. H. Drieger. 1956. Vitamin, mineral and approximate composition of frozen fruits, juices, and vegetables. J. Agr. and Food Chem., 4:418–425.

Buttrose, M. S., C. R. Hale, and W. M. Kliewer. 1971. Effect of temperature on the composition of Cabernet Sauvignon berries. Amer. J. Enol. Vitic., 22:71–75.

Caldwell, J. S. 1925. Some effects of seasonal conditions upon the chemical composition of American grape juices. J. Agr. Res., 30:1133–1176.

Casale, L. 1937. Esame critico, Tecnico e practico della varietà delle uve da vino coltivate in Piemonte, in Lombardia ed in Liguria. R. Staz. Enol. Sper. Asti, 2:67–104.

———, and E. Garina-Canina. 1937. Recerche sugli enzimi del vino e del mosto. R. Staz. Enol. Sper. Asti Ann., II, 2:239–250.

Cassignard, R. 1966. La polyphénol oxydase et la vinification des moûts de raisins blancs en Bordelais. Vignes et Vins, numéro spécial 1966:13–17, 24–25.

Castor, J. G. B. 1953a. The B complex vitamins of musts and wines as microbial growth factors. Appl. Microbiol., 1:97–102.

―――. 1953b. The free amino acids of musts and wines. I. Microbiological estimation of fourteen amino acids in California grape musts. Food Res., 18:139–145.

―――, and T. E. Archer. 1956. Amino acids in must and wine, proline, serine, and threonine. Amer. Jour. Enol., 7:19–25.

Chaudhary, S. S., R. E. Kepner, and A. D. Webb. 1964. Identification of some volatile compounds in an extract of the grape. Vitis vinifera var. Sauvignon blanc. Amer. J. Enol. Vitic., 15:190–198.

―――, A. D. Webb, and R. E. Kepner. 1968. GLC investigation of the volatile compounds in extracts of Sauvignon blanc wines from normal and botrytised grapes. Amer. J. Enol. Vitic., 19:6–12.

Chen, T. F., and B. S. Luh. 1967. Anthocyanins of Royalty grapes. J. Food Sci., 32:66–74.

Colagrande, O. 1959. Formazione and evoluzione degli acidi organici durante la maturazione dell'uva. Ann. Microbiol., 9:62–72.

―――. 1960. Recerche sulla composizione chimica e sulla naturazione delle uve nel piacentino. Revista Vitic. Enol., 13:331–342.

Coombe, B. G. 1960. Relation of growth and development to changes in sugars, auxins, and gibberellins in fruits of seeded and seedless varieties of Vitis vinifera. Plant Physiol., 35:241–250.

Cordonnier, R. 1956. Recherches sur l'aromatisation et la parfum des vins doux naturels et des vins de liqueur. Ann. Technol. Agr. 5:75–110.

Crane, J. C., and R. M. Brooks. 1952. Growth of apricot fruits as influenced by 2, 4, 5-trichlorophenoxyacetic acid applications. Proc. Amer. Soc. Hort. Sci., 59:218–224.

―――, E. D. Dekazos, and J. G. Brown. 1956. The effect of 2, 4, 5-trichlorophenoxyacetic acid on growth, moisture, and sugar content of apricot fruits. Proc. Amer. Soc. Hort. Sci., 68:105–112.

Crisci, P. 1930. Intorno alla pretesa proporzionalita fra il ph e il sapore acido delle subizioni acquose con speciale riguardo ai vini Ann. Chim. Appl., 20:566–583.

Daniel, E. P., and H. E. Munsell. 1932. The vitamin A, B, C, and G content of Concord grapes. Jour. Agr. Res., 45:445–448.

Di Castro, G. 1953. Vitamin and essential biological principal contents of cool stored fruits and vegetables. Atti sec. Cong. Nazl. Freddo, pp. 69–79. (See Chem. Abs., 49, 8522d.)

Drawert, F. 1961. Über Anthocyane in Trauben, Mosten, und Weinen. Vitis, 2:288–304.

―――, and A. Rapp. 1966. Über Inhaltsstoffe von Mosten und Weinen. VI. Gaschromatogrophische Untersuchung der Aromastoffe des Weines und ihre Biogenese. Vitis, 5:351–376.

―――, and H. Steffan. 1966. Biochemisch-physiologische Untersuchungen on Traubenbeeren. III. Stoffwechsel von zugeführten C^{14} Verbindungen und die Bedeutung des Säure-Zucker-Metabolismus fur die Reifung von Traubenbeeren. Vitis, 5:377–384.

Development and Composition of Grapes

Durmishidze, S. V. 1955. Tannin compounds and anthocyanins of grape vine and wines. [Trains. title.] Moscow, Izd. Akad. Nauk. SSSR.

———. 1969 Tannins and anthocyans in the grape vine and wine. Amer. J. Enol. Vitic., 10:20–28.

Ferenczi, S. 1966. Étude des protéines et des substances azotées. Teur évolution au cour des traitements oenologiques. Conditions de la stabilité protéique des vins. Bull. O. I. V. (Office Intern. Vigne Vin) 39:1311–1336.

Flanzy, M. 1959. Mise au point des characteristiques que doivent présenter des raisins, France. Bull. Off. Internatl. du Vin, 31:25–46.

———, and L. Deibner. 1956. Sur la variation des teneurs en fer dans les vins obtenus en présence ou en absence d'une terre ferrugineuse. Ann. Technol. Agr. (Paris), 5:69–73.

Flanzy, C., and C. Poux. 1965. Note sur la teneur en acides aminés du moût de raisin et du vin en fonction des conditions de l'année (maturation et fermentation). Ann. Technol. Agr., 14:87–91.

Follenberg, von., Th. 1914. Über des Ursprung der Methylalkohols in Trinkbranntweinen. Mitt. aus dem Geb. der Lebensmtl. Untersuch. u. Hyg., 5:172–178.

Françot, P., and P. Geoffroy. 1956. Repartition du cuivre dans les moûts et vins au cours du pressurage champenois. Le Vigneron Champenois, 7:45–49.

Garina-Canina, E. 1928. Le sostanze pectiche e la tecnica enologica. Ann. R. Accad. d'Agr. di Torino, 71:49–68.

———. 1946. La catalosi nell' uva e nel mosto. Ann. R. Accad. d'Agr. di Torino, 88:95–97.

Gatet, L. 1939. Recherches biochemiques sur la maturation des fruits. Ann. Physiol. Phys. Biol., 15:990–1020.

Geisler, G., and F. Radler, 1963. Entwuklungs- und Reifevorgänge on Trauben von Vitis. Ber. Deut. Botan. Ges., 76:112–119.

Genevois, L. 1938. Formation et évolution biologique des acids organiques dans les raisins. Rev. de Vitic., 88:102, 121, 382, 447.

———, A. Maurie, A. Peynaud, and J. Ribéreau-Gayon. 1954. Evolution des acids organiques chez la vigne. Inter. Cong. Bot., Paris; Rfat & Commun., 8(sec. 11 & 12):36–37.

———, and J. Ribéreau-Gayon. 1947. Le vin. Paris, Hermann et Cie.

Gerber, C. 1897. Recherches sur la maturation des fruits charnus. Annales Sci. Nat. Bot. 8, Série 4:1–6.

Girard, A., and B. Lindet. 1898. Recherches sur le développement progressif de la grappe de raisin. Bull. Min. Agri., 14:694–782.

Golodriga, P. Ya., and K. Pu-Chao. 1963. Rannespelost' vinograda i nekotorye biokimicheskie pokazateli. Tr. Vses. Nauchu. -Issled Inst. Vinodeliya i Vinogradarstva Magarach, 12:74–83.

———, and I. A. Suyatinov. 1966. Onekotorykh faktorakh vliyayuschchikh na nakoplenie krasyashchikh veschestv v yagodakh. Vinodelie i Vinogradarstov SSSR, 26(4):29–32.

Greenblau, N., and J. P van der Westhuyzen, 1956. An improved preliminary treatment for the routine estimation of lead in wines and related products. Jour. Sci. Food Agr., 7:186–189.

Development and Composition of Grapes

Guichard, C. 1954. Contribution à l'étude des glucides de la vigne et de certains fruits. Thése Science Naturelles, Bordeaux.

Haagen-Smit, A. J., F. N. Hirosawa, and T. H. Wong. 1949. Chemical studies on grapes and wines. I. Volatile constituents of Zinfandel grapes. Food Res., 14:472–480.

Hale, C. R. 1962. Investigations on translocation in the grapevine using carbon-14-labeled carbon dioxide. II. Studies on the origin and translocation of organic acids. Doctors Thesis, University of California, Davis.

———. 1968. Growth and senescence of the grape berry. Aust. J. Agri. Res., 19:939–945.

———, B. G. Coombe, and J. S. Hawker. 1970. Effects of ethylene and 2-chlorophosphonic acid on the ripening of grapes. Plant Physiol., 45:620–623.

Hall, A. P., L. Brinner, M. A. Amerine, and A. F. Morgan. 1956. The B vitamin content of grapes, musts, and wines. Food Res., 21:362–371.

Harborne, J. B. 1967. The comparative biochemistry of the flavonoids. New York, Academic Press.

Hardy, P. J. 1968. Metabolism of sugars and organic acids in immature grape berries. Plant Physiol., 43:224–228.

———. 1969. Selective diffusion of basic and acidic products of CO_2 fixation into the transpiration stream in grapevine. J. Expt. Bot., 20:856–862.

Harel E., and A. N. Mayer. 1971. Partial purification and properties of catechol oxidases in grapes. Phytochem., 10:17–22.

Harris. J. M., P. E. Kriedemann, and J. V. Possingham. 1968. Anatomical aspects of grape berry development. Vitis, 7:106–119.

Haslam, E. 1966. Chemistry of vegetable tannins. London, Academic Press.

———. 1967. Gallotannins. XIV. Structure of the gallotannin. Jour. Chem. Soc. (C), 1967:1734–1738.

Hawker, J. S. 1969a. Insoluble invertase from grapes: an artifact of extraction. Phytochem., 8:337–344.

———. 1969b. Changes in the activities of enzymes concerned with sugar metabolism during the development of grape berries. Phytochem., 8:9–17.

———. 1969c. Changes in the activities of malic enzyme, malate dehydrogenase, phosphopyruvate carboxylase and pyruvate decarboxylase during the development of a non-climacteric fruit (the grape). Phytochem., 8:19–23.

Heide, von der, C., and Schmitthenner. 1922. Der wein. F. Braunschweig, Vieweg und Sohn.

Hennig, K. 1943. Bilans de l'azote dans les moûts et les vins nouveaux en fermentation. Bull. Off. Internatl. du Vin, 16(159):82–86.

———. 1955. Der Einfluss der Eiweiss- und Stickstoffbestandteile auf den Wein. Deut. Wein-Ztg., 91:377–380, 394–397.

———, and R. Burkhardt. 1951. Die polargraphische Bestimmung Apfel-säure in Wein. Z. Lebensmtl. Untersuch. u. Forsch., 92:245–252.

———, ———. 1957. Über die Gerbstoffe und Polyphenole der Weine. Naturwissenshaften, 11:328–329.

———, ———. 1958. Die Nachweis phenolartiger Verbindungen und hydro-

aromatischer oxycarbonsäuren in Traubenbestandteilen Wein und Wein-
ähnlichen Getränken. Weinberg Keller, 5:542–552, 593–600.

————, and P. Venter. 1958. Der qualitative Nachweis der Ammosäuen im
frischen und gärenden Traubenmost. Naturwissenschaften, 46:130.

————, and F. Villforth. 1942. Die Aromastoffe der Weine; ein Beitrag zur
Untersuchung der Duft-ader Bukettstoffe der Weine. I. Isolierung der
Aromastoffe. II. Die Ester, Ihre Komponenten. Vorratspflege u. Leben-
smittlforsch, 5:181–199, 313–333.

Herrmann, K. 1963. Über die phenolischen Inhaltsstoffe der Trauben und des
Weines (Flavonoide, Phenolkarbonsäure, Farbstoffe, Gerbstoffe). Weinberg Keller, 10:154–164, 208–220.

Hussein, A. A., and W. V. Cruess. 1940. Properties of the oxidizing enzymes of
certain *vinifera* grapes. Food Res., 5:637–648.

Ibarra, H. P. T. 1941. Ascorbic acid in 26 samples of grape juice. Univ. Repub.
Urug., Res. Fac. Agron., No. 25, pp. 109–115. (*See also* Bio. Abs.,
17:15720.).

Ivanov, T. P. 1967. Sur l'oxydation du moût de raisin. I. Activité de la polyphenoloxydase du raisin des cepages "Muscat rouge", "Dimiat", "Riesling"
et "Aligote". II Étude comparee de anhydride sulfureux et de la bentonite
en tant qu'inactivateurs de la polyphenoloxydase du moût de raisin. Ann.
Technol. Agr., 16:35–39, 81–88.

Iwahori, S., R. J. Weaver, and R. M. Pool. 1968. Gibberellin-like activity in
berries of seeded and seedless Tokay grapes. Plant Physiol., 43:333–337.

Jensen, F. L. 1953. Coloring Emperor grapes. California Farmer, 199(3):109.

Kliewer, W. M. 1964. Influence of environment on metabolism of organic acids
and carbohydrates in *Vitis vinifera*. I. Temperature. Plant Physiol., 39:869–
880.

————. 1965a. Changes in the concentration of malates, tartrates, and total
free acids in flowers and berries of *Vitis vinifera*. Amer. J. Enol. Vitic.,
16:92–100.

————. 1965b. Changes in concentration of glucose, fructose, and total soluble
solids in flowers and berries of *Vitis vinifera*. Amer. J. Enol. Vitic., 16:101–
110.

————. 1956c. The sugars of grapevines. II. Identification and seasonal changes
in the concentration of several trace sugars in *Vitis vinifera*. Amer. J. Enol.
Vitic., 16:168–178.

————. 1966. Sugars and organic acids of *Vitis vinifera*. Plant Physiol., 41:923–
931.

————. 1967. The glucose-fructose ratio of *Vitis vinifera* grapes. Amer. J. Enol.
Vitic., 18:33–41.

————. 1968a. Changes in the concentration of free amino acids in grape berries during maturation. Amer. J. Enol. Vitic., 19:166–174.

————. 1968b. Effect of temperature on the composition of grapes grown under
field and controlled conditions. Proc. Amer. Soc. Hort. Sci., 93:797–806.

————. 1969. Free amino acides and other nitrogenous substances of table
grape varieties. J. Food Sci., 34:274–278.

————. 1970a. Free amino acids and other nitrogenous fractions in wine
grapes. J. Food Sci., 35:17–21.

————. 1970b. Effect of time and severity of defoliation on growth and composition of Thompson Seedless grapes. Amer. J. Enol. Vitic. 21:37–47.

————. 1970c. Effect of day temperature and light intensity of coloration of *Vitis vinifera* L. grapes. J. Amer. Soc. Hort. Sci., 95:693–697.

————. 1971. Effect of day temperature and light intensity on concentration of malic and tartaric acids in *Vitis vinifera* L. grapes. J. Amer. Soc. Hort. Sci., 96:372–377.

————. 1973. Berry composition of *Vitis vinifera* cultivars as influenced by photo- and nycto-temperatures during maturation. J. Amer. Soc. Hort. Sci., 98:153–159.

————, and A. J. Antcliff. 1970. Influence of defoliation, leaf darkening, and cluster shading on the growth and composition of Sultana grapes. Amer. J. Enol. Vitic., 21:26–36.

————, L. Howarth, and M. Omori. 1967a. Concentration of tartaric acid and malic acid and their salts in *Vitis vinifera* grapes. Amer J. Enol. Vitic., 18:42–54.

————, and L. A. Lider. 1968. Influence of cluster exposure to the sun on the composition of Thompson Seedless fruit. Amer. J. Enol. Vitic., 19:175–184.

————, ————. 1970. Effects of day temperature and light intensity on growth and composition of *Vitis vinifera* L. fruits. J. Amer. Soc. Hort. Sci., 95:766–769.

————, ————, and H. B. Schultz. 1967b. Influence of artificial shading of vineyards on the concentration of sugar and organic acid in grapes. Amer. J. Enol. Vitic., 18:78–86.

————, and A. R. Nassar. 1966. Changes in concentration of organic acids, sugars, and amino acids in grape leaves. Amer. J. Enol. Vitic., 17:48–57.

————, and C. S. Ough. 1970. The effect of leaf area and crop level on the concentration of amino acids and total nitrogen in 'Thompson Seedless' grapes. Vitis, 9:196–206.

————and H. B. Schultz. 1964. Influence of environment on metabolism of organic acids and carbohydrates in *Vitis vinifera*. II. Light. Amer. J. Enol. Vitic., 15:119–129.

————, and R. E. Torres. 1972. Effect of controlled day and night temperatures on grape coloration. Amer. J. Enol. Vitic., 23:71–77.

————, and R. J. Weaver. 1971. Effect of crop level and leaf area on growth, composition, and coloration of 'Tokay' grapes. Amer. J. Enol. Vitic., 22:172–177.

Koblet, W. 1967. The importance of leaf area for the development of colour and flavor in grapes. Schweiz. Z. Obst- u. Weinb., 103:771–773.

————. 1969. Wanderung von Assimilaten in Rebtrieben und Einfluss der Blattfläde auf Ertrag und Qualität der Trauben. Wein-Wiss., 24:277–319.

Koch, J. 1963. Protéines des vins blancs. Traitements des précipitations protéiques par chauffage et à l'aide de la bentonite. Ann Technol. Agr., 12(numéro hors série I):297–311.

————, and E. Breker. 1955. Über die Bestimmung von Schwermetallen in Traubensaften (Traubensüsmost). Ind. Obst. u. Gemüseverwert., 40:252–256.

————, H. Fretter, and E. Sajak. 1959. Über das Auftreten der "löslichen" Proteine im Saft der Früchte. Z. Lebensmtl. Untersuch. u. Forsch., 109: 395–399.

Kriedemann, P. E., W. M. Kliewer, and I. N. Harris. 1970. Leaf age and photosynthesis in Vitis vinifera. Vitis, 9:97–104.

Kursanov, A. L. 1962. Metabolism and transport of organic substances in the phloem. Advances in Bot. Research, 1:209–278.

Lafon-Lafourcade, S., and G. Guimberteau. 1962. Évolution des amino-acides au cours de la maturation des raisins. Vitis, 3:130–135.

————, and E. Peynaud. 1959. Dosage microbiologique des acids aminés des moûts de raisins et des vins. Vitis, 2:45–56.

Larkin, O., M. Page, J. C. Bartlet, and R. A. Chapman. 1954. The lead, zinc, and copper content of foods. Food Res., 19:211–218.

La Rosa, W. V. 1955. Maturity of grapes as related to pH at harvest. Amer. Jour. Enol., 6:42–46.

Lavollay, J., and J. Sevestre. 1944. Le vin, considéré comme une alimente riche en vitamin P. Compt. Rend. Acad. d'Agr. de France, 30:259–261.

Leopold, A. C. 1958. Auxin uses in the control of flowering and fruiting. Ann. Rev. Plant Physiol., 9:281–310.

LeRoux, M. S. 1953. Color experiment with table grapes. So. Africa Fr., 28: 375–376.

Leverton, R. M., J. Ellison, N. Johnson, J. Pazur, F. Schmidt, and D. Geschwenden. 1956. The quantitative amino acid requirement of young women. I. Threonine, 59–81; II. Valine, 83–93; III. Tryptophane, 341–353; and Leucine, 355–365. Jour. Nutrition, Vol. 58.

Loewus, F. A. 1963. Tracer studies on ascorbic acid formation in plants. Phytochem., 2:109–128.

Loomis, N. H., and J. M. Lutz. 1937. The relationship of leaf area and leaf area fruit ratios to composition and flavor of Concord grapes. Proc. Amer. Soc Hort. Sci., 35:461–465.

Loomis, W. E. 1945. Translocation of carbohydrates in maize. Science, 101: 398–400.

Lott, R. V., and H. C. Barrett. 1967. The dextrose, levulose, sucrose, and acid content of the juice from 39 grape clones. Vitis, 6:257–268.

Marsh, G. L., and G. A. Pitman. 1930. Pectin content of grapes. Fruit Prod. Jour., 9:187–188.

Marteau, G. 1956. Evolution de la teneur en glucides solubles dans divers organes de le vignes au cours de la maturation des raisins. Compt. Rend. Acad. d'Agr. de France, 41:193–198.

May, P., N. J. Shaulis, and A. J. Antcliff. 1969. The effect of controlled defoliation in the Sultana vine. Amer. J. Enol. Vitic., 20:237–250.

Maynhardt, J. T. 1963. Assimilation of ^{14}C-labelled carbon dioxide by Barlinka grape berries. Proc. National Conference on Nuclear Energy, South Africa, 456–463.

————. 1965. Biosynthesis of dicarboxylic acids through carbon dioxide fixation by an enzyme extract from Barlinka grape berries. S. Afr. J. Agri. Sci., 8:381–392.

Morand, P., and J. Silvestre. 1960. Contribution a l'étude d'une huile vegetale a base d'acides gras polyinsature: L'huile de pepen de raisin, caracteres analytiques qualitics alimentaires et dietetiques. Ann. Falsification, Paris, 53:193–203.

Moreau, L., and E. Vinet. 1932. Contribution a l'étude du phénomène de veraison (au Gamay). Compt. Rend. Acad. d'Agr. de France, 18:198–202.

Morgan, A. F., L. Kinnel, A. Field, and P. F. Nichols. 1935. Vitamin content of Sultanina (Thompson Seedless) grapes and raisins. Jour. Nutrition, 9: 369–382.

Muller, C. J., R. E. Kepner, and A. D. Webb. 1971. Identification of 3-(methylthio)-propanol as an aroma constituent in 'Cabernet Sauvignon' and 'Ruby Cabernet' wines. Amer. J. Enol. Vitic. 22:156–160.

——, ——, ——. 1972. Identification of 4-ethoxy-4-hydroxybutyric acid α lactone [5-ethoxydihydro-2 (3H)-furanone] as an aroma component of wine from *Vitis vinifera* var. Ruby Cabernet. Agric. Food Chem., 20:193–195.

Müller-Thurgau, H. 1898. Abhäñgigkeit der Ausbildung der Traubenbeeren und einiger anderer Früchte von der Entwicklung der Samen. Landow. Jahrb. Schweiz, 12:135–205.

Muradov, A. G. 1966. Vitaminnyĭ sostav vinogradnogo soka Azerbaĭdzhara. Konserv. Ovoshchesushil. Prom., 21:28–29.

Naito, R. 1964. Studies on coloration of grapes. V. Influence of light intensity on the coloration and pigmentation in some black and red grapes. J. Japan. Soc. Hort. Sci., 33:213–220.

——. 1966. Studies on the coloration of grapes. VII. Behavior of anthocyanins in the skin of some black and red grapes as affected by light intensity. J. Japan. Soc. Hort. Sci., 35:225–232.

——, S. Kyo, and T. Sumi. 1965. Studies on the coloration of grapes. VI. Effects of shading on the color and pigmentation of Muscat Bailey A. J. Japan. Soc. Hort. Sci., 34:145–151.

Nassar, A. R., and W. M. Kliewer. 1966. Free amino acids in various parts of *Vitis vinifera* at different stages of development. Proc. Amer. Soc. Hort. Sci., 89:281–294.

Négre, E., and R. Cordonnier. 1953. Les origines du fer des vins. Prog. Agr. et Vit., 139:160–164.

Nitsch, J. P. 1953. The physiology of fruit growth. Ann. Rev. Plant Physiol., 4:199–236.

——, C. Pratt, C. Nitsch, and N. Shaulis. 1960. Natural growth substances in Concord and Concord Seedless grapes in relation to berry development. Amer. Jour. Bot., 47:566–576.

Novak, J. 1958. The influence of reducing the leaf surface of vines on the amount and quality of the crop. [Trans. title.] Arkiv. Za. poljop. Nauk., 9:82–92. (*See also* Wein-Wissenschaft., 14:117–129.)

Onokhova, N. P. 1937. Grapes as a source of vitamin C. [Trans. title.] Bull. Appl. Bot. Genet. Pl. Breeding USSR. Suppl. 84 (II):195–200. (*See also* Chem. Abs., 33:1367[6].)

Ough, C. S. 1968. Proline content of grapes and wines. Vitis, 7:321–331.

————, and R. E. Kunkee. 1968. Fermentation rates of grape juice. V. Biotin content of juice and its effect on alcoholic fermentation rate. Appl. Microbiol., 16:572–576.

————, L. A. Lider, and J. A. Cook. 1968. Rootstock-scion interactions concerning wine making. I. Juice composition changes and effects on fermentation rate with St. George and 99-R rootstocks at two nitrogen fertilizer levels. Amer. J. Enol. Vitic., 19:213–227.

Ournac, A. 1965. Étude du dosage de l'acide ascorbique dans les vins et dans les jus fortement colorés. Ann. Technol. Agr., 14:341–347.

————, and M. Flanzy. 1957. Localisation et évolution de la vitamine B_1 dans le raisin, au cours de la maturation. Ann. Technol. Agr., 6:257–292.

————, and C. Poux. 1966. Acide ascorbique dans le raisin au cours de son développement. Ann. Technol. Agr., 15:193–202.

Pallavicini, C. 1967. Distribuzione degli enzimi fenolasi, fosfatasi, proteinasi e saccorasi nelle parti constituente gli acini di 4 uve e nei vini proveninti dalle une stesse. Ind. Agr., 5:603–606.

Pantanelli, E. 1910. Ein proteolytisches Enzym in Most überreifer Trauben. Zentbl. f Bakt. Abt. II, 31:545–559.

Perlman, L., and A. F. Morgan. 1945. Stability of B vitamins in grape juice and wines. Food Res., 10:334–341.

Peynaud, E. 1939. Sur les variations de l'azote du raisin au cours de la maturation. Rev. de Vitic., 90:189–195, 213–225.

————. 1947. Contribution a l'étude biochemique de la maturation cu raisin et de la composition des vins. Lille, Imp. G. Santi et Fils.

————, and S. Lafourcade. 1955. Inositol in grapes and wines. Ann. Inst. Natl. Res. Agron., Ser. E, 4:381–396.

————, ————. 1956. Sur la teneur en biotine des raisins et de vins. Compt. Rend. Acd. Sci., 243:1800–1802.

————, ————. 1957. Sur les teneurs en thiamine des vins et des jus de raisin. Inds. Aliment. et Agr. (Paris), 74:892–904.

————, ————. 1958. Évolution des vitamines B dans le raisin. Qual. Plant. Mater. Végétabiles, 34:405–414.

————, and A. Maurié. 1953. Evolution des acides organiques dans le grain de raisin au cours de la maturation en 1951. Ann Technol. Agr., 2:83–94.

————, ————. 1958. Synthesis of tartaric and malic acids by grape vines. Amer. Jour. Enol., 9:32–36.

————, and P. Ribéreau-Gayon. 1970. The grape. In "The biochemistry of fruits and their products." Vol. 2. A. C. Hulme, ed. London, Academic Press.

Pool, R. M., and R. J. Weaver. 1970. Internal browning of Thompson Seedless grapes. J. Amer Soc. Hort. Sci., 95:631–634.

Power, F. B., and V. K. Chestnut. 1921. The occurrence of methyl anthranilate in grape juice. Amer. Chem. Soc. Jour., 43:1741–1742.

Prillinger, F., A. Madner, and J. Kovacs. 1968. Die flüchtigen Inhalsstoffe des Aepfel- und Traubensaftes. Mitt. Rebe u. Wein, Obstbau u. Früchteverwertung. (Klosterneuburg), 18:98–105.

Puissant, A. 1960. Étude sur la variotion de la teneur en NH_4, K, Ca, Mg de quelques raisins au cours de la maturation. Ann. Technol. Agr., 9:321–330.

———, and H. Léon. 1967. La matière colorante des grains de raisins de certains cépages cultives en anjou en 1965. Ann. Technol. Agr. Paris, 16:217–225.

Radler, F. 1957. Untersuchungen über den Gehalt der Moste einiger Rebensorten und -arten an den Vitamin Pyrodoxin, Pantothensäure, Nicotinsäure, und Biotin. Vitis, 1:96–108.

———. 1965a. The main constituents of the surface waxes of varieties and species of the genus *Vitis*. Amer. J. Enol. Vitic., 16:159–167.

———. 1965b. The surface waxes of the Sultana vine (*Vitis vinifera* cv. Thompson Seedless). Aust. J. Biol. Sci., 18:1045–1056.

Rankine, B. C. 1964. Heat extraction of colour from red grapes for wine. Australian Wine, Brew. Spirit Rev., 82(6):41–42.

———, R. E. Kepner, and A. D. Webb. 1958. Comparison of anthocyan pigment of *vinifera* grapes. Amer. Jour. Enol., 9:105–110.

Ribéreau-Gayon, G. 1966. Étude du métabolisme des glucides, des acides organizues et des acides aminés chez *Vitis vinifera* L. Thèse Sciences Physiques, Paris.

———. 1968. Étude des mechanismes de synthese et de transformation de l'acide malique, de l'acide tartrique et de l'acide citrique chez *Vitis vinifera* L. Phytochem., 7:471–1482.

Ribéreau-Gayon, J., and E. Peynaud. 1960–61. "Traite d'oenologie", 2 vol., p. 753, 1065. Paris, Librairie Polytech. Beranger.

———, ———. 1971. Traité d'ampelologie sciences et techniques de la vigne. Tome 1. Biologie de la vigne sols de vignobles. Paris, Durod.

Ribéreau-Gayon, P. 1958. Les anthocyannes des raisins. Qual. Plant et Mat. Veg., 3/4:491–499.

———. 1959. Recherches sur les anthocyannes des vegetaux application au genre *Vitis*. Rev. Gen. de Bot., 66:531–559.

———. 1963. Les anthocyannes des fruits. Méthodes d'identification et applications. Meses Point Chim. Anal., Org., Pharm., Bromatol., 11:189–220.

———. 1964. Les composés phenoliques du raisin et du vin. Ann. Physiol. Végétale, 6:119–147; 211–242; 259–282.

———, P. Sudraud, and P. M. Durquety. 1955. Relations entre génétique et nature chimque des pigments anthocyaniques de la baie dans le genre *Vitis*. Rev. Gen. Botan., 62:667–674.

Robinson, W. B., N. Shaulis, and C. S. Pederson. 1949. Ripening studies of grapes grown in 1948 for juice manufacture. Fruit Prod. Jour., 29(2): 36–37, 54, 62.

Rose, W. C., and R. L. Wixom. 1955. The amino acid requirement of man. XVI. The role of nitrogen intake. Jour. Biol. Chem., 217:997–1004. (*See also* Parts I–XV, in the same journal.)

Saito, K., and Z. Kasai. 1968. Accumulation of tartaric acid in the ripening process of grapes. Plant & Cell Physiol., 9:529–537.

———, ———. 1969. Tartaric acid synthesis from L-ascorbic acid-1-^{14}C in grape berries. Phytochem., 8:2177–2182.

Scarborough, H. 1945. The nature of vitamin P and the vitamin P potency of certain foodstuffs. Jour. Biochem., 39:271–278.

Semichon, L., and M. Flanzy. 1926. Sur les pectines des raisins et le moelleux des vins. Acad. des Sci. Compt. Rend. Hebd., 183(6):394–396.

Shaulis, N., H. Amberg, and D. Crowe, 1966. Response of Concord grapes to light exposure, and Geneva double curtain training. Proc. Amer. Soc. Hort. Sci., 89:268–280.

———, and P. May. 1971. Response of 'Sultana' vines to training on a divided canopy to shoot crowding. Amer. J. Enol. Vitic., 22:215–222.

———, and W. Robinson. 1953. The effect of season, pruning severity, and trellising on some chemical characteristics of Concord and Fredonia grape juice. Proc. Amer. Soc. Hort. Sci., 62:214–220.

Singh, R. K. N., and R. W. Campbell. 1964. Some aspects of 4-thianaphthene-acetic acid ripening of Concord grapes. Proc. Amer. Soc. Hort. Sci., 84: 257–262.

Singleton, V. L. 1966. The total phenolic content of grape berries during the maturation of several varieties. Amer. J. Enol. Vitic., 17:126–134.

———, and P. Esau. 1969. Phenolic substances in grapes and wine and their significance. Advances in Food Research, Supplement 1. New York, Academic Press.

Smith, R. M., and B. S. Luh. 1965. Anthocyanin pigments in the hybrid grape variety Rubired. J. Food Sci., 30:995–1005.

Solms, J., W. Buchi, and H. Deuel. 1952. Untersuchungen über den Pektinge-halt einiger Traubenmoste. aus dem Geb. der Lebensmittl. Untersuch. u. Mitt. Hyg., 43:303–307.

Stafford, H. 1959. Distribution of tartaric acid in the leaves of certain angio-sperms. Amer. Jour. Bot., 46:347–352.

———, and F. A. Loewus. 1958. Fixation of $C^{14}O_2$ into tartaric and malic acids of excised grape leaves. Plant Physiol., 33:194–199.

Stevens, K. L., J. L. Bomben, A. Lee, and W. H. McFadden. 1966. Volatiles from grapes. Muscat of Alexandria. J. Agr. Food Chem., 14:249–252.

Swanson, C. A., and E. D. H. El-Shishiny. 1958. Translocation of sugars in the Concord grape. Plant Physiol., 33:33–37.

Terčelj, D. 1965. Etudes des composés azotés du vin. Ann. Technol. Agr., 14: 307–319.

Torres, R. E. 1971. Effect of temperature and light on coloration of *Vitis vinifera* L. grapes. M.S. thesis, Univ. of California, Davis.

Tukey, H. B. 1936. Development of cherry and peach fruits as affected by destruction of the embryo. Bot. Gaz., 98:1–24.

Usseglio-Tomasset, L., V. Astegiano, and M. Matta. 1966. Il linalool composto responsabile dell'aroma delle uve a dei vini aromatico. Ind. Agr., 4:583–584.

Van Wyk, C. J., A. D. Webb, and R. E. Kepner. 1967. Some volatile com-ponents of *Vitis vinifera* variety White Riesling. 1, 2, 3. J. Food Sci., 32:660–664, 664–668, 669–674.

Ventre, J. 1930. Traite de vinification practique et rationelle. I. Le raisin; les vinifications. Montpellier, Libraire Coulet.

Wali, Y. A. and Y. M. Hassan. 1965. Qualitative chromatographic survey of the sugars prevailing in some horticultural crops. Proc. Amer. Soc. Hort. Sci., 87:264–269.

Watt, B. K., and A. L. Merrill. 1950. Composition of food—raw, processed, and prepared. U.S. Dept. Agr., Agriculture Handbook, 8:1–147.

Weaver, R. J. 1955. Use of benzothiazole-2-oxyacetic acid to delay maturity of grapes. Bot. Gaz., 116:266–273.

———, M. A. Amerine, and A. J. Winkler. 1957. Preliminary report on effect of level of crop on development of color in certain red wine grapes. Amer. J. Enol. Vitic., 4:157–166.

———, and S. B. McCune. 1960. Influence of light on color development in *Vitis vinifera* grapes. Amer. J. Enol. Vitic., 11:179–184.

———, and R. M. Pool. 1971, Effect of (2-chloroethyl) phosphonic acid (ethephon) on maturation of *Vitis vinifera* L. J. Amer. Soc. Hort. Sci., 96: 725–727.

Webb, A. D. 1967. Wine flavor: Volatile aroma compounds of wines. In, "Symposium on foods: Chemistry and physiology of flavors" (H. W. Schultz, E. A. Day, and L. M. Libbey, eds.), Westport, Conn., Avi Publishing Co.

———. 1970. Anthocyan pigments in grapes and wines. Suomen Kemistilehti, A43:67–74.

———, and R. E. Kepner. 1956. Volatile aroma constituents of *Vitis rotundifolia* grapes. Amer. Jour. Enol., 7:8–18.

———, ———. 1957. Some volatile aroma constituents of *Vitis vinifera* var. Muscat of Alexandria. Food Res., 22:384–395.

———, ———, and L. Maggiora. 1966. Gas chromatographic comparison of volatile aroma materials extracted from eight different muscat-flavored varieties of *Vitis vinifera*. Amer. J. Enol. Vitic., 17:247–254.

———, and C. J. Muller. 1972. Volatile aroma components of wines and other fermented beverages. Advances in Applied Microbiology, Vol. 15: 75–146.

Webster, J. E., and F. B. Cross. 1942. The uneven ripening of Concord grapes: chemical and physiological studies. Oklahoma Agr. Expt. Sta. Tech. Bull. T-13:5–48.

Willaman, J., and Z. I. Kertez. 1931. Enzymatic clarification of grape juice. New York (Geneva) Agr. Exp. Sta. Tech. Bull., 178:1–15.

Williams, W. O. 1946. California vineyard fertilizer experimentation. Proc. Amer. Soc. Hort. Sci., 48:269–278.

Willstätter, R., and E. H. Zollinger. 1915. Anthocyans. IV. Liebig's Ann. d. Chem., 408:83–109.

———, ———. 1916. Anthocyans. XVI. Liebig's Ann. d. Chem., 415:195–216.

Winkler, A. J. 1930. Relation of number of leaves to size and quality of table grapes. Proc. Amer. Soc. Hort. Sci., 27:158–160.

———. 1932. Maturity test for table grapes. Calif. Agr. Exp. Sta. Bull., 529: 1–35.

———. 1954. Effects of overcropping. Amer. Jour. Enol., 5:4–12.

————, and W. O. Williams. 1936. Effect of seed development on the growth of grapes. Proc. Amer. Soc. Hort. Sci., 33:430–434.

————, ————. 1939. The heat requirement to bring Tokay grapes to maturity. Proc. Amer. Soc. Hort. Sci., 37:51–54.

Zimmerman, W., L. Malsch, and R. Weber. 1940. Die Veränderung des Vitamin-C-gehaltes von Süssmosten. Vorratspflege u. Lebensmtlforsch., 3(1/2):1–7.

9

Propagation

Grapevines may be propagated from seeds, cuttings, layers, or grafts. Normally, new vines grown from seeds differ markedly from the parent vine and from each other. Since most seedlings are inferior to the parent vines in vigor, productivity, and quality of fruit, seed propagation of vines is impractical for vineyards. The seeds are useful, however, in producing new varieties. Propagation by cuttings, layers, buds, or grafts, in contrast, produces vines identical with the parents in all varietal characteristics.

Cuttings or rootings of the desired fruiting variety, bench grafts, and resistant stock rootings may be used to plant a vineyard—though not always interchangeably. The choice is governed by several factors: presence or absence of phylloxera; presence or absence of nematodes; location of the vineyard and climatic conditions; skill of the grower or labor available for field budding or grafting; and availability (Jacob, 1944).

CUTTINGS

Nearly all grape varieties, whether for fruiting or rootstocks, are propagated by cuttings. These are usually grown in a nursery for one year to produce rootings. The cuttings may be grafted before being planted in the nursery, to produce bench grafts. Occasionally, unrooted cuttings are planted directly in the vineyard. A few varieties whose cuttings are difficult to root are propagated by layering.

A cutting is a piece of a parent plant (stem, root, or leaf) that will develop into a new plant when placed under conditions favorable for growth. For grape cuttings, segments of dormant canes are almost always used. The vine can also be easily propagated from green or softwood cuttings using specialized greenhouse techniques; and where sources of wood are scarce, this practice has found limited commercial usefulness (see p. 202).

Selecting the parent vines.—Dormant cuttings should always be taken from healthy, vigorous vines having well-matured canes. Vineyards of mixed varieties are best avoided unless the vines of the desired variety are carefully marked during the summer, when they can be clearly identified. The best cuttings come from mature vines that have made a good growth, have borne a good crop, are free of disease, and have not been pinched or topped or severely injured in other ways. Cuttings are poor from vines that have suffered from drought or disease, or that have been defoliated by insects or frost before the wood is mature. Wood from one- or two-year-old vines is often immature, and wood from vines that have borne excessive crops may be in a poorly nourished condition.

So long as the vines from which cuttings are made are of the desired variety and true to name, little can be gained by mass selection of parent vines on the basis of past performance. Most variations in size of crop, size of berry, shade and intensity of color, and time of maturing are caused by differences in climate, soil, and cultural practices; thus, the new vines will vary in the same ways, according to the conditions under which they are grown. In an investigation at the California Agricultural Experiment Station conducted by Bioletti (1926), production records were kept for five consecutive years for individual vines in a Muscat vineyard. Then one lot of cuttings was made from the heaviest-yielding vines in the vineyard and another lot from the lowest-yielding vines. A new vineyard established with the vines produced from these two lots of cuttings failed to show any correlation between the productivity of the parent and the progeny vines.

Sports (bud mutations) do occur, however, in vines, as in all other plants, and have been the source of some important variations. Most such mutants are poorer than the originals; very few are better. By recognizing and propagating the latter, new and superior clones may result (Rives 1961 and Sartorius, 1928). The promising clones, when found, should be preserved for thorough testing. Occasionally these finds make for marked improvement in productivity and quality. They afford the observant individual an opportunity to help himself and the breeder by fostering the improvement of varieties.

Some mutants that are poor yielders are vigorous growers. Since there is a natural tendency to choose the vigorous vines, in making cuttings one must be alert to avoid the vigorous vines that are poor producers. Otherwise, the new vineyard may have more undesirable vines than the old one. Mixed varieties may sometimes occur in a vineyard; the undesirable ones, too, must be aovided. To avoid poor producers, undesirable mutants, and mixed vines, it is always good practice to go over the vineyard carefully while the crop is on the vines, marking those that should not be used for cuttings. Further, it is highly important that vines with virus disease be avoided (see p. 484).

Time to make cuttings.—For general propagation, grape cuttings are always made from vines that are dormant. It is usually considered good practice to make the cuttings during late fall or early winter. If for any reason the cuttings must be made from weak vines or poorly ripened wood, cuttings will be better if not made until most of the severe winter weather is past; the weak canes will have been killed during the winter and thus eliminated. The grower will do well to leave the cuttings on the vines until they are to be planted. Whenever the cuttings are made, precaution must be taken to prevent drying.

Selecting wood for cuttings.—Well-nourished, well-matured current-season wood (canes) from any part of the vine is suitable for cuttings. There seems to be no reason to avoid water sprouts and other canes that bore no crop, or even laterals of good quality from primary canes. The most desirable canes for cuttings are of medium size, with internodes of moderate length (fig. 36). Very short internodes usually indicate disease or poor growing conditions. Very long internodes indicate very rapid growth; such canes are usually soft and poorly nourished, hence *low in stored reserves* * (starches and sugars). The outer bark should be of clear color—light brown or purplish brown according to the variety—and without dark blotches, dead streaks, or immature areas. When the cane is cut, the inner bark should appear green and full of sap; the wood firm, well stored with reserves, and free from dark specks; the pith of moderate size, clear, and light-colored. Canes that are unusually flat or angular in cross section should be avoided.

With *vinifera* varieties, cuttings are most commonly one third to one half of an inch in diameter. Those less than one quarter of an inch at the small end should, usually, be avoided. Those larger than three quarters of an inch are often looked upon with disfavor, yet the only valid objection to them would seem to be their bulkiness. When only well-matured, normally developed canes are used for cuttings, the wood is seldom too thick. American and rootstock varieties usually have thinner canes, and wood of average and smaller size is acceptable.

Making cuttings.—The length of cuttings used for nursery plantings

---

* When ordinary tincture of iodine, diluted with an equal volume of water, is applied to the freshly cut surface of a cutting well supplied with starch, a deep bluish-black staining should appear throughout the wood of the cut surface, and a very dark staining in the vascular rays. In cold weather much of the starch is converted to sugars and the iodine test is then less reliable; as the weather becomes warmer the sugars are reconverted to starch.

Propagation

varies from 12 to 18 inches. The most common length is 12 to 16 inches from the base to the top bud for fruiting varieties, and 16 to 18 inches for rootstocks to be budded in the vineyard. The cutting should be long enough that, when the rooting is planted in the vineyard, the main roots at the base of the original cutting are below plow depth. Unless wood of the particular variety is very scarce, therefore, the cuttings should seldom be less than 12 inches long. For direct planting in the vineyard, a practice which requires considerable extra care in the field to obtain a good stand, the cuttings should be longer than for nursery planting. In very open, porous soils the cuttings should be longer than average; and in tight, heavy soils, they should be shorter.

The cut at the base (lower end) of the cutting should be made nearly straight across, close below a node; the top is cut at an angle of about 45°, 1 to 1.5 inches above a node, to avoid injuring the top bud and to help orient the cuttings in handling and planting. Grape cuttings planted upside down will not grow.

Bundling and storing.—To facilitate handling, the cuttings are put in bundles of 100 or 200 each, with the basal ends even, and are tied with two wires, one near the top and one near the bottom. Each bundle should carry a durable label tied to a cutting where it is not likely to be torn off by accident. The label should show the name of the variety, the number of cuttings, the place obtained, and any other information needed for identification. Wooden tree labels, painted white on one side and attached with copper wire, will serve well. The label can be wired to a cutting on the outside of the bundle in such a position that it will stay under the top tie-wire of the bundle.

If the cuttings are to be held for a long period before planting, they should be stored in a cool place, neither too wet nor too dry. Under no circumstances should they be held in open air (Stachelin, 1954). Burying in

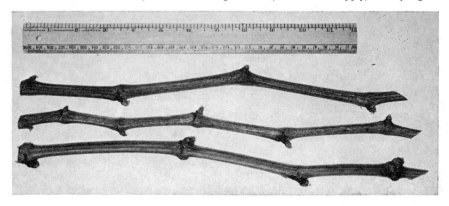

FIGURE 36: Grape cuttings of normal length and desirable character.

Propagation

moist sand or sawdust in cold storage (40° to 45° F.) is ideal. If cold storage is unavailable, the cuttings may be buried in a pile of moist sand in a cellar or shed, or in a pile of sand out in the open. In the latter case, the pile should be covered with boards, straw, or other material, to prevent the sand from drying out or becoming too warm. This last precaution is particularly necessary if the planting must be delayed until late spring; otherwise, the buds may start growth, which greatly increases the care and cost of planting and may considerably reduce the stand.

If the cuttings are to be held for only a few weeks, they may be buried 3 to 4 inches deep in the soil in any well-drained location (Alley and Christensen, 1970). It may be necessary to sprinkle them during warm periods if the soil is very sandy (see table 17).

In a well-drained soil, particularly in the warm regions of California, the best time to plant is at the time the cuttings are made or as soon thereafter as possible. In the hot, dry regions the best possible place to hold cuttings through the winter is the nursery row, in well-drained soil. Much experimental work has been done on the stimulation of cuttings by chemical agents (see p. 221), callusing, and heat before planting; in nearly every instance, however, planting the cuttings in the nursery immediately after making them gives results equal or superior to the best obtained by artificial stimulation. For varieties that are rooted with considerable difficulty, such as the Champini varieties and Berlandieri hybrids, which are used as grafting stocks, the cuttings must not be allowed to become dry. Planting them immediately in a wet furrow has given the best results.

Planting the vineyard with cuttings.—The use of cuttings to plant a vineyard is not to be encouraged, because the resulting stands are often poor; yet, experienced growers using extra care during the first season can be quite successful. The practice does sometimes have advantages: if handled properly to avoid contamination, the cuttings are free of phylloxera and nematodes; they are slightly less susceptible to injury from drying in handling; they are cheaper in first cost, and they may be available when rootings of the desired variety are not. If a vineyard must be planted with cuttings, every precaution should be taken to secure a good stand. Only the best cuttings should be used; those to be preferred are medium-large ones taken from the base (the part of the cane immediately off the old wood). Although cuttings from the base have given the best results under California conditions, Cosmo (1948) found that cuttings of resistant stock taken from a median position on the cane gave better results than either apical or basal cuttings. Calma and Richey (1931), using American grapes, obtained their most vigorous vines from the middle and basal parts of the canes. Early planting is advisable. Deep holes are advantageous, and the soil must be packed firmly around the cuttings. Only the top bud should be above the soil level, and it should be completely covered with a mound of loose soil. In the interior valleys of California an immediate irrigation is needed, followed by shallow irrigations every ten days to two weeks to keep the soil thoroughly moist until the cuttings have rooted and made a fair top growth. If dibbles or planting machines are used in the planting, or if water injection probes are used to make the holes, the soil must be firmed carefully around the full length of the cuttings.

Resistant-rootstock cuttings.—Rootstock cuttings may be taken from any vigorous canes of the desired variety. These cuttings should be longer than those of the fruiting varieties for nursery planting, so that when they are set in the vineyard 4 to 5 inches of the rooting will be above ground for budding or grafting. A convenient length is 16 to 18 inches. *Before a cutting is planted in the nursery, all buds except the one at the top should be removed by a deep incision made with small pruning shears, wire wheel or a special motor-driven saw,* unless it is known that the rootstock used is not prone to sucker. Such disbudding is essential to avoid suckers in the vineyard; removing suckers is laborious and costly. If disbudding is not done before the cuttings are planted in the nursery, the rootings must be disbudded before being placed in the vineyard. Failure to disbud may result in a short-lived vineyard and also, because of sucker growth from the rootstocks, one extremely expensive to maintain. Disbudding the rootings is much more difficult and costly than disbudding the cuttings. Direct planting of rootstock cuttings in the vineyard is a *very poor practice* because many will fail to grow.

Green or soft-wood cuttings.—The grapevine can be readily duplicated from segments of the green shoots collected at any time during active growth. However, the specialized greenhouse technique, using intermittent fogging or misting over the cuttings while they are striking root is necessary. Stoutemeyer and O'Rourke (1943) defined the environmental limits of this technique for many horticultural plants. The principal advantage of using soft-wood cuttings is the huge number of plants that can be duplicated from one mother-vine in a single season. Goheen and Nyland (1971) have shown that with this procedure several thousand rootings can be produced in one season from a single vine.

In recent years a great demand has arisen for planting stock of wine varieties certified to be free of known virus diseases (see p. 11). The scarcity of wood from these highly preferred vines has given impetus to this means of rapid propagation. Several commercial nurseries have supplied mist-propagated vines for thousands of acres of new vineyards in California.

The cuttings used are one node segments of green wood which can be collected from current season's growth of the mother-vines anytime during the growing season. These are rooted in a greenhouse. Bottom-heat and overhead intermittent mist are employed and literally 100 per cent rooting success is obtained within fifteen to twenty days. The misting cycle usually approximates 10 seconds *on* and 90 seconds *off*; however, combinations which keep the relative humidity around the cuttings at 100 percent is satisfactory. This misting effectively maintains air temperatures in the range of 75° to 80° F., with literally no transpiration stress on the green cuttings while they root. Automatic controls are used, and misting is usually discontinued at night. The rooting medium must be very well drained to remove any excess moisture that might accumulate from this misting. Although bottom heat is suggested, the temperature of the rooting medium should not be more than a few degrees higher than the air temperature around the cuttings. A rooting hormone treatment, such as an indolebutryic acid dip, can be used; however, green wood grape cuttings root so readily under intermittent mist to make this unnecessary. Details of the design and operation of misting systems have been described by Hartmann and Kester (1968).

When rooting is accomplished the vines are taken out of the misting environment—transplanted to four-inch plastic pots and held in the greenhouse or, if the temperature allows, in an outdoor lathhouse. During the first few days after transplanting, reduced light, moderate temperature and highly humidity are vital to the survival of the tender plants. After four to six weeks, the plants have re-established themselves in the pots. They are then hardened-off in a partially shaded outdoor location for a few days prior to planting in the vineyard. Thus the entire process, from cutting to field-planting requires only 50 to 60 days.

The post-planting care of these small plants is critical. They are actively growing and their roots must become established in the vineyard soil; hence, shallow frequent irrigations and intensive weed control are necessary during the first summer.

LAYERS

Layering as a means of propagating vines is recommended under two conditions: when the purpose is (*a*) to multiply vines of varieties whose cuttings can be rooted only with great difficulty, or (*b*) to replace occasional missing vines in an established vineyard.

Layering for varieties difficult to propagate by cuttings.—Varieties whose cuttings strike root poorly can be propagated by simple layers, trench layers, and mound layers. The simple layer is a cane bent down into moist soil for a part of its length, with the tip end exposed. The cane is usually shortened so that only 1 or 2 buds project above the ground. To make the trench layers, trenches 8 to 20 inches deep are dug in early spring, radiating from the parent vine. A cane is bent down into each trench, held in place by pegs, and covered with 1 or 2 inches of soil. As the shoots arising from the buds of the buried cane grow, soil is filled in around them until the trench

Propagation

is full. The cane strikes root at each node. During the next winter, plants are obtained by digging up the cane and cutting it into rooted sections. Mound layers are made by covering the heads of low-headed vines with soil during the growing season, leaving the tips of the growing shoots exposed. Each shoot strikes root near its base and during the next winter can be removed from the parent stock as a rooted vine. These methods are particularly useful in propagating varieties of the *rotundifolia* group: Scuppernong, Flowers, Eden, James, and others.

Layering to replace missing vines.—By far the most important use of layers in the vineyards of California is to replace occasional missing vines in established vineyards where competition with older vines makes it difficult to fill in the vacancies with rootings. For this purpose the simple type of layer is used. A long, vigorous cane from a vine adjacent to a missing vine is bent down into a hole or trench about 10 inches deep. The tip end projecting after the hole is filled should be exactly in position to replace the missing vine. It may be shortened to one or two buds above the ground or headed at the height where branches are desired. Layering can be done during the winter whenever the soil can be worked. A wire should be placed around the cane, between the parent vine and the buried part of the cane, and be twisted until it is snug. As the cane grows, the wire becomes tight and acts as a girdle, increasing the rate of development of the new vine. The girdle prevents the movement of elaborated foods from the new vine

FIGURE 37: Replacing a missing vine by means of a layer from an adjacent vine.

back to the parent vine, but does not stop the movement of water and dissolved minerals to the new vine.

The only care needed by these layers during the growing season is to prevent all growth on the layered cane except the part that will form the trunk and arms or branches of the new vine, and to tie these appropriately to give the new vine the desired form (fig. 37). All buds that start on the cane between the parent vine and the ground should be rubbed off. The new vine must be trained in the year in which the layer is made.

The new vine produced from a layer should be allowed to bear little or no fruit in the first year, and only a limited crop the second. Thus enabled to devote all its energies to growth of stem and root, the vine will be able by the third year to compete successfully with its older neighbors. The new vine should not be separated from the parent for several years unless there is danger of virus infection. Layering to replace missing plants in grafted vineyards requires approach grafting, a very difficult technique and one seldom used in vineyards today.

GRAFTS

Any grafted plant consists of three essential parts: the stock, the scion, and the union. The stock consists of the roots—the underground stem. The scion consists of all the rest, always including the leaf-bearing and fruit-bearing parts. The union is the place or region where stock and scion are joined.

Purpose of grafting.—Vines are grafted for any of the following purposes: (*a*) to obtain vines of the desired fruiting variety on roots resistant to phylloxera or nematodes; (*b*) to correct mixed varieties in an established vineyard; (*c*) to change the variety of an established vineyard; (*d*) to increase a supply of new or rare varieties rapidly; or (*e*) to obtain vines on roots tolerant to certain soil conditions such as high lime.

Most varieties that produce fruit of desirable character are susceptible to the attacks of phylloxera and nematodes. The only known practical means of growing susceptible varieties in badly infested soils is to graft them on immune or resistant rootstocks.

Requirements for successful grafting.—The most important factors governing success in grafting vines are compatibility or affinity between stock and scion; favorable conditions of moisture, temperature, and aeration; contact or close proximity of the cambium layers of the stock and scion; mechanical rigidity to maintain the position of stock and scion until the union is formed; youth of scion and stock, particularly the scion; and a healthy degree of vegetative activity in stock and scion.

Compatibility, referring to the capabilities of the stock and scion to exist together, involves structural and chemical similarity. Usually, varieties of the same botanical species graft readily on one another. Thus, almost all *vinifera* grape vareties—Muscat, Thompson Seedless, Tokay, Carignane, Zinfandel, and the like—are easily intergrafted. The results of grafting one species on another of the same genus are less certain. Occasonally, such grafts are nearly perfect—and sometimes they are impossible. An example of a nearly perfect interspecific graft is Carignane (*Vitis vinifera*) on St. George (*V. rupestris*). An example of a more difficult interspecifie combination of grapes is Muscat of Alexandria (*V. vinifera*) on Scuppernong (*V. rotundifolia*). Compatibility is usually lacking between different genera of the same family. Some effects of partial or incomplete compatibility are failure to unite, imperfect or structurally weak unions, overgrowth of the stock or scion, decrease in longevity, decrease in vigor, increase or decrease of fruitfulness, and changes in the quality of the fruit.

Callus formation, the first step in the growing together of the tissues, requires favorable conditions of temperature, moisture, and aeration. It takes place best in an atmosphere nearly saturated with moisture at a temperature of 75° to 85° F. Grape grafts are usually not waxed, as is done in grafting most other plants. Drying out is prevented, and aeration is provided, by covering the graft with some moist porous material—soil, sand, moss, or sawdust.

Union between stock and scion is made primarily by outgrowths of the respective cambium layers, bridging the gap between the stock and the scion. The narrower the gap to be bridged, the more rapid the union. The process is facilitated, therefore, by the closest proximity and the most complete coincidence possible of the respective cambiums. Not only must the cambiums of the stock and the scion approach each other very closely, but this proximity must be maintained until stock and scion are firmly grown together. If the union, once formed, is broken by movement of the scion or the stock, the bridging of the gap must start all over again. Consequently, mechanical rigidity is as essential as a good fit. After the gap is bridged, the growing tissue differentiates to form the xylem (wood) and phloem (bark) tissues.

Generally, the younger the parts to be grafted together, the more successful is the grafting—provided, of course, that the requirements of good fit, mechanical rigidity, moisture, temperature, and aeration are met and maintained. Herbaceous (green) grafting of vines is not at all difficult, but proper conditions for union are more difficult to maintain with soft green tissues than with mature tissues. Young vines are easier to graft than old vines. Seldom, if ever, should growth older than the current season be used for scions.

With dormant scions, results are best if the work is delayed until the stock starts growth, or near that time. The scions should be kept dormant by storing them in a cool place. Summer grafting or budding is most successful when the stocks are growing vigorously.

Propagation

Influence of grafting on the characters of stock and scion.—Grafting may alter the nutrition of the plant, thus affecting the characters of either stock or scion that are susceptible to influence by changes in nutrition. Grafted vines may be either more or less vigorous or more or less fruitful, produce larger or smaller berries of darker or lighter color, and ripen their fruit earlier or later than ungrafted vines of the same variety. These are influences of the same nature as those caused by variations in soil, climate, and cultural conditions. No changes in varietal characteristics have been produced by grafting. A Muscat grape retains its muscat flavor, no matter what stock it is grown on, and, similarly, the St. George retains its resistance to phylloxera, regardless of the scion variety grafted on it. There is no exchange or intermingling of characters between stock and scion. Since, however, the usually slight changes in vigor, fruitfulness, and character of the fruit that do occur with grafting may seriously affect the profitability of a vineyard of grafted vines, the stock selected should be well suited to the particular variety under the given conditions.

The most extensively utilized influence is the effect of the rootstock on the vigor of the scion. A weak-growing rootstock retards the growth of a scion of stronger-growing varieties. As a rule, weak-growing rootstocks are in demand in the cold northern areas of grape production since they tend to advance ripening. Owing to their more limited root system, these rootstocks do not supply so much of water or mineral elements in midsummer as do the strong-growing; growth is thereby checked, carbohydrates accumulate, and maturation is hastened. Strong-growing rootstocks, in contrast, increase vine growth. Large vines with an abundance of foliage that may delay maturation in hot areas will tend to produce fruit of improved balance, because of a lower summation of heat during the ripening period. In wide spacing, strong-growing rootstocks are necessary if the vines are to make full use of the soil area allowed to each vine.

BENCH GRAFTING

In the past, bench grafting (indoor grafting) has been the most common method of producing grafted vines of the desired fruiting varieties on roots resistant to phylloxera or nematodes. The work is carried on in a well-lighted place, usually indoors, during the late winter and early spring. The newly made grafts are stored or callused in sand or in a hot room, and are grown for a year in the nursery before being planted in the vineyard. Single-bud scions of the desired fruiting variety are grafted on either unrooted cuttings or one-year-old rootings of the desired stock variety. Those grafted on rootings may be planted directly in the vineyard.

The wood for the scions and unrooted-stock cuttings should be selected acording to the directions given for cuttings to be planted in the nursery. The canes for scions and those for stock cuttings are often made up in lengths of 30 to 45 inches or more. Then, when the grafting is done, the long pieces are cut into the desired lengths—about 14 inches for the stocks, and single-bud pieces for the scions.

Rootstock and scion material for bench grafting may be stored in sand, as are cuttings for nursery planting; but they must be washed free of sand before use. To avoid this troublesome washing and to ensure freedom from anything apt to damage the cutting edge of the grafting machines, cuttings for bench grafting are usually stored in some other medium—wood shavings, sawdust, rice straw that is free from water grass and tules, or clean rice hulls will serve. To prevent mold growth, the cuttings may be dipped in lime-sulfur solution before being stored. The lime-sulfur solution is made by diluting 1 gallon of the concentrated liquid with 12–15 gals. of water.

Preparing the stocks and scions.—Just before being grafted, the stock and scion materials are removed from storage, washed clean, and, if at all dry, soaked for a few hours in water. Then the stocks are cut to the desired length (about 14 in.), with the basal cut immediately below the lowest node and the upper cut 1.5 to 2 inches about a node. They are next disbudded (all buds completely removed) with small pruning shears or a special saw (fig. 38) to prevent the growth of stock suckers in the nursery and, later, in the vineyard. The disbudded stock cuttings are then graded according to diameter *at the top*, where the graft is to be made. The grading may be done by eye into three or four sizes; but if it is done

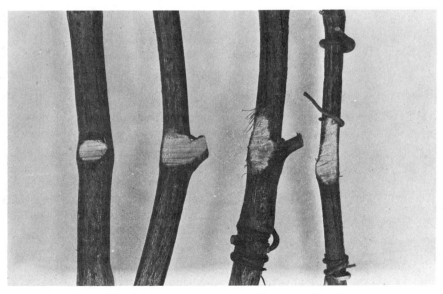

FIGURE 38: Disbudded resistant rootstock cuttings: A, disbudded by a mandrel of saws; B, disbudded by a motor-driven wire wheel.

accurately with a slot or notch grader, as many as six or seven sizes may be obtained. Accuracy in grading greatly facilitates and speeds the grafting job.

The scions are cut to a single eye, with not over a half inch of internode above the bud and only 1.5 to 2 inches of internode below. They are sorted according to diameter *at the bottom* into the same series of grades used for the stocks. Economical and successful bench grafting of cuttings requires that stocks and scions be of similar diameters.

Actual grafting may be done by hand, but machines are more often used. When made by hand, the short whip graft is employed. When made before conditions are favorable for planting, the grafts are held in moist sand and afterward planted directly into the nursery when conditions are favorable.

Long whip grafts.—The cuts for the long whip graft are shown in figure 39. The cut surface is two-and-a-half to three times the diameter of the stock or scion. This cut should be straight; that is, its surface must be flat and smooth. Only an experienced grafter can make such a cut regularly. Paring the cut is not permissible, since this makes an irregular or wavy surface, preventing a good fit between stock and scion. The cut is made most readily with a sliding motion, moving the knife lengthwise with, as

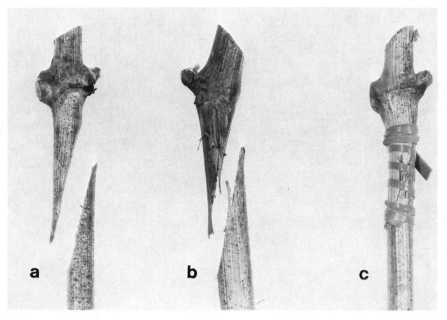

Figure 39: The long whip graft: a, the sloping cuts made on the stock and the scion; b, the tongue cut and opened out; c, the completed graft, tied and ready for planting.

well as across, the stock or scion. The tongue is made with a slow, slightly rocking motion of the knife. The tongue should extend across the middle third of the cut surface. This cut should be straight, not split, making a thin tongue. The knife is carefully withdrawn to avoid breaking the tongue; and just before it is free of the cut the tongue is gently bent out to open the cut. This facilitates placing stock and scion together.

The stock and scion are now placed together with the tongues interlocking; and, if everything has been done properly, no cut surface will be visible, and neither stock nor scion will project over the cut surface of the other (fig. 39c). It is much better that the points should not quite reach the bottom of the cut surface than that they overlap, since the unions will be more nearly perfect and the scions less apt to throw out roots. If the points do overlap, the overlapping part should be cut off. If the fit is not good and the graft not firm, the cut should be remade completely.

After the stock and scion are put together, the graft is tied with string, grafting rubber, or raffia; the latter is the best. The tying material is passed two or three times round the point of the scion, to hold it down firmly; then with a wide spiral the material is taken to the point of the stock, which is fastened with two or three more turns.

When early grafts are to be stored in sand, it is best to bluestone the raffia to prevent rotting before the grafts are planted. The bundles of raffia are soaked a few hours in a 3 per cent solution of bluestone (copper sulfate) and then hung up to dry. Before being used for tying, the raffia should be washed quickly in water to remove the bluestone crystallized on the outside, which might injure the graft if it were not removed.

Some grafters prefer waxed string, strong enough to hold the graft and weak enough to be broken by hand. Number 18 knitting cotton is a convenient size. The balls are soaked in melted grafting wax for several hours. A good wax for this purpose is made by melting together one part of tallow, two parts of beeswax, and three parts of rosin. When tying is done with raffia or string, the end is passed under the last turn.

If used correctly, grafting rubber is satisfactory. If, however, the entire unions are so closely wrapped that the air is excluded, many of the grafts may fail. The rubber must be cut and removed the first time the scion roots are cut in the nursery, and great care must be taken lest the union be injured.

Short whip graft.—The cuts for the short whip graft are made like the corresponding cuts for the long whip, except that the cut surface is only one-and-a-half times the diameter of the stock or scion. The tongue covers the middle half of the cut surface. In addition to being longer in proportion to the cut surface, it is also heavier than the tongue of the long whip. It must be cut, not split, and should be about half as thick as it would be if the knife were allowed to follow the grain of the wood. This

Propagation

graft is not tied. The heavy tongue holds the stock and scion firmly together until they can be packed into boxes for hot-room callusing.

Machine grafting.—In California, vine grafts are usually made by machine. The primary reasons are these: there are few experienced hand grafters, and labor costs are high. Both the commercial nurserymen and the individual growers, who make their own grafts, use machines.

A very successful machine, designed by Jacob (1936) and modified by Alley (1957), consists essentially of four 8-inch circular saws, each one-sixteenth of an inch thick, mounted in a gang head on a ball-bearing shaft that is belt-driven at 5250 r.p.m. by a one-half-hp electric motor (fig. 40). The saws are separated by spacer disks so that the width of the space between the saws is the same as their cutting edges. The spacer disks also limit the depth of the cuts. The stocks and scions are pushed endwise (radially) against the saws. Spacer disks 7 inches in diameter with the 8-inch circular saws limit the depth of the cuts to a half inch. Thus a slip-joint consisting of one, two, three, or four tenons, according to the diameter of the stock (or scion) and the corresponding slots, is formed on the upper end of the stock and on the lower end of the scion. The table or guide is so constructed and adjusted that a good fit is obtained by cutting the stock against the right-hand guide and the scion against the left-hand guide, or vice versa—provided, of course, that they are of the same size

FIGURE 40: A multiple-saw type of grafting machine.

Propagation

and that the end of each has been cut square across before the slip joint is sawed on the machine (fig. 41). A small stream of water must flow on the saws to prevent gum from collecting on them. For the best results, grafts are tied in the same way as in long whip grafting. However, in some commercial nurseries an ordinary lightweight wire paper stapler has been employed. The tightly fitted tongue and groove cuts made by the machine have more stability than the hand-made long whip graft and the staple is much faster. Different length staples are used depending on the diameter of the wood. In all cases, the staple should penetrate all the way through the graft union and clinch slightly on the opposite side.

With this machine, three reasonably skilled men can make 500 to 1,000 grafts an hour. Necessary to the fastest work is good, straight, hard wood, carefully graded according to size. During several years' observations, the

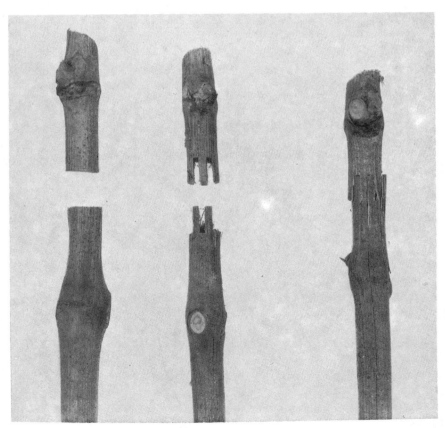

FIGURE 41: Showing cuts in scion and stock made by saw-type grafting machine.

average percentage of machine-made grafts that grew into first quality rooted one-year-old grafted vines has been found to be slightly less than the average of skilled hand grafts—probably because nearly all defective stocks and scions are noticed and discarded in hand work, whereas some will escape detection in the more rapid machine operation.

Other saw machines are also in use. One of these, which makes a saddle-type graft, has a very efficient centering device. It is a simple V-shaped guide that automatically centers the stock or scion, regardless of size. A drawback is that two machines are required, one for cutting the stock and another for the scion (this machine is patented by Lafata Brothers, of St. Helena, Calif.) A number of machines use mounted knives. These usually make a whip-type graft, in which case the grafts will ordinarily require hot-room callusing.

Bench grafting of rootings.—If one-year-old rootings are to be bench grafted, they must first be washed clean. Then the rootings are shortened to a uniform length of about 12 to 14 inches; the roots are cut back to short stubs, not more than 1 inch long, to facilitate handling. One-bud scions are grafted on them by the long whip or machine method. They are usually planted directly in the vineyard, but, if they are small, replanting in the nursery is advisable.

Since certain good rootstocks—particularly some of the *berlandieri* hybrids—root poorly from cuttings, bench grafts of their unrooted stock cuttings give very low nursery yields. It is sometimes more economical to root the cuttings first and then do the grafting. Also, when stock cuttings are made, there is always much wood that is too small in diameter to be bench grafted, although perfectly sound and well matured. This wood becomes excellent stock material after one year in the nursery.

Sand callusing.—When the grafts are made, the stocks and scions are nearly or completely dormant; under favorable conditions of moisture, temperature, and aeration, however, they begin growth processes that bring about the rooting of the stock, the sprouting of the scion, and the uniting of one with the other. If these favorable conditions do not exist in the nursery at the time of grafting, the grafts must be stored.

The long whip grafts are usually stored in moist sand. Storage is the primary purpose, but these will callus if conditions are favorable and if they are stored for some time. First, they are tied in bundles of 25 to 50 each, for convenience and economy in handling. Raffia treated with bluestone is excellent for tying. Two ties are best, one near the bottom and one near the top. The bundle must be securely labeled. Clean, fine sand is suitable for storage. It must be moist enough to support plant growth, but not too wet to be worked easily between the bundles of grafts. The sand bed may be a pile of sand in an open shed or on the south side of a building. If in the open, it should have a glass, canvas, board, or other type of cover so that it can be protected during rainy or cold weather and uncovered during warm weather.

The bundles of grafts are placed in the sand in a nearly vertical position, scions up, and the sand is worked in between the bundles. A layer of sand 2 or 3 inches deep is spread before the grafts are placed in position, and the tops of the grafts are covered 3 or 4 inches deep with a uniform layer of sand. The top sand must occasionally be moistened slightly to replace water lost by surface evaporation. Care must be taken to wet only the sand that has dried out.

If the temperature of the sand is about 75° F., the unions will callus over and the buds and roots begin to grow within three or four weeks. Higher temperatures will hasten the process; lower temperatures will retard it. Temperatures above 85° cause profuse, soft callus tissue, which is objectionable. Below 70°, callus formation is very slow; below 60° it practically stops. The long whip and the stapled or tied machine grafts should be planted in the nursery as soon as the conditions favor planting, whether they have callused or not.

Hot-room callusing.—When the short whip or similar untied machine grafts are made, they must be callused before planting. Ordinarily a heated room is used. As the grafts are made, they are packed into boxes, in moss or sawdust charcoal. The boxes may be of any size, except that they should be 8 to 10 inches taller than the grafts. A convenient size is 16 by 19.5

FIGURE 42: A callusing box showing method of filling. (*From Calif. Agr. Ext. Ser. Cir. 101*)

inches (inside); such a box will hold 500 grafts of average size. When the boxes are made, spaces of one eighth to three sixteenths of an inch should be left between the individual boards to allow for drainage. It is also well to perforate the bottom with several rows of small holes. To facilitate packing and unpacking, one side of the box should be hinged.

The best inexpensive packing material is a mixture of three parts of coarse sawdust to one part of "fine chick" charcoal. Since the water-holding capacity of this material is not very great, the boxes should be lined on the sides and bottom with a 1-inch layer of sphagnum moss. The moss, besides holding water, prevents the sawdust-charcoal mixture from sifting out through cracks or holes in the boxes.

For filling, a box is laid on its unhinged side and the hinged side is propped open (fig. 42). A layer of wet moss about 1 inch deep is spread over the side that is down and also upward several inches on the vertical sides and bottom. Then a light layer of wet sawdust and charcoal is sprinkled over the moss, and a layer of grafts is placed horizontally on the sawdust-charcoal layer, with the ends of the stocks about 2 inches from the bottom of the box and with the scions all at exactly the same distance from the top of the box. It is convenient to fit a loose board temporarily into the box so that, during filling, the tops of the scions can be butted against the board. More of the sawdust-charcoal mixture is added to cover the grafts, and another layer of grafts is put in place. The box is filled to within an inch of the open side with alternate layers of grafts and the sawdust-charcoal mixture, the moss being built up on the sides and bottom as necessary. After a layer of moss has been put on top (the open side of the box), the hinged side is closed and fastened. When full, the box is set upright, and the tops of the scions are then covered to a depth of 2 inches with the sawdust-charcoal mixture. The filled boxes may be placed in the callusing room or stored in a cool place for a few weeks if necessary.

Just before the boxes are placed in the callusing room, they should be warmed to 75° or 80° F. by being dipped in warm water to just below the unions, care being taken to avoid submerging the unions. After the box is removed from the dipping tank, the top of the box should be sprinkled copiously with warm water (80° F.). If the packing material settles appreciably, more of the material should be added. As soon as the box has drained, it should go into the callusing room.

The hot room for callusing may be any well-ventilated room of convenient size and shape in which the temperature can be held within a range of 75° to 80° F. and which is neither too wet nor too dry. Any heating system that maintains an even temperature throughout the room may be used.

After the boxes of grafts have been in the hot room from ten days to two

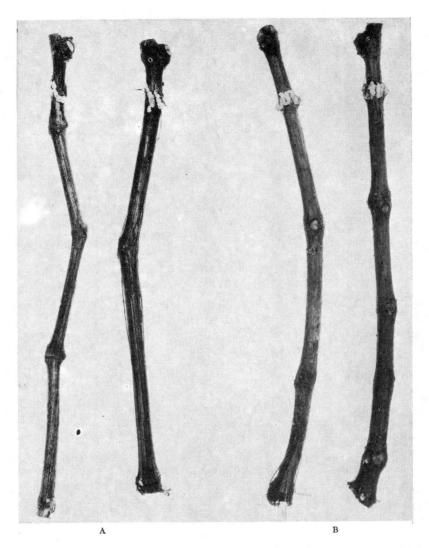

A   B

FIGURE 43: Callused bench grafts: A, hand-made short whip; B, machine-made. (*From Calif. Agr. Exp. Sta. Cir. 101*)

Propagation

weeks, they should be removed and diped in warm water (75° to 80° F.) in order to aerate them. They should be lowered carefully, so that the water fills the box nearly to the unions, which it should not reach. The boxes are then allowed to drain and are replaced in the hot room.

When callusing is complete all around the cuts, the boxes are transferred to a room where the temperature is fairly constant, but is about 10° F. below that of the callusing room. At this stage the best grafts should show callused unions, indication of root formation, and swelling of the buds (fig. 43). After a week or ten days at the lower temperature, the grafts may be planted in the nursery if weather and soil conditions permit. Otherwise, they may be stored longer in any cool, protected place, such as an open shed.

Greenhouse forced bench grafts.—The prosperity of the wine industry has accelerated the rate of vineyard planting in most grape districts of California. The limited supplies of the new clonal selections, vines free of known virus diseases, and the vines that have undergone heat therapy have led to modification in the conventional grafting procedure to save time. In the modified procedure the machine-made grafts are wire stapled, callused in the usual manner described above, and then coated with a low melting point paraffin to retard water loss. The paraffin should be held at a temperature just above its melting point so it will not injure the delicate callus tissue or the new shoot growth. Grafting wax including a small amount of resin, and beeswax has been found useful to insuring a uniform and lasting coating at greenhouse temperatures. If the scion bud has grown several inches, it should be cut back to about one-half inch.

After waxing, the grafts are placed in a planting tube made from inexpensive milk carton paper or commercial plastic impregnated paper. They also can be made by hand by rolling 6 or 8 inch squares of light-weight roofing paper. Tubes 2 to 2½ inches in diameter and 6 to 8 inches high are satisfactory. A light potting soil mix is used in setting the grafts in the tubes. If the roots have grown extensively into the callusing material, they should be trimmed back to fit freely in the planting tube. This will avoid entangled primary roots on the graft when it is moved to the vineyard. The tubed grafts are usually set tightly together in greenhouse flats to facilitate watering and handling (fig. 44).

The potted grafts are then held under carefully-controlled greenhouse conditions for four to six weeks. During this time the scion produces a shoot of 4 to 6 inches and the stock develops more roots. Weinberger and Loomis (1972) describe in detail the care necessary in the greenhouse. Strict humidity, temperature, and light control during several days following the waxing and transplanting is vital to the grafts' survival. They recommend a temperature of 85° F., a relative humidity of above 70 per cent, and strongly stress that the light be reduced down to about 30 per

FIGURE 44: Tubed grafts in flats during forcing in greenhouse. (*From Weinberger and Loomis, 1972*)

cent of normal sunlight. The callus which developed in complete darkness is very sensitive to full greenhouse light. For the first two or three weeks after planting in the tubes over-head shades of burlap or plastic saran should be used. Placing cheesecloth or single sheets of newspaper directly over the flats of waxed grafts for the first few days will further reduce light and permit easier control of humidity. Some variations in these techniques have been developed and used in Europe. Becker (1971) has summarized their experience and describes the practices generally used by their propagators.

The post-planting care of these tender green, growing grafts is critical to the stand obtained at the end of the first summer. Since the grafts cannot be set in the field until the danger of spring frosts is well over, planting in the coastal valleys of California must be delayed until late May or June. This subjects the young grafts to the possibility of hot, dry days soon after planting. An ample supply of soil moisture is vital to their survival. Frequent thorough irrigations, one at planting and up to once a week for the early part of the summer may be necessary to insure well developed plants. For this reason, the most successful plantings of these greenhouse-forced grafts have been those set in sites equipped with an adequate irrigation

Propagation

system, especially where over-head sprinkling was used. With good management this procedure will save a year in bringing the vineyard into bearing.

PLANTING AND CARE OF THE NURSERY

The site selected for the vine nursery should be one of well-drained, fertile soil, well leveled for uniform irrigation, and free of phylloxera, nematodes, and noxious weeds. For bench grafts, friable sandy-loam soils are preferred. Adequate irrigation is essential. In preparation for planting, the soil should be deeply plowed or subsoiled 12 inches deep when the degree of moisture allows it to break up into a loose, friable condition without large clods.

Planting cuttings.—The method of planting varies with the size of the nursery, the equipment at hand, and the availability of irrigation. If water can be had at planting time, a large nursery of cuttings can be planted most economically by using a modified subsoiler to form the rows. A furrowing shovel or a pair of small lister wings may be attached to the standard of the subsoiler, about 10 or 12 inches above the shoe, to make a furrow in which water is run to fill the subsoiler cut and soften the soil. While the water is in the furrow, the cuttings are pushed into the soft soil, leaving the top bud on each cutting 2 or 3 inches above the general level of the soil (fig. 45). When the row is finished, the cuttings are covered with a wide ridge of loose soil. The wet soil settles firmly around

FIGURE 45: Planting cutting in a subsoiler cut.

the cuttings and gives them an excellent chance to grow. Planting in a dry subsoiler cut is not advisable unless irrigation can follow in a day or two.

Another good method of planting—preferable to that described above if irrigation water is not available at planting time—is begun by using a turning plow to make a deep furrow (about 10. in.), with the land side of the furrow in the position where the row is to be. Then the bottom of the furrow is loosened 3 or 4 inches deeper by going through it with a second, smaller plow—a subsoiler or other suitable implement. The loose soil thus formed in the bottom of the furrow is not removed. The cuttings are stuck into the loose soil so that they rest against the vertical side of the furrow. The soil around the base of the cuttings is firmly packed by tramping. Then most of the soil thrown out of the furrow is turned back into it and again tramped firmly around the cuttings. The ridge of loose soil completely covering the cuttings is raised by making a turn to the row with a turning plow. If the soil is in ideal condition, the land side of the furrow will stand up and the cuttings may be planted without a planting line or board. If the soil is not in ideal condition, the land side of the furrow breaks down and a board (fig. 46) must be used to obtain a straight row. Irrigation should follow within a few days unless the soil has been thoroughly wet by rain in the meantime.

In a fertile soil that is frequently irrigated, the cuttings may be spaced as closely as 2 inches in the row, with the rows 5 feet apart. In a less fertile soil, especially one that cannot be well irrigated, wider spacing in the row will produce larger and better rootings.

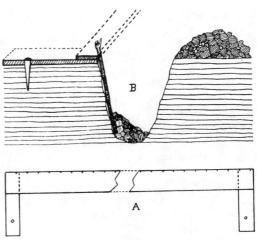

FIGURE 46: A, planting board; B, diagram showing use of planting board with bench grafts.

Propagation

According to Winkler (1927) early planting has regularly produced the highest percentage of, as well as the best, rootings at Davis. For identical lots, designating the rooting of December-planted cuttings as 100 per cent, the rooting was 90 per cent for January, 89 per cent for February, 53 per cent for March, and 38 per cent for April. Quinn (1931) in Australia found that early planting also produced the strongest rootings. Alley and Christensen (1970), working at the Kearney Horticultural Field Station near Fresno, California showed, however, that late (April) planted cuttings of Thompson Seedless when properly stored gave the highest percentage of rooting as well as the largest rootings (table 17).

Improving rooting.—Branas, *et al.* (1934) summed up the situation on improving the rooting of cuttings by stating that it is not practical to attempt to increase the rooting of varieties that root poorly. They felt that breeding was the solution to this problem. Since that time a great deal of work has been done, especially with certain rootstocks. Jacob (1932) showed a slight improvement in grafts by soaking the stocks for twenty-four hours in a 0.001 molal $MnSO_4$ solution and then for ten to twenty minutes in water at 122°F., and afterward holding the stocks ten days in callusing boxes at 75 to 85°F. before grafting. Others have applied bottom heat in the nursery by burying electric cables below the rows of cuttings or grafts. Priess (1955), using grafts of Sylvaner on Kober 5 BB, obtained rooting of 53 per cent with day-and-night heat from May 12 to 30, whereas the average for an unheated lot was 38 per cent.

TABLE 17

EFFECT OF STORAGE CONDITIONS AND PLANTING TIME ON PRODUCTION OF
ROOTINGS OF THOMPSON SEEDLESS

Type of storage	Position in storage	Planting dates (1966)					
		Feb. 15		Mar. 15		April 14	
		No. of rootings *	Mean wt. of rooting †	No. of rootings *	Mean wt. of rooting †	No. of rootings *	Mean wt. of rooting †
Sand	top up	11.4	1.62	11.4	1.66	14.4	2.07
	top down	11.1	1.67	12.0	1.67	14.8	2.38
	horizontal	12.0	1.69	12.1	1.52	14.2	1.90
Refrigerator	top up	11.6	1.64	10.9	1.36	11.2	1.52

SOURCE OF DATA: Alley and Christensen (1970).

* Value is mean of 10 replicates of 15 cuttings, dug January 1967.

† Value is mean fresh weight, in Kgs. of the 10 largest rootings in each of 10 replicate due January 1967.

Growth regulators have received much attention as a means of improving rooting. Improvements have been reported by workers in several countries (Alley, 1961; Anliker and Kobel, 1945; Harmon, 1943; and Kordes, 1937). The most promising regulators have been the auxins and heteroauxins. Wilhelm and Zillig (1938) showed that differences in wood maturity greatly affected rooting percentage, storage conditions of the cuttings, concentration of the regulator, timing of the treatments, conditions in the nursery, and the like have caused the results to vary greatly between workers and between varieties and rootstocks at the same location. It is evident that rooting can be influenced, but much more work under rigidly controlled conditions will be required before recommendations can be made with confidence. In limited tests at Davis by Weaver (1956) it was found that cuttings treated with various plant regulators produced a profuse growth of roots compared to that of controls. Up to the present, however, cuttings treated with regulators have given no higher percentages of rooting in the nursery than untreated cuttings.

Planting grafts.—More care is necessary in the planting of grafts than of cuttings. The soil should be warm, moist, and well pulverized. The weather should be mild—not cold, not very hot, and not windy.

As the grafts are unpacked, either from the sand or from the callusing boxes, they are carefully inspected. All suckers from the stocks and all roots from the scions must be broken out. Any scion shoots more than an inch long should be cut back to that length. Grafts that are hot-room callused are best hauled to the nursery in the callusing boxes and unpacked there. The grafts must be kept covered with wet burlap or other suitable material between the time they are removed from the callusing boxes or sand and the time they are planted. In all operations they must be handled very carefully in order to avoid breaking the unions.

For planting in a dry furrow, a planting board is indispensable. A board 16 feet by 6 inches by 1 inch, marked with shallow notches at the spacing desired in the row, and with an 18-inch crosspiece at each end, is convenient. A hole in the end of each crosspiece, through which a small iron bar or a heavy spike can be thrust, holds the board in place. The board is laid in position on the edge of the furrow, which is at least as deep as the length of the stocks. Each graft is placed opposite a notch, with the union just above the board (fig. 46). The trench is half or two thirds filled with soil, which is firmly packed around the stocks by tramping. The trench is then filled with loose soil and the planting board is moved to a new position, immediately after which the scions are carefully covered 2 or 3 inches deep with fine soil. The ridge of soil covering the grafts should be broad and regular (fig. 47)—a narrow ridge dries out too quickly. An irrigation should follow within a day or two, but should not wet the tops of the ridges.

FIGURE 47: A newly planted nursery of bench grafts. The two rows in the foreground have been partially uncovered.

A planting distance of 3 inches in the row is sufficient in a fertile sandy loam or loam soil that can be well irrigated. In a poorer soil, or where irrigation water may be limited or lacking late in the summer, a wider spacing of 4 or 5 inches in the row will produce larger and better vines. The rows may be spaced as close as 3 feet, but spacing of 4 or 5 feet will make planting, cultivation, irrigation, and digging easier.

If irrigation water is available at the time of planting, an alternate method of planting grafts can be used. With a large lister, a V-shaped furrow is made—about 10 inches deep, as measured from the level of the undisturbed soil. The furrow is then filled with water to just above the general soil level. As soon as most of the water has soaked into the soil, the grafts are laid against one side of the furrow, with all of the unions exactly at the water line, the stocks in the mud, and the scions above the wet soil. The grafts should be covered immediately, by hand, care being taken to avoid breaking any of the unions. The covering ridge should be 2 to 3 inches above the scions and wide enough to ensure against injurious drying-out between irrigations early in the season.

In the coastal valleys of California one need give the grafts little or no further attention for some time except to control weeds and carefully break the crust that forms after rain. In the hot interior valleys care must be taken not to permit the ridges to dry out badly enough to injure the scions. An additional irrigation may be required before the shoots come through the soil.

Removing scion roots, stock suckers, and tying materials.—As soon as the grafts are growing vigorously, the unions should be examined and all roots that have started from the scions should be removed. This will need to be done at about the beginning of July in the warmer districts, and at the end of July in the cooler districts.

The scion roots are useful to the graft for a while in keeping the scion alive and allowing the union to become perfected; hence they should not be removed too soon. The stocks usually start more slowly than the scions, partly because they are deeper in the soil, where the temperature is lower. Scion roots, however, take the nourishment elaborated by the scion leaves, thereby starving the stock roots. If the scion roots are removed too late, the stock roots may be unable to supply sufficient water to support the scion growth and the graft may die.

At the same time that the scion roots are removed, the tying material (raffia, string, or rubber), whichever has been used, should be cut and removed on all the grafts where it has not rotted. With rubber, waxed string, or bluestoned raffia, this operation is essential; otherwise the growth of the union will be constricted.

Stocks properly disbudded before grafting will produce no suckers. If suckers have developed, however, they should be removed as soon as they show above the ground, and any found when the scion roots are removed should be carefully broken out. To perform these several operations it is necessary to dig down beside the grafts to below the unions. The soil should be replaced around the grafts as soon as these operations are performed. An irrigation should follow immediately.

The grafts should be examined again about two months later, and any new scion roots or stock suckers should be removed. After this second removal of scion roots, the soil need not be replaced about the scions, but again the grafts should be irrigated.

Irrigating the nursery.—Except for the irrigations at or immediately after planting, which have already been discussed, the frequency of application and the quantity applied at each irrigation will be determined in each case by the soil and climate. The lighter the soil and the hotter the weather, the more frequently is water needed. Until the cuttings have rooted, the soil of a nursery of cuttings should not be allowed to dry more than 2 or 3 inches deep. When growing vigorously, they should be irrigated only often enough to maintain a vigorous growth until late July or early August. Thereafter, irrigation should cease in order to check the vigorous growth and force the wood to ripen.

The soil around the unions of grafted vines must be kept moist until the unions are solidly grown together and the grafts are growing with water absorbed by the stock roots. This condition will be found a week or two after the first removal of the scion roots. Thereafter the irrigation of a nursery of bench grafts does not differ from that of a cutting nursery.

Digging the nursery.—The vines in the nursery can be dug in the autumn as soon as they have lost their leaves. In a small nursery one may conveniently use a turning plow to remove as much soil as possible along the rows of vines on one side, and then take out the vines with a shovel or nursery spade. In large nurseries the vines are dug with a nursery digger drawn by a tractor. The digger cuts the roots and loosens and lifts the vines so that they can be easily pulled out by hand. If the vines have made a large top growth, the tops may be cut back to a length of a few inches to facilitate digging and handling.

Storing rooted vines.—Since rooted cuttings and bench grafts are injured more easily than are cuttings, they must be handled more carefully and are best stored in cool, moist sand or soil. A shaded place, on either the north side of a building or under large evergreen trees, is appropriate for storage. The sand or soil must be well drained. A pile of sand or sandy soil raised a foot or two above the soil level will ensure good drainage.

The rootings or grafts are usually sorted into bundles of 25 or 50. The bundles of vines are "heeled in" in an inclined position. The soil about the roots must be firmly packed by tramping, after which the vines should be nearly covered over with the sand or soil. In dry weather the soil should be settled thoroughly with water after the vines are heeled in and before they have a chance to dry out. Sawdust or wood shavings may be used instead of sand or soil and are much easier to handle; with these, however, more care is required to prevent drying out.

Field Budding

Owing to the expense and skill required in the making and handling of bench grafts, many vineyards on resistant rootstocks in California are now established by planting the rooted rootstocks and then field budding them to the desired fruiting variety. Grafted vines, of course, must still be used in locations where conditions in the late summer are unfavorable for field budding.

In field budding, mature scion buds and actively growing stocks are prime requisites for success. The budding is done, therefore, as early as mature buds of the desired variety can be obtained—August in cool regions on unirrigated soils, September in warm regions on irrigated soils. Although this period usually yields best results, some degree of success, as shown by Snyder and Harmon (1941), can be obtained at any season of the year. If the budding is done in spring with buds from cold storage, the top of the stock must be removed or the bud may not push. The usual cause of failure is working with green buds or on dry stocks that have stopped growing.

The buds should be plump and taken from well-developed canes having light-brown bark color and whose leafstalks (petioles) will break in a normal, mature manner. The bark over the nodes and on the tendrils opposite the buds should be uniformly brown, since green areas on these parts, even though the bark elsewhere is brown, usually indicate insufficient maturity, poor nutrition, or disease. Buds at the base of large laterals should be avoided; those at the base of very small laterals are not objectionable. The leaves are removed from the bud sticks as soon as they are cut from the vines. The bud sticks must be kept fresh in moist packing material until used. The stocks must be actively growing. Irrigation in early or middle August, where possible, will contribute to good stock condition.

A special form of chip bud (fig. 48a) is commonly used. To remove the bud from the cane, the first cut is made deep into or through the bud stick, beginning three sixteenths to one quarter of an inch below the bud and sloping downward at an angle of about 45°. The second cut is started about three eighths to one half of an inch above the bud; the knife travels in a nearly straight plane behind the bud to the first cut, removing a wedge-shaped piece one sixteenth to one eighth of an inch thick at the lower end (fig. 48b). Some workmen reverse the order in which the cuts are made.

A notch into which the bud will fit is made in the stock 2–4 inches above the soil surface in the vineyard, and preferably on the side of the vine from which most of the top growth arises. The work is facilitated by first removing the soil around the vine to a depth of several inches. The angle made by the two cut surfaces of the notch in the stock is somewhat more acute than the angle formed by the cut surfaces of the bud piece. This technique ensures intimate contact between the lower end of the chip and the corresponding cut surface of the stock when the bud piece is pushed firmly into place. (fig. 48c). The chip must fit well in the notch. It is then tied securely in place with budding rubber or raffia (fig. 48d). In tying, two or three wraps should be made round the top end of the bud, thus holding it firmly in place. Then, with a long spiral, the tie is finished with two or three turns round the lip of the stock over the base of the bud. Waxing is unnecessary.

Immediately after being tied, the bud is covered with moist, well-pulverized soil, and this in turn is covered with 4 to 8 inches of well-pulverized soil that may be either moist or dry. If the soil is fairly moist, a covering 4 inches deep may be adequate; if dry, 8 inches is better. In very dry soil, from about a fourth to a third of the top growth of the vines may be cut off at the time of budding. The bud "calluses in"—that is, grows fast to the stock—within several weeks. It usually remains dormant, however, until the next spring.

During the winter, field-budded vines need no treatment except staking or trellising, if that work has not already been done. To avoid damaging the buds in driving the stakes, it is best to stake the vineyard before planting. The next spring, when the buds on the rootstock vines are just starting growth, the scion buds should be uncovered. The usual procedure is, first,

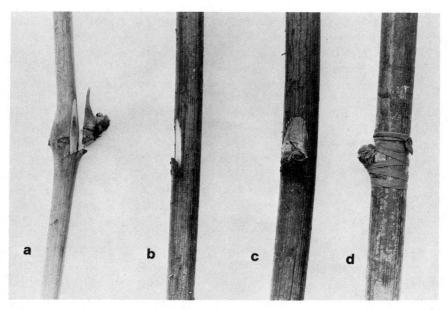

FIGURE 48: Steps in field-budding vines: A, the bud removed from the bud stick; B, notch made in the stock to receive the bud; C, the bud in place; D, finished and tied, ready to be covered with moist soil.

to cut the rubber or raffia used for tying. Then the scion on each vine should be examined carefully, to ascertain whether it is alive and grown fast to the stock. One need not hesitate to apply pressure to the bud chip —it can hardly be dislodged by one's fingers if the union is firm. If the scion bud seems to be well united with the stock and is beginning to grow, the stock should be cut off at about 1 or 1.5 inches above the bud. A building-paper sleeve about 1.5 or 2 inches in diameter and 9 inches long is placed over the end of the stock and the scion bud, and 3 or 4 inches of loose soil is banked round the lower end of the sleeve to prevent the wind from blowing it away. Suitable sleeves may be made by rolling 9-inch squares in the form of tubes. Sleeves protect the buds and scion shoots from damage by wind, cutworms, rabbits, and drifting soil. They also force the scion shoots to grow upright, thereby facilitating training. As soon as the scion shoot emerges from the sleeve, it should be tied to the stake. All stock suckers and scion roots whenever they appear, should be removed. If the scion bud is defective, the vine may be whip-grafted immediately; or it may be pruned back to one or two buds and left for rebudding in early summer or the fall. When the vines are large, grafting is to be preferred; when the vines are small, it is best to rebud.

Stocks are often killed by being cut off when the scion buds are imperfect. Unless one is experienced, it is not easy to find all the poor unions.
Rootstock rootings properly disbudded before planting will grow only from
the top or from the scion bud; hence, if the top is cut off and the scion
bud fails to grow, the vine must be rebudded or grafted, or it is lost. To
avoid this danger, one proceeds by uncovering the vines to expose the scion
buds at about the time the rootstock buds begin to break. Then, all the
canes on each rootstock are pruned back to the base buds. One should
cover the scion bud lightly with about an inch of loose soil, or else place
a building-paper sleeve over it. One should watch the vines closely, going
over the vineyard about once a week. As the scion buds start, the tops of
the rootstocks are cut off at an inch or more above them. As the scion
shoots grow, they should be tied carefully to the stakes, as in the training
of any other vines. Thereafter, one keeps the soil away from the base of the
scion shoot, so as to discourage scion roots, and removes all suckers that
start from the rootstocks.

Each time, in going over the vineyard, one should remove all shoots
from stocks on which the scion buds have not started. Sometime in May
the scion buds that have not started and are thought to be defective are
uncovered and examined. Thereafter, the shoots on all stocks that have
defective scion buds are allowed to grow. These can be rebudded in the
fall.

Bench grafting and field budding compared.—Using uniform scions of
ten fruiting varieties, Snyder and Harmon (1943) bench grafted a number
of each to uniform St. George rootstocks. At the time the grafts were
planted in the nursery, enough St. George cuttings of the same lot were
planted to produce an equal number of rootings. The next spring, five
bench grafts of each variety were planted in alternate spacing with five
St. George rootings. The rootings were field-budded in the fall with buds
of the same ten scion varieties. During the summer of the next year the
scions of both the bench-grafted and the field-budded vines were trained
for the same system of pruning. The figures in table 18 indicate that

TABLE 18
Comparison of Development of Bench-Grafted and Field-Budded Vines

Measurements	Bench grafted vines	Field-budded vines
Trunk circumference increase, cm., annual (for 5 years)	7.31	7.39
Average weights of pruning, lbs. (for 4 years)	2.85	3.02
Average weight of fruit, lbs. (for 3 years)	5.97	5.01

SOURCE OF DATA: Snyder and Harmon (1943).

Propagation

growth and fruit were essentially the same for the ten varieties. Similar results have been observed in a comparison of field-budded and bench-grafted Cabernet Sauvignon on AxR #1 rootstock. This trial was set out in a two acre non-irrigated site in Napa Valley in 1970. Significant from this study, is that a more complete stand was obtained at the end of the second year where bench-grafts were used. Unpublished data from this trial also indicates that as a result of the more uniform stand early crop production in the planting will be greater with bench grafts.

GRAFTING TO CHANGE VARIETIES

Vines three quarters of an inch or more in diameter may be cleft grafted. Those of large diameter are notch or bark grafted. The vines are sawed off so that about 2 inches of smooth, straight grain is left at the top of the stock, so a straight split will be obtained. If one must saw where the grain of the wood is crooked or curly, as may be the case with vines on resistant stocks, the notch graft should be used.

Vines of fruiting varieties, grafted merely to change the variety, are usually sawed off 2 to 4 inches below the ground level. *When resistant stocks are grafted to a fruiting variety, however, the graft must be put in above the level of the ground.* If the grafting is done below the ground, scion roots will form and the resistant stocks may die. Resistant stocks are, therefore, cut off above ground level. The cuts are the same whether the graft is made below ground, above ground, or higher up on the vine trunk. Either the cleft, notch, or bark graft may be used, depending on the character of the vine trunk where it is cut off and the experience of the grafter.

Cleft grafts.—In cleft grafting the trunk is split to a depth of 1 to 1.5 inches with the broad edge of a special grafting tool; a carpenter's chisel may be used instead, but is less convenient. After the stump is split, the grafting tool is removed and the small end or chisel is placed in the cleft to pry it apart for insertion of the scion.

The scion is cut in wedge form, a little thicker on the side that is to be placed nearest the bark of the stock. The length of the wedge depends on the character and size of the cleft in the stock. The wedge—usually with a long taper—is inserted so that the cambium of the scion coincides with the cambium of the stock (fig. 49C, cuts on scions and scions in place). Since the bark is thicker on the stock than on the scion, the outer surface of the scion will be set in slightly from that of the stock. Although the cambiums of the stock and scion will seldom correspond exactly, the union is satisfactory if they rest very near together or cross in one or two places. Most grafters insert the scions at a slight angle—in at the bottom and out at the top.

The scion should be cut with a sharp knife and inserted in the stock immediately, before even the surface dries. Scions of one or two buds are ordinarily used.

If the vines are an inch or less in diameter, one scion to each vine is sufficient. For larger vines, two scions are preferable whenever both can be made to fit securely. If both grow, the weaker is removed as soon as the growth from the other is tied to the support.

To hold the scions firmly in place, vines less than an inch in diameter should be tied with a few tight wrappings of raffia or string around the top of the stump. Larger vines need not be tied.

Notch grafts.—The notch graft differs from the cleft graft in the shape of the scion and the method of insertion. Instead of being wedge-shaped and inserted in a cleft or split, the scions are shaped to fit into a narrow V-shaped notch on the side of the stock extending from the top of the stump downward for 1.25 to 1.75 inches. The width and depth at the

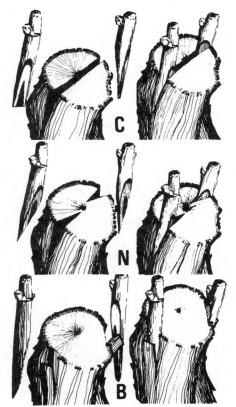

FIGURE 49: C, cleft grafting. At left showing cleft in stock with cut scions; at right scions in place.

N, notch grafting. At left noches in stock with cut scions; at right, scions in place.

B, bark graft. At left bark slit, strip loosened at top and cut scions; at right, scions in place.

(*Agric. Ext. Ser. leaflet, Fresno and Tulare counties*)

top of the notch should be approximately the same as the diameter of the scion to be used (fig. 49N). The notch tapers to a point at the bottom. The scion should be fitted into it so that the cambium layers of scion and stock will, as nearly as possible, coincide.

One can form the notch in the stock most conveniently by first making a saw cut as long and as deep as the notch is to be. Then, with a knife, the notch is widened at the top and tapered to a point at the lower end (fig. 49N, left). When finished, the cut surface should be smooth and straight, for a rough and irregular surface prevents a good fit with the scion. The angle formed by the cut surfaces of the notch should be just wide enough to accommodate the scion.

The scion should be so shaped that when it is placed in the notch, the cambiums of the stock and scion fit together. The angle that the cuts of the scion make with one another may be slightly more obtuse than the angle of the notch. Thus, when the scion is placed on the stock, the contact will be firm at the line of the bark, ensuring close contact of the cambium layers. In figure 49N, right, the scions are in place.

After insertion in the notch, the scion must be held firmly in place until the tissues grow together. When the notch is just wide enough to receive the scion, it will be held firmly. If necessary, it may be held in place by driving in one 1-inch, 19-gauge, flat-headed wire nail through the scion into the trunk.

Bark grafting.—In recent years bark grafting has been employed on large vines, especially when the unions are well above the ground. It requires the least skill. It cannot be done until the bark slips—probably in early May in the interior valleys and later in the cooler areas.

After the vine is sawn off, the rough bark is removed where the scion or scions are to be placed. The bark is slit forming a strip as wide as the diameter of the scion and is peeled back at the top. Then, the scion is prepared by making a straight, slanting cut about 2 inches long. Usually the bud of a one-bud scion or the lower bud of a two-bud scion is opposite the slanting cut (fig. 49B, left). The scion is then inserted under the strip of bark. Some grafters shorten the strip of bark by a half-inch or so. Two one-inch, flat head 19-gauge wire nails are then driven through the scion into the vine trunk to stabilize it until a union is formed (fig. 49B, right).

Covering the grafts at ground level.—As soon as the grafts are finished a stake should be driven close to the vine. The graft is then carefully covered at once with a wide mound of moist, well-pulverized soil. No wax, and no covering other than moist soil, need be used. The soil immediately around the scion should be put in place very carefully, so that the position of the scions will not be disturbed. The scions are completely covered. If the weather is cool and moist and likely to remain so until the scions grow, merely covering them to their tips is sufficient. In the hot, dry weather of the interior valleys, however, scions should be covered 2 or 3 inches deep, so that they may not become even slightly dry. When finished, each graft will be in the middle of a wide mound of soil; narrow mounds do not remain moist enough to ensure growth of the graft.

The mounds must not be disturbed by hoe or cultivator until the unions are well formed. If the scions are completely covered and the mounds form a hard crust, the crust should be broken carefully.

Jacob (1936) and Hartmann and Kester (1968) stress that with grapevine grafts, there is an apparent high oxygen requirement for callus formation; thus, the success with a simple covering of soil of below-ground-level grafts.

Grafts above ground have been used in the San Joaquin Valley with varying degrees of success, for many years. Jensen (1971) using both cleft and notch grafts and Alley (1964) used the three types of grafts as described above, at 3 to 4 feet above ground had a high percentage of success. In each case the grafts were *thoroughly coated with grafting wax and then covered with either whitewash or white latex paint. Proper waxing and, possible rewaxing if cracks develop, plus the white covering to control temperature at the union are necessary.*

The advantage of high level grafting is primarily that of retaining the established trunk of the vine. This saves the time of retraining and permits the cultural operations in the vineyard to proceed as usual. It will also result in normal fruit production earlier, since the growth of the scion or scions is at the level to form the new fruiting surface of the vine.

Suckering grafted vines.—Many large, vigorous shoots may develop from the stock. When the grafts have started to grow vigorously, so that the shoots can be tied to the stake or trellis, it is safe to begin suckering. At this stage the workman can sometimes pull up the suckers by hand without removing any soil. Unless he is sure, however, that they are not entangled with the scion, he must carefully remove some soil and ascertain how to detach them without disturbing the union.

If grafts are slow in starting and the suckers are vigorous, one must remove the suckers before the scion has made much growth. One can do this safely on surface bench grafts only by removing soil and by using extreme care.

Training grafted vines.—When the union is complete, the growth of the grafts on large vines is generally rapid—often an inch a day; many canes grow 15 feet or more by the end of the season. Unless this vigorous growth is properly managed, its benefits are lost and it will cause great trouble during the next year. The shoots are managed in exactly the same manner as those on exceptionally vigorous own-rooted vines. Topping to force growth where it can be used the next year as fruiting wood will usually be desirable.

Other Methods of Grafting and Budding

Although the methods already described are the most widely used for propagating grapevines on resistant rootstocks or replacing missing vines, there are numerous others. Several of these are useful at times. They, like those described, are not new; only minor changes have been made in any of the methods during the past century.

Green-wood grafting.—No method of green-wood or herbaceous grafting is practical in unirrigated vineyards in California. As the name implies, both stock and scion are in an active growing condition when the grafts are made. This method of grafting has been used in New Zealand (Woodfin, 1931), in the San Joaquin Valley of California (Harmon and Snyder, 1952), and in some European countries. It is useful for regrafting field-budded vines when the bud fails. It is, however, somewhat more expensive than budding, owing to the care the stocks require before grafting and the added irrigation.

The vines are irrigated two or three days before grafting and again immediately after. A simple bevel (sloping cut) graft, with the cut 2.5 to 3 times the diameter of the stock, is as good as any other kind and is the easiest and quickest to make. The rootstock vines to be grafted are trained to a single shoot in the spring. This shoot should be about one third of an inch in diameter, and hardened and lignified, but still green, when grafted. The portion of the stock below where it will be grafted should be defoliated and disbudded at least four days before the grafting operation. The wounds thus have time to plug with gum, so that they will not lose water under the root pressure that develops when the top is removed at grafting. The stage of growth of the scion may vary from tender to firm. For ease in handling, lignified scions with green bark and white pith are best. Scions can be cut as needed or kept one or two days in damp, cool packing material. The leaf is removed by cutting the petiole.

In making the graft, a sloping cut 1 to 1.5 inches long is made on the rootstock vines in removing the top. A similar cut is made below the bud of a one-bud scion of the same diameter. The cuts of the stock and scion are immediately placed together and tied firmly by closely wrapping the entire length of the graft with cotton string or strips of grafting rubber. The top of the scion is cut off an inch or so above the bud. Sap exuding from the top of the scion soon after grafting is a good indication that it will grow. Scions that do not exude sap do sometimes grow, but they are less certain to form unions. Stock suckers must be removed.

Harmon (1954), working near Fresno, California, obtained 84 to 98 per cent success with green-wood grafting. The earlier in the spring that the grafting can be done, the greater is the growth of the scion, although good satisfactory unions have been obtained from June up to mid-August.

This method of grafting is not successful in the Sacramento Valley, where desiccating winds occur during the period at which the work should normally be done. Results at Davis were most irregular. A strong, drying wind had destroyed many grafts after they seemed to be established.

Shield budding.—This type of budding, also known as T budding, is commonly used by nurserymen for deciduous fruit trees. It is not so well adapted to grapes, because the buds are much larger and the shield is consequently wide and rigid. The wide, flat back surface of the bud piece does not fit on the round stock on which it is placed; the edges of the bud piece cannot be forced down for contact unless the stock is quite large. The method may be useful, however, on vines that are too large (1 in. or more in diameter) for field budding. Ordinarily, the bark on such large vines is thick and will separate readily from the wood, even in August and September. The gentle curve of the surface of these large stocks makes possible a fairly close fit with the flat back surface of the bud piece, especially if the bud is cut from a cane of comparatively small size.

A bud, with a thin layer of wood, is sliced from a bud stick that is mature, and it is placed beneath the bark of the stock. To remove the bud, start the cut three eighths to one half of an inch below the bud and draw the knife straight upward just beneath the bud to three eights to one half of an inch above the bud; then cut off the shield-shaped bud piece straight across near the top of the first cut. The back side of the bud piece must be smooth and straight. On the stock, make a T-shaped incision through the bark. To insert the bud, peel back the bark on each side of the vertical cut and just below the horizontal cut. The bud piece is then pushed down until it is entirely covered by the bark of the stock, with only the bud projecting through the vertical slit. Tie with budding-rubber strips, beginning at the top and wrapping downward, so that the bud will be held firmly in place. Then cover with a mound of soil, as with chip or field budding. When well matured buds are put on vigorous stocks in August or September, successful union should be obtained. The care of such buds the following spring is the same as that for chip or field buds.

Shield budding may be used on green shoots in early summer if very small buds, such as those from small lateral shoots or seedlings, are used. This type of budding, when done on established vines, is useful for obtaining the rapid multiplication of a rare variety or for obtaining early fruiting of seedlings. The budded shoots are pinched at the time the buds are made, and ten days later the shoot is cut back severely, but some of the mature foliage must be left for shade. About 50 per cent of such buds may be expected to grow, although skilled workers may have success with 80 per cent or more. The earlier the budding can be done, the greater will be the growth that year. Harmon and Snyder (1939) and Snyder and Harmon (1936) stress that heat and drying winds are factors that may markedly affect the percentage that grow.

Layer grafts.—The layer graft, also known as the approach graft, provides a method of replacing missing vines in mature vineyards on resistant rootstocks. A newly planted rootstock vine is grafted into a long cane from an adjacent vine, which nourishes the replant until it becomes large enough to compete successfully with the neighboring mature vines. Although feasible, the technique of layer grafting is almost never used by grape growers.

PROPAGATION BY SEEDS

Vines are propagated by seed for only one purpose—to produce new varieties. Until phylloxera destroyed many of the *vinifera* vines of Europe, most varieties were unplanned. Even before that time, however, some breeding work had been done to develop new varieties. The propagation of the crosses and hybrids resulting from this work naturally involved the use of seeds. The coming of the phylloxera gave impetus to vine breeding because of the need to develop varieties that would resist this insect. Such work gave prominence to the seed as a means of propagating the vine. Thus, seeds have been employed extensively in the introduction of new varieties for both fruit and grafting stocks. A great deal of European experimentation has been aimed toward the breeding of direct producers—that is, varieties whose fruit is suitable for wine making or table use and whose roots resist phylloxera. Nearly all the rootstocks that resist phylloxera (and nematodes) have resulted from the hybridization of American species with other American species or with *vinifera* varieties.

Variability of seedlings.—Seedlings grown from the seed of the same vine can differ greatly from each other. The reason is that the *species* of *Vitis* are quite heterozygous and seedling offspring show wide genetic variability. It is amongst this variability that the plant breeder selects for new varieties. By controlled pollinations and with a high degree of selection, the undesirable segregants are eliminated and the few remaining desirable seedlings can be carried on into field trials for further eliminations. Ultimately, the final few selections with their complex array of desirable characteristics are ready for release as promising new grape varieties.

Variability of seedlings may also result from open-pollination. Each different kind of pollen that happens to fertilize the ovules of a flower will induce variations. Naturally, only one kind of pollen (a single grain from a single variety) can fertilize a single ovule. But, each ovule in a flower may be fertilized by the pollen of a different variety. The variability in seedlings resulting from open-pollination, therefore, may be considerable where different varieties are grown near one another.

Seedlings vary not only in the qualities of their fruit, but in vegetative vigor. The variation in vigor is so great that it is impossible to establish a uniform vineyard by using seedlings. This is as true with seedlings used for rootstocks as with seedlings of fruiting varieties. Because of these unpredictable variations, seeds are not used in propagating vines for vineyard purposes.

BIBLIOGRAPHY

Alley, C. J. 1957. Mechanized grape grafting. Calif. Agr., 11:3, 12.

――――. 1961. Factors affecting the rooting of grape cuttings. II. Growth regulators. Amer. J. Enol. Vitic., 12:185–190.

――――. 1964. Grapevine propagation 1: a comparison of cleft and notch grafting; and bark grafting at high and low levels. Amer. J. Enol. Vitic., 15:214–217.

――――, and L. P. Christensen. 1970. Rooting of 'Thompson Seedless' cuttings. Amer. J. Enol. Vitic., 21:94–100.

Anliker, J., and F. Kobel. 1945. Wuchsstoffversuche mit Rebenveredlungen. Landw. Jahrb. Schweiz, 59:203–248.

Becker, H. 1971. Aspects modernes des techniques de conservation des boutres et des plants et de production des Areffes-soudes. Off. Int. Vignes Vin Bull., 449:223–237.

Bioletti, F. T. 1926. Selection of planting stock for vineyards. Hilgardia, 2:1–23.

Branas, J., G. Brenon, and M. Laporte. 1934. Recherches sur les portegreffes. Prog. Agr. et Vitic., 101:251–257, 284–287.

Calma, V. C., and H. W. Richey, 1931. Growth of Concord grape cuttings in relation to vigor, chemical composition, and relative position on the cane. Proc. Amer. Soc. Hort. Sci., 28:131–136.

Cosmo, I. 1948. Ricerche sulla correlazione tra topofici e precentuale di ripresa della talee di vitigni portinnesti. Ann. Sperim. Agrar. (Rome), 2(3):383–396.

Goheen, A. C., and G. Nyland. 1971. The big break-through: mist propagation. Wines & Vines, 52:25–27.

Harmon, F. N. 1943. Influence of indolebutyric acid on the rooting of grape cuttings. Proc. Amer. Soc. Hort. Sci., 42:383–388.

――――. 1954. A modified procedure for green-wood grafting of *vinifera* grapes. Proc. Amer. Soc. Hort. Sci., 64:255–258.

――――, and E. Snyder. 1939. The "T" bud method; an aid to grape propagation. Proc. Amer. Soc. Hort. Sci., 37:663–665.

————, ————. 1952. Some factors affecting the success of greenwood grafting of grapes. Proc. Amer. Soc. Hort. Sci., 52:294–298.

Hartmann, H. T., and D. E. Kester. 1968. Plant propagation, principles and practices. 2nd ed. Englewood Cliffs, New Jersey, Prentice-Hall. 702 p.

Jacob, H. E. 1932. Stimulation of bench grafts. Proc. Amer. Soc. Hort. Sci., 29:356–358.

————. 1936. Propagation of grapevines. Calif. Agr. Exp. Sta. Cir., 101:18–19.

————. 1944. Vineyard planting stock. Calif. Agr Exp. Sta. Cir., 360:1–12.

Jensen, F. 1971. High level grafting of grapevines. Amer. J. Enol. Vitic., 22: 35–39.

————, M. Bailey, and C. Lynn. 1970. Grafting grapevines. Univ. Calif. Agr. Ext. Ser. Leaflet (Fresno and Tulare Counties). p. 1–27.

Kordes, H. 1937. Bedeutung der Wuchsstoffe für die vegetative Vermehrung der Rebe, ins besondere für di Rebenveredlung. Angew. Bot., 19:543–544.

Priess, F. 1955. Essais de chauffage du sol en pépinières dans le nord-est. Ann. Soc. Nat. Hort., 1:50–52.

Quinn, G. 1931. Influence of season of planting on the rooting of grape vine cuttings. J. Dept. Agr. So., Australia, 35:420–430.

Rives, M. 1961. Bases génétiques de la sélection clonale chez la vigne. Ann. Amélior. Plantes, 11(3):337–348.

Sartorius, O. 1928. Über die wissenschaflichen Grundlagen der Reben-selektion in reinen Beständen. Zeit. Pflanzenzu., 13:79–86.

Snyder, E., and F. N. Harmon. 1936. Hastening the production of fruit in grape hybridizing work. Proc. Amer. Soc. Hort. Sci., 34:426–427.

————, ————. 1941. Time limits of the grape bud-graft method. Proc. Amer. Soc. Hort. Sci., 38:373–374.

————, ————. 1943. Comparison of bench-grafted and field-grafted *vinifera* grape vines. Proc. Amer. Soc. Hort. Sci., 42:389–390.

Stachelin, M. 1954. Quelques considérations sur la maturité et la conservation des bois à greffer. Rev. Rom. Agr. Vitic. Arbor., 10(2):14–15.

Stoutemeyer, V. T., and F. L. O'Rourke. 1943. Spray humidification and the rooting of greenwood cuttings. Amer. Nurs. 77:5–6, 24–25.

Weaver, R. J. 1956. Plant regulators in grape production. Calif. Agr. Exp. Sta. Bull., 752:1–26.

Weinberger, J. H., and N. H. Loomis. 1972. A rapid method for propagating grapevines on rootstocks. Agricultural Research Service, U.S. Dept. of Agriculture, ARS-W-2:1–10.

Wilhelm, A. F., and H. Zillig. 1938. Die Kennzeichen der Holzreife bei Weinreben und Untersuchungen darüber an wichtigen Rebsorten. Gartenbauwiss., 11:413–430.

Winkler, A. J. 1927. Some factors influencing the rooting of vine cuttings. Hilgardia, 2:329–349.

Woodfin, J. C. 1931. Green grafting of the grape vine. New Zealand Jour. Agr., Nov., 356–358.

10

Establishing the Vineyard

Essential to success in any vineyard is a favorable combination of locality, variety of grapes, and proper utilization of the crop. The famous Riesling wines of Germany, the splendid Ohanez grapes of Spain, and the Thompson Seedless raisins of California cannot be easily duplicated in other parts of the world. They are supreme in their respective fields largely because of the varieties and the natural advantages possessed by the regions where they are produced.

CHOICE OF A LOCATION

In chapter 4 the climatic requirements for grape growing are discussed in detail. It may be assumed here that only a region meeting the general requirements is under consideration. One must then make a study of the region in order to choose the district best suited to the *class* of grape to be grown. If one already has a tract of land, study of conditions is required to determine what *type* of grapes can be grown with the greatest likelihood of success. If grapes are already being grown in the district, the necessary information can probably be gained by observing the success of the local industry and the difficulties encountered, and then comparing these with similar observations made in other districts. If new land or a new district is being developed, other means must be found for getting the needed information.

Climatic factors.—Temperatures and exposure are the first consideration. Temperature data, if not known, can be secured best by making a daily record of the maximum and minimum temperatures for each day at the site. The longer these records have been kept for a given place, the more valuable they become. To be reliable, temperature records must cover several years.

The amount, nature, and season of rainfall are important. Some varieties of grapes can be grown in cool regions with 15 inches of water, and occasionally less. The hotter the climate and the shallower the soil, the greater is the water requirement. Late-ripening table grapes in Tulare County in California need 36 inches of water or more each year. Irrigation with good water is an acceptable substitute for rainfall. Hence, where rainfall is deficient, irrigation water of good quality is essential. Grapes of the *vinifera* varieties thrive best if no rain falls between blooming and harvest.

Strong winds are particularly damaging to table grapes, since their appearance is important. Strong winds scar the berries. Appearance of wine and raisin grapes is of less importance. Strong, excessively hot winds such as the sirocco of North Africa, make grape growing impossible in exposed positions. When the irrigation water contains salts, strong winds may cause marginal burn of the leaves with sprinkler irrigation (see p. 486).

Unseasonable frosts are very harmful. Late spring frosts may reduce or destroy the crop, and early fall frosts prevent maturation of the wood. Severe frosts in the early autumn frequently kill above-ground vine parts, particularly in young vines.

Soil conditions.—Factors to be considered are topography, cost of clearing, depth, texture, and composition. In unirrigated vineyards, rolling topography is not objectionable and may be advantageous. The rougher the terrain is, however, the greater the cost of all operations. Land to be irrigated must be well leveled or be adaptable to sprinkler irrigation.

The depth, texture, and composition of the soil affect yields, quality, and cultivating costs. Deep, fertile soils favor heavy crops and lower the costs of production. Such soils should be planted to heavy-yielding varieties in order to utilize both soil and vines to best advantage. Shallower and less fertile soils cannot compete with deep, fertile soils in the production of low-cost grapes, but the less fertile soils often produce grapes of finer quality and should generally be planted to varieties with a potential of higher quality. Deep soils need less frequent irrigation than shallow soils. Avoid alkali soils; the grape vine is only moderately tolerant of salt. (See chapter 17 for injurious soil constituents.)

Other considerations.—The presence of specific vine pests or diseases should be considered. In phylloxera-free regions vines are grown on their own roots. In badly infested regions the fruiting varieties must be grafted onto phylloxera-resistant rootstocks. Nematode-resistant rootstocks will be necessary in sandy soils badly infested with root-knot and other nematodes. When nematodes or oak root fungus are present the soil must be fumigated prior to planting. (See p. 545 and p. 460). It is only good practice to fumigate soils that have been in vineyards prior to replanting them to vines. Fumigation has not proven successful in ridding soil of phylloxera. Most fungus diseases are so widespread that they can hardly be avoided except by choosing a climate unfavorable to them (see chap. 18).

Size of planting.—On the steep, rocky slopes of the middle Moselle district in Germany a vineyard of 2 or 2.5 acres will support a grower and his family and keep them busy. Much of the labor is done by hand, and the product, though not great in quantity, is very valuable. In most grape-growing districts a larger vineyard acreage is required. In California, where hand labor must be held at a minimum and living costs are high, 40 to 160 acres of vines are necessary to support a family. With a minmum acreage, the grower and his family must do all of the work except the harvesting and pruning—aided, of course, by a tractor and other suitable equipment. Beyond the minimum, the size of planting depends on one's finances and ability to work or manage. An average California vineyard represents an investment of some $5,000 per acre, ranging from $3,000 to $9,000. A newly planted vineyard will not come into commercial bearing until the third year in the warm, interior valley areas and the fourth year in the cool, coastal areas. Hence, in addition to the cost of land, planting stocks, and stakes, a grower planting a new vineyard must have at his disposal enough capital to care for the planting for two to three years without returns from the vines. Intercrops among young vines may produce worthwhile returns if irrigation water is ample.

PREPARATION OF THE SOIL

Clearing the land includes the removal of trees, stumps, rocks, and any other obstructions that would interfere with the care of the vineyard, and also the eradication of noxious weeds and rodent pests. Cultivated land that has been well farmed may require little or no clearing. New or virgin, land always requires much labor to prepare it for use.

Weeds and pests.—Cultivated land that has been poorly farmed usually contains noxious weeds. In California the chief noxious weeds are perennial morning-glory, bermuda grass, johnson grass, and puncture vine. Most of the other weeds can be eliminated by clean fallow or by growing a clean cultivated crop before planting the vines. Noxious weeds are eradicated by procedures using chemicals or special methods of cultivation.

Buidweed (*Convolvulus arvensis*) is killed by applying the appropriate hormone weed killers—herbicides—in the years before planting the vines. Bermuda grass (*Cynodon dactylon*) is most easily dealt with by very deep plowing (10 in. or more) when the soil is very dry. The plowed soil should be left rough, so that it will dry out as much as possible. If all the underground stems can be thoroughly dried out, eradication will be complete. Or, both it and johnson grass (*Holcus halepensis*) can be killed with dalapon, and glyphosate. Puncture vine (*Tribulus terrestris*) is most easily overcome by repeated applications of oil sprays (stove distillate) that kill both the plants and the burrs. (See weed control chap. 15).

Worst among the rodent pests are gophers, ground squirrels, and rabbits. These are not often seriously troublesome in land that has been under cultivation, but virgin land may be badly infested. Of these rodents, gophers and squirrels may best be poisoned; rabbits are got rid of by hunting or kept out by fences. A 2-inch netting fence, 2.5 feet high, with the lower edge buried 4 inches in the ground, is effective against rabbits. If poison is used, permission for using it should be obtained from the proper regulatory authority, such as the agricultural commissioner of the county. Rodents are not usually a serious problem in a mature vineyard. Gophers, on occasion, do gnaw on and kill mature vines.

Drainage.—Since vines are deep rooted good drainage is necessary. In rolling lands the slopes are usually drained adequately by natural downflow. The draws and low places can be drained by tiles, or by deep, narrow open ditches if the land is not too valuable and if ditches do not interfere with cultivation and care. Flatlands present greater difficulties. If gravel or porous sand strata underlie level land, it is only necessary to tap these strata by means of open drains, tiles, or even pumps to get rid of the surplus water. Where no gravel or porous sand strata are present, a regular system of tile drains may be necessary, spaced uniformly under the entire vineyard. Minor excesses of salts may be kept down or removed by an effective drainage system. Vineyard soils should be drained to a depth of at least 4 feet in cool climates and 6 feet in hot climates. On many soils judicious irrigation will forestall the need for drainage.

Most unirrigated soils of California do not require drainage. Where seeps occur, they can usually be handled by spot drainage.

Leveling.—Land that is to be irrigated and is of a depth and contour that permits leveling should be leveled before planting. For uniform surface irrigation the land must be flat or gently sloping at a uniform grade in the direction of the water flow. Vineyards planted on steep or irregular slopes must be watered by sprinklers, which will entail more labor unless a solid-set sprinkler system is installed which, in turn, will require more capital than surface irrigation. Careful leveling is of greatest importance in arid regions, where practically all of the needed water is applied artificially. It is of least importance where the rainfall is nearly enough for the needs of the vines. Unirrigated vineyards on gentle slopes should be leveled only where filling the gullies will facilitate cultivation and transport. Where slope grades are more than 10 per cent, terracing is necessary to secure moisture penetration without erosion, whether the land is irrigated or not. Because of the added difficulty of cultivation, the use of such steep slopes may be questioned.

In humid regions, and particularly on shallow soils, no leveling should be done, since the topsoil is the most fertile. If topsoil is removed from the high spots to fill low areas, poor soil is thereby exposed.

Fertilization.—If the soil is reasonable fertile and has been growing good crops of other kinds, fertilization before planting is not needed. If the soil is known to be very poor, the best preparation is to grow a heavy leguminous cover crop (alfalfa, vetch, cowpeas, etc.) the year before planting and to plow it under well in advance of planting the vines. A light application of commercial fertilizer may help the cover crop achieve a good growth to turn under. The nitrogen fixed by the cover crop will become available to the vines as the organic matter decomposes.

New land, especially desert land, will grow a better vineyard if it is farmed to other crops for a few years before being planted to vines. Alfalfa is especially beneficial. The alfalfa must be destroyed before vines are planted.

Preparing the soil.—The depth to which the soil should be broken up depends on its nature and previous treatment. Where it is uniform in texture and not depleted in fertility and has no plow sole, ordinary plowing from 8 to 10 inches deep is adequate. The plowed surface should be smoothed to facilitate laying out the vineyard and planting the vines.

If poor practice has permitted the development of a plow sole or heavy use for cattle has formed a hard layer, subsoiling or deep plowing should be used to break these up. Where the plow sole is not dense enough to interfere with water penetration, it will disappear in a few years if the depth of plowing is changed or if the land is cultivated with other implements.

Subsoiling is not generally done in vineyards. Yet, where the soil lacks uniformity, the subsoiler can be used to good advantage. Hard spots are broken up, water penetration is improved, and vine growth is more vigorous and uniform. The effect, however, may be only temporary.

When the soil is non-uniform in depth, or if water penetration is non-uniform, the irrigation system must be designed to meet these irregularities and the water applied accordingly. If this is not taken into account, the shallow soils will be over irrigated to build up a water table or the deep soils will not be used to their full potential owing to lack of water. The same is true of soils that take water at different rates; those that take it fast will be over-irrigated and the others will not be wet to their entire usable depth.

Trenching has been a common practice in Europe. As has already been said, these soils have been farmed for centuries, and the available nutrients of the subsoil have been partially exhausted. Only nitrogen reaches the subsoil from surface applications. In the trenching operation the fertile surface soil, together with added organic matter or other fertilizers, is placed down in the root zone, and the exhausted subsoil is brought to the surface to be enriched by natural weathering and fertilizer application. Trenching is usually done to a depth of 2 to 3 feet. It would be interesting to know whether results equivalent to trenching could be obtained by injecting a water solution of the needed fertilizer elements deep into the soil through a pipe fastened to the rear edge of the standard of a subsoiler. Trenching is not practiced in California.

PLANNING THE VINEYARD

Where all work is hand labor and natural rainfall is sufficient, the only advantages that a well-arranged vineyard has over one less well planned are uniformity in exposure and nutrition of the vines (plus better appearance, of course). Where power implements and irrigation are used, economical handling demands careful planning.

Values of good planning.—Long rows, uniformly spaced, with adequate turning spaces at the ends, make cultivation easier. Widely spaced vines are cheaper to cultivate than closely planted vines, since larger implements can be used. The planning of irrigated vineyards should take into consideration the uniformity of the soil texture, the uniformity of depth, the slope, and, in regard to water, the available volume, means of distribution, and system of application, so that irrigation may be done so as to wet the usable soil evenly and economically. Light, porous soils can be surface-irrigated most nearly uniformly when the rows are short—about 320 feet—with a moderate slope and a fairly large head of water. Heavier soils may have longer rows; with gentle to nearly flat slope; these can be irrigated well with a smaller flow of water than the lighter soils would need. Distribution of water to various parts of the vineyard demands consideration of the source and volume of the supply.

Vine spacing.—Vine spacing varies greatly in the different grape-growing countries of the world. A number of factors influence spacing, such as temperature, soil fertility, moisture supply, variety, means of cultivation, and the like. In the Champagne region of France vines are planted 3,000 or more to the acre, to ensure full yields in this cool region. Near Almeria, Spain, there are only several hundred vines per acre, owing to the hot climate and scant moisture. Factors such as these have an influence, but not so direct or drastic a one as is sometimes asserted. In general, and especially in the present era of mechanization and restricted labor supply, by far the most important single factor determining vine spacing is cost.

Wide spacing of vines, particularly between the rows, makes for ease and economy of operation. The per acre cost of cultivation, for example, is determined more by the number and length of rows than by the actual acreage in the vineyard. Harvest labor and costs are materially reduced if the grapes can be hauled out from between the rows rather than carried to the avenues by hand. The cost of pruning disposal is nominal if the brush can be disked or shredded, but becomes a considerable item when this material must be carried or hauled away. Power equipment for dusting or spraying can be used only if the rows are far enough apart to let the power machines move through the vineyard. Irrigation is facilitated when there is adequate open space in which to prepare for and manage the flow of water. The initial costs—of vines, planting, stakes, and training—are directly proportional to the number of vines, not the acreage. Generous spacing between the vines within the row will materially improve the efficiency of the operation of row plows. It also overcomes crowding between vines and improves leaf exposure to light.

Almost the only point in favor of close planting is the fact that first few crops are usually larger. This is of only minor importance, however, unless wide spacing is carried to extremes, as spacing trials have demonstrated at both Davis (unpublished data) and Oakville (Winkler, 1959, 1969) in California. Malan (1959) indicates similar results with Alphonse Lavallée and Waltham Cross varieties in South Africa, and Moser (1950) has demonstrated the economy of row spacing of 3 to 3.5 meters (about 10 to 12 ft.) in Austria.

In the past, when minor increases in spacing were tried in the old grape growing countries, the benefits were slight, since most of the hand operations had to be continued. However, Boubals and Pistre (1962) in the south of France showed that a reduction in number of vines from 4,444 per hectare (2.5 acres) to one-half that number still produced as much fruit of equal quality when the fewer vines were trained high instead of the traditional low training of the former. The higher training, no doubt, contributed to the increased yield per vine owing to improved leaf exposure, but the larger soil mass per vine also promoted greater vine capacity for growth and crop. Pavlov and Stoev (1965) state that plant spacing has no effect on grape quality and that regulating the number of retained buds per unit area at pruning is more important than number of plants.

The most desirable spacing, therefore, is the widest that can be had without reducing the crop of the mature vineyard or upsetting normal vineyard operations. For the interior valleys and desert areas of California the generally recommended spacings are 6 by 12 feet and 8 by 12 feet per vine—in a solid planting, these spacings result in 622 and 453 vines per acre. Varieties of moderate growth are planted at the closer spacings; the wider spacing is proper for the vigorous varieties. Most wine grapes of vigorous growth, and practically all table grapes, do well at 8 by 12 feet. At wider spacing than 8 by 12 feet the surface of the usual three-and-four-wire sloping-top trellis is inadequate for carrying the required fruiting wood.

In the cooler coastal areas the recommended spacings are 6 by 12 feet (540 vines per acre) for varieties of moderate growth and 8 by 12 feet (410 vines) for vigorous varieties—when 10 per cent of the area is used for roads and avenues. This spacing is based on the results of spacing trials by Winkler (1969) in the Napa Valley and on vine-thinning trials by Sisson

(1959) in commercial vineyards. In the latter trials, non-irrigated vineyards spaced at 7 by 7 feet were thinned 50 per cent by removing alternate rows on the diagonal. Three years later, they produced as much as they did before. There was definitely no loss in quality from the increased crop of individual vines at the wider spacing. The use of still wider spacing in the coastal areas would lead to more costly supports, as well as to difficulties in the pruning and management of the larger amount of fruiting wood required.

At present, with the very high costs of establishing vineyards, some thought has been given to closer spacing to obtain the benefit of slightly larger crops in the early years of the vineyard: that is, until the root system of the wider spaced vines have completely occupied the soil mass available to them. The spacing in the rows can hardly be reduced without causing crowding and shading between vines which will reduce leaf efficiency. Narrowing the row spacing also has its limits if and when mechanical harvesters are to be used—9 or 10 foot spacing is about the minimum. The higher and modified trellises required for mechanical harvesting (see p. 264) will improve leaf exposure and thereby not only make the closer row spacing more tolerable but also increase production. Beyond this the overhead support (arbor) for Almeria (Ohanez) has proved to be economical. The larger development and retention of permanent wood in this variety favors the larger storage of reserves which leads to the formation of more fruitful buds.

Vigorous vines will fully utilize 100 square feet of soil after they are mature. The first few crops may be less per acre than with closer planting, but the economies effected by the wider spacing in staking, trellising, cultivating, and harvesting during the life of the average vineyard far more than compensate for the few smaller crops when the vines are young. In the light of the experience of growers in California, it seems likely that growers in other countries could profit by spacing their vines farther apart. This would enable them to increase their use of power implements and reduce hand labor.

Spacing American grapes.—In the eastern United States, varieties derived from native American species are generally spaced at 8 by 9 feet or less. On the basis of trials over a ten-year period Shaulis and Kimball (1955) concluded that 8 by 9 feet is the widest spacing at which yields will be maintained. In the state of Washington, Snyder (1951) and Bryant *et al.* (1959) recommended spacings of 8 by 8 feet to 10 by 10 feet, depending on the fertility of the soil, with a general preference for the closer spacing. In California the American grapes are spaced the same as the *vinifera* varieties.

Avenues and roadways.—Large vineyards are always planted in blocks separated by avenues or roadways. The length of the rows across the blocks varies from 300 to 1,000 feet (including an avenue) and may even be longer when sprinkler irrigation is used. When rows are 12 feet apart, avenues paralleling the rows are unnecessary, since the row spacing is sufficient to permit the passage of vineyard implements. Main avenues should be at least 20 feet wide, to allow for turning around. Minor avenues in trellised vineyards are not intended to provide turning spaces, and may be only 16 feet wide. These narrow avenues are crossed in cultivation. Their purpose is to provide easy access to all parts of the vineyard and to facilitate irrigation and harvesting. The distribution systems for irrigation—pipelines or open ditches—should in general conform to the avenue arrangement.

Direction of the rows.—In surface-irrigated vineyards the slope of the land largely determines the direction of the rows. The rows should follow a grade that will permit a suitable flow of water. They may or may not parallel the general slope. If the slope is too steep, the rows may angle across the general slope to secure a more suitable grade.

In raisin vineyards, an east-west direction of the rows facilitates drying the raisins in the vineyard. The grapes are spread on trays between the rows of the vines. The east-west direction allows the direct rays of the sun to strike the drying grapes throughout the day. If the rows run from north to south, the vines will shade the trays during much of the day. Raisins, therefore, will dry appreciably faster between east-west rows than between north-south rows.

In trellised vineyards of early table grapes in California, sunburn could be lessened by running the rows northeast to southwest. For late table grapes the reverse might be true. Sunburn usually occurs during the early and middle afternoon. If the rows run northeast to southwest, the sun's rays will strike the tops of the vines at this time and the fruit will be protected. However, because of base survey lines, the rows usually run in an east-west or north-south direction in California.

The type of support is a factor in reducing sunburn. The single wire trellis used widely for raisin and wine grapes exposes much of the fruit directly to the sun after the shoots assume a drooping position; hence when conditions are right for sunburn, the fruit may burn. Even a 2-wire vertical trellis offers more protection, especially when the fruiting wood is on the lower wire. Better protection has been provided by the 2-wire, wide-top trellis with a third wire below to support the fruit canes. The higher and modified trellises that are being developed for mechanical harvesting should provide even greater protection from sunburn. (See p. 264.)

LAYING OUT THE VINEYARD

When the site has been chosen and prepared, the laying-out of the vineyard is begun by determining the base lines. Then measuring lines are prepared, and are used in locating the desired positions of the rows and vines.

Base lines.—Base lines are straight lines in two directions from which all measurements are made in placing the vines. One base line must parallel the rows, and the other must parallel the line formed by the first vine in each row. Base lines at right angles to each other are common and convenient, but are not essential. On most tracts of land the boundaries may be used as base lines if they are already located and are straight lines, or the first row and the line of the first vine in each of the rows may be used as base lines for the remainder. Base lines should be located accurately, for the regularity of the planting depends largely on the accuracy of the base lines and the care used in working from them. In large plantings the base lines for each block, and at least the corner stakes marking the ends of these lines, should be located with surveying instruments. In plantings of 40 acres or less the work can be done accurately enough by measuring with a steel tape or well-made planting lines.

Planting lines.—Two special measuring chains or lines are almost indispensable in the economical laying out of a vineyard. Any grower can make his own lines. One of these lines has buttons or other markings on it spaced accurately according to the distance between rows. This may be called the *row line.* The other line, the *planting line,* is accurately marked according to the distance between the vines in the row. Of the two, the row line is by far the more important with which to be accurate. Appearance may be important in both cases, but a few inches error within the row spacing really means little, while a few inches out of line in the row may cause considerable trouble in cultivation and perhaps in mechanical harvesting. Ordinary smooth galvanized wire of No. 11 gauge is satisfactory for these lines. To make a line, first stretch out a considerable length of the wire, 100 feet or more, then lay a taut 100-foot steel measuring tape alongside the wire. At the proper points on the wire, set on buttons of solder about three eighths of an inch to a half inch in diameter. A small piece of wood having a depresssion in it is convenient to use as a mold for forming the solder buttons. Wetting the wire where the button is to be formed with hydrochloric (muriatic) acid or with acidified zinc chloride, such as is used by tinsmiths, causes the solder to fuse onto the wire so that the buttons will not slip. A 3-inch harness ring at each end of the line makes it convenient to handle in the field.

If it is desired, the vines may be planted to the planting line without first pegging each row. This, however, usually proves to be false economy. It usually results in crooked rows through accidental moving of the line in planting the vines. Furthermore, the pegs are needed as markers to facilitate cultivation before the vines have grown enough to be readily visible.

Sometimes the permanent stakes or trellises are put in before the vines are planted. This is advisable in very hot regions, where the vines can often be trained the first season. Where this is done, permanent stakes instead of marker pegs are driven at the buttons.

When sprinkler irrigation is to be used, the stakes supporting the risers must be set prior to planting. This is imperative when one-bud, potted, mist-propagated vines are planted. Beyond this, the time of placing the permanent stakes is open to discussion. With present high costs, delaying of the capital investment for permanent stakes is a minor item. Especially so, when consideration is given to the greater protection the stakes provide for the vines during year *one* and to the more nearly perfect stand obtained. They must be in place for training the vines in the second year.

CHOICE OF VARIETY, PLANTING STOCK, AND PLANTING

It is necessary to consider the grape variety along with the climate, soil, and other factors. Of course, everyone wants to grow the grapes that sell to best advantage. It is much more important, however, that the variety be suited to the location, or vice versa. Demand may change, and so may supply; and price will change with demand and supply. In general, these temporary market conditions should be discounted in favor of the more permanent condition of suitability of variety to the environment; the kind of grapes to grow is usually the kind that does best in the particular locality. In the older grape-growing regions of the world, varieties have become highly localized, and in some of these the varieties that may be planted are restricted by law. Experience has furnished the information as to which are best. In new districts—and most parts of California are still comparatively new with regard to experience in grape growing—the list of varieties grown is usually longer than in those where the vine has long been cultivated. The prospective planter will do well to study carefully the behavior of all the varieties being grown locally, and should consult his Farm Advisor in order to be able to make the wisest choice. At all times, however, he should keep in mind that heavily-producing hot regions and fertile, deep soils should be planted with heavy-yielding varieties, and that cool regions with less fertile soils, which are incapable of producing large yields but do produce grapes of high quality, should be planted with fine varieties. In heavily-producing regions of the hot interior valleys the fruit of the fine varieties may be of only mediocre quality.

Rootings, grafts, potted vines, or unrooted cuttings may be used according to circumstances. Rootings are cuttings that have grown for one year in the nursery. They may be of the desired fruiting variety, or of the root-stock variety if they are to be grafted later. Rootings of the desired fruiting variety should always be used unless special rootstocks are required because of phylloxera, nematodes, or other conditions. Only good rootings are worthy of planting.

Grafts or rootings of a suitable resistant-rootstock variety should always be used in phylloxera-infested territory. Grafts or rootings of nematode-resistant rootstocks are necessary in soils heavily infested with nematodes.

Some varieties may occasionally give better results under certain conditions when grafted onto suitable stocks (Gladwin, 1932). (For the production handling of potted vines, rootings, and grafts see chap. 9.)

Unrooted cuttings should be used only when rootings of the desired variety cannot be obtained and it is known that cuttings of the variety strike root readily. The planting of unrooted cuttings is always hazardous, usually resulting in poor stands. If good rootings or grafts are well planted in good soil, the stand should always be better than 95 per cent. Stands from unrooted cuttings, except when the planting is handled as carefully as in a nursery, will not average more than 85 per cent, and will often be less than 60 per cent. The replanting made necessary through the use of unrooted cuttings is expensive and will result in an uneven vineyard. Second-year vines seldom catch up with those of the first-year planting.

Disease-free planting stock.—A number of virus diseases of grapevines are found in California vineyards as in most grape-growing areas of the world (Hewitt, 1954). Some of these kill the vines within a few years; others bring about gradual decline, reducing production and shortening the life of the vineyard. These viruses are transmitted in the propagating wood —buds, cuttings, rootings, or grafts. The most effective control is to avoid propagating or planting infected materials. When a new planting is contemplated, the propagating wood—buds, cuttings, rootings, or rootstocks— should, by all means, be certified to be free of viruses and true to variety.

Planting the vineyard.—The rootings, or grafted vines, are pruned before planting; the tops are cut back to a single good spur of one or two buds. For convenience in planting, the roots are usually shortened to 3 or 4 inches (fig. 50) for holes that are dug or made with a power-driven auger, and to about 1 inch for holes made with hydraulic pressure or when planted by machine.

L. A. Lider and J. A. Cook (unpublished data, 1966) pruned away the roots of vines as dug with a nursery digger, so that the retained roots were ½, 4, and 6 inches in length. The tops were uniformly cut back to 1 spur of 2 buds. Using the growth of the rootings of Chenin blanc vines with 6-inch roots as the basis of comparison, it was found that cutting the roots to 4 inches reduced total growth 22 per cent and that cutting them to ½ inch reduced growth 32 per cent during the first season. Very similar results were obtained in the above ground growth of St. George rootstock rootings, when the rootings were pruned to the same degree. Von Kiefer and Hofmann (1970), who pruned the top growth of vines on resistant rootstocks to 1 spur with 1 bud and the roots to three lengths (0.079, 0.79, and 1.97 inches), found that the plants with very short and medium length roots made 64 and 32 per cent, respectively, less top growth than the lot with 1.97 inch roots during the first two seasons. Martin and Georgescio (1968), who pruned to 3 different lengths of both top and roots—that is, short tops and short roots, medium tops and medium roots, etc.—obtained results very similar to the above. (They state that the short pruning as compared to the medium and long pruning delayed production by at least one year.) These trials definitely indicate that retaining more roots on the rootings at planting favors more rapid vine development during the first year or years in the vineyard. This probably results from the smaller removal of stored carbohydrates in the rootings with the longer roots, the greater number of new roots that develop, and the larger, early contact between roots and soil. The economy of handling these rootings, which require a larger hole for planting, is, as yet, undetermined.

All roots within 8 inches of the top of the pruned vines are removed entirely. While the vines are being prepared for planting, all poor or defective ones should be discarded. It is questionable whether these discards

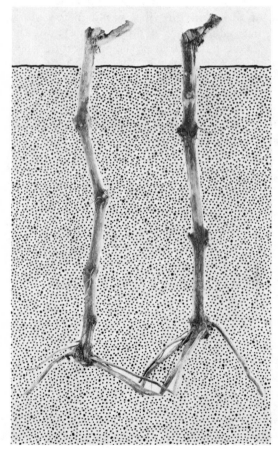

FIGURE 50: One-year-old rooted vines pruned for planting. The dotted area shows the approximate planting depth.

should be placed in a nursery to provide replants for the next season. Tests have shown that two- and three-year-old rootings suffer greater mortality in transplanting than do one-year-old rootings (Capucci, 1939). The vines must be carefully protected from drying out in all handling operations— from their removal from the nursery to their planting in the vineyard. When planting in well-drained soils, it is good practice to move the vines directly from the nursery to their permanent places in the vineyard. If the rootings are stored, they should be heeled-in (partially or completely buried) in moist sand or soil in a cool place. While being moved from the nursery or storage place in the vineyard they must be well covered with moist sacks or canvas, or, better still, hauled in tubs containing 2 or 3 inches of water. The planters carry the vines in picking buckets or planting cans (often made from five-gallon paint buckets or oil cans). Two or three inches of water in the planting cans will keep the roots wet. The holes for the vines are all dug on the same side of the planting pegs or stakes in the row, and are so dug that the side or corner of the hole slopes away from the peg and at the bottom is 2 to 4 inches distant from it, but in the line of the row. The hole should be slightly deeper than the vine is long. The vine is dropped into the hole with the top close to the peg. Then the hole partly filled—one half or two thirds of its depth—with moist topsoil; the vine is raised to the proper height and held against the peg or stake while the *soil is solidly packed* about the roots; next, the hole is filled almost completely, and again the soil is packed firmly; then the hole is completely filled and the top of the vine is covered, leaving the soil over the top well

FIGURE 51: A newly planted wine grape vineyard in region II.

pulverized yet loose (fig. 51). Vines planted in holes made by hydraulic means are also covered.

When the work is completed, the top of the vine should be exactly at the side of the peg or stake, and the roots 2 to 4 inches away. All vines must be on the *same* side of the peg or stake, so that the permanent stakes, if not put in before planting, may be placed close to the vine on the side toward which the top slants without danger of breaking the vine.

Rootings of the fruiting varieties are planted so that the two buds left after pruning are just above the general level of the ground on flat land, but in contour planting they should be 2 to 5 inches above, depending on the slope. Bench-grafted vines are planted with the union 2 or 3 inches above ground level. Rootstock rootings that are to be budded or grafted in the field should have 4 or 5 inches of the main stem above the ground level, so that the bud or graft union will be above the surface of the soil, thus preventing the development of scion roots. The tops of all are covered a half inch to two inches deep with a mound of loose soil to prevent drying before growth starts.

Greenhouse potted vines.—In the rapid multiplication of own rooted vines certified to be free of known viruses the plants are delivered to the grower in 4-inch plastic pots (see chapter 9, p. 202). These vines should be planted at the bottom of a wide hole or preferably in a lister furrow, in the position of the vine row, *so the root crown will be 6 to 8 inches below the surface of the soil.* Unless this is done, the roots may be injured, by row plows or by chemicals used in weed control under the vine rows, in future years. The stakes should be in place and the growing shoot tied to keep the future below ground trunk of the vine in the desired position. As the vines grow and mature their wood, the soil is worked back around them to fill the furrow by years end.

BIBLIOGRAPHY

Boubals, D., and R. Pistre. 1962. Resultats d'essais de vignes hauts a grand écartement obtenus dans l'Aude. Prog. Agric. Vitic., 157:280–284.

Bryant, L. R., W. T. Clore, and C. G. Woodbridge. 1959. Factors affecting yield of Concord grapes and petiole composition in some vineyards in the Yakima Valley. Proc. Amer. Soc. Hort. Sci., 73:151–155.

Capucci, C. 1939. Alcuni fattori che influis cono sullo sviluppo delle viti durante il primo anno vegetazione a dimora. Riv. Frutticoltura, 3:249–270.

Gladwin, F. E. 1932. Grafting American grapes on vigorous stocks. New York Agr. Exp. Sta. Bull., 607:1–28.

Hewitt, W. B. 1954. Some virus and virus-like diseases of grapevines. Bull. Calif. State Dept. Agri., 43:43–64.

Kiefer, von, W., and E. L. Hofmann. 1970. Untersuchung über verschiedene Methoden beim Pflanzen von Pfropfreben. Weinberg Keller, 17:267–299.

Malan, A. H. 1959. Wider espacement of table grapes advisable. Fm. So. Africa, 35:19–26.

Martin, T., and M. Georgescio. 1968. The influence of the degree of pruning of one- and two-year-old rooted vines on their rate of development with a view to early bearing. Lucari Sliintifice (Bucharest) Ser. B, 11:253–261.

Moser, Lenz. 1950. Weinbau, einmal anders. Krems, Austria, Joseph Faber.

Pavlov, N., and K. Stoev. 1965. The influence of planting density of Gamza vines. (Bulg. with French and Russian sum.). Grad. Lazar. Nauka, 2:81–101.

Shaulis, N., and K. Kimball. 1955. Effect of spacing on growth and yield of Concord grapes. Proc. Amer. Soc. Hort. Sci., 66:192–200.

Sisson, R. L. 1959. Yield and quality response of some respaced North Coast vineyards. Amer. J. Enol. Vitic., 10(1):44–47.

Snyder, J. C. 1951. Growing grapes in Washington. State College of Washington, Ext. Bull., 271:1–34.

Winkler, A. J. 1959. The effect of vine spacing at Oakville on yield, fruit composition, and wine quality. Amer. J. Enol. Vitic., 10(1):39–43.

———. 1969. Effect of vine spacing in an unirrigated vineyard on vine physiology, production and wine quality. Amer. J. Enol. Vitic., 20:7–15.

II

Supports for Vines

Grapevines cannot be grown satisfactorily without some form of support. Until the early 1920's some vineyards in California were still being developed without supports, but the extra costs involved in labor, delayed bearing, and operating a vineyard of poorly formed vines were greater than the expense of suitable stakes or trellises. Moreover, greater skill and experience were required.

The supports needed are of two kinds, short-time and permanent. Both kinds make it possible to obtain, quickly and economically, a well-formed vine with a strong, straight trunk, a vine that does not interfere with cultivation and other vineyard operations, and that is free of the defects and large wounds that diminish vigor and longevity. Short-time supports, used with head-pruned vines, provide support until the vines are large and rigid enough to stand alone—six to ten years, depending on the variety, height of head, and region of production. Permanent supports, in the form of trellises, are required for economic and consistent performance by vines that are either cane-pruned or cordon-trained.

With an industry as old and extensive as grape growing, it is not surprising that greatly varied forms of supports have been devised and used. The most practical forms, however, may be classified into four groups: stakes, vertical trellises, wide-top trellises, and arbors. Except where local conditions, such as available materials, frosts, or methods of harvesting, demand special consideration, one or the other of the forms described here may be used. Each has been throughly proved in use. They are suited to nearly all the varieties and conditions of the grape-growing districts in California, and they do the job with less expense than any other types tried or widely used.

Supports for Vines

In choosing a system of support for a California vineyard several factors must be considered. The variety is of greatest importance because of its fruiting habit which determines, to a degree, the kind of bearing units (spurs or canes) required; its size of cluster which may require extra spread; and its vigor which may require added height or width to provide adequate leaf exposure (Winkler, 1945). The method of harvesting—hand or by machine—must also be given high priority. Shaulis *et al.* (1953) showed that both the height and spread of the support influence vine size and yields of Concord grapes. Similar results have been obtained in our state and Australia. The economic advantages of machine harvesting have made it a determining factor in the choice of the support for wine and raisin grapes.

SUPPORTS FOR VARIETIES REQUIRING HEAD-TRAINING AND CANE-PRUNING

Cane-pruned vines require permanent supports for the annually renewed fruit canes. The most generally used permanent support is the trellis. Its construction varies with the purpose for which the fruit is grown. For example, for raisin and wine grapes, in which the appearance of the fresh fruit is of minor importance, a simple 1- or 2-wire trellis is usually employed, whereas for table grapes, whose appearance is of great importance, a multiple-wire wide-top trellis is preferable.

In years past, the support for the Thompson Seedless variety, *for raisin production*, was the simple 2-wire trellis (fig. 52). It consisted of a 2-inch-

FIGURE 52: A two-wire trellis for cane-pruned vines.

by-2-inch stake, 6 feet in length, placed at each vine, with two No. 11 or No. 12 smooth galvanized wires stretched along the row at 34 and 48 inches above the ground. The wires were held taut by 4-inch-by-5-inch split redwood posts or reinforced concrete posts, 8 feet in length, firmly set 4 feet deep at the ends of the rows.

When this trellis was first introduced, the fruit canes were placed or tied on the lower wire, and the upper wire served as a support for the shoots as they developed in the spring. All of the fruit was placed at the same level, which made for uniform exposure, and the shoots on the support above the fruit provided some protection under severe conditions of wind and temperature. The advantage of uniform exposure of the fruit, however, did not offset the inconvenience of harvesting the fruit from the level of and below the lower wire; consequently, many growers place the fruit canes on both wires, and more recently it has become common practice to place them on only the upper wire. The shift to placing all canes on the upper wire was speeded by the fact that when canes were placed on both wires, those on the lower wire were densely shaded and their productivity was markedly reduced. Besides, the placing of all the canes on the upper wire lifted the fruit to where it could be harvested more conveniently, with only slightly less uniform exposure. Thus, at present many Thompson Seedless vines, if the fruit is grown for the production of raisins or wine, are commonly supported on a single-wire trellis at the height of 48 inches. This trellis is constructed like that described above, except that the lower wire is omitted. To simplify maintenance of the shape of the vines, they should be headed just below the wire.

If a Thompson Seedless raisin vineyard is making unusual growth, its capacity for production will be better utilized by replacing the upper wire of the 2-wire trellis with a horizontal cross arm of 24 to 30 inches, with a wire at each end. The fruit canes are spread by tying them to the wires on the cross arm, one or more in each direction. The foliage is also spread and affords better leaf exposure to light. This type of support not only facilitates hand harvesting but also provides the possibility of machine harvesting when the cross arm is semi-flexible. It is adapted for the vertical impacter type machine. When the crop is to be machine harvested, the few clusters that form in the head of vines should be removed by flower cluster thinning.

A number of *wine grape varieties* that produce very small clusters, such as Cabernet-Sauvignon, Pinot noir, White Riesling, and Sauvignon blanc, are cane-pruned in order to obtain normal crops. In sites where vigor is low these varieties are usually supported by a single-wire trellis. In this case the wire is likely to be somewhat lower; nevertheless, it should be high enough (36 to 42 in.) for easy harvesting and pruning. In windy areas a 2-wire trellis is preferable for these wine varieties; the canes are then

Supports for Vines

placed on the lower wire, and the upper wire reduces wind breakage of the shoots. Where high vegetative vigor is anticipated, the use of a foliage supporting cross arm can be advantageous to increase production. However, the height and length of the cross arm must be considered carefully if mechanical harvesting is to be used.

In some older unirrigated vineyards, where yields are only moderate, some varieties requiring cane pruning are supported with stakes. The canes are arched over the top of the vine and tied to the stake at their middle. They are bent down and tied in the case of high-headed vines, or are simply taken up along the stake and tied. These methods however, are defective, since they tend to mass the fruit together; fruit ripening is irregular and, unless the canes are tied down, maintaining of the shape of the vine is difficult. Except where the canes are tied down, the best growth is at the tip part of the erect canes and on the high part of the bowed canes, and the growth below is weakened by shading.

HEAD-TRAINED AND CANE-PRUNED TABLE GRAPE VARIETIES

Table grape varieties are supported most satisfactorily with a sloping wide-top trellis. This trellis was introduced in 1930 to the growers of Emperor, a cordon-trained, spur-pruned variety, by W. E. Gilfillan, farm adviser of Tulare County. It also provides an ample surface for tying the canes of cane-pruned varieties singly on the wires and thereby spreading the

FIGURE 53: Four-wire sloping-top trellis for cane-pruned vines.

clusters to ensure exposure. The clusters hang free below the wires and the leaves furnish an even covering over the top of the trellis.

This type of trellis is begun by placing at each vine a 2-inch-by-2-inch grape-stake 6 or 7 feet in length. Then a crossarm (2 in. by 2 in. by 3.5 ft.) is tied near the top of each stake, for vine spaces farther than 6 feet apart, and is braced at a slope of about 30° from the horizontal. The short, lower part of the crossarm is about 12 inches long, and the upper part 30 inches. In placing the crossarm, a single nail may be driven through it into the stake; then, with the crossarm in a horizontal position, a wire is taken over the long part, around the stake, and under the short part, and its ends are twisted together until the wire is snugly taut. The tie becomes very tight as the long part of the crossarm is raised to the desired angle. This type of tie prevents the wind from lifting the trellis. A wire or metal brace from the stake to the short end of the crossarm maintains the desired slope. Four No. 12 wires are spaced equally on the upper side of the crossarm and held in place by one-and-a-quarter-inch staples. The wires are held taut by firmly set posts at the ends of the row (fig. 53); these measure 4 inches by 5 inches by eight feet.

FIGURE 54: A two-story trellis for table grapes. It provides more uniform shade for the fruit and a greater expanse of the leaf surface. (*Courtesy of H. B. Richardson*)

Supports for Vines

The head of the vine should be just below the wire nearest the stake. The fruit canes are tied on the two middle wires, equally divided in each direction along the trellis. This arrangement brings most of the clusters between the top and bottom wires of the trellis. With this type of support and fruit distribution, it is easy to get at the canes for girdling and at the clusters for thinning and harvesting.

About 1950, in the vineyards of the southern San Joaquin Valley a second crossarm with three wires was added to trellises of the above type. The second crossarm is usually 12 to 15 inches above the first. This variation and also a two-story, flat-top, 6-wire trellis (fig. 54) are now being used quite extensively for both cane- and cordon-pruned vines. When the vines are spaced 8 feet or more in the row, there should be a lower and upper crossarm at each vine. The crossarms are attached and held in position in the same way as for the sloping-top trellis. These trellises provide a better exposure of the fruit to light than those discussed above while still shading it adequately, and give greater expanse to the leaf surface of the vines. The data available indicate a small increase in yield with this two-story trellis.

SUPPORTS FOR CORDON-TRAINED AND SPUR-PRUNED VARIETIES

The varieties trained to cordons require permanent supports. Cordons more than 2 feet long rarely become rigid enough to remain horizontal without some support.

For *wine grapes* that are cordon-trained, the usual support is the 2-wire trellis (fig. 55). The cordon is placed on the lower wire; the upper wire protects the shoots against wind damage and, of equal or greater importance, provides a place to tie shoots in the early life of the vineyard, so as to prevent the cordon from turning over under the weight of its shoots and their fruit (see p. 283) and provides some protection from sunburn.

Sometimes the top wire of the 2-wire trellis is replaced by a horizontal crossarm of 24 to 36 inches, with a wire near each end. This type of trellis keeps the shoots upright until they have grown above and between the upper wires, and thereby offers more protection to the fruit. It does not materially ease hand harvest, however, since the shoots bend down over the wire in early summer and the picker must work through them. Also, since the shoots are semiupright toward the wire, the fruit must be harvested from between them, but this added difficulty can usually be eased by picking from both sides of the row.

The same type of flat-top trellis, with somewhat longer crossarms (30 to 42 in.), is also commonly used for *table grapes* (fig. 56). In this case a

FIGURE 55: A two-wire trellis for cordon-trained, spur-pruned vines. (*Courtesy of A. N. Kasimatis*)

stake 7 feet long is desirable, so as to elevate the fruiting surface of the vine and thereby facilitate getting at the fruit clusters for thinning and harvesting, these operations being done from both sides of the row.

Cordon-trained, spur-trained table grapes may also be supported by a sloping wide-top trellis. This trellis differs from that described for cane-pruned table grape varieties only in that one wire is dropped down to support the cordons—thus leaving three wires, equally spaced, on the sloping crossarm. The supporting wire is attached to the stake at 12 to 14 inches below the crossarm. Such a trellis, like that in figure 53, spreads the clusters effectively for easy access in thinning and harvesting. The fruit is uniformly exposed to the light, the even covering of leaves on top of the trellis provides protection from abnormally high temperatures, and the thinning and harvesting operations may be done from one side.

SUPPORTS FOR HEAD-TRAINED, SPUR-PRUNED VARIETIES

New planting of vines head-trained and spur-pruned with a single stake at each vine, are rare in California in spite of their several advantages (see chapter 13 p. 328). This system is the most depressing on vine capac-

Supports for Vines

FIGURE 56: Three-wire flat-top trellis for cordon-trained, spur-pruned vines. (*Courtesy of A. N. Kasimatis*)

ity. Even with modern irrigation and fertilizer practices, growers have found it disappointing in both growth and yields. Then, too, the vines so trained can not be efficiently harvested by machine.

Head-trained vines require short-time supports. When they have developed a stout, straight trunk 3 to 4 inches in diameter, they stand alone. The higher the head, the thicker the trunk must be before the vine will safely stand alone. The less vigorous the variety and the less favorable the soil and the climate, the longer must artificial support be provided.

The usual support for head-trained vines consists of two-inch-by-two-inch-sawed pine or fir or split Coast Redwood stakes from 4 to 6 feet in length, one stake to each vine (fig. 57). The stakes are placed at the buttons on the vine-planting line when the vineyard is laid out, and are set up beside the vines in the holes for planting when these are made with a mechanical auger, or they are later driven into the holes occupied by the pegs to which the vines were set—this staking being done during the first winter after the vineyard is planted. The shorter stakes are driven 12 to 18 inches into the ground, and the longer 15 to 22 inches, depending on the firmness of the soil.

FIGURE 57: Support for head-trained, spur-pruned vines.

BROAD-TOP SLOPING TRELLIS

Although broad-top sloping trellises have been used extensively abroad, their use in California is still very limited. In much of Italy, various forms of such trellises are used. One of these is shown in figure 11. In South Africa, Le Roux (1957, 1960) and Malan (1953) indicated that table grapes are commonly supported by a trellis 6 feet wide or more (fig. 58A). The only form of this trellis now used in California was developed by Ray van Buskirk, of Lodi. He takes two long grape-stakes (7 to 8 ft.) and forms a hip support over the middle between two rows of vines (fig. 58B). In this trellis the west or south slope, according to the direction of the rows, is used to support the bearing wood, shoots, and fruit, and the other slope is left open to provide better light. If most of the slope on one side of the trellis is to be used for fruiting wood, the high point of the hip should be not more than 7 feet. The hip pieces are attached to the regular grape stakes in the vine row at about 4 feet from the ground. Large nails and taut wire ties hold the trellis pieces together and in position. Four or more wires, equally spaced, are strung on the side carrying the crop, and two near the base on the other side.

FIGURE 58: "Y"-type trellis for table grapes: A, in South Africa; B, on Tokay vines in California. (*Courtesy of K. E. Nelson*)

ARBORS AND PERGOLAS

An arbor is a structure on which the vines are trained overhead on a crosspiece supported at both ends. A pergola is a similar, but narrower, structure on which vines are trained overhead, usually in a garden or about a dwelling. The construction in either case is like that of a high, flat, wide-top trellis, except that more wires are used on the top.

The structural details of arbors are variable. Arbors must be high enough (usually 6.5 to 7 ft.) not to interfere seriously with the necessary vineyards operations. They must be strong and rigid enough to carry the load of foliage and fruit and withstand the rocking effect of strong winds. A structure such as illustrated in figure 59 represents one of the cheapest satisfactory types.

In commercial vineyards, arbors are used only when other types of support do not permit the vines to grow to sufficient size. In California the Almeria (Ohanez) variety is the only one for which arbors are used extensively. This variety, it seems, must be allowed to develop very large vines, to accommodate a large storage of reserve materials, in order to produce large crops of good-quality table grapes.

The limited use of over-head supports in California is due principally to their high cost of installation and maintenance. Vine management also is more complicated when fruit and growth are supported 6.5 to 7 feet above the ground. It is becoming increasingly difficult to find labor to do the tedious over-head hand work involved. Recent reports (personal communication) indicate that the over-head support—parral—in Argentina is also losing favor. Furthermore, with vines which grow quite vigorously, the dense, horizontal canopy of foliage which often develops on these

Figure 59: An arbor covering two rows.

over-head arbors can interfere with the activity of leaves deep in the canopy and the heavy shade cover can complicate fungus disease control on the fruit as it matures.

Most of the recently constructed arbors extend across one middle—the space between two rows and from 2 to 3 feet over the adjacent middles (fig. 59). This leaves an open strip of 6 to 8 feet in every other middle. The added exposure so provided is believed to improve the coloring of the fruit. The uprights and cross supports are of any appropriate wood; the top that carries the fruiting wood and shoots consists of wires spaced 12 inches apart.

Supports for American Vines

In the eastern United States and in the state of Washington the vines of American varieties and hybrids are supported by vertical and wide-top trellises. Examples of these are briefly discussed and illustrated in chapter 13, p. 329 to 332. The Geneva double curtain system of support has brought about both improved fruit maturity and higher yields which tend to offset the added costs.

Supports for Vines to be Harvested by Machine

Mechanization of the harvest of wine and raisin grapes is rapidly being accepted by industry. During the 1972 harvest, in California alone, more than 113 machines were operating.

Just 20 years ago experiments were initiated by Winkler (unpublished report to American Society of Agricultural Engineers) to position the fruiting wood of a number of varieties for machine harvesting. The first trellis was an inverted L shape with 4 wires on the underside of the long portion of the crossarm. The clusters, after fruit-set, were disengaged from the shoots and wires so they would hang free. Winkler and Lamouria (1956) had a cutter-bar type machine operating in 1954. Improvement were made each year in the design of the harvester until the mid-1960's, when it became evident that stem length was an unsurmountable limiting factor. Many clusters were cut through with the basal part remaining on the vine. At that time, the direction of development was shifted by Olmo *et al.* (1968) to the vibratory or impactor type machine which offered greater promise and with less hand labor. Progress with this type of machine has been most satisfactory with raisin grapes when the harvest was preceeded by cane cutting (see p. 625), and with minor changes in machine design the harvest of wine grapes is improving.

In the meantime extensive work had been done by Shepardson *et al.* (1962) on a similar type harvester in the eastern part of the United States. Their problem was less difficult owing to the brittle stems of the Concord and its natural tendency to form an abscission layer at the attachment of the berries. The perfect support to position these grapes for machine harvesting was developed by Shaulis *et al.* (1966)—the Geneva double curtain trellis. With this support the vines are trained to a bilateral cordon and short-cane pruned. The cordons are tied to trellis wires which are supported on 4 foot crossarms at 5.5 to 6 feet above the ground. As shown in figure 87, p. 332, the vines have two or more trunks which make for flexibility. The cordons are tied in opposite directions on one of the wires. At present over 90 per cent of the grapes of this, their principal variety, there and in the state of Washington are harvested by machine.

Wide-top support.—Olmo *et al.* (1968) proposed a wide-top trellis, somewhat similar to the Geneva double curtain, for California vineyards. It consists of two wires supported on a 3 to 4 foot semi-rigid crossarm (fig. 60). They suggested cane-pruning, with the fruit canes being attached to the two wires, while the shoots arising from the head of the vine produce canes for the following year. They called this support the "Duplex system." The fruit of the canes on the wires was to be harvested by a vertical impactor machine. But this left the fruit in the head of the vine to be forgotten, to be harvested by hand, or to be removed as flower clusters or as clusters soon after set. In either case, the cost of establishing such a trellis and the expense of retraining mature vines for it, together with the hand work involved in de-florating and suckering the head of the vine, has discouraged grower acceptance.

A possible way to utilize this trellis would require that the vines have

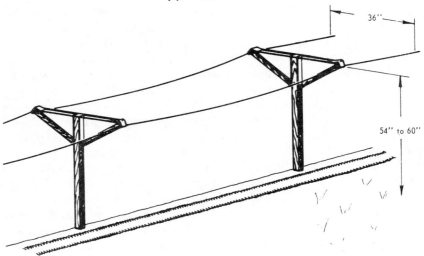

FIGURE 60: "Duplex" system of vine support with flexible crossarm for machine harvesting. (*From Olmo* et al., *1968*)

multiple trunks which would be flexible for a number of years. Then the fruiting wood tied to the wire would produce not only fruit but also wood for next year's canes. This system is being used with success by a few growers.

Vertical supports.—In the late 1960's several of the companies manufacturing grape harvesters adapted their machines to operate as horizontal impactors. These could operate on existing 2-wire, vertical support. And with only minor reworking of mature vines and existing trellises the fruiting wood could be positioned to make the fruit accessible to the harvestor. This gave added impetus to mechanical harvesting in the transition from old mature vineyards to newly established plantings.

In the newly established vineyards the most common support is a 3 wire vertical trellis; that is, 7 to 8 foot stakes with the lowest wire at 36 to 42 inches and the second and third wires at either 12 or 14 inches higher (fig. 61). With head-trained, cane-pruned varieties, the head of vines should be just below the lowest wire and the fruit canes should be tied to the middle wire. This will keep most clusters in a band between the highest and lowest wires where the machine can reach them without seriously injuring the permanent parts of the vine.

This type of support is also adapted for cordon-training and cane-pruning. It may be of special value with some of the small clustered wine varieties that fruit better on short 2 to 3 foot canes than with 3.5 to 4 foot canes. A bilateral cordon with cordons of 2 to 2.5 foot is supported on the lowest wire. Arms are developed just beyond the bend and at the

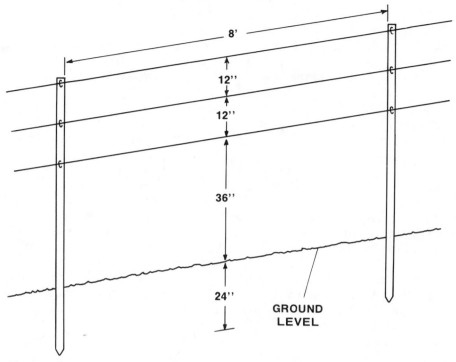

FIGURE 61: A 3-wire vertical trellis for machine harvesting on 7 foot stakes. A similar trellis on 8 foot stake is also being used, in which the bottom wire is higher and other wires spaced a bit wider. Such a trellis is adapted for the slapper or horizontal impactor type harvester. To spread the foliage more or to protect against wind a 2 to 2½ foot crossarm with a wire near each end may be added at the top.

end of the cordon. Canes from the arms are tied to the middle wire. This positions the fruit in a band between the top and bottom wires of the trellis. Renewal spurs must be retained on each arm to keep the vines in shape. Added arms may be developed on the cordons.

In windy locations the shoots may be protected by a crossarm with a wire near each end. The crossarm must be 16 to 18 inches above the middle wire. To make such an arrangement successful the harvester should have a canelifter which lifts the cane up, to remove their interference with impactors, and then drops them again. Such a device will also keep most of the leaves intact.

TYPES OF STAKES USED IN CALIFORNIA

In the past, split coast-redwood was the most popular grape stake used in California. As the virgin stands of this wood become depleted, the quality of the stakes has declined. Stakes from second-growth timber and sapwood are commonly used for vineyard supports today, and these are especially subject to attack by rot organisms. The best redwood stakes may last twenty or more years in the dry interior valleys, but in some coastal valleys they rot and break off in less than half that time.

Since stakes are expensive and replacement adds to the expense, treating them with a suitable wood preservative is advised (Neubauer and Kasimatis, 1959). This is especially so with the lower quality redwood available today. Soaking the stakes in undiluted wood-preservative creasote or in a 5 per cent solution of pentachlorophenol in deisel oil for 24 hours is effective. Only the part of the stake that goes into the ground need be treated. Stakes treated with these preservatives must not be placed close to young vines until the preservative has thoroughly dried. This may require a month or more. A good practice is to treat the stakes during the late summer preceding their use. Thus a thorough penetration of the preservative is ensured, and there will be ample time for drying before placing them in the vineyard (Neubauer and Kasimatis, 1966).

In recent years California growers have begun to use sawed pine and fir stakes. Also, supports from imported hardwoods from the Orient, and especially, from the forests of the Malay peninsula, have been adopted. Stakes of these woods must be treated with a preservative throughout their length. This is generally done by commercial processors using copper compounds in a closed pressure treating system.

Some use of steel supports is finding its way into the California industry. Various patented designs are available, some galvanized, others protected with non-corrosive paints. These metal supports perform quite satisfactorily in most vineyard situations. As the available supply of good quality domestic woods decreases and the costs increase, there will be a continued interest in the use of metal supports.

PLACING THE STAKES

The stakes may be driven in with a heavy hammer, but driving can be done more easily and with less damage to the stakes with a device similar to that shown in figure 62*a*, or by placing them in a hole made with a simple device utilizing water under several hundred pounds of pressure, as in figure 62*b* (La Vine, 1959). When large areas are to be planted, even more economical driving can be had by employing a tractor-mounted driver or press, shown in figure 62*c*. Most of the tractor-mounted stake drivers take two rows in one pass.

PLACING THE WIRES

In the past, smooth galvanized fence wire of the desired gauge (11 to 13) has been used for trellises. With mechanical harvesting, however, it is not

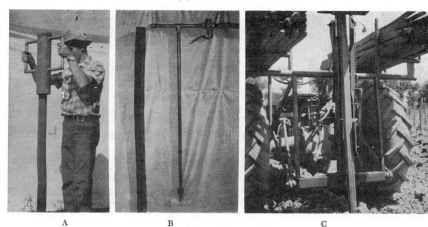

A   B   C

FIGURE 62: Placing stake supports for vines: A, with a section of large pipe; B, a hydraulic hole maker; and C, a tractor-mounted stake driver.

only necessary that the trellis wires be taut, but that they stay so. This requirement is being met, to a high degree, by the use of "high tensile" galvanized wire.

After the end posts of the trellis are firmly in place, the wires can be strung. When the trellis is erected at the time the stakes are being driven, it is well to put one wire in place—usually the lowest or another that is stapled to the stakes—to serve as a guide in aligning the stakes as they are driven.

A reel is very convenient for unrolling the wire as it is strung along the row. Then the wire is passed round the post at the far end of the row in a loop about 3 feet long. It is held at the proper height by a 1.5-inch partially driven staple on each side of the post. The wire being loose at this time, it is difficult to make either a tight wrap or a back wrap to prevent the loop from slipping shut as the wire is stretched. To overcome this difficulty it is possible, and perfectly practical, to tie the loop at this end of the wire with a bowline knot. The knot is fashioned as with a string or rope, and then is cinched up with a sharp jerk of the wire. Making the knot is much faster than making a wrap on loose wire.

The wire is pulled by hand to remove the slack; then it is brought to the height on the post at the near end of the row and stapled lightly to hold it there. The wire is cut beyond the post to leave enough to make a loop of about 3 feet. The end of the wire is grasped with pliers and pulled until it is sufficiently taut; then the end is brought round the post and wrapped on the main wire to form the loop. To make the wrap, one proceeds to (*a*) make a sharp bend about 3 inches from the end of the wire, (*b*) place both wires of the loop together and grasp firmly with pliers, just behind the bend made in the loose end, and (c) wrap the loose end round the main wire. The wrapping is done most easily by using a small wrapper tool—a flat piece of iron, about 1 inch wide, 5 inches long, and three sixteenths of an inch thick, with a hole near the end just large enough to slip over the wire. The loose end of the wire is put through the hole in the wrapper tool and then wrapped around the main wire by rotating the tool; at the same time both wires are held firmly with pliers. After the wrap is completed, a back twist must be made to prevent slipping. To do this, one places the wrapper between the wire of the loop just adjacent to the wrapped end, grasps both wires of the loop firmly with the pliers about 3 inches from the wrapper, and then twists the two wires firmly together by rotating the wrappers in a direction opposite to that taken in wrapping the end.

Once the wire is in place, it is fastened to the stakes with 1.5-inch staples at the predetermined height. The staples are driven not quite tight, so that the wire can be drawn through them when the trellis is being tightened in years to come. It is best to have the wire on the windward side of the stakes, so that the staples will not be pulled out by strong winds.

The other wires are put on in the same way. Those on top of the trellis do not carry as much weight, so they may be one gauge smaller, but should never be less than No. 13. If on a vertical trellis, these upper wires are stapled as were the lower ones. The wire on top of the wide and sloping-top trellises is attached with 1-inch staples. None of the staples is driven tight.

BIBLIOGRAPHY

La Vine, P. D. 1959. Stakes set with water. Amer. Fruit Grower, 79(11):19–20.

Le Roux, M. S. 1957. Table grapes do well on the broad slanting trellis. Farming So. Africa, 33:13–16.

———. 1960. Wide trellises pay dividends in Barlinka grape cultivation. Farming So. Africa, 36(7):37–38.

Malan, A. H. 1953. The slanting trellis. Farming So. Africa, 28:61–64.

Neubauer, L. W., and A. N. Kasimatis. 1959. Preservative treatment for grape stakes and posts. Calif. Agr. Ext. Ser., unnumbered leaflet, Oct.

———, ———. 1966. Chemical treatment of grape stakes may weaken young vines. Calif. Agric., 20(7):14–15.

Olmo, H. P., H. E. Studer, A. N. Kasimatis, and the Grape Farm Advisors of Fresno, Kern, Madera and San Joaquin Counties. 1968. Training and trellising grapevines for mechanical harvesting. Calif. Agric. Ext. Ser. AXT-274:1–15.

Shaulis, Nelson, Herman Amberg, and Donald Crowe. 1966. Response of Concord grapes to light, exposure and Geneva double curtain training. Proc. Amer. Soc. Hort. Sci., 89:268–280.

———, K. Kimball, and J. P. Tomkins. 1953. The effect of trellis height and training systems on the growth and yield of Concord grapes under a controlled pruning severity. Proc. Amer. Soc. Hort. Sci., 62:221–227.

Shepardson, E. S., H. E. Studer, N. J. Shaulis, and J. C. Moyer, 1962. Mechanical grape harvesting, research progress and development at Cornell. Amer. Soc. Agric. Eng., 43:66–71.

Winkler, A. J. 1945. Pruning *vinifera* grapevines. Calif. Agr. Ext. Ser. Circ., 89:1–56.

———, and L. H. Lamouria. 1956. Machine harvesting of grapes. Calif. Agric., 10(5):9, 14.

———, ———, and G. H. Abernathy. 1957. Mechanical grape harvesting problems and progress. Amer. Jour. Enol., 8:182–187.

12

Training Young Vines

In establishing a commercial vineyard, the purpose of training is to produce vines (*a*) of a shape that facilitates cultivation, insect and disease control, pruning, and harvesting and, therefore, are (*b*) economical to maintain and (*c*) capable of producing fruit of the desired type and in good quantity. In a well-trained vineyard the aims of any system of pruning are (*a*) to facilitate pruning and harvesting; (*b*) to permit carrying out cultivating operations, including insect and disease control, with power equipment; (*c*) to spread the fruit so as to prevent its forming masses of interlocked clusters; (*d*) to hold the bearing surface at a height that provides good leaf exposure; and (*e*) to keep the permanent parts of the vines free of large wounds. Figures 84, 85, and 86 (chap. 13) show well-shaped mature vines of the types generally used in California.

Forming Head-Trained Vines

While training and pruning the young vines, the grower must know the form desired in the mature vine. Otherwise he will make mistakes, and the mature vine will be defective. Poorly-formed vines can, in some instances, be corrected, but correction is costly and it always necessitates large wounds.

Planting and care the first summer.—When vines are planted on their own roots, only the two-bud spur of the rooting should be above the surface of the ground (see fig. 50); with grafted vines the graft union must be above the surface. As a rule, in moderately warm to cool regions no summer pruning will be done, and staking will be optional. Where heat,

Training Young Vines

soil, and water favor very rapid growth, however, the first two seasons of work can be done in one season and, therefore, the treatment for the second year, described here for more usual conditions, will be done in the first year.

First winter pruning.—At the end of the first growing season the young vine should have made an above-ground growth of at least one or more canes 1 to 3 feet long, and it should have a strong, widely spreading, and penetrating root system.

The vines are pruned in winter after the leaves have fallen. Only one cane is reserved, and this is usually cut back to two buds (fig. 63). If large, this cane may be so cut as to retain more buds. The young vineyard will be more uniform, however, when all the vines are treated alike.

After pruning, therefore, the vine above the ground usually looks almost as it did when it was planted in the previous spring. Yet its condition is very different. It now has a well established root system and is prepared to make a much larger growth in the second season.

The vine's primary work during the second season is to produce a single strong cane that can be developed into a trunk. To do this, the vine requires not only favorable conditions for growth, but also support and training during the spring and early summer.

As soon as possible after pruning, if it was not staked at planting, the vineyard should be set with stakes that are long enough to support the vine at the height desired for the head or cordon, and the trellis.

Well before the vines start to bud in the second spring, a single furrow should be turned along and away from each side of each row, and then the ridge should be hoed away at the vines. This procedure will expose suckers and surface roots, which must be removed without leaving stubs—since

FIGURE 63: A one-year-old vine: a, before pruning; and b, after pruning.

stubs would produce more suckers and surface roots in later years. If this work is neglected or done improperly, much trouble and expense may result. Vines properly suckered and surface-rooted during the first two years give no such trouble later.

Second-summer treatment.—In the second spring, the vines will produce several or more shoots (fig. 64). When the longest of these on most of the vines are about 12 to 18 inches long, the first disbudding and tying should be done. Disbudding is the rubbing-off or breaking out of all the shoots or swollen buds except the one that is best placed for tying to a support. This single shoot will form the trunk of the young vine. It should be tied loosely and very carefully to the stake with a piece of strong string.

These single shoots from a well-established root system will grow rapidly, often as much as one inch per day, and since the retained shoots should be tied at 8 to 12 inch intervals, the vines must be reworked within the next week or ten days. At this time the vines with growth too short for tying on the first pass may now be disbudded and tied up.

Only excess buds and shoots arising from the winter-pruned part of the young vine should be removed at the early tyings. Later, as the trunk shoot goes up the stake, side shoots (laterals) will start on vigorous shoots in the axils, the angles where the leaves are attached to the shoot. For all types of today's training all of these laterals should be broken out up to a

A   B   C   D

FIGURE 64: Training the second summer. From left to right: (a) before disbudding; (b) after disbudding; (c) manner of tying the reserved shoot; (d) topping reserved shoot with part removed shown at the left of picture (d). Note that the laterals arising on lower part of the reserved shoot (d) have been removed.

minimum height of two feet as soon as they appear, but the leaves sub-tending them should be left to help support the trunk shoot. When the trunk shoot has grown 18 to 24 inches above the height where the head or cordon is desired, it should be topped (cut back). The cut should be made exactly through the first node above the height at which the vine is to be headed or cordoned and in such a way that the bud at that node is de-stroyed, but the enlarged stem portion is retained as an aid in tying (fig. 64d). Topping in this severe manner stimulates uniform lateral growth where it is desired, for the several nodes below the cut.

Up to this stage the training of young vines for all the pruning systems used in California is identical. From here on there is only slight variation in the development of head-trained cane- and spur-pruned vines but that for cordon-training vines is distinctly different.

Height of head.—Vines have been trained high for years in California. The standard height of head for table, raisin, and, recently planted wine grapes is about 4 feet. This height has favored vineyard operations—such as cultivation, disease and insect control, pruning, and harvesting—and has improved the quality and quantity of the fruit owing to the better leaf exposure. At present there is definite interest in still higher training and wider supports to further improve leaf exposure. R. J. Weaver *et al.* (un-published data) have shown a definite increase in growth and production of Thompson Seedless vines with increasing heights of head from 4.5 to 5.5 to 6.5 feet, and that a 2 wire wide-topped trellis is better than a single wire support.

Of course, costs increase as vines are trained higher and the trellises made wider; hence, the type of growth a vine makes should be considered. A vine with relatively short upright-growing shoots will likely not respond as favorably to an increase in height and width of trellis as a variety that produces long shoots that droop.

FORMING HEAD FOR CANE- AND SPUR-PRUNED VINES

Second-winter pruning.—After the leaves have fallen, at the end of the second growing season, these vines should receive their second-winter pruning. In frosty locations the pruning should be deferred until a few days before the buds start in the spring.

Each vine will consist of a single straight cane tied vertically to the stake, together with its laterals. If well grown, this cane should be cut off at the node above the level at which the head is desired. The cut should destroy the bud and leave the enlargement of the node, thereby facilitating secure tying (fig. 65).

If the cane is less than three tenths of an inch thick at the desired height of the head, the vine should be cut back to two buds, as at the first-winter

FIGURE 65: The second winter pruning: left, an average vine; right, a vigorous vine. Also note the tying after this pruning.

pruning or to where the trunk cane is thick enough to produce a strong growing shoot.

To permit close cultivation and other vineyard operations, the trunk should be as nearly straight and vertical as possible; hence before the buds swell in the spring, the pruned cane that will become the trunk should be tied securely to the stake. A single hitch, double half hitch, or clove hitch is made round the cane just below the enlargement of the node that was cut through; the string is tied round the stake as tightly as possible with a firm square knot (fig. 66). One or two loose ties are then placed round the stake and cane, depending on its length. These ties should not pass between the cane and the stake, lest the vine be girdled. If two fingers can be inserted between the cane and the stake, the danger is avoided.

When suckers and surface roots develop again during the second summer, they should be removed thoroughly and carefully, as in the previous year.

Third-summer treatment.—During the second summer a cane was produced that will develop into the permanent trunk. During the third summer a small or medium crop will be produced and the development of the head begun.

To complete the head will require several seasons, unless the growing

FIGURE 66: The first disbudding during the third summer.

conditions are unusually favorable. An attempt to form the head too rapidly will result in loss of crop and an ill-shaped vine.

During the summer all new shoots on the lower two-thirds of the trunk cane are to be removed as soon as possible after they start (fig. 66). A second disbudding is usually necessary (fig. 67). All new shoots on the upper one-third should be allowed to grow without interference. Only when the upper shoots grow so rapidly that they are in danger of being broken by the wind do they need attention; then it is usually sufficient to top them lightly.

Completing the head of cane-pruned vines.—At the end of the third

FIGURE 67: The second disbudding during the third summer. All shoots below those desired for forming the head of the vine have been removed.

season, after the leaves have fallen, a vine of average vigor will consist of a well-developed trunk 1 to 2 inches thick, bearing on its upper part 4 to 10 strong, well-matured, healthy canes.

The pruning during the third winter will consist in the retention of renewal spurs and fruit canes. The renewal spurs should be given priority at this time, since they are the base on which the permanent arms of the vine will develop. They should be so placed that the arms will extend in the direction of the trellis. The mature, cane-pruned vine will usually have two arms on each side. The arms should be just below the lower trellis wire.

After the renewal spurs have been selected, 1, 2, or 3 canes depending on the size of the vine, are chosen for fruit canes. These are pruned in accordance with their length and wood maturity. Care should be exercised not to overcrop the vine.

During the summer no pruning will be needed except the prompt removal of all shoots that start below the bottom cane and all suckers that come from below the ground. In windy situations the vigorous shoots may have to be topped when they are 12 to 20 inches long.

At the end of the fourth growing season, each renewal spur of the last winter pruning should have produced one, two, or more canes large enough to serve for renewal spurs or fruit canes. Again, priority should be given to the position of the renewal spurs so the head of the vine will be completed. By now the vine should be large enough to carry 3 or 4 fruit canes (see fig. 68).

FIGURE 68: Forming the head of head-trained, cane-pruned vine.

For the pruning of mature, cane-pruned vine, see page 321.

Completing the head of spur-pruned vines.—At the end of the third growing season, after the leaves have fallen, a vine of average vigor will consist of a well-developed trunk 1 to 2 inches thick bearing on its upper 12 to 15 inches, well matured, healthy canes.

Enough of these canes should be cut back to spurs to bear the crop that the vine is judged capable of producing without injury to its vigor or to the proper maturing of the grapes. The spurs will usually range in number from three to six, according to the capacity of the vine. Each spur should be cut back to two, three, or four buds, according to the size of the cane from which it is retained. These spurs should be as near the top of the vine as is possible. On very vigorous vines it may be necessary to space the spurs over a foot or two of the trunk cane at this pruning in order to have enough crop to control the growth of the vines (fig. 69a).

During the summer no pruning will be needed except the prompt removal of all shoots that start below the bottom spur and all suckers that come from below the ground. In windy situations the vigorous shoots may have to be topped when they are 18 to 20 inches long.

At the end of the fourth growing season, each spur of the last winter pruning should have produced one, two, or more canes large enough to

A   B   C

FIGURE 69: Forming the head of head-trained, spur-pruned vine. (a) the third winter pruning; (b) the fourth winter pruning; (c) the fifth winter pruning.

serve for spurs. Beginning as near the top of the vine as is desirable, the spurs should be spaced evenly around the trunk and as nearly as possible in a horizontal plane—that is, at the same distance from the ground. Enough buds should be retained to bear the crop that the vine is judged capable of producing. Spurs of the previous year that were left too high or too low are removed when sufficient spurs can be had at the height desired for the head (fig. 69b, c). On vigorous vines the spurs may be left long and the crop controlled by thinning, thus spreading the head more rapidly and creating a large framework on which to produce the fruit early in the life of the vine. All growth rising from the trunk below the spurs should be removed. Usually all the spurs on the upper third of the vine will be left.

The summer treatment in the fifth growing season is the same as that in the fourth. No topping, or even pinching, should be done unless it is needed to prevent serious wind damage.

The fifth-winter pruning is a continuation of the method of the fourth. Spurs should be chosen at the top of the vine in such a way as to give the head and arms approximately the desired form; they should be numerous enough to bear a crop commensurate with the size—the capacity—of the vine.

For the pruning of mature, head-trained, spur-pruned vines, see page 327.

FORMING CORDON-TRAINED VINES

The treatment of cordon-pruned vines during the first year is exactly the same as that for head-pruned vines. Since all cordon-pruned vines have long trunks, the canes from which they are formed must be vigorous.

For proper training, cordon vines require more careful and skilled handwork during the second, third, and fourth years than do the headed vines. If the training is not carried out skillfully and carefully, with full knowledge of the method, faulty development of the vines is more likely to occur with cordons than with other forms. Although there is nothing very difficult about establishing a cordon properly, the grower must be sure to understand the method and do everything necessary for success.

Forming the trunk of bilateral horizontal cordons.—The treatment of the bilateral cordon vine is identical with that of the training of cane- and spur-pruned vines to the middle of the second summer when the vines are topped; see page 275 and fig. 64a to d. Following the topping, two well placed laterals are permitted to grow on the trunk shoot, 6 to 10 inches below the wire of the trellis that will support the cordon. All other laterals are removed. After the two chosen laterals, which should be on opposite sides of the trunk cane parallel to the vine row, have made 12 to 18 inches of growth they are tied upright to the stake. When the selected laterals have grown about 1 foot above the top of the stake (fig. 70a), all ties are taken off except those on the trunk cane. A lateral is then bent over, in a gentle turn, in each direction along the trellis and tied loosely to the support wire (fig. 70b).

Each lateral shoot is tied once or twice again as it lengthens. The tie should be well back of the growing tip since elongation may be checked by bringing the tip into a horizontal position. The shoots are topped after

FIGURE 70: Placing the growing shoots of a horizontal bilateral cordon on the wire.

282

Training Young Vines

they have grown 12 to 18 inches beyond the halfway point to the next vine.

Pruning the trunk canes of bilateral horizontal cordons.—At the end of the second season, after the leaves have fallen, the two branch canes of the trunk should be cut back to the place where they are at least three-eights of an inch thick. If they have grown sufficiently, they should be allowed to extend to within 8 to 12 inches of the branches of the adjoining vines. Should either of the branch canes not be large enough to reach a moderate distance on the wire beyond the bend, it must be cut back to a lower-side bud within a few inches of the point at which the trunk was divided, and more rigorous canes must be grown the next year. It is a mistake to use canes that are too small. All laterals on the trunk below the point of branching are removed entirely, and, unless the vines are extremely vigorous, no spurs are left on the branches.

Tying the trunk canes of horizontal cordons.—In the cordon system the canes are straightened by turning, or rather weaving them, one or one-and-a-half times round the support wire (fig. 71). They should be wrapped

FIGURE 71: The completed trunk of a horizontal bilateral cordon vine tied to the wire—second winter.

round the wire no more than is necessary to make them straight. If wrapped more, they will be broken the next year when they are untwisted, and if they are not untwisted the wire will be broken as the cordons thicken.

The ends of the branch canes should be tied firmly to the wire round the one internode projecting beyond the end bud. If, then, any parts of the canes are not close to the wire, these should be straightened by other ties. The horizontal part of the canes must be straight. The ties, except the tie at the end of the trunk cane, should be loose enough to allow the cane to grow to an inch or more in diameter during the summer.

Establishing the arms.—During the first season that the cordons are on the wires, the first crop will be borne and the vine will produce canes from which to start its arms.

Two serious dangers should be avoided. One, overproduction, will result in poor-quality grapes and in weakening which will prevent the vine from producing the good canes necessary for spurs the next year. If too much fruit sets, it should be thinned to what the vine can mature normally. The other danger is the development of shoots on the lower rather than on the upper side of the trunk cane.

While the buds are starting in the spring, the vineyard should be examined several times and any shoots found starting on the underside of the canes should be rubbed off. This disbudding will remove half the shoots and leave the other half spaced 8 to 12 inches apart on the upper side. It should be done promptly; no shoot that is to be removed should be allowed to grow more than a few inches. At the same time, all shoots starting on or below the bend should be removed (fig. 72).

Because the shoots grow at uneven rates, some of those retained on the upper side of the cordon will soon become much longer than the others. These long shoots are usually either near the bend or at the end of the cordon. They should be pinched as soon as this can be done without injuring the flower clusters, which are usually at the fourth and fifth nodes. This pinching will check the growth of the long shoots and allow the weaker shoots to catch up.

On branch canes that do not extend the full length, a shoot should be allowed to grow from near the end to complete the trunk. This shoot should be tied to the wire to make the extension of the trunk cane as straight as possible. Best for this purpose is a shoot from the underside of the cane.

As soon as the shoots are long enough (fig. 72), one or two of them should be tied to the upper wire. If this is not done, the shoots on the upper side of the trunk cane, together with their fruit, will be so heavy as to twist the trunk completely over and leave the upper side bare, with the shoots all pointing toward the ground. If this happens and is not corrected immediately, the vine can never be made into a good cordon. The tying of supporting shoots is usually necessary in only the first year— occasionally in the second; thereafter, the trunk is thick and rigid enough to prevent turning.

Pruning the completed cordons.—The third winter pruning, after the trunk canes have been completed on the wire, consists in leaving spurs along the upper side of the horizontal part of the trunk. These spurs should be spaced as evenly as possible, 8 to 12 inches apart. Their length will be one to four buds, according to the capacity of the vine and the individual canes. If there is no cane on the upper side where a spur is needed, a cane from the lower side may be taken if there is one at the proper place. By cuttings this back to one bud, a strong shoot will be obtained that, when it is long enough, can be tied to the upper wire so that it will provide a vertical cane for a spur the following year.

Although not here-to-fore done, cordon vines may also be cane-pruned for mechanical harvesting and to permit the use of shorter canes. For this purpose a short bilateral cordon with branches of 2 to 2.5 feet long and with arms developed just beyond the bend and at the end of the branch are used. The fruit canes arising from the arms are tied on a wire 10 to 12 inches above the cordon, thus the slapper or horizontal impactor type harvester can be set up to get the grapes without injuring the permanent parts of the vine. By taking fruit canes from the arms at the bend and at

FIGURE 72: A horizontal bilateral cordon, first year on the wire. After first disbudding, shoots ready for tying to the upper wire.

the ends of the branches of the cordons, they can be cut shorter and still utilize all the space between vines spaced at 8 to 10 feet in the row. Shorter fruit canes (2 to 3 feet) of some of the premium quality wine varieties produce better clusters than canes of 4 to 5 feet. Renewal spurs must be retained on the arms.

For the pruning of mature, cordon-pruned vines, see page 324.

TRAINING GRAPEVINES ON ARBORS AND WALLS

Arbors are little used commercially in California. They are popular, however, for shading the entrances to houses or as covers for porches and garden walks. To meet these needs, they vary greatly in design and size.

Since vines can be trained to almost any form, it is possible by proper training and pruning to fit them to any arbor. Because of their vigor, certain varieties will cover an arbor more rapidly than others; but medium- or weak-growing varieties can also be used if they are properly trained and not forced to compete with vigorous growers.

In the training of arbor vines, one must develop a strong root system before attempting to form a long trunk. Without such a root system the growth of the vine, even when forced into a single shoot, will not be great enough by the end of the season to be retained for a trunk cane.

Overhead arbors.—The procedure for training vines on an overhead arbor is the same as that for forming head-pruned vines (figs. 65, 66, and 67), except that the trunks are longer. To favor the growth of the trunk shoot, care should be exercised in pinching all the laterals on the lower part of the main shoot. During the third summer all new shoots on the lower three fourths of the trunk cane should be removed. By the end of the third summer the vines should have developed a number of strong canes at or near the top of the arbor. At the third winter's pruning and in subsequent years a head or cordons will be formed.

Arbors over walks.—An arbor over a walk may have horizontal laths or wires spaced 18 to 24 inches apart on the supports on one or both sides of the walk. If so, it may be desirable to cover the side or sides as well as the top of the arbor with leaves and fruit. This arrangement requires different vines, trained to different heights; that is, some vines are trained to the top and others to the different levels at which growth is desired on the sides of the arbor. To attempt to develop side arms at different levels on the trunks of vines that are also taken to the top of the arbor will result in failure, for the reasons indicated in discussion of the vertical cordon (see p. 326).

Training of the vines is the same for this type of arbor as for the overhead arbor. Some vines will be headed at the desired levels on the side of the arbor, and others will be taken to the top. If the variety fruits well on spurs, the vines for the sides of the arbor are divided into bilateral horizontal cordons at the desired height or heights and those for the top of the arbor are trained to cordons at that level. The vines requiring cane pruning are trained into heads with arms at the side levels or on the top of the arbor, according to the part of the arbor they are intended to cover.

Garden walls.—Vines on walls should be trained to bilateral horizontal cordons. The procedure in training is the same as that for forming cordon-pruned vines. When growth and fruit at several levels are desired, different vines should be used for each level. It is impossible to maintain two- or three-story vines.

13

Pruning

Pruning comprises the removal of living canes, shoot, leaves, and other vegetative parts of the vine. The removal of dead wood, although desirable, is not regarded as pruning, since it in no way affects the physiological behavior of the vine. The removal of flower clusters, immature clusters, or parts of immature clusters is *thinning*. The removal of ripe fruit, of course, is *harvesting*.

The purposes of pruning are: (*a*) to help establish and maintain the vine in a form that will save labor and facilitate vineyard operations, such as cultivation, control of diseases and insects, thinning, and harvesting; (*b*) to distribute the bearing wood over the vine, among vines, and over the years in accordance with the capacity of the spurs (or canes) and vines, so as to equalize production and get large average crops of high-quality fruit; and (*c*) to lessen or eliminate thinning in the control of crop. Pruning is the cheapest way of reducing the number of clusters.

PRUNING AND TRAINING

Training includes certain practices that are supplementary to pruning and necessary in shaping the vine. It consists chiefly in attaching the vine and its growth to various supports. Whereas pruning determines the number and position of the buds that develop, training determines the form and direction of the trunk and arms, and the position of the shoots that develop from the buds retained at pruning.

When the vine is young, the vineyardist's interest centers primarily on developing a single strong shoot having several well-placed laterals that will form a permanent framework; he sacrifices some of the plant's energy in order to obtain a well-shaped vine as cheaply and as early as possible. In contrast, when the vine is mature and bearing, the pruner must consider both wood and crop, since a proper balance between them is necessary for the development of good fruit and the continued production of large crops. For this reason, training (the development of a young vine of desirable form) is distinguished from pruning (maintenance of the established form and regulation of the fruiting).

VIGOR AND CAPACITY

In discussing the characteristic responses of the vine to pruning, one needs two terms: vigor and capacity. *Vigor* is the quality or condition that is expressed in rapid growth of the parts of the vine. It refers essentially to the rate of growth. *Capacity*, in contrast, is the quantity of action with respect to the total growth and total crop of which the vine or a part of it is capable. The term refers to ability for total production rather than to rate of activity.

A young vine may show great vigor in the qualitative sense and yet, in the quantitative sense, have much less capacity for growth and fruiting than an old and relatively mature vine. If a vine is pruned severely, the number of shoots it produces is reduced and the shoots will be more vigorous (will grow faster) than those of a lightly pruned vine. The severely pruned vine will be the more vigorous of the two, but, having fewer shoots and fewer leaves, it will make less total growth and therefore have less capacity for growth and fruiting than the one lightly pruned. In a single shoot, vigor and capacity for production vary together; a vigorous shoot has large capacity, and a weak shoot small capacity.

The influence of pruning on vigor is exploited in developing the desired form of trunk in the training of young vines. Once a vineyard is established, however, the grower is primarily concerned with obtaining large crops of good fruit for many years. The capacity to produce fruit depends on the production of wood; hence, to produce heavily over a long period, a vine must be capable not only of maturing a satisfactory crop each year, but also of maturing a good growth of wood.

THE RESPONSE OF THE VINE TO PRUNING AND CROP

Vine pruning was well established as an art long before the scientific method came into being. Near the beginning of the Christian Era, Vergil and Pliny gave directions for the training and pruning of vines. In many areas their directions are still followed in our time, except for minor empirical changes, such as the length and position of bearing units (spurs) brought about by Guyot in the nineteenth century. Without an understanding of the physiological basis, it has been common practice to remove 85 to 98 percent of the annual growth of the vine at pruning, and it is still the opinion of many viticulturists that this is beneficial to the vine.

Early in the present century, however, plant physiologists provided the scientific basis for the concept that the active leaf area of the vine is the unit that determines the amount, composition, and quality of the crop. This relationship, together with observations on the behavior of other fruit plants when pruned long and the outstanding productivity of very large, well-known individual historic vines in California that carried many bearing units, led the senior author and others at the California Agricultural Experiment Station to question the procedure in vine pruning in general. It was apparent that basic information was needed, and research was begun to determine (*a*) the effect of pruning on vine growth, (*b*) the effect of crop on vine growth, and (*c*) the effect of pruning on capacity for production.

The fruiting habit of the vine made it an ideal plant for this investigation. It is a prolific producer of clusters, and thus there is always an overabundant crop potential. Yet the fruit buds develop only to the primordia of the individual flower in the year in which they are differentiated. The floral parts—the caylx, corolla, stamen, and pistil—are not formed until after the vine leafs out in the spring. Therefore it is possible to regulate or eliminate the crop even before the flowers are formed.

Using vines with no crop, three levels of pruning were established, the first being no pruning at all, the second the normal pruning of the commercial type for the varieties used, and the third a severe pruning in which the spurs were retained in the usual number but were cut to the base bud. Crop was eliminated by removing the flower clusters as soon as they appeared after the vines leafed out in spring. This series was paralleled by another series of vines, none of which was pruned, but which had three levels of crop: maximum potential crop, part crop, and no crop. The vines with maximum potential crop carried all the clusters they produced to maturity. In the case of the part-crop vines, flower clusters were removed as they appeared, so as to balance the crop with what experience indicated was the vine's capacity for production. On the no-crop vines all the flower clusters were removed as they appeared.

In figure 73 the bars at the left of the control—the nonpruned, no-crop vines—show that vine growth was depressed 25 per cent by normal spur-pruning and 31 per cent by severe pruning (all spurs cut to base buds). This is the physiological response of the vine to pruning. Similarly, the bars to the right of the control show that the growth of the nonpruned, part-crop vines was depressed 22 per cent and that of the nonpruned maximum-potential-crop vines 36 per cent. This represents the response of the vine to the burden of crop production.

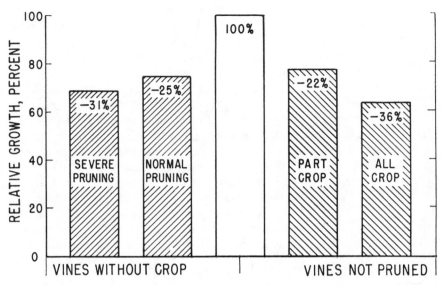

FIGURE 73: The depressing effect of pruning and crop on vine growth relative to non-pruned no-crop vines (the center bar graph).

The greater capacity of less severely pruned vines is illustrated in figure 74. Here the growth, as measured by the weight of the vine, of vines with crop at different levels of pruning is compared with that of the nonpruned, no-crop vines (Winkler, 1931).

Nonpruned vines, evidently, have a greater capacity for fruit production than pruned vines. Although the nonpruned vines produced an average crop of 51 pounds a year, their growth was only 2 per cent less than that of the normally pruned vines, which were producing average crops of 23 pounds—less than half that of the nonpruned vines. The severely pruned vines, with a very small yearly crop, were limited in growth to almost the same degree as the vines that received no or normal pruning and were bearing heavy or moderate crops. In cane pruning, some flower clusters were removed to limit the crop to what experience indicated was the vines capacity. It seems, however, that the effect of lighter pruning on the vine's capacity for production was underestimated: despite the relatively heavy average crops, the cane-pruned vines produced the greatest total growth of any of the vines with crop. These data indicate the limiting effect of pruning, as well as of crop, on the vine's capacity. In these experiments crop and pruning had approximately equal effects in diminishing the capacity of the vines for growth. That is, growth was depressed about the same amount with minimum pruning and maximum crop (fig. 74, *right*) as with maximum pruning and minimum crop (fig. 74, *left*). With lighter pruning,

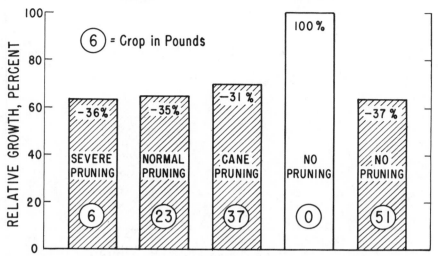

FIGURE 74: The effect of pruning on the capacity of the vine for growth and production relative to non-pruned no-crop vines.

capacity (growth plus crop) was increased so that the larger crops of these vines, when kept within suitable limits by flower-cluster removals, were no more depressing to vine growth than were the small crops of the severely pruned vines whose capacity had been greatly reduced by pruning (Winkler, 1931).

This difference in capacity of vines unpruned or pruned to different levels is explained by the number of leaves produced and the length of time during which the leaves were active. Pruning not only reduced the total weight of the leaves developed by the vine during the growing season; (see fig. 75) it also delayed the attainment of maximal leaf area until well beyond midsummer. It thus reduced both the total leaf area and the length of time during which most of the leaves functioned.

The graphs show that the less the amount of wood removed at pruning, the more rapidly the leaves develop and the larger the total leaf area produced during the growing season. Considering only the total weight of leaves at the end of the growing season, the total leaf weight was reduced 23 per cent by cane pruning, 61 per cent by normal pruning, and 65 per cent by severe pruning. In view of the marked delay in leaf development of the more severely pruned vines, the loss in leaf activity is shown more correctly by the combination of the weight and the time during which the leaves functioned.

The beneficial influence that a large leaf area exerts on the set, development, and quality of the fruit of Muscat of Alexandria is shown in figure

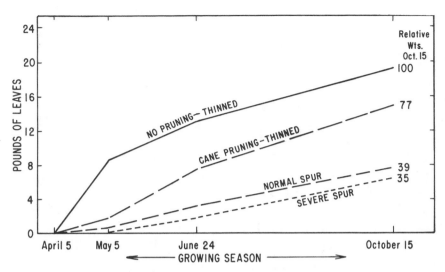

FIGURE 75: The weight and relative activity of the leaves of vines pruned to different levels.

FIGURE 76: The effect of the number of leaves to a vine on the setting and development of the berries of Muscat of Alexandria.

76. The clusters at the left, from cane-pruned, part-crop vines with 1,700 leaves each at bloom were well filled with normal berries of uniform size. The clusters in the middle, from normally pruned vines with 760 leaves each, did not set so well; the berries that did set were less uniform in size and there were many shot berries. The clusters at the right, from normally pruned vines that were defoliated two weeks before bloom, shattered badly and showed an even greater tendency to set shot berries; also, many of the berries with seeds were undersized (Winkler, 1929).

It is thus evident that the unpruned vines' greater capacity for growth and production was the result of a more abundant supply of available carbohydrates, the product of the larger leaf area. This was confirmed by analyses of basal segments of canes and shoots from vines unpruned and pruned to different levels. The results of these analyses, as total available carbohydrates (sugars and starch), are shown in figure 77.

These graphs show the normal maxima and the two minima in the level of available carbohydates during the year. The severely pruned vines, however, showed no noticeable late spring maximum. In the unpruned and cane-pruned vines total carbohydrates were increased, respectively, 18 and 15 per cent at the winter maximum, and 36 and 44 per cent at the late spring maximum, over that of the normally pruned vines. In the normally and severely pruned vines the level of total carbohydrates was about the same for each. The graphs indicate that the larger leaf surfaces of the nonpruned and cane-pruned vines, which also functioned over a greater part of the growing season, very definitely provided these vines with a more abundant supply of available carbohydrates. These leaf area, yield, and

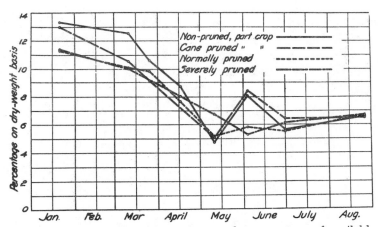

FIGURE 77: The effect of pruning on the percentage of available total carbohydrates in the basal portion of canes and shoots during the period January to August.

fruit quality relationships are more thoroughly discussed by Winkler (1958). The large increase in available carbohydrates at the late spring maximum is of especial significance in relation to improvement in the set of the fruit and the subsequent quality of the fruit of varieties such as Muscat of Alexandria, in that critical nourishment is provided during the latter stages of flower development and fruit set.

Although the percentage differences in favor of the lightly pruned vines are only moderate for the winter maximum, the differences in the total available carbohydrates in the vines at the beginning of the growing season are marked. This is indicated by the data of table 19.

The weight of total carbohydrates in the unpruned vine is four times that in the normally pruned and ten times that in the severely pruned. The difference in total amount of available carbohydrates again seems to be a significant factor in flower development and fruit set. Other varieties (Emperor and Almeria), when pruned so as to produce vines with a greater bulk of permanent wood, have shown very definite, though less marked, improvement in the set of fruit.

From these data it is evident that the physiological response of the vine to pruning remained obscured because the effect of the crop set was not separated from that of pruning. Thus any attempt at lighter pruning met with failure because in most varieties the depressive effect of the increase in crop, when uncontrolled, more than offset the benefit of the retention of more wood. This situation led to the belief that pruning is stimulating and invigorating, since severe pruning, which drastically reduces the crop, increases the rate of individual shoot growth. Not until this study was made, was the effect of the crop eliminated or controlled to reveal the true effect of pruning—namely, that *less severe pruning increases vine capacity for both growth and production.*

These findings provide a clear understanding of the physiological responses of the vine to pruning and to crop; they also indicate the possibilities of definite improvement in the quality of the fruit when less severe

TABLE 19

WEIGHT OF VINE AND AVAILABLE CARBOHYDRATES
CONTAINED AT BEGINNING OF GROWTH
(In pounds, all vines of same age without crop)

Substance	Non-pruned	Normally pruned	Severely pruned
Vines, dry weight	86.0	27.9	9.9
Carbohydrates per vine	11.4	3.0	1.1

SOURCE OF DATA: Winkler (1958).

pruning is accompanied by appropriate thinning (see chap. 14). Application of these findings can lead both to increased production and to improved quality of the fruit, if vineyard economics permits. As is the case in many agricultural operations, however, the pruning of grapevines is governed more by cost than by the physiological responses. This indicates that some compromise must be made between physiological responses and the economics of vineyard operation.

POSSIBLE COMPROMISES IN THE USE OF LONGER PRUNING

To arrive at what seems a logical conclusion concerning the application to practice of the general principles established in the investigations discussed above, each type of pruning (except removing all the crop) is considered here and the merits or demerits of each are indicated. To facilitate comparison, the growth and production with the different degrees of pruning and cropping are shown in figure 78.

The two extremes, severely pruned all-crop vines (at left) and nonpruned all-crop vines (at right) are easily eliminated. The severely pruned vines (fig. 78, A) had their capacity for production reduced to such an extent that the crops were insufficient to be considered commercial. Besides

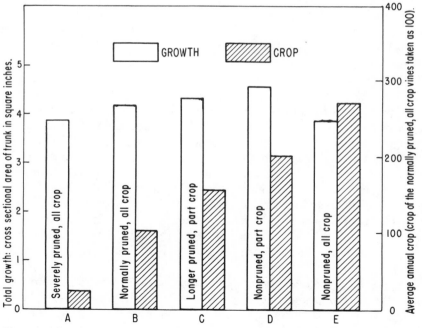

FIGURE 78: The growth and production of vines pruned to different levels.

the low yields, the fruit quality was only fair; the degree Brix was high, but the clusters were small and the percentage of abnormal berries was large. The poor set was owing to competition for food materials between the developing flowers and the very rapidly growing shoots. In other words, vigor was high, but capacity was low.

The nonpruned all-crop vines (fig. 78, E), at the other extreme, produced the largest crops, but the fruit quality was the poorest. The clusters were reduced in size for the variety, the degree Brix was low, and the berries were small. These vines were low in vigor but high in capacity.

Between the two extremes are intermediate treatments indicating possible balances in pruning, growth, and crop that favor maximum production of high-quality fruit, together with other treatments that are more adaptable to vineyard practice, yet not quite so favorable from the standpoint of yield and quality.

Crop regulation entirely by thinning.—The responses of the nonpruned part-crop vines (fig. 78, D) are considered first. In this treatment, crop is controlled entirely by thinning. These vines produce twice as much as the normally pruned vines. The fruit also was of superior quality—large clusters of uniformly large berries, with a high degree Brix. In addition, these vines made the most growth of any of the vines with crop. Both vigor and capacity were high.

By all odds, this is the most favorable compromise from the point of view of the vine, but it is not practical on a commercial scale. The supports (arbors) would be very expensive, and of even greater cost would be the removal of excess clusters by thinning. The thinning would be impossible at present labor costs.

Crop regulation entirely by pruning.—Another compromise is represented by the normally pruned, all-crop vines (fig. 78, B). It is a heritage of the past. In this treatment, crop is controlled entirely by pruning. The fruit is of fair to good quality, but the quality is not equal to that produced by the nonpruned part-crop vines and the yields are much smaller. In this treatment, pruning, crop, and growth are balanced only at a considerable loss in vine capacity. It is a means whereby fair crops of average-quality grapes can be produced with most varieties; when it is used, for Muscat of Alexandria, Ribier, and similar varieties, the fruit is of poor quality in some areas. This treatment cannot be said to be efficient with regard to the vine, yet it is economical. It should continue to be the usual practice where cost of production rather than appearance and quality of the fruit is the determining factor of profit or loss.

Crop regulated by longer pruning plus thinning.—The third compromise is that of moderate pruning accompanied by flower-cluster, cluster, or berry thinning to regulate crop. The response with cane-pruning and flower-cluster thinning is shown in (fig. 78, C) improvement in fruit quality and vine capacity may be obtained with moderate pruning—extra buds on half or more of the spurs of a vine, or an extra cane on a cane-pruned vine—when accompanied by appropriate thinning. The shape of the vine is maintained or improved, a top limit is placed on the cost of thinning, and the fruit is of excellent quality, with large berries of uniform size and high degree Brix. The vines are of good vigor and high capacity.

This is the best compromise whenever it is ecnomically feasible. It is being used by many table grape growers. The degree of longer pruning may consist of a few extra buds or an extra cane, according to the variety. Nevertheless, the retention of more buds, with crop controlled by thinning, produces an earlier and larger leaf surface which improves the nutrition of both vine and fruit.

PRINCIPLES OF PRUNING

To accomplish the purposes of pruning, one must consider certain principles of plant behavior as they apply to the vine. These principles are based on knowledge of the vine's response to the removal of vegetative or fruiting parts and on present understanding of its growth and fruiting habits.

The physiological response of the vine to pruning and crop, already discussed, supplies the basis for the first four of the following principles of pruning:

1. *Pruning has a depressing or stunting effect on the vine; the removal of living vegetative parts at any time decreases the capacity or total productive ability of the vine.* Capacity is largely determined by the number, size, and quality of the leaves and the length of time during which they are active. Pruning during the dormant season reduces the total number of leaves that will be formed during the growing season by restricting the number of shoots, and also delays the formation of the main leaf area until well into the summer. It thus reduces both the total leaf area and the length of time during which most of the leaves function. In consequence, smaller quantities of carbohydrates (such as sugar and, finally, starch) will be formed and the amounts available for nourishing the roots, stems, shoots, flowers, and fruit will be less (figs. 75 and 76, and table 19).

Thus, to the grower, pruning has two pronounced effects: it concentrates the activities of the vine into the parts left, but it diminishes the total capacity of the vine for growth and fruit production. Correct pruning consists in achieving the first effect to the extent required, while minimizing the second as much as possible.

2. *The production of crop depresses the capacity of the vine for the following year or years.* Growers recognize that vines with a very heavy crop grow less vigorously than vines with a light crop, and also that vines that overbear in one year are likely to have a lighter crop the next year. This effect has been indi-

cated very definitely in the irregularity of cropping that has been the rule for certain varieties in California. The crops of 1938, 1943, 1946, 1951, 1955, and 1971 were outstanding in volume. Each of these years of excessive over-cropping was followed by lower yields. Owing to other conditions, such as unusually favorable weather, better management, etc., the years of lowest yield did not always follow the heaviest crops immediately. But they did follow. A vine severely depressed by a heavy overcrop one year may be further depressed the next year by what might usually be considered a normal crop. The effect of crop, as such, on vine growth, however, has not been clearly understood, mainly because under vineyard conditions it is impractical to separate the effects of crop and pruning. This effect is illustrated in figure 73 (right side), which shows the growth of a series of vines treated alike in every respect except crop. The bar graphs show very definitely, within the limits of the trials, that the growth of the vines falls off with the increase in crop.

3. *The capacity of a vine varies directly with the number of shoots that develop.* The total active leaf area, not the rate of elongation of the shoots, determines capacity. A severely pruned vine having only a few shoots that elongate very rapidly will seem vigorous; yet it will be excelled in production by another vine that, having numerous shoots of slower growth, makes no great show of vigor yet nevertheless produces a larger total leaf area. This relation is illustrated by figures 73 and 75. On the average, the severely pruned vines had 23 shoots each, the normally pruned had 33, the cane-pruned thinned had 42, the nonpruned part-crop had 48, and the nonpruned all-crop had 49.

4. *The vigor of the shoots of a vine varies inversely with the number of shoots and with the amount of crop.* The fewer the shoots permitted to develop and the smaller the crop, the more vigorously (rapidly) each shoot will grow. The first part of this principle is illustrated by the response of Muscat of Alexandria and Monukka vines that were not permitted to bear (Winkler, 1934). On severely pruned vines the average number of shoots that developed was only 22 per vine and the average length of shoots was 6.8 feet; on the non-pruned vines the average number of shoots that developed was 64 per vine and the average length of shoot was 4.2 feet. How crop affects shoot growth is indicated by the length of the shoots on nonpruned vines of the same varieties. The shoots of the no-crop vines made an average length growth of 4.2 feet; those of the part-crop vines, with 25.4 pounds of fruit to a vine, made 3.7 feet; and those of the all-crop vines, with 63.5 pounds of fruit, made 3.2 feet. Similarly, the normal spur-pruned vines without crop made an average shoot growth of 5.8 feet, whereas the shoots of the vines with a crop made an average growth of 4.7 feet.

The inverse relation between number of shoots and rate of growth finds special application in the development of young vines. The main object at this period in the vine's life is to develop a single, strong, vigorous shoot with which to form the permanent trunk; hence only one shoot is permitted to grow.

In a broader application, this principle applies to the arms of the mature vine as well as to its fruit. The fewer the number of arms, the more vigorous each will be. To obtain large clusters, one must limit their number; if large berries are wanted, there must not be too many on a cluster.

5. *The fruitfulness of a vine, within limits, varies inversely with the vigor of its shoots.* Within the limits of good commercial practice, methods that increase vigor favor fruitfulness. Failure to reckon with this fact (to maintain a proper balance between vigor and crop) leads, by the one extreme to excessive vigor, to reduced fruitfulness and, by the other extreme to overbearing, with poor quality of fruit and depression of the vine's capacity to a point beyond which there is again a reduction in fruitfulness. A proper balance is one that maintains a desirable vigor without diminishing the crop.

This relation of vigor to fruitfulness is illustrated in figure 79. The reduction in length of the shoots at the left reflects a weakened vine condition resulting from poor vineyard management. In other words, a vine that is weakened by overbearing, insects, diseases, or other causes cannot form as many flower clusters as a normal vine.

The shoot growths shown in the figure should not be considered as average for locations other than Davis; the average length of shoots under other conditions and with other varieties will differ from these. Thomas and Barnard (1937) reported a similar correlation for Sultana (Thompson Seedless) in Australia, first positive and then negative. Using total growth rather than cane length as a measure of vigor, bud fertility increased with an increase from poor to normal growth and decreased with very vigorous growth.

6. *A large cane, arm, or vine can produce more than a small one and therefore should carry more fruit buds.* As already pointed out, capacity is directly proportional to total growth. A cane of large size, therefore, has greater capacity than a small one but its buds are likely to be less fruitful (see principle 5). This being the case, a large cane should be pruned so that the spur or fruit cane retained from it will carry more buds than a spur or fruit cane from a small cane.

The same is true of arms or vines. If one arm on a vine has large canes and another the same number of small ones, more buds should be retained on the

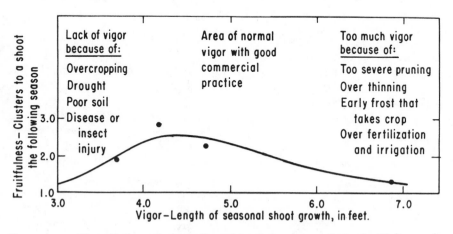

FIGURE 79: The relation of vigor (length) of shoot growth to fruitfulness of the buds of Muscat of Alexandria and Alicante Bouschet.

arm with the large canes. Similarly, a vine with large canes should be pruned so as to keep more or longer spurs or fruit canes than would be kept on a vine with canes that are small for the variety.

7. *A given vine in a given season can properly nourish and ripen only a certain quantity of fruit; its capacity is limited by its previous history and its environment.* Within the limit of a vine's capacity to bear fruit, the date of ripening is determined mainly by the seasonal accumulation of heat and cannot be hastened by further reduction in crop. The maximum crop that a vine will bear *without delaying maturity* is, therefore, an index to its bearing capacity. This is its normal crop. As the crop is increased beyond this point, the first effect is delayed maturity. Further successive increases in crop result in low sugar and acid content, "water berries," and drying of the tips of the clusters, reduced vine growth, and poor fruit-bud formation. The last will limit the next year's crop. These effects are the same, no matter whether the overcrop resulted from too long pruning, underthinning, shortage of moisture in the soil, disease or insect injury, or some other cause. Furthermore, overbearing not only results in poor fruit (Galley *et al.*, 1960), but also reduces the vine's capacity for future growth—both in top and root (Eremeev, 1960) and in production. Thus, every vine must be pruned on the basis of its own condition. A vine that has borne too heavily must be protected from a recurrence of overproduction and consequent exhaustion. Growers usually attempt to overcome the weakening effects of overbearing by severe pruning which limits the crop of the next season by reducing the number of fruitful buds retained. This is the cheapest method of guarding against overbearing and exhaustion. Since, however, severe pruning is in itself weakening (see principles 1 and 3), the more rational method would be to prune less severely and then limit the crop by removing some flower clusters as soon as possible after leafing out, or by thinning soon after the berries have set. This procedure rehabilitates the vines faster and places the operation of crop limitation at a time when the vines are in leaf and when a better estimate of crop in relation to leaf area is possible.

In addition to the above principles, the following relationships of growth and fruiting will be observed and exploited by the careful pruner.

Conditions of good vine carbohydrate nutrition, moderate shoot growth, and normal crops favor both the early maturing of the shoots and the abundant formation of fruitful buds. In contrast, continued rapid shoot growth and other abnormal conditions of nutrition will interfere with both shoot maturation and fruit-bud differentiation. The wood of mature canes is firm and carries a large storage of reserve materials, such as starch and sugars. The color of the bark is characteristic for the variety almost to the ends of such canes. In canes that are only partly mature, because of overbearing or for other reasons, the distal part, in contrast, never becomes woody, does not color normally, and usually freezes and dries up before pruning time. Such partly mature canes carry only a moderate storage of reserves, and the weaker canes are deficient in these materials.

Length of internode is another index of the type of growth that the canes have made and is significant of the fruitfulness of their buds. Shoots forming at the beginning of the season and making regular growth will have internodes of normal length for the variety. The fact that a cane has internodes of normal length, other conditions being favorable, indicates good bud development and a well-matured condition of its wood. Long internodes indicate excessively vigorous growth, a characteristic of shoots that form late in the growing season; such shoots often grow until checked by cold weather, and both their buds and their wood are likely to be immature. Very short internodes, on the other hand, indicate slow growth—the result of poor nutrition or, more often, disease, especially viruses, or insect injury or drought.

Observation has indicated that buds are generally fruitful on one-year-old canes that arise from two-year-old wood. On this basis many pruners select for spurs and fruit canes only the canes that come from two-year-old wood. Yet time and character of growth—normal length of internodes and normal maturing of the wood—are more revealing of bud condition than a cane's position of origin. For example, when the growth and maturing of water sprouts parallel those of the shoots arising from the spurs or fruit canes, their wood and buds will mature normally and they are, therefore, suitable for spurs or fruit canes. If, however, the water sprouts grow rapidly and late, their buds are poorly nourished and will mostly remain sterile. To the inexperienced pruner or the laborer who prunes only occasionally, position of origin of the cane may be the simplest means of selecting wood that usually has good buds, but the careful pruner should select the canes to be cut to spurs and fruit canes by their conditions. This provides a greater choice, which will not only result in better spurs and canes, but will also be an aid in maintaining the shape of the vines.

The first growth in spring usually comes from the buds nearest the ends of canes or spurs and those on the highest parts of the vine. Earlier starting gives the shoots from such buds an advantage over later-starting shoots. Besides, a vertical position of canes or growing shoots, through its effect on polarity, tends to retard the development of buds on the middle and lower parts of the canes and of laterals on the shoots. In the training of young vines, these effects of position on growth are utilized—the shoot selected to form the trunk of a vine is tied to a stake or other support to keep it erect. In the pruning of mature vines, efforts are made to neutralize the effects of position on growth. The spurs of head-pruned vines are formed and maintained near a common level or equal exposure. The parts of the trunks or branches of cordon vines that bear the spurs are formed and maintained in a horizontal position, with the spurs all at a common level; vertical cordons cannot be maintained, because the lower arms weaken, owing to unequal competition and shading, and after some years must be removed. Long fruit canes, with cane pruning are bent down and tied in a horizontal position on the trellis.

Near the northern limit of *vinifera* grape growing in Europe, where growth is limited, the shoots of bearing vines that will be used for fruit canes the next year are tied erect to a stake. The fruit canes are tied in a bow or horizontal position, and the shoots arising from them are allowed to droop. The erect shoots grow vigorously, and their capacity as fruit canes for the next year is increased.

DORMANT PRUNING

The principal pruning is done while the vine is dormant, between leaf-fall in autumn and the starting of the buds in spring. In large vineyards it may be necessary to spread the pruning over most of this period; in smaller vineyards it is usually possible to prune in the month that the grower considers most favorable.

Time of pruning.—In deciding upon the best time for pruning, one must consider the facilitation of other vineyard operations and also the possible effect on the health and bearing of the vine. Early pruning usually fits in best with the other operations. Pruning in December or January allows ample time to dispose of the prunings, to tie the vines and fruit canes, to do the winter cultivation, and, where necessary, to irrigate before the starting of the buds.

Past generations of viticulturists assumed that the time of pruning materially influenced the amount of reserve foods (sugars and starch) stored in the trunk and roots. This assumption was based on supposedly rapid translocation of the stored reserves between the above-ground and below-ground parts of the vine.

Investigations on both American (Richey and Bowers, 1924 and Schrader, 1924) and *vinifera* varieties (Antcliff *et al.*, 1958; Winkler and Williams, 1945; and Eifert *et al.*, 1961) have shown, however, that there is no appreciable transfer of sugars or starch from the canes to the roots after leaf-fall in the autumn. The basic reason for the absence of movement of reserve foods was clarified by Esau (1948), who found that the phloem of the vine is inactive at Davis from late November (after frost) until mid-March. During this period, the sieve plates are coated with a thick layer of callus. A marked reduction in starch in the canes takes place in late autumn and is accompanied by an almost equivalent increase in sugars. Thus, the changes hitherto observed are changes from one form of carbohydrate to another, not in the total amount of reserve food. The changes in starch and sugar occurring in the canes of vines during the dormant season at Davis are shown in figure 80. The graphs of this figure, with similar data (Winkler and Williams, 1945) for other parts of the vine, support the conclusion that the food materials accumulate as stored reserves in all parts of the vine during summer and fall. They remain stored, without appprecciable movements after leaf-fall until the following spring, when they are

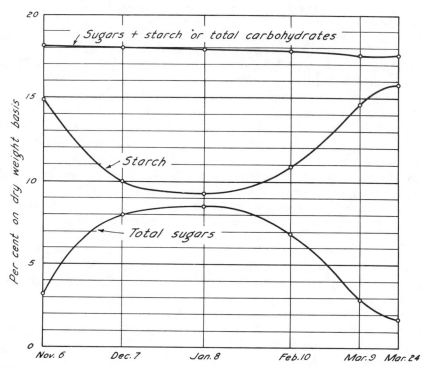

FIGURE 80: The change from starch to sugars and sugars back to starch in the canes of the vine during the dormant season, while total carbohydrates remain almost constant. (*Calif. Agr. Ext. Ser. Cir. 89*)

utilized in the starting of new growth. Considering these results, one may safely say that pruning at any time after leaf-fall and before the start of growth in spring can have little or no effect on the amount of the carbohydrate reserves of the vine.

Within the dormant season, the time of pruning has little or no effect on vigor of growth or on the crop, except when frost occurs soon after the buds start growth in the spring. Vines pruned very late in the season usually start growth slightly later than those pruned in mid-dormancy. Pruning when the upper buds on the canes have grown several inches will retard growth on the bearing units as much as a week to ten days if the weather remains cool. Such a delay in starting growth may avoid damage by late spring frosts (see frost protection p. 493).

Except in a few areas in southern California and the central coastal counties, differences in yield caused by pruning at different times between December 1 and March 1 are negligible. In these areas late pruning (after

March 15) has resulted in marked increases in yield. The reason is not fully understood; it seems to be related in some way to a late summer and fall drought condition associated with low to minimal boron nutrition.

Vigorously growing vines pruned before leaf-fall may be weakened, since pruning removes the leaves and stops the accumulation of reserves. It has been reported in Russia (Basan'Ko and Truzhova, 1953) that the leaves are still very active in October. In fact, the rate of photosynthesis was reported to be greater in early October than in mid-September or earlier in the season. In tests made at Davis, no injurious effects were observed when vines that had ceased length growth, but still retained most of their leaves, were pruned during the third week in October several weeks before frost.

As shown by the figures of table 20, the sugars and starch in the basal part of the canes increased only slightly after October 7.

The vines pruned September 7 leafed out at once—their buds must not have been in profound rest—and some made 6 to 10 inches of growth. A few buds grew after the September 21 pruning. The October 7 and later prunings were not followed by growth. There was no deleterious effect on the growth or fruiting of the vines pruned after October 7 in the following year. By this time the Valdepeñas vines had dropped one third of their leaves and the canes of St. Emilion were brown over 75 per cent of their length. This work should be followed over a number of years. (Caution is given against early pruning of vines that have been over-cropped and have a low level of carbohydrate reserves.)

Pruning late, after the roots are active, causes bleeding—loss of liquid from the pruning cuts. In fact, bleeding may occur at pruning in mid-winter if the vine roots have been stimulated into growth by an irrigation

TABLE 20

LEVEL OF SUGARS AND STARCH IN THE BASAL PART OF VINES PRUNED
DURING EARLY AUTUMN

| Dates of pruning | Total sugars and starch, in per cent of dry weight | | | |
| | Valdepeñas [a] | | St. Emilion [b] | |
	At pruning	Next Feb. 15	At pruning	Next Feb. 15
September 7	14.2	14.4	11.5	13.4
September 21	16.4	15.5	16.2	16.0
October 7	16.9	16.5	18.0	17.4
October 21	16.9	17.1	19.0	18.0
November 7	17.3	16.9	18.4	17.5

SOURCE OF DATA: A. J. Winkler (Unpublished data).

[a] The canes of Valdepeñas were entirely mature, but retained most of their leaves, and the fruit was 25 degrees Brix on September 7.

[b] The canes of St. Emilion were brown over only 10 per cent of their length and the fruit was 21 degrees Brix on September 7.

with warm water or following several warm sunny days. Ordinarily, the vines are not injured by this loss of liquid. By recutting the tips of canes every other day, as much as 19 liters of liquid have been collected from a single large vine, yet its growth and productivity were not affected. Normally the liquid contains 2 to 4 grams of dry matter per liter, about two thirds organic matter and one third inorganic matter (Dvornic, 1954, and Negrul and Nikiforva, 1958). After a frost the liquid may for a short while contain three to four times as much dry matter, which gives it a slightly sweet taste. According to Kás and Hanousek (1946), a liter of the liquid of bleeding vines contained 3.5 gm. of reducing sugar, 0.35 gm. of polysaccharides, 0.04 gm. of nitrogen, 0.356 gm. of potassium, 0.148 gm. of calcium, 0.013 gm. of phosphate as oxides, and a trace of iron. More recently Skene (1967) and Skene and Antcliff (1972) have shown that significant amounts of the plant hormones, gibberellin and cytokinins, occur in the bleeding sap of grapevines.

Amount of pruning.—An average vine before pruning may have 25 canes, with 30 buds on each (a total of 750 buds). Even though the vine remains unpruned, not all of these will start—that is, produce shoots. Probably only 100 to 150 will do so. If the canes are pruned back, leaving only 100 or 150 buds, almost the same number of shoots will be produced. The primary effect will be that buds nearer the bases of the canes will start instead of buds farther up on the canes. If the vine is pruned still shorter to leave only 40–60 buds, fewer shoots will be produced. Since this small number will have a proportionately larger storage of reserves for each shoot, as well as the same root system to supply water and soil nutrients, each shoot will grow more vigorously and become larger (see principle 4, p. 298). Fewer bunches will be produced, but each may have its flowers somewhat better developed. Although the total weight of the crop will be less than that of an unpruned or very lightly pruned vine, the quality will be much better.

To increase the severity of the pruning—that is, diminsh still further the number of buds left—will increase the vigor of the individual shoots at the expense of total growth and crop. There are two reasons for this. First, severe pruning decreases cluster size, since the clusters in the basal buds are often smaller, without causing a corresponding increase in berry size. Second, the excessive vigor given to the shoots is unfavorable to fruiting, often causing excessive dropping of the flowers at blooming. The pruner, therefore, when crop is controlled by pruning, should leave just enough fruit buds to furnish the number of clusters that the vine can bring to perfect maturity. Beyond this point, total growth and crop are diminished, quality is reduced, and vigor of the individual shoots is correspondingly increased. This increase in vigor results not alone from the reduced number of buds, but also from crop curtailment, which leaves the vine more energy for the work of vegetative growth. Heavy winter pruning, therefore, invigorates the vine by diminishing the crop. Light winter pruning increases the crop. If this increase is represented by more clusters than the vine can properly nourish, the crop will be inferior in quality and the vine will be weakened by overbearing.

Vines that have been pruned moderately long for years and then are pruned short to curtail crop will often produce numerous water sprouts. Many of the basal buds that remained latent under moderately long pruning will be stimulated to grow by the temporary imbalance between top and roots brought on by the shorter pruning. In varieties of which the basal buds are fruitful the growth of water sprouts may largely or wholly offset the desired reduction of crop. When such a condition arises, it should be corrected by judicious head suckering before the water sprouts are more than a few inches long. Head suckering for one to three years will bring the vine into balance again and remove the tendency to throw water sprouts.

Amount of wood to retain.—On a mature vine that has produced good crops and shows normal vigor, the pruner should leave the same number of bearing units and fruit buds as in the year before. If the vine seems abnormally vigorous, he should leave more fruit buds in order to divert more energy to producing the crop. If, however, the vine seems weak, he should prune it more severely than in the year before—that is, leave fewer fruit buds—in order to strengthen it by diverting more of its energy from crop production to growth and to replenishing the store of reserve food materials. Or, better yet, the vine may be pruned moderately, provided some of the flower clusters are removed before or shortly after bloom depending on the variety. Under this treatment the result will be a greater total growth than under severe pruning (see principle 1, p. 297). Any attempt to make a weak vine bear a large crop by longer pruning without crop thinning can result only in further weakening and the production of inferior grapes. If a weak vine is pruned for a small crop, or is pruned moderately and crop is reduced by removal of flower clusters, the grapes will be of good quality and the vine will be invigorated so that it can produce normal crops under normal pruning in subsequent years (Winkler, 1934).

Thinning, however, is not usually economical in the production of raisin and wine grapes. Thus, pruning will continue to be the principal means of regulating the crop of these varieties, even though it results in lower quality in some years. When pruning is the sole control of crop, and if normal production is to be obtained over the years, the vines must overproduce to a degree in some years and underproduce in others. Recently Lider *et al.* (1973) initiated work to determine whether or not a system of pruning, based on the weight of previous year's cane growth, would provide a better balance of crop and growth. To date the results have not been as striking as those obtained by Shaulis (1960) in the "balanced pruning" of American grapes, especially Concord (see p. 332).

Forecasting crop potential.—Research on bud fruitfulness was initiated in Australia by Barnard (1932) and Barnard and Thomas (1933). Further studies were made by Antcliff *et al.* (1957, 1958) and by Antcliff and Thomas (1955) in Austrialia, Kondo (1955) in Russia, Alleweldt (1958, 1960) in Germany, and Immink (1958) in South Africa. Microscopic examinations were made of the buds on a number of representative canes from a given area in early fall. A high correlation was found between the number of cluster primordia and potential crop. Years of experience in forecasting crop yield in Australia, where bud fruitfulness of Thompson Seedless varies from 30 to 65 per cent between years, convinced the researchers that this procedure is worthwhile for that variety in their country.

In areas of Europe bud fruitfulness was determined by Wurgler *et al.* (1955) and Briza and Milosavljevic (1954, 1958) by taking segments of canes similar to those to be retained at pruning and forcing them into growth. In the early fall, however, the buds are in deep rest, thus to get them to grow, the segments were subjected to ethylene chlorohydrin (15 g/m^3) for 24 hours. The basal end of the segments were then placed in fresh water at 20° to 25° C. in the greenhouse. After three or four weeks, the buds had pushed enough that their clusters were visible.

The value of either of the above procedures with Thompson Seedless in central California, where the percentage of fruitful buds is always high, is questionable. It might have some value in the desert area, where the fruitfulness of its buds is lower. There, pruning, however, is such that it places an upper limit on potential crop and the final load is actually controlled by cluster and berry thinning after blooming.

Tests of this procedure at Davis have not been encouraging, largely owing to the fact that in California, where the winters are mild, pruning is started as soon as the leaves are off, or even earlier.

Units of pruning.—When a vine has reached the stage of full bearing, pruning consists of removing all the growth except (*a*) *bearing units* for the production of fruit and new wood or fruit only, (*b*) *renewal spurs* for renewal or the production of wood for the next year, and (*c*) *replacement spurs*, in the older vines, for the replacing or shortening of arms.

The length of the bearing units is largely determined by the fruiting habit of the variety to be pruned—that is, by the location of the fruitful buds on the canes and by the size of the clusters. On varieties having fruitful buds to the base of the canes, short bearing units are retained. This is called *spur-pruning*. On varieties whose buds toward the base of the cane are sterile (unfruitful), or whose clusters are small, long bearing units must be used in order to secure a full crop. This is *cane-pruning*. Occasionally, bearing units of intermediate length are retained—*half-long pruning*. Because the shape of vines so pruned is difficult to maintain, this last method is not recommended. The treatment of a single arm by spur-pruning and cane-pruning is used here to illustrate the units of pruning and their use in each method.

The units of pruning in short, or spur, pruning are illustrated in figure 81, which shows a long arm about twelve years old. At the end of the arm is the two-bud spur, S_2, of the previous year, bearing two canes, C_1 and C_2. Nearer the base of the arm, a single water sprout, WS, is growing out of the old wood. Such an arm would normally bear other water sprouts, since they would all be removed entirely at pruning, they have been taken away to simplify the figure.

In the pruning of such an arm, one of the canes growing from S_2 (the spur of the previous year) is cut back to form a new spur for producing fruit and wood this year; the other cane is removed entirely. In deciding which cane to use for the new spur, one that is well ripened and moderately thick and has well-formed buds is chosen. Among canes that fulfill this condition, the one that is most likely to preserve or improve the form of the vine should be chosen. This cane, in most cases, will be the one nearest the base of the spur of the previous year (C_2 in fig. 81),

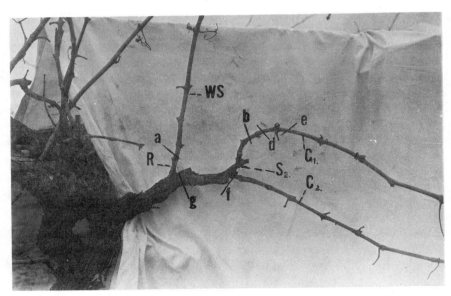

FIGURE 81: The units of short, or spur, pruning. S_2, two-bud spurs; C_1 and C_2, canes; WS, water-sprout; R, replacement spur. The lines at a,b,c,d,e,f, and g indicate where cuts are to be made as explained in text.

because it increases the length of the arm the least. If this one is weak, however, or its direction of growth is unsuitable, as in this case, then C_1 or some other cane must be chosen.

When a cane arising from the base bud of the spur of the previous year is chosen for the new spur, the arm is lengthened imperceptibly. A spur from the first bud (C_2) will lengthen it, usually, a little over an inch; one from the second bud (C_1), 2 or 3 inches. In any case, the arm finally becomes too long, like that in the figure. It should then be shortened or replaced. One may use a conveniently placed water sprout for a replacing spur, as at R in the figure, and cut back the arm in the place indicated by the line g. If the water sprout is not well matured, the cutting back of the arm should be deferred until the following year. Meanwhile the fruit spur from cane C_1 will bear a crop; the replacing spur R will produce fruit wood for the following year.

The chosen cane C_1 is cut at b, d, or e, leaving a fruit spur of two, three, or four fruit buds, in accordance with its capacity and the fruiting habit of the variety, and the cane C_2 is removed entirely by a cut at f. The more vigorous the variety and the particular cane, the more buds should be left. As a general rule, a spur retained from a cane as thick as one's thumb should be cut to three or sometimes four buds, whereas a spur from a cane thinner than a lead pencil should have only one bud. Four-bud spurs should be used sparingly since the first and possibly the second bud also on such long spurs usually fail to grow. If at all possible, it is more desirable to leave two spurs; one of two buds and the other of three buds. However, it is only by retaining more buds on the pruning unit or units of a large cane or arm that its potential for crop can be fully utilized and its growth brought into balance with the rest of the vine. The base buds are not counted; the first bud counted should have a definite internode between it and the base of the cane. The water sprout is cut back at a, leaving a replacing spur of one bud when the cane is small, or of two or three buds when the cane is large and well matured. Of course, a replacing spur is left only when the arm is too long and should be shortened.

The units in short (or spur) pruning, therefore, consist of a single fruit spur of one to three fruit buds and, when occasion arises, a replacement spur of one, two, or three buds. In the latter case the arm is shortened immediately.

Figure 82 shows the units of pruning in long, or cane, and half-long systems. S_2 represents the renewal spur of two years before. On it was left a fruit cane, F_2, which produced the crop of the past season and a renewal spur, S_1, which has produced fruit wood for the coming season.

In pruning, the fruit cane F_2 is removed entirely at g. The upper cane, C_2, of the renewal spur (S_1) is used for a new fruit cane and shortened to about f for half-long pruning and to about f_1 or f_2 for cane pruning.

The diameter and length of a cane should determine the length of the fruit cane retained from it—with Thompson Seedless, from eight buds for a small cane to fifteen buds for a larger cane. To leave longer canes will result in numerous buds remaining dormant, in overloading the canes, and in increasing the cost of getting the canes off the trellis at pruning. The lower cane, C_1, is cut back to two buds at *a* to form a renewal spur, S, which will produce the new wood for the next winter pruning—one-bud to produce a new fruiting cane: one bud to produce another renewal spur.

Often this procedure must be modified. If the cane C_2 is unsuitable because of lack of size, another cane (such as C_1, or even B, D, or E) near the base of the old fruit cane may be used for a new fruit cane. In the same way, any suitably placed cane may be used for a renewal spur. Water sprouts from three-year, four-year, or older wood may also be used.

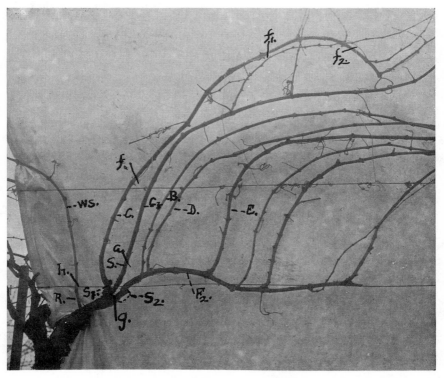

FIGURE 82: The units of long, or cane pruning. S_1, and S_2, are renewal spurs of one and two years ago, and S will be the renewal spur of the coming season; F_2, fruit cane; C, C_1, B, D, and E, canes; WS, water-sprout; R, replacing spur. The lines at a, f, f_1, f_2, g, and h indicate places where canes are to be cut according to different systems explained in the text.

Pruning

Preferably, the renewed spur will be below the fruit cane—that is, nearer the trunk.

Replacing spurs for shortening the arms are occasionally needed, as in spur pruning; but the same spur can usually be used both for renewal and for replacing. The water sprout R may be used for this purpose, being cut at *h*.

In either cane or half-long pruning, therefore, the units of pruning consist of the fruit cane, the renewal spur, and the replacement spur.

Restriction and treatment of wounds.—The possible length of life of a vine is seemingly unlimited. Actual profitable life varies from a few years to fifty or more. Vines may be killed by some disease or by unfavorable conditions, such as severe freezing or prolonged drought. Most vines fail and become unprofitable because of an accumulation of small injuries. Among the chief of these are pruning wounds, which not only destroy wood, bark, and other conducting tissues, but also allow the entrance of boring insects and wood-destroying fungi.

All pruning wounds, therefore, should be as small as possible, especially on the main body and other permanent parts of the vine. By using foresight one can largely avoid the necessity of making large wounds.

Useless canes should be removed while they are small, and necessary renewals of arms or branches should be made before the part to be suppressed becomes too large. The vine heals its wounds from the inside by producing gummy matter—tyloses—that fills up the ducts and tissues and so prevents loss of sap. It may cover the above-ground wounds with healing tissues from the outside, but not so easily nor so quickly as many fruit trees do: wounds more than an inch in diameter seldom heal over completely. Small, close wounds are engulfed as the vine grows.

By careful and skillful use of the pruning tools one can keep harm from necessary wounds to a minimum. All cuts should be made clean, and those of canes and spurs should be smooth. The shears should be sharp. If they are held at the proper angle, there will be no splitting or cracking of the wood. Canes for spurs should be cut at a slight angle, not at a right angle to the grain. In cutting off a cane or spur entirely, place the blades of the shears against the vine and cut without unduly bending the part removed. This will ensure a clean, close cut and the very short stub will dry back sufficiently to prevent the growth of undesirable shoots from its basal buds. Stubs left when canes are removed never heal over; and they usually prevent the making of clean cuts at future prunings. Where large arms or parts are removed, a short stub with a length equal to one-half the diameter of the part removed should be retained. This permits the wound to heal (plug) without drying out so far inward that conducting tissue in either the wood or bark is seriously interrupted.

The cuts at the ends of spurs and canes should be made about a half inch above the last bud. This procedure leaves enough wood beyond the last bud to prevent drying out and reduces the exposed pith to a minimum. It leaves the woody diaphram intact to protect the spur from injury. If a long piece of internode is left beyond the last bud, it dies and offers entrance and harbor for wood-boring insects which may destroy the bud below. In some countries the cut is made through the bud above the last one of the pruner desires to have grow. This procedure leaves the diaphragm intact with no pith exposed. It requires skill obtained through long practice and is not recommended in California.

Disposal of prunings.—Although the pruning brush has no particular fuel, feed, or fertilizer value, its influence upon the texture of the soil has sometimes been found of value. The prunings improve the texture more as the soils become heavier and tighter. For this reason the practice of incorporating prunings into the soil is becoming general where the spacing of the vines is wide enough to permit the necessary implements to pass. A heavy (cover-crop) disk is usually satisfactory for reducing the prunings in size and incorporating them into the soil. Where available, brush-shredding machines are excellent for breaking up the brush into small fragments at relatively low cost. The shredder takes the brush from the ground if the pruners have put the brush in the middle of the space between the rows. Where it is impractical, for any reason, to incorporate the prunings into the soil, they may be burned in a brush burner in the

Figure 83: Power pruning. Left, pneumatic shear; right, power unit to supply air under pressure and to carry boon which carries air lines to 3 to 5 rows on either side. The power unit is self-guiding and moves along at a convenient rate.

vineyard or removed by means of a tractor-mounted buck rake, to be burned or used outside the vineyard.

Pruning tools.—For decades one-hand shears have been used in pruning unirrigated vines and short two-hand shears on the large vines in irrigated areas. Recently, pneumatic shears (fig. 83) have gained favor in some vineyards. This type conserves the energy of the pruner and is well adapted for spur-pruned vines. In some areas upwards of 25 per cent of the vines are now pruned with pneumatic shears.

SUMMER OR HERBACEOUS PRUNING

Summer pruning, of which there are many forms, consists in removing buds, shoots, or leaves while they are green, or herbaceous. Thus, it is done while the vine is growing or active.

The effects are similar to those of winter pruning in some ways, and opposite in others. If a part of a cane is removed in the winter, the vine is weakened through diminishing its latent possibilities of growth; yet indirectly this weakening effect is offset appreciably by diminished bearing. If, on the contrary, a growing shoot is removed in the summer, the vine is weakened through removal of the leaves, its chief manufacturing organs, to which it owes its vigor and capacity. This weakening effect is greatest in the middle of summer, when the vine is most active, its reserve food materials at their lowest level, and when it is most in need of carbohydrates supplied by the leaves. Removal of many leaves by defoliating insects at this time will destroy the crop and may seriously injure the vine. The danger is not so great in the early spring, before the reserve food materials stored in the vine during the previous season have been much reduced. At that stage some shoots or leaves can be removed without serious injury. In fact, vines struck by spring frosts often become more vigorous; the weakening caused by leaf removal is more than counterbalanced by the strengthening that results from the development of fewer shoots and the lack of or reduced crop.

The removal of growing shoots or parts of shoots also has an effect similar to that of winter pruning, in that the growth of the vine is concentrated in the remaining parts. This concentrating effect and the weakening effect occur in inverse ratio and will vary according to the time of pruning. In early spring, at the starting of the shoots, the weakening effect is slight and the concentrating effect is almost as marked as that of winter pruning (see principle 4, p. 298). In early summer, with the vines in full growth, the weakening effect may be sufficient to neutralize the concentrating effect completely—that is, the removal of some of the shoots may so weaken the vine that here will be no acceleration of growth in those that are left (Vega and Mavrich, 1959).

Uses of summer pruning.—Summer pruning has various uses, principally as follows:

To direct the growth into the parts that will form the permanent framework of the vine, such as the trunk, branches, and arms, and to keep these parts active and healthy. This is accomplished by such operations as disbudding, pinching, and suckering.

To alleviate wind damage by topping. This procedure reduces the surface exposed to the wind and checks length growth temporarily; the basal part of the shoot has time to become hardened and tough, so that it is broken off less easily.

To increase the shade on the fruit by topping, which promotes an upright position of shoots and growth of laterals.

To open the vines and thus expose the fruit more favorably to light and air.

Disbudding—Young vines are disbudded during their development. Disbudding consists of removing the swollen buds and young shoots from the lower part of the stem in order to concentrate the growth in one or more shoots which will be near the top where they can be used to develop branches of the cordon or arms of head trained vines. By this operation one can prevent the production of canes low on the trunk and avoid making wounds by cutting off such canes the next winter. The sooner the young shoots are removed, the better. Early removal prevents their using much of the reserves of the vine and comes when the concentrating effect of their removal is at its maximum. On younger vines that have not yet formed a stem, it consits in removing all the buds and young shoots but one. Thus, all the growth becomes concentrated into the single shoot that is to form the stem or trunk of the vine.

Late disbudding, done when the young shoots are more than 6 to 12 inches long, is better called shoot thinning. It is inferior to disbudding in that the vine is more weakened and the concentrating effect is correspondingly less.

Topping young vines.—Disbudding during the second year (or, in very hot regions, the first year) concentrates all the growth into a single shoot, making it grow with great vigor. When it is 12 to 20 inches above the top of the stake—that is, above the height at which the head will be developed —it should be topped, cutting through the next node above the desired height so a secure tie may be made below the swollen node. Topping in this severe manner stimulates the growth of laterals where they are desired; these may be used, at the next winter pruning, as fruit spurs and as the beginnings of permanent arms. If this topping is not done, there may be very few laterals on the mature trunk cane in the region where the grower desires to make the head. It will then be difficult to find buds in the proper place for developing the arms and to produce the crop that the vine should yield during the third season.

Suckering.—Suckering is the removal of the undesired shoots that originate on the trunk and below the ground. Neglect of suckering diminishes the vigor of the whole above-ground part of the vine. The suckers grow vigorously and appropriate food materials that should nourish the whole vine. Finally, the top is weakened so more and more of the growth goes into the suckers, and all the benefits of a properly trained vine are lost. One can renovate such a vine only by cutting off the old trunk and building up a new vine from vigorous sucker.

With grafted vines the consequences are even more serious. Suckers coming from the stock divert food materials from the top even more easily, since the top is connected to the root by the grafting union, which to some extent impedes the passage of water and food materials. A grafted vine seriously weakened by the prolonged growth of rootstock suckers is useless and cannot be renovated.

Suckering should be done with the greatest care and thoroughness during the first two to four years. This will save a great deal of expensive and troublesome work later. Vines properly cared for in this respect will produce very few suckers during the fourth and fifth years, and usually no suckers thereafter. If, on the contrary, the suckering has been done imperfectly during the first three years, numerous underground shoots will be produced year after year.

Suckering, like disbudding, should be done as early in the season as possible, for the reasons already given. There is another and even more important reason: especially where suckers are allowed to grow the entire summer, will promote the formation of mature base buds that may remain dormant, only to produce suckers in later years.

Young vines must be suckered two or three times during the spring. This is done every time the vines are visited for tying up. When soft and succulent, the suckers are easily pulled off without cutting. They must be removed completely at the base. When they become a little tough, one must dig down to their point of origin. To remove part of a sucker is bad practice. The part left behind forms an underground spur or arm—a source of perennial trouble.

Head suckering.—This suckering consists in the removal of shoots from the permanent parts of the vine, especially the water sprouts—shoots which arise from buds in older than one-year wood in the head of the vine. Suckering will prevent growth in places where growth is not wanted, will open the head of the vine in order to improve the quality of the fruit, or will concentrate growth in parts where growth is wanted. The removal of all sterile shoots, however, on the theory that they are useless, is a mistaken practice.

The regular growth of a large number of water sprouts, or the production of many sterile shoots, is usually a sign that an insufficient amount of the vine's capacity is being used for producing the crop or that the method of pruning is incorrect. The remedy is less severe pruning, or a type of winter pruning that is better adapted to the fruiting habit of the variety. The production of sterile shoots on what ought to be fruit wood often indicates some error in vineyard management that results in excessively vigorous growth or in too late growth of the vine in autumn.

Sterile shoots and water sprouts are by no means useless. Research, both here by Winkler (1932) and by Dvornic (1954) and by Negrul and Nikiforva (1958) abroad, shows conclusively that the products of their foliage nourish the vine and the clusters on the fruitful shoots. Then, too, they may be needed for the use as bearing units, renewal spurs, or replacement spurs, for which purpose their position often makes them a better choice than fruitful shoots. Studies by Huglin (1955, 1959) and Mel'nikov (1957) definitely prove that, when well matured, the buds of water sprouts are just as fruitful as those of regular canes.

Water sprouts are sometimes troublesome. They may grow through the clusters, making it impossible to harvest the crop without cluster injury, or may make the heads of the vines too dense. These results are especially harmful with table grapes. By removing the undesirable shoots early in the season, while they are small, one may overcome this trouble for the season. Suckering at that time will not appreciably weaken the plant, and it can be done for a small fraction of the cost of pruning off the excess canes. The removal of excess shoots also enable those retained to develop into better fruiting wood for the following year. Care must be taken not to remove too many shoots directly over the head of the vine. Exposure of the large branches and arms to the direct rays of the sun during midsummer will result in sunburn in the hotter regions.

The tendency of water sprouts to grow through the clusters may be minimized or overcome by changing to a wide-topped trellis or modifying the shape of the vine at the winter pruning, or both, so that all the clusters may hang free. Improvement may also be obtained by a better balance between wood growth and capacity to produce and the following season.

Pinching.—Pinching is removal of the growing 3 to 6 inch tip of a shoot with thumb and finger. Its weakening effect is very slight, since no expanded leaves and only a little material are sacrificed. The immediate effect is to arrest elongation of the shoot. If this is done when the shoot is 15 to 18 inches long, the shoot can toughen sufficiently to resist the wind before becoming long enough to afford the wind much pressure surface. Shoots pinched as early as this will usually produce, from a lateral, a new growing tip which later cannot be distinguished from an original growing tip.

It has been reported by several investigators, Le Roux and Malan

(1945), Skene (1969), and Coombe (1970), that the pinching of fruiting shoots at the beginning of blossoming induces a better fruit set (see chap. 14). The increase in fruit set on tipped shoots is believed to be due to reduced competition between developing leaves and ovaries for available organic nutrients.

Topping bearing vines.—Topping consists in removing 1 to 2 feet or more from the end of growing shoots, usually in June, July, or later. In some regions topping is practiced regularly, twice or even three times, during the season. When this is done, it is injurious to the vine and delays coloring and maturing of the fruit (Huglin, 1955, and Vega and Mavrich, 1959).

Topping tends to keep the canes upright and, by causing the development of laterals, to increase the shade. In very windy districts topping may be advisable. To cut off part of the young shoot and save the remainder is better than to have the wind break off the entire shoot. The later the topping is done, the more the practice weakens the vine.

Since topping removes mature leaves, it is weakening. Winkler (1949) reported that the removals of 20, 40, and 50 per cent of the leaves of Emperor and Aramon vines in early June reduced the coloring of the fruit 11, 20, and 36 percent and delayed maturity for one, two, and two-and-a-half weeks, respectively, in that year. In the next year, when no leaves were removed, the crops of the same lots of vines were reduced 15, 46, and 70 per cent, respectively. The loss of crop in the second year was owing to poorer development of fruit buds in the season when the leaf removals were made; the result was a marked reduction in the number of clusters and flowers that formed.

However, under certain conditions, topping may not cause so much weakening as expected. Repeated topping is a custom in many European vineyards, but there the spacing both within the vines and between the rows is such that many mature basal leaves are shaded, and therefore not producing. Topping exposes these leaves to the sun and their renewed photosynthetic activity offsets to a considerable degree the loss of the upper-most leaves.

The usual opening of the center of the vine as the shoots elongate and bend downward is an advantage, promoting the coloring of the grapes that require light for color development and making the control of mildew easier. Sometimes, however, it increases the sunburn of the grapes. Sunburn may be caused by excessive heat or by desiccation. After a protracted cool period, a severe hot spell with temperatures of 104° F. or more may cause damage even to fully shaded grapes. The fruit is not all equally sensitive to heat injury; fruit constantly exposed on the outside of the vine will withstand more heat than that protected by continuous shade. Perhaps the commonest form of sunburn—often found in dry vineyards—

is caused by an excess of evaporation over sap supply to the fruit; this is essentially a temporary drought effect. Such injury seldom occurs when vines have ample water, but a deficiency of soil moisture may prevent the vine from absorbing enough water to replace that lost by evaporation from the leaves and fruit, thereby making the fruit more liable to injury. Large crops reduce the carbohydrate nutrition of the roots through competition, which in turn lessens the ability of the roots to forage for water. Sunburn is usually worse, therefore, on vines with heavy crops than on vines with normal crops. Increasing the shade by topping is merely a palliative, and any practice that further weakens the vine may increase the trouble.

If the growing shoots are topped lightly before they are 3 feet long, the shade is increased in two ways. First, since they are relieved of the weight of the growing top, they grow more upright until they are lignified enough to retain their upright position. Second, they produce laterals that increase the number of leaves near the base and over the head of the vine. Topping done later is less effective in these respects; moreover, since it involves the removal of mature leaves, it may weaken the vine so much that it increases susceptibility to sunburn.

Removing mature leaves.—Removing the basal leaves on table grape vines permits the clusters to hang free, so that the berries are free of wind scarring and the bloom is not rubbed away. Removing the leaves below the clusters in June is usually sufficient.

In varieties that require light for color formation (see p. 161), coloring can be promoted by opening the vines. One means of doing this is to remove some of the leaves. For this purpose only, leaves in the heads of staked vines and those on the lower parts of the north or east sides of trellised vines should be removed. The number of leaves to be taken away depends on the size and vigor of the vines. The removal of one eighth to one fourth of the leaves in this part of the vine will usually give the desired results. More drastic treatment will weaken the vines and may stop development of the fruit.

Removal of the interior leaves may sometimes be useful for protecting very late varieties from molding after rains. It allows sun and air to reach the grapes freely and helps to evaporate the moisture quickly from their surfaces.

Allowing sheep or other animals to eat the leaves immediately or soon after the harvest of early varieties is undoubtedly a bad practice. It removes the leaves before they have fulfilled their important duty of providing the reserve food to be stored up in the canes, trunk, and roots for the growth of the next spring. "Sheeping" the vineyard in late fall, however, after the vines are thoroughly mature, does no harm.

The systems of pruning are numerous. They differ in the form given to the body of the vine and in the number and length of the pruning units retained. Some of the differences depend on variations in the nature of the vines, on the cultivating and growing conditions of the district, and on the objectives of the grower. Others are merely matters of taste. The best system is the one most adapted to all conditions of the particular vineyard. Any system is defective if it does not take into account the nature of growth and fruiting habit of the variety.

The essential differences among the pruning systems are few; on the basis of these, the systems may be classified according to: arrangement and amount of old wood; length of the units of bearing wood; and management and placement of the bearing units. According to the arrangement and amount of the old (permanent) wood, the systems may be divided into two groups. In the first, the trunk has a definite head, from which all the branches or arms rise symmetrically at nearly the same level. This is *head-training* with *spur-* or *cane-pruning*. The group includes the systems of spur-pruning and cane-pruning as used in California, the Guyot system, the Médoc system, and similar systems used in the various grape-growing countries. In the second group the trunk is elongated 4 to 8 feet or more and the arms are distribtued regularly along all or most of its length. Because of the ropelike form of the trunks of such vines, this is called *cordon-training* with *spur-* or *cane-pruning*. It is represented by the vertical, the unilateral, and the bilateral horizontal cordon systems in California, South Africa, and Australia, and by similar systems in the other grape-growing countries.

The headed vines are classed, according to the length of the vertical trunk to the lowest arm, into: high, 4 to 6 feet; medium, 2 to 4 feet; and low, 1 to 2 feet. In headed vines trained on arbors the trunk may be 6 to 7 feet long. The arms of a headed vine may be arranged symmetrically in all directions or only in the direction of the trellis and may rise at angles varying from near o to about 45 degrees. This form, or some modification of it, has been used in many vineyards.

The cordons are vertical or horizontal, according to the direction of the trunk. The horizontal ones may be single (unilateral) or composed of two branches extending in opposite directions (bilateral). Double and even multiple vertical and horizontal cordons occur, as in the espalier system, but these have no advantages in the commercial vineyard and are inadvisable. On the vertical or upright cordon the arms are arranged at as regular intervals as possible on all sides of the trunk, from the top to within 15 to 20 inches of the bottom. On the horizontal cordon the arms are spaced at regular intervals, but as nearly as possible on the upper side only of the horizontal part of the trunk.

Each of these pruning systems may again be divided into two types, according to the length of the bearing units. In the most severe types, some of the canes retained for bearing units are cut back to one- and two-bud spurs. This is *short-spur* pruning. In *long-spur* pruning the bearing units are three and four-bud spurs. In the other systems long canes are left for fruit production. This is *cane-pruning* or *long-pruning*. In *short* or *half-long* pruning canes of five-to-eight-bud bearing units are retained. In cane-pruning, each fruiting cane is usually accompanied by one short renewal spur. These must also accompany half-long pruning. Systems that leave only long canes without renewal spurs are usually defective, in that they make it impossible to maintain a desirable form of the vine. In all systems, replacing spurs are left wherever and whenever needed.

In long-pruning the management or positioning of the bearing units varies greatly. The differences depend on variations in the cultivating and growing conditions of the grape-producing regions and the type of support.

In California, if a trellis is used, the canes are distributed equally in the two directions of the trellis from the vine. For years raisin growers have tied the canes to a single wire trellis. This exposes the fruit unduly to sunburn after the shoots take on a drooping position. A two-wire vertical trellis with all the canes tied to the lower wire overcomes most of the tendency to sunburn since the shoots that attach themselves to upper wire provide shade over the fruit. Better yet, would be a three-wire wide-top trellis with the canes tied to the lower wire which is stapled to the stakes. The shoots grow up between the two wires on the crossarm, then droop, thus covering the fruit but exposing more leaf surface to the sun.

In this practice the head of the vine should be formed at a height that is below the wire to which the canes are tied. For table grapes a multiple wire, wide-top trellis with the canes tied separately to the wires is better (fig. 84). With a wide-top trellis, the head should be formed just below the wires. Forming the head within 6–8 inches of the crossarm height favors growth and development of the shoots rising from the renewal spurs. If the head is low, the renewal spurs are certain to be shaded and will often fail to produce siutable fruit canes for the following season.

With certain wine-variety grapes that are cane-pruned, the canes are often tied across the head of the vine in the form of a basket; sometimes they are tied vertically to a stake. Both methods are defective. Vigorous vines that are cane pruned should be trellised; vines that are not vigorous seldom need cane-pruning. For the latter, long spurs (4 to 5 buds) can be made to suffice. When long spurs are used for this purpose, the vine should be headed high enough that the spurs with their fruit will not interfere with cultivation after the weight of the crop bends them downward. Such long spurs should be accompanied by renewal spurs.

COMMERCIAL SYSTEMS OF PRUNING

The systems of pruning that are used extensively in commercial vineyards of California may be grouped into three general types; convenient names for these three types are cane-pruning, cordon-pruning, and head-pruning. There are various subtypes, each having advantages for special conditions. The first general type and its subtypes take their name from the bearing unit—the fruit cane—and from the position of the bearing units on the supports. The other two of the general types (and their subtypes), in which the retained annual growth is usually reduced to spurs, are distinguished by the form given to the more permanent parts of the vine.

Cane-pruning.—With the advent of mechanical harvesting cane-pruning is rapidly becoming the most generally used system in California. The

FIGURE 84: A mature head-trained, cane-pruned vine.

long bearing units are readily positioned on the trellis so the machine has ready access to the fruit.

In cane-pruning, the vine is given an upright trunk similar to that used in head-pruning. The head of the vine spreads in the direction of the trellis (fig. 84). This arrangement is necessary for convenience and economy of cultivation, which can take place in only one direction. Furthermore, the large number of shoots rising from a fruit cane will produce more fruit than will the few shoots of a spur. Thus, on cane-pruned vines, few canes are needed and few arms are necessary to produce them. Two arms on each side of the head are all that are usually required by a vine in full bearing.

In cane-pruning, the fruit cane bears the fruit, while the production of canes for the following year is left largely to the renewal spur. The renewal spur is usually cut to 2 buds. The cane produced by one of these can be cut back the next year to 8 to 15 buds, according to its size, while the cane from the other can be cut to 2 buds for a new renewal spur. Each year the fruit cane that has borne a crop is cut off and replaced by a new one. Thus, cane-pruning consists of head training and the retention of both fruit canes and renewal spurs at each annual pruning.

Pruning mature cane-pruned vines.—The amount of fruiting wood (canes) to be retained on mature vines depends on the capacity of the individual vine. One can best determine the capacity by observing the number of the previous season's canes and the growth they made, and by noting the amount of fruiting wood left on the vine the previous year. A vine with canes of normal size should be pruned to have about the same amount of fruiting wood as was left the year before. When a vine has canes larger than is normal, more fruiting wood should be left. If the canes are below normal size, the vine should be treated to bear less crop.

The length of the fruit canes should be 8 to 15 buds. Small canes will have about 8 buds; very large canes, about 15 buds. Only well-ripened wood, of good thickness but not overgrown, should be used. In hot regions, where the growth is usually very vigorous, some of the laterals with well-matured buds should be left on the canes and cut back to spurs. The thicker and longer the canes, the longer should be the fruit cane retained from them. The number of fruit canes to be retained will vary from none, for very weak vines, to 3 or 4 for vines of average vigor, and 5 to 6 for very large, vigorous vines.

At each winter pruning, the fruit canes that produced the previous season's crop are cut off and replaced by new ones. If, as often happens when they are poorly exposed, the renewal spurs fail to give a sufficient number of suitable fruit canes, then well-matured water sprouts on the arms of the vine or canes from near the base of the fruit canes of the previous year may be utilized. The latter should be used as seldom as possible, because this practice tends to make the arms elongate more rapidly. On most varieties, including Thompson Seedless, a water sprout that has developed early in the season and is well matured will make a satisfactory fruit cane. To prevent the arms from elongating too rapidly one should, whenever possible, have the renewal spurs nearer the head of the vine than the fruit cane. If a renewal spur points at right angles to the line of the row, it should be cut short (to one bud), so that it will not be broken during cultivation. If the vine is vigorous, base buds will grow, and such a spur will supply the two canes needed—one for use as a fruit cane and another for a renewal spur. In number, the renewal spurs should equal the fruit canes. When desirable, a replacement spur may also serve as a renewal spur.

The fruit canes should be so tied that most of the weight will fall on the wire of the trellis and not on the string with which they are tied. This is accomplished by giving the cane about one turn round the wire and tying firmly at the end. No other tie is needed. The canes, when tied, should not be wrapped several times round the wire, because wrapping makes it difficult to remove them at the next winter pruning. Weaving the canes on the wire may be simpler to do and like-wise easier to remove at pruning.

Advantages of cane-pruning.—The most generally recognized advantage of cane-pruning is the possibility of obtaining full crops on varieties whose buds are sterile near the base of the canes. The pruning of Thompson Seedless illustrates the use of cane-pruning for this purpose. Similarly, long pruning is also used for wine varieties with very small clusters to ensure full crops. In fact, until a few years ago these were the only merits of this system of pruning that were widely recognized.

With the use of thinning to regulate the crop, however, cane-pruning offers two other advantages over other systems. First, it permits spreading the fruit over a larger area. Whereas in cordon-pruning the fruit is spread only in the vine row, in cane-pruning the fruit can be spread laterally as well. The wide-top trellis greatly enhances these possibilities. Second, if accompanied by flower-cluster thinning several weeks before blooming, cane-pruning reduces the tendency of varieties such as Muscat of Alexandria to produce shot berries or straggly clusters. Cane-pruning allows the vine to make a greater development early in the season than any other system. At blooming time, other conditions being equal, cane-pruned vines will have produced half again to several times as many leaves as spur-pruned vines. With the same number of clusters to a vine, the flower clusters on the cane-pruned vines will be better nourished.

Cane-pruning is the least severe system now in general use; it allows the greatest yearly development of the vine. Cane-pruned vines will produce more fruit than spur-pruned vines and, other conditions remaining the same, will still make an equal amount of growth.

Disadvantages of cane-pruning.—Cane-pruning any variety that has been producing full crops under spur-pruning will result in overcropping and poor quality of fruit unless the vines are thinned severely. The explanation is that more buds are retained under this system, and that the buds on the canes of practically all varieties become more fruitful from the base upward over much of the length usually retained in cane-pruning.

To obtain the benefits of spreading the fruit, together with its favorable influence on quality, one must have a trellis, which adds to the cost. Supporting the canes without a trellis is unsatisfactory, since the clusters then tend to mass close together.

Cane-pruning is the most difficult system. Since the units retained are relatively few, each must be more nearly perfect if regular full crops are to be produced. The selection of one poor cane may mean the loss of a fourth of the fruit of the vine. For this reason, one must be very careful in choosing the wood to be retained. Much care is also required, with this system, to maintain the form of the vine. In spur-pruning, the units are relatively short and the vine cannot get out of shape quickly. This is not true of cane-pruned vines. Here the units may become very long. If the pruner is careless in selecting wood, the vine will be out of shape in a few years. Then, finding suitable wood for renewal spurs and fruit canes close to the head of the vine may be very difficult if not impossible.

Cordon-training.—The distinguishing characteristic of cordon-training is the much elongated trunk, which bears arms over the greater part of its length. Instead of the usual 2 to 4 feet, or at most 5 feet, the trunk is extended 6 to 8 feet or more. In practice, three types of this system are used—namely, the bilateral and unilateral horizontal cordons and the vertical cordon (step system). The trunk of the bilateral cordon rises to 42 to 48 inches or more and is then divided into two parts, each continuing through a quarter circle to the desired height and then extending horizontally in opposite directions toward the next vine (fig. 85). In the unilateral horizontal cordon the trunk is bent in a quarter circle beginning at the desired height, but extending in only one direction, with its end approaching the bend of the next vine. The trunk of the vertical cordon is erect over its entire length. It is not adapted to machine harvesting with present day machines.

The vines of the cordon system have no definite head. The arms are distributed over the greater part of the trunk at intervals of 8 to 12 inches. In the horizontal cordons the arms should rise only on the upper side of the horizontal part of the trunk; otherwise the fruit will not be exposed uniformly to light and air. The arms of the vertical cordon are distributed round the trunk from its top to within 15 to 20 inches of the soil. At the ends of the arms, at each winter pruning, spurs are left. These produce shoots that bear the next crop of fruit and supply wood for the next year's spurs. This system, therefore, consists of cordon-training and spur-pruning.

Cordon vines may be, and in some regions are, cane-pruned. This procedure may have value with mechanical harvesting. It will permit the use of shorter canes and still have canes occupying all of the trellis. Canes may be retained near the bend of the cordon and at its end 2 or 2½ feet out. A relatively short bilateral cordon is favored. In this case the canes would be tied to a wire above the cordon, thus protecting it in machine harvesting.

Pruning mature cordon-trained vines.—Since the annual pruning of the cordon vine generally consists in the leaving of spurs, it resembles head-pruning or any other system of spur-pruning. In choosing the wood and estimating the number of buds to be left, the pruner proceeds as in cane-pruning (p. 321). To maintain the capacity of the individual arms at the same level, one must carefully regulate the length of the spurs in accordance with the size of the canes of which they are the basal parts. Long spurs, retained from large canes, should be accompanied by renewal spurs of one bud; otherwise the arm may soon become too long. The use of canes as indicated above will require the use of renewal spurs.

Advantages of cordon-training and spur-pruning.—The long trunk of the cordon-pruned vine with either spurs or short canes distributes the crop well; the clusters should not touch each other. In horizontal cordons the

FIGURE 85: A mature horizontal bilateral cordon-trained, spur-pruned vine.

shoots do not come against or grow through the clusters. The clusters are thus more nearly perfect and can be more easily harvested without injury. These cordons place all the clusters at about the same distance from the ground. This arrangement favors uniform development of the factors that constitute quality, such as color, size, and sugar content.

The extension of the trunk in cordon-pruning increases the permanent wood of the vine and thus enlarges the reservoir for the storage of reserves. It seems that this greater volume of mature wood, with its possible greater reserves of food materials, tends to make the buds on the lower parts of the canes more fruitful. Some varieties that require long spurs under head-pruning will bear normal crops on spurs of normal length when trained to the cordon system.

Pruning cordon vines to spurs reduces pruning cost to the minimum. In fact, the pruning of a well-trained cordon vine is perhaps the simplest, and therefore the least expensive, of the systems requiring a trellis.

Disadvantages of cordon-training and spur-pruning.—The greater length of vine trunk makes the cordon, of the three systems, the most laborious to establish. Not only is more work required to establish the vines: those who do the work must have much more skill and must exercise greater care than is necessary for head- and cane-pruning. The work, skill, and care required for the training of horizontal cordon vines makes them initially the most expensive. Of the three types of cordons, the vertical is the least difficult, and the unilateral the most difficult, to establish.

The vertical cordon, however, has defects that perhaps overshadow its advantages. The fruit is subjected to varying degrees of temperature and shading at different levels on the vine, so that ripening and coloring are often uneven. A more vital defect is that the cordon cannot be maintained permanently. Each year the arms and shoots at the top of the trunk become more vigorous, and the lower arms and shoots, because of shading, become weaker, until finally little or no growth is obtained below. After a time, therefore, most of the vines lose the character of cordons and become simply headed vines with rather long trunks; they may be weak and short-lived because of the large wounds where the lower dead arms were removed.

Because of this loss of form by the vertical cordons, the present practice in the Emperor vineyards of the San Joaquin Valley, where this system was formerly used, is to develop the vines to a high, bilateral cordon. Similarly, around Lodi, many vineyards of Tokay in which the bearing surface was extended upward—resembling a vertical cordon—in the late 1920's were reduced, at great expense and some loss of the crop, to the original form of headed vines after fifteen to twenty years.

The horizontal cordons, beside being difficult to establish, require trellising, which further increases the cost.

Head-training and spur-pruning.—In the various systems of head-pruning, the vine is given the form of a small upright shrub (fig. 86). The mature vine consists of a vertical stem or trunk bearing at its summit a ring of arms or short branches. At the ends of the arms, at each winter pruning, the spurs are left; these consist of the basal parts of canes, which are the matured shoots from the previous summer. These spurs produce shoots which serve the *dual* purpose of bearing the crop of fruit *and* supplying wood for next year's spurs. Thus the system consists of head-training and spur-pruning. The point or region where the trunk divides into or bears the arms is the *head*.

This type of pruning is often called *vase* or *goblet* pruning. The vase-like arrangement of the arms, although common, is not universal or essential; hence the term "head-pruning" seems preferable. In regions of very high temperatures and low relative humidity, the head of the vine may be sunburned if the "vase" opening permits the sun to shine directly on the base of the arms. Under such conditions enough growth should be maintained directly above the head to shade this part of the vine.

Pruning mature head-trained, spur-pruned vines.—On a mature head-pruned vine enough spurs to bear a normal crop should be left. This will favor the production of quality fruit and will also maintain vigor of growth. The number of buds left should be in proportion to the vine's capacity, and the buds should be distributed on the spurs in proportion to the size of the canes that were cut back to form the spurs. The spurs should be so distributed that the form of the vine will be maintained or improved and the fruit will be uniformly exposed.

To determine how many buds or spurs should be left on a mature vine, one may roughly count the spurs left from the year before and observe the size of the canes. A vine that produced a good crop and whose canes are of normal size should be pruned so as to leave about the same num-

FIGURE 86: A mature head-trained, spur-pruned vine.

ber of buds and spurs as it had during the previous bearing season. If the canes are abnormally large for the variety, this condition indicates that the canes were very vigorous during the previous summer, and more buds should be left in order to utilize this capacity in fruit production. One may leave more buds by increasing either the number or the length of the spurs. The method selected for increasing the number of buds should be the one that best retains the desired shape of the vine and that also distributes the fruit uniformly. If the canes seem weak—that is, small for the variety—fewer buds should be left. To reduce the number of buds, one may reduce the number of spurs retained or may cut the spurs shorter. In every case, the spurs from large or vigorous canes should carry more buds than those from small or weak canes.

What has been said above applies to varieties that produce regular and full crops with head-pruning. If the crops of the previous years have been small and the vine growth large, perhaps the basal buds of the variety are not very fruitful. In that case the spurs should be left longer. If full crops do not result, some type of cane-pruning may be necessary.

Advantages of head-trained spur-pruning.—The advantages of head-pruning are simplicity of form, ease of training, and low cost of supports. The headed vine is the easiest type to establish, largely because of its natural growth form, its rather short trunk, and its relative small amount of permanent wood in comparison with that of the cordon type. The fact that the trunk is upright over its entire length also simplifies training.

Because headed vines are usually rather small, the cost of supports, a stake at each vine, is relatively low. Stakes are necessary during the development period, but the trunks or stems become rigid enough to support the vine after six to ten years. This type of support permits cross cultivation—an advantage whenever weeds are a problem.

Disadvantages of head-trained spur-pruning.—Head-pruning allows the least development of the vine; hence it is the most depressive. When the crop is controlled entirely by pruning, as it is with most head-pruned varieties, the pruning must sometimes be almost severe in order to prevent overbearing. The vines remain small and the capacity for both growth and production is depressed.

The necessity of pruning to short spurs tends not only to reduce the capacity of the vine, but also to keep the head too compact. The fruit may be inferior because of unequal exposure to light and air. As the vines become old and the arms increase in length, this defect becomes less serious. Long spur-pruning, with some form of thinning to regulate the crop, practiced for a number of years beginning the third or fourth year after planting, helps overcome the tendency to crowd the fruit and lessens the depressive effect of the pruning.

In some varieties, notably Muscat of Alexandria, the fruit of head-pruned vines is poor as a result of shattering (shelling) and the setting of shot berries. Investigations in a number of vineyards have shown a definite relation between these troubles and the restriction of leaf development early in the season with this type of pruning (Winkler, 1929).

In still other varieties the crops are small and irregular with head-pruning because the buds near the basal ends of the canes are not always fruitful, or because the clusters are small. Slight variation in the fruitfulness of the buds of a single variety may occur from year to year and may sometimes account for irregular bearing. Long spur-pruning, with some form of thinning to regulate the crop in the years when more clusters develop than the vine can mature perfectly, may overcome this situation and appreciably increase the average yield over a period of years. If the spurs must be left very long, however, it will be difficult to maintain the form of a vine unless care is taken to retain a short renewal spur close to the base of each long spur.

The pruning systems of other grape growing countries are discussed in the 1961 issues of the Bulletin l'Office International de la Vigne et du Vin (Decker, 1961).

SYSTEMS OF PRUNING AMERICAN GRAPES

Practically all American grape varieties are cane-pruned. Several general systems of cane-pruning are employed. These differ in the shape given to the trunk and the management of the fruit canes (Shaulis, 1960). The systems are Geneva double curtain, umbrella-Kniffin, Kniffin, Keuka, and Chautauqua.

The *Geneva Double Curtain* is the most generally used system of supports for American grapes in New York and adjacent states. It was developed by Shaulis *et al.* (1966) at the Geneva Agricultural Experiment Station.

In this system the vines are trained to a bilateral cordon and are short-cane-pruned. The cordons are secured to trellis wires which are supported on 4 foot crossarms at 5½ to 6 feet above the ground. As illustrated in figure 87, the vines have two (or more) trunks, which make for flexibility, and are tied in opposite directions on one of the wires. The trunks are alternately attached on the two wires. The wires are held in position by wood or metal supports attached to sturdy posts, spaced every third or fourth vine depending on the spacing in the vine row.

Training these vines is similar to the development of bilateral cordon vines described in chapter 12. At pruning, the canes arising from the arms which hang vertically on the cordons are cut to 4 to 6 buds with the usual renewal spurs (see middle vine in fig. 87). The fruiting units are spaced about a foot apart on the cordons.

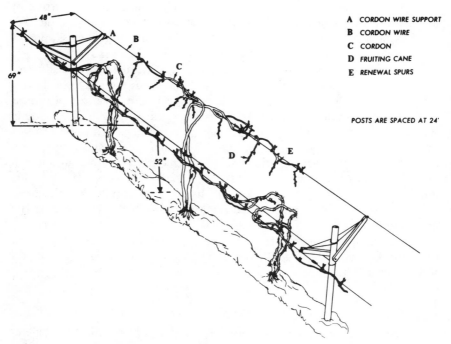

A CORDON WIRE SUPPORT
B CORDON WIRE
C CORDON
D FRUITING CANE
E RENEWAL SPURS

POSTS ARE SPACED AT 24'

FIGURE 87: Diagrammatic sketch of Concord vines trained to the Geneva double curtain system of vine support. Canes with renewal spurs are shown only on the middle vine in the space between the two trellis posts. (*From New York Exp. Sta. Bull. 811, Geneva*)

Vines so trained and supported position the fruit well for a vertical impactor mechanical harvester.

In *Umbrella-Kniffin pruning,* the head of the vine is high between the top and middle wires of the three-wire vertical trellis with the wires being spaced 18 inches apart. The height of the top is 54 to 72 inches up according to wishes of the grower. The canes retained at pruning are bowed sharply over the top wire, spread along the trellis, and tied to the middle or lower wire (fig. 88). This is the next most extensively used system for Concord grapes.

In the *Kniffin system* the vine has two arms in the plane of and just below the middle wire of a three-wire trellis and is headed into another two arms just below the top wire. If the vine has sufficient capacity, one fruit cane is retained on each of the four arms. Two of the canes are tied in opposite directions on the middle wire, and the other two, in the same manner, on the top wire. Renewal spurs are retained on the arms.

There are several systems of training and pruning under the name "high renewal." The *Keuka* system has been the most extensively used of these. In it the vine is headed just below the bottom wire of the three-wire vertical trellis. New fruit canes, one in each direction, are placed on the lower wire each year. If more fruit canes are required, these are placed on the middle wire. Renewal spurs for the development of canes for next year's fruit canes are retained. The new shoots must be tied up to the middle and upper wires as they develop.

The *Chautauqua* system is essentially a bilateral cordon. The vine is headed just below the bottom wire of the three-wire trellis. Two strong canes, one in each direction, are tied horizontally on this wire. These are permanent arms or branches of the trunk. Canes arising from them are retained as fruit canes and are tied in a vertical position to the middle and top wires. Renewal spurs are left on the arms to produce fruiting canes for the next year.

Amount of wood for American grapes.—Partridge (1925), indicated the

FIGURE 88: An American grapevine pruned to the umbrella system. (*From New York Ext. Sta. Bull. 805, Cornell*)

relation of growth to capacity for production in Concord. Later, Shaulis (1948, 1953) developed a procedure whereby the number of buds to be retained at pruning was related directly to the weight of prunings removed. To accomplish this, an estimate of the weight of the prunings must be made so that enough buds will be retained; then, after pruning, the removed brush is weighed and a downward adjustment in the number of buds made accordingly. After pruning a number of vines, the experienced pruner finds it necessary to check this estimate only occasionally—say, every tenth or fifteenth vine. This procedure, termed "balanced pruning," has been fairly generally accepted for Concord grapes in New York State. Consistently better cropping has also been reported by Partridge (1925) with its use in Michigan and by Bell *et al.* (1958) in Ohio.

CHOICE OF A PRUNING SYSTEM

Whatever the system of pruning adopted, the choice must be made before the vineyard is planted if all possible benefits are to be obtained. In deciding upon a system, one should consider its advantages, disadvantages, probable cost, returns and practicality, as well as the variety of the vines, the soil, the climate, and the use to be made of the fruit.

Head-training and cane-pruning.—Cane-pruning should be used with varieties of which the lower buds on the canes are usually sterile, such as Thompson Seedless (Sultanina or Sultana), or of which the clusters are small, such as those of Cabernet Sauvignon, Pinot noir, White Riesling, Chardonnay, Sauvignon blanc and Black Corinth, and also Concord, Salvador, and most varieties of American origin. The varieties with unfruitful basal buds bear very little when spur-pruning is used on either head- or cordon-trained vines, and likewise those with small clusters produce only small crops while the vines are young.

With the varieties producing small clusters, cane-pruning should be used regularly. With cane-pruning only a few arms are developed, and the head of the vine is kept restricted in the line of the trellis.

The crop of such varieties as Muscat of Alexandria and Red Malaga, which are subject to excessive shatter or the setting of shot berries with spur-pruning, can be improved by long spur or short cane-pruning accompanied by flower-cluster thinning. With varieties subject to shatter, this type of pruning, which results in a greater development of leaves before blooming, causes the flower clusters left after thinning to set more perfectly.

Where shatter is the result of a deficiency of zinc (little leaf) or a virus condition, longer pruning and flower-cluster thinning will not improve the set. A favorable response to the application of zinc has been obtained with the Muscat of Alexandria in various locations in the San Joaquin

Valley (Hewitt and Jacob, 1945); hence, where little or no improvement in fruiting is secured with longer pruning and flower-cluster thinning, the efficacy of zinc should be tested. A virus condition cannot be corrected.

Cane-pruning is being used for more and more varieties because it permits positioning the fruit for machine harvesting better than the other systems. Its use in California will continue to increase along with machine harvesting.

Cordon-training and spur-pruning.—Certain varieties of table grapes, such as Tokay, Malaga, and Cornichon, are usually pruned to a high head. This is generally satisfactory, except where they are grown in very rich soil with abundant water and heat, in which case the fruit fails to color uniformly or satisfactorily because of the dense foliage and the crowding of the clusters. Under such conditions cordon-pruning should produce better-quality fruit, since the clusters then are spread along the entire trunk and are separated from each other. In fact, cordon-pruning should be satisfactory with most of the varieties of very large-clustered table grapes that set fairly perfect clusters with spur-pruning, such as Cardinal, Emperor, Red Malaga, Ribier, and Tokay. With all these varieties, the character of the clusters, their uniformity, and the general quality of the fruit are improved by the retention of extra buds at pruning and by final regulation of the amount of crop through the appropriate method of thinning.

The Almeria (Ohanez) has fruited most successfully when much permanent wood was retained, as with a multiple cordon (several long branches) trained over an arbor. This system of training, with the retention of long spurs or short fruit canes, has usually produced enough flower clusters for a full crop each year. The amount of crop should be regulated by flower-cluster thinning, which will further improve the quality of the fruit.

The uniformity and condition of the fruit of wine varieties with large clusters is improved under cordon-training. This system spreads the fruit and will facilitate harvesting if the cordon is 42 to 54 inches above the ground. Wine varieties that have done well with such training are Aramon, Burger, Carignane, Grenache, Mission, Muscat of Alexandria, and Palomino.

Head-training and spur-pruning.—For the most economical production of all varieties of grapes that produce medium-sized clusters on shoots rising from buds at the base of the canes, and where appearance of the fruit is not of foremost importance, head-pruning should be used. This system is satisfactory with most varieties of wine grapes, such as Zinfandel, Mataro, Sauvignon vert, Folle blanche, and the varieties of Muscadine grapes (on arbors) (Loomis, 1943). By leaving longer spurs and employing the requisite method of thinning for the variety, head-training with spur-pruning has given very good results with such table grapes as the

Tokay, Muscat of Alexandria, Dattier, and Malaga. It requires the least outlay of capital for supports and is economical in cost of pruning.

Practicality.—Head-training with spur-pruning is the system most generally understood; if it is improperly or unskillfully applied, the results are less disastrous than with the other systems. No system is profitable, however, unless it is carried out properly. If the owner of a vineyard will take pains to understand a system and follow it carefully, there is very little more difficulty with one system than with another. Head-training with cane-pruning perhaps requires the most experience.

Pruning Grapevines on Arbors

The pruning of vines on overhead arbors is either to spurs or canes, according to the fruiting habit of the variety. Such varieties as Tokay, Muscat, Malaga, Ribier, and the varieties of muscadine grapes (Loomis, 1943) are spur-pruned; such varieties as Almeria and Thompson Seedless are cane-pruned. On an arbor, the head of the vine must be high enough not to interfere with cultivation; thus the arms may be developed into cordons that extend over the top of the arbor. This disposition of the arms and bearing wood with spur-pruning permits the clusters to hang free of one another. The Almeria fruits well, with the large volume of permanent wood that serves as reservoir for storage of carbohydrate reserves, when pruned to short canes. Care must be exercised, however, to have the pruning units spaced regularly, so that no part of the head is altogether devoid of foliage cover. In hot regions, unshaded sections of the cordons will sunburn. With varieties requiring cane-pruning, a definite head may be maintained and the fruit canes may be spread over the top of the arbor.

Varieties that fruit on spurs—that is, those that can be pruned to short spurs—are best adapted to growth on walls. With varieties that require cane-pruning, the fruit canes should be tied downward in order to develop, near the base of the fruit canes, some vigorous shoots that may serve as fruit canes the next year.

BIBLIOGRAPHY

Alleweldt, G. 1958. Eine Frühdiagnose zur Bestimmung der Fruchtbarkeit von Reben. Mitis, 1:230–236.

————. 1960. Untersuchungen über den Austrieb der Winterknospen von Reben. Vitis, 2:134–152.

Antcliff, A. J., P. May, and W. J. Webster. 1957. Studies on the Sultana vine; IV. A pruning experiment with number of buds per vine varied, number of buds per cane constant. Aust. Jour. Agr. Res., 7:401–413.

————, ————, ————. 1958. Studies on the Sultana vine; VI. The morphology of the cane and its fruitfulness. Aust. Jour. Agr. Res., 9:329–338.

————, and W. J. Webster. 1955. Studies on the Sultana vine; I. Fruit bud distribution and bud burst with reference to forecasting potential crop. Aust. Jour. Agr. Res., 6:565–588.

Barnard, C. 1932. Fruit bud studies; I. The Sultana: An analysis of the distribution and behavior of the buds of the Sultana vine, together with an account of the differentiation and development of the fruit buds. Aust. Jour. Coun. Sci. and Indus. Res., 5:47–52.

————, and J. E. Thomas. 1933. Fruit bud studies; II. The Sultana: Differentiation and development of the fruit buds. Aust. Jour. Coun. Sci. and Indus. Res., 6:285–294.

Basan'Ko, A. A., and M. P. T. Turzhova. 1953. Determination of the time of pruning of grape vines, taking into account the assimilative activity of the leaves. [Trans. title.] Vinodelie i Vinogradarstvo, SSSR, 13(11):29–31. (See Hort. Abs., 24:1279.)

Bell, H. K., R. P. Larsen, and A. L. Kenworthy. 1958. Balanced pruning of the Concord grape. Quart. Bull. Michigan Agr. Exp. Sta., 40:915–919.

Briza, K., and M. Milosavljevic. 1954. Determining the fruitfulness of vine buds during dormancy. [Tran. title.] Zborn. Rad. Poljopriv. Fak. (Belgrade), 2(2):214–217. (See Hort. Abs., 25:2546.)

————, ————. 1958. A method of forecasting vine yields. [Trans. title.] (Yugoslav with German summary) Zborn. Rad. Poljopriv. Fak. (Belgrade), 6(1):151–158. (Hort. Abs. 29:1219.)

Coombe, B. G. 1970. Fruit set in grape vines: the mechanism of the CCC effect. J. Hort. Sci., 45:415–425.

Decker, K. 1961. Systems rationnels de conduite et de taille. Bull. l'Office Interna'l. vigne et vin, 34(361):26–30; See also: *ibid* (362):5–54, (363): 4–34, (364):3–48, (365):4–37, (366):4–20, (367):3–34, and (368):4–27.

Dvornic, V. 1954. Rational pruning of the vine. [Trans. title.] (English, French and German summaries) Gradina, Via si Livada, 3(7):67–69.

Eifert, J., M. Panczel, and A. Eifert. 1961. Änderung des Stärke—und Zuckergehaltes der Rebe während der Ruheperiode. Vitis, 2:257–265.

Eremeev, G. N. 1960. Growth of absorbing roots of fruit trees in relation to soil conditions. [Trans. title.] Dokl. Akad. Nauk. SSSR, 130:36–38.

Esau, K. 1948. Phloem structure in the grapevine, and its seasonal changes. Hilgardia, 18:217–296.

Galley, R., H. Leyvroz, and J. L. Simon. 1960. Influence de la charge de raisin sur la qualité de la vendange. Rev. Rom. Agric. Vitic., 16:48–51.

Hewitt, W. B., and H. E. Jacob. 1945. Effect of zinc on yield and cluster weight of Muscat grapes. Proc. Amer. Soc. Hort. Sci., 46:256–262.

Huglin, P. 1955. Sur la fertilité des yeux des "gourmands" de quelques cépages de *vitis vinifera*. Acad. d'Agr. de France Compt. Rend. Hebd., 41(16): 1709–1711.

————. 1959. Recherches sur les bourgeones de la vigne; initiation florale et développement végétatif. Thèses Insti. Natl. Rec. Agron. (Paris), pp. 13–174.

Immink, R. J. 1958. Sultana crop estimate months in advance. Farming in South Africa, 33(11):32.

Kás, V., and J. Hanousek. 1946. Bleeding of the grapevine. [Trans. title.], Czechoslovakia. Sbornik Ceské Akad. Zemedělskí, 19:268–272.

Kondo, I. N. 1955. Rest period of grape buds. [Trans. title.] Dokl. Akad. Nauk. SSSR, 102:633–636.

Le Roux, M. S., and A. H. Malan. 1945. Experiments on the topping of vines. Farming in South Africa, 20:543–548.

Lider, L. A., A. N. Kasimatis, and W. M. Kliewer. 1973. Effect of pruning severity and rootstock on growth and yield of two grafted, cane-pruned wine grape cultivars. J. Amer. Soc. Hort. Sci., 98(1):8–11.

Loomis, N. H. 1943. The influence of time and method of pruning on yields of Muscadine grapes. Proc. Amer. Soc. Hort. Sci., 42:418–420.

Mel'nikov, V. I. 1957. On the fruit bearing ability of the main and suckering shoots. [Trans. title.] Vinodelie i Vinogradarstvo, SSSR, 17(3):27–37. (Bio. Abs. 36:35278).

Negrul, A. M., and L. T. Nikiforva. 1958. Concerning the transfer of materials between different parts of the vine. [Trans. title.] SSSR Izv. Timiryazer. Seljsk. Akad., 1(20):73–84. (See Hort. Abs. 28:2269.)

Partridge, N. L. 1925. Growth and yield of Concord grape vines. Proc. Amer. Soc. Hort. Sci., 22:84–87.

Richey, H. W., and H. A. Bowers. 1924. Correlation of root and top growth of the Concord grape and translocation of elaborated plant food during the dormant season. Proc. Amer. Soc. Hort. Sci., 21:33–39.

Schrader, A. L. 1924. Seasonal changes in the chemical composition of Concord grape vines. Proc. Amer. Soc. Hort. Sci., 21:39–44.

Shaulis, N. 1948. Some effects of pruning severity and training on Fredonia and Concord grapes. Proc. Amer. Soc. Hort. Sci., 51:263–270.

——. 1953. The effect of season, pruning severity, and trellising on some chemical characteristics of Concord and Fredonia grape juice. Proc. Amer. Soc. Hort. Sci., 62:214–222.

——. 1960. Cultural practices for New York vineyards. New York State Col. Agr. Ext. Bull., 805:3–47.

——, H. Amberg, and D. Crowe. 1966. Response of Concord grapes to light, exposure and Geneva double curtain training. Proc. Amer. Soc. Hort. Sci., 89:268–280.

——, E. S. Shepardson, and T. D. Jordan. 1966. Geneva double curtain for Concord grapes. New York, Agric. Exp. Sta. Bull., 811.

Skene, K. G. M. 1967. Gibberellin-like substances in root exudate of *Vitis vinifera*. Planta, 74(3):250–262.

——. 1969. A comparison of the effects of "cycocel" and tipping on fruit set in *Vitis vinifera* L. Aust. J. Bio. Sci., 22(6):1305–1311.

——, and A. J. Antcliff. 1972. A comparative study of cytokinin levels in bleeding sap of *Vitis vinifera* (L.) and the two grapevine rootstocks, Salt Creek and 1613. J. Exp. Botany, 23(No. 75):283–293.

Thomas, J. E., and C. Barnard. 1937. Fruit bud studies; III. The Sultana: Some relations between shoot growth, chemical composition, fruit bud formation, and yield. Aust. Jour. Coun. Sci. and Indus. Res., 10:143–157.

Vega, J., and E. P. Mavrich. 1959. Effectos fisiológicos de la poda herbacea en vid. Rev. Invest. Agric. (Buenos Aires), 13:183–206.

Winkler, A. J. 1929. The effect of dormant pruning on the carbohydrate metabolism of *Vitis vinifera*. Hilgardia, 4:153–173.

———. 1931. Pruning and thinning experiments with grapes. California Agr. Exp. Sta. Bull., 519:1–56.

———. 1932. The lateral movement of elaborated foods in the grapevine. Proc. Amer. Soc. Hort. Sci., 29:335–338.

———. 1934. Pruning *vinifera* grapevines. California Agr. Ext. Ser. Cir., 89: 1–68.

———, (ed.) W. B. Hewitt, N. W. Frazier, and J. H. Freitag. 1949. Pierce's disease investigations. Hilgardia, 19:207–262. (See p. 258.)

———. 1958. The relation of leaf area and climate to vine performance and grape quality. Amer. J. Enol. Vitic., 9:10–23.

———, and W. O. Williams. 1945. Starch and sugars of *Vitis vinifera*. Jour. Plant Physiol., 20:412–432.

Wurgler, W. H., and Leyvraz and A. Boley. 1955. Peut-on prévoir le rendement de la vigne avant le debourrement? Annuaire Agr. Suisse, 56: 783–786.

14

Means of Improving
Grape Quality

The production of good-quality grapes pays. That was the very definite indication given by studies of the movement of grapes through a number of the large Eastern markets of the United States made during several seasons by members of the College of Agriculture, University of California (Nelson *et al.*, 1963, 1972 and Nelson and Richardson, 1967). It was true of all varieties studied and all market conditions. The higher the prices, the wider were the market preferences for fruit of good quality.

Good quality in table grapes represents a combination of medium-sized clusters of uniformly large, perfect berries with the characteristic color, pleasing flavor, and texture of the variety.

Many factors of grape growing enter into the production of quality. Some of these are the more general factors, such as choice of variety, climatic location, and soil type, along with the operations of cultivation, irrigation, and insect and disease control. Other factors are those that affect the vine and its fruit more directly, such as pruning, amount of crop, thinning, girdling, sprinkler cooling, and the use of plant growth regulators. Although all of these factors are of importance, only the latter, more direct ones are discussed here. The general factors influencing quality, including pruning, are discussed in other chapters.

THINNING

Since less severe pruning, in the absence of excess crop, increases vine capacity for both growth and production (Winkler, 1931), thinning has a definite place as a means of improving quality. With less severe pruning and with crop control achieved by thinning, the quality of the grapes is improved owing to the increase in the ratio of leaves to crop (Winkler, 1958; Kliewer and Weaver, 1971). This, as was indicated in discussion of the response of the vine to pruning, improves the nutrition of both the vine and the fruit.

The removal of flower clusters before blooming and of immature clusters or parts of such clusters after the fruit has set is *thinning*. Like pruning, thinning consists in the removal of living parts and, like pruning, it concentrates the activities of the vine into the parts left. In other respects, however, thinning has the opposite effect of pruning—it strengthens the vine by limiting the crop without diminishing the leaf area, actual or potential. Thinning offers far greater possibilities for improvement of quality than does pruning. In winter, when pruning is done, the probable crop is estimated on the basis of experience. After the cluster forms appear, however, the potential crop can be seen; hence pruning accompanied by thinning permits a better balance of capacity and crop than does pruning alone.

Thinning makes it possible to grow as many grapes as the vine can bear without sacrificing quality. With thinning, it may actually be possible to increase bearing capacity, since vines that are to be thinned may be pruned longer to produce a greater leaf surface, which is not possible when crop level is determined by pruning alone.

Compared with that from unthinned vines, fruit from thinned vines is less likely to decay, and the decay that occurs is less likely to be overlooked in trimming at harvest. Also, properly thinned fruit is less costly to pick, because the clusters are more uniformly colored and less time is required in selecting the clusters to be harvested (see table 23, below).

Even so, not all varieties set their fruit equally well; with normal pruning, some tend to set straggly clusters; other, near-perfect clusters; and still others, overcompact clusters. To obtain maximum improvement in quality within these variations in set, three different methods of thinning were developed for use in combination with light pruning; each is adapted to a given type of fruit setting. The methods are: flower-cluster thinning, for varieties that tend to set straggly clusters; cluster thinning, for those that set near-perfect clusters; and berry thinning, for those that set overcompact clusters.

Flower-cluster thinning.—Flower-cluster thinning, which is done between leafing-out and blooming, reduces the number of flower clusters without changing the number of leaves. With this increase in the ratio of leaves to clusters, the flowers on the retained clusters are better supplied with the food materials—carbohydrates—that are manufactured in the leaves. As a result, the flower parts (anthers and pistil) that are formed after the vines leaf out will develop more perfectly, the set will be better, and there will be a larger percentage of normal berries per cluster. Flower-cluster thinning, done as early as possible, provides the retained clusters with the benefit of the larger ratio of leaves to cluster over a longer period. At this stage the flower clusters are readily visible above the foliage and can be removed with the thumb and finger nails. Figure 89 shows the proper stage of development for flower-cluster thinning.

This method of thinning is adapted to such varieties as Muscat of Alexandria, Ribier (Alphonse Lavallée), and Cardinal, and possibly Emperor on the lighter soils. In Cardinal and Ribier the heavy tip of the retained flower clusters should be pinched off.

Table 21 shows the beneficial effects of light pruning, with flower-cluster thinning to control crop, on the quality of the fruit of Muscat of Alexandria (Winkler, 1927, 1958).

Considering normally pruned, unthinned vines as standard, the table shows that, with flower-cluster thinning, the cluster weight was increased 80 per cent on long-spur-pruned vines and 132 per cent on cane-pruned vines. The increases in cluster weight were accompanied by increases in cluster length. Light pruning combined with flower-cluster thinning is the

FIGURE 89: A single cane of Muscat of Alexandria showing the proper stage of development for flower-cluster thinning.

Means of Improving Grape Quality

TABLE 21

INFLUENCE OF LIGHT PRUNING PLUS FLOWER-CLUSTER THINNING ON THE
WEIGHT AND LENGTH OF CLUSTER AND THE NUMBER OF
NORMAL BERRIES OF MUSCAT OF ALEXANDRIA

Type of pruning and degree of thining	*Crop per vine*	*Cluster weight*	*Cluster length*	*Number of normal berries*	*Germin- ability of pollen*
	pounds	*pounds*	*inches*		*per cent*
Normally pruned vines, no thinning	30.0	0.43	7.8	43	10
Long-spur pruned vines, thinned to 3 clusters per 4 or 5 shoots	29.5	0.74	9.5	86	26
Cane-pruned vines, thinned to 1 cluster per 2 shoots	32.1	1.00	10.5	115	42

SOURCE OF DATA: Winkler (1958).

only known means, other than treatment with gibberellin (see p. 361), of increasing the cluster length under given environmental conditions without reducing crop. The increase in the number of normal berries per cluster reflects the improved development of the flowers as indicated by germinability of the pollen.

This same method of thinning should be employed to rehabilitate weakened vines. By removing most or all of the flower clusters, the greater part or all of the energy of the vine can be diverted into vegetative growth.

Cluster thinning.—In cluster thinning, entire clusters are removed after the berries have set. This method has no direct effect on the percentage set or on cluster length. It is essentially a grading and sorting of fruit clusters at an early stage. Undesirable clusters—those that are undersized, misshappen, or oversized—are removed. Thus, the early thinning provides a more favorable condition for nutrition of the retained clusters, giving them larger berries. It is adapted to such varieties as Malaga and, on heavy soils, Emperor.

Cluster thinning is the easiest and best means of reducing the crop on overloaded vines of highly productive wine- or raisin-grape vineyards in order that the remainder of the crop may develop and mature properly. By leaving enough fruiting wood (spurs or canes) at pruning time to produce a good crop in years of poor set, and then reducing the overload in years of good set by cluster thinning, large regular crops may be produced year after year. However, cluster thinning is a time consuming and expensive operation and growers should not leave more fruiting wood than can be economically thinned.

Berry thinning.—Berry thinning, as practiced in California, consists of removing parts of clusters after the shatter of impotent flowers (Coombe, 1959, 1962). The rachis (main stem) of the cluster is cut far enough back from the apex of the cluster to retain only the desired number of berries. Retention of 4 to 8 of the long branches at the base of the cluster, depending on their size, is usually ample. These branches are usually long enough to give way to each other as the berries grow, so that the cluster will not be overcompact. The branches farther out on the rachis not only are shorter, but also arise nearer each other and have less space for spreading; it is here that the clusters of some varieties become too compact. The Tokay, when grown for table fruit, should be regularly berry thinned. Besides preventing compactness, berry thinning done at different times has characteristic size effects, as shown in table 22 for Tokay and Malaga berries.

The increase in weight of berry (30 per cent) in these seeded varieties is greatest when the thinning is done immediately after set—following the shatter of impotent flowers after bloom. With a delay of about a week the increase in berry size is one third less, and with a delay of about two weeks the increase in berry size is two thirds less. The greater effectiveness of the early thinning arises from the fact that it coincides with the still-active cell division in the pericarp of the berries (Coombe, 1960), with the rapid normal berry growth, and with the summer maximum of carbohydrates in the shoots.

The proper stage of development for berry thinning for size increase and the number of branches to retain on a typical Tokay cluster are shown in figure 90. Retention of 80 to 100 berries per cluster will suffice to produce clusters of 1 to 1.5 pounds, provided the thinning is timed properly. Uniformity of coloring in the Tokay (Winkler, 1930) and Red Malaga (Weaver, 1952; Weaver and McCune, 1959a) is enhanced by berry thinning at any time up to the beginning of ripening. The square centimeters of leaf

TABLE 22

INFLUENCE OF BERRY THINNING AND TIME OF BERRY THINNING ON
THE WEIGHT OF BERRY
(In grams)

Variety	Control, not thinned	Thinned		
		Immediately after set	7 to 10 days later	15 to 20 days later
Tokay	4.9	6.4	5.8	5.3
Malaga	3.8	6.0	4.6	4.2

SOURCE OF DATA: Winkler (1930).

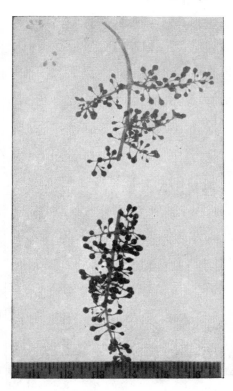

FIGURE 90: Clusters of Tokay showing both the proper stage of development for berry thinning and the
amount of berries that should be removed.

area per gram of fruit needed for producing maximum berry size, fruit
maturity and coloration of Tokay grown at Davis was 11 to 14 (Kliewer
and Weaver, 1971). This was equivalent to 24 to 26 leaves per cluster with
an average weight of 1.35 pounds.

The effect of the more uniform coloring on rate of harvest is shown in
table 23.

The table shows the marked increase in the rate at which the thinned
fruit was harvested; the increase ranged from 16 per cent above to several
times the rate for the unthinned control vines. Comparable increases have
been obtained over and over by Tokay growers. This speed-up in harvesting
tends to offset some of the cost of thinning.

The very nature of berry thinning, as described here, indicates that the
character of the clusters is changed materially (fig. 90, 91). This is the
only method by which the thinning can be done economically in vineyards.
Removing individual berries or small clumps, as is done in hothouses in
Europe, is prohibitive in cost. So long as the berries are large, uniform, and
well-colored, the consuming public has not objected to the atypical globular
clusters.

TABLE 23

EFFECT OF BERRY THINNING ON THE COLORING OF TOKAY AS INDICATED
BY RATE OF HARVEST

	Pounds of fruit harvested per hour per man	
Picking	Control vines, not thinned	Thinned vines
Plot No. 1:		
First	108	168
Second	270	342
Plot No. 2:		
First	54	222
Second	60	216
Plot No. 3:		
First	84	118
Second	165	191

SOURCE OF DATA: Winkler (1930).

Berry thinning is not an effective means of increasing the size of berries of seedless varieties. Because the effect is slight, thinning is impractical for this purpose. It is, however, very important in the production of table fruit of seedless varieties for preventing overcompactness of clusters when berry size is increased by either girdling (table 25, below) or the use of plant growth regulators (see tables 27, 28, and 29, and fig. 96). The method of berry thinning indicated for Tokay is also used for Thompson Seedless and other seedless varieties of which the long upper branches of the cluster do not become overcompact even with large increases in berry size. An older method consists of tipping the cluster and clipping the branches off one side or both sides of the cluster. Seedless clusters of 150 to 200 berries will weigh 1 to 1.25 pounds. If economics will permit, tipping the very long basal branches of large clusters will foster more uniform development and maturation. With the Perlette variety, either or both of the above methods must be used; additional thinning is usually required on the retained branches.

Since berry thinning has little effect on the berry size of seedless varieties (Winkler, 1953), the timing of the thinning of these varieties is less important (see table 24). It should, however, be done before the "bloom"— the waxy coating—has formed on the berries, or this coating will be rubbed off where the berries are touched.

Investigations on, and industry experience with, thinning clearly indicate the possibilities of improvement in the quality of the fruit when moderate pruning is accompanied by appropriate thinning. These practices can lead to both increased production and improved fruit quality. Because of the

FIGURE 91: Proper stage for berry thinning of Thompson Seedless and amount of cluster removed.

cost, at its lightest the pruning must be severe enough to fix a top limit on the amount of thinning. In the case of wine and raisin varieties, it must, in all but exceptional cases, be severe enough to control crop. Moderate pruning accompanied with cluster thinning might be economical when a grower is producing premium wine varieties during years when the price of grapes is exceptionally high.

If thinning is to produce the desired results, it must control crop (Winkler, 1954). Thinning that does not prevent overcropping should not be expected to improve quality. For maximum results, the crop retained after thinning must not be more than is normal for the vine. In the case of seeded varieties, or where thinning accompanies the girdling of seedless varieties or the application of growth regulators to them, crop control must make allowance for the potential increase in berry size resulting from these treatments.

GIRDLING

Girdling, also called ringing or cincturing, is an old practice. Its use to improve set and advance maturing was first reported by Lambry (1817). It was introduced into Greece by accident, as a means of improving the set of Black Corinth, in 1833. According to a letter by Dr. U. X. Davides, professor of viticulture in the University of Athens, a mule was staked to a grapevine, the rope girdled the trunk by rubbing off the bark, and the vine thus accidentally girdled set much better than any others. The earliest record of girdling in the United States appears in the report of the state horticulturist of Massachusetts for the year 1887 (Maynard, 1887). Its further use down through the years is recorded by Branas, *et al.* (1946). Its longest and most extensive use has been with Black Corinth, which until recently had been grown successfully only when set was induced by girdling. The next widest use of girdling is for increasing berry size in seedless varieties, such as the Thompson Seedless when grown for table fruit. Girdling for this purpose has been practiced for many years in California, but the results were erratic until Jacob (1931) established the relation of time of girdling to increase in size of berry. Girdling to advance maturation has been of minor importance.

Girdling, as practiced in commercial vineyards, consists of removing a narrow ring of bark entirely round some member of the vine. The common width is about three sixteenths of an inch. The ring may be removed from the trunk, the arms, or the fruit canes or spurs. Girdling on the arms is not advisable, first, because of the difficulty and expense of doing the work, owing to the knotty, gnarled nature of the arms and their coverings of rough, hard outer bark, and, second, because of the slow and imperfect healing of the wounds. Girdling the spurs is also costly. Thus, with nearly all of the varieties, girdling is done on either the trunk or the individual fruit canes. Girdling the trunk affects the entire vine, whereas girdling a cane affects only the part of the cane above the girdle.

It is essential that the ring of bark be *completely* removed. If only a small section of the ring of bark is left, there may be little or no response. The immediate effect of a complete girdle is to interrupt the normal movement of food materials so that the level of carbohydrate materials (sugars and starches) and plant hormones increase in the parts above the wound. If a small section of bark is left, the transfer of materials is not interrupted enough to produce the desired effects.

The girdling should be done in such a way that the wounds will heal over within a short time. This is especially true where the trunk is girdled, in which case failure to heal results in the death of the vine. Where only the fruit canes are girdled, failure of the wounds to heal does not result in the death of the vine, since the root system will receive nourishment from the shoots that grow from the renewal spurs and other parts of the head of the vine basal to the wounds; the food material so received, however, is usually insufficient to allow the root system its full development, and some weakening results. Removing wood below the bark in girdling injures the vine.

Means of Improving Grape Quality

Objectives of girdling.—Vines are girdled to accomplish one or more of three things: to improve the set of berries, to increase the size of the individual berries, and to advance maturation. Each of these effects may be obtained within certain limits by complete girdling at the proper time. It is quite evident, from study of experimental data now available, that the effectiveness of girdling decreases very rapidly as the wounds heal over. Girdling must, therefore, be done at such a time when the wounds will be open and effective while the particular phase of development to be influenced is occurring. The stage at which the operation is performed is probably the greatest single factor in determining the nature and magnitude of the effect obtained.

The crop is increased both from an increase in the number of berries to a cluster and from an increase in the size of the berries. These are the real reasons for girdling the Black Corinth variety, which is a very shy bearer without girdling. With most varieties, however, except certain wine grapes, the increase of crop obtained in this way is too costly, owing to the loss of quality of the fruit resulting from the increased number of shot berries and the reduced vigor of the vines.

1. *To improve the set of berries.*—All cultivated varieties of grapes usually produce so many flowers that, if each flower should set and produce a berry, all of the cluster would be too compact. Many flowers fail to set because of lack of pollination, lack of fertilization, or other causes. In most varieties the unfertilized flowers fall very soon. Other varieties produce small, round seedless berries (shot berries) from some of the pollinated but unfertilized flowers. The setting and maturation of shot berries varies greatly among varieties. Most varieties mature very few, but some others, such as the Black Corinth, rarely produce anything but shot berries. Shot berries in clusters of normally seeded varieties of table grapes are a serious defect, since they detract from eye appeal, but those of Black Cornith are its chief merit, provided they are normal and are numerous enough to fill the cluster. The setting and subsequent development of the seedless berries, either on Black Corinth vines or on vines of other varieties, can be greatly influenced by girdling (see the clusters in fig. 92). The setting of normally seeded berries, in contrast, is influenced very little by girdling. Girdling the normally seeded varieties at any time after the beginning of bloom does not materially improve the set of berries with seeds, but it may increase the number of shot berries (Coombe, 1960; Jacob, 1934, 1941).

Thompson Seedless and similar varieties, such as Perlette, Monukka, and Delight, in which set is by stenospermocarpy and which contain only rudiments of seeds, will respond to girdling in a manner very similar to that of Black Corinth (Jacob, 1931).

Wine grape varieties, such as Pinot Chardonnay, which occasionally produce only straggly clusters, can be made to yield larger crops by girdling

FIGURE 92: Effect of girdling on increasing set and size of berries in Black Corinth. Left, cluster from ungirdled vine; right, cluster from girdled vine.

(Lider and Sanderson, 1959). The additional fruit consists mostly of seedless berries. This, however, is not at all objectionable in wine varieties.

Girdling increases the set of shot berries primarily by reducing the extent of the drop, which normally occurs very soon after blooming (see set of Black Corinth, p. 347). Obviously, therefore, to be effective in increasing the number of berries, girdling must be done before this normal drop occurs —that is, during or immediately after bloom. It is most effective when done during bloom (table 24). The increase in crop results from heavier berries as well as better set.

The figures of the table show the influence of girdling on berry set, weight of berry, crop, and maturity at harvest. The rather uniform degrees Brix readings indicate that none of the vines was overcropped. These

Means of Improving Grape Quality

TABLE 24

IMPROVEMENT IN THE SET OF BLACK CORINTH BY GIRDLING

Time of girdling	Crop to a vine	Berries to a cluster	Weight of 100 berries	Maturity at harvest
	pounds		*ounces*	*degrees Balling*
Beginning of bloom	24.0	361	1.23	25.9
End of bloom	23.6	351	1.23	25.6
Berries, one-fourth grown	13.9	328	0.95	26.3
Control (not girdled)	7.1	266	0.60	26.3

SOURCE OF DATA: Jacob (1931).

data point up the benefit of girdling as well as the effect of proper timing.

2. *To increase berry size.*—Enlargement of seedless berries can be hastened and their ultimate size appreciably increased by a girdling timed to be effective during the period of rapid berry enlargement. Increased berry size is very desirable in Thompson Seedless and other seedless varieties grown as table grapes. The data of table 25 show that the berry weight of Thompson Seedless is greatest if girdling is done as early as possible after the normal drop of impotent flowers. Girdling during the drop will increase the number of berries that set, but it makes the clusters more compact and raises the cost of thinning. The increase in berry size is less with each successive delay in girdling. Only with the two earliest girdlings shown in table 25 was there enough increase in berry weight to make the fruit of desirable table quality. Berry weight was increased only slightly when girdling was delayed three weeks. From these data it is apparent that girdling to obtain maximum increases in berry size of Thompson Seedless and other seedless

TABLE 25

EFFECT OF GIRDLING, TIME OF GIRDLING, AND TIME OF THINNING ON
AVERAGE BERRY WEIGHT OF THOMPSON SEEDLESS

Date of girdling	Date of Thinning and Weight of Berries, in grams					
	Lot 1		Lot 2		Lot 3	
	Thinned	Weight of berry	Thinned	Weight of berry	Thinned	Weight of berry
June 9	June 9	3.00	June 9	2.92	July 1	3.06
June 15	June 9	2.80	June 15	2.62	July 1	2.64
June 23	June 9	2.04	June 23	2.04	July 1	2.14
July 1	June 9	1.55	July 1	1.53	July 1	1.66
Control—Not berry-thinned or girdled. Drop was about June 5–8.						1.40

SOURCE OF DATA: Winkler (1953).

Means of Improving Grape Quality

FIGURE 93: Thompson Seedless berries. Left, from vine berry-thinned and girdled; center, from control vine; right, from vine berry-thinned, but not girdled. (*Calif. Agr. Ext. Ser. Cir. 56*)

sorts must be done immediately after the normal drop following bloom. The greater effectiveness of the earliest girdling arises from the fact that it coincides with the rapid cell division in the pericarp that occurs between the fifth and tenth days after anthesis (Coombe, 1960), with the time of very rapid normal berry growth, and with late spring maximum in the level of available carbohydrates.

The increases in size of seedless berries from girdling shown in figure 93 are typical of those of all seedless varieties as well as of the shot berries of seeded varieties.

The effect of girdling in increasing berry size is markedly reduced by an increase in crop above normal. The depressive effect of 1.3 tons more crop per acre on berry size increase was greater than that of a week's delay in girdling (see table 26). For practical purposes, girdling was ineffective with a 10-ton crop at Davis; the berries were still too small.

Thinning is always necessary when the vines of seedless varieties are girdled. The increase in total crop, without thinning, is roughly proportional to the increase in berry size; hence vines that are girdled and not thinned are nearly always overloaded, with consequent poor quality of fruit and weakening of the vines. As a rule, the clusters from ungirdled vines of

TABLE 26
EFFECT OF CROP (AND TIME OF GIRDLING) ON AVERAGE BERRY WEIGHT AND TIME OF MATURING, THOMPSON SEEDLESS

	Time of girdling and weight of berry					Date reaching 18° Balling
Crop	June 6	June 13	June 20	June 27	Control [a]	
tons	grams	grams	grams	grams	grams	
6.0	3.03	2.85	2.50	2.10	1.57	August 30
7.3	2.66	2.54	2.15	1.89	1.56	September 8
10.0	2.01	....	....	1.52	1.42	October 1

SOURCE OF DATA: Winkler (1953).
[a] Not girdled.

these varieties are normally well filled to compact. Since girdling increases the size of the berries without affecting the length of the stem parts, it increases the compactness of the clusters, often making them too compact.

The method of thinning used will be determined in each instance by the character of the clusters. Cluster thinning should be used to eliminate the least desirable clusters—those too compact, too small or too large, misshapen, or otherwise defective—leaving the required number of the best. Any of the remainder that are too compact must be berry thinned. Even when the clusters are loosely filled, the forked tip ends should be cut off. Ordinarily, one or the other of the methods of berry thinning shown in figures 90 and 91 is used. In short, practice usually combines the cluster-thinning and berry-thinning methods.

The girdling of seeded varieties has regularly failed to produce increases in berry size comparable to those obtained with the seedless sorts. Jacob (in unpublished data) reported a range from zero to increases up to 14 per cent, and Coombe (1960) obtained an increase in berry size in three of five experiments in which the vines were girdled near the end of bloom, the increases ranging from 6 to 11 per cent. These increases in berry size were not large and, in general, the girdling of seeded varieties is of questionable value. At times, however, when berries of these varieties are naturally large, girdling to add this small increase may make them outstandingly attractive. Under such conditions, girdling would probably be worth while. Usually, however, berry or cluster thinning, or both, should achieve an increase in size equal to or greater than that obtained by girdling, and without risk of injuring the vine.

3. *To advance maturation.*—If girdling is to improve color and hasten ripening, the girdles must be open and effective during the early part of the ripening period, which is the period of the most rapid increase in sugar. The effectiveness is also influenced by level of crop, vine growth, and seasonal conditions. Girdling improves the coloring of Cardinal, Red Malaga, and Ribier, and speeds the ripening of most seeded varieties—such as Malaga, Muscat of Alexandria, Red Malaga, and Ribier. To improve color and hasten ripening, the girdle should be made just before ripening starts, when the first traces of color appear in the fruit (Jacob, 1928, 1941; Sharples, *et al.*, 1955; Weaver, 1955; Weaver and McCune, 1959a). Best results are obtained from normal vines bearing light to moderate crop. With an overcrop, very active growth, or cool weather, there may be little or no response.

Girdling to hasten ripening is of doubtful economic value except in the very early districts, where a few days' advance in maturity may mean a great difference in price—enough to compensate for the reduced crops, added expense, danger of killing or weakening the vines, and risk of failure.

Girdling at the beginning of ripening usually has little or no effect in advancing the maturity of seedless varieties, such as Thompson Seedless

Means of Improving Grape Quality

(Jacob, 1928) and Perlette. With proper thinning, girdling after set to increase berry size may hasten maturing under some conditions. This effect seems to be greatest in the hot areas, where the elapse of time from set to maturity is short. When the girdle fails to heal, maturation is advanced, but the fruit is soft, poorly colored, and liable to sunburn.

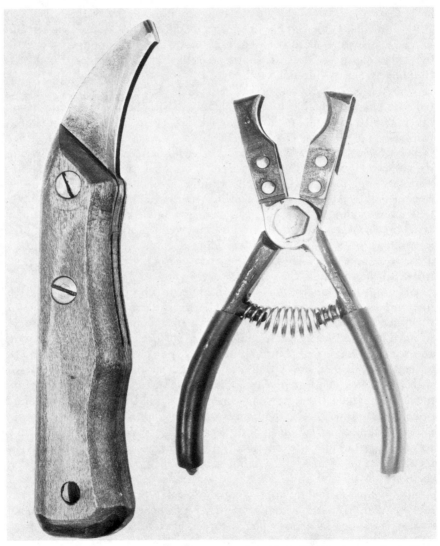

FIGURE 94: Tools for girdling. Left, the double-bladed knife for trunk girdling; right, a plier-type tool for cane girdling.

Means of Improving Grape Quality

Making the girdle.—Various types of double-bladed knives are used in girdling trunks. Work done with a single-bladed knife usually is less effective and requires much more time. In trunk girdling the tip of the two-bladed knife is pressed into the bark and pulled to remove a strip about 1 inch long. Then the tip is placed where the previous cut ended, and is pulled again. This is repeated until a strip of bark is removed entirely round the trunk.

Cane girdling is best performed with girdling pliers, which have double blades on each side. With pliers, such as those shown in figure 94, a cut is made through the bark by pressing the handles and releasing the pressure; the pliers are rotated on the cane, then, and another section of the ring is cut by pressing the handles. This process is continued until the ring of bark has been cut completely round the cane. The ring of bark is loosened by rotating the pliers, under slight pressure, round the cane. The bark removed will stick between the double blades, but with further use of the tool will pass on through between them. A spacing of three sixteenths of an inch between the double blades is usually recommended.

In making the girdles, only the bark is removed. Again, if a narrow strip of bark is left, the effect of the girdle will be greatly reduced. Girdles that are not complete are easily detected, since the retained bark tissue turns brown or dark in ten minutes or less. Cutting deeply into the wood is injurious; it destroys many of the most active conducting vessels in the outer layers of wood and thus may cause a lack of water above the girdle. Improper sharpening of the hook at the point of the two-bladed knife usually leads to deep girdling. Repeated deep girdling year after year makes the removal of a ring beneath the bark all the more damaging.

Weakening effect of girdling.—Girdling stops the downward movement of organic food materials—especially growth regulating substances—past the wound until after healing. Unpublished data by J. A. Cook show that upward movement of mineral nutrients is also interrupted. Top growth is checked, and the leaves tend to become yellowish (Coombe, 1960; Jacob, 1931). The longer the wounds remain open, the more serious is the weakening effect. Trunk girdles that do not heal during the growing season cause the vines to die. Cane girdles that fail to heal are less serious, because only the portion above the girdle will die. Girdles made during or soon after blooming and not more than three-sixteenth-inch wide will usually heal in three to six weeks; those made later or cut wider, or reopened to influence ripening, will heal more slowly and have a greater weakening effect.

Good care in cultivation, particularly in irrigation and in thinning to regulate the crop, will make the girdle less weakening. Although little more water need be applied, the time between irrigations should be cut in half while the wounds are open. Girdling in unirrigated vineyards must be practiced with caution; a single knife-cut or a one-sixteenth-inch girdle should suffice.

Overcropping of girdled vines is to be avoided. This is done with Black Corinth by pruning, and with Thompson Seedless and all other table varieties by thinning, to the extent that the girdled vines will have not more than two thirds to three fourths of the maximum crop they could mature if not girdled.

If properly thinned and well cared for, Thompson Seedless vines may be girdled year after year. One lot of irrigated mature vines in Stanislaus County, California, has been girdled and thinned for eleven consecutive years with no apparent decrease in crop or growth. Girdling of unirrigated vines, in contrast, may be very weakening if moisture is insufficient while the wounds are open.

TOPPING AND PINCHING

Topping (removing 12 inches or more of the shoot tip) and pinching or tipping (removing 3 inches or less of the succulent shoot tip) have for many years been referred to as means of increasing set. Branas, *et al.* (1946) cited twenty-nine reports on this practice between 1863 and 1931. Tests have continued, with possibly less conclusive results. Even well before the end of the above period, Bioletti and Flossfeder (1918) found that topping young Tokay and Carignane vines gave a slight increase in yield the first year, decreased yield in the second year, and severely weakened the vines. Thomas and Barnard (1937), in Australia, obtained no improvement in yield of Sultana (Thompson Seedless) by topping. They indicated that it was detrimental to vines of below-normal vigor. Working with the Ribier variety in South Africa, Le Roux and Malan (1945) showed that pinching at the beginning of blooming improved the crop in quality as well as in quantity. In their work, topping increased the crop markedly the first year, although coloring and maturation were delayed, and decreased the crop in subsequent years. Serpuhovitina (1955), using four varieties in Russia, reported a generally reduced flower drop and increased yields following pinching. He indicated a difference between varieties. In trials at Meridian, Mississippi, using seventeen paired vines, Loomis (1949) found that pinching only the terminal bud during or just after bloom increased the yield of Champanel, an American variety, significantly in the first year, but not significantly in any of the next four years. Coombe (1959), working in California, found that pinching increased set 10 to 20 per cent above that of the controls in six of seven trials, and that topping during bloom also increased set and yield. In these trials with Muscat of Alexandria and Ribier, pinching increased the set of shot berries 39 per cent and seeded berries 18 per cent; topping resulted in respective increases of 77 and 14 per cent. The increase in the set of shot berries in table grapes would be objectionable. In later experiments, Coombe (1962, 1965, 1967, and 1970) showed that tipping during bloom or the application of the growth retardant CCC (2-chloroethyltrimethylammonium chloride) to shoots before bloom increased fruit set in several seeded wine and table grape varieties. The increase in fruit set is believed to be due to reduced competition for carbohydrates and other nutrients between the shoot tip and the developing ovaries, since both treatments reduce shoot elongation. Similar findings and conclusions were reached by Skene (1969), using Cabernet-Sauvignon vines.

The early European trials were usually with wine grape varieties in which total yield was the only consideration. In California this has not been the case. In unreported earlier toppings by Jacob, as in the trials by Coombe (1959), increases in the number of shot berries in the table varieties very noticeably outweighed increases of normal seeded berries. On the basis of the available data, topping and pinching cannot be recommended for improving the quality of table grapes in California. Topping in this state is rare, a noteworthy difference from practice abroad.

PLANT GROWTH REGULATORS

Within the last two decades plant growth regulators have become established as possible aids in the field of viticulture.* Weaver and Williams (1950) reported the beneficial effects of a number of these substances on the set of Black Corinth. Similar results were obtained with the same substances in Australia by Coombe (1953). Since these early reports, research has moved forward rapidly. As a result, the following four compounds have been singled out as the most promising: the auxin, 4-chlorophenoxyacetic acid (4-CPA), the retardant, 2-chloroethyl trimethylammonium chloride (CCC), gibberellin, and 2-chloroethylphosphonic acid (ethephon). The first three of these plant growth regulators, applied properly, produce effects similar to girdling. When they are combined with girdling, even greater responses are often obtained. In addition, gibberellin stimulates rapid enlargement or elongation of actively growing vine parts, including the berries. Ethephon, applied at the proper time, hastens maturation and color development in grapes (Hale *et al.*, 1970). Numerous other growth substances, including auxins, cytokinins, and inhibitors, have

* This discussion of growth regulators is simply to give information on what may be expected of them, provided their use does not conflict with the provisions of the Miller Amendment, the Food and Drug Laws, or the regulations of the federal and state Departments of Agriculture. This discussion should not in any way be construed to be a recommendation for their use.

produced various growth responses in grapevines, but generally of lesser magnitude or at greater risk of injury to the vine (Weaver, 1972). New growth regulators are continually being found and there is little doubt that additional compounds will appear on the market in the future.

INCREASING FRUIT SET

4-Chlorophenoxyacetic acid (4-CPA).—During the 1950's 4-CPA was widely used in California to replace girdling in increasing fruit set in Black Corinth grapes. To achieve good set with this auxin, the clusters must be thoroughly sprayed with a solution of 2 to 10 ppm 4-CPA three to six days following full bloom. Set is usually equal to or greater than that obtained by girdling, and the berries produced are equal in size or larger (Weaver, 1956; Blommert and Meynhardt, 1955). Spraying at full bloom or earlier causes many berries to form hard seeds. The hard seeds are usually empty and will not germinate; they are, however, very objectionable in dried currants used in the baking industry. Concentrations of 4-CPA higher than those recommended are very injurious to the vine, forming stunted leaves and abnormal veins similar to leaves damaged with 2, 4-D. In addition, spraying with 4-CPA sometimes results in compact clusters that are subject to rotting, especially if vines are planted in heavy soils. For these reasons *gibberellin* has replaced 4-CPA as a girdling substitute for Black Corinth in California and, further, 4-CPA is no longer cleared for use on grapevines by the Environmental Protection Agency. Gibberellin applied to Black Corinth at full bloom to 3 days later markedly increases berry size (see fig. 95), but either decreases or has no effect on fruit set (Weaver and McCune, 1959c).

Gibberellins.—Bukovac et al. (1960) found that application of gibberellin to *Vitis labrusca*, variety Concord, either during or shortly after anthesis, resulted in a slight increase in fruit set. This finding contrasts with results obtained with Carignane, a seeded variety of *Vitis vinifera*, in which set was sharply reduced by bloomtime application of gibberellin (Christodoulou et al., 1968) and also with Tokay and Zinfandel (Weaver and Pool, 1971a).

2-Chloroethyl trimethylammonium chloride (CCC).—Application of the growth retardant, CCC, to either the foliage or the fruit cluster from one to three weeks before bloom increased fruit set by more than 20 per cent in several seeded and seedless *vinifera* grape varieties (Coombe, 1965, 1967, 1970; Skene, 1969). In addition to greater berry set, spraying shoots with CCC often resulted in darker green leaves, shortened internodes, retarded tendrils, increased number of inflorescences differentiated on lateral shoots and smaller size berries. In New York State, Barritt (1970) showed that application of CCC at concentrations of 750 to 1,250 ppm to the seedless *labrusca* hybrid, Himrod, increased fruit set and cluster weight.

The mechanism of the effect of CCC on increasing fruit set is believed to be due to inhibition of shoot growth, whereby organic nutrients are diverted from the shoot tip to the developing ovaries. This explanation is supported by the finding that CCC is almost without effect on set when the shoot tip has been removed (Coombe, 1970). Gibberellin is able to reverse the shoot stunting effect of CCC (Weaver and Pool, 1971c).

Another growth retardant, succinic acid—2, 2-dimethylhydrazide, has also been shown to increase fruit set in two *labrusca* grape varieties, Himrod and Concord (Tukey and Fleming, 1967, 1968), but has not generally been as effective as CCC in *vinifera* varieties. What long term stunting effects growth retardants have on vine capacity and crop yields has not yet been fully evaluated.

INCREASING THE SIZE OF SEEDLESS BERRIES

The effect of proper application of selected growth regulators to increase the size of seedless berries is very similar to the effect produced by girdling. When application of the compounds is combined with girdling, berry size is increased even more. Black Corinth and Thompson Seedless are the two varieties in which hormones have been most widely used to increase berry size.

In the early 1960's sprays of gibberellin at concentrations of 2.5 to 5 ppm applied at 90 per cent capfall (separation of calayptra from flowers) to Black Corinth cluster replaced 4-CPA in California. Relatively loose clusters

FIGURE 95: Black Corinth clusters 59 days after being sprayed on May 31 at concentrations of 5 (C) or 20 ppm (D) gibberellin. (A) is the untreated control and (B) was girdled but unsprayed. Note that the gibberellin sprayed berries are larger than both the girdled and the control berries. (*Courtesy of Weaver and McCune, 1959c*)

with berries of suitable size for currant-making are produced (figure 95). Care must be taken not to use too high a concentration of gibberellin or berries too large for commercial use will result. In Australia, El-Zeftawi and Weste (1970) found that a mixture of 4-CPA at 20 ppm and gibberellin at 0.5 ppm produced yields of Black Corinth about equal to that obtained by girdling. They also found that applications of gibberellin at 1 ppm plus CCC at 100 ppm produced higher yields than the mixture of gibberellin and 4-CPA. Evidently, the retardant CCC increased fruit set and gibberellin maintained berry size.

In the 1950's the auxin 4-CPA at concentrations of 5 to 15 ppm was applied by some California growers to Thompson Seedless clusters at the time of berry shatter. However, grower acceptance of this auxin on Thompson Seedless was slower than on Black Corinth because it sometimes resulted in a delay in maturation, and it often failed to produce as uniform and as large a berry size as did girdling (Weaver and Winkler, 1952).

By 1961, within four years after the first experiments of gibberellin on grapes (Weaver, 1957; Stewart *et al.*, 1958), nearly all the Thompson Seedless fruit being used for table grapes was sprayed with gibberellin at concentrations of 20 to 40 ppm at the fruit set stage, immediately after shatter of impotent flowers. This resulted in berry size increases larger than that obtained by girdling alone. Some of these clusters were very compact, subject to bunch rot, and difficult to pack in shipping lugs, since sufficient berry thinning usually had not been done to compensate for the greatly enlarged berries. In order to overcome this problem two applications of gibberellin are now used on Thompson Seedless grapes used for table fruit (Christodoulou *et al.*, 1968).

The first application of gibberellin (2.5 to 20 ppm) is made at bloom

TABLE 27

EFFECT OF DIFFERENT CONCENTRATIONS OF GIBBERELLIN APPLIED AT
BLOOM ON THE WEIGHT, SHAPE, CLUSTER LOOSENESS, AND
MATURITY OF THOMPSON SEEDLESS BERRIES *

Concentration of gibberellin applied at bloom	Weight per berry (g)	Berry width (cm)	Berry length (cm)	No. of berries per cm of laterals	Soluble solids (° Brix)
0 ppm	2.69 [a]	1.45 [a]	1.84 [a]	5.0 [a]	19.8 [a, b]
2.5	2.97 [a]	1.48 [a]	1.91 [a, b]	4.3 [a, b]	20.6 [a, b]
5	3.10 [a, b]	1.47 [a]	2.11 [b, c]	3.8 [b]	20.7 [a, b]
10	3.47 [b]	1.52 [a]	2.19 [c]	3.7 [b]	21.1 [b]
20	3.49 [b]	1.50 [a]	2.22 [c]	3.7 [b]	21.3 [b]
40	3.60 [b]	1.47 [a]	2.34 [c]	3.4 [b]	19.2 [a]

SOURCE OF DATA: Christodoulou *et al.* (1968).
* Within any one column, values with different letter superscripts differ at the 5% level.

Means of Improving Grape Quality

TABLE 28

EFFECT OF GIBBERELLIN APPLIED AT BLOOM AND/OR FRUIT SET
ON THE WEIGHT, SHAPE, CLUSTER LOOSENESS, AND MATURITY
OF THOMPSON SEEDLESS BERRIES *

Concentration of gibberellin and stage of cluster development	Weight per berry (g)	Berry width (cm)	Berry length (cm)	No. of berries per cm of laterals	Soluble solids (° Brix)
20 ppm at bloom	3.28 [a]	1.49 [a]	2.20 [a]	3.5 [a]	19.6 [a]
40 ppm at fruit set	4.02 [b]	1.61 [b]	2.30 [b]	4.9 [b]	15.2 [b]
20 ppm at bloom plus 40 ppm at fruit set	4.75 [c]	1.65 [b]	2.57 [c]	3.1 [c]	17.3 [c]

SOURCE OF DATA: Christodoulou *et al.* (1968).

* Within any one column, values with different letter superscripts differ at the 5% level.

time when capfall is between 20 and 80 percent (table 27). This thins the cluster by reducing berry set and also increases berry size (see also table 28). A second application of gibberellin (20 to 40 ppm) is made on the same vines at the fruit-set stage (berry shatter), usually 10 to 14 days after the initial application, to further increase the size of the berries (fig. 96, table 28). In addition, girdling is still usually performed on gibberellin-treated vines at the fruit-set stage to further increase size and uniformity of berries (table 29). Thompson Seedless clusters sprayed with gibberellin at bloom and again treated with gibberellin and girdled at fruit-set are usually 2 to

TABLE 29

BERRY WEIGHT OF THOMPSON SEEDLESS GRAPES AT HARVEST FROM VINES
THAT WERE GIRDLED AT VARIOUS TIMES AND SPRAYED OR NOT SPRAYED
WITH GIBBERELLIN

Date of Girdling	Berry diameter (mm) at girdling time		Berry weight at harvest (g)	
	No gibberellin	Gibberellin [a]	No gibberelin	Gibberellin [a]
June 2	3–4	3–4	3.20	4.94
June 9	6–7	7–8	3.25	4.51
June 16	7–8	9–10	3.21	4.29
June 23	9–10	11–12	2.93	4.10
June 30	11–12	13–14	2.25	3.57
July 7	12–13	14–15	2.25	3.36
July 14	12–13	14–15	2.00	3.46

SOURCE OF DATA: Weaver and Pool (1971d).

[a] Clusters were treated with 15 ppm gibberellin at bloom and 40 ppm at fruit set.

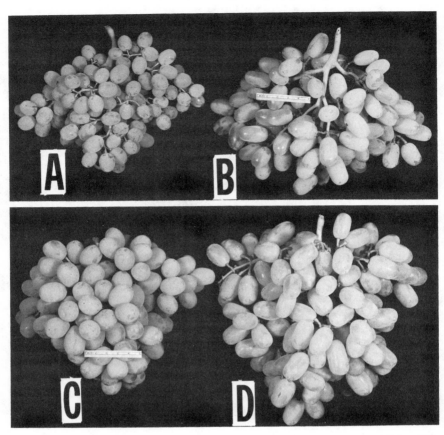

FIGURE 96: Response of Thompson Seedless berries to 20 ppm gibberellin applied at bloom, 40 ppm applied at fruit-set stage or both. A, unsprayed; B, gibberellin applied at bloom; C; gibberellin at fruit-set; and D, gibberellin applied at bloom and fruit-set. Unsprayed cluster (A) is loose and has small berries. Bloom sprayed clusters (B, D) were loose, while cluster sprayed at fruit-set stage only (C) was compact. The largest berries were produced by the double spraying (D). (*Courtesy of Christodolou, Weaver, and Pool, 1968*)

3 times the size of berries not treated with gibberellin nor girdled (see fig. 96 and table 28). The bloom-time thinning spray tends to change the shape of the berry from the typical oval to a longer configuration; however, the consumer has generally not objected to the change in berry shape. Similar effects of gibberellin on the shape of seeded grapes have also been found (Katar'yan *et al.*, 1960; Wurgler, 1961).

The increase in berry size resulting from gibberellin applications on other seedless varieties, such as Perlette, Black Monukka, Delight, Beauty Seedless, and Seedless Concord is generally similar to that of Thompson Seedless (Weaver, 1972). However, the proper timing of applying gibberellin to Perlette clusters to increase berry size without producing overly compact clusters is much more critical than with Thompson Seedless (Kasimatis *et al.*, 1971).

CHEMICAL THINNING

Because of the cost of hand thinning, much effort has been expended in attempts to develop means of thinning by the use of chemical sprays. In the past, hand thinning has been economically feasible for table grapes only. However, with high prices of some varietal wine grapes, cluster thinning by hand after set may be economical in some areas. A method of spray thinning clusters with plant hormones or some other chemicals would greatly reduce labor cost and might make more possible the thinning of wine and raisin grape varieties. With such thinning, leaving more and longer spurs or more canes might be economical and the added foliage could nourish a large crop. At the present time gibberellin is commercially used in California as a prebloom spray on some tight clustered seeded wine grape varieties to elongate and loosen the clusters and thus reduce bunch rot damage. It is also used as a bloom spray on Thompson Seedless clusters to reduce fruit set, resulting in less compact clusters, and to increase berry size (*see* p. 359).

Thinning compact-clustered wine varieties with gibberellin.—Bunch rot in seeded wine grapes that produce compact clusters may be very high in some years. Compactness of such clusters may be reduced by prebloom spraying with gibberellin, which produces a lengthening of clusters parts, especially the pedicels (Alleweldt, 1959; Rives and Pouget, 1957; Shaulis, 1959; Weaver and McCune, 1959b). In California, vines are sprayed when shoots are 15 to 20 inches long, which is usually two or three weeks before bloom. Clusters should average 3 to 4 inches in length and may range from 2 to 5 inches. The concentration of gibberellin used depends on the variety — 1 to 2½ ppm for Tinta Madeira and Palomino; 2½ to 5 ppm for Carignane, Valdepeñas, and Aleatico; and 5 to 10 ppm for Zinfandel, Petite Sirah and Chenin blanc. Loosening of the cluster is a result of reduced set, cluster elongation, and/or production of shot berries (figure 97 and table 30). At 10 ppm gibberellin or less, crop was not reduced. However, at higher concentrations yields may decrease (Weaver and McCune, 1959b; Weaver *et al.*, 1962). The severity of bunch rot varies from year to year; therefore, a prebloom application of gibberellin to tight clustered wine varieties is considered a form of insurance.

Seeded varieties of grapes may be injured if too high a concentration of gibberellin is used, resulting in markedly decreased bud growth the following spring. This is in sharp contrast to seedless varieties, which appar-

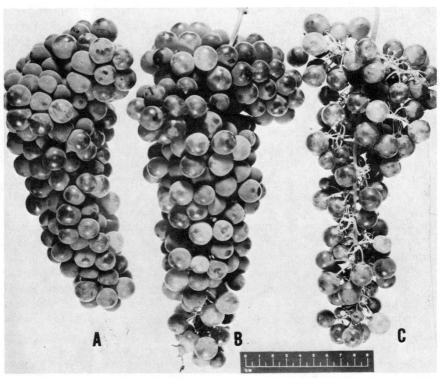

FIGURE 97: Zinfandel clusters at harvest, taken from vines that were sprayed at prebloom stage (April 15) with gibberellin when shoots were 10 to 20 inches long. A, unsprayed; B, with 10 ppm; C, 25 ppm. (*Courtesy of Weaver and McCune, 1959c*)

ently suffer no ill effects from gibberellin, even at concentrations over 50 ppm (Weaver and McCune, 1959b, d; Weaver, 1960). Gibberellin should not be applied to seeded *table* grape varieties for thinning purposes because the shot berries that develop as a result of the application detract from the appearance of the cluster.

Gibberellin bloom sprays to thin Thompson Seedless clusters for table fruit.—During the early 1960's the commercial practice in California was to spray gibberellin on Thompson Seedless once at the fruit-set stage to increase berry size and at the same time to girdle the vines to further increase berry size. The large-berried clusters that subsequently developed had to be heavily berry-thinned to reduce compactness. To reduce this over compactness gibberellin is now sprayed twice; once at bloom for a cluster loosening and berry sizing effect and again at fruit set for an additional berry sizing effect. Christodoulou *et al.* (1968) found that application of

TABLE 30
EFFECTS OF GIBBERELLIN ON ESTIMATED CLUSTER
LOOSENESS AND ROT

Concentration of gibberellin ppm	Estimated increase in looseness per cent	Average number of clusters with rot per vine
0	0	9.5
10	15	0.6
25	31	1.6
50	50	0.3

SOURCE OF DATA: Weaver and McCune, (1959b).

gibberellin at levels of 2.5 to 20 ppm at 30 to 80 per cent capfall was most effective in loosening clusters (table 28). Loose clusters are less subject to summer bunch rot and are easier to pack.

Working in Israel with the varieties Queen of Vineyards and Chasselas doré, Samish and Lavee (1958) reported that a water spray at the time of bloom produced the desired amount of thinning. The addition of 5 ppm of the auxin, alpha-naphthaleneacetic acid, to the water spray at the time of bloom did not increase its effectiveness. Spraying with a 5 ppm solution of this compound immediately after fruit-set, however, produced good results. Spraying with a 10 ppm solution overthinned the bunches. They reported that spray thinning increased the proportion of the desired (moderately loose) bunches by 20 to 50 per cent; that the number of solid, compact bunches was reduced to negligible proportions; and the number of very loose, straggly bunches was doubled. Crop was not reduced.

BERRY SHRIVEL IN EMPEROR AND CALMERIA TABLE GRAPES

Berry shrivel in Emperor and Calmeria grapes is a condition in which some fruit loses turgidity approximately one month before harvest, resulting in appreciable crop loss every year in the San Joaquin Valley. Jensen (1970) found that application of gibberellin at a concentration of 20 ppm to Emperor one to two weeks following the fruit-set stage decreased the amount of berry shrivel and increased average berry size somewhat (figure 98). The increase in crop was mainly a result of increase in size of seedless or shot berries in Emperor clusters. In Calmeria there was no increase in berry size; however, gibberellin did reduce losses caused by berry shrivel.

ENHANCING FRUIT COLORATION AND RIPENING OF GRAPES

In the warm interior valleys of California the level of pigmentation in the skin of some red and black grape varieties is less than that desired for max-

FIGURE 98: Berry shrivel in 'Calmeria' clusters. Left, cluster from vine sprayed with gibberellin; center and right, clusters from vines not sprayed with gibberellin. (*Courtesy of Jensen and Weaver, 1972*)

imum consumer appeal of table grapes and for wine. Australian workers found that ethylene or 2-chloroethylphosphonic acid (ethephon), a compound that slowly releases ethylene, when applied to Shiraz or Doradillo berries just before the start of the second growth phase (see figure 28, p. 139), advanced maturation by 4 to 6 days, increased fruit coloration, and increased the sugar/acid ratio (Hale *et al.*, 1970). However, when fruits were treated with ethephon during the first berry growth phase or at the start of the slow growth phase, it delayed ripening. In California, application of ethephon at concentrations of 200 to 2,000 ppm to Emperor and Carignane fruits shortly after the initiation of coloring (veraison) resulted in increased fruit coloration and total soluble solids and decreased total acidity (Weaver and Pool, 1971b). The optimum time for treatment was two weeks after the beginning of coloring.

Ethylene has been shown to accelerate the ripening of many fruits and there is strong evidence that it is a fruit-ripening hormone (Burg and Burg, 1965; Pratt and Goeschl, 1969). Ethephon is commercially used to hasten the ripening of bananas, mangos, and honeydew melons and to degreen citrus fruits before marketing. It is also used to help bring field-canning tomatoes that are mechanically harvested to uniform maturity and thereby increase the percentage of fruit acceptable for canning. Further research is needed with ethephon, to determine whether it will have commercial use in increasing fruit coloration and maturation of grapes, and to obtain more complete data on its over-all long term effects on the grapevine.

DELAYING RIPENING

In general, it is desirable to have grapes mature at the period normal for the variety. Other things being equal, this ensures the best balance of the constituents of the fruit. Other things, however, are not always equal: table grapes of some early-ripening varieties bring high prices if they are offered late in the season; and the harvest of wine grapes can proceed more economically if some of the varieties ripen at different times over a long period instead of ripening mostly about the same time. To meet the situation at present, maturation is delayed by overcropping the vines. This, in either table or wine grapes, is unsatisfactory, since the oxidation of the acidity is not slowed in proportion to the delay in the accumulation of sugar. In other words, the grapes become flat in taste and the wines made from them are unbalanced: the Brix-acid ratio becomes too high.

In trials at Davis (Weaver, 1956; Weaver and McCune, 1954, 1957) with Thompson Seedless, Ribier, and Zinfandel, using 2.5 and 25 ppm of the auxin, benzothiazol-2-oxyacetic acid, immediately after set or later, delayed maturation by two to three weeks without an appreciable change in the balance of the fruit at maturity. The delay in coloring parallels that of maturing. Unfortunately, there are no patent rights on this compound and little interest has been shown by chemical companies to invest the large amount of funds necessary to clear this compound through various government protection agencies before it can be applied commercially to vineyards.

SPRINKLER COOLING GRAPEVINES

In the interior valleys of California exessively high temperatures from June through September are a major concern to viticulturists. Maximum temperatures in these areas consistently exceed 90° F. and may reach as high as 116° F. in hot spells, with daytime relative humidities usually below 25 per cent. During these hot spells, sunburn damage of exposed grapes may be high, especially on varieties easily subject to sunburning, such as Tokay. Temperatures above 90° F. during the bloom-fruit set period markedly reduce berry size and weight, due to both fewer and smaller size cells per berry (Harris *et al.*, 1968; W. M. Kliewer and Jirair Carapetian, unpublished data). High temperatures during the ripening period greatly decrease total acidity especially malic acid (Kliewer and Lider, 1970; Kliewer, 1973), which generally lowers the quality for making dry table wines. For these reasons there is considerable interest in seeking ways to cool vineyards when temperatures are excessively high.

Means of Improving Grape Quality

One approach is the use of overhead sprinklers to cool vineyards at high temperatures, but information on this subject is limited. Gilbert *et al.* (1970) reported that intermittent overhead sprinkling in a commercial vineyard with conventional sprinkler nozzles lowered leaf and fruit temperatures by 7 to 25° F., and air temperatures by 7 to 10° F. Kliewer and Schultz (1973) used mist type sprinkler nozzles to cool potted Cardinal, Carignane, and White Riesling grapevines at Davis when air temperatures exceed 86° F. Berries from sprinkler-cooled vines were significantly larger and heavier, and the berry juice was higher in acidity and lower in pH than unsprinkled fruits at harvest. Fruit maturity (total soluable solids) was little affected by the sprinkler cooling. Sprinkler cooling also significantly increased the coloration of Cardinal fruits compared to unsprinkled fruits. Fruits from vines continuously sprinkled when air temperature exceeded 86° F. were usually significantly larger and higher in acidity than intermittently sprinkled fruits. Sprinkler cooling between bloom and veraison was the most effective period for increasing berry size; however, for increasing acidity of berry juice, sprinkling from veraison to fruit maturity was most effective.

The cultural conditions and plant material used in this work differs considerably from that of field-grown vines. Several problems have been reported in vineyard sprinkler cooling trials. These include excessive bunch rot, rapid vegetative growth during fruit ripening resulting in delayed fruit maturity, and susceptibility of wines to early over-oxidation. Before sprinkler cooling of vineyards can become a commercial practice these problems must be solved.

BIBLIOGRAPHY

Alleweldt, G. 1959. Forderung des Infloreszenwachstums der Reben durch Gibberellinsäure. Vitis, 2:71–78.

Barritt, B. H. 1970. Fruit set in seedless grapes treated with growth regulators Alar, CCC and gibberellin. J. Amer. Soc. Hort. Sci., 95:58–61.

Bioletti, F. T., and F. C. Flossfeder. 1918. Topping and pinching vines. California Agr. Exp. Sta. Bull., 296:1–14.

Blommert, K. L. J., and J. T. Meynhardt. 1955. Preliminary experiments with hormone sprays as a substitute for girdling of Zante currants. Farming in South Africa, 30:367–368.

Branas, J., G. Brenon, and L. Levadoux. 1946. Éléments de viticulture générale. Montpellier, École Nationale d'Agriculture de Montpellier. (*See* p. 400.)

Bukovac, M. J., R. P. Larsen, and H. K. Bell. 1960. Effect of gibberellin on berry set and development of Concord grapes. Quar. Bull. Mich. Agr. Exp. Sta., 42:503–510.

Burg, S. P., and E. A. Burg. 1965. Ethylene action and the ripening of fruits. Science, 48:1190–1196.

Christodoulou, A., R. J. Weaver, and R. M. Pool. 1968. Relation of gibberellin treatment to fruit-set, berry development, cluster compactness in *Vitis vinifera* grapes. Proc. Amer. Soc. Hort. Sci., 92:301–310.

Coombe, B. G. 1953. Setting currants by spray with P.C.P.A. South Australian Jour. Agr., 57:107–110

———. 1959. Fruit set and development in seeded grape varieties as affected by defoliation, topping, girdling, and other treatments. Amer. Jour. Enol. Vitic., 10:85–100.

———. 1960. Relationship of growth and development to changes in sugars, auxins, and gibberellin in fruit of seeded and seedless varieties of *Vitis vinifera*. Plant Physiol., 35:241–250.

———. 1962. The effects of removing leaves, flowers and shoot tips on fruit set in *Vitis vinifera* L. J. Hort. Sci., 37:1–15.

———. 1965. Increase in fruit set of *Vitis vinifera* by treatment with growth retardants. Nature (London), 205:305–306.

———. 1967. Effect of growth retardants on *Vitis vinifera* L. Vitis, 6:278–287.

———. 1970. Fruit set in grape vines: the mechanism of the CCC effect. J. Hort. Sci., 45:415–425.

El-Zewtawi, B. M., and H. L. Weste. 1970. Effects of some growth regulators on the fresh and dry yield of Zante currant (*Vitis vinifera* var.). Vitis. 9: 47–51.

Gilbert, D. E., J. L. Meyer, J. J. Kissler, P. D. La Vine, and C. V. Carlson. 1970. Evaporation cooling of vineyards. Calif. Agri., 24:12–14.

Hale, C. R., B. G. Coombe, and J. S. Hawker. 1970. Effects of ethylene and 2-chloroethyphosphonic acid on the ripening of grapes. Plant Physiol., 45: 620–623.

Harris, J. M., P. E. Kriedemann, and J. V. Possingham. 1968. Anatomical aspects of grape berry development. Vitis, 7:106–119.

Jacob, H. E. 1928. Some responses of the seedless varieties of *Vitis vinifera* to girdling. Proc. Amer. Soc. Hort. Sci., 25:223–229.

———. 1931. Girdling grape vines. California Agr. Ext. Ser. Cir., 56:1–18.

———. 1934. The response of the Hunisa grape to girdling. Proc. Amer. Soc. Hort. Sci., 32:386–388.

———. 1941. Girdling table grapes to hasten maturity of the grapes. Blue Anchor, 18(3)24–25, 42.

Jensen, F. L. 1970. Effects of post-bloom gibberellin applications on berry shrivel and berry weight on seeded *Vitis vinifera* table grapes. M.S. Thesis, Univ. of Calif., Davis, Calif.

Kasimatis, A. N., R. J. Weaver, R. M. Pool, and D. D. Halsey. 1971. Response of 'Perlette' grape berries to gibberellic acid application applied during bloom and at fruit set. Amer. J. Enol. Vitic., 22:19–23.

Katar'yan, T. G., M. A. Drboglav, and M. V. Davydova. 1960. The effect of gibberellic acid on different varieties of grapes. Plant Physiol., 7(3):284–287: (Trans. of Fixiol. Rastenii, p. 345–347, 1960).

Kliewer. W. M. 1973. Berry composition of some *Vitis vinifera* cultivars as influenced by photo- and nycto-temperatures during maturation. J. Amer. Soc. Hort. Sci., 98.

———, and L. A. Lider. 1970. Effect of day temperature and light intensity on growth and composition of *Vitis vinifera* L. fruits. J. Amer. Soc. Hort. Sci., 95:766–769.

———, and H. B. Schultz. 1973. Effect of sprinkler cooling of grapevines on fruit growth and composition. Amer. J. Enol. Vitic., 24:17–26.

———, and R. J. Weaver. 1971. Effect of crop level and leaf area on growth, composition, and coloration of 'Tokay' grapes. Amer. J. Enol. Vitic., 22:172–177.

Lambry, M. 1817. Exposé d'un moyen misen pratique pour empêcher la vigne de couler et hâter la maturité du raisin. 2d. ed. Paris, Imprimerie Labrairie Madame Huzard.

Le Roux, M. S., and A. H. Malan. 1945. Experiments on the topping of vines. Farming in South Africa, 20:543–548.

Lider, L. A., and G. W. Sanderson. 1959. Effects of girdling and rootstock on crop production with the variety Chardonnay. Proc. Amer. Soc. Hort. Sci., 74:383–387.

Loomis, N. H. 1949. The effect of pinching off the terminals on yield and cane growth of Champanel grapes. Proc. Amer. Soc. Hort. Sci., 54:181–182.

Maynard, S. T. 1887 and 1890. Report of the horticulturist. Massachusetts Agr. Exp. Sta. Bull., nos. 1, 7.

Nelson, K. E., J. W. Allen, and H. G. Schultz. 1972. Effect of grape maturity, sample order, and sex of the taster on the flavor response of supermarket customers. Amer. J. Enol. Vitic., 23:86–95.

———, G. A. Baker, A. J. Winkler, M. A. Amerine, H. B. Richardson, and Francis R. Jones. 1963. Chemical and sensory variability in table grapes. Hilgardia, 34:1–42.

———, and H. B. Richardson. 1967. Relationship between flavor and maturity in consumer acceptance of Thompson Seedless. Blue Anchor, 44(2):43–45.

Pratt, H. K., and J. D. Goeschl. 1969. Physiological roles of ethylene in plants. Ann. Rev. Plant Physiol., 20:265–302.

Rives, M., and R. Pouget. 1957. Action de la gibberelline sur la compacité des grappes de deux varietiés de vigne. Acad. d'Agr. de France Compt. Rend. Hebd., 45:343–345.

Samish, R. M., and L. Lavee. 1958. Spray thinning of grapes with growth regulators. Ktavim, 8:273–285.

Serpuhovitina, K. A. 1955. Effect of pinching on flower drop and yield of vines. [Tran. title.] Viodelia i Vinogradarstvo S.S.S.R., 15:23–25. (See Hort. Abs., 26:296).

Sharples, G. C., R. H. Hilgeman, and R. L. Milnes. 1955. The relation of cluster thinning and trunk girdling of Cardinal grapes to yield and quality of fruit in Arizona. Proc. Amer. Soc. Hort. Sci., 66:225–233.

Shaulis, N. 1959. Gibberellin trials for New York grapes. New York Agr. Exp. Sta. Farm Res., 25:11.

Skene, K. G. M. 1969. A comparison of the effects of "Cycocel" and tipping on fruit set in *Vitis vinifera* L. Aust. J. Biol. Sci., 22:1305–1311.

Stewart, W. S., D. Halsey, and F. T. Ching. 1958. Effect of the potassium salt of gibberellic acid on fruit growth of Thompson Seedless grapes. Proc. Amer. Soc. Hort. Sci., 72:165–169.

Thomas, J. E., and C. Barnard. 1937. The influence of tipping, topping, cincturing, and disbudding on growth and yield in the Sultana vine. Jour. Coun. Sci. and Indus. Res. (Australia), 10:64–78.

Tukey. L. D., and H. K. Fleming. 1967. Alar, a new fruit setting chemical for grapes. Pa. Fruit News, 46(6):12–13.

——, ——. 1968. Fruiting and vegetative effects of N-dimethylaminosuccinamic acid on 'Concord' grapes, *Vitis labrusca* L. Proc. Amer. Soc. Hort. Sci. 93:300–310.

Weaver, R. J. 1952. Thinning and girdling of Red Malaga grapes in relation to size of berry, color, and percentage of total soluble solids of fruit. Proc. Amer. Soc. Hort. Sci., 60:132–150.

——. 1955. Relation of time of girdling to ripening of fruit of Red Managa and Ribier grapes. Proc. Amer. Soc. Hort. Sci., 65:183–186.

——. 1956. Plant regulators in grape production. California Agr. Exp. Sta. Bull., 752:1–26.

——. 1957. Gibberellin on grapes. Blue Anchor, 34: 10–11.

——. 1960. Toxicity of gibberellin to seedless and seeded varieties of *Vitis vinifera*. Nature, 187:1135–1136.

——. 1972. Plant growth substances in agriculture. San Francisco, W. H. Freeman and Company.

——, A. N. Kasimatis, and S. B. McCune. 1962. Studies with gibberellin on wine grapes to decrease bunch rot. Amer. J. Enol. Vitic., 13:78–82.

——, and S. B. McCune. 1954. Effect of benzothiazol-2-oxyacetic on the development of Black Corinth grapes. Bot. Gaz., 115:367–371.

——, ——. 1957. Response of Thompson Seedless grapes to 4-chlorophenoxyacetic acid and benzothiazol-2-oxyacetic acid. Hilgardia, 27:189–200.

——, ——. 1959a. Girdling; its relation in carbohydrate nutrition and development of Thompson Seedless, Red Malaga, and Ribier grapes. Hilgardia, 28:421–435.

——, ——. 1959b. Effect of gibberellin on seeded *Vitis vinifera*, and its translocation within the vine. Hilgardia, 28:625–645.

——, ——. 1959c. Response of certain varieties of *Vitis vinifera* to gibberellin. Hilgardia, 28:297–350.

——, ——. 1959d. Effect of gibberellin on seedless *Vitis vinifera*. Hilgardia, 29:247–275.

——, and R. M. Pool. 1971a. Thinning 'Tokay' and 'Zinfandel' grapes by bloom sprays of gibberellin. J. Amer. Soc. Hort. Sci., 96:820–822.

——, ——. 1971b. Effect of (2-chloroethyl) phosphonic acid (ethephon) on maturation of *Vitis vinifera* L. J. Amer. Soc. Hort. Sci., 96:725–727.

——, ——. 1971c. Effect of succinic acid—2, 2-dimethylhydrazide and (2-chloroethyl) trimethylammonium chloride on shoot growth of 'Tokay' grapes. Amer. J. Enol. Vitic., 22:223–226.

————, ————. 1971d. Berry response of 'Thompson Seedless' and 'Perlette' grapes to application of gibberellic acid. J. Amer. Soc. Hort. Sci., 96:162–166.

————, and W. O. Williams. 1950. Response of flowers of Black Corinth and fruit of Thompson Seedless grapes to applications of plant growth-regulators. Bot. Gaz., 11:477–485.

————, and A. J. Winkler. 1952. Increasing the size of Thompson Seedless grapes by means of 4-chlorophenoxyacetic acid, berry thinning, and girdling. Plant. Physiol., 27:626–630.

Winkler, A. J. 1927. Improving the fruiting of the Muscat of Alexandria grapes by less severe pruning. Proc. Amer. Soc. Hort. Sci., 24:157–163.

————. 1930. Berry thinning of grapes. California Agr. Exp. Sta. Bull., 492:1–22.

————. 1931. Pruning and thinning experiments with grapes. California Agr. Exp. Sta. Bull., 519:1–56.

————. 1953. Producing table grapes of better quality. Blue Anchor, 30(1):28–31.

————. 1954. Effects of overcropping. Amer. Jour. Enol., 5:4–12.

————. 1958. The relation of leaf area and climate to vine performance and grape quality. Amer. Jour. Enol., 9:10–23.

Wurgler, W. 1961. Effect de l'acide giberellique sur certaines variétés de raisin de table. Ann. Rpt. Agricole de la Suisse, 62:229–231.

15

Cultivation, Chemical Weed Control, and Erosion Control

In agriculture the term "cultivation" is most commonly applied to the loosening, turning, or stirring of soil, by mechanical means, around and between growing plants. It is used here, in this narrow sense, to include all of the various mechanical manipulations of the soil of a vineyard after the vines have been planted.

Cultivation is practiced in some form in most commercial vineyards. Frequency and depth vary widely. Cultivation is beneficial in some respects and detrimental in others. It is beneficial to the extent that it accomplishes the purposes for which it is intended more easily, cheaply, and satisfactorily than do other means. It may be detrimental, in breaking down favorable soil structures and developing unfavorable structures, such as puddled surface soil and compacted subsurface layers (plow soles). The present trend is to cultivate only as often and only as deeply as is necessary.

PURPOSES OF CULTIVATION

The general purposes of vineyard cultivation are: to destroy weeds; to facilitate such vineyard operations as irrigation, harvesting, and the drying of raisins; to prepare the soil as a seedbed for cover crops; to incorporate cover crops and manures and fertilizers into the soil; to help control certain pests (see chap 19); and to promote the absorption of water where other vineyard operations have compacted or puddled the surface.

Cultivation, Chemical Weed Control, and Erosion Control

Weeds must be kept under control. In unirrigated vineyards in California, control means complete elimination soon after the winter rains are over and before the weeds have robbed the soil of moisture needed to carry the vines through the rainless summer. Where water is ample throughout the summer, as irrigation or summer rains, control of weeds means that they are held in check sufficiently that they do not compete seriously for soil nutrients or interfere with such operations as pest control and harvesting. Clean cultivation is not practiced in all situations, nor is it advisable for all.

In itself, cultivation does not conserve soil moisture. Evaporation from the surface dries out the top 4 to 8 inches of soil, whether cultivated or not. In a well-drained soil, moisture below the upper 8 inches of soil is removed mainly by the roots of plants, not by evaporation from the soil surface. Veihmeyer (1927) showed in a study of moisture losses from bare soils, both cultivated and uncultivated, in tanks and in field plots that tillage of the soil did not save water. The soil dried out to the same extent, and practically to the same depth, whether it is cultivated or not. When water removal by plants was compared with water lost by surface evaporation, a tank of soil containing field bindweed (*Convolvulus arvensis*) lost 120 pounds of water in twenty-three days, whereas a similar tank of bare uncultivated soil lost only 57 pounds in more than four years. Although the tank of bare soil was not irrigated after the initial wetting, it still contained available water at the end of the four-year period. Cultivation conserves moisture only by destroying weeds that would use up the water. Destroying the weeds by other means has exactly the same effect on moisture conservation. If no weeds or plants other than vines are present in the vineyard, cultivation cannot conserve any moisture.

Furrows or ridges are needed to distribute irrigation water effectively. The furrows or ridges interfere, more or less, with harvesting and with the drying of raisins between the rows. Especially where the raisins are dried on paper trays, smoothing the soil (by cultivation and dragging) is essential before harvest. In vineyards of table and wine grapes the rough ground is less objectionable. In table grape vineyards extensive stirring of the soil in preparation for harvest is avoided in order to reduce dust deposit on the fruit; a light disking is sometimes done to knock down any high weeds and to reduce the roughness of the soil.

Where cover crops are planted to improve the soil or prevent destructive eroison, cultivation to prepare for planting is usually necessary for a good stand. Also, cultivation is needed to incorporate the cover crop into the soil, if for no other purpose than to prevent fires. Fertilizers other than nitrogen and boron tend to become fixed in the surface soil. To be useful to the vines, such fertilizers must usually be placed, by mechanical means, below the depth of the ordinary cultivation.

Breaking up a compacted or puddled surface-layer by cultivation may increase the soil's permeability to water, but this effect lasts only a short time. Repeated cultivation tends to decrease permeability. Natural channels formed by cracking of the soil, decaying roots, earthworm burrows, etc., enable the soil to absorb water more rapidly than is the case when these natural channels have been broken up by tillage. Cultivation, particularly when the soil is wet, tends to form plow sole—a more or less impervious, compacted layer of soil that forms just below the depth of tillage. The chances of forming a plow sole are lessened if only necessary cultivations are given and the soil is cultivated only when it is dry enough not to be compacted or puddled by the implement used. When a plow sole has been formed, deep tillage is often used in attempts to overcome it; but experience has shown that leaving the soil untilled or cultivating it infrequently, shallowly, and only when dry is often the best remedy.

CULTIVATION IN UNIRRIGATED VINEYARDS

In the unirrigated vineyards of California the only water available to the vines throughout most of the growing season is that stored in the soil from the winter rains. Any weeds in the vineyard after most of the winter rains have fallen will use part of the water; hence such weeds and any cover crop should be destroyed before they can rob the vines of appreciable amounts of soil moisture. The growth of summer weeds must be prevented. Since cultivation is usually the most practical means of destroying or preventing weeds, unirrigated vineyards are cleaned in early spring as soon as the soil is dry enough to work. The winter cover crop, beneficial up to this time in reducing soil erosion and preventing loss of soil nutrients by leaching, is incorporated into the soil by plowing or disking.

The timing of the first spring cultivation is very important. The winter cover crop should be knocked down and all but destroyed during the first period in spring when the soil is dry enough to work well. The cover crop need not be incorporated into the soil at this time. Getting it down largely stops its use of moisture, while its presence on or in the surface of the soil with many of its roots in place still checks erosion. The need for this early cultivation arises from the fact that in some years the early dry spell extends on into the summer. It is under such a condition that an intact and growing cover crop takes moisture at the expense of the vines.

Thus, the cover crop is turned under completely when the rainy season is normally at an end, and the cultivation is repeated often enough to destroy or prevent further weed growth. In the absence of perennial noxious weeds, such as field bindweed and johnson grass, the cultivation usually may be discontinued as soon as the surface soil becomes too dry for seed germination; where perennial weeds are present, however, it must be continued as late and as often as is necessary to control them. The method of cultivation is unimportant so long as it eliminates weeds, discourages erosion, and does not injure the vines. Working the soil when it is wet and plastic enough to be puddled or packed by the implement should be avoided. Rarely should the maximum depth of cultivation exceed 6 inches.

CULTIVATION IN IRRIGATED VINEYARDS

The conservation of water is of less importance in irrigated than in unirrigated vineyards, because additional water may be supplied to replace that removed by both vines and weeds. Irrigated vineyards are usually cleared of weeds in the spring, and subsequent weed growth is controlled during the period of rapid vine growth to reduce or eliminate competition for soil nutrients. After the beginning or middle of summer, if enough irrigation water is available, weed control is aimed mainly at preventing interference with the various vineyard operations. In raisin vineyards using natural sundrying, the soil between the rows is leveled and smoothed by cultivation and by dragging in order to prepare a place for the trays on which the grapes are dried. In table grape vineyards cultivation is often discontinued early in the summer, or by midsummer, and a cover crop of grasses or other plants is allowed to grow, and, if necessary, is controlled by mowing. The same furrows or ridges are used repeatedly for irrigations in such vineyards. Factors favoring this system are the comparative freedom from dust and, on shallow soils, a somewhat earlier beginning of maturation (with a susbsequent more desirable color at maturity) and a firmer texture of the fruit. The disadvantages are the greater requirements for water and, possibly, for nitrogen.

TILLAGE IMPLEMENTS FOR VINEYARDS

Useful in cultivating between the rows of vines are plows, disks, chisel-tooth cultivators, harrows of various kinds, including the revolving and spring-tooth types, and plank or steel drags. The choice of tools is governed by the nature of the soil, the power available for pulling the implements, the distance between the rows, the nature of the cover crop, the manner of pruning-brush disposal, and the preferences of the operator. The same tools will not serve all conditions. In close-planted vineyards with vine rows spaced at 8 feet or less, the main implement for spring cleanup is the moldboard plow. Where a heavy winter cover crop grows in close-planted vineyards, the soil is usually turned toward the vines by shallow plowing, covering the weeds in the row, as soon as soil conditions permit after the heavy winter rains are past (late February or March). Spring rains often cause another crop of grasses and weeds to start after the first plowing. When the spring rains are mostly over, but before the soil becomes too dry to work easily, the soil is turned back to its original position by a second, slightly deeper, plowing and then is smoothed by harrowing. Later cultivations are usually done by disk, weed-cutter, or spring-tooth harrows. The double plowing procedure may, at first thought, seem unnecessary, but as yet no easier or cheaper way has been found for doing the job under the conditions defined. Disks that are small enough to be used in close-planted vineyards are ordinarily too light to do the work of turning under a heavy cover crop as economically as it can be done by plowing.

Vineyards with rows 10 to 12 feet apart are rarely plowed. The spring cleanup and practically all of the summer cultivations are done by disking. Large, heavy disk harrows can turn cover crops of almost any size and also chop up light to normal prunings, which are incorporated into the soil along with the cover crop. To prevent such disks from cutting too deeply for summer cultivation, the use of hydrolically adjusted disks is recommended.

With head-pruned vines and square planting (rows and vines in the rows spaced the same distance apart), cross cultivation (cultivating in both directions) is frequently used to clean the spaces between the vines in the rows. With avenue planting (rows spaced farther apart than the vines in the rows), trellised vines, and often even where cross cultivation is possible, the vine rows are cleaned by special tools. Of these special tools, the initial effective one was the "Kirpy" plow (sometimes also called the French plow or horse hoe). More recently, several types of row plows have been developed. Some of these are completely automatic; others depend to some extent on the vine or stake to move them out of the row. The various automatic row plows are not all equally well adapted to different soil types. To ensure good performance the purchaser should demand a demonstration in his vineyard. When the Kirpy plow is still used, two plows, one right-hand and one left-hand, are often drawn by a light tractor, and the workmen who operate the plows ride sleds also drawn by the tractor. Sometimes these plows and the sleds are attached to the ends of the back section of the disc. Hand hoeing may occasionally be needed to remove small islands of broken but unturned soil immediately adjacent to the vines. The automatic or mechanical row plows are as effective as the hand-operated types, or more so—they cultivate a little more deeply and are more thoroughgoing in their action (fig. 99).

If row plows are to work at their best, the strip of unstirred soil underneath the vine rows must not exceed 15 inches in width, and preferably should be not more than 12 inches wide. The strip should be bordered on either side by a furrow or depression into which the soil from beneath the row can be turned. Some row plows have a moldboard plow that makes this furrow. The ordinary disk harrow, operated by a skillful tractor driver, will go close

Cultivation, Chemical Weed Control, and Erosion Control

FIGURE 99: A row plow. This and similar plows practically eliminate hand hoeing. (*Courtesy of C. Lynn, Visalia, California*)

enough if the vines are headed above 18 inches and the rows are straight. Some of the older vineyards are neither spaced nor headed to permit mechanical cultivation to this extent and will need either more hand work or chemical weed control.

WEED CONTROL WITH OIL

Because of the detrimental effects of cultivation on the grape roots in the topsoil, occasional injury to vine trunks, and the spreading of dust on the fruit, oil sprays have been used to limited extent for controlling weeds. Where weeds are controlled entirely by oil sprays, a permanent system of ridges or basins is constructed for irrigation. This means of total weed control is limited at present.

Weeds in the vine row only can also be controlled by oils or oil emulsions containing an added toxicant, with mechanical cultivation in the centers between rows. An emulsion currently in use contains 10 to 20 gallons of oil, such as Diesel oil or an aromatic weed oil, to which is added 2 or 3 pints of dinitro secondary butyl phenol (55 per cent strength), and this is diluted to 100 gallons with water. Currently registered use for California vineyards permits 150 gallons of such spray per acre, with as many as four applications per year—but not permitted within 30 days before harvest. This fortified oil emulsion is used quite effectively in very young vineyards as a directed spray. A shield is often used to reduce leaf injury during the growing season. Straight or unfortified oil is used at 40 to 100 gallons per acre and is most effective when the weeds are only 1 or 2 inches high. Oils are also used as a spot treatment to control noxious perennial weeds during the late spring and early summer.

Cultivation, Chemical Weed Control, and Erosion Control

CHEMICAL WEED CONTROL

In recent years, two herbicides, simazine and diuron, have been used to control annual weeds in vineyards. Generally the chemicals are applied for control only in the vine row, though effective overall control can be attained without danger to the vines. The overall spraying technique is practiced in some limited vineyard areas today, for example, in most plantings in Switzerland. Field trials conducted by Julliard and Ancel (1969) on complete non-tillage, for a 10-year period, have been favorable. However, recent non-tillage trials in California in a non-irrigated vineyard in Napa Valley and in an irrigated planting near Fresno showed that this practice markedly reduced water infiltration as compared to the cultivated plots. At present it appears that the principal use of herbicides will be for weed control in the vine row—a practice now adopted in nearly 20 per cent of the vineyards of California (Lange *et al.*, 1968).

Simazine and diuron are not toxic to weed seeds until they begin to germinate (Leonard, *et al.*, 1969). Weed seedlings pick up the herbicides through their roots. If the herbicides are applied and leached into the soil prior to seed germination, most annual weeds are killed during their emergence (figs. 100 and 101).

In established vineyards, at 2 to 5 pounds per treated acre (80 per cent active ingredients), both simazine and diuron are effective against germinating seedlings for from 3 months to a year. Both herbicides are used as

FIGURE 100: Weed control in a contoured hillside vineyard after two years of treatment using diuron at the rate of four pounds per treated acre.

food or energy sources by microorganisms and are ultimately broken down (Kaufman and Kearney, 1970; Knuesli *et al.*, 1969; and Aeissbuler, 1969). The breakdown is most rapid in warm, moist soils. Simazine undergoes chemical degradation in the soil more rapidly than diuron.

These two herbicides are generally ineffective in controlling well-established annual weeds or perennial weeds at the rates given above. Leonard and Lider (1969) showed that considerably higher rates—up to 25 pounds per acre—resulted in a high degree of control of field bind-weed, *Convolvulus arvensis*, without injury to the grapevines. However, such a high dosage is risky, judged by the occasional injury to vines treated at lower rates in the sandy, arid areas of California. In these sandy areas where minimum rates are recommended incomplete control of annual weeds often results. Under these conditions alternating the use of simazine and diuron is helpful. For example, wild oats, *Avena fatua*, and the common groundsel, *Senecio vulgaris* are more tolerant of diuron, while barnyard grass, *Echinocloa crusgali*, is more tolerant of simazine.

One of the most persistant noxious annual weeds in vineyards in many parts of California is the puncture vine, *Tribulus terrestris*. In heavily infested vineyards the seed pods can be quite irritating to workers, especially at harvest time. Fortunately, this weed is quite readily controlled with applications of either of the chemicals discussed above.

In order to kill established annual weeds at the time of application of simazine or diuron, either paraquat or amitrole is added to the spray. At

FIGURE 101: Weed control in a vineyard after one year of treatment using simazine at the rate of four pounds per treated acre.

present, in the United States, the federal Food and Drug Administration does not permit the use of amitrole in vineyards. Amitrole is picked up by the foliage and transported throughout the plant, and is most effective against young weeds. This herbicide, however, is rapidly broken down by microorganisms and by chemical means in warm, moist soil. Paraquat kills green foliage but is not transported in the plant. However this herbicide is tied up in the soil and is slow in decomposing. Both chemicals—paraquat and amitraole—are commonly combined with simazine for weed control in European vineyards.

An economical method of controlling field bindwood, *Convolvulus arvensis* and *C. sepium*, a noxious perennial weed, in unirrigated vineyards is with an amine form of 2, 4-D or MCPA. Currently 2, 4-D is permitted for use in vineyards in the United States by the federal Food and Drug Administration, while MCPA currently has only a pending registration. It seems that both compounds effectively control bindweed, but the grapevine is only about one-fourth as sensitive to MCPA as it is to 2, 4-D. Great care should be taken to keep both of these chemicals off the vines' foliage to prevent leaf malformation and injury to developing clusters. It is recommended that the applications be made after shatter following bloom. If the vines' canes are trailing, they should be lifted before spraying. Every effort must be made to minimize spray drift when using these materials.

Bermuda grass, *Cynodon dactylon*, and johnson grass, *Holcus halepensis*, in the vine row can be controlled with dalapon (Leonard *et al.*, 1969). The herbicide should be applied monthly, using 4 pounds of dalapon in 100 gallons of water containing 8 to 16 ounces of a surfactant or wetting agent. Care should be taken to keep dalapon spray off the grapevines. Excessive run-off of the spray from treated weeds onto the soil should be avoided. Dalapon should be applied soon after an irrigation to allow as much time as possible between the application and the next irrigation since it is water soluble and can be leached into the soil where it will be picked up by vine roots. The vines themselves should not be sprayed, for they are quite sensitive to dalapon. Dalapon injury is expressed by leaf symptoms—marginal leaf chlorosis quite similar to boron toxicity, leaf cupping, shoot stunting, and the setting of shot berries. It is advisable to consider dalapon for use as a spot treatment rather than as a material to use as a complete coverage spray in the vine row.

RECENT RESEARCH WITH HERBICIDES

A note should be made of the rapid advances being made in the development of several promising new herbicides. A few of these chemicals are currently being tested in California for their potential in the control of both annual and perennial weeds in vineyards.

Cultivation, Chemical Weed Control, and Erosion Control

Dichlobenil is registered by the federal Food and Drug Administration for use in the United States, while chlorthiamid, which decomposes into dichlobenil in the soil, is being used to a limited extent in Europe. Lider and Leonard (1968) found that both of these herbicides effectively controlled field bindweed, *Convolvulus arvensis*, when applied as a sub-surface layer 3 inches deep, without injury to the vines. In subsequent studies in Europe by Leach *et al.* (1971) it was found that a breakdown product, 2, 6-dichlobenzamide, causes a marginal leaf chlorosis but does not have appreciable vine toxicity.

Another compound, trifluralin, which controls field bindweed, as well as most annual weeds, when applied as a subsurface layer, was reported on by Lange *et al.* (1972). It is now registered for use in vineyards. Trials at the University of California are underway to attempt to find a means for effective subsurface chemical applications in established vineyards (figure 102). This would be an important achievement since there appears to be no phytotoxicity of this herbicide to the established grapevine. Lange *et al.* (1972) showed that effective weed control in young vineyards can be achieved with trifluralin. In these trials, the chemical was applied in the

FIGURE 102: Blade for subsurface application of herbicides.

Cultivation, Chemical Weed Control, and Erosion Control

vine row, close to the vines, as a subsurface layer 3 to 4 inches deep, by using a specially designed blade with closely spaced injector nozzles below. A well-mulched soil is necessary for this application to be effective. In a recent trial in Napa County (Lange *et al.*, 1972), a narrow, deep furrow was opened through the layer of chemical, and rooted vines were planted, followed with an application of water down the furrow. Subsequently, sprinkler irrigation was used in the trial. Weed control was excellent, and no injury to the rootings was noted. At Davis, recent vineyard studies showed that rooted vines can be planted through the layer of trifluralin using a 4-inch auger hole and following with sprinkler irrigation. Again, weed control was excellent with no injury. There is keen commercial interest in this procedure for new vineyard plantings as well as for established vineyards, but the method of application is still not perfected. Good control of bindweed and annuals is achieved except around the vine trunks.

A possibility for controlling field bindweed around the trunks following a subsurface application of trifluralin is repeated treatments with an oil emulsion containing dinoseb. For such use a mixture containing 10 pounds of dinoseb, 4 gallons of dormant oil, and water to make 100 gallons has resulted in good control when the established bindweed was thoroughly wetted. Repeat applications would be necessary, using perhaps 3 sprayings in the spring and early summer followed by another after harvest, concentrating on the "islands" of bindweed left around the vines following the trifluralin application. A vine cane-lifting device would be necessary in making the early summer and post-harvest applications to avoid damage to the vines. The field bindweed should be under effective control after 2 or 3 years of this treatment.

Finally, of great interest is the potential of a new chemical for control of perennial weeds—bindweed, johnsongrass and bermuda grass. Preliminary tests (Lange *et al.*, 1973a, 1973b) underway at the University of California at Davis with N-(phosphonomethyl) glycine, also known as glyphosate, show real promise for effective control of these perennials with no vine damage sustained and relatively little danger from residual toxicity in the soil. Glyphosate is a readily translocated, non-selective herbicide, killing all plant species yet tested. However, it has a very low mamalian toxicity, is adsorbed or fixed rapidly in the soil and appears to break down completely into nontoxic products. It seems to be an environmentally safe compound.

SOIL EROSION CONTROL

On rolling lands in semiarid regions, and even on gentle slopes in humid regions, soil deterioration is mainly the result of soil erosion. The erosion may be insidious, passing unnoticed for some years, but ruinously cumulative in time—as with sheet erosion; or it may be spectacular—as when gullies are deeply cut, often by a single storm.

When rain falls on unprotected ground faster than the soil can absorb it, the pelting drops stir the surface soil into the rain water, and the soil particles, suspended in the water, run off with the water in surface drainage. This is sheet erosion. It does not occur if the rain falls so slowly that none runs off the surface, or if the surface is covered with vegetation that breaks the pelting forces of the raindrops.

Gullies are caused by the rapid flowing of large quantities of water. Any circumstances or provisions that reduce the volume that collects in the flow, or that reduces the velocity of the flowing water, will slow the formation of gullies. Spreading the flow, by vegetation, and slowing the velocity, by vegetation or by cross-slope collecting ditches or checkdams, will reduce or eliminate gully erosion.

The judicious use of cover crops in vineyards on land subject to erosion cannot be too strongly emphasized. The cover crop is most valuable if it is well established and growing during the periods of heavy rains; yet it is still effective if heavy rain falls in the spring after it has been disked to check its growth or kill the plants.

Cover crops reduce or prevent erosion in at least three ways. First, as has been pointed out, the top growth covers and protects the surface, breaking the force of the raindrops before they reach the soil surface and reducing the velocity of flow of the surface runoff. Second, the roots bind the soil, more or less, in a mass of fiber that tends to hold the soil in place. Third, cover cropping, after a year or two, increases the rate of water penetration. The roots, on decaying, leave channels through dense layers and deep into the subsoil. Also, the incorporation of coarse vegetable matter into the topsoil makes the surface more porous, so that surface sealing is prevented or reduced. In a cover-crop experiment at Davis, Proebsting (1958) showed that a 6-inch watering disappeared from the surface of a cover-cropped irrigation basin in less than twenty-four hours, whereas in an adjacent clean-cultivated basin used for comparison the time required was a week.

In California the cover crop for a vineyard may be composed of native self-seeding plants, such as grasses, wild mustard, bur clover, or filaree; or it may be a seeded crop of grasses or legumes, or both. Whatever the nature of the plants, it is important that they be established early in the rainy period, so that the soil will be covered with vegetation before it becomes saturated with water to the point that surface runoff occurs and before the heavy rains of midwinter occur. Native plants, and also those that are broadcast-seeded, will grow over the whole area—between the vines, around the vines, and into the vines. The cleaning up of a vineyard with an over-all weed growth is expensive, and the cost of the spring cleanup has discouraged many vineyardists from the use of cover crops. If, however, a cover crop is sown in strips between the rows, most of the extra expense of cleaning around the vines is avoided and most of the benefits of preventing soil erosion are realized. Excellent for the purpose is a mixture of grass—barley, oats, or rye—and purple vetch (*Vicia atropurpurea*), subterranean clover (*Trifolium subterraneum*) or bur clover (*Medicago hispida*). The latter two seem particularly suited to general vineyard use. About 25 pounds of grain and 20 to 30 pounds of vetch or 4 to 6 pounds of subterranean clover per acre are drilled between the rows and across the slope of the soil in strips from 4 to 8 feet wide, according to the distance between the rows. The soil in the row is left unseeded, and hence it remains relatively clean. In California the seed is drilled into the dry soil at any time in early autumn, but it does not start to grow until the soil is wet by the seasonal rains. Except on fertile soils that are not already eroded, a light application of fertilizer may be needed in the first two or three years to stimulate a rapid early growth. Usually 100 pounds of ammonium sulfate per acre, or its equivalent in nitrogen (20 to 21 lbs.) in some other form of fertilizer, is adequate; occasionally phosphorous, especially where legumes such as vetch and sub-clover are to be planted, may be beneficial. The fertilizer is best drilled into the soil by a fertilizer attachment on the seed drill. The strip of heavy vegetation so obtained prevents damaging soil erosion and interferes very little or not at all with normal vineyard operations. In unirrigated vineyards the cover crop must be destroyed by disking or plowing as soon as the heavy winter rains are past. If a heavy rain should unexpectedly fall after the cover crop is worked down, the presence of the stems and roots will still largely prevent damaging erosion. If strip cover crops are permitted to go to seed, the benefits of the strip effect are soon lost unless herbicides are used in the vine row.

According to Shaulis and Jordan (1960), in vineyards of American grapes in the eastern United States the soil must be protected against erosion during the winter. A cover crop is usually planted in late summer. A common practice is to drill domestic rye grass in alternate middles between the vine rows. A straw mulch may be spread in the other middles, or the prunings may be placed in these middles to be shredded. Studies conducted in Europe by Schrader and Steinlein (1961) indicate that the primary purpose of the covers is to retard or prevent erosion; yet under humid conditions the straw, prunings, and cover crop, on being added to the soil, are factors in building up its humus content. Further, there are some indications that the straw mulch, if present during the summer, may promote root growth in the top 6 inches of soil by both its cooling effect and its protection from moisture loss. This could be of importance on shallow soils.

BIBLIOGRAPHY

Geissbuhler, H. 1969. The substituted ureas. *In* Degradation of herbicides. P. C. Kearney and D. D. Kaufman, eds. New York, Marcel Dekker, Inc. pp. 79–111.

Julliard, B., and J. Ancel. 1969. Enseignement de quelques essais de desherbage chimique de la vigne. Extrait des Comptes Rendus des Journées d'Etudes sur les herbicides. COLUMA:900–904.

Kaufman, D. D., and P. C. Kearney. 1970. Microbial degradation of s-trizine herbicides. In, Residue reviews. F. A. Gunther and J. D. Gunther, eds. New York, Springer-Verlag. Vol. 32. pp. 235–265.

Knuesli, E., D. Berrer, G. Dupuis, and H. Esser. 1969. s-triazines. In, Degradation of herbicides. P. C. Kearney and D. D. Kaufman, eds. New York, Marcel Dekker, Inc. pp. 51–78.

Lange, A. H., H. Agamalian, D. R. Donaldson, C. L. Elmore, W. D. Hamilton, O. A. Leonard, and H. M. Kempen. 1972. Bindweed control in vineyards. Agric. Ext. Ser. Univ. of Calif. MA-41, 3/72.

Lange, A., D. Donaldson, and C. Elmore. 1972. Layered trifluralin for bindweed control. Res. Prog. Rpt., West. Soc. Weed Sci., pp. 4–5.

———, B. Fischer, D. Hamilton, and H. Agamalian. 1968. Weed control in California vineyards. California Agriculture 22(10):6–7.

———, H. Kempen, W. McHenry, and O. Leonard. 1973. Roundup— a new perennial weed killer. California Agric., 27(2):6–7.

———, C. Elmore, B. Fischer, F. Swanson and D. Donaldson. 1973. Glyphosate for perennial weed control in trees and vines. Agric. Ext. Ser. Univ. of Calif. MA63 5/73.

Leach, R. W. A., N. L. Biddington, A. Verloop, and W. B. Nimmo. 1971. A side effect of chlorthiamid and dichlobenil herbicides. Ann. Appl. Biol., 67:137–144.

Leonard, O. A., and L. A. Lider. 1969. Response of grapes to several years application of soil-applied herbicides. Abstracts of Weed Sci. Soc. Amer. for 1969. Paper 51.

———, ———, and A. H. Lange. 1969. Weed control in grapes. Calif. Agric. Expt. Sta. -Ext. Ser. Leaflet 203:.

Lider, L. A., and O. A. Leonard. 1968. Morning glory control in vineyards with dichlobenil and chlorthiamid. California Agriculture 22(5):8–10.

Proebsting, E. L. 1958. Fertilizer and cover crops for California orchards. California Agr. Exp. Sta. Ext. Ser. Cir., 446:1–19.

Schrader, T., and B. Steinlein. 1961. Neue Erfahrungen mit der Gründüngung im Weinbau. Weinberg Keller, 8:137–151.

Shaulis, N. J., and T. D. Jordan. 1960. Cultural practices for New York vineyards. New York State College of Agric., Cornell Ext. Bull., 805:1–35.

Veihmeyer, F. J. 1927. Some factors affecting irrigation requirements of deciduous orchards. Hilgardia, 2:125–291.

16

Irrigation

All soil particles hold water (more strictly, a water solution) on their surfaces. The coarse particles hold only a small amount in proportion to their own mass; the very small clay particles, in contrast, hold much water in proportion to their mass. Additionally, all natural soils contain organic matter, living organisms, air, and substances in solution in the water or precipitated in the form of salts. The water containing dissolved substances is held as a film on the surface of the particles and, in the form of continuous films of varying thickness, between the surfaces of closely associated very small particles. Air is also held in the spaces, or pores, between the particles. The amount of water held by a soil fluctuates within a considerable range, and the amount of air varies approximately inversely with the water content. The pore space (space not occupied by the particles themselves) constitutes 30 to 50 per cent of the volume of most soils suited to vineyard use.

THE SOIL AND SOIL MOISTURE

When the pore space in the soil is completely filled with water, the soil is said to be *saturated*; no more water can be put into it. If drainage takes place, part of the water from a saturated soil will move downward by gravity. The amount of water retained by the drained soil is called the *field capacity* of that soil. Although each soil particle holds a film of water over its entire surface, most of the water is held between the soil particles in the form of variously shaped wedges. Plants get most of their water from these wedges.

Field capacity is a critical point in soil-water relations. It represents the point at which further downward movement of liquid water through the soil becomes negligible. It usually represents the upper limit of the water readily available to plants. The field capacity of well-drained soils of uniform texture may vary from less than 5 per cent (by weight) in coarse sandy soils to more than 35 per cent in clay soils. It may be even higher in soils containing much organic matter.

During the growing season, plants remove water from the zone of soil occupied by their roots (the root zone) until the moisture content diminishes to a point at which many plants wilt and do not recover unless water is added to the soil. When this condition is reached, the soil in the greater part of the root zone is at the *permanent wilting percentage* (Hendrickson and Veihmeyer, 1945). Thus, the permanent wilting percentage is the soil moisture content below which plants cannot readily obtain water. Wilting probably does not begin at a specific moisture content, but for an individual soil it does begin within a very narrow range of soil moisture. When soil moisture is reduced to near the permanent wilting percentage, plants show distress by wilting in late afternoon or by stopping growth. With a further slight reduction, they remain wilted all night. The permanent wilting percentage is essentially the same for different kinds of plants grown in the same soil under different atmospheric conditions.

Growth and other plant functions cannot proceed normally when moisture content is at the permanent wilting percentage, though most plants can still very slowly extract additional water from the soil. This small amount may be enough to carry them through periods of drought. The permanent wilting percentage is, therefore, a critical point in the relation of soil moisture to plant growth. In agricultural soils it varies from less than 1.5 per cent to more than 21 per cent. In general, the lowest values are found in sandy soil; the highest, in clay loams and clays.

As the wetted soil becomes drier, the tenacity with which water is held by the soil particles becomes greater, though not at a uniform rate. When moisture content is greater than field capacity, the free water—that which will drain away—is obviously held with a net force less than that of gravity; otherwise it would not drain away. Between field capacity and the permanent wilting percentage, the force or tension with which water is held increases as the soil moisture is depleted. This tension is dependent upon surface forces and includes the force arising from the presence of dissolved mineral elements in the soil solution. The graphs of figure 103 illustrate the increase in soil moisture tension in normal soils—sand to clay—as the available moisture is depleted (Hagan, 1955, 1957). In sandy soils the tension does not begin to build up until as much as 85 per cent of the available moisture is released; then it increases rapidly. In clays, in contrast, the tension begins to increase as soon as moisture is withdrawn,

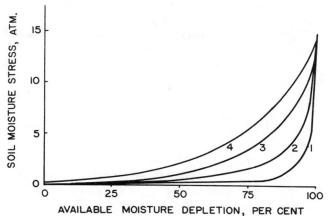

FIGURE 103: Moisture retention curves for non-saline sandy soil (curve 1), loam soil (curve 2), and two clay soils (curves 3 and 4). (*From Hagan, 1955*)

and the rate of increase accelerates as the permanent wilting percentage is approached. Richards and Weaver (1941) indicate that the force required to extract additional water beyond the permanent wilting percentage is equal to 15 atmospheres.

The presence of excess salts increases the force which plants must exert to extract water at any particular soil moisture percentage. Thus, under this condition irrigation is required more frequently and in larger volume.

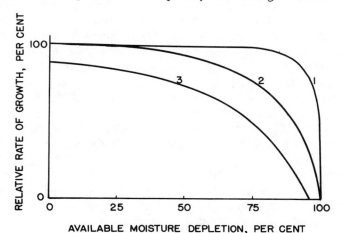

FIGURE 104: The effect on plant growth of the tension with which water is held by different soils: 1, sands; 2, clays; 3, saline soils. (*From Hagan, 1955*)

The additional water dilutes the salts and, where drainage is possible, washes them beyond the root zone.

Figure 104 shows the effect on plant growth of the tension with which water is held by different soils (Hagan, 1957). In sandy soils (curve no. 1) growth is retarded little until nearly all of the available water is depleted. In clay soils, in contrast, some slowing of growth should occur after about 30 per cent of the water is depleted (curve no. 2). In saline soil (curve no. 3) slower growth would be expected at near field capacity, for growth would decline even in the upper half of the available moisture range.

Attempts have been made to increase the soil's ability to hold readily available water by adding organic matter. Proebsting (1937) and Veihmeyer (1938) found, however, that additions far in excess of amounts feasible in commercial practice were not effective.

How Soils Are Wetted

Rain or irrigation water moves downward into the soil, wetting to full capacity (or temporarily beyond full capacity) the soil it passes through. When the rainfall or irrigation is over, water continues to move only so long as the water content of some of the soil is higher than field capacity. If the soil is uniform in texture and structure, so that there are no open channels, such as cracks or tunnels, and no impeding layers, such as plow sole or hardpan, the water moves downward almost uniformly over the area wetted. A light rain or a small application of irrigation water simply wets a shallower depth of soil to its field capacity more than a heavier one does. It does not establish a moisture content less than field capacity; soils cannot be partially wetted, but must be wholly so or not at all. The boundary between the wet soil and the drier soil will be fairly sharp. A second rain, or a second application of irrigation water, does not increase the water content of the already moistened soil beyond field capacity for more than a very short period; instead it wets to field capacity a layer of soil immediately beneath the layer first wetted.

Lateral movement of water in a well-drained soil of uniform texture and structure is slight in comparison with downward movement, seldom exceeding a few inches unless free water is allowed to stand for some time in the furrows. If the furrows are too far apart in a porous soil, some of the soil between the furrows will remain dry because of the limited lateral movement. Impervious plow sole, hardpan, or dense clay subsoil diverts water to a greater lateral movement. In a well-drained soil the upward movement of water is negligible.

The Soil as a Reservoir for Water

The ability of a vineyard's soil to function as a reservoir of water for use by the vines is determined by the available moisture—the difference between field capacity and the permanent wilting percentage—in the soil where most of the roots are growing.

The water in the cultivated surface soil is mostly lost by surface evaporation. Thus, the root zone may be regarded as starting just below the cultivated layer and extending to a depth at which root growth is limited by hardpan, dense clay subsoil, water table, or lack of aeration. In coarse sandy or gravelly soils, grape roots go down 10 to 20 feet or more if no obstructions are present. Not many roots will be found below 8 to 12 feet in sandy loam soils, 5 to 8 feet in loams, or 2 to 3 feet in clays. The depth of rooting in a clean-cultivated vineyard can be easily determined by soil borings made in late summer or fall after lack of available water has checked the growth of the vines. The roots may be assumed to have gone at least as deeply as the soil has been dried out. The approximate amount of water readily available to the vine roots, beginning with field capacity, can then be determined by measuring the minimum quantity of water required to rewet the soil just to the depth which has dried out. The final borings should be made two or three days after the water has disappeared from the surface, at which time all of the wetted soil will be at field capacity. Such measurements are not precise from the irrigation engineer's standpoint, but they are accurate enough for all practical purposes of the vineyardist. The reservoir capacity of the soil varies from about 0.7 to 3.0 inches of water per foot of soil, depending on the texture and structure of the soil.

Absorption of Water by Vines

Plants growing in soil take in water almost exclusively through the absorption zone of the small rootlets, close by the tip of a growing root. A root that is not growing absorbs almost no water. As the rootlet extends itself in the soil, the absorption zone moves along with it, always remaining just behind the growing point. The older parts of the rootlets become covered with a corky layer. In early spring this layer on rootlets formed the previous year may still be incomplete, permitting some absorption of water (Filippenko, 1958); later, however, the layer becomes fully suberized, losing its ability to absorb water.

Theoretically, as water is withdrawn from the small area of soil in the immediate vicinity of the absorption zone of a rootlet, more water should move into that area from the adjacent soil mass. Probably this does occur to a limited extent, but the movement is too slow to be of much value to the vine. Actually, the rootlet gets more water because it continues to grow into areas where available water remains. So long as the roots are able to grow into soil that contains available water, the vine continues to function normally. Each time the soil is wetted by rain or irrigation, the whole soil mass again becomes a region for exploration by new rootlets.

Large vines, having a larger leaf area, use more water than small vines. Since water is lost almost entirely through the leaves, the total amount of water needed by the vine is not materially influenced directly by its fruit load. The fruit load may, however, through its effect on the nutrition of the vine, influence the foraging capacity of the roots and, hence, their ability to get water. The developing fruit competes with the growing shoots and roots for the food materials manufactured in the leaves. The roots of heavily-loaded vines are, consequently, not so well nourished as those of similar vines with a normal or light crop and not so capable of exploring the soil rapidly or thoroughly. Therefore, a vine with a large crop may show distress from lack of water when vines carrying less crop experience no shortage.

Vine Responses to Soil Moisture Conditions

Under favorable conditions of soil moisture, nutrition, temperature, and vineyard care, the seasonal growth cycle of bearing vines is characterized by a very rapid and succulent growth of the shoots in spring and early summer, a rapid slowing of shoot growth as the berries rapidly enlarge, and a gradual slowing of shoot growth toward the ripening period, with many shoots stopping growth by the time the grapes are ripe. During and after harvest the vines should make little new shoot growth, but should retain their leaves, which may remain green or change to yellowish green or red and green, according to the variety; at the same time the bark color of the canes should change from green to light, medium, or reddish brown, according to the variety.

Hendrickson and Veihmeyer (1950) found that grapevines, corresponding to the behavior of deciduous fruit trees and other plants, showed no marked differences in growth and fruiting from differences in the moisture content of the soil so long as the moisture content was above the permanent wilting percentage in *all parts* of the root zone (saturated soils were not considered). Not all of the soil within the root zone is equally populated with roots, however, and the parts containing the most roots are likely to be depleted of readily available moisture sooner than the parts—usually deeper—that contain fewer roots. Vines continue to take water from the regions less densely populated with roots, but the amount of water obtained may be insufficient for maintaining normal growth. Under such conditions the vines cannot get as much water as they would take if all of the root system were in soil containing readily available water. Thus it is true that vines function normally, within only small variations, so long as the soil in all parts of the root zone contains readily available moisture; but it is equally true that vines may evidence lack of water if extensive parts of the root zone reach the permanent wilting percentage while some other parts still contain readily available moisture.

SYMPTOMS OF INSUFFICIENT MOISTURE

An abrupt and severe reduction in the water supply to a growing vine causes wilting of the leaves and succulent shoots. Such wilting occurs with vines growing in pots or cans when the soil reaches the permanent wilting percentage; under field conditions it sometimes occurs in hot weather with vines growing on sandy or shallow soils when the permanent wilting percentage is reached in all parts of the occupied soil at about the same time. Wilting seldom occurs on deep soils, because not all of the soil reaches the permanent wilting percentage at the same time or within a very short period. As the readily available water is exhausted in successive parts of the soil, the vine adjusts itself, by lessened shoot growth, to the limitations imposed by the reduced, though not altogether exhausted, water supply.

A restricted supply of water, with readily available water exhausted from only some parts of the root zone, causes characteristic symptoms that the experienced vineyardist easily recognizes. Early in the season, while vines are growing rapidly, a soft, yellowish-green appearance is imparted by the rapidly elongating shoot tips. This condition persists until after the grand period of growth, provided none of the soil below cultivation depth is depleted of its readily available water. But, as increasingly larger parts of the soil become dry, the rate of growth diminishes, and the appearance gradually changes from the long, soft, yellowish-green to shorter, yellow-green growing tips and then to the harder, darker, or grayish green of the mature leaves. This change in appearance is caused altogether by a shortening of the actively growing tips and may be accompanied by the drying-up of the tendrils at the shoot tips. When enough of the soil becomes depleted of readily available moisture, growth stops (Vaadia and Kasimatis, 1961). Still further reduction in water supply causes drying of the shoot tips and curling of the leaves; mid-cane leaves, well exposed to the sun, develop unpatterned areas of necrosis. The older leaves, at the base of the shoots, become desiccated and die, eventually dropping from the vine. Under these conditions of gradual reduction in the water supply, vines do not wilt in the commonly accepted sense of drooping of the leaves. From the appearance of the vines an observant grower can detect a water shortage before injury results.

Insufficient water during the early period of rapid berry enlargement prevents the attainment of normal berry size (Vaadia and Kasimatis, 1961), and applying water after this period of growth is past will not enable the undersized berries to become normal. This effect has been utilized successfully in some wine grape vineyards to restrict berry growth, thereby reducing cluster compactness and avoiding bunch rot. A severe shortage of readily available water during ripening delays maturity, gives the fruit a dull color, and often allows sunburn. A slight shortage just as maturity is approached may, in contrast, actually hasten ripening, probably because of its effect in limiting shoot growth and its tendency to reduce berry size by shrinkage, which increases the sugar concentration in the juice of the berries.

After the fruit is ripe, and particularly after the crop is harvested, vines seem to be able to adjust to a very limited water supply. Under moderate climatic conditions they will make little or no further shoot growth, but will retain their leaves and ripen their canes even though the soil throughout the greater part of the root zone is at the permanent wilting percentage.

In hot desert regions, however, only early-ripening varieties—mostly Cardinal, Perlette, and Thompson Seedless—are grown. These ripen and are harvested for table grapes during late May and June. Neglect of such vines for the remainder of the long growing season often causes serious damage: most of the leaves drop, and then, when cooler weather in early autumn reduces the moisture stress, new leaves are formed that use stored carbohydrate reserves without ever becoming mature enough to produce replaceable food materials. Such vines will enter the dormant period poorly supplied with reserves, and their buds may fail to grow the next spring or may leaf out irregularly. Vines grown under severe desert conditions will require one or more irrigations after harvest—not to renew active growth, but to keep the leaves functioning normally. Such post-harvest maintenance irrigations might often be recommended as alternate-middles applications.

POSSIBLE EFFECTS OF TOO MUCH WATER

If the soil is saturated for prolonged periods during the growing season (a few weeks or longer in hot weather), roots in the saturated soil may die from lack of aeration. If the greater part of the roots should be thus killed, the vines may actually show symptoms characteristic of insufficient water, caused by the inability of the few remaining healthy roots to meet the needs of the vine, even from the very wet soil.

It has already been stated that new shoot growth should not occur late in the season. Vineyard experience indicates that vines will continue to grow or start new vigorous growth after harvest if supplied with readily available water. This late growth utilizes carbohydrates that should remain as stored reserves, and because the new shoots fail to mature properly, they are subject to injury by early frosts or even by cold winter weather. Such vines are likely in the following year to have bud failure and less crop than vines that ceased growth early and matured their wood well. This is particularly true for cane-pruned varieties. Vines one or two years old, not yet bearing, have a greater tendency than bearing vines to grow vigorously into the late fall. This late growth can usually be prevented by avoiding late—after midsummer—irrigation that is not necessary.

Quantity of Water Needed by Vineyards

California vineyards require from 16 to 54 inches of available water, depending on climate, soil, variety, and cultural conditions, for maximum crops of grapes. In the cool parts of the coastal valleys (region I), supplemental irrigation is unnecessary on soils that hold 12 inches or more of readily available water within the root zone, provided the total rainfall exceeds 16 inches, with 2 inches or more occurring in April and early May. Under such conditions the vines grow well, bear good crops, and keep their leaves until frost. The water required to wet the cultivated 5- to 6-inch top layer of soil is unavoidably lost by surface evaporation; the vines also do not get benefit from any part of the rainfall that is lost by surface runoff and drainage or used by weeds or cover crop after the spring rains are over. Regardless of total rainfall, only the water held by the soil and available to plants is useful. Hence, supplemental irrigation may improve growth and yields even in cool districts that receive considerably more than 16 inches of rainfall if the vineyard is planted on shallow soil, on gravelly soil, on heavy clay soil in which vines do not root deeply, or where vines are too closely planted for the soil depth and/or total rainfall. On the other hand, grapes have been grown without irrigation in the Livermore Valley, with an average rainfall of 14.6 inches, and near Soledad, in the Salinas Valley, with less than 10 inches annually. Vines are able to adjust themselves to limited water supplies by early cessation of growth, small crops, and by dropping their leaves in late summer; obviously, the crops are not as large as they would be with additional water.

Many of the vineyards on the rolling lands bordering the coastal valleys of California would yield larger crops if additional water could be supplied in early or midsummer. Only in rare instances, however, is irrigation water available to these rolling lands at a cost low enough to be economical. Vineyards on the deep, fertile coastal valley soils, for which cheap water might be available, generally do not respond to supplemental irrigation, because these soils hold enough water to supply the vines throughout the season. Some of such vineyards are irrigated in seasons of abnormally low rainfall, in seasons lacking the usual spring rains, or in areas of low rainfall.

In the warmer vineyard areas of the state summer irrigation is practiced almost everywhere that water is available. Table 31 gives the approximate total seasonal needs (rainfall plus supplemental irrigation) for maximum crops of best-quality grapes as produced by successful vineyardists. Vineyards having more rainfall than the total needed for maximum crops may or may not respond to supplemental irrigation, depending on whether the soil holds enough water in the root zone, either by soil texture or by soil depth, to supply the needs of the vines throughout the season. If ordinarily the vines grow until the beginning of the ripening period of the fruit and retain nearly all of their leaves in a healthy green condition until late in the fall, little benefit is likely to be derived from supplemental irrigation. If, however, the vines cease growth by midsummer and drop many leaves before the middle of September, additional water in early summer would increase both growth and crop.

The amount of irrigation water needed in regions of low rainfall can be estimated by subtracting the effective rainfall for the season or the available-water-holding capacity of the soil, whichever is less, from the appropriate figure of table 31. For deep loam soils the minimum figure of the table may be used; the higher figures should be used for shallow or light sandy soils that require three or more irrigations.

GENERAL PRINCIPLES OF VINEYARD IRRIGATION

From the foregoing discussion certain objectives for vineyard irrigation practices can be formulated. During the dormant season—winter or early spring—all parts of the root zone should be wet to the field capacity of the soil by rainfall or irrigation. In regions of low rainfall this usually requires more water than technical calculations show as the minimum required to wet the soil. The reason is that no soil is uniform (nonuniformity is the rule, not the exception), and the water applied must thoroughly wet the parts of the soil that hold the most water or take the water most slowly. In achieving this thorough wetting, varying quantities of water will percolate below root depth and be lost as drainage in the parts that offer least resistance to the percolation of water. The depth of water penetration can be measured with an inexpensive soil auger or a more expensive soil-sampling tube or by strategically-placed tensiometers.

After growth starts in the spring, no additional water is required until some of the soil within the root zone is dried out almost to the permanent wilting percentage. The vines will not benefit from earlier application. Nevertheless, the grower may have to start irrigating earlier, so as to cover

TABLE 31
APPROXIMATE AMOUNTS OF AVAILABLE WATER REQUIRED FOR MAXIMUM
PRODUCTION OF GRAPES IN VARIOUS REGIONS OF CALIFORNIA AND ARIZONA

Region	Wine grapes [a]	Raisin grapes [a]	Table grapes [a]
Cool areas: Cooler parts of the north coastal valleys and rolling lands (region I); heat summation less than 2,500 degree-days [b]	16–20 inches [c]	. . . [d]	. . . [d]
Moderately cool areas: Middle parts of the north coastal valleys (region II); heat summation 2,501 to 3,000 degree-days	16–24 inches	. . . [d]	. . . [d]
Moderately warm areas: Warm parts of the coastal valleys (region III); heat summation 3,001 to 3,500 degree-days	20–30 inches	. . . [d]	. . . [d]
Warm areas: Southern California valleys (except the deserts), middle and lower Sacramento Valley, lower San Joaquin Valley, and the intermediate valley area between the Sacramento and San Joaquin Valleys (region IV); heat summation 3,501 to 4,000 degree-days	24–30 inches	24–30 inches	30–36 inches
Hot areas: Middle and upper San Joaquin Valley, middle and upper Sacramento Valley (region V); heat summation over 4,000 degree-days	30–36 inches	30–42 inches	36–42 inches
Hot desert areas: Coachella, Borrego, Imperial, and Palo Verde valleys of California; Salt River and Yuma valleys of Arizona; heat summation over 6,000 degree-days	. . . [d]	. . . [d]	42–54 inches

SOURCE OF DATA: Jacob (1950) and Pillsbury (1941).

[a] Class of grapes according to intended use, not strictly on the basis of variety.

[b] Heat summation as degree-days above 50° F. For the period April 1 to October 31.

[c] Acre-inches per acre, including rainfall held in the soil of the root zone and supplemental irrigation. Water that runs off the surface or percolates below root depth is not included.

[d] Such grapes not grown in this region.

the vineyard before the vines irrigated last become too dry. The change in vine appearance caused by slowed growth is a good index of when a considerable extent of the soil has reached the permanent wilting percentage. When this stage is reached with vines growing on very shallow soil, such as San Joaquin loam or Penryn loam, the water available may be only enough to carry the vines for a few days longer without serious injury. On deep soils no serious injury is likely to occur within a week or longer after the first appearance of the symptoms of water shortage. If the vines show evidence of depletion of available water early in the season, it is exceedingly important that water be applied soon. Except in the hot desert regions, the situation is less critical after the fruit is ripe. Where only a small head of water is available, the time needed to cover the vineyard may be so long that the vines that are irrigated last may be seriously injured unless irrigating is started before it is really necessary.

Each early irrigation should, if possible, wet all of the soil to the depth at which most roots occur, even though the lower layers still contain some readily available water. After midseason it may not be necessary or desirable in some vineyards to wet all of the soil. Wetting a part of the soil—alternate middles between the rows, for example—or wetting the soil only 1.5 or 2 feet deep may be enough to furnish the water needed to mature the crop and carry the vines through the remainder of the season. Two or more such partial or light irrigations during ripening may sometimes be used to advantage in producing early-ripening table fruit of good color and quality.

When there are large amounts of salts in the soil or the irrigation water, special irrigation treatment may be necessary to keep the concentration below the toxic level. Large quantities of water may have to be used to leach the salts downward from the root zone, or water may have to be applied more frequently to keep the moisture in most of the soil well above the permanent wilting percentage at all times. On the other hand, if there is a hardpan or other impervious layer within 5 or 6 feet of the surface, drainage may be impaired or blocked. What does one do in that case?

While it is true that *dormant, mature* vines have an unusually high tolerance to water-logged soils (one or two year old vines may develop collar-rot if kept too wet too long into the early growing season), it is equally true that vines, like most other plants, will suffer significant damage if, during the growing season, the roots are subjected for any considerable period to water-logged or saturated soil conditions.

With a salt problem in either the irrigation water or the soil or both on poorly drained soils, it is best not to plant vines in the first place. However, if such is the situation, irrigations during the growing season should be limited to just enough water to wet the soil to the impervious layer.

Then, during the dormant season, excess water should be applied so as to leach out the season's accumulation of salt—even though at a slow rate during the dormant season. If very good quality water is available for irrigation of such soils then, obviously, the emphasis on winter leaching can be ignored. Irrigation with good water need not be beyond that needed to wet the soil to the depth of the impervious layer.

TIME AND FREQUENCY OF IRRIGATIONS

The time to irrigate, the number of irrigations required, and the amount of water to be applied at each irrigation are determined by soil type and depth, climate, the kind of grapes grown, and the time of ripening.

In the mild climates of the coastal valleys of California (regions I and II) the deep, heavy soils store enough of the average winter rainfall to supply all the water the mature vines need. If irrigation water is available in seasons of short rainfall, or where the usual spring rains are lacking, one irrigation that wets most of the soil sometime in early summer would benefit vineyards on deep soils, and two such irrigations would usually be ample for soils 2 to 3 feet deep. (Grapes should not be grown on soils less than 2 feet deep.)

In the warmest parts of the coastal valleys (region III) most vineyards will benefit from irrigation in most summers. On the deep soils a single irrigation in early summer is enough. The shallow soils may need two irrigations, one in early summer and one in midsummer. Many of the vineyards in these areas are not regularly irrigated, and, probably for this reason, do not produce maximum potential crop.

The vineyards in the great interior valley of California (the Sacramento and San Joaquin valleys and the intermediate valley area lying between them), and those in southern California are nearly all irrigated. The few that are not irrigated probably would be if water were available. The coolest of the vineyard areas of these regions—those of the intermediate valley—receive enough winter rainfall to wet the shallow soils to the depth of rooting, but the deep soils are fully wet only in seasons of heavy rainfall. The summers are rainless. Irrigation is, therefore, needed almost every year. Without it the vines remain small, bear poor crops, and drop their leaves from drought before fall. Irrigation practices vary. The deep sandy loam and loam soils may be filled to field capacity sometime during the winter or early spring and receive no summer irrigation. This practice gives satisfactory results only on soils that hold 15 to 20 inches of available water in the root zone. Other soils require summer irrigation; some of moderate depth and texture are irrigated only once, in early summer; those that are sandier or shallower need one irrigation in early summer and another in midsummer; those that are very shallow (Penryn loams) are irrigated regularly from late spring until the grapes are almost ripe. On the very shallow soils, furrows or basins are placed in the vineyard in late May for use throughout the season; no cultivation is done thereafter. The early irrigations are given at intervals two to three weeks apart, depending on the weather.

The central and northern parts of the Sacramento Valley (region V) are hot, but in most years there is enough winter rain to wet the soil fully. Winter irrigations are not usually needed. Summer irrigation is essential for best results; one to four applications will be needed, depending on soil conditions and the varieties grown. In the northern part of this region, on deep soils, there are a few vineyards that receive late spring rains and are not irrigated.

The central and southern San Joaquin Valley (region V) receives less rain—about 10 inches at Madera, 9 inches at Fresno, and 6 inches at Bakersfield. In general, rainfall increases slightly to the east of the axis of the valley and decreases to the west. Summer temperatures are high. Nearly all the vineyards of the valley are irrigated. Winter or early spring irrigation is common. The number of summer irrigations varies from one to ten, mainly according to soil conditions and the kind of grapes grown, but also increasing slightly toward the upper (southern) end of the valley. A few vineyards of early table grapes on very sandy soils in the hottest areas are irrigated after the crop is harvested (a recommendation, at least in alternate middles), but the practice is not general. The interval between irrigations is shorter in table grape vineyards than in raisin and wine grape vineyards. Many of the table grape vineyards are on shallow soils (Madera, Exeter, and San Joaquin series) from which water is removed at about the same rate throughout the root zone. Because the reserve of readily available water is very limited after a part of such soil reaches the permanent wilting percentage, and because complete depletion before the fruit is ripe has serious consequences, it is good practice to irrigate such vineyards before the soil reaches the point where the vines really need water. Otherwise, some vines are almost certain to suffer before all can be watered. Until near the beginning of the fruit-ripening period, table grapes, even on deep soils, are usually irrigated before much of the soil reaches the permanent wilting percentage; most growers feel that, despite the cost, the more frequent irrigations are preferable to the risk of injury from the soil's becoming too dry. During the ripening period, however, most vineyards on deep soil are not irrigated at all, or only a part of the soil is wet if an application is required.

When there are several pickings of table grapes, the harvest may extend over a long period, so that irrigation becomes necessary on some soils. If the stress for moisture is great, a deep irrigation may cause the berries of such varieties as Ribier and Red Malaga to crack across the apical end.

To guard against too rapid uptake of water, with resultant berry cracking, a shallow irrigation should be applied in every other middle. If more water is thought necessary, it should be applied in the alternate middles some days later.

Raisin and wine grape vineyards are, in general, irrigated when the vines indicate, by a slight characteristic change in appearance that the readily available water has been depleted from a part of the root zone. Irrigation ceases a week to three weeks before the beginning of harvest, depending on the type and depth of the soil. In very hot late summers, raisin vineyards may benefit from an alternate-middle irrigation after harvest.

QUANTITY OF WATER REQUIRED FOR AN IRRIGATION

The quantity of water applied at each irrigation varies greatly. Until near the beginning of fruit ripening, the soil of the entire root zone should be re-wet completely. This quantity must be determined for each soil type. A probe (iron rod with a handle) or a soil auger is the only equipment needed. In soils of uniform texture, a probe can usually be pushed 5 to 6 feet into saturated soil. After the soil drains, however, an auger is usually needed. Neither the probe nor the auger will penetrate hardpan—nor will roots. The amount of water needed to re-wet the soil varies, inversely, of course, with the amount of water remaining.

Regular and extensive use of the probe or the auger at each application is recommended for learning the extent of water pentration of a particular vineyard. Various sections of the vineyard should be tested, because penetration changes with differences in the soil. No general rule can be given for the amount of water required to wet a soil. Some soils hold less than 1 inch of water per foot of soil depth; others hold more than 3 inches. Once a grower is familiar with the penetration rate and the amount of water required by the various sections of his vineyard, he need make fewer probes to check his irrigations.

More sophisticated equipment, such as tensionmeters, may be used instead of augers and probes. However, they are relatively expensive, require a considerable number of locations and depths, and require more attention, maintenance, and interpretation than most growers wish to consider (Veihmeyer *et al.*, 1943).

QUALITY OF IRRIGATION WATER

Irrigation waters contain a complex array of salts and vary widely in composition. In large part, the salts that are brought to the soil by the irrigation water are left behind when plants and evaporation remove the water.

Unless the salts are leached out, they accumulate in the soil solution of the root zone, sometimes reaching toxic levels of concentration. Other conditions being equal, the higher the salt content of the irrigation water, the sooner the concentration can become injurious. Many factors, however, modify the accumulation of salts in the soil, and water that might be dangerous for irrigation under some conditions might be safe under others. Such factors include the texture, composition, and underground drainage of the soil; the amount of rainfall; the amount of irrigation water applied; and the kind of crop grown. Grapes are among the crops that are moderately tolerant to high salt concentration, being slightly more so than citrus crops and most deciduous tree fruits (Bernstein, 1965). Injury may be caused by too high a concentration of total salts or by a toxic concentration of particular substances, such as borates or chlorides. Also, water that contains too much sodium in proportion to its content of calcium and magnesium may cause the calcium and magnesium to leach out of the upper layers of soil. When this occurs, with the subsequent build-up of sodium in these layers, the soil often puddles (runs together) after irrigation, becoming difficult to work, difficult to cultivate, and unfavorable for plant growth.

The term "white alkali" usually refers to the total salts accumulation, which sometimes forms a white deposit on the surface when the soil becomes dry. "Black alkali" refers to the accumulation of sodium carbonate.

Although it is impossible to assign definite critical or toxic limits for the various irrigation-water constituents, it is helpful to indicate probably safe limits and probably injurious concentrations of some, with the understanding that what might be safe under some conditions might be injurious under others. The information in table 32 is to be regarded with such an understanding. In general, though with some exceptions, the figures in the "increasing problems" column are close to the maximum that may be used with reasonable safety in arid regions to supply practically all of the water used by the vines. If one or more of the constituents of a water are higher than is indicated in this column, its exclusive and long-continued use is likely to result in crop injury. It must be emphasized that where irrigation water of doubtful quality is used, good drainage—to facilitate good flushing away of accumulated excesses of salt and boron—is essential.

Water containing one or more constituents in concentrations as indicated in the middle column is likely to cause serious injury if used for many years in arid regions to supply all of the water used by the vines. In regions of moderate rainfall, where half or less of the total water is supplied by irrigation, such water may have no pronounced ill effects.

So far as is known, the waters of all the major perennial rivers of California are suitable for vineyard irrigation. Some of the small rivers and creeks, particularly those fed in part by hot springs, contain too much of

TABLE 32

WATER QUALITY FOR IRRIGATION OF GRAPES: TENTATIVE LEVELS.
INTERPRETATION OF CHEMICAL ANALYSIS IS RELATED TO TYPE OF PROBLEM
(SALINITY, PERMEABILITY, OR TOXICITY) AND SEVERITY EXPECTED
(NO PROBLEMS, INCREASING PROBLEMS, OR SEVERE PROBLEMS).

Type of problem	No problems	Increasing problems	Severe problems
Salinity (total salt) [a]			
EC (in millimhos)	Below 0.75	0.75–3.0	Above 3.0
Permeability			
EC (in millimhos)	Above 0.5	0.5 down to 0	—
SAR (sodium hazard) [b]	Below 6	6 to 9	Above 9
HCO$_3$—[c]	—	—	—
Toxicity [d] of specific ions			
Furrow or flood irrigated:			
Sodium (related to SAR)	SAR below 8	8 to 18	Above 18
Chloride, me/L.	Below 4	4 to 15	Above 15
Boron, ppm	Below 1	1 to 3	Above 3
Sprinkler irrigated: [e]			
Sodium, me/L.	Below 3	3 to 7.5	Above 7.5
Chloride, me/L.	Below 3	3 to 7.5	Above 7.5
Miscellaneous			
HCO$_3$ me/L.[f]	Below 1.5	1.5 to 7.5	Above 7.5
NO$_3$—N ppm	0–5	5 to 30	Above 30
pH	6.5 to 8.4	Below 6.5 or above 8.4	—

[a] Assumption is made that rainfall and inefficiencies of normal irrigation will supply evapo-transpiration needs plus a 10 to 20% Leaching Requirement for salt control.

[b] Permeability problems related to SAR are more likely to occur with low salt water than with high SAR.

$$SAR = Na / \sqrt{\frac{Ca + Mg}{2}} \quad \text{in m.e. per liter}$$

[c] Relatively high values may result in penetration problems related to decreased calcium (due to precipitation) and resultant increase in ESP (Exchangeable Sodium Percentage) of the soil.

[d] Differences in variety tolerances are reported but have not been adequately evaluated.

[e] Problems are too much leaf absorption of chloride and, perhaps, sodium, resulting in leaf burn.

[f] Bicarbonate causes white deposits on fruit and leaves. Not toxic but reduces market acceptability of table grapes.

Adapted from Ayers (1973).

boron or other minerals to be used for irrigation during periods of low stream flow. Many of the small streams flowing out of the Coast Range are of this character. The waters of the large streams flowing out of the Sierra Nevada are among the purest of river waters, and may, because of this purity, lead to boron deficiency by excessive leaching of sandy soils with such pure water.

Wells vary greatly in water composition. Most of those in the Coachella Valley and in the eastern half of the great Central Valley (San Joaquin and Sacramento valleys and the intermediate area between them) north of Kern County deliver good irrigation water. Some well waters in Kern County and, generally, in the western half of the San Joaquin Valley contain too high concentrations of boron and other minerals (Eaton, 1935). Many well waters of the coastal valleys are likewise unsuited for vineyard irrigation. This is especially true in parts of the Hollister area and the Livermore Valley.

Unless the source of water—stream or well—is known to be above suspicion, the water should be analyzed by a competent chemist and found to be safe before it is regularly used for vineyard irrigation.

DISTRIBUTION OF WATER

Irrigation is done by surface application and by sprinklers. Uniform and economical distribution of water on the surface of vineyards is possible only if the land is properly leveled and the system for controlling the water is well laid out. In both surface and sprinkler irrigation the system should be laid out before the vines are planted. The spacing of sprinklers must be close enough for uniform wetting of the soil.

Furrow irrigation.—In most of the irrigated vineyards of California the water is distributed in furrows (fig. 105). The vine rows are usually spaced 12 feet apart, and two broad-bottom or three regular furrows are used in a middle between rows. The water is held in the furrows only so long as is necessary for wetting the soil to the desired depth. Lateral penetration between furrows varies with the soil. It is usually least in sandy soils of uniform texture. The time required to wet as deeply as the roots go varies with soil texture.

Soils of uniform sandy or sandy loam texture that are free of tight layers are best irrigated by filling the furrows from end to end fairly rapidly, then cutting the flow of water into the furrow down to the point that maintains water in the furrow from end to end without overflowing. Only in this way can furrow application of water be reasonably uniform on such soils. If water is run slowly down the furrows in such soils and shut off when it reaches the farther end, too much water goes into the soil near the head of

FIGURE 105: Irrigation in regular furrows. (*Courtesy of Wine Institute*)

the furrow, with resultant leaching and waste, and too little is applied toward the other end.

To avoid the accumulation of salts at the surface of soils that contain such material in excess, broad-bottom furrows may be preferable (fig. 106). These furrows are 3 to 3.5 feet wide—two to a middle between the vine row—and have level bottoms. This system covers more of the soil surface and materially aids in the leaching of salts, and, additionally, reduces the rise of salts which occurs by capillary action.

Where the slope is too great for irrigation through regular or broad-bottom furrows, in many California vineyards a unique system of furrow blocking is used to check the flow of water. The scheme employs three furrows, with cross connections between the furrows. The furrows, the blocks in the furrows, and the cross connections are made simultaneously with specail equipment. This modification of furrow irrigation is especially useful on steep or nonuniform grades. For reasons of economy or because of shallowness of soil, the slope is sometimes greater in some parts of the vineyard than in others. In such instances the furrows are left free in any flat parts, and blocks and cross connections between furrows are used in parts that slope. The main effect of the furrow blocks and cross connections is to hold the water at each block until it backs up to and flows through the cross connection above the block. This ponding of the water makes for more uniform penetration. The distance between the blocks and cross connections is, of course, determined by the grade.

Strip-check irrigation.—In very coarse sandy soils the downward percolation of water is so rapid and lateral penetration so limited that furrow irrigation is impractical. This condition calls for either the strip-check method of irrigation, like that commonly used for alfalfa, or irrigation by sprinklers. The width and length of the checks will be governed by the nature of the soil and the head of water available. Once a piece of land is laid out for check irrigation, the amount of water to be applied can be changed only by varying the amount of water turned in at the inlet. It is, therefore, very important that proper consideration be given to the size of the checks in relation to the soil type and the head of water available. Experience with sandy soils has shown that a flow of 20 cubic feet per second for a check of 1 acre gives a rapid flushing of the water over the ground and, consequently, a light application. The ratio between flow (in cubic feet per second) and the area of check (in acres) is 20 to 1. Applying this ratio to a pump discharging 900 gallons per minute (2 cub. ft. per sec.), the proper size of the check would be one tenth of an acre (Brown, 1942). The head of water turned in at the upper end of the check must be of such volume that the water will have reached the lower end of the check by the time the soil at the upper end has been wetted to the desired depth. The water is then shut off. When the flow is so regulated, there will be enough water in the check at the time it is shut off to wet the soil almost uniformly—to the same depth—from end to end of the check. Under such soil conditions, however, sprinkler irrigation should find favor as providing an even more nearly uniform wetting of the soil.

Basin irrigation.—On vineyard soil of varied textures the basin system gives the most nearly uniform irrigation. With large heads of water and large level areas of regular texture, 30 or more vines may be included in a basin, whereas with a small head of water or a soil of varying types or

Figure 106: Irrigation in broad-bottom furrows. (*Courtesy of Wine Institute*)

steep slope, a basin may contain as few as 2 or 3 vines. Ridges are thrown up between the vine rows in both directions, enclosing the desired number of vines in each basin. Each basin is quickly filled to the desired depth and then closed. A definite amount of water is thus applied to each different area. Much labor is required for forming the basins and distributing the water. Basin irrigation is not adapted to trellised vineyards because it requires cross-cultivation to make the basins.

Sprinkler irrigation.—Sprinklers can be used when land that is to be irrigated is unsuitable for leveling or when the cost of leveling would be too great. Very open, porous soil can also be irrigated more uniformly by sprinkling than by surface application. Under such conditions the added cost of the original installation may be justified. The water requirement for sprinkling is about the same as that for other systems, and the same requirements as to uniformity of distribution and penetration must be met if equally good results are to be obtained.

In California, with usually low relative humidity, sprinkler irrigation has had no influence on disease or insect control. Powdery mildew control has remained the same. Sprinkler irrigation of almost mature or mature fruit should be avoided, because of the likely increase in bunch rot.

Figure 107 shows a portable system, quite common in the past decade, which operates from permanently installed main lines and primarily for

FIGURE 107: Portable sprinklers which are attached to solid set underground main lines.

irrigation purposes. Today the practice is more toward the solid-set system with all parts permanently installed—risers with the sprinkler heads most often at about every fourth vine in every fourth row with the usual 8 by 12 foot spacing (figure 108).

And it is more for frost protection than as a means of irrigation that sprinkler installations have become more popular in recent years. Recent experiences have shown that at least 5 degrees of frost protection may be obtained from a good sprinkler system delivering 0.1 inch per hour. Although the cost is high (Burlingame *et al.*, 1971), the currently high prices of wine grapes has changed the picture. Marginal water sources become practical. More important, locations in the cool coastal areas which were formerly questionable because of frost hazard are now—with the use of sprinklers as frost protection—potential and realistic grape planting sites (Meyer and Marsh, 1972). And, of course, an advantage of the sprinkler system for frost protection is that it can be used for the dual purpose of irrigation even if the water supply is such that perhaps only one irrigation may be possible.

In efficient frost control by sprinklers the dew point is a guide to when the sprinklers should be turned on. The following data (Meyer and Marsh,

FIGURE 108: A permanent or "solid set" sprinkler system for irrigation, frost control, or heat control. Here the system is operating for spring frost control. (*Courtesy of Almáden Vineyards*)

1972) show the relationship of dew point and starting temperature for turning on the sprinklers.

Dew point temperature	Starting temperature of sprinklers
26°F. and above	34°F.
24–25°F.	35°F.
22–23°F.	36°F.
20–21°F.	37°F.
17–19°F.	38°F.
15–16°F.	39°F.

Further precautions: Run sprinklers until all ice is melted. It takes heat to melt ice. What you don't want is to have the vine supply this heat at the expense of a crop in vine temperature below 32°F. Melt all the ice and wait until the temperature outside the sprinkled area is over 32°F. If it is windy it would be safer to wait until the temperature is over 34°F.

Sprinkler irrigation also offers the possibility of uniform application of fertilizers, especially micro-nutrients such as zinc and boron, and pest and disease control materials—any and all of which might be added to the source water. Yet, as of now, little if any clear data are available as to the efficacy or success of these modifications.

The use of sprinklers—to cool vines and fruit in hot regions—has received much publicity in recent years. Theoretically, intermittent sprinkling (a few minutes at intervals of perhaps 15 minutes) during afternoon hours of excessively high temperatures should cool the fruit, maintain acidity, and thus improve wine quality. A number of trials have proved disappointing—sugar and acid levels have not been affected significantly. However, very recent work by Kliewer (1973), in which the sprinklers ran continuously so long as the temperature was above 86°F. did result in fruit of higher acidity.

Drip irrigation.—Another innovation—its true value for vineyards yet to be proven by a number of trials now in progress—in the so-called drip system of irrigation (Goldberg *et al.*, 1971; Kenworthy, 1972; Gustafson *et al.*, 1972). Theoretically, this technique, in which water is applied very slowly (about one gallon per hour) in a very limited area near the plant, will conserve water while still promoting good vine growth and yields. However, installation costs are high, careful maintenance is required, and there may be salt effects from the interface zone between the wetted and dry zones. Experience will tell.

BIBLIOGRAPHY

Ayers, R. S. 1973. Personal communication from California Agric. Ext. Lab. guidelines.

Bernstein, L. 1965. Salt tolerance of fruit crops. USDA Agric. Information Bull. 292.

Brown, J. B. 1942. The irrigation of alfalfa, border or check method. California Agric. Ext. Cir. (unnumbered), pp. 1–8.

Burlingame, B. B., A. N. Kasimatis, B. E. Bearden, J. V. Lider, R. L. Sisson, and R. A. Parsons. 1971. Frost protection costs for north coast counties. AXT 127 (revised 10/71), Agric. Ext., Univ. of Calif.

Eaton, F. M. 1935. Boron in soils and irrigation water and its effects on plants with particular reference to the San Joaquin Valley of California, United States Dept. Agr. Tech. Bull., 448:1–113.

Filippenko, I. M. 1958. Water uptake by roots during the movement of sap in the spring. [Trans. title.] Fisiol. Fost., 5:175–177. (See Hort. Abs., 28:3430).

Goldberg, D., B. Gornat, and Y. Bar. 1971. The distribution of roots, water, and minerals as a result of trickle irrigation. J. Amer. Soc. Hort. Sci., 96 (5):645–648.

Gustafson, C. D., A. W. Marsh, R. L. Branson, and S. Davis. 1972. Drip irrigation experiments with avocados in San Diego County. Calif. Agric., 26(7):12–14.

Hagan, R. M. 1955. Factors affecting soil moisture-plant growth relations. Rept. XIV Internatl. Hort. Cong. (The Hague). pp. 82–102.

———. 1957. Water-soil-plant relations. California Agr., 11(4):9–12.

Halsey, D. D., J. R. Spencer, and D. Mulder. 1970. Reclamation of a Coachella Valley Ranch. California Agr., 24(9):4–6.

Hendrickson, A. H., and F. J. Viehmeyer. 1945. Permanent wilting percentages of soils obtained from field and laboratory trials. Plant Physiol., 20:517–539.

———, ———. 1950. Irrigation experiments with grapes. California Agr., Exp. Sta. Bull., 728:3–31.

Jacob, H. E. 1950. Grape growing in California. Calif. Agr. Ext. Ser. Cir., 116:1–79.

Kenworthy, A. L. 1972. Trickle irrigation—the concept and guidelines for use. Research Report No. 165, Farm Science., Michigan State Univ., East Lansing, Michigan.

Kliewer, W. M. 1973. Berry composition of some *Vitis vinifera* cultivars as influenced by photo- and nycto-temperatures during maturation. Proc. Amer. Soc. Hort. Sci., 98:153–159.

Meyer, J. L., and A. W. Marsh. 1972. A permanent sprinkler system for deciduous orchards and vineyards. Calif. Agr. Ext. (AXT) n-70.

Pillsbury, A. F. 1941. Observations of use of irrigation water in Coachella Valley, California. California Agr. Exp. Sta. Bull., 649:1–48.

Proebsting, E. L. 1937. The effects of cover crops on nitrogen and field capacity in orchard soils. Proc. Amer. Soc. Hort. Sci., 35:302–305.

Richards, L. A., and L. R. Weaver. 1941. Moisture retention by some irrigated soils as related to soil-moisture tension. Jour. Agr. Res., 69:215–235.

Vaadia, Y., and A. N. Kasimatis. 1961. Vineyard irrigation trials. Amer. Jour. Enol. Vitic., 12:88–98.

Veihmeyer, F. J. 1938. Evaporation from soils and transpiration. Trans. Amer. Geophys. Union, 19:612–619.

———, N. E. Edlefsen, and A. H. Hendrickson. 1943. Use of tensiometers in measuring availability of water to plants. Plant Phys., 18:66–78.

———, and A. H. Hendrickson. 1950. Soil moisture in relation to plant growth. Ann. Rev. Plant Phys., 1:285–304.

17

Fertilizer Elements Required by the Vine

Grapevines can adapt themselves to a wide range of soil fertility. They are less exacting than many other horticultural crops in the quantitative level of soil nutrients required and, if depth, texture, and water conditions are favorable, will survive and sometimes bear paying crops on soils where the fertility is so meager that other fruit crops would fail. The root system of the vine explores the subsoil, as well as the surface soil, to depths determined primarily by the physical character of the soil. The roots are active from early spring to late autumn and, therefore, have a long time to absorb the required soil nutrients. The leaves, and usually the prunings, constituting about 90 per cent or more of the annual growth, are returned to the soil. Since carbon dioxide, from the air, and water compose more than 99 per cent of the raw material for the fruit, the crop removes comparatively small quantities of soil nutrients from the vineyard. Thus it is not surprising that practical results from fertilizing vineyards have been limited. Instances of the deficiency of fertilizer elements are rare, and only four elements have been shown, by reason of their deficiency or excess, to present problems in California. These are nitrogen and potassium and two micro nutrients, zinc and boron.

CHEMICAL ELEMENTS ESSENTIAL TO PLANT GROWTH

Although chemical analyses of plant tissues reveal that most of the elements are used in one plant species or another, only sixteen elements are known to be absolutely necessary for normal growth and fruiting of green plants: carbon, hydrogen, oxygen, nitrogen, phosphorus, potassium, sulfur, iron, calcium, magnesium, boron, manganese, copper, zinc, molybdenum, and chlorine. These have been shown to be necessary for so many different kinds of plants that they are generally recognized as probably essential for all.

The carbon used by green plants is obtained from the carbon dioxide of the air. Hydrogen and oxygen come mainly from water, absorbed from the soil along with dissolved elements. An element is essential only if lack of it can be shown to result in injury, abnormal development, lack of growth, poor fruit set, or non-viable seeds.

The first ten elements named above, being used in relatively large amounts, are often called the major or macro elements; the others, required in only very small amounts, are sometimes called the micro, or trace, elements. It would seem unwise, however, to place much emphasis on the relative amounts needed, because all are presumed to be indispensable.

FUNCTIONS OF THE ELEMENTS

The role or roles of each element in the plant's metabolism have been assigned largely from observation of what happens when a particular element is withheld or restricted. Most of the assignments are substantiated by experimental evidence, some by indirect experimental evidence, and some by deduction. Most of this work has been done on plants other than grapes, but it may be fairly assumed that the results generally apply also to grapes.

The various elements may be classified as follows:

1. Constituents of compounds that form part of the living material, or protoplasm; play a part in the plant structure (as, in the cell walls); and serve as sources of energy for various processes.

2. Agents that have influencing or regulating functions, but in the process do not enter into the composition of any known specific compound. Such functions include regulating the osmotic pressure of cells and the permeability of cell membranes; regulating the acidity and buffer action of plant fluids; serving as catalizers of various reactions, including hydration of the cell colloids; and carrying other elements or ions in chemical combination.

Carbon, hydrogen, and oxygen are constituents of most plant materials. They are essential parts of the protoplasm and cell walls, and they compose the principal energy materials—carbohydrates, fats, and oils. Along with nitrogen and some other elements, they are components of all proteins. Hydrogen and oxygen constitute water, which functions as a building material for other compounds, as a solute, as a transport medium, and in numerous other ways.

NITROGEN

Nitrogen is a component of proteins, which form an essential part of all protoplasm. It is also a constituent of the amino acids, lecithins, and chlorophyll, and it seems to be needed in processes that form such substances as essential oils and resins, though it is not a part of the final product. Nitrogen deficiency is reflected in reduced growth of the vine and paling of the green leaves.

The decomposition of organic materials, such as vegetation and soil organisms, accounts for most of the native (original) nitrogen in the soil. A small amount is fixed by organisms that form nodules on the roots of leguminous plants. It matters not whether the nitrogenous material in the soil is present in the form of fertilizer applications of ammonium sulfate, urea, and the like, or as decomposing leaves and prunings or dead soil organisms. The soil organisms oxidize the various nitrogenous compounds to nitrates, the form in which they are most readily available to plants. Thus, most of the nitrogen removed from the soil by the vine, except for ammonia compounds or urea soon after application, is in the form of nitrates, such as KNO_3 and $Ca(NO_3)_2$. The nitrogen supply at a given time may not be sufficient to supply the vine's needs for long, but during the growing season, the supply is continually being replenished.

Of the major elements, nitrogen is the most likely to be deficient. Vines, however, unlike most crop plants, do not readily manifest a need for nitrogen. Yields may be reduced long before deficiency symptoms are evident.

Numerous field trials (Cook and Kishaba, 1956a; W. O. Williams, 1943) over many years suggest that about one of every four vineyards in California is not getting enough nitrogen to produce the best yields of which it is capable. About one in five, in contrast, is being fertilized so heavily with nitrogen that crop production is reduced by poor set and the formation of fewer clusters.

Determining the need for nitrogen.—With the Thompson Seedless variety, the most reliable rapid method of determining nitrogen status is the nitrate color test. For this test, 20 representative petioles are taken adjacent to the flower clusters at bloom time from an area not greater than five acres (Cook and Kasimatis, 1959). While the petioles are fresh, a half-inch to 1-inch lengthwise cut is made through the bulbous base of each, and one drop of indicator solution is applied and watched for about five seconds. If 15 or more of the 20 petioles show no blue color, need for nitrogen is indicated. (The indicator is pure, colorless diphenylamine, 1 gm. per 100 cc. of concentrated (36N) sulfuric acid.) Extreme caution must be observed in the use of this reagent!

Since the nitrogen requirement differs among varieties, the color test procedure must be altered for the other leading varieties. Research is not yet complete, and only general suggestions can be made, applying to all varieties. However, Carignane and Zinfandel fall into the same nitrate level class with Thompson Seedless. In general, the vineyards that have shown the largest yield increases from experimental nitrogen fertilization have been on soils that are shallow, soils subject to extreme leaching, and light sandy soils with a long history of very little or no application of any nitrogen fertilizer. On such soils the yields of heavy-producing wine and raisin varieties may be profitably increased with 40 to 70 pounds of actual nitrogen per acre per year.

For colored table varieties, particularly Tokay and Emperor, 20 to 40 pounds of actual nitrogen per acre are recommended, since high-quality, well-colored fruit is wanted, rather than maximum tonnage. Young, non-bearing vines that seem low in vigor should receive nitrogen at about this same rate, but the method of application will be different. Broadcasting is preferable for mature vines, whereas in young vineyards the application should be in a three-foot area around each vine or in a surface band about one foot from the vine row.

Form of nitrogen to use.—Several large-scale trials have indicated that the form or type of nitrogen applied makes no measurable difference in the effect on the vines. Therefore one generally applies the cheapest form —with a few possible exceptions. For instance, the nitrate form may leach excessively in some coastal areas where total rainfall is heavy and the monthly rate is unpredictable; the best form or compromise for these areas seems to be urea or ammonium nitrate, ensuring fair downward movement in dry winters and avoiding excessive leaching in very rainy winters (Cook and Kishaba, 1957).

When nitrogen should be applied.—The grapevine is similar to most tree fruits in its seasonal demands for nitrogen, the greatest amounts being needed during early spring growth and through the period of blooming. After the crop has set, the nitrogen supply should be only great enough to provide for an adequate, but diminishing, shoot growth and a healthy leaf surface. Excess nitrogen during ripening tends to divert the sugar produced by the leaves to continued shoot growth. In such cases, especially when excess nitrogen is combined with abundant water supply, vegetative growth may continue so late into the fall that the vine does not have time to mature its shoots before frost occurs and a serious die-back of canes may result. Also, since the grape's root system is deep and widespread, controlling nitrogen availability is more difficult with vines than with shallow-rooted annual plants. Thus, late spring or early summer applications should usually be avoided.

Nitrogen should be in the root zone when spring growth begins. The time of application for any particular area will be influenced by soil texture, rainfall, and the practicality of getting into the vineyard with equipment. In coastal counties subject to high rainfall the ideal time for applying urea or ammonium nitrate is during a dry period in February. Since, however, a dry period cannot always be counted on, the best alternative time seems to be just before the rainy season begins. This latter is the best time for application in unirrigated low-rainfall areas, where the total season's rainfall may be needed to move the nitrogen into the root zone (Cook and Kishaba, 1957).

In the San Joaquin Valley all forms of nitrogen may be applied in January and February. Where a midwinter irrigation is the rule, it is best to apply the nitrogen one or two weeks before irrigation. This allows the soil microorganisms time to convert all forms to nitrate, which will then move downward with the water.

Midwinter applications may use the cheapest form of nitrogen available. If for some reason application is delayed until bud-break, ammonium sulfate or ammonia forms should be avoided, since movement of this material into the root zone may be delayed. Urea, if irrigated within one or two days, and nitrate forms will move downward as soon as water is applied, whereas ammonium forms and ammonia gas are not free to move downward with water until they are wet enough to stick to the soil particles and have undergone microorganism oxidation to nitrates, which requires one to two weeks.

Good steer manure averages about 1.5 per cent nitrogen. Thus, in one ton of dry weight (about 2 cub. yd.), the grower may hope to get 30 pounds of nitrogen if turned under immediately after application. Manure is recommended only when the costs of the nitrogen it contains and the labor of application are no more expensive than the costs of applying an equivalent amount of commercial fertilizer. Poultry manure on light sandy soils has frequently, for some as yet unsolved reason, caused zinc deficiency.

Pomace, the grape seeds and skins left over from winery operations, is equal to good manure (Jacob, 1947) as a vineyard fertilizer, providing the price is reasonable.

Cover crops.—No long-term data are available on the value of cover crops as fertilizers in California vineyards. The conclusions and recommendations presented below are based on a thirty-year cover-crop study with various fruit trees at Davis (Proebsting, 1958), University of California trials on the amount of nitrogen fixed per year by various leguminous cover crops (W. A. Williams *et al.*, 1954), and the known effects of high temperatures on the rate at which organic matter decomposes.

It is very difficult, if not impossible, to raise soil organic matter to, and maintain it at, a higher level than existed naturally before the soil was brought under cultivation. The nitrogen supplied by an interplanted winter-legume cover crop will vary from 10 to 35 pounds per acre, but the cost of seeding and irrigating the cover crop usually exceeds the cost and application of an equal amount of commercial nitrogen. Interplanting a cover crop may have one or more undesirable aspects in vineyards: *a*) irrigating the seed bed in the early fall, when the temperatures are still favorable for vine growth, may stimulate succulent vine growth just before frost; *b*) in unirrigated vineyards careful timing is required to determine how long the cover crop may be allowed to grow in the spring before it will affect the soil's water reserve for vine growth; and *c*) plowing under a heavy, succulent green-manure crop in early spring may cause soil nitrogen to become very low when the vine needs it most—just before and during blooming—and, later, be released in rather large amounts at the time when the supply to the vine should be reduced—during maturation of fruits and shoots.

For these reasons the general recommendation is to plant cover crops only where plow sole has created a water penetration problem or where erosion must be controlled in hillside vineyards (see erosion control, p. 381).

Summer cover crops.—In many irrigated table grape vineyards grasses and other plants are allowed to grow after the early part or middle of the summer. The fruit produced in such vineyards is clean—that is, mostly free of dust—and begins to ripen earlier, colors better, and ships better than fruit from clean-cultivated vineyards. These differences are greatest on shallow soils and least, or nonexistent, on deep, fertile soils. The effects of the summer cover crop on the character of the fruit are usually explained on the basis of competition: the cover crop competes with the vines for soil nutrients, especially nitrogen and water, so that the amounts available for vegetative vine growth during the fruit-ripening period are less than where clean tillage is practiced. Although plausible, this explanation has not been proved.

In unirrigated vineyards lacking summer rainfall, any summer-growing plants other than the vines are detrimental, using water needed to carry the vines through the season.

POTASSIUM

For more than a hundred years potassium has been known to be an essential element for plants. Despite the great amount of research carried out on this element, however, there is little definite information on its function. One of the difficulties in assigning a specific role to potassium in plants is that it is not known to occur in any organic compounds except the salts of organic acids and proteins. It is not a constituent of any of the structural materials of the vine.

There is evidence that potassium in some way activates enzymes in the

Fertilizer Elements Required by the Vine

synthesis of proteins and possibly in the synthesis of fats also. This is in keeping with E. J. Hewitt's opinion (1951) that potassium, possibly along with calcium, has a function in maintaining cell organization, hydration, and permeability, and hence directly or indirectly influences many enzyme systems. Some workers have emphasized the importance of potassium in the formation of carbohydrates; others have reported that a deficiency of potassium results in an accumulation of carbohydrates. The view that potassium increases the development of color in the fruit has been stressed all too often. To the contrary, if enough potassium is present to prevent the development of definite foliage-deficiency symptoms, there is good evidence that adding potassium will not improve the brightness or depth of color of the fruit; the quality of the fruit, too, will remain unchanged (Williams, 1946).

All fruit crops place a heavy demand on the potassium supply of the soil. This is comparable to, or perhaps even greater than, the demand for nitrogen, yet the vineyards in California that are deficient in potassium are relatively few. The reason is, in part at least, the greater original supply of potassium in the soil—the rock from which it was derived. In addition, potassium leaches from the soil much more slowly than nitrogen.

FIGURE 109: Stages of early-season potassium deficiency in Carignane variety, shortly after bloom time.

Fertilizer Elements Required by the Vine

Potassium deficiency.—The visual symptoms of potassium deficiency begin to appear in early summer, usually showing first on leaves on the middle part of the shoots. First the leaf color fades, beginning at the leaf margin. As the fading continues, it moves into the areas between the main veins, gradually decreasing as it approaches vein areas in the leaf center. Marginal burning and upward or downward curling of the leaf edges follow the development of the pale green color (fig. 109). Leaf fall is premature, especially with vines carrying a heavy crop, and can be so extensive that the fruit will fail to ripen. In such cases, weak secondary growth may begin on the defoliated shoots in a manner similar to that which occurs when defoliation is caused by red spiders. Vines with advanced potassium deficiency carry small, tight clusters of small, unevenly ripened berries.

Low soil potassium, as distinct from other indirect causes of potassium deficiency in California, has been associated with very sandy soils in certain vineyard areas that have been scraped in land-leveling operations. A very high correlation between soil depth and water-soluble and replaceable potassium has been demonstrated for orchard soil in California (Lilleland and Brown, 1937). Of 100 soils studied, 94 had less potassium in the fourth foot of soil than in the first; 72 of the 100 had only half as much —sometimes less than half—in the fourth foot as in the surface soil, even though most of these soils were of alluvial origin and exhibited no noticeable profile changes in texture. Many of the interior valley soils were originally smooth to slightly undulating, but leveling for irrigation often removed surface soil to a depth of several feet in small areas. It is in such areas that symptoms of potassium deficiency are most likely to develop. Potash applications have effected vine recovery, but, unfortunately, the doses must be heavy and deeply placed. A *minimum* application of about 1,500 pounds of potassium sulfate per acre—3 pounds per vine—should, when properly applied, correct the deficiency in the second year after treatment; 4 to 6 pounds per vine will usually be required for correction during the first year (Cook and Kishaba, 1956, b). Spray applications have not been effective (Gerber and Peyer, 1959).

The recommended fertilizer is potassium sulfate (sulfate of potash). Potassium chloride (muriate of potash) applied at these high rates may cause chloride toxicity in vines. Most mixed fertilizers are so low in potassium that unreasonably large amounts would have to be used to supply enough potassium, and what they contain beside potassium may contribute nothing beneficial and may even delay the recovery of the vines if applied in large amounts. For best results the potassium sulfate should be placed as near the root zone as possible. If special equipment is not available for deep placement, a plow furrow should be made as close to the vine row and as deeply as is possible without causing serious root injury. The potash, placed in the bottom of the furrow, dissolves slowly and in many soils is fixed (inactivated) to a great extent. Therefore the furrow should be left open for maximum wetting from winter rains, or the first irrigation should be down this furrow.

ZINC

Although zinc is essential for plants, it is not a part of the molecules of carbohydrates, proteins, or fats. It seems to have a function in the catalyzing of certain processes—such as the system producing trytophane, which is a precursor of auxin (Tsui, 1948a). A deficiency of zinc results in a deficiency of auxin and a failure of the shoots to grow normally. The lack of normal shoot growth may well be associated with the decrease in the water content of zinc-deficient plants (Tsui, 1948b). Shatter of flowers and a set of straggly clusters, with many shot berries, as indicated by W. B. Hewitt and H. E. Jacob (1945), is also likely to be due to the lack of auxin. However, according to Skoog (1940), zinc is required not so much for the synthesis of auxin as for its maintenance in an active state.

Zinc deficiency (*"little leaf"*).—Zinc deficiency probably ranks second to nitrogen deficiency in the number of acres affected in California vineyards. Deficiency symptoms are frequently found in vineyards on sandy soils; in vineyards grafted onto the nematode-resistent rootstocks, Salt Creek and Dogridge; and in locations previously used as corrals (feed lots, stockyards, poultry pens) for long periods. The symptoms usually appear in early summer, at about the time when secondary shoot growth starts. The primary and secondary shoot tips are affected first, with the symptoms illustrated in figure 110. The principal symptoms of zinc deficiency are the chlorotic pattern, the location and small size of the affected leaves, and particularly the widened petiolar sinus (the leaf indentation where the petiole is attached). Because one or more of these symptoms is associated with other deficiencies or diseases, one can diagnose zinc deficiency only when all the symptoms listed are present.

With some varieties, particularly Muscat of Alexandria, the first effect of zinc deficiency is very straggly clusters. Berries on the straggly cluster may range in size from very small undeveloped shot berries, through undersized berries with one or two seeds, to normal-sized berries with the normal number of seeds. With other varieties, particularly Salvador, leaf symptoms may be moderate or even severe before poor berry set is observed.

Supplying zinc to vines.—Zinc is a micro, or trace, element, and vines need only a very small amount of it—a half pound per acre at most. Yet, according to Cook (1958), it is difficult to get even this small amount of zinc into the vine. Most soils will "fix" such large quantities of zinc sulfate that soil applications are impractical. On very sandy soil, however, 1 to 2 pounds of zinc sulfate per vine will give fair success when applied

FIGURE 110: Little-leaf symptoms of zinc deficiency in variety Muscat of Alexandria, midsummer. (*Courtesy of W. B. Hewitt*)

in the manner described above for potash. For spur-pruned varieties the most common, and by far the most successful, treatment is to daub the pruning cuts with a zinc sulfate solution. Pruning must be so timed that little or no bleeding occurs. Results are best when pruning cuts are daubed immediately, but may be profitable even after delays of as much as 24 hours (Snyder and Harmon, 1954). The usual solution is 1 to 1.5 pounds of zinc sulfate (23 per cent metallic zinc) per gallon of water. With 36 per cent metallic zinc, 1 pound per gallon is sufficient; higher concentrations severely injure the dormant buds on the spurs.

Daubing the pruning cuts of cane-pruned varieties is not effective. This is particularly true of Thompson Seedless. The zinc moves inward only a few inches at most. Foliage sprays are more promising, though at best only moderately successful. Foliage sprays containing zinc should be applied two to three weeks before bloom, with as much wetting of the undersurface of the leaves as is possible. When obtaining berry set is the problem, one spray may suffice; when vine growth is stunted, a second spray is needed several weeks after bloom. Spray concentrations can vary from

4 to 10 pounds of zinc sulfate per 100 gallons of water. To prevent foliage burn, however, all concentrations in this range *require* an addition of half as much spray lime as zinc sulfate. A normal proportion would be 6 pounds of zinc sulfate to 3 pounds of spray lime in 100 gallons of water. A good wetting agent should be included (Cook, 1962).

BORON

Some years ago the hypothesis was presented that, in the translocation of sugar, boron had a function in a sugar-borate complex that would pass from cell to cell more readily than nonborated sugar (Gauch and Duggar, 1952). Other studies, however, instead of supporting this hypothesis, have shown that boron-deficient stem and root tips are not necessarily deficient in sugar and that the application of sugar to these terminals does not alleviate the symptoms of boron deficiency (McIlrath and Palser, 1956). According to Skok (1957), the role of boron in sugar translocation is indirect, seeming to stem from its effect on cellular activity rather than from the direct enhancement of diffusion through membranes by formation of a sugar-borate complex. This view is supported by Whittington (1959), who found the primary effects of a deficiency of boron to be a cessation of cell division and an enlargement of the apical cells. Whittington suggested that the cell division ceases because abnormalities in the formation of the cell wall prevent the cell from becoming organized for mitosis. These views are further supported by recent studies (Dyer and Webb, 1961) which indicate that boron plays an essential role in the biosynthesis of auxin in the meristems of the plant and that translocation occurs as a result of growth rather than the reverse.

Boron deficiency.—In grapes, lack of boron prevents the normal development and germination of pollen, thus drastically reducing set of fruit (Gärtel, 1956).

Grapes seem to have a higher requirement for boron than do most other perennial deciduous fruit crops. Its deficiency in vineyards has been reported in New Zealand by Askew (1944), in Australia by Jardine (1946), in France by Branas and Bernon (1956), in Germany by Wilhelm (1952), in Portugal by Dias (1953), and in the southeastern U.S. by Scott (1944). Wherever V. *vinifera* varieties are grown on acid or slightly acid soils subject to high rainfall leaching, they are likely to show need for boron fertilization.

With the great concern in California about excess boron and with the generally basic soils, the possibility of boron deficiency was overlooked until it was belatedly discovered to occur here also (Cook *et al.*, 1960). As elsewhere, deficiency symptoms are found where vines are planted in soils subject to severe leaching with water of very low boron content. Low

Fertilizer Elements Required by the Vine

sandy areas on the east side of San Joaquin Valley—which are irrigated with the low-boron water from reservoirs of the Sierra Nevada mountain range—and upland vineyards in the high-rainfall coastal counties have shown the most frequent need for boron. It is known that boron deficiency becomes worse under drought conditions, and this fact adds to the likelihood of deficiency in the vineyards on unirrigated shallow soils in the coastal areas of California.

Leaf symptoms of boron deficiency, in general, may resemble either early season Pierce's disease symptoms or Spanish measles. But Pierce's disease affects the basal leaves first, whereas boron deficiency is first manifested in the terminal leaves of the primary shoots. Measles causes a characteristic speckling of the fruit, whereas lack of boron, depending on the variety, may result in a very light set, with many flower clusters drying up; a set with a high percentage of shot berries; or a seemingly normal set that shatters severely about midsummer. The shot berries resulting from boron deficiency fail to elongate properly and thus tend to be round or even oblate in shape, whereas in zinc deficiency the berries have the normal shape for the variety, though they are smaller than the normal size. The symptoms of boron deficiency are the above fruiting characteristics and the following vegetative or foliage symptoms: death of the pri-

FIGURE 111: Leaf symptoms of boron deficiency on Thompson Seedless variety: progressive stages, from normal leaf, in upper left.

mary shoot tip, with subsequent growth of numerous laterals that may have normal appearance; abnormally short internodes near the tip of the primary shoot; a characteristic chlorosis, in some varieties initially almost white and later turning red (fig. 111); necrotic areas in the tendrils; and swollen areas in the terminal portion of the primary shoot that sometimes resemble lesions (Cook *et al.*, 1960). Not all of these symptoms are always found. The poor set or flower shatter seems to result from lack of sugars or probably more directly from lack of auxin.

Boron deficiency is easy to correct, but, as with most trace elements, overdoses are a danger. Many boron materials are available, varying in strength from about 35 to 65 per cent boric oxide, B_2O_3. One ounce per vine of any of the less concentrated boron fertilizers, or a half ounce of stronger materials, should provide enough boron. This is equivalent to about 10 pounds of B_2O_3 per acre in California vineyard spacing (Cook, 1962). In small areas this very low rate may be surface broadcast by hand with a 1-ounce measure at any convenient time during the year. When large areas are to be treated, it has been found to be most economical and practical to use a spray rig and apply the boron fertilizer during the dormant season, calculating the pounds per 100 gallons and spray application per acre to give the correct dosage of about 10 pounds of B_2O_3 per acre, at intervals of 3–4 years between treatments. Where large areas are deficient the application may be and is made by airplane.

Boron toxicity.—In California the problem of boron is more likely to be an excess than a deficiency of this element. Parts of Kern County and the coastal vineyard areas—the Santa Clara, Livermore, Sonoma, and Napa valleys—have incidences of boron toxicity. Eaton (1944) reported that Malaga and Thompson Seedless vines in culture solution grew best with 1 part ppm boron and that 5 ppm reduced growth markedly and caused the symptoms characteristic of injury. An excess of boron seems to stop or slow the growth or expansion of the edges of young vine-leaves, while the middle parts keep on growing. The leaves consequently pucker, or wrinkle, and cup. Leaves that have reached full size before boron levels become toxic show little cupping. The general symptoms may sometimes be confused with those of excess of dalapon, a weed killer. The more specific symptoms begin as a sprinkling of necrotic (black or brown) specks near the leaf margin (fig. 112). These specks later become so numerous that they seem to be continuous from the edge inward.

Excess boron may come from the soil or from irrigation water. The only practicable remedy known at present is to flush out the excess with a generous supply of low-boron irrigation water. Recent studies conducted by the University of California on soils of the western side of San Joaquin Valley show that as much as 9 acre feet of good water may be necessary to leach the excess boron to acceptable levels. Boron excess can be

FIGURE 112: Symptoms of boron toxicity on the variety Carignane in midsummer. Notice the speckling and downward cupping of mature leaves and extreme puckering and cupping of immature small leaves.

confirmed by analysis of the tissue of mature leaves that show the discolored areas next to the margin. Affected leaves will contain 200 to 300 or more ppm of boron on a dry-weight basis (Gärtel, 1954; Saur, 1958).

PHOSPHORUS

An average crop of fruit will remove from the soil about 3 to 6 pounds of phosphorus per acre per year (Perold, 1927). Vines obtain this much phosphorus from most soils, so it is not surprising that no need has been shown for this element in any of numerous tests in the commercial vineyards of California.

In the plant, phosphorus enters into the composition of phospholipids and nucleic acids. Chemical combinations of the nucleic acids with proteins result in the formation of nucleoproteins, which are important constituents of the nuclei of cells. Phosphorus is necessary not only for photosynthesis, but also for transforming sugars to starch and starch to sugars (Akazawa, 1965). It is also indispensable in respiration.

A deficiency of phosphorus in tree fruits causes reduced growth, dark green leaves often with some purpling of main veins, and premature fruit ripening (Chandler, 1965). The last disagrees with the often repeated statement that abundant phosphorus hastens ripening. Theoretically, abundant phosphorus could hasten ripening indirectly by reducing nitrogen intake to the point of deficiency, which hastens ripening. Such an effect is attained only when the nitrogen supply is rather low. The depressant effect of added phosphorus on nitrogen intake by grapes is so slight (or mild) that the effect on earlier ripening, if any, cannot be measured in field trials. When both phosphorus and nitrogen were present in adequate supply, very large amounts of added phosphorus showed no effect on ripening, color development, or shipping and keeping quality (W. O. Williams, 1946).

MAGNESIUM

The only mineral constituent of the chlorophyll molecule is magnesium. It is also part of a compound that may be a precursor of chlorophyll and that functions as an activator of numerous enzymes. Lack of magnesium causes a characteristic chlorosis of the older leaves. The large veins of affected leaves retain their color longest, whereas the areas between these become pale green, yellow, or creamy white.

Only a few instances of magnesium deficiency have been observed in California vineyards. These have been found on young vines planted on sandy soil—especially where fills were made when the land was leveled for irrigation. According to J. A. Cook (unpublished data), the symptoms usually disappear within a few years, when the roots have penetrated subsoil layers of higher magnesium content. Because the effect is transient and few acres are involved, no studies have been made of corrective procedures in California.

Where the deficiency is severe, the best recovery has been obtained with three or four applications each season of a 1 per cent magnesium oxide or 2 per cent magnesium sulfate spray, beginning in June (Lott, 1952). Soil applications give slow improvement, since the magnesium is fixed (Scott and Scott, 1952).

An abundance of potassium in the soil tends to reduce the intake of magnesium. Many vineyards in Europe have received generous applications of potassium for years. It would be of interest to determine the effect of heavy potassium fertilization on the deficiency of magnesium in some of these older grape-growing countries.

IRON

Iron is indispensable in the synthesis of chlorophyll, even though it does not enter into the chlorophyll molecule. The form of the iron in plant tissues often governs its influence in chlorophyll synthesis. Chlorosis from iron deficiency is sometimes found in leaves that contain as much iron as green leaves; the iron present is in an unavailable form. In such instances it has probably been precipitated and is stored in insoluble compounds. Some of the enzymes and carriers that function in the respiratory mechanism of living cells are iron compounds. Some of these are catalase, peroxidase, and cytochromes, which have important roles in cellular metabolism.

The amount of iron in the plant tissue is very low. It is also one of the least mobile of all elements in plants, with little if any redistribution from one tissue to another.

Chlorosis.—A lack of usable iron in the vine tissues causes a characteristic yellowing of the foliage. When severe, entire shoots, usually all of the shoots on an affected vine, may be yellow to yellowish-green. Usually the first leaves that form in the spring are of normal green and only the later growth is chlorotic. There is usually no lack of iron in the soil, but some soil conditions, such as high lime content or overwetness, make the iron insoluble or otherwise unavailable to the vines. Chlorosis of this kind is, therefore, a symptom of iron deficiency, either direct or indirect.

The vineyard soils of California rarely contain more than five per cent of calcium carbonate—too low a proportion to cause an iron deficiency problem with *vinifera* varieties on their own roots. Therefore, iron deficiency is rarely encountered in California vineyards. On occasion, however, vines may show iron deficiency for a few weeks in early spring. This is usually a result of late spring rains plus poor drainage, and the symptoms disappear with warmer weather and cessation of rainfall.

Many varieties of native American species, including the most important variety, Concord, are much more sensitive to lime-induced chlorosis than are the varieties of *vinifera*. Early attempts to use American vines as rootstocks against phylloxera in Europe resulted in a great increase in the incidence of iron deficiency on the high lime soils of central and northern France.

On the other hand, one American species, V. *berlandieri*, found in the limestone hills of central to southwest Texas, grows very well on such soils. This species and its various hybrids when used as rootstocks have provided the most effective and practical control of lime-induced chlorosis. From work done in Mexico on vineyards with lime-induced chlorosis, J. A. Cook and R. Mancilla (unpublished data) found that foliar sprays, whether iron sulfate or chelated iron, must be applied several times to obtain appreciable correction. Greening occurs only where each droplet falls on the leaf, i.e., there is no apparent translocation within the leaf from the immediate point of absorption. Thus new growth must be sprayed if the chlorosis is severe. Chel 138 (Fe-EDDHA) when added to the irrigation water for flood (basin) application gave only partial control at a rate of 10 kilos per hectare (1 g per square meter). However, when Chel 138 was applied dry in the irrigation furrow at a rate of 15 g per vine (spacing at 1.5 x 3 meters), effective control was obtained over at least two growing seasons.

MANGANESE

Manganese is another element that is essential in the synthesis of chlorophyll. It is not a constituent of the pigment. It also plays an important part in oxidation-reduction reactions, since it functions as an activator of certain enzymes, such as dehydrogenase and carboxylase. Manganese has another important role in the reduction of nitrate to organic forms, specifically the conversion of nitrite to hydroxylamine; the latter is further reduced to ammonia.

Iron is commonly absorbed as the ferric ion and reduced in the cells to the ferrous state unless some oxidizing agent is present to prevent this reaction. According to Somers and Shive (1942), manganese plays the role of such an oxidizing agent. An excess of manganese may thus induce symptoms of iron deficiency by converting available iron into the physiologically inactive ferric state.

There are no known instances of manganese toxicity in California vineyards. Deficiency symptoms to a mild degree appear in many vineyards throughout the state; but severe symptoms, which might affect yields, are extremely rare. Perhaps the greatest importance of the widespread but mild symptoms is the likelihood of confusion with zinc deficiency. The leaf pattern of chlorosis or lack of green color is similar. The basic difference is that manganese deficiency shows on the basal leaves and does not affect the basal sinus; zinc deficiency shows first on the terminal leaves and causes a widening of the sinus.

SULFUR

Sulfur is a constituent of the amino acid cystine, which in turn is a constituent of proteins, and of thiamine and biotin, which are important vitamins in plants. It is also a constituent of the mustard oil glucosides, which impart characteristic odor and flavors in certain plants.

In the plant the sulfur of organic molecules may be reconverted into organic sulfur, such as the sulfate ion, and then be redistributed within the plant and reutilized in the formation of other organic sulfur compounds.

Sulfur applied to certain forage crops on certain soils has greatly improved growth, but sulfur is not likely to be deficient in soils suitable for grape production. The regular dusting of vineyards with sulfur to control powdery mildew (oïdium) offers further insurance against a deficiency of this element.

COPPER

Copper is toxic to plants except in very dilute concentrations. Its need by plants was revealed in a stimulus from fungicidal sprays containing copper. It is now well known that copper constitutes the nonprotein part of certain oxidizing enzymes, such as ascorbic acid oxidase and tyrosinase. In trace amounts it is a natural constituent of grapes.

Reports of copper deficiency in vineyards are rare; in part, perhaps because fungicides containing copper, notably the Bordeaux mixture, are used throughout much of the grape growing world. More common are reports of copper toxicity—symptoms similar to lime-induced chlorosis, i.e., iron deficiency—as reported by Gärtel (1957) for Germany, Delmas (1963) for France, and by Suit (1948) on the Concord grape in the eastern U.S.. Since California vineyards do not have the problem of downy mildew (Peronospora), copper sprays are not used here; further, as yet, there have not been any recognized instances of copper deficiency with grapes in the state. However, there have been a few reports of copper deficiency in orchards, almonds for example, and it may be that in time there will be cases of deficiency in vineyards also.

Teakle *et al.* (1943) reported a response to copper treatment of a vineyard in West Australia. The deficiency symptoms included poor root development, small pale-green leaves, rough bark, short internodes, and reduced yields. The leaves contained 4 ppm or less of copper. Both spray and soil treatments were used, but there was no response to either until the second year when vine growth greatly improved.

MOLYBDENUM

Molybdenum seems to have a part in the reduction of nitrate to nitrite, among other possible roles. Minina (1960) reports that it effects nitrogen fixation as well as the activity of ascorbic acid oxidase. Molybdenum-deficient soils have been found in Australia, California, New Jersey, and central Europe. As yet, no deficiency has been observed in grapes in California.

CALCIUM

Calcium is usually thought of as a soil addition to reduce acidity and improve water penetration in soils of high sodium content. It is also necessary for normal metabolic processes in plants and, therefore, plays an important role in plant nutrition. It is necessary to the continued growth of apical shoot and root meristems, aids in the translocation of carbohydrates, has a role in nitrogen utilization by plants, and, as calcium pectate in the middle lamella, is a constituent of the cell wall.

Calcium deficiency has not been observed in California vineyards, and there is no reason to suspect that calcium is lacking as a plant nutrient. Heavy calcium applications in the form of gypsum (calcium sulfate) are, however, a standard recommendation for treatment of high-sodium soils. Such soils are characterized by unusual stickiness when wet and by water penetration noticeably slower than is normal for a soil of a given texture.

SODIUM

Although sodium is not an essential element, it can be a factor in grape production. It may have beneficial effects, as in the case of high acidity, but these are rare; other elements usually meet the needs more aptly. The harmful effects of sodium are the effects of real interest. In some vineyard soils the sodium content may be high enough to cause a typical leafburn pattern and general vine stunting. The scorch begins at the margin of leaves and progresses inward, producing symptoms that can easily be mistaken for potassium deficiency.

Another effect of excess sodium is to reduce soil permeability to water. The soil is deflocculated by the excess of sodium; the clay particles become dispersed and excessively hydrated when wet, swelling and interrupting water movement through the soil. Although this is a physical condition, the basic cause is chemical, and a chemical process is required to correct the trouble.

When gypsum is applied to such soils, the calcium it contains replaces the sodium on the soil clay particles; then the sodium can be removed by leaching with large amounts of irrigation water. Gypsum is useful in improving water penetration only if the cause of poor penetration is high sodium content. As often as not, the cause of poor water penetration is physical rather than chemical. Bad soil-management practices—such as cultivating when the soil is too wet, and indiscriminate and frequent use of heavy equipment in the vineyard—will in time result in compaction or the development of a plow sole, or both. Water penetration is thus impaired by physical causes, and in such cases gypsum is not a corrective. The recommended remedies are deep-rooted cover crops; cultivation only when necessary, and then only when the soil is dry; and a minimum of traffic by heavy equipment. Such practices have proved effective in improving soil structure and permeability to air and water.

NITROGEN, POTASSIUM, AND PHOSPHORUS REMOVED FROM THE SOIL

In most California vineyards the leaves and the prunings are returned to the soil. The fruit harvested per acre varies from less than 2 tons to more than 20 tons. Irrigated vineyards average about 7 tons of fruit per acre; the non-irrigated coastal vineyards average about 3 tons.

The content of nitrogen, phosphorus, and potassium of ripe grapes also varies between wide limits. For specific data, see Colby (1893), Bioletti (1894), and Jacob (1942). Summarizing these references, it seems reasonable to assume that ripe California grapes contain from about 0.12 to 0.24 per cent nitrogen, 0.02 to 0.04 per cent phosphorus, and 0.16 to 0.32 per cent potassium.

Thus, if all leaves and prunings are returned to the soil, a crop of 7 tons of grapes may be expected to remove 16.8 to 33.6 pounds of nitrogen, 2.8 to 5.6 pounds of phosphorus, and 22.4 to 44.6 pounds of potassium. Mature grape canes, which constitute most of the prunings, contain about 45 per cent water, 0.25 per cent nitrogen, 0.04 per cent phosphorus, and 0.25 per cent potassium (W. O. Williams, unpublished data). An unirrigated vineyard that produces 3 tons of fruit per acre should produce about 0.6 ton of brush. A crop of 3 tons of fruit and 0.6 ton of brush may therefore be expected to remove from the soil about 9.8 to 17.5 pounds of nitrogen, 1.6 to 2.9 pounds of phosphorus, and 12.7 to 22.3 pounds of potassium. In comparison to nutrient removal by other crops, amounts of the major elements removed by grapes are not large, which may account in part for the frequent failure of vineyards to respond to fertilizer applications.

RESPONSE TO MAJOR FERTILIZER APPLICATIONS ELSEWHERE

European vineyards generally respond to applications of nitrogen and, in lesser magnitude, to potassium and phosphorus added with nitrogen. Published results of favorable responses to all three elements are far too numerous and too well authenticated to permit doubt. Of the three elements, nitrogen usually gives the greatest response, but that response seems to be enhanced by the addition of potassium or phosphorus, or both. But potassium deficiency in European vineyards is not so common as is the incidence of leafroll virus (Scheu, 1936), and the great similarity of visual symptoms of the two (Cook and Goheen, 1961) frequently results in unnecessary applications of potash. This unbalance of excess potassium

(Gärtel, 1960; Levy, 1967) often causes magnesium deficiency—symptoms of which are often seen in high rainfall, acid-soil areas of Europe.

Vineyards of American grapes east of the Rocky Mountains seem to be generally more responsive to fertilizer applications than California vineyards and somewhat less so than European vineyards. Well-planned tests have often, though not always, shown response to nitrogen applications and, less often, to potassium. According to Shaulis (1954), a moderate percentage of the vineyards of New York responded to potassium applications and about 5 per cent showed serious deficiency symptoms when potassium was withheld. Generally, there was no response to calcium or phosphorus, and magnesium deficiency was of only minor importance. It was indicated that 1.6 per cent (dry weight) of total nitrogen in the leaf petiole in late June and 0.4 per cent potassium in late August would be enough for normal growth and production (Shaulis and Kimball, 1956). Reporting on a five-year fertilizer trial with Concord grapes, Larsen *et al.* (1959) concluded that higher yields could be maintained in Michigan with less nitrogen than is usually applied; that phosphorus and magnesium were not required; that annual applications of potassium were not needed; and that excess potassium induced magnesium deficiency. A survey of the nutrient-element status of Concord grapes in Ohio (Beattie and Forshey, 1954) found that the concentration of nitrogen and potassium in the leaf petiole was correlated significantly with average yields, whereas calcium and phosphorus concentrations were not. Of the minor elements, manganese alone showed occasional positive deficiency symptoms. Analyses suggested that the petiole levels of nutrients in July necessary to obtain a yield of 3.5 tons per acre of grapes were as follows: nitrogen, 0.77 per cent; phosphorus, 0.14 per cent; potassium, 2 per cent; calcium, 0.70 per cent; and magnesium, 0.15 per cent. From a fertilizer trial in Texas, Randolph (1944) concluded that nitrogen applied alone or in combination with potash did not influence production; but phosphorus in combination with nitrogen or potassium, or both, increased yields markedly; so did large quantities of manure (8 tons per acre) on a sandy, non-irrigated soil. Was this indeed a direct response to added phosphorus—one of very few well-replicated ones on record? Or was it an indirect effect? Randolph stated that the winter covercrops of oats, wheat, and barley did not grow well without fertilizers; thus one-half of the annual phosphorus application was worked into the soil when the covercrop was planted. The maximum rate of phosphorus application was 47 pounds per acre, yet one-half of this was applied to benefit the covercrop. The 18 pounds of nitrogen per acre could hardly be considered a real test for nitrogen response. One could then argue that the additional covercrop growth, as a result of the phosphorus addition, was about equal to the organic matter of the 8-ton manure treatment—and that both caused increased crop through greater water-holding capacity in this sandy, non-irrigated soil. In this case, tissue analysis, to show an increase in phosphorus uptake, would have been enlightening.

Many vineyard tests in California and elsewhere have shown a low percentage of profitable responses to any fertilizer. Seldom do such results find their way into print, but they must not be ignored on that account.

DETERMINING THE NEED FOR FERTILIZER

The few examples of responses to vineyard fertilization given in the preceding section show that the fertilizer problem has no single solution for all conditions and that results in one place are not necessarily applicable elsewhere. A review of mineral nutrition of grapes, more complete than can be presented here, has been published by Cook (1966). However, no fertilization program in California vineyards can logically be based on European responses, nor can recommendations for New York growers be based on fertilizer tests in California or Texas. Further, vine growth alone is not always a good index of fertilizer needs. Growth can be too vigorous for best production; also deficiencies of some nutrients such as nitrogen may begin to limit yields before growth is reduced.

Soil analysis, which in the beginning of the scientific approach seemed the logical way to determine plant nutrient needs, had lost favor over the years, especially for such deep-rooted and perennial crops as trees and vines. Representative sampling is time-consuming, thus expensive; laboratory extraction methods usually show poor correlation with plant performance; and finally, so far as vineyards of the U.S., particularly those of California, are concerned, there are practically no experimental data to correlate soil analysis with vine response to any nutrient element. True, soil analyses can be informative concerning possible toxicities of salt and boron, and knowledge of the pH can be useful in predicting mineral nutrition problems, but beyond these factors, the chemical analysis of soils is of very little practical value.

The work done by Cook (1966) indicates that the leaf petiole is almost an ideal vine part for determining the nutritional status of the grapevine. Petioles are easily handled in relatively large numbers (allowing for a very representative sample with little effort) and need little or no washing.

The most important question is the location on the shoot from which to take the petiole and the time of the year the sample should be taken. For the most reliable interpretation, it would be best, of course, to take samples throughout the growing season, plot these, and base the diagnosis on both the periodic levels and the seasonal behavior. However, from the practical viewpoint, samplings must be kept at the minimum per year. This has been a question for debate, for investigation, and for modification over the years. In summary: the French, in their Diagnostic Laboratory at Montpellier (which is at the service of the 3 million acres of French vineyards) take a leaf-plus-petiole opposite the first cluster at end of bloom and another at the beginning of ripening and average the two results (J. F. Levy, personal communication). In the laboratory at U.C., Davis, the bloomtime sample has proven to be the most important, taking only petioles at the cluster position, with follow-up samples taken on questionable vineyards at approximately one month after bloom.

The above procedure is for survey or routine sampling: the other aspect is "troubleshooting" to determine the cause of vine disorders. Both deficiency and toxicity symptoms most commonly appear in mid-season or early harvest time. For such situations, samples are taken of the affected leaves, regardless of location on the shoot. When no reasonable clues are recognized, samples are taken of both the petioles and blades, but analyzed separately; if Na and/or Cl are highly likely, only the petioles are analyzed (these two elements accumulate in the petioles even though the blades may show the symptoms); for excess boron, the blades where the much greater levels will be found, are taken. The variety, sampling date, approximate stage of fruit development, and location on the vine of the abnormal leaves should be noted.

Naturally, the larger the sample, the more representative the analysis will be; but for minimum and maximum collected amounts, the following limits apply:

	Min.	Max.
Shoot tips, 2–3″ long	20–30	80–100
Petioles (small, early spring)	30–40	80–100
Petioles (normal, bloom and mid-summer)	20–30	80–100
Leaf blades	20–25	40–50

Petioles do not usually need to be washed unless the vineyard is unusually dusty. Leaf blades, noticeably dirty, should receive a quick rinsing in distilled water containing a very small amount of detergent. Remember, however, that some elements—sodium, potassium, and chloride, in particular—can be leached quite easily from necrotic or dead tissue. Therefore, make the washing very quickly and do a thorough job of shaking and blotting off the excess water. All samples should be dried in a forced air-draft oven at approximately 70° C. for 48 hours, and ground to 20 mesh fineness.

Interpretation.—Tissue analysis is just another tool to aid in establishing guidelines for indicating the mineral nutritional levels of vines; that is, deficiencies or excess of the various elements. The deficiency range is of most practical importance, since at this level economic response to fertilizer applications is general. The sufficiency level cannot be expected to be so precise.

Fertilizer Elements Required by the Vine

The following are the approximate percentage or parts per million amounts of the various elements at several levels of nutrition of vines under conditions found in California. They are based on data for only a few important varieties, notably Thompson Seedless, which accounts for about 50 per cent of California's grape yield. The data are for leaf petioles taken from opposite clusters at full bloom, unless otherwise stated. In all cases a $\pm$ value of about 10 per cent should be allowed.

Nitrogen (*Nitrate*): Deficient, less than 0.15 per cent NO_3 or 350 ppmN; normal, 0.25 to 0.50 per cent or 600 to 1200 ppm; more than necessary,* over 0.75 per cent or over 1800 ppm; and excess, over 2400 ppmN.

Nitrate as a diagnostic aid is limited in several ways: varieties differ in "native" level; rootstocks also make a difference; and rainfall or irrigation seems to affect. Trials are underway to see if arginine, an amino acid, in harvest-time juice might be a better guide to nitrogen needs.

Phosphorus.—No deficiency symptoms have been identified in California vineyards, and there have been no measurable responses in yield or fruit quality in California vineyard trials. With rare exceptions, bloomtime values lie between 0.3 and 0.6 per cent total phosphorus. The negative-response trials have included vineyards with levels of 0.25 per cent; perhaps applications at levels lower than this will bring response—still to be tested.

Probably deficient, less than 0.15 per cent; questionable, 0.15 to 0.20 per cent; and normal, 0.30 to 0.60 per cent.

Potassium.—Some precautions in interpretations: varietal differences exist for potassium also, although not so great as for nitrate. Potassium level is easily affected by any condition that might reduce the effectiveness of the root system: drought, overcropping, shallow-rooting, nematodes, or phylloxera. Positive response to potash applications in such situations has often been negative. The most striking responses have been in areas with low soil potassium, usually scraped areas. A big, unanswered question: why does tissue level of K vary so greatly (30–50 per cent) from year to year in the same, untreated vineyards!

Deficiency, less than 1.0 per cent; questionable 1.0 to 1.20 per cent; normal, 1.5 to 2.5 per cent; and toxic, over 3.0 per cent—not observed in California.

Magnesium.—Most of our California soils have high K/Mg in surface samples, but gradually reversing with depth. Thus, the few instances of

---

* For Thompson Seedless, values between 0.50 and 0.75 per cent Nitrate may result in some reduction in total crop, but may be justified in areas where extra foliage is desirable to prevent sunburn of fruit. Observational experience indicate that over 1.0 per cent nitrate at bloomtime in Thompson Seedless is associated with various detrimental effects—excessive growth, perhaps fewer clusters formed, frequently reduced set of fruit, and poorly matured canes for next year's crop.

Mg deficiency have been with newly-planted (shallow-rooted) vines or instances where there have been deep fills of top-soil. In the latter situations, within 3 to 4 years the vines usually grow through to the Mg-rich lower soil. In short, there seems to be no real problem of magnesium deficiency in California grape vineyards.

The bloomtime values range from 0.3 to 0.8 per cent and petiole levels almost always increase, on a dry weight basis, as the season progresses. With the extreme sensitivity of vines to the K/Mg ratio in tissue the problem is much more one of Mg *toxicity* than of Mg *deficiency*.

Likely deficient, less than 0.3 per cent (very rare in California); normal, 0.5 to 0.8 per cent; and likely toxic, over 1.0 per cent (might lead to potassium deficiency).

Zinc.—The emphasis has been on attempts to correct the *visual* symptoms of deficiency. Until this can be done easily and practically on cane-pruned varieties, survey analyses and normal levels are of secondary importance.

Deficiency symptoms less than 15 ppm; questionable symptoms, 15 to 20 ppm; and normal, 25 to 50 ppm.

Boron.—In California both deficiency and toxicity occur. There are many more acres of toxicity, but the effects are much more disastrous with deficiency. With deficiency, petioles and blades show about the same levels; with toxicity, boron accumulates very much more in the blades than in petioles.

Deficiency, less than 25 ppm; questionable, 25–30 ppm; normal, 40 to 60 ppm; and toxic, over 300 in blades.

Chloride.—Of the three elements likely to be toxic under California conditions, (Na, Cl, B), chloride seems to be the most serious in that it reduces total vine growth. Varieties (and rootstocks) differ greatly in tolerance. Chloride continues to accumulate with the growing season, and does so predominately in the petiole even though the symptoms show in the blades.

Normal, 0.05 to 0.15 per cent; and excess, 0.50 per cent if it continues to rise as the season progresses up to over 1.0 per cent.

Sodium.—Since chloride is almost always associated with high sodium, we have no real quantitative data as to what level is a toxic level (if any) of sodium. At this time, we would say that a bloom-time level of over 0.50 per cent Na might be suggestive of problems, especially if potassium is relatively low.

FERTILIZER RECOMMENDATIONS (WHEN DEFICIENCY IS SUSPECTED)

Nitrogen: Apply 50 to 75 pounds actual N during dormant season; use cheapest form (per pound of actual N), and apply according to recommendations—usually broadcast before February 1 in California.

Potassium: Apply one to two pounds of potassium sulphate per vine in deepest and closest furrows possible during dormant season; leave the furrows open for winter rains or for first irrigation.

Boron: Apply about 10 pounds of *actual Boron* per acre about every three years.

Zinc: For spur-pruned varieties, there does not seem to be any better way than the daubing of pruning wounds immediately after pruning with one pound of zinc sulfate per gallon of water; if bleeding occurs, wait one to two hours before application.

Each grower should make tests and observe results in his own vineyard in order to find out whether he can use fertilizers profitably and which kinds he may need, if any. Fortunately, such field tests can be very simple, requiring no unusual technical knowledge or skill. They do, however, require care and accuracy in laying out the test plots, applying the fertilizer, labeling the vines or rows that are treated, and observing the results. Haphazard methods or careless technique can easily lead to erroneous conclusions.

In laying out such tests, the manner of harvesting should be considered in choosing the vines to be included in the individual lots. If each row is ordinarily harvested separately, then one row across a block of vines, in the direction followed in harvest, constitutes a convenient unit. If the fruit from two rows is placed together, as is often done in wine vineyards, the two rows are best used as a unit, so as to simplify the keeping of crop records. In all cases untreated (guard) units of two or more rows should separate the units that are fertilized. For evaluation of fertilizer treatments, control units are absolutely essential. The control units should be strictly analogous to the fertilized units except that they receive no fertilizer. They must be separated from fertilized vines by enough guard rows in order to eliminate the possibility of penetration by the roots of the controls into the soil of the fertilized rows or of underground lateral movement of the nutrient—especially so with micro nutrients such as boron. Finally, no test is conclusive unlesss sufficient replications are established. The required number of treated vs. non-treated plots varies, of course, with the size of plot, but generally, 4 to 6 comparisons of 40 or more vines per plot are necessary for reliable conclusions. Differences in the quality of the fruit, particularly in its color, and differences in vine growth must usually be estimated. If the differences are too small to be recognized visually, they are probably too small to be important.

BIBLIOGRAPHY

Akazawa, T. 1965. *In* Plant biochemistry. Bonner and Varner, eds. New York & London, Academic Press. p. 276.

Askew, H. O. 1944. A case of combined K and B deficiencies in grapes. New Zealand J. of Sci. Tech., 26:146–152.

Beattie, J. M., and C. G. Forshey. 1954. A survey of the nutrient element status of Concord grapes in Ohio. Proc. Amer. Soc. Hort. Sci., 64:21–28.

Bioletti, F. T. 1894. The ash of grapes. California Agr. Exp. Sta. Rept. for the years 1892–93 and part of 1894, Sacramento, State Printing Office, pp. 322–326.

Branas, J., and G. Bernon. 1956. La clarence de bore dans les vignobles francais. Prog. Agr. et Vitic., 146:259–270, 334–343, 356–361, 388–394, 414–419.

Chandler, W. H. 1965. Deciduous orchards. 3rd ed. Philadelphia, Lea & Febiger. *See* p. 178.

Colby, G. E. 1893. On the quantities of nitrogenous matters contained in California musts and wines. Univ. California, Rept. of the vitic. work during the seasons 1887–1893, part II, pp. 422–446.

Cook, J. A. 1958. Field trials with foliar sprays of Zn-EDTA to control zinc deficiency in California vineyards. Proc. Amer. Soc. Hort. Sci., 72:158–164.

———. 1962. Micronutrients in vines. Western Fruit Grower, 16(2):17–18.

———. 1966. In Fruit nutrition. 2nd ed. N. F. Childers, ed. Rutgers, New Brunswick, New Jersey, Hort. Pubs. pp. 777–812.

———, and A. C. Goheen. 1961. The effect of a virus disease, leafroll, on the mineral composition of grape tissue and a comparison of leafroll and potassium deficiency symptoms. In Plant analysis and fertilizer problems. Walter Reuther, ed. Am. Inst. Biol. Sci. Pub. No. 8, pp. 338–354.

———, and A. N. Kasimatis. 1959. Predicting nitrogen response in vineyards (The petiole test). Univ. California Agr. Ext. Ser., leaflet, May.

———, and T. Kishaba. 1956a. Petiole nitrate analysis as a criterion of nitrogen needs in California vineyards. Proc. Amer. Soc. Hort. Sci., 68:131–140.

———, ———. 1956b. Using leaf symptoms and foliar analyses to diagnose fertilizer needs in California vineyards. VIème Congrès Internatl. Sci. du Sol. (Paris), pp. 158–176.

———, ———. 1957. Nitrogen fertilization of unirrigated vineyards in the north coastal area of California. Amer. Jour. Enol., 8(3):105–112.

———, C. D. Lynn, and J. J. Kissler. 1960. Boron deficiency in California vineyards. Amer. Jour. Enol. Vitic., 11:185–194.

Delmas, J. 1963. Toxicity of Cu accumulated in the soil. Agrochimica, 7:258–288. (In French) Abstract only seen. Chem. Abst., 59:9270 f.

Dias, H. F. 1953. Informacao sobre "Marombo" do Douro. Bolet da Casa Douro, 8:1167–1169.

Dyar, J. J., and K. L. Webb. 1961. A relation between boron and auxin in C[14] translocation in bean plants. Pl. Physiol., 36:672–676.

Eaton, F. M. 1944. Deficiency, toxicity, and accumulation of boron in plants. Jour. Agr. Res., 68(6):237–277.

Gärtel, W. 1954. Untersuchungen über Borschäden an Reben. Weinberg u. Keller, 1:329–335.

———. 1956. Untersuchungen über die bedeutung des bors für die rebe unter besonderer berücksichtigung der befructung. Weinberg u. Keller, 3:132–139, 185–192, 233–241.

————. 1957. Untersuchunger über den Kupferghalt von Weinsbergund Rebshulboden. Weinberg u. Keller, 3:221–228.

————. 1960. Die verteilung von kalium und magnesium in reben unter normalen ernährungsbedingungen und bei kaliummangel. Weinberg u. Keller, 7(12):481–489.

Gauch, H. G., and W. M. Duggar, Jr. 1952. The role of boron in the translocation of sucrose. Plant Physiol., 28:457–466.

Gerber, H., and E. Peyer. 1959. Blattbespritzung gegen Kalimangel bei Reben der sorte "Blauer Burgunder" in der Bunder Herrschaft. Schweiz. Ztschr. f. Obst. u. Weinbau, 68:463–466.

Hewitt, E. J. 1951. The role of the mineral elements in plant nutrition. Amer-Rev. Plant. Phys., 3:25–52.

Hewitt, W. B., and H. E. Jacob. 1945. Effect of zinc on yield and cluster weight of Muscat grapes. Proc. Amer. Soc. Hort. Sci., 46:256–262.

Jacob, H. E. 1942. The relation of maturity of the grapes to the yield, composition, and quality of raisins. Hilgardia, 14:321–345.

————. 1947. Fertilizer value of pomace. Grape Grower, 1(6):12, 23.

Jardine, F. A. L. 1946. The use of borax on Waltham Cross grapes in the Stanthorpe district. Queensland Agr. Jour., 62(2):74–78.

Larsen, R. P., A. L. Kenworthy, H. K. Bell, E. J. Benne, and S. T. Bass. 1959. Effects of nitrogen, phosphorus, potassium, and magnesium fertilizers on yield and petiole nutrient content of a Concord grape vineyard. Quart. Bull. Mich. Agr. Exp. Sta., 41:812–819.

Levy, J. F. 1967. L'application du diagnostic foliaire à la détermination des besoins alimentaires des vignes. Vignes et Vins 157:23, 25, 27, 29, 31.

Lilleland, O., and J. G. Brown. 1937. The potassium nutrition of fruit trees; I. Soil analyses. Proc. Amer. Soc. Hort. Sci., 35:327–334.

Lott, W. L. 1952. Magnesium deficiency in Muscadine grape vines. Proc. Amer. Soc. Hort. Sci., 60:123–131.

McIlrath, W. J., and B. F. Palser. 1956. Responses of tomato, turnip, and cotton to variations in boron nutrition; I. Physiological responses, II. Anatomical responses. Bot. Gaz., 118:43–70.

Minina, E. I. 1960. On the physiological role of molybdenum in plants. [Trans. title.] Doklady Akad. Nauk., SSSR, 130:32–35.

Perold, A. I. 1927. A treatise on viticulture. MacMillan & Co. pp. 517–518.

Proebsting, E. L. 1958. Fertilizers and covercrops for California orchards. Calif. Agr. Exp. Sta. Ext. Ser. Cir., 466:1–19.

Randolph, W. A. 1944. Effects of phosphate fertilizers upon growth and yield of the Carmen grape in north Texas. Proc. Amer. Soc. Hort. Sci., 44:303–308.

Saur, M. R. 1958. Boron content of Sultana vines in the Mildura area. Australian Jour. Agr. Res., 9:123–129.

Scheu, G. 1936. Mein Winzerbuch. Berlin, Reichsnährstand Verlags G.m.b.H.

Scott, L. E. 1944. Boron nutrition of the grape. Soil Sci., 54:55–67.

————, and D. H. Scott. 1952. Further observations on the response of grapevines to soil and spray applications of magnesium sulfate. Proc. Amer. Soc. Hort. Sci., 60:117–122.

Shaulis, N. 1954. Potassium deficiency in the vineyard and its cure. New York Agr. Exp. Sta. Farm Res., 20(2):4.

———, and K. Kimball. 1956. The association of nutrient composition of Concord grape petioles with deficiency symptoms, growth, and yield. Proc. Amer. Soc. Hort. Sci., 68:141–156.

Skok, J. 1957. Relationship of boron nutrition to radiosensitivity of sunflower plants. Jour. Plant Physiol., 32:648–658.

Skoog, F. 1940. Relationship between zinc and auxin in the growth of higher plants. Amer. Jour. Bot., 27:939–951.

Snyder, E., and F. N. Harmon. 1954. Some responses of *vinifera* grapes to zinc sulphate. Proc. Amer. Soc. Hort. Sci., 63:91–94.

Somers, I. I., and J. W. Shive. 1942. The iron-manganese relation in plant metabolism. Jour. Plant Physiol., 17:582–602.

Suit, R. F. 1948. Effect of copper injury on Concord grapes. Phytopathology, 38:457–466.

Teakle, L. J. H., H. K. Johns, and A. G. Thurton. 1943. Experiments with micro-elements for the growth of crops in Western Australia. J. Dept. Agric. W. Aust., 20:171–184.

Tsui, C. 1948a. The role of zinc in auxin synthesis in the tomato plant. Amer. Jour. Bot., 35:172–179.

———. 1948b. The effect of zinc on water relations and osmotic pressure of the tomato plant. Amer. Jour. Bot., 35:309–311.

Whittington, W. J. 1959. The role of boron in plant growth; I. The effect on general growth, seed production, and cytological behavior, II. The effect on growth of the radicle. Jour. Exp. Bot., 8:353; 10:93–103.

Wilhelm, A. F. 1952. Bormangel bei der Weinrebe *Vitis vinifera*. Phytopath. Ztschr., 19(2):129–159.

Williams, W. A., D. Ririe, H. L. Hall, and F. J. Hills. 1954. Preliminary comparison of the effects of leguminous and non-leguminous green manures on sugar beet production. Amer. Soc. Beet Tech., 8:90–94.

Williams, W. O. 1943. Initial results from grape fertilizer plots. Proc. Amer. Soc. Hort, Sci., 42:421–424.

———. 1946. California vineyard fertilizer experimentation. Proc. Amer. Soc. Hort. Sci., 48:269–278.

18

Grape Diseases and Disorders

Grapes are susceptible to a number of diseases, some so serious that vine-yards cannot be maintained where climate particularly favors the disease. In other cases, weather conditions may often limit the kinds of grapes that can be grown. In general, the more humid the summer weather, the more difficult are some diseases to control. This is so especially for fungus and bacterial diseases, except powdery mildew. Particularly harmful are frequent summer rains—especially when accompanied by high tempera-tures. In contrast, the absence of summer rains, even when temperatures are high, as in California, eliminates many of the more serious diseases and assists the control of most of the remainder.

Fungus parasites cause the largest number of grape diseases. Virus and/or virus-like diseases spread by insects, such as Pierce's disease, or those spread in the soil (by nematodes), such as fanleaf, are the most de-structive and are difficult to control. Most other virus diseases, however, can be prevented if care is taken to plant stock free of virus and virus-like pathogens. Bacterial diseases are, except in certain areas, few and relatively unimportant. Nutritional disturbances are sometimes of local importance, but these are often easy to remedy, once their cause is known. Insects are the direct cause of a few diseases and are of critical importance as vectors (agents in dissemination) of viruses. Direct injuries from unfavorable weather—frost, hail, excessive heat, and winter freezing—do not fall within the common concept of diseases, but are logically treated in con-nection with them.

The following discussions are designed to give a description of the symp-toms of each disease and of the effects of disorders and injuries, so that each may be recognized; to indicate its importance; and to list the known measures for control or remedy.* Technical descriptions of the causal organisms are avoided; descriptions of the organisms and their life histories can be found in any good textbook on plant pathology or in the references cited. Information on diseases in humid regions and their control is presented by Lafon *et al.* (1959).

FUNGI ATTACKING BOTH THE VINE AND ITS FRUIT

Although there are a number of fungus diseases of the vine and its fruit, only four fungi are generally recognized as being destructive on a worldwide basis. These are the fungi that cause powdery mildew (Oïdium); anthracnose; black rot; and downey mildew (Peronospora), usually called mildew outside California. Of these diseases, only powdery mildew is present in California vineyards, where it is called mildew.

POWDERY MILDEW (OïDIUM)

Unlike most other fungus diseases of the grape, which are favored by moist conditions, powdery mildew grows well in dry climates. It is probably present wherever grapes are grown, and it is by far the most troublesome fungus disease of the grape in California.

* Because new fungicides and insecticides are being rapidly introduced, the Extension Service of the University of California annually revises its list of recommended control materials and procedures for vine diseases and insects. Residents of California may obtain a copy of this leaflet at the office of their Farm Advisor or by writing to the Public Service Office, College of Agriculture, Davis, California and asking for Leaflet (P5332L) KB, revised. The newest revision becomes available early in each year.

CAUTION: The suggestions made here for pest control are based on the best information currently available for each pesticide listed. If followed carefully, they should give satisfactory control and should not leave residues exceeding established tolerances. To avoid excess residues on the harvested crop, directions should be followed carefully as to dose levels, number of applications, and minimum intervals between application and harvest.

Certain chemicals may cause plant injury if used at the wrong stage of plant development or when temperatures are too high. Injury may also result from excessive amounts of the wrong formulation or from mixing incompatible materials. To AVOID INJURY, FOLLOW RECOMMENDATIONS PRECISELY. Plants may be injured by inert ingredients, such as wetters, spreaders, emulsifiers, diluents, and solvents. Thus, since formulations are often changed by manufacturers, it is possible that plant injury may result even though none occurred in previous seasons.

THE GROWER IS RESPONSIBLE both for residues on his own crop and for problems caused by chemicals that drift to other properties or crops.

CAUTION: The fungicides listed as control agents for the various diseases discussed here have proved to be effective and are registered for use in some grape producing country or countries. Make sure they are registered for use in your country before you apply them. For this, read the label or see your Farm Advisor or Agricultural Commissioner.

Grape Diseases and Disorders

The fungus parasite *Uncinula necator* Burr. attacks all green parts of the vine, at first producing a very fine, light, translucent, cobweb-like growth that radiates from the spot where the fungus spore began to grow. According to Delp (1954), the fungus starts to produce spores in about eight to fourteen days, depending on the temperature. The spores, called conidia, are produced on short stalks that stand upright on the surface of the affected part of the vine. The large number of the spores gives a powdery appearance to the fungus. It is at about this stage that the very careful observer will first notice the disease in the vineyard. Generally, some secondary spread will have taken place already. The conidia (spores) are spread through the air by wind. Those that land on the same or other vines develop into new fungus colonies. The spores germinate overnight and infect the plant by sending rootlike projections, called haustoria, into the surface cells of the leaves, shoots, or fruit; through these organs the fungus absorbs food from the grapevine for its growth.

After some three to five weeks of development on the vines, the colonies of the fungus, and perhaps its musty odor, can be readily observed and recognized. If not controlled, the fungus will continue to develop and spread in the vineyard during the summer and fall, when temperatures favor its growth. In the fall, overwintering spore cases, called cleistotheca, are produced. These appear as small black specks on the surface of the affected tissues. Cleistotheca usually begin to form in late September or early October. They may develop in the mycelium on any of the infected leaves, shoots, or other green tissues. These spore cases are spherical (about one sixty-fourth of an inch in diameter), with long appendages, and are dark brown in color. During the winter, other spore cases, called asci, are formed inside the cleistotheca. Each ascus usually contains 4 to 8 ascospores.

The powdery mildew fungus may survive the winter in two ways: as fungus in the buds between the bud scales and as overwintering cleistotheca. The fungus grows down between the bud scales on infected shoots in the summer, remains dormant there in the buds through the winter, and in the spring grows over the new shoot. The overwintering spores may cling to pieces of canes or bits of leaves, or they may be free in the soil. Although the spores in these cases have not been experimentally germinated in California, it is assumed that they do germinate and cause infections in the spring (Hewitt, 1957a). The spores probably are discharged into the air, where they are transported by wind.

Development of powdery mildew.—Temperature is one of the most important factors limiting the growth and development of this fungus. The disease is favored by cool weather. Delp (1954) showed that the fungus spores would germinate and infect grapes at temperatures as low as 45° F.; development was most rapid between 70 and 85° F. For instance, in experiments with grapevines in chambers, the time from the seeding of spores on grape leaves until the resulting colonies produced new spores was twelve days at 55° F. and only five days at 78° F. The maximum leaf temperature for infection was about 92° F., though spores germinated at higher temperatures. Vigorously growing mildew colonies that developed under optimum conditions were killed in six hours at 104° F.

In the same studies, the powdery mildew fungus grew well at 70 to 90° F., the spores still germinating at relative humidities approachng zero. Thus, moisture seems to have little effect on germination, infection, and development of powdery mildew.

The disease develops much more abundantly in shade or diffused light than in bright light. Long exposure to the direct sun may destroy the fungus.

These studies show that the powdery mildew fungus will grow very well at moderate temperatures, even under dry conditions; that its development is slowed or arrested at high temperatures; and that the colonies may die at temperatures above 104° F.

Symptoms.—The development of powdery mildew first becomes apparent as whitish patches of cobweb-like growth on the surface of the green parts of the vine. Soon the patches take on a grayish, powdery appearance, caused by the formation of numerous spores. Affected areas later darken to reddish-brown or black, owing to injury of the vine tissues. These areas are particularly conspicuous on the fruit and dormant canes (fig. 113). Severely affected young leaves become distorted and discolored,

A   B

FIGURE 113: Powdery mildew (Oidium). A, on a leaf; B, on the fruit. (*Courtesy of W. B. Hewitt*)

sometimes giving the vines a wilted appearance. A badly affected vine emits a mildew odor.

Flowers may be attacked, with the result that they fail to set fruit. Berries that are attacked when very small drop off. Large berries that are attacked develop irregularly into abnormal shapes; sometimes they crack or become badly scarred. Berries that are ripening or already ripe are not attacked. Powdery mildew on the stems of the clusters makes them weak and brittle; it also interferes with the nutrition and ripening of the fruit.

Control.—Control is divided into prevention and eradication. The most effective and most reasonable control practice is prevention. Sulfur dust gives excellent protection if grapevines are kept properly dusted throughout the season. This means keeping the green foliage and fruit covered with a very fine coating of sulfur. The degree of protection will depend upon the proper timing and thoroughness of applications. The sulfur particles prevent development of the fungus mainly by destroying the germinating spores.

For effective results it is essential to have a good dusting machine that will mix sulfur dust with the air and give good uniform distribution over the shoots, fruit, and foliage. The following schedule for dusting has given effective control under conditions very favorable for development of the disease:

Apply sulfur dust when the shoots are 6, 12, 18, and 24 inches long, and every 14 days until several weeks before harvest.

Apply dust every 14 days in each row middle or every 7 days in alternate middles.

The first two applications are particularly important; they are made irrespective of temperature and are repeated after heavy rains. They must not be delayed in anticipation of rain. From 5 to 10 pounds of sulfur per acre, according to the equipment used and its operation, will be required for each of the applications. Heavy application, 15 pounds or more, may cause injury at temperatures above 95° F. Applying sulfur when the temperature is 100° F or higher is likely to cause burning of immature leaves and exposed fruit.

Eradication.—Once the powdery mildew fungus becomes established on the vine and starts producing spores, it is no longer susceptible to sulfur dust. An eradicant spray is then necessary to kill the fungus. Sprays should also be used if the first two dustings were omitted. If only the first dusting was omitted, but the mildew was bad the previous season, an eradicant spray is necessary. The eradicant spray solution consists of 1 to 2 pounds of wettable sulfur to 100 gallons of water and enough of a good wetting agent to ensure that leaves and berries submerged in the solution will be thoroughly wet when removed. To be effective all foliage (both the upper and the lower surfaces of the leaves), the canes, and the fruit must be wet very thoroughly. This is often difficult to accomplish. Average vines generally will require from 200 to 300 gallons of spray per acre early in the season and from 300 to 400 gallons in the middle or late season. The wetting agent and water eradicate the fungus, and the sulfur forms a protective coating over the foliage until the next dusting time. In cool areas up to 3 pounds of sulfur per 100 gallons may be used. When the vines are very vigorous, removing leaves in the dense parts of the vines will improve the spray coverage.

All of the eradicant sprays, even plain water, leave spots of spray residue or caked dust on the grapes. Hence, grapes that are sprayed after they are one-third grown can seldom be marketed as table fruit. The residue is less objectionable on raisin and wine grapes.

All *vinifera* varieties are susceptible, in slightly varying degrees to powdery mildew. Among the more susceptible are Carignane, Muscat of Alexandria, and Sylvaner. For good control, all dust applications should be given every season to all *vinifera* varieties grown in the coastal valley of California and to all table grapes grown in any section of the state except the Coachella and Imperial valleys. The fourth and sixth applications may be omitted for raisins and wine grapes grown in the interior valleys if the other applications are properly done. Where frequent irrigations are applied, additional dusting may be necessary, because the vines will continue to make new growth that must be protected.

The American varieties are generally more resistant than the *vinifera* varieties. Under conditions especially favorable to the disease, however, Concord and other American varieties may be damaged severely. These varieties are, moreover, sensitive to sulfur and may be badly burned if too much is applied in hot weather. In California the American varieties seldom require any treatment. If they do, an organic fungicide, such as maneb may be used.

In California, sulfur dust is as effective as liquid sprays in preventing powdery mildew if coverage is equally good. If a spray is preferred, use 1.5 pounds of wettable sulfur per 100 gallons of water with a suitable spreader. Thorough coverage is essential. Winter control treatment is ineffective.

ANTHRACNOSE

Anthracnose has been known in Europe since ancient times. It is a problem in the eastern United States but not known to be present in California. The spores of the fungus are disseminated mainly by rain and dew. It is present in all grape-growing regions having summer rains, but it is not usually serious unless rains are frequent in spring and early summer. Varieties differ in their susceptibility. The Muscadine grapes seem immune; Champanel is highly resistant; Concord is moderately resistant; most other American varieties are more susceptible than Concord; and most, though not all, *vinifera* varieties are highly susceptible.

Symptoms.—Cankers are produced on the shoots, tendrils, clusters, stems, leaf veins, and berries. At first the lesions are pin point in size, brown or grayish-black, depressed in the center, and raised at the border; as the spots become older they enlarge and elongate lengthwise of the vine part. The bark on the shoots is finally destroyed, and the underlying wood turns grayish. Isolated leaf spots are pale gray, with reddish-brown or purple borders. The spots may run together and eventually drop away, leaving a ragged leaf. On berries the spots are small and dark brown at first; as they enlarge they remain circular, becoming grayish in the center, with the border remaining dark. Between the gray center and the dark border a bright-red or purple band develops; the appearance thus produced has given rise to the common name, "bird's-eye rot." Severely affected berries finally dry into mummies, which retain the outline of the original spot.

Cause.—The causal fungus is *Gloeosporium ampelophagum* (Pass) Sacc., which attacks all parts of the vine.

Control.—For control of anthracnose (McGrew and Still, 1972), the vines are sprayed during the dormant season with commercial lime-sulfur solution diluted 1 to 8 parts in water. The prunings are burned and the vineyard is plowed in spring to turn under all disease-bearing leaves and mummied fruit. During the growing season, the vines are sprayed five times with Bordeaux mixture or with copperoxychloride: when the shoots are 7 to 8 inches long; just before bloom; immediately after bloom; seven to ten days later; and when the berries are about half grown. The control should be varied to fit the severity of the disease under local conditions. Application of ferbam (Fermate) (as recommended for black rot below) also might improve control.

BLACK ROT

Black rot, caused by the fungus *Guignardia bidwellii* (Ellis) Viala & Ravaz, is indigenous to eastern North America. It was introduced into Europe before 1885 and is now present in all grape-growing regions that have frequent summer rains. It is not present in California; if it is present in Australia and other regions having only occasional summer rains, it is not serious. This fungus grows best in hot, moist weather; rain helps disseminate the summer spores; and droplets of water, as from rain or dew, seem to be necessary for spore germination. It is probably the most destructive disease in vineyards of the United States east of the Rocky Mountains, where it virtually prevents success in growing *vinifera* varieties. It is also very destructive in parts of southern France.

Symptoms.—Black rot attacks all green parts of the vine and is particularly destructive to the fruit. On the leaves it produces reddish-brown, irregularly-shaped spots, with the black fruiting bodies of the fungus sometimes forming more or less concentric rings within the spots. On the shoots, tendrils, cluster stems, petioles, and large leaf veins it produces small elliptical, dark-colored cankers. The berries are usually attacked between the time they are half grown and the beginning of ripening. The infection spot, which first appears as a small blanched area, soon changes to a whitish area having a brownish line around the margin, enlarges rapidly, and becomes sunken. The black-rot spots are sometimes mistaken for spots of anthracnose, though with anthracnose the center remains gray and is surrounded by a bright-red or purple ring, whereas black-rot spots soon turn brown or black. Within twenty-four to forty-eight hours numerous brown or black fruiting bodies (pycnidia) of the fungus appear within the previously light-colored area, causing the whole spot to turn reddish-brown or black. The affected berries shrivel and dry, and in about a week become hard, black mummies that cling tenaciously to the cluster stem. The mummies are covered with small pimple-like structures that contain spores.

Control.—An effective control material, used on American grapes, is ferbam. Not only is it more effective than Bordeaux mixture; it does not injure the vines. According to McGrew and Still (1972), three or four ferbam sprays are sufficient. Applications should be made when the shoots are 18 to 24 inches long; just before bloom; immediately after bloom; and seven to fourteen days later. Especially important are the applications before and after bloom. Under very favorable conditions for the fungus additional sprays may be required.

The fungus overwinters in mummified fruit, affected canes, and tendrils. Control is assisted by burning the prunings and plowing the vineyard in the spring to turn under mummified fruits and other disease-carrying material.

DOWNY MILDEW (PERONOSPORA)

The fungus *Plasmopara viticola* Berl. & Toni, which causes downy mildew, is native to eastern North America. It was carried to Europe before 1878, probably on American vines imported as grafting stock to combat phylloxera. It is now probably present in most grape-growing regions of the world, though unknown in California. Its seriousness in any region or season depends on the humidity and on the frequency and duration of summer rains or heavy dews. A physiologic form of this fungus has been found in abundance in some years in California on the native wild grape, *Vitis californica*. Inoculation trials by Santelli (1957) showed that this California strain does not reproduce on varieties of *Vitis vinifera*. It attacks

Vitis californica, V. girdiana, V. arizonica, and V. *treleasei,* but these are also injured—and more severely—by the true *P. viticola.*

Symptoms.—The first evidence of infection is the appearance of light-yellow translucent spots on the upper leaf surface. The leaves in the center of the vine are infected first. Soon patches of white mildew form on the underside of the leaf. These patches are caused by spore-producing organs of the fungus growing out through the stomata. If the spots are numerous, most of the leaf surface may be involved. The tissues of affected portions are killed, later turning brown. Badly affected leaves finally become dry and crumpled and drop from the vine. In wet seasons varieties that are poorly cared for may be completely defoliated by late summer or early fall; defoliated vines cannot ripen their fruit or mature their canes. Early in the season succulent shoots, petioles, and tendrils may be attacked; the affected parts have a water-soaked and slightly swollen appearance and may later be covered with a downy growth of the fungus. Flowers and young fruits may be attacked and killed; afterward they fall from the cluster. Late-infected berries wither, turn brown, and finally shrivel into mummies that shatter easily from the cluster. All varieties of *Vitis vinifera* are very susceptible. All cultivated varieties of American grapes are more resistant than the *vinifera* varieties, and some are not severely damaged except under conditions very favorable to the disease. The muscadine varieties are attacked but little, if at all.

Control.—The fungicide still most widely used for control of downy mildew has been Bordeaux mixture. On American grapes in the eastern United States a 4-4-100 concentration is generally satisfactory. Three sprayings are usually sufficient: just before bloom; just after bloom; and eight to twelve days later. The concentration and number of applications, however, will depend on the susceptibility of the variety and the conditions favoring the fungus. Earlier and later sprayings may be required.

In recent years a number of organic fungicides, such as zineb, maneb, and captan, have been used with success against downy mildew in the countries where they are registered for grapes. They may not be as effective, but they appeal to the grower because they are less toxic than Bordeaux mixture to leaves, flowers, and newly set berries (Suit, 1948).

The fungus overwinters in old, affected leaves on the ground. During wet weather in late spring, spores are released and are carried to the living leaves by rain splash or wind; if the leaves are wet, the spores germinate, and the fungus grows into the leaf tissues through the stomata.

DEAD-ARM

The dead-arm disease of grapevines occurs in certain vineyard districts of California in the interior valleys from Tulare County northward. It has been particularly severe in Sacramento and San Joaquin counties when there was rainfall after the start of growth. It has been reported in the eastern United States, Canada, several European countries, and South Africa.

Cause.—Dead-arm disease is caused by a fungus identified by Pine (1958), to be *Phomopsis viticola* (Reddick) Sacc.

Symptoms.—The disease is named from the killing of spurs and arms, which usually becomes apparent when the buds fail to push in the spring. Other ·symptoms develop on the leaves, shoots, and cluster stems. They are most frequent on the lower part of the shoot (fig. 114). Numerous small spots usually develop on the leaf blade, evident on both sides. These

FIGURE 114: Dead-arm in the variety Tokay. Symptoms on shoot and leaves. (*Courtesy of W. B. Hewitt*)

spots first show within three to four weeks after a rain. They are often light green, with brown to black pinpoint centers that have yellow borders. When very numerous, the spots run together, forming large spots having many dark specks and when this occurs, together with appreciable wind, the dead areas are torn out, giving a ragged appearance to the leaf. Some leaves develop blackened areas along the veins, and parts of the leaf blade die as the leaves mature. The leaf stems often show similar spots, with dark centers or larger dark-brown areas that crack open.

The shoot stems develop small spots with black centers very similar to those on the leaves. These are the first evidence of the disease. Often, many of these spots run together and form irregular black crusty areas that crack. Some cause the shoot to split open, forming long longitudinal cracks into the tissue. Severely affected shoots are often dwarfed. In fall and winter these affected areas become bleached, with many black raised specks scattered over the surface.

The cluster stems and the pedicels of berries are often affected, especially on shoots with diseased leaves. The spots resemble those on the petioles and shoots. Late in the season some of the spots on cluster stems may grow into the berries and rot the fruit.

During fall or winter, the dead parts of canes, shoots, and leaf stems become infected. These parts usually develop whitish bark, with numerous small black specks scattered over the surface. Almost all varieties of grapes grown commercially, both *vinifera* and American species and hybrids, are susceptible to the dead-arm disease.

Climate and the disease.—The dead-arm fungus is favored by cool weather, and when the pycnidia are wet by rains or the dripping moisture of heavy fog or dew, the spores are ejected profusely. As the spring warms up, the fungus slows down; during much of the summer, growth seems to stop. As the days cool in the fall, the fungus resumes activity, and the spots on canes and leaves enlarge. During winter, the dead-arm fungus is very active in the canes, spurs, and arms of the vine. It produces numerous pycnidia in the bark.

Control.—Early pruning is recommended for removing as many of the diseased canes as is practical. This should be done as soon as the leaves drop, or in California not later than November before the winter rains begin. The prunings should be burned.

Spraying with benomyl or captan has given very good control. During most seasons, a single spray when the shoots are about 1 inch long will suffice. This spray has given effective protection of the first 6 to 8 nodes of shoots. In seasons when late rains are forecast, however, it may be advisable to apply a second spray when the shoots are about 6 to 8 inches long.

Hewitt (1951) found that spraying with sodium arsenite to control black measles may also give fair control of dead-arm.

BLACK MEASLES

This disease is known by various names, such as Spanish measles, black mildew, esca, and apoplexy, in different localities. In California the names black measles and Spanish measles are generally associated with the speckling that occurs on the skin of the berries.

Symptoms.—According to Chiarappa (1959b), the symptoms may develop in any season, but frequency is highest in midsummer. Leaf symptoms vary from small chlorotic areas between the primary veins, which gradually enlarge and become necrotic, to the stage in which the only green tissue of the leaf is along the main veins. In red and black grape varieties the interveinal necrotic areas have a dark red margin. Some leaves show no chlorotic clearing; instead, their normal green color is replaced by numerous bronzed areas scattered throughout the blade. In still other instances, though less commonly, there is clearing of the small veins in the interveinal tissue and bulging of the tissue. These areas later become necrotic, while the rest of the leaf remains normal.

Symptoms on the fruit also vary. They usually consist of dark purple spots or blotches on the surface of the berries (fig. 115). They may become apparent at any time between berry set and the beginning of ripening. The spots may be all over the berries or only in scattered areas. Some clusters may be affected while others appear normal. Severely affected berries may crack and dry on the vine; in less severe cases the fruit remains turgid and normal in shape. At times a characteristic pungent taste is detectable in spotted fruit of varieties that are otherwise neutral in taste.

There is no direct correlation between symptoms in leaf and fruit. Symptoms may be present in one and not in the other. Single shoots or entire vines may be affected. Symptoms may be present on individual vines one year and not the next. According to Hewitt (1957b), a low or moderate percentage of affected vines may show symptoms every year for several years in succession. Further, there is no pattern of distribution of this disease in vineyards.

Black measles is rare in young vines. In older vineyards both frequency and severity increase with the age of the vines. Vines without heart rot in the head of the vine never show symptoms of black measles. This indicates that decayed areas are necessary to the disease.

Cause.—Chiarappa (1959b) found that the soft, spongy decay of vine wood seems to be identical with the white rot described in the literature as caused by *Fomes igniarius* (L. ex Fr.) Kickx—one of the most destructive of wood-rotting fungi, attacking both the heartwood and sapwood of many species of trees. Chiarappa considers this fungus to be the causal organism. He further indicates that *Cephalosporium* sp. may have some function in the decay process and eventually in the black measles syndrome.

Grape Diseases and Disorders

His data very definitely show that the organism, *Stereum necator* Viala, long thought to be associated with black measles, is not involved.

Control.—The treatment for black measles is to spray or swab the trunk and arms during the dormant season with a solution of 3 quarts of a prepared sodium arsenite solution (containing 32.5 per cent, or about 4 lb., of arsenic trioxide per gal.) to 100 gallons of water. Special care should be

FIGURE 115: Black Measles in the variety Thompson Seedless. (*Courtesy of W. B. Hewitt*)

taken to wet all old wounds thoroughly and to avoid as much as possible the wetting of the one-year-old wood. The treatment is applied only after the vines have become thoroughly dormant. In seasons when the vines do not become fully dormant, experience shows it is best to delay treatment to another year. The spray may be applied before or after pruning. If after pruning, the treatment should be delayed until at least three weeks after pruning and be completed before the buds begin to swell in the spring. If a spray machine is used, a moderate pressure is recommended. To prevent arsenic injury to canes through the leaf scars, the spray must be directed towards the trunks and arms of the vine.

Sodium arsenite is very poisonous, and care must be taken to keep it away from people and animals and to avoid getting it on the skin or in the mouth and nose of the persons applying the spray.

Experience shows that control is much more effective if all vines in the vineyard are sprayed. Spraying only diseased vines does not much reduce the number of diseased vines, since not all diseased vines show symptoms every year.

Successive annual sprays with sodium arsenite, according to Nelson (1952), may tend to reduce the yield in some varieties. It is therefore advisable to skip one, two, or more years between sprayings. Spraying every three or four years may be necessary to keep the disease under control.

Fungi Attacking the Fruit

Many of the fungi discussed above attack both the vegetative parts of the vine and its fruit. Some do more damage to one or the other, but under favorable conditions for their development they attack both. The organisms discussed below, in contrast, attack only the maturing or mature fruit.

BLUE-MOLD ROT

The common blue-mold fungus (*Penicillum* sp.) that causes this rot is a weak parasite, and infection begins in fruit injuries from rough handling, too tight packing, or other causes. Under conditions of high humidity like those in a packed box, the fungus, once well established, is able to spread to sound berries in contact with decaying ones. In cold storage or in transit the fungus frequently forms a rather heavy growth on the stems if grapes have not been fumigated with sulfur dioxide; it seems to grow into the berries by way of the pedicels. The tissues of decaying fruits become slightly brown and soft. The mold growth is white at first and becomes bluish green when the fruiting bodies of the fungus form in profusion on the surface of affected stems and fruits. All fruits thoroughly infected with it have a moldy odor and taste.

If thinning has been properly done, this rot is not of great importance as a field disease of table grapes. In the principal areas of table grape and raisin grape production the temperature is too high for its best development. In wine grape varieties with compact clusters in cooler regions, however, it continues to be a serious disease.

The control in harvested table grapes consists in careful handling and packing, followed by proper fumigation with sulfur dioxide (0.5 per cent SO_2 in air for 20 min.) and prompt precooling and cold storage, with repeated fumigation at regular intervals (see p. 598). At present there is no effective treatment against this fungus in wine grapes if the clusters are so compact that berries are crushed or pushed loose from the stem as the maturing berries enlarge.

BLACK-MOLD ROT

In some varieties the clusters are so compact that the pressure of the berries against each other as they grow becomes sufficient to break the skin of some berries or detach them from the pedicels. Such breaks in the skin of ripening berries, together with the juice leaking from them, furnish a favorable medium for germination of the spores of the black-mold fungus. Insect injury—for example, that of the raisin moth in the San Joaquin Valley—may also provide favorable conditions for the fungus to start growing in compact clusters.

Cause.—Black-mold rot is caused by *Aspergillus niger* Van Tiegh., a thermophilic organism; hence it occurs most frequently in hot regions. The spores of this organism seem to be present everywhere, but they are able to infect grapes only when there are skin breaks or punctures, or when the ripening grapes are wet—as, by rain or sprinkler irrigation during maturing. The rot spreads to adjoining berries only when the berries are in contact or when the skin of a sound berry is wet by the juice of a decaying berry. All varieties with compact clusters are susceptible; loose-clustered varieties are seldom attacked except during or immediately after rainy periods. High temperatures—70 to 100° F.—favor development of the organism.

Symptoms.—The black-mold rot is a watery, odorous decay, characterized by masses of powdery black or dark purplish-brown spores (fig. 116). By the time the grapes are harvested, the decayed berries are often only shells and the spores of the fungus so numerous that small clouds of dust-like spores are released when these valueless clusters are handled. Occasionally brown, buff, and green mold rots caused by other species of this organism occur.

Control.—Of the many fungicides that have been tried, none controls this type of bunch rot. Berry thinning to reduce the compactness of the clusters, as used with table grapes, is usually too expensive for use with most raisin and wine grapes. Pruning and managing the bearing unit to spread out the fruit may tend to reduce the damage. Since irrigation and other

FIGURE 116: A cluster of Perlette showing bunch rot caused by *aspergillus niger*.

operations that increase berry size favor the fungus, judicious use of water just after set and as the fruit approaches maturity may prove worth while. Christodoulou *et al.* (1968) found that a 10 ppm spray of gibberellic acid at 50 per cent capfall reduced the berry set of Carignane by over 50 per cent. This virtually eliminated black-mold rot. In different climatic regions or on different varieties the concentration of the gibberellin may have to be adjusted up or down to obtain the desired degree of berry thinning. The reduction in set can be compensated for by leaving more buds at pruning (*see* chemical thinning, p. 361).

The black-mold rot is primarily a vineyard disease of ripening grapes and does not develop further after packed grapes are cooled to refrigeration temperatures (32 to 40° F.). Prompt cooling and fumigation with sulfur dioxide give effective control in shipping.

RHIZOPUS ROT

Rhizopus rot has a wide distribution. It is of importance on grapes, peaches, berries, and strawberries (Harvey and Pentzer, 1960).

Cause.—The organism that causes this rot in grapes is *Rhizopus nigricans* Ehrenb. ex. Fr. This, like the black-mold fungus, is a thermophilic organism which, in California, occurs most frequently in the warm interior valleys. Rhizopus gains entrance to the fruit through cracks or breaks in the skin of the berries caused by excess pressure of the berries against each other during enlargement just before and during ripening. This rot causes juice to drip from the attacked clusters. As a result, the organism is much more damaging to wine grapes than to table grapes, since proper thinning of the latter reduces or eliminates the possibilities of skin injury. Rough and careless handling of table grapes, however, will damage the berries, providing conditions that favor development of this fungus.

Symptoms.—On grapes, Rhizopus causes the berries to become soft. As the fungus spreads through the berry, it breaks down the tissues and allows the juice to escape and leak from the clusters. Under the usual conditions of moisture and temperature of the San Joaquin Valley, the fungus is characterized by a heavy growth of coarse white mycelium and small, sperical, spore-bearing heads (sporangia), at first white and shiny, later becoming dull and black. In cold storage and in refrigerator cars the growth of mycelium is scant and the sporangia are dense gray or black masses close against the fruit.

Control.—Berry thinning in table grapes with compact clusters reduces infection. Beyond this, development of the organism is retarded by thorough trimming to remove injured and infected berries, fumigation with sulfur dioxide, and prompt cooling. A delay in precooling is especially serious, since it gives the fungus time in which to become established. *See* use of gibberellin in chemical thinning (p. 361).

BOTRYTIS (GRAY-MOLD) ROT

According to its degree of development and the variety of grapes, the gray mold may enable the wine maker to make a highly esteemed wine, or it may be a serious disease of ripe grapes in the vineyard, in transit, or in cold storage. In the Sauternes region of France, and in certain areas of Germany, grapes are left on the vines until late in the season in order to develop this mold, the "noble rot." There, under favorable weather conditions, the fungus, *Botrytis cinerea* Pers., causes the grape skins to crack and the berries to turn brown and dry into a sort of moist raisin with low acid, low nitrogen, and very high sugar content (30 to 40 per cent). Such berries are picked, separately or as parts of clusters, and from them are made highly aromatic natural sweet wines. Fortunately or unfortunately, according to the point of view, proper natural conditions for the development of the noble rot do not exist in California, but its beneficial effect has been produced by Nelson (1957), using a procedure of infecting harvested grapes with a culture of Botrytis and then holding them under favorable conditions of temperature and humidity for the fungus to do its work. The feasibility of this procedure has been demonstrated on a modest scale in several wineries.

Development of Botrytis rot.—Free moisture on the surface of fruit, from rain or cracked berries, is most conducive to infection, though infections will take place readily, according to Nelson (1951), in an atmosphere of very high relative humidity (92 to 97 per cent). Insect injuries to berries also provide places for infection. Infection will take place within eighteen hours at about 60 to 70° F. and during longer periods at higher and lower temperatures—for example, about thirty-six to forty-eight hours at 40° F. and about seventy-two hours at 35° F. Development at low temperatures indicates why this is one of the most serious diseases of grapes in transit or storage.

Grapes harvested early in the season usually have less Botrytis rot than those harvested later. The reason may be the generally lower susceptibility of berries of low sugar content. Also, in late season the weather is cooler and periods of high humidity are longer. If dry weather follows the infection, berries may dry up on the cluster or remain firm yet turn brown; they do not become soft enough to cause marked collapse of the tissues. If the weather remains wet, however, the rot may spread rapidly and involve most of the cluster—especially in the compact clusters. Cool weather, instead of checking the rot, seems to favor it, probably by limiting the growth of other fungi that may be present.

Symptoms.—Areas of skin that slip freely from the grape characterize early stages of Botrytis rot. The first signs of the disease in colored grapes are 2–3 mm., circular, faintly cleared spots, usually beginning to show about seventy-two hours after inoculation. Rubbed with the fingers, the skin under these spots slips from the berry leaving the firm plup exposed. Nelson (1956) found that if one presses the skin over the infection it will crack. After infection has developed for about five to seven days, the fungus grows out through cracks in the skin of berries and produces large masses of gray to buff-colored spores (fig. 117). It is in this stage that the disease is called gray mold. Boxes of fruit in storage, if not fumigated to prevent the mold, may be severely damaged and have large, compact masses of rotten fruit covered with gray mycelium and spores.

Control.—Most infections that develop in transit or storage originate in the field. McClennan (1972) and McClennan *et al.* (1973) found that

FIGURE 117: Gray-mold rot in the variety Tokay caused by *Botrytis cinerea*.

infection may occur at bloom: the spores then remaining dormant until the fruit begins to ripen. In storage the fungus develops and spreads from the field-infected berry to others around it. In trials designed to prevent this field infection Harvey (1955, 1959) and Harvey and Pentzer (1960) found captan to be effective. Three or four applications of captan dust are recommended, beginning about July 1 while the clusters are still open, and followed by applications at intervals of three to four weeks. This is a type of insurance. In years that favor Botrytis, dusting repays Emperor growers well. Stellwaag-Kittler's (1969 and 1970) results indicate promise of Botrytis control with benomyl in a number of wine grape varieties. Captan and benomyl are effective against this organism.

If shipment of table grapes not treated with captan or benomyl is to be resumed after a rain, one should delay picking for several days to a week to let infected berries become brown, so that they can then be found and be trimmed from the clusters before the grapes are packed. In storage the standard control of this fungus is fumigation with sulfur dioxide immediately after packing and at appropriate intervals thereafter.

SUMMER BUNCH ROT

This disease continues to be a problem on grapes in the San Joaquin Valley from Madera south. Strobel and Hewitt (1964) have identified the causal organism as *Diplodia natalensis* P. Evans. Infection of the fruit occurs during blooming, but the fungi remain inactive until the berries begin to ripen. This fungus can attack sound berries. The rotting produced by it, like that of *Rhizopus*, causes the affected fruit to leak or drip. This organism also causes cane blight. It lives in the soil; hence, when the shoot tips touch the soil or are buried in it by cultivation, they become infected. Infected canes may be killed back severely. No chemical is known for the control of summer bunch rot. Best control is to cut canes to prevent cane blight; the fungus will die out in soil in about 3 years and infection will drop to very low level.

CLADOSPORIUM ROT

Cladosporium rot, caused by *Cladosporium herbarum* Pers., occurs on grapes held for long periods in cold storage. According to Delp *et al.* (1951), it may be found at normal storage temperatures, the infections developing at 39 to 86° F.

Symptoms.—This rot occurs periodically as sharply delimited dark spots of decay beneath the skin that spread very slowly, do not penetrate deeply, and are firm and comparatively dry. The affected tissue, being firmly attached to the skin, is readily removed with it. Although the dark spots develop on the berries in storage, growth of the fungus is not usually apparent until the fruit is held at room temperature, when a sparse olive-green development of conidia takes place.

Control.—Fumigation with sulfur dioxide reduces post-harvest infection of grapes by this fungus and slows the spread of the decay to sound berries in transit or storage. Damage from this fungus, however, is usually not serious enough to justify the cost of applying the fungicides.

ALTERNARIA ROT

Decay caused by species of *Alternaria* and *Stemphylium* may develop in Emperor and other varieties during storage. Infection seems to take place during harvest, even in the absence of rain. The fungi gain entrance to the berry through the pedicel, causing a localized tan or brown decayed area. Attachment of the berry is weakened, so that affected berries are readily shaken from the cluster. Fumigation with sulfur dioxide reduces development and spread.

RIPE ROT AND BITTER ROT

Grapes are sometimes attacked when ripening or ripe by the fungus that causes bitter rot in apples, *Glomerella cingulata* (Stoneman) Spauld. & Schrenk. It is not known to be in California, even on apples, and is not a factor in any region of practically rainless summers. In the East, Southeast, and Middle West it occasionally causes heavy losses. Berries, canes, and fruit pedicels may be attacked, but ripe rot is of importance only on ripening or ripe fruit. The diseased flesh of the affected berry becomes reddish brown or rose-colored, and the surface is sunken. The lesions enlarge in concentric zones until they involve the whole berry, which becomes a brown or purple mummy that shatters easily from the cluster. Affected berries are not bitter.

Another rot, called bitter rot, is caused by the fungus *Melanconium fuligineum* (Scrib. & Viala) Cav. It produces similar symptoms, except that the decayed pulp has a bitter taste.

Both ripe rot and bitter rot are usually controlled with the sprays applied to control black rot. If experience shows later sprays to be needed, copper acetate (4 lb. to 100 gal. of water, with a suitable spreader) is preferred to Bordeaux mixture because it leaves less residue on the fruit.

WHITE ROT

The fungus causing white rot, *Charrinia diplodiella* (Speg.) Viala & Ravaz, is probably native to the eastern and central United States, although first reported from Italy. Occurrences are not often serious anywhere in the United States and are not known in California. This fungus occasionally causes heavy damage in Europe when hot, humid weather favors its development. White rot may attack the shoots and, rarely, the foliage of the vine; the principal damage is done to the clusters, stems, and berries. The fungus, according to Perold (1927), enters through wounds, such as those produced by hail. Stems of the clusters are attacked, and brownish depressed cankers are formed that may enlarge to girdle the stem. Then the entire cluster or the part beyond the girdle withers and dries, and may drop. Affected berries become very juicy and afterward turn whitish-gray and dry up, with brown or brownish-black conidia appearing on the surface.

Special control measures are seldom necessary. The sprays for black rot or downy mildew should also control white rot. An application of copper acetate as recommended for ripe rot, is advisable immediately after any hail damage.

FUNGI ATTACKING THE ROOTS OF GRAPEVINES

OAK-ROOT FUNGUS (ARMILLARIA ROOT ROT)

Many kinds of plants, especially trees and shrubs, are susceptible to a root rot caused by the fungus *Armillaria mellea* (Vahl) Quelet. It was first observed on grapes in California about 1887. The regions most infected in the United States are in the central, southwestern, and Pacific Coast areas. The fungus is native to California, on oak trees and other woody plants. It survives in the soil on decaying roots and wood fragments for some years after the aerial parts of the trees or shrubs are gone. It is carried from place to place on infected wood or infected nursery trees. Once established, the parasite may slowly spread from one plant to another by means of dark brown, cordlike fungus strands (rhizomorphs) growing out from infected roots—for several yards through loose soil and for lesser distances in firm soil. The tip of a growing rhizomorph is white. When a tip comes in contact with a susceptible root, it penetrates the surface by force. After the tip makes contact with living tissue, the strands flatten out and exude enzymes that destroy the cells of the host in advance of the plaques. Under favorable conditions the fungus also produces toadstool- or mushroom-like fruiting bodies. It is doubtful that the spores from these fruiting bodies are able to infect healthy plants. They may, however, establish the parasite in rotting stumps or other favorable situations, from which the fungus can grow to living plants. This may be a form of spread in forests, but it would hardly occur in cultivated vineyards. Once the fungus is established, it lives from one year to the next in the tissue of the host and in the soil.

Symptoms.—Vines attacked by Armillaria root rot show a gradual decline in vigor as parts of the root system are progressively destroyed. Vines may linger on for several years before dying, or, without showing marked symptoms of distress, may suddenly collapse and die when the fungus girdles the underground stem or large roots. When the bark is removed from an affected root, the inner bark and cambium layer are found to be replaced by white or cream-colored mycelium in the form of conspicuous, fanlike plaques or sheets of fungus growth. The wood is also invaded. In late stages the normal consistency of the root is entirely changed, first becoming as if water-soaked and afterward soft and decaying. The odor of the decaying bark and wood has a sharp, rather agreeable, mushroom-like odor; it is not sour or putrid. The white mycelium is never found in nature on the surface of the root, being always buried within or beneath the bark. The rhizomorphs that grow out from diseased areas under favorable conditions resemble small roots, but they branch in a different manner and are smooth and shiny.

No varieties of grapes are known to resist oak-root fungus. Land known to be infested should not be planted to vines without prior thorough fumigation.

Control.—The most promising remedy is soil treatment with carbon disulfide or methyl bromide. Although expensive, it is worth while in vineyards that have relatively small infected areas from which the fungus is spreading or where the value of the land and crop potential warrants the expenditure. Either of the treatments, properly applied, is effective.

SOIL FUMIGATION

Application of either carbon disulfide or methyl bromide should be made in summer or early fall when the soil is fairly dry. A low moisture content is particularly advisable in heavy soils and for deep penetration. The area to be treated is cleared by removing all vine trunks and roots to a depth of 12 inches.

With carbon disulfide.—The surface is pulverized to form a loose mulch and, if possible, is wet 2 or 3 inches deep by sprinkling in order to form a seal that will prevent the escape of the gas from the soil. While the surface is still wet, the carbon disulfide is injected at a depth of 12 inches in holes 18 inches apart and staggered in rows 18 inches apart. The application is 2 ounces by weight (one and three fifths ounces by volume) of carbon disulfide in each hole, the hole afterward being plugged by packing the soil with the heel of the shoe. As soon as the treatment is completed, the entire surface is packed down by dragging or rolling, and, when sprinkling can be done, the surface should be rewet.

The carbon disulfide may be injected in various ways. A simple way is to make the holes with a bar gauged to the proper depth and then pour a measured 2 ounces into the hole through a funnel. Hand-operated applicators are available that will inject measured quantities of the liquid into the soil at the desired depth. Automatic, power-pulled machine applicators are available for hire from distributors of carbon disulfide. When the carbon disulfide is applied with power equipment, the soil is not wet before treatment or after, but the surface is firmed with a cultipacker or roller (most power units have a heavy roller mounted in back of the drill). The grower should allow a minimum of 300 gallons per acre.

The treatment should kill the fungus to a depth of 5 to 6 feet in sandy or loam soils. If vine roots go deeper, the dose must be increased accordingly or part of the dose applied at 30 inches.

The effectiveness of this treatment is hard to determine until three or more years after replanting. In some vineyards where the method has been used, parts of the area have had to be treated again. In others, diseased vines at the margins of the treated plots have indicated that the application did not include all of the affected vines.

With methyl bromide.—In soils with gravel or stones, however, carbon disulfide may be ignited by sparks when the applicator strikes a stone. In such soils methyl bromide may be used. Again, since A. *mellea* is found in the pithy center of the trunk and larger roots, these parts of the vines must be removed. The soil should be dry to or near the wilting point. According to Munnecke, Kolbezen, and Wilbur, Department of Plant Pathology, University of California, Riverside (personal communication), 2 pounds of methyl bromide as liquid, gel formulation, or in chilled cans are placed at a depth of 3 feet in otherwise undisturbed soil (600 pounds per acre). The injection hole must be tightly compacted to prevent escape of the gas. Avoid placing the charge in less compacted soil where vines have been removed. It is better to apply it in an area of undisturbed soil near the vine locations. Random application at 12 x 12 feet pattern gives adequate dosage in the entire intervening soil mass from 1 to 10 feet deep or more. To provide a lethal dosage in the upper foot of soil the entire treated area must be tarped. The tarp should remain intact for at least a week. The use of a water seal has not yet been proved adequate.

According to Munnecke *et al.* (1970), A. *mellea* is not killed outright by this fumigation but is sufficiently stressed so that it is killed by the biological complex in the soil in three weeks or more.

OZONIUM ROOT ROT, COTTON ROOT ROT, OR TEXAS ROOT ROT

In parts of Texas, Oklahoma, and states westward, including a few local areas in southeastern California, the Ozonium root rot attacks the roots of many plants, including the grape. It is caused by the fungus *Phymatotrichum omnivorum* (Shear) Duggar, which requires high soil temperature, abundant moisture, and alkaline soils. Since grapes are not an important crop in most regions infested with this fungus, the disease is economically much more important on cotton, alfalfa, and other crops. It could probably assume great importance in the vineyards of the San Joaquin Valley if it should become established there. It is of great importance in the vineyards of Mexico.

Early symptoms of the disease are a dull, yellowish appearance of the foliage and a tendency to wilt during mid-afternoons. Badly affected vines may die suddenly, as a result of extensive killing and decay of the roots. A network of buff-colored fungus strands, characterized by 90° branching, is abundant on the surface of diseased roots. When frequent rains keep the soil surface moist, the fungus grows on the surface of the soil, where it may produce conspicuous spore mats, cottony white at first, becoming buff-colored and powdery later. Grapes should not be planted in infested areas.

DEMATOPHORA ROOT ROT

In European vineyards Dematophora root rot is found mainly in local areas of poorly drained soil. It is of little or no importance in open, well-drained soils. Although the casual fungus occurs in California, this root rot has never been reported in California vineyards. This would indicate that it is less serious on grapes than on apples and some other fruits. If present in poorly drained soils, it may attack grapes and appear on the dead and diseased vines in patches or in spots resembling the spots caused by phylloxera or oak-root fungus. The disease is caused by the fungus *Rosellinia necatrix* (Hart.) Berl., which, under favorable conditions, attacks both large and small roots, causing them to die and rot. The fungus grows between the bark and wood, and into the wood. In manner of killing and the superficial appearance, Dematophora root rot somewhat resembles oak-root fungus (*Armillaria*), but its growth between the wood and bark is more delicate, and it does not form the dense, fanlike plaques of mycelium or the rhizomorphs produced by the oak-root fungus. Further, it produces no toadstool-like fruiting bodies. The mycelium that develops on the surface of affected roots is at first white and cobwebby, later turning black. During wet weather a delicate, pure-white mold growth may be seen on the surface of the bark and in the soil around the base of the plant. The most reasonable control on grapes is removal of the conditions favoring this rot, i.e., improving the drainage.

ROOT ROT

Root decay of grapevines caused by *Pythium oligandrum* Dreschsler was observed by Williams and Hewitt (1948) in solution cultures at Davis. Some years ago a decline of vines in areas of the irrigated vineyards of the interior valleys of California was found by Chiarappa (1959b) to be caused by fungi of the genera *Pythium* and *Phytophthora*.

Symptoms.—According to Chiarappa (1959a), delayed and weak growth characterize affected vines; sometimes they are said to be "running out," or degenerating. The foliage of these vines is restricted, pale in color, mottled, and subject to burning during midsummer. Fruit set is poor. The canes do not mature properly in autumn; often they are killed back severely by early frost. The roots reveal abundant necrosis and abnormal branching; a reduction in feeder roots is always associated with the decline.

Control.—The use of certain resistant rootstocks is indicated as a control measure. The rootstock 1613, the only one used in Chiarappa's studies, showed little to no injury by *Pythium ultimum*. Further tests will be required, however, before definite recommendations can be made. If rootstocks are tried on a test basis where this decline occurs, the 1613 should be included. Some control may result from greater attention to the use of water, especially preventing overirrigation.

Van der Merwe and Matthee (1972) report that *Phytophtora cinnamoni* is responsible for the decline and death of vines in several districts of South Africa. Young vines suddenly die in summer even though they had an extensive root system and appeared healthy the previous year. The leaves turn yellow or red and the roots are mostly dead. This disease may occur in nurseries as well as mature vineyards. In the vineyard, vines die singly or in patches. The trouble appears to be more prevalent in heavy soils, that at times may be water logged. Some rootstocks, such as Richter 99, Richter 110, and Rupestris du Lot, are more susceptible than Jacques, 101-14, or 143-B. The authors also report this form of root rot in India and Australia.

COLLAR ROT (STEM GIRDLING)

Young vines, one to four years old, are occasionally attacked in the spring by a species of *Pythium* that causes a wet, sour-smelling lesion to form at or just below the surface of the soil. Cool, wet conditions favor its development. As the soil becomes warm and dry, the fungus stops growing. Under favorable conditions the lesion enlarges rapidly and may destroy the cambium and phloem, girdling the vine (fig. 118). Completely girdled vines suddenly wilt and die in late spring and early summer. Those partially girdled are weakened and stunted to various degrees, depending on the extent of girdling. Most of the partially girdled vines

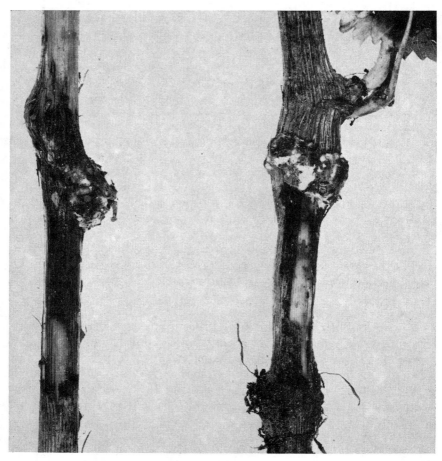

FIGURE 118: Collar rot at ground level in young vines. (*Courtesy of W. B. Hewitt*)

Grape Diseases and Disorders

recover, and the wound eventually heals. Recovery and healing, however, may require several years.

Vines in soils that tend to remain wet late in the spring seem to be affected by collar rot more often than those in porous, well-drained soil. Collar rot sometimes occurs when wet soil is plowed against the trunks just as the vines are starting growth. Some varieties seem more susceptible than others, and vines grafted onto Rupestris St. George rootstock are attacked more often than ungrafted vines or those grafted onto other varieties of rootstocks. Old vines are seldom affected.

Control is effected by removing the soil (taking care not to injure the vines in the operation) to a depth of 3 or 4 inches around the base of the vines, to allow the bark to dry. When the rainy season is over, the soil will become dry and can be crowded back to the vines, as will occur in normal cultivation.

BACTERIAL DISEASES

Bacteria have been associated with vine diseases, but doubt arises in most cases as to whether the bacteria were the primary cause or simply a secondary phenomenon. Only two seem worthy of discussion.

BLACK KNOT, CROWN GALL

In this disease, galls or overgrowths form on the trunk and arms of the vines and, in sandy soil, on parts of the roots. The galls are caused by the organism, *Agrobacterium tumefaciens* (Smith & Town) Conn., which is ever present in the soil. The infection points are injuries or wounds from any cause. Entry is often made through cracks in the bark of the trunk or arms caused by freezing. Rains splash soil laden with the bacteria into these wounds, and bacteria may be washed onto wounds from other galls or from the rough bark of the vine. Infection in California usually occurs only during the winter.

Lehoczky (1968, 1971) and Melenin (1969) indicate the nature of the attack of the pathogen, show that it may be present in the vascular system of the vine, and that it may be spread by cuttings and grafts of vines that are infected in certain areas of Europe.

Symptoms.—Gall development becomes apparent in the cracks when growth begins in the spring. When young, the galls are soft, cream to greenish in color, with no bark or covering. As they age, the tissue darkens to brown; the surface becomes open-textured, moderately hard, and very rough. The surface tissue of the gall turns black as it dies (fig. 119).

Control.—The disease is not generally serious in California vineyards except where winter freezing causes the trunks and arms to crack. The only control measures normally needed are to avoid cutting into the galls

FIGURE 119: Black knot, following winter freezing injury. (*Courtesy of* W. B. *Hewitt*)

with pruning tools, lest the disease be spread to healthy wood subsequently cut with the contaminated tools. Most of the galls disappear after one to several years if left alone. There is no chemical registered for use on grapes to control crown gall in the United States. For control in other countries see Zinca and Rajkov (1969).

BACTERIAL BLIGHT

"*Tsilik marasi*" of Greece, "*Ulamsickte*" of South Africa, "*mal nero*" of Italy and Sicily, "*gelivure*," "*gommose bacillaire*," "*la maladie d'Oleron*" (Prunier, 1970) of France, and "bacterial blight" are all one and the same disease. This blight is not known in the United States. Until Panagopoulos (1969) succeeded in isolating *Xanthomonas ampelina* Sp. Nov.

from disease grapevines and then produced bacterial blight by artificial innoculation, it was thought that this disease was caused by *Erwinia vitivora*. He also demonstrated that *Erwinia vitivora* has no pathogenic ability.

Among the varieties regarded as fairly resistant are Malbec, Cabernet-Sauvignon, Carignane, Ribier (Alphonse Lavallée), and Folle blanche; more susceptible varieties include Alicante Bouschet, Grenache, Muscat of Alexandria, Dattier (Waltham Cross), and Black Corinth. Most American varieties are resistant.

The bacteria enter the vine through wounds made in pruning, topping, suckering, fruit thinning, and otherwise. Symptoms on young shoots show first near the base, as small, pale, yellowish-green spots without definite margin. The spots soon become grayish-black and expand slowly along the shoots, producing dark stripes or streaks that ultimately extend the entire length. On more mature shoots the discolored areas may not be continuous. The tissues beneath the discolored areas disintegrate and crack, sometimes as deep as the pith. Very young shoots may be totally invaded, blackened, and killed before they are more than 4 inches long. Late-infected shoots may die back from the tips, ripen poorly, or develop cankers at the nodes, though they do not crack deeply. If infected canes are retained for spurs or fruit canes, the buds on them may be infected and not start, or the shoots may be badly stunted. Infection may pass into the main portion of the vine. Ultimately the vine may be killed. Roots may be infected when diseased scion material is used in grafting.

The disease may pass from infected shoots into the leaves through the petiole, causing black discoloration of the infected veins and yellowish or reddish-brown dried areas in the surrounding tissues. Primary infections on the leaves cause fairly well-defined, dark brown spots surrounded by a yellow border. Infected leaves drop early, often causing partial or complete defoliation of the shoots. Clusters or cluster parts that become infected are killed; usually they drop off.

Control is effected by using resistant varieties. With susceptible varieties there should be careful pruning to remove infected canes, sterilizing of pruning tools and cuts with a suitable disinfectant, and prompt burning of the prunings.

According to Matthee *et al.* (1970) the regular copper sprays recommended in the standard vine disease control program have largely controlled this disease in South Africa.

RICKETTSIA-LIKE DISEASE

Pierce's disease.—This disease, was listed and discussed as a virus disease in the earlier book. Work by Goheen *et al.* (1973) and Hopkins and Mollenhauer (1973) show a Rickettsia-like organism to be associated with the diseased grapevines. This separates it from the diseases caused by a virus, but its symptoms, transmissions, and potential destructiveness remain unchanged. Usually only a very, very low percentage of vines is infected each year, but under very favorable conditions for its spread, whole vineyard areas have been destroyed—example are the destruction of vines in Southern California, 1883–1886 and in the San Joaquin Valley in 1937–1944.

This disease, which is confined to the United States and northern Mexico, has been found in most vineyard regions of California except the hot desert. Although it is active in certain areas, the number of vines destroyed each year is small—probably less than 0.1 per cent. In a study of its host range, Freitag (1951) found that the pathogen infests many host plants, including shrubs, grasses, and weeds; it also causes alfalfa dwarf. According to Frazier (1965), the disease is spread naturally by three or more species of sharpshooter leaf hoppers and by spittle insects. As recorded by Winkler *et. al.* (1949), the development and epidemic spread of this disease is related to periods of high rainfall which favor the growth of host plants and the number of insect vectors. Because of the poor maturity of the wood of affected vines, this disease is rarely spread by cuttings. These usually fail to root. Buds from affected vines that are budded or grafted into healthy vines, however, may transmit the disease even though they fail to grow.

The first symptoms of Pierce's disease are scalding and burning of the leaves in late summer. Scalding is characterized by a sudden drying of a part of the leaf while it is still green. The tissue around the margins and the tips of the large veins dries up and later turns brown. The area of scalding varies from a small part to as much as half of the leaf (fig. 120). Leaf burning is usually preceded by a yellowing of tissue before the leaf dries and becomes brown. This starts at the margin of a part of the leaf and progresses, sometimes in concentric zones, toward the point of attachment to the petiole. In the early stage of the disease these symptoms may occur on only one shoot or on a lateral shoot of partially mature canes arising from a single arm or branch of a vine. All of the symptoms become more severe as the season advances. Severely affected leaves drop, leaving the petiole attached to the shoot or cane. The fruit on shoots showing early leaf symptoms may be checked in growth and then wither; if scalding occurs late in the season, however, the fruit may color prematurely, become soft, and wither.

In the next and later seasons Pierce's disease is characterized by delayed growth in the spring, followed by very slow growth of the shoots of affected parts of the vine. The first 4 to 8 leaves on the shoots often show interveinal chlorosis or mottling. The mottling is most intense in the first leaves, becoming less so in each successive leaf formed on the shoot. The first leaves

FIGURE 120: Pierce's disease in the variety Palomino. A, leaf scalding; B, irregular maturing of canes. (*Courtesy of W. B. Hewitt*)

may also be deformed. As the season advances, the leaves will show more severe scalding and burning and will drop; in severely affected vines the shoots may die back from the tips. The fruit withers before harvest. The canes fail to mature uniformly: irregular patches of green bark remain on parts that in regular maturing would be of normal cane color. The decline of the root system of affected vines closely follows that of the top.

According to Hewitt (1958), the culture of *vinifera* grapes for a hundred years in the areas of California where Pierce's disease first occurred indicates that the virus is not indigenous. This deduction is further supported by the fact that V*itis girdiana* and V. *californica*, the native grapes of California, are very susceptible to this disease. On the other hand, since grape species native to the Gulf Coastal Plain region in the United States, where Pierce's disease is also found, have resistance to the disease and in some instances immunity, the indication is strong that it is indigenous to that region. It might very well have been the principal cause of the failure of the extensive planting of *vinifera* varieties on the Tombigbee River in Alabama in the 1820's. Crall and Stoner (1957) have shown it to be the cause of the decline of those varieties in Florida. Diseased vines should be removed and replaced with layers, layer grafts, or rootings.

MYCOPLASMA-LIKE DISEASE

Flavescence dorée (not known in the United States).—A disease identified by Caudwell (1964) as being caused by a virus. More recently he and his co-workers have shown it to be caused by a mycoplasma-like pathogen. Caudwell *et al.* (1971b) transmitted the causal agent from vines to herbaceous plants and back to vines, using its vector, the leafhopper, *Scapoideus littoralis* Ball.

Caudwell and Schvester (1970) reported that it can be transmitted by budding or grafting. To date, natural spread of this disease was thought to occur only in the southwest of France where the leafhopper, *S. littoralis*, is present. Now a very similar yellows disease—"bois noir"—is known in Burgundy. It is not transmitted by *S. littoralis* (Caudwell *et al.*, 1971a). These workers have also identified another yellows disease with identical symptoms. They suggest that these diseases, which are caused by the same infective agent be called "vine yellows." *Vitis* was formally thought to be its only host, but that is no longer true.

Vines infected with flavescence dorée are stunted in growth. Buds may fail to grow, there is a progressive shortening of the internodes, and certain parts of the leaf blade may fail to develop. In the more susceptible varieties the shoots are rubbery and assume a weeping posture. The leaves harden, with edges rolling downward, and overlie one another to produce a scale-like appearance. The shoots fail to mature and remain green over their entire length. A golden-yellow area shows on the hard and brittle leaves where they are exposed to the sun. Creamy-yellow spots then appear along the leaf veins. The spots rapidly become necrotic giving the diseased vine a characteristic appearance. Early infection causes the flower-clusters to dry up and drop off. When the infection is late, the grapes wrinkle before the cluster stems are dry. The berries have a bitter, fibrous pulp.

VIRUS DISEASES

A number of viruses infect grapevines. Hewitt (1971) described a number of these and appended an extensive bibliography. Some of the viruses cause a gradual decline that reduce yields and fruit quality and shorten the life of vineyards (Boubals, 1971). Others are more deleterious for the reason that they often do great damage to a vineyard before a grower discovers the cause. Even more serious, however, as shown by Hewitt and Delp (1953), is the fact that fanleaf, yellow mosaic, vein banding, and yellow vein become established in the soil, so that, at least for a number of years, the soil is unfit for replanting to vines unless it is fumigated.

Cause.—Virus diseases are caused by an infective agent that may be transmitted by budding or grafting wood from a diseased vine on to a healthy vine. To determine whether a pathological condition of a vine is caused by a virus, the vine is "indexed". The first step is to prove, by culturing and microscopic examination, that there are no microorganisms present that may cause the disease. Then, buds or scions from the diseased vine are budded or grafted onto healthy, but very sensitive, vines. If the budded or grafted vines develop symptoms similar to those of the original diseased vine, buds and scions of these new diseased vines are taken at some distance from the original buds or grafts and are budded or grafted onto a second series of healthy vines. If these vines also develop the same symptoms, it is evident that the infective agent causing the disease was transmitted by buds and grafts. It is also evident that the causal agent, assumed to be virose in nature, increased in these vines and spread through them. These same criteria and transmissions by vectors have been used and accepted to indicate the presence of other pathogens such as Rickettsia-like and mycoplasma-like pathogens of plants. The electron microscope is presently used to identify the presence of the latter two types of plant pathogens.

Spread.—A prime mode of spread of virus diseases between vineyards is by man. Consequently, great care should be exercised in selecting buds, scions, rootings, and grafts to make sure that they are free of disease. Natural vectors—insects, mites, nematodes, and fungi—are also important modes of spread of viruses and virus-like diseases. Modes of spread of all viruses of vines have not been determined. The following viruses are known to be spread in the soil: fanleaf, yellow mosaic, vein banding, yellow vein, arabis mosaic, and Hungarian chrome mosaic.

Virus Diseases Spread in the Soil

Fanleaf.—Brought to California from abroad many years ago, fanleaf was identified by Hewitt (1939) as a virus disease. The early spread was by propagating wood taken from affected vines. More recently Hewitt *et al.* (1958) found that the endemic spread is by *Xiphinema index* Thorne & Allen, an ectoparasitic nematode. No aerial vector is known. In France this disease is called *court-noué* and is one of the chief contributors to *dégénérescence infectieuse*. In Italy it is called *arricciamento* or *roncet*; in Portugal, *urticado*; and in Germany, *reisigkrankheit*. It is present in all countries of Europe, in North Africa, and elsewhere.

The common symptoms of fanleaf, according to Hewitt (1950) are: stunted early shoot growth; shoot and leaf deformity; light mottling of the

Grape Diseases and Disorders

young leaves; shelling of flowers; and distinctly invigorated vine growth from midseason on. The shoots are slow to start growth, and they continue to grow slowly for a time; they are also slender and have a tendency to zigzag at the nodes. The leaves are usually small and folded upward along the center vein, and on the young shoots they tend to stand upright along the shoot axis. At maturity the leaves assume a normal position and unfold, and after early summer they are of full size. The early leaves on the shoots show varying degrees of deformity: in some varieties the petiolar sinus—the inlet in the blade where the petiole is attached—opens to as much as 200 degrees, giving the leaf veins the effect of a closing fan; in other varieties, the leaf surface becomes rough and pitted; in still others the leaves develop deeply serrated, nettle-like margins (fig. 121). It is common for many leaves to be asymmetrical. In addition to the deformities already listed, the leaves may show various patterns of mottling, such as variegated shades of green, veinlet clearing, speckling, rings, and oak-leaf-shaped areas. In some instances the mottling seems to leak from the veins into the leaf tissue, forming lighter green blotches of various shapes.

In the early stages of fanleaf the mature canes may be almost normal in length, because of the increase in the rate of growth after midsummer. The base of the canes may usually be zigzagged, with enlarged nodes, short

FIGURE 121: Fanleaf in the variety Mission. (*Courtesy of W. B. Hewitt*)

internodes, and sometimes double nodes. Double nodes and short internodes may be found on normal vines, though much less often than on diseased ones. Since vines with fanleaf disease carry little or no crop, the canes mature ahead of healthy vines carrying full crops. This fact has led unsuspecting vineyardists, who wanted to do early field budding, to take buds from such vines. At that season the diseased vines do not show their condition, yet an inspection of the crop and of the condition of the growth at the base of the canes would reveal the distinguishing symptoms of fanleaf.

The flower clusters on vines with fanleaf disease are usually smaller than those on healthy vines; they shell badly, are straggly, and poor clusters are the rule. In advanced cases the vines fail to set fruit—the flower clusters wither away.

Since this disease is transmitted by nematodes, it stands to reason that healthy vines will become infected if planted in soil from which diseased vines have been removed and where *Xiphinema index* nematodes are present. The soil will be unsafe for at least as long as the roots of the removed vines remain alive in it, which may be a number of years.

Yellow mosaic.—A few vineyards of California have had yellow mosaic for many years. Hewitt (1935) proved it to be a virus disease. At that time it was appearing in young plantings. This disease is widely distributed in the older grape-growing countries of the world. Although it does not seem to kill vines, it markedly stunts them and reduces crops.

Yellow mosaic is caused by a virus that is readily transmitted from diseased to healthy vines by budding or grafting. Diseased propagating wood—scions, rootstocks, or cuttings—are the primary means of spread into new plantings. Hewitt *et al.* (1958a) showed that *Xiphinema index* nematodes spread it in the vineyard in an expanding circular pattern. Recently, Sohn *et al.* (1970) have shown that X. *Italiae* is a vector of this virus. The virus is retained in the roots of diseased vines left in the soil and is transmitted from them to the roots of the new vines. How long the virus may remain active in the soil is unknown.

This disease is characterized by chrome-yellow leaves in striking contrast to the bright-green foliage of healthy vines in spring. The shoots, leaves, stems, and flower clusters may be yellow. The degree of yellowing will differ with variety, season, and the strain of the virus. The flowers usually shell off, so that little or no crop is produced.

The leaves of vines with yellow mosaic disease may show several patterns of symptoms. The mottling may range from a slight flecking of yellow or cream color about the small veins to a marked clearing or yellowing along the large veins, and from a slight speckling and spattering of light or pale yellow, to complete yellowing (fig. 122). As the leaves age,

FIGURE 122: Yellow Mosaic in the variety Grand noir. (*Courtesy of W. B. Hewitt*)

some of the yellow is replaced by green and some of it fades to a cream color that is later bleached. The bleached areas usually burn and dry up later in the season.

Vein banding.—Another soil-borne virus is characterized by light green or chrome-yellow banding of the veins of the leaf (fig. 123). The symptoms usually develop after midsummer and are most conspicuous in early autumn. Some leaves may be asymmetric and free of yellowing along the veins. Many flowers shell off, followed by the set of a few small, seedless berries along with some normal berries to give the clusters a straggly appearance.

The vein banding virus is soil-borne. Goheen and Hewitt (1962) present strong circumstantial evidence indicating its vector to be *Xiphinema index*. Its natural spread is outward from an infected vine or area. This virus has

FIGURE 123: Vein banding in Thompson Seedless variety. (*Courtesy of W. B. Hewitt*)

been wide spread by propagation wood in Europe and to a lesser extent in California, South Africa, and Australia.

Yellow vein.—Yellow vein was shown by Hewitt (1956) to be transmissible by budding or grafting. No other method of spread has been identified, though there is indication of a slow spread from infected areas. Gooding and Teliz (1970) found that *Xiphinema americanum* is a vector for yellow-vein in herbaceous plants. It has been found in many varieties and in at least one rootstock in California. Vines affected with yellow vein, except for seedless varieties, are prone to produce very straggly clusters, with some shot berries or only shot berries, and some may become entirely fruitless (fig. 124).

The leaf symptoms range from a yellow speckling in the palm of the leaf to a distinct yellow vein banding. The vein banding first becomes apparent as a mild chlorosis along the veins, turning yellow as the leaves mature. These symptoms develop most frequently in the lower 10 to 15 leaves on the shoot, but yellow veining has been found in the tip leaves of shoots of some varieties. The disease tends to be unnoticed since the symptoms are not very striking early in the season and usually appear on only a very few of the lower leaves.

Arabis mosaic (not known in the United States).—The symptoms are indistinct in old vines in Germany and France where this disease was

FIGURE 124: Yellow Vein in the variety Emperor: lower, fruit symptoms; upper, leaf symptoms. (*Courtesy of W. B. Hewitt*)

first observed. There its symptoms are masked by those of fanleaf and yellow mosaic. In young vines of some varieties, according to Hewitt (1965), it causes the formation of broad, dark yellow stripes along the primary leaf veins. He reported such symptoms in Hungary, Chile, and Argentina. Its spread is primarily by infected propagating wood and probably by the nematode *Xiphinema diversicaudatum* (Stellmach, 1970).

Hungarian chrome mosaic (not known in the United States).—It has been present in Hungary for many years where it was confused with iron deficiency. According to Martelli *et al.* (1970), this disease has been found in vineyards north of Lake Balaton and southwest of Budapest.

The characteristic symptom is the chrome-yellow or whitish color of the leaves in early spring, which differs from yellow mosaic in that it does not fade or burn. The color may cover the entire leaf or only sections next to veins. Sometimes only single arms of the vine are affected. Leaves may be deformed and the canes have double nodes and short internodes.

There is strong evidence that this disease is soil borne; that is, when healthy vines are planted where diseased vines have been removed they contract the disease. The dagger mematode, *Xiphinema vuttenezii,* is found in the areas of diseased vines.

VIRUS DISEASES APPARENTLY AIR-BORNE

The diseases discussed here appear to be air-borne, yet no vector has been identified. They are leafroll, asteroid mosaic, corky bark, and necrosis of the grapevine.

Leafroll.—Leafroll is characterized by a rolling downward of the leaf margins, reduced fruit color, and a markedly lower sugar content of the fruit at the normal time of harvest. The causal virus is readily transmitted from infected to healthy vines by budding or grafting. Scheu (1936) states that it has been present in central Europe for hundreds of years; it was so widespread, in fact, that it was not recognized as a disease and was accepted as the normal condition. For many years there was confusion about this disease and what was called the white-Emperor condition. Now, as the result of work by Goheen *et al.* (1959), leafroll and the white-Emperor condition are recognized as one and the same disease. Leafroll is spread in propagation by the use of infected wood. Goheen *et al.* (1958) report that there is evidence of some natural spread in central Europe, but none in California.

Vines with leafroll are usually less fruitful than healthy vines. The affected vines of different varieties show differing degrees of loss of vigor and productivity. Some varieties evidence little effect; others, such as Melon, decline and become unfruitful. Harmon and Weinberger (1956) found that the development of color in the fruit of the affected vines of thirty-five varieties was only about one third that of the fruit of adjacent healthy vines, and that the Brix reading of the expressed juice was 6 below that of mature normal fruit. The difference in acidity (0.46 as against 0.43 per cent) was negligible; thus the lower color and lower total soluble-solids value could not be attributed altogether to a delay in maturation of fruit.

A distinct downward roll of the leaf margins and leaf chlorosis characterize this disease in most varieties. The rolling shows first on the oldest leaves, near the base of the shoots. Rolling usually does not occur before early August. Then, as the season progresses, the rolling becomes more pronounced, so that by late September most of the mature leaves on infected vines show this deformity (fig. 125). The new leaves at the ends of the shoots rarely show the rolling. Chlorosis of the leaf margins and interveinal tissue—yellow for white varieties, red for black varieties—becomes apparent as rolling advances. The large veins usually remain green.

Symptoms of leafroll and potassium deficiency are somewhat similar. In leafroll, however, the early rolling of the leaves takes place in the basal leaves on the shoot, whereas in potassium deficiency the leaves along the middle length of the shoot are the first to show the symptom.

No vector for leafroll has been found, yet it is the most wide-spread virus disease in California. According to Goheen (1970), there are two reasons for this: (1) the virus does not interfere with propagation, so there is no natural elimination of infected stocks, and (2) the virus does not produce symptoms in grape rootstocks that may carry it.

Asteroid mosaic.—Hewitt and Goheen (1959), demonstrated that asteroid mosaic can be transmitted by budding or grafting. The symptoms are distinctly different from those of the other grape viruses in California. The leaf symptoms are characterized by small transparent veins that often coalesce to form starlike spots (fig. 126). When these spots are numerous, they form translucent areas, most frequently between the primary and secondary veins. Marginal serrations are cut more deeply than is normal, and blisters of normal green tissue occur in the leaves of some varieties. In most varieties the symptoms tend to become less severe during summer.

FIGURE 125: Leafroll in the variety Burger. (*Courtesy of* W. B. *Hewitt*)

Grape Diseases and Disorders

FIGURE 126: Asteroid Mosaic in the variety Merlot. (*Courtesy of W. B. Hewitt*)

The affected vines are stunted and produce little fruit. The incidence of this virus is very low in California vineyards. Asteroid mosaic is also found in Italy and South Africa.

Corky bark.—The disorder was first recognized by Hewitt (1954) in California. It has been transmitted to healthy vines by grafting. Transmission trials by Beukman and Goheen (1970) have been negative with both herbaceous and woody plants other than grape. It has been identified in Mexico, Yugoslavia, Italy, and South Africa. It seems to be specific for *Vitis*.

Many grape varieties show no symptoms of corky bark except reduced vigor. Budding out in spring is delayed and some vines have dead spurs. Shoots tend to droop while the tips are upright. The shoots are limber and mature irregularly with green areas interspersed with normal lignified areas.

The leaves of diseased vines are smaller, become pale early, roll downward, and persist on the vines after those on normal vines have abscised (the leaves of red fruited varieties turn red). In some varieties the young leaves at the shoot tips are light yellow. The bark of the current season's growth splits into longitudinal cracks that become pronounced fissures as the shoots mature into canes. With aging of the wood retained at pruning, the bark continues to split, instead of dropping off in shreds, and acquires a very rough appearance (fig. 127). Affected vines are low in vigor and productivity.

The spread to date has probably been by infected cuttings, rootings, or grafts.

Necrosis of the grapevine (not known in the United States).—According to Fic and Vansk (1970), this disorder appears in several vineyard areas in Czechoslovakia. It has a circular pattern of spread, suggesting a virus. Spread has been by diseased propagating wood. Leaves may be asymmetric. Greenish-yellow spots appear between the veins, which gradually shade into the green vein-banding tissue. This tissue then becomes necrotic, turns brown, and breaks out, leaving only the petiole and main veins with a border of leaf tissue. The vines are stunted and production falls.

FIGURE 127: Rough bark in the variety Petite Sirah. (*Courtesy of W. B. Hewitt*)

A number of vine conditions somewhat resembling the appearance and effect of virus infections have not responded to the usual techniques of identifying viruses (Hewitt, 1954). These are carried along in the propagating wood and show in the progeny vines. They are enation, legno riccio, and shoot necrosis.

Enation.—Enation is characterized by the formation of very small, leaf-like outgrowth—enations—from the lower surface of leaves, usually along the larger veins (fig. 128). The growths are most frequently on leaves at the base of the shoots. Besides enations there may be contortion or bulging of the tissue between the large veins near the base of the leaf. Many leaves do not have enations, but are smaller, more leathery, and thicker than is normal.

Affected vines are often slow to leaf out in spring. Internodes near the base of the shoots may be very short, giving the vine a bushy appearance.

FIGURE 128: Enation in the variety Tokay. (*Courtesy of* W. B. *Hewitt*)

In addition, according to Graniti *et al.* (1966), the base of the shoots may be flattened and bear furrows and ridges. The axillary buds fail to develop normally, tending to be over size, and produce abnormal outgrowths. The shoots have a tendency to downward rather than upright growth. They are not limber or rubbery. The vines are stunted, and the crop is less than that of normal vines.

Grapevine yellow speckle.—A newly recognized, graft-transmissible disease of grapevines. It is present in California, but does not show symptoms, and in Australia, where its symptoms are conspicuous. According to Taylor and Woodham (1972), the symptoms consist of small yellowish-green irregular speckles ranging in size from pinpoint to 1 mm on exposed mature leaves. The speckles are usually along the main and smaller veins, but may be scattered in the interveinal tissue. Sometimes only 1 or 2 and rarely more than 20 leaves on a vine show symptoms. The symptoms usually develop in mid-summer and may intensify in early autumn and become chrome yellow. Young vines sometimes show speckling in late spring. The symptoms vary widely among varieties, age of vines, and environmental conditions. As indicated above, no symptoms develop in California, yet varieties taken from California to Australia developed symptoms there.

The authors cited above state that there are no obvious effects of this disease on growth, fruit set, or production. Spread is by grafting or cuttings. There is no known natural spread. Healthy vines growing beside diseased vines do not become infected.

This disease does not respond to heat treatment. The authors cited above exposed plants of Mission and Sultana (Thompson Seedless) to 37–38° C. (99–100° F.) for as long as 396 days, yet they showed typical symptoms during their first 2 years of growth.

Some varieties imported into Australia many years ago and which have always been propagated on their own roots show typical symptoms. Luhn and Gold (1970) report a similar situation in Mission in California. Thus it would seem likely that grapevine yellow speckle originated in Europe.

Legno Riccio.—Legno riccio (known as bark and wood-pitting disease in California) was observed in this state for the first time by Hewitt and Neja (1971) in June, 1971. It also occurs in southern Italy, Hungary, Israel, and likely in South Africa (Engelbrecht and Nel, 1971). According to Graniti and Martelli (1966), it causes vine decline with progressive reduction of crops. Leafing out in spring may be delayed several weeks. In grafted vines there is a marked enlargement at the union and overgrowth of the scion. Leaves are distorted and the bark is rough. Scions of Primotivo di Gioia on 420-A rootstock die off in a few years, but the stock develops shoots, while in other combinations both stock and scion die. In some combinations the wood and bark of both scion and stock are pitted and ribbed in the cambial region, while in others only the stock is affected. The bark is usually thicker.

In California the disease showed strong symptoms of bark and wood-pitting in the variety Pinot noir grafted on Emerald Riesling vines. The Emerald Riesling were planted in 1963 and top worked to Pinot noir in 1968. It appears the virus was present in the Emerald Riesling since the Pinot noir scions came from vines that had been indexed and found to be free of known viruses (Hewitt and Neja, 1971).

Field evidence seems to indicate that this disease is soil borne. *Xiphinema index* was always present in soil where natural spread occurred. This appears to be a combination situation; that is, the stock may be a carrier of the virus but it does not show symptoms until combined with certain varieties.

Shoot necrosis (not known in the United States).—Martelli and Russo (1966) state that this disease occurs only near Apulia, Italy. Its origin can be traced to a single vine. Many young shoots are killed and ultimately the vines die. The principal symptom is the formation of minute brownish spots and lesions on the basal shoots. The lesions may be 10 to 15 centimeters long, they coalesce, and a large part of the bark tissue becomes necrotic. This may be followed by longitudinal splitting of the shoot to form fissures. The fissures heal, but the scars remain and give the canes a scaly and rough appearance. Aerial roots may develop from the arms. Cane maturing may be irregular. So far, transmission has been limited to diseased propagating wood. A virus is suspected but, as yet, unproved.

VIRUS-LIKE CONDITION

Spindle shoot.—Hewitt (1954) named this disease spindle shoot. The cause is not known. It causes unfruitfulness. The young shoots are not really spindly, but they seem so because the leaves are very small, puckered about the margins, and rolled downward. The symptoms are strong in early spring. They become less obvious to normal as the vine grows in late spring or early summer. This disorder has been observed in the French Colombard. The varieties Salvador, and Tinta Madeira show a similar but somewhat different disorder.

SPREAD AND CONTROL OF VIRUS DISEASES

Most of the virus diseases that concern the California vineyardist are known to exist in vineyards in Europe. How long they have been incident has not been determined. There is good evidence, however, that some of these diseases have been present in California for seventy or more years. They were brought in with imported vine-propagating wood. Unfortunately, these same viruses, and possibly others, are still being spread through exchange of wood among countries of the world. California has regulations controlling grape wood imports from abroad. Permits to import must be obtained from the Bureau of Plant Quarantine, State Department of Agriculture, Sacramento. Then, before the imported vines are released in California, they must be indexed to determine if they are free of viruses.

The distribution and potential seriousness of these viruses in California were not realized until the 1940's, though some were recognized before then. As early as 1912, in anticipation of Prohibition, the planting of wine grapes dropped sharply. There was a flurry of planting in the early 1920's, but it consisted almost entirely of own-rooted vines of common varieties for fruit to be shipped to markets in the eastern United States for home winemaking. Beyond this, the new vineyards and replants from 1920 to 1940 were largely of table and raisin varieties, again largely on their own roots. There were some diseased vines in these varieties, but the spread of virus diseases was slow and for the most part went unnoticed.

After the repeal of Prohibition, growers in the table-wine-producing areas of the State again became interested in planting premium quality wine varieties. These areas required rootstocks resistant to phylloxera. Scion wood of fruiting varieties and wood for rootstocks were both scarce. At the same time, little care was taken in selecting propagating wood. Cuttings for resistant stocks were taken from vines in old vineyards where the fruiting tops had died for some reason, probably because of disease or a virus, but the rootstocks, being more tolerant, had survived and were producing masses of canes, as they are today. Buds or scions of the fruiting varieties were also taken without selection. Often the bud wood was taken from vines that matured their wood early. In some instances the early maturation was owing to little or no crop. These haphazard means of collecting propagating wood resulted in the rapid and widespread dissemination of a number of virus diseases. This unfortunate situation did, however, arouse interest in and concern for the production and longevity of the vineyards.

Control.—The best control of these diseases is the avoidance of infected propagating wood. Wood for propagation should be certified to be free of virus diseases. Rootstocks, if such are to be used, must also be certified.

In view of the rapid spread of these diseases, the Department of Viticulture and Enology and the Department of Plant Pathology, University of California, with the support of the grape industry, in 1952 initiated a project for the production of vine-propagating wood that is free of known viruses, true to name, and of good productivity. Adequate amounts of virus-free wood of most fruiting varieties, as well as rootstocks, are now in the hands of nurserymen and private growers. If not available, by placing the order as early as possible it can be filled by means of rapid mist-propagation before the season for planting is over (see p. 202). These must carry the certificate of the State of California Nursery Service as to their freedom from viruses. Even with the present flurry of planting, be it fruiting sorts or rootstocks, it is only wise to use certified vines and plant in soils known to be free of grape virus diseases.

Elimination.—Gifford and Hewitt (1961) found that it was possible, through a combination of heat treatment and shoot-tip (mesophyll) culture, to rid vines of viruses. Potted vines are placed in a suitable chamber at a constant 100° F. (38° C.) and kept there for 60 to 90 days; then, shoot-tips ½ to 2 inches long that grew while in the hot chamber are removed and rooted under mist culture. Plants so produced are free of known viruses, as well as of some viruses that may not have been indicated in the usual indexing. Rives (1970) persued this research further and found that an entire young plant can be ridded of fanleaf. He used rooted cuttings taken from fanleaf vines of St. George and grew them in a special hydroponic pot at 38° C. (100° F.) for 163 days. The vines were then indexed and found to be free of virus.

Note.—It is difficult to determine the presence of all viruses in grapevines. Although the vines listed as being free of virus diseases have been indexed on a known susceptible host, heat treated, etc., there remains the possibility that some selections are not free of all viruses. However, using the techniques and indicator plants employed at the University of California, the selections are free of diseases under our conditions. We do not guarantee freedom from all viruses or from viruses that may show diseases in other locales or countries.

Soil fumigation.—The work of Vuittenez (1960) indicated that DD was the most effective of the chemicals being tested. It gave satisfactory control of *Xiphinema index* in the shallow soil of France. Some reinfestation occurred in soils deeper than 3.5 feet. Hewitt (1962) also found that the early recommended dosages of DD did not control *X. index* in the deep soils of the Napa Valley of California. Where virus-infected vines were removed, root pieces remained alive and produced new roots for some years. Hence, the surviving nematodes—some did survive—had a ready source of the virus. This led Raski *et al.* (1971) to apply the fumigants at higher dosages and/or at split levels. They achieved excellent control with carbon bisulfide at 250 gallons per acre placed at 8 inches deep on 18 inch centers and with 1, 3-dichloropropane at 200 gallons at 30 inches on 18 inch centers plus 50 gallons at 8 to 10 inches deep on 12 inch centers. Soil preparation is an important factor; it should be worked to seedbed condition. The effectiveness of this soil treatment may be further insured by ridding the soil of live root pieces. This was achieved to a high degree by spraying the vines to be removed with a concentrated solution of 2,

4-D; 2 gallons of 2, 4-D solution to 100 gallons of water. With 5 grams of the chemical applied to a vine, in full leaf, immediately after harvest, the roots were killed to a depth of 9 feet.

The ultimate success of this control procedure remains to be proved. Even if fumigation does not end all possibility of immediate reinfection, it may very materially reduce the waiting period between the removal of a diseased vineyard and the time when replanting is safe. The effect of soil type on the effectiveness of the fumigant must be considered.

NONPARASITIC DISORDERS

Salinity injury.—Salinity injury caused by high total salts can develop in arid regions or from continued use of irrigation water that is high in chlorides. The injury first appears as a marginal chlorosis, which is followed by progressive necrosis of the leaf blade toward the petiole until only the main veins remain green. The line of demarcation between the green and the brown tissue is sharp. The grape is rather tolerant to salt, but all varieties are susceptible to salinity injury, though not equally so. Ehlig (1960) found the Cardinal and Black Rose to be more severely injured than the Perlette or Thompson Seedless when these varieties were grown side by side in the same sand beds. The Cardinal and Black Rose accumulated chloride two to three times as rapidly as the Perlette and Thompson Seedless.

Woodham (1960), in Australia, found that the chloride content of the petiole of the Sultana (Thompson Seedless) increased rapidly as the season advanced. A content of 1.9 per cent in December or 2.5 per cent in January was associated with severe burning of the basal leaves, restricted growth, and poor yields. In Israel, Ravikovitch and Bidner (1937) found that vines of Chasselas and Muscat Hamburg deteriorated and died when the accumulation of chloride in the dried leaves ranged from 1.5 to 3.8 per cent. Working under controlled conditions in large sand beds, Ehlig (1960) demonstrated that 1.93 to 2.27 per cent of chloride in the dried leaves caused marginal burn and that hot weather accelerated the burn.

(For control of salinity injury see "Alkali injury," below.)

Alkali injury.—Another trouble of arid regions is caused by too high a concentration of sodium. The symptoms are indefinite and confusing. Vines growing in alkali soils are usually smaller than vines in clean soil; the shoots tend to have shorter internodes; the leaves are usually smaller and will often show burning similar to that associated with salinity injury, beginning at the margin if the soil becomes dry in hot weather; and, sometimes the leaves show large chlorotic areas between the larger veins. The discolored areas are whitish yellow, fading at the margins into the normal green of the surrounding tissue. Sometimes the vines show no symptoms other than smallness and poor crops. In other instances the vines may grow fairly well for one or more years; then, in midsummer, the leaves of some may burn suddenly, while growth stops. The worst-affected vines may die; others may be partly or completely defoliated. Cooler weather or an irrigation may cause the vines to start new growth, which may not mature, being killed by winter freezing. Such vines often die in subsequent seasons. Thus, alkali areas in the vineyard are usually characterized by weak or missing vines.

Control.—The remedy for salinity injury and alkali injury is to reduce the salt content of the soil. Usually drainage and leaching are required, and in the case of alkali the treatment includes certain soil amendments—for example, the application of gypsum, lime, or sulfur. Frequent irrigations to keep all parts of the soil moist may help temporarily, but frequent irrigation without good drainage is likely to increase, rather than decrease, the concentration of salt in the upper layers of soil: the increased evaporation from the soil surface increases capillary movement of the salt solution to the surface.

Coulure, shelling, and shot berries.—Flowers that fail to develop into berries usually drop from the cluster within a week or ten days after opening. A heavier than normal drop of flowers, creating loose or straggly clusters, is called shelling or coulure. Often, flowers that might drop remain on the cluster and develop into small, round, seedless berries (commonly called shot berries) instead of normal berries.

Winkler (1926) showed that flowers may fail to develop into normal berries because of poor pollination or fertilization, defective flower parts, or poor carbohydrate nutrition of the flowers before bloom. An excess of flowers in relation to leaves results in poor nutrition of the flower parts, and in some varieties, such as Muscat of Alexandria, the undernourished flowers set poorly. In such cases flower-cluster thinning is the remedy (see p. 339). A deficiency of zinc or boron creates in the vine a condition that prevents normal flower development and set (see "Little leaf" and "Boron deficiency"). When deficiencies are the cause of shelling and shot berries, correcting them will improve set. There is no known means of overcoming these disorders in vines infected with viruses.

Red cane.—Bright reddish canes in autumn are symptoms of the disorder called red cane. This condition occurs when the shoots fail to mature and their bark remains green until late in autumn, when it is turned pink to red by the lower temperature. It is not uncommon for the tips of shoots to fail to mature and become woody; however, when most or all of the shoots fail to mature, the level of the next crop will be seriously affected. This condition usually occurs when an overcrop delays the ripening of the fruit until very late and the season is over before the shoots mature into canes. The only widespread occurrence of red cane in California was in the southern San Joaquin Valley in 1938, following the un-precedentedly heavy crops of 1937 and 1938.

Red canes are characterized by low levels of reserve carbohydrate materials. Analyses (unpublished data) revealed that the reducing sugar content of red canes was only 50 per cent, and total sugars 30 per cent, of that of normally matured canes. Starch content was practically nil. Because of the poor storage of reserve materials, red canes are killed by frosts. Since not all canes on the vines are affected equally, late pruning, after the poor canes or parts of canes have been killed by frost, makes it easier to select the better wood for bearing units. The remedy is to control the crop so that both crop and shoots will mature normally and on time.

Bud failure.—Bud failure or a delay in bud growth in spring follows poor bud development caused by only partial wood maturity in the previous year. It is closely related to red cane, though less severe, since most of the basal parts of the canes that might be used for spurs or fruit canes usually mature to the color normal for dormant wood of the variety. Vines so affected are subject to varying degrees of injury by lower winter temperatures, depending on their state of bud development and wood maturity. The more nearly mature the wood, the less is the damage.

The delay of bud growth and extent of bud failure are also affected by how severe the low temperature is, when it occurs (early or late), and how long it lasts. If wood maturity is very poor, there will be bud delay and failure even without damage from low temperature.

Failure of wood to mature normally may be caused by any of the following conditions: overcropping; vigorous late growth owing to excess nitrogen and water in the soil; defoliation of the vines by insects or diseases in summer, followed by rapid new growth in late summer and fall; lack of potash; or disorders that upset the annual cycle of vine development, such as virus diseases.

Compared to most crops, grapes have a low requirement for nitrogen. Medium-textured and heavier soils probably have enough nitrogen between the surface and the first 6 feet of depth to supply most vine needs, if not all. Growers who add large amounts of nitrogen to vineyards on these soils are inviting problems in bud development, pre-bloom flower shatter, low counts of flower clusters, and bud failure.

Usually bud delay or failure occurs only in certain areas of a vineyard. This fact in itself is perhaps the best guide to the means of controlling the condition. A comparison of the vineyard operations, the water conditions, the soil conditions, nitrogen level, and crop level of the affected area with those of normal areas should indicate a solution.

Water berry.—There are two conditions of interrupted berry development called water berry. In one condition the affected berries are largely confined to the tip of the rachis; in the other conditions they may be scattered throughout the cluster.

Grape Diseases and Disorders

The first condition was described by Bioletti (1923) as a condition where the berries lack normal sugar, color, flavor, and shipping quality. He attributed this condition to overcropping, which prevented proper nourishment and complete development of the affected berries. The most common cause of undernourishment is overcropping. This form of water berry usually occurs at the tips of the clusters and, in more severe cases, in berries at the tips of large laterials of the clusters. In mild cases only a few berries at the tips of the clusters are lower in total soluble solids, higher in acid, and somewhat soft in texture. In severe cases the berries of part of the cluster tip may become dull in color and watery, shriveling as the season advances and then drying up entirely. In colored varieties this condition is called *red berry*, from the retarding of the coloring of the berries. Except for poor color development, the symptoms of red berry are identical with this type of water berry. In some cases this type of water berry has been reduced by potash application.

The second condition, in which the affected berries may appear in all parts of the clusters (fig. 129), is not associated with overcropping, nor with lack of potash. In fact, in the southern San Joaquin Valley, where this condition has been most frequent, Kasimatis (1957) found it most prevalent on thoroughly thinned, vigorous vines carrying crops well within their capacity. The evidence incriminates stresses induced within the vine by hot spells while girdling wounds are still open. The stresses seem to re-

FIGURE 129: Water berry; affected berries develop in all parts of the cluster. (*Courtesy of A. N. Kasimatis*)

sult from competition between the fruit and the vegetative parts, especially the leaves, for materials in short supply. Kasimatis showed that this condition was directly associated with plugging of the xylem vessels in the pedicel by tyloses. The extent of tylose development and its influence on the passage of water and other materials seemed to determine the degree of deterioration in berry development. When obstruction is nearly complete, the pedicel becomes necrotic, and both it and the berry dry up. When obstruction is only partial, the pedicel may continue to keep the berry alive, but the berry becomes a water berry—in this case the phloem vessels are also obstructed, and sugar is not moved to the berries.

On the basis of present information it is evident that both overly vigorous vines and excessive thinning of such vines should be avoided. When girdling is done on them, the cut should not injure the wood. Further research will be required for more definite directions for control.

Stem necrosis.—Stiellähme or *dessichement de la rafl* in central Europe was found by von Theiler (1970) to have its beginning in the stomata. From there it spreads into the surrounding tissue. As cells die, polyphenols are oxidized in the cells and cellwalls, which with enlargement of the adjacent live cells produces the characteristic necrotic condition.

This condition develops more often on very fertile soils in dry period following ample moisture. According to Koblet and Lauber (1968), Stellwaag-Kittler (1969), and Hartmiar (1971), it is owing to magnesium deficiency; that is, spraying the clusters with magnesium markedly reduces the instances of necrosis. Magnesium sulfate is more effective than the chloride because it may be used at higher concentrations without burning. From 0.5 per cent magnesium chloride to 5.0 per cent magnesium sulfate have been recommended. Calcium chloride or an antioxident may increase the effectiveness of the spray. Some have suggested a spray before and after bloom, while others recommend one or more applications beginning in August. The late spray should be directed on the clusters. Removal of leaves in the fruit zone may be advisable to facilitate this application.

WEATHER INJURIES

Spring frosts.—The succulent shoots and flower clusters of the vine may be killed by temperatures below 31° F. in spring. If warm weather and rapid growth have immediately preceded a frost, some killing of the most rapidly growing shoots is likely to occur if the temperature falls to 30° F., but if the temperatures are not lower than 30° F. and if they are of short duration and occur in periods of cool weather, damage is slight. A temperature of 26° F. or lower for a few hours will kill all green shoots and flower clusters—and even buds that are partly open. Between 26° and 30° F. the extent of the damage varies directly within the duration of the low temperature period, the daytime temperature preceding the frost, the rate of growth, the variety of grape, and, of course, the minimum temperature reached.

The reduction in crop caused by a severe spring frost will depend on how many fruitful buds have started growth at the time of the frost and on the fruiting habits of the variety. The first buds to grow are those uppermost on the vine, at the ends of the spurs. The lower buds and the basal buds of the spurs start later, if at all. Vines pruned very late tend to start growth later than vines pruned early. A very early frost catches only a small proportion of the fruitful buds in growth, causing less damage than a later frost that catches more buds in active growth.

Varieties that produce fruitful shoots from basal buds and from side growing points in dormant buds on the spurs always suffer less crop reduction from frost than varieties whose basal buds are not fruitful. Certain varieties—Zinfandel, Sauvignon vert, and Muscat of Alexandria, for example—regularly produce fruitful shoots from basal buds. Even basal buds left on the old parts of these vines by careless pruning in past years, or basal buds that have been dormant for some years (latent buds), may start growth after a severe late frost and produce nearly a full crop if handled properly. In contrast, varieties such as Thompson Seedless, which seldom have fruitful basal buds or fruitful side growing points in the dormant buds, may suffer almost complete loss of crop when a severe late frost occurs, for, then, only the buds on the spurs and fruit canes not yet in growth will have crop potential, and these only if they grow following the frost.

The probability of damage from spring frost is one of the major factors limiting the areas suited to grapes. Areas that have frequent frosts after the bud break should be avoided. Few regions, however, are entirely free from unseasonable weather. Accurate weather records, maintained over many years, furnish the best basis for predicting the frequency of damaging frosts in a given region. Areas adjacent to large bodies of water, such as oceans, lakes, and very large rivers—particularly areas on the leeward side in the seasons of frost—are less subject to frost than areas farther removed. Frost hazard is reduced if protection from continental winds is afforded by high mountains. In local areas the low-lying lands are more subject to frost than slightly higher adjacent lands because cold air, being heavier than warm air, tends to flow into the low spots.

Prediction of minimum temperatures for various locations in California is a function by the Weather Bureau stations of the federal Department of Commerce. Reports are released by newspaper and radio, and in some instances by telephone, each late afternoon and evening during the spring, and special warnings of impending damage are sent out if frost is expected. These predictions, based on reliable criteria, are far more accurate than the grower can make for himself on the basis of wet- and dry-bulb thermometer differences. Each grower must, however, know how the temperature in different parts of his vineyard varies above or below that of the Weather Bureau prediction if he intends to use the predictions as a basis for timing protective measures.

Protection from frost can be obtained by covering, heating, sprinkler or surface irrigation, and very late or double pruning. Covering with straw mats, muslin, or other material may be feasible in the back yard; it is impractical in large vineyards, though it is used in parts of Europe.

Heating is a common practice in citrus and deciduous fruit orchards, less common in vineyards. Grapes start growth later than citrus, pome, and stone fruits, thereby escaping most of the frosts. Furthermore, losses from frosts are usually less extensive with grapes, because of the fruit that may come from side growing points of the axillary buds or latent buds of many varieties after frosting. With some exceptions in a few areas, most California vineyardists in years past have considered the cost of equipment and preparation for heating to be greater than the crop loss from frost, averaged over the years. At present the higher prices of grapes, however, have made protection against frost profitable.

If the use of heating or wind machines is contemplated, a careful study of the cost and the probable benefits should be made. At present the cost of forty heaters, probably the minimum number per acre, for protection against the average frost hazard, would be about $400. Fuel for a single filling of the heaters must be held in storage for emergencies; this costs about $50 per acre. Normal depreciation and interest amounts to about 10 per cent, and to this must be added the annual cost of placing, filling, emptying, gathering up, and storing the heaters, even if the heaters do not have to be lighted. The most common fuel is oil; other fuels must be avoided because they fail to burn cleanly. Only the heat generated is of value; smoke smudge gives little or no protection. Modern oil-burning orchard heaters are constructed and adjusted to burn with minimum smoke; they are more efficient and also less objectionable to the community than any other type.

Wind machines may or may not be of value, depending on the temperature and the height of the inversion ceiling. Used in combination with heaters, they may reduce the number of heaters needed. The usual stationary wind machines add $300 to $500 per acre to the capital investment. Portable and less costly types are also available. In either case the machines must be depreciated over a short period; they are expensive to operate, and they must be well maintained if they are to operate when needed.

Sprinkler irrigation is the principle method of protecting against frost in California. (*See* p. 406 in chap. 16).

Very late pruning delays the starting of the buds on the retained wood. Pruning after some of the upper buds have grown 1 to 3 inches on the unpruned vines will sometimes delay the starting of the lower buds as much as a week to ten days. Delaying all pruning so long is, of course, impractical in large vineyards. With spur-pruned vines, results almost equally good can be obtained by cutting back the canes to be retained for spurs to lengths from 15 to 20 inches and removing all other canes. This is done at the regular pruning time. Later, when the uppermost buds have grown 2 to 3 inches, the spurs may be quickly cut back to the normal length. Similar results can be obtained with cane-pruned vines if the fruit canes are left 2 feet longer than usual and are temporarily tied in a vertical position. The uppermost buds will start first. When these have grown from 1 to several inches, the canes are cut back to normal length and tied in the usual horizontal position. This practice is called double pruning.

The first autumn frost seldom freezes ripe fruit. Damage to mature fruit by freezing is usually in the form of frozen cluster stems. The damaged clusters are unfit for table fruit, because the fruit soon develops a stale flavor, but they are acceptable for wine if used immediately. The temperature at which the berries freeze is governed by their sugar content.

In the autumn of 1971 a number of vineyards were protected from frost by sprinklers. This is common practice in some European countries. Californians have feared the possibility of bunch rot. However, by keeping sprinkler time to a minimum, rot has not increased. In 1971 maturing was late and a severe frost came early, so fruit on protected vines matured normally, while that on the frosted vines, with no functioning leaves, did not.

WINTER INJURY

Severe winter cold may kill the aboveground parts of vines. The degree of cold that the vines will stand differs according to the variety, the maturity of the wood, and the weather pattern preceding the freeze. All *vinifera* varieties, if the vines are fully dormant, will withstand temperatures down to 10° F. (−12° C.), but vines that are not well matured may be killed by less severe temperatures. At zero F. (−18° C.), *vinifera* varieties are usually damaged seriously, though a report by Vidal (1933) from France indicated that Folle blanche and Colombard, as well as certain red varieties, were but little damaged by temperatures of −2° F. (−19° C.) and −4° F. (−20° C.) Similar results were reported by Caramete (1960) from Romania. However, the senior author saw a number of vineyards in Europe that were virtually destroyed by a low temperature of −4° F. (−20° C.) in February, 1956. This freeze followed a period of moderately warm weather. Experience in New York indicates that Concord and most other American varieties are severely damaged by temperatures between

—8° F. and —18° F. (—22° C. and —28° C.). A few varieties, notably Alpha, Beta, Dakota, and similar varieties produced for Minnesota conditions, will withstand even lower temperatures without special protection.

Any sort of covering—snow, earth, straw, cornstalks, etc.—over the vines gives them some protection from cold weather. In cold areas where grapes are grown, the vines are kept small and close to the ground. Each fall a trench is plowed close to the vines, and they are laid over into the trench and covered with soil. As soon as the danger of freezing is past in the spring, they are uncovered and straightened. If the trunk and arms are completely killed by winter freezing, the vines must be re-built by using suckers that grow from the base of the vine; the underground part is seldom killed. Grafted vines may be killed to the union; rehabilitation is then impossible except by regrafting.

HEAT INJURY

A sudden rise in temperature after a cool period in late spring, when vine growth is very rapid, may kill the tips of the shoots. This injury is more likely to occur when a drying wind accompanies the sudden rise in temperature. The damage is usually limited to the tips of the shoots. As a rule, such damage is of minor importance, since the flowers are rarely injured. It merely checks growth for a time.

Injury may result from a spell of hot weather at any time from bloom to harvest. The type and amount of injury will vary. Single berries, parts of clusters, or entire clusters may shrivel and dry. Sometimes only berries directly exposed to the sun are injured. The condition is commonly, and properly, called sunburn. The affected berries shrivel, turn brown, and dry up. Other injury may occur on clusters that seem to be partly or totally shaded. Such injured clusters often have only a few berries, or none, that are obviously sunburned. The first symptom to be noted is a wilting of the berries, followed by shriveling and drying. In many instances the primary injury seems to be to the stem. Within a few days after the direct injury, parts of the stems become dry, and other parts show injured areas or streaks that turn brown or black. The part of the cluster beyond the injured area of the stem is the part that shrivels and dries. If the injury occurs early in the summer, the dried part may drop off or be broken off before the fruit matures. If it occurs later in the season, the affected clusters, or parts of clusters, may hang on until the fruit is harvested. In other instances the berries will shrivel without apparent stem injury. Within a few days the entire cluster, including the stem, becomes dry. These several conditions have been given various names: "grape shrivel" is probably the most common. No pathogen is involved. The injury usually appears soon after a hot spell that follows moderate or cool weather. A gradual increase in temperature as the season advances usually does not cause damage.

Similar injury has been produced experimentally (unpublished data) by raising the temperature of shaded fruit to between 104° and 106° F. The Tokay was particularly susceptible to such injury; Muscat of Alexandria was only slightly less susceptible than Tokay; Thompson Seedless and the other varieties included in the experiment were injured, though less readily.

Good pruning, adequate trellis, and good irrigation practices all tend to keep vines vigorous and reduce damage from sunburn and heat injury. Neglect usually increases it.

Almeria spot.—Another form of heat injury is called "Almeria spot," characterized by sunken areas in the surface of green and mature berries of the Almeria (Ohanez) and other heat-sensitive varieties. The spots are irregular in size and shape, have sharp margins, and in extreme cases may cover much of the berry. The affected tissues collapse, so that the area becomes noticeably depressed. The spot may darken nearly to black or may remain green. This trouble can be reduced by good vineyard care.

RING SCARRING

Ring scarring and buckskin-type corky areas have occurred in recent years on Perlette and Thompson Seedless that had been treated with growth regulators. Years of prior use absolved the growth regulators as causal agents. So Weaver et al. (1971) tested the effects of three wetting agents that had been used to obtain better coverage.

One wetting agent caused no scarring at 0.3 per cent or less, another caused a few light rings at 0.1 per cent, while the third was more toxic, causing distinct ring scars at 0.1 per cent. At higher concentrations all three agents caused increased scarring. Seldom, however, are wetting agents used in concentrations as high as 0.1 per cent (about one pound per 100 gallons).

HAIL

A severe hailstorm in summer can destroy an entire crop, defoliate the vines, and even drastically reduce the crop of the following year—by reducing leaf surface and thereby restricting fruit-bud formation (see p. 111). No practical protective measures are known that are applicable to vineyards. Close-mesh wire netting stretched above the vines is used occasionally to protect a few vines. Commercial vineyards should not be planted in areas that lie in the usual path of hailstorms. Hail damage is rare in the grape-growing regions of California and, when it occurs, is very limited in extent.

If serious hail damage occurs early in the season (May or June), the defoliated shoots should be cut back to spurs in order to produce several good new shoots for the next year's fruit wood instead of many weak laterals. If the damage occurs after midsummer, no special treatment is of much value.

LIGHTNING

On rare occasions lightning may strike a vineyard. If the vines in a small area show severe injury or suddenly die after an electrical storm, it may be easy to identify the cause of the injury or death as lightning. Sometimes shattered stakes assist identification of the trouble. More often, however, the vines reveal only necrotic areas along the shoots, with or without excretions, and wilting or shriveling berries, while the appearance of the leaves is almost normal. The bark of the shoots may be entirely brown, or brown over most of the area between the nodes, the nodes remaining green. Some shoot tips may be dead. This type of injury may occur in small irregular areas in staked vineyards or along an entire row in trellised vineyards (the lightning having traveled along the trellis wires). When the areas of destroyed cambium are small, the vine part or shoot will continue to grow, but when the injury is sufficient to girdle a vine or part of a vine, the part above the girdle will die, though it may remain active for some time. Thus, the degree of injury determines whether a struck vine can be rehabilitated. Unless the strikes are severe, most vines will remain alive.

OZONE STIPPLE OF LEAVES

Ozone stipple of leaves appears as small lesions—brown to black dotlike specks—on the upper leaf surface. Leaf fall is premature in areas polluted by air-borne ozone. In California this condition has been confined to vineyards near the large industrial areas—Los Angeles and San Francisco; in New York it occurs in areas near the Great Lakes (Shaulis *et al.*, 1972). According to Richards *et al.* (1959), the typical primary lesions, varying in size from 01. to 0.5 mm., are confined to groups of pigmented palisade cells bounded by the smallest veins. Aggregates of these minute, dotlike lesions produce the typical stipple appearance which distinguish this trouble from other grape diseases. The condition has been observed in numerous varieties.

In controlled trials on Zinfandel with ambient (smog) air and the same air filtered through activated carbon, Thompson *et al.* (1969) found that, in addition to premature leaf drop, the smog air reduced the chlorophyll content of the leaves 43 per cent, leaf weight 13 per cent, berry weight 26 per cent, sugar content 20 per cent, crop 13 per cent, and pruning weight 120 per cent. In very smoggy areas there is no efficient control.

BIBLIOGRAPHY

Beukman, E. F., and A. C. Goheen. 1970. Grape Corky Bark. Virus diseases of small fruits and grapevines handbook. Univ. of Calif., Div. Agric. Sci., pp. 207–209.

Bioletti, F. T. 1923. Black measles, water berries, and related troubles. California Agr. Exp. Sta. Bull., 358:1–15.

Boubals, D. 1971. Importance economique des viroses de la vigne. Circonstances favorisant leur propagation lutte contre ces maladies. (Economic importance of vine virus diseases. Conditions favoring their spread). Bull. Off. Int. Vin, 44:1–39.

Caramete, C. 1960. Frost injury to main grape varieties. [Trans. title.] Grandina, Vía sí Lívada, 9(12):13–18.

Caudwell, A. 1964. Identification et étude d'une nouvelle maladie à virus de la vigne: la flavescence dorée. Am. Epiphyties, 15(1):June 9.

————, A. J. Giannotii, C. Kuszala, and J. Larrue. 1971a. Étude du role the particules de type "mycoplasme" dans l'etiologue de la flavescence dorée de la vigne. Examen cytologie des plants malades et des cícadelles infectienses. Ann. de Phytopathologie, 3(1):107–123.

————, J. Larrue. C. Kuszala, and J. C. Bachelier. 1971b. Pluralite des jaunisses de la vigne. Ann. de Phytopathologie, 3(1):95–105.

————, and D. Schvester. 1970. Flavescence dorée. Virus diseases of small fruits and grapevines, handbook. University of California. Div. Agric. Sci., pp. 201–207.

Chiarappa, L. 1959a. The root rot complex of *Vitis vinifera* in California. Phytopathology, 49:670–674.

————. 1959b. A study of some of the fungi causing root rot and wood decay of *Vitis vinifera* L. in California and their effect on the host. Phytopathology, 49:510–519.

Christodoulou, A. J., R. J. Weaver, and R. M. Pool. 1968. Relation of gibberellin treatment to fruit-set, berry development, and cluster compactness in *Vitis vinifera* grapes. Proc. Amer. Soc. Hort. Sci., 92:301–310.

Crall, J. M., and L. H. Stoner. 1957. The significance of Pierce's disease in the decline of bunch grapes in Florida. Phytopathology, 47:518.

Delp, C. J. 1954. Effect of temperature and humidity on the grape powdery mildew fungus. Phytopathology, 44:615–625.

————, W. B. Hewitt, and K. E. Nelson. 1951. Cladosporium rot of grapes in storage. Phytopathology, 41:937–938.

Ehlig, C. F. 1960. Effects of salinity on four varieties of table grapes grown in sand culture. Proc. Amer. Soc. Hort. Sci., 76:325–331.

Engelbrecht, D. J., and A. C. Nel. 1971. A graft-transmissable stem-grooving of grapevines in the Western Cape Province (S.A.) resembling legno riccio. Phytopathology, 3(2):93–96.

Fic, V., and G. Vanek. 1970. Necrosis of grape. Virus diseases of small fruits and grapevines, handbook, Univ. of Calif, Div., Agric, Sci., pp. 214–217.

Frazier, N. W. 1965. Xylem viruses and their insect vectors. Proc. Int. Conf. on Virus and Vectors on Perennial Hosts, Davis, Calif. pp. 91–99.

Freitag, J. H. 1951. Host range of the Pierce's disease virus of grape, as determined by insect transmission. Phytopathology, 41:921–934.

Gifford, E. M., and W. B. Hewitt. 1961. The use of heat therapy and *in vitro* shoot tip culture to eliminate fanleaf virus from the grapevine. Amer. J. Enol. Vitic., 12:129–130.

Goheen, A. C., 1970. Grape leafroll. Virus diseases of small fruits and grapevines, handbook. Univ. of Calif., Div. Agric. Sci., pp. 209–212.

———, F. N. Harmon, and J. H. Weinberger. 1958. Leafroll (White-Emperor disease) of grapes in California. Phytopathology, 48:51–54.

———, and W. B. Hewitt. 1962. Vein banding—a new virus disease of grapevines. Amer. J. Enol. Vitic., 13:73–77.

———, ———, and C. J. Alley. 1959. Studies of grape leafroll in California. Amer. J. Enol. Vitic., 10:78–84.

———, G. Nyland, and S. K. Lowe. 1973. Association of a rickettsialike organism with Pierce's disease of grapevines and alfalfa dwarf and the heat therapy of disease in grapevines. Phytopathology. 63:341–345.

Gooding, G. V., and D. Teliz. 1970. Grape yellow-vein. Virus diseases of small fruits and grapevines, handbook. Univ. of Calif., Div. Agric. Sci., pp. 238–241.

Graniti, A., and G. P. Martelli. 1966. Further observations on Legno riccio (rugose wood). A graft-transmissible stem-pitting of grapevine. Proc. Int. Conf. Virus Diseases and Vectors on Perennial Hosts, with special reference to *Vitis*. Univ. Calif., Div. Agric. Sci., Dept. Plant Pathology, Davis, California, pp. 168–179.

———, ———, and F. Lamberti. 1966. Enation disease of grapevine in Italy. Proc. Int. Conf. Virus Diseases and Vectors on Perennial Hosts, with special reference to *Vitis*. Univ. of Calif., Div. Agric. Sci., Dept. Plant Pathology, Davis, California, pp. 293–306.

Harmon, F. N., and J. H. Weinberger. 1956. Foliage burn of *vinifera* grapes as a symptom of White-Emperor disease. Plant Disease Reptr., 40:300–303.

Hartmair, V. 1971. Mahrjährige versuche über der Stiellähme der Trauben und deren Bekämpfung. Mitteilungen. Reben Wein, 31(3):171–182.

Harvey, J. M. 1955. Decay in stored grapes reduced by field application of fungicides. Phytopathology, 45:137–140.

———. 1959. Reduction of decay in storage grapes by field application of captan. Plant Disease Reptr., 43:889–892.

———, and W. T. Pentzer. 1960. Market diseases of grapes and small fruits. United States Dept. Agr., Agr. Marketing Ser., Agr. Handbook No. 189, pp. 1–37.

Hewitt, W. B. 1935. A graft transmissible mosaic disease of grapevines. Plant Disease Reptr., 19:309–310.

————. 1939. A transmissible disease of grapevines. Phytopathology, 29:10. (Abstract.)

————. 1950. Fanleaf—another vine disease found in California. California State Dept. Agr. Bull., 39:62–63.

————. 1951. Grape dead-arm control. Plant Disease Reptr., 35:142–143.

————. 1954. Some virus and virus-like diseases of grapevines. California State Dept. Agr. Bull., 63:47–64.

————. 1956. Yellow vein, a disease of grapevines caused by a graft-transmissible agent. Phytopathology, 46:15. (Abstract.)

————. 1957a. Powdery mildew of grapevines. Mimeograph Univ. Calif. Dept. Plant Pathology, Davis, California.

————. 1957b. Some manifestations of black measles of grapevines. Phytopathology, 47:16. (Abstract.)

————. 1958. The probable home of Pierce's disease virus. Amer. J. Enol. Vitic., 9:94–98.

————. 1962. Summer bunch rot of grapes. Wines & Vines, 43(2):17.

————. 1962. Virus diseases of grapevines and a control for most of them. Wines & Vines, 43(2):18–20.

————. 1965. Las enfermedades y otros problemas de los vinedos Chilenos. F.A.O., Rpt. No. 1962, p. 28, Rome.

————. 1971. Les maladies a virus de la Vigne. Symptoms. Mode de dissemination et repartition géographique. Bul. Off. Int. Vin, 44:97–125. *See also* Rev. Appl. Mycol., 47(9):433–455, 1968.

————, and C. J. Delp. 1953. Yellow mosaic of grapevines and evidence of retention of virus in the soil. Phytopathology, 43:475. (Abstract.)

————, and A. C. Goheen. 1959. Asteroid mosaic of grapevines in California. Phytopathology, 49:541.

————, and R. Neja. 1971. Grapevine bark and wood pitting disease found in California. Pl. Disease Repts., 55(10):860–861.

————, D. P. Raski, and A. C. Goheen. 1958. Nematode vector of soil-borne fanleaf virus of grapevines. Phytopathology, 48:586–595.

Hopkins, D. L., and H. H. Mollenhauer. 1973. Rickettsia-like bacterium associated with Pierce's disease of grapes. Science, 179(4070):298–300.

Kasimatis, A. N. 1957. Some factors influencing the development of water berries in Thompson Seedless grapes grown for table use. Unpublished Master's thesis, Univ. of California, Davis, California.

Koblet, W., and H. P. Lauber. 1968. Weitere Untersuchunger über die Steillähme der Trauben. Schweiz. Z. Obst. u. Weinb., 104:223–230.

Lafon, J., P. Couillaud, and R. Hude. 1959. Maladies et Parasites de la Vigne. I. Maladies Cryptogamique. Paris, Baillière et fils, p. 205.

Lehoczky, J. 1968. Crown gall, a serious disease of vines. [Trans. title.] Russian and English summaries. Orrz. Szol. Bor. Kut. Int. Evk., 13:115–126.

————. 1971. Further evidences concerning the systemic spreading of *Agrobacterium tumefaciens* in the vascular system of grapevines. Vitis, 10:215–221.

Luhn, C. F., and A. H. Gold. 1970. Viruses in early California grapevines. Pl. Dis. Reptr., 54:1055–1056.

Martelli, G. P., J. Lehoczky, and A. Quaquarelli. 1970. Hungarian chrome mosaic. Virus diseases of small fruits and grape vines, handbook, Univ. of Calif., Div. Agric. Sci., pp. 236–237.

———, and M. Russo. 1966. Shoot necrosis of *Vitis vinifera* L. Razaki, a virus-like disease. Proc. Int. Conf. Virus Diseases and Vectors on Perennial Hosts, with special reference to *Vitis*. Univ. of Calif., Div. Agric. Sci., Dept. Plant Pathology, Davis, California, pp. 287–292.

Matthee, F. N., A. J. Heyns, and D. H. Erasmus. 1970. Present position of bacterial blight (Vlamsiekte) in South Africa. Dec. Fruit Gr., 20:81–84.

McClellan, W. D., and W. B. Hewitt. 1973. Early Botrytis rot of grapes: Time of infection and latency of *Botrytis cinerea* Pers. in *Vitis Vinifera* L. Phytopathology, 63:1151–1157.

———, H. B. Hewitt, P. La Vine, and J. Kissler. 1973. Early Botrytis rot of grapes and its control. Amer. J. Enol. Vitic., 24:27–30.

McGrew, J. R., and G. W. Still. 1972. Control of grape diseases and insects in the Eastern United States. U.S.D.A. Farmers Bull. No. 1893:1–24.

Melenin, I. 1969. Some histological and morphological changes in *Vitis vinifera* induced by *Agrobacterium tumefaciens*. [Trans. title.] Grad. Lozar. Nauks., 6(6):69–76. (French and Russian summaries.)

Munnecke, D. E., W. D. Wilbur, and M. J. Kolbezen. 1970. Dosage response of *Armillaria mellea* to methyl bromide. Phytopathology. 60:992–993.

Nelson, K. E. 1951. Effect of humidity on infection of table grapes by *Botrytis cineria*. Phytopathology, 41:859–864.

———. 1952. Some responses of grapevines to sodium arsenite spray applied for black measles control. Phytopathology, 42:158–161.

———. 1956. The effect of botrytis infection on the tissue of Tokay grapes. Phytopathology, 46:223–229.

———. 1957. The use of *Botrytis cineria* Pers. in the production of sweet table wines. Hilgardia, 26:521–563.

Panagopoulos, C. G. 1969. The disease "Tsilik marasi" of grapevine; its description and identification of the causal agent (*Xanthomonas ampelina* Sp. Noo). Ann. L'inst. Phytopath. Benaki N.S., 9:59–81.

Perold, A. I. 1927. A treatise on viticulture. London, Macmillan and Co. (*See* pp. 478–479.)

Pine, T. S. 1958. Etiology of the dead-arm disease of grapevines. Phytopathology, 48:192–196.

Prunier, J. P. 1970. La necrose bacterienne de la vigne. Prog. Agric. Vitic., 170:316–322.

Raski, D. J., W. B. Hewitt, and R. V. Schmitt. 1971. Controlling fanleaf virus-dagger nematode disease complex in vineyards by soil fumigation. Cal. Agric., 25:11–14.

Ravikovitch, S., and N. Bidner. 1937. The deterioration of grape vines in saline soils. Empire Jour. Agr., 5:197–203.

Richards, B. L., J. T. Middleton, and W. B. Hewitt. 1959. Ozone stipple of grape leaf. California Agr., 13(12):4, 11.

Rives, M. 1970. Complete cure of a whole plant of *Vitis rupestris* cu. Du lot (St. George) of grapevine fanleaf by thermotherapy. Pl. Dis. Reptr., 54: 915–916.

Santelli, V. 1957. A physiologic form of *Plasmopara viticola* found for the first time. Phytopathology, 47:3. (Abstract.)

Scheu, G. 1936. Mein Winzerbuch. Berlin, Reichsnährstand Verlags, G.M.b.H.

Shaulis, N. J., W. J. Kender, C. Pratt, and W. A. Sinclair. 1972. Evidence for injury by ozone in New York vineyards. HortScience, 7:570–572.

Sohn, E., E. Tanne, and F. E. Nitzany. 1970. *Xiphinema italiae* a new vector for grapevine fanleaf virus. Phytopathology, 60:81–82.

Stellmack, G. 1970. Arabis mosaic in *Vitis*. Virus diseases of small fruits and grapevines, handbook, Univ. of Calif., Div. Agric. Sci., pp. 233–234.

Stellwaag-Kittler, F. 1969. Stiellähme der Trauben. Hessische Lehr. u. Forschungsanstalt für Wein. Obst. u. Gartenbau, Geisenheim, Jahresbericht, Germany, pp. 119–120.

———. 1969 and 1970. Benlate (benomyl) for the control of Botrytis. Hessiche Lehr. u. Forschungsanstalt für Wein-, Obst., u. Gartenbau, Jahresbericht, pp. 115–117 and 95–96. See also Obstbau und Weinbau, 7(4): 110–112.

Strobel, G. A., and W. B. Hewitt. 1964. Time of infection and latency of Diplodia viticola in *Vitis vinifera* var. Thompson Seedless. Phytopathology, 54:636–639.

Suit, R. F. 1948. Effects of copper injury on Concord grapes. Phytopathology, 38:457–466.

Taylor, R. H., and R. C. Woodham. 1972. Grapevine yellow speckle—a newly recognized graft-transmissible disease of *Vitis*. Aust. J. Agric. Res., 23: 447–452.

Theiler, von R. 1970. Anatomische Untersuchungen an Traubenstielen im Zusammenhang mit der Stiellähme. Wein Wissenschaft., 25:381–417.

Thompson, C. R., E. Hensel, and G. Kats. 1969. Effect of photochemical air pollutants on Zinfandel grapes. Hort Science, 4:222–224.

Van der Merwe, J. J. H., and F. N. Matthee. 1972. Phytophthora—root rot of grapevines in the Western Province. Deciduous Fr. Gr., 22:268–269.

Vidal, J. L. 1933. Les gelées de fin Décembre dans le vignoble Charente. Prog. Agr. et Vitic., 111:71–72.

Vuittenez, A. 1960. Nouvelles observations sur l'activité des traitements chimiques du sol pour l'éradication des virus de la dégénérescence infectieuse de la vigne. Acad. d'Agr. de France Compt. Rend. Hebd., 46:89–99.

Weaver, R. J., A. N. Kasimatis, and R. M. Pool. 1971. Effect of wetting agents on Thompson Seedless and Perlette grapes. Amer. J. Enol. Vitic., 22:40–43.

Williams, W. O., and W. B. Hewitt, 1948. Control of grape root rot in solution cultures. Proc. Amer. Soc. Hort. Sci., 52:279–282.

Winkler, A. J. 1926. The influence of pruning on the germinability of pollen and the set of berries in *Vitis vinifera*. Hilgardia, 2:107–124.

———, H. W. Hewitt, N. W. Frazier, and J. H. Freitag. 1949. Pierce's disease investigations. Hilgardia, 19:207–264.

Woodham, R. C. 1960. The chloride status of the irrigated Sultana vine and its relation to vine health. Aust. Jour. Agr. Res., 7:414–427.

Zinca, N., and E. Rajkov. 1969. Tumeurs bacteriennes de la vigne (*Agrobacterium tumefaciens*). Bull. Off. du Vin, 42:1159–1179.

19

Grape Pests

Various kinds of insects and mites attacks grapes. Some, like the phylloxera, are specific to the grape and cannot live on any other host; others, like
cutworms and grasshoppers, feed on many kinds of plants. The mites are
not true insects. Certain nematodes—true worms—as well as rodents and
birds are also discussed here.

There are about fifty insects and other pests that attack the grapevine
and its fruit, but of these only some thirty are found in California. Fewer
than half of these are likely to be serious. Those with the potential of doing great damage are the grape leaf hopper, grape leaf roller, Pacific mite,
Willamette mite, nematodes, phylloxera, grape mealy bug, grape bud beetle, grasshoppers, hoplia beetle, and sphinx moth.

Not all the insects listed here are distributed throughout California.
Their distribution is influenced by soil, climate, isolation, and parasites.
For example, as a result of climate conditions, soil texture, and isolation of
producing areas, only about 20 per cent of California's vineyards require
rootstocks resistant to phylloxera. The grape leaf hopper, a serious pest in
the San Joaquin Valley, is of only limited importance in the desert and
coastal areas. Then, too, certain pests have a changing history. For example, the sphinx moth was a serious pest during the late 1920's and middle 1950's, but it was hardly observed at other times, probably because of
parasitism.

Natural predators on a number of the grape pests are important factors
in variations in their popualtion from year to year. These predators, natural
enemies of the pests, are the friends of the grape growers. Without their
coöperation, grape growing would be more difficult than it now is and

might, in fact, be impossible in some areas. When a predator reduces the population of a pest to nearly zero, it thereby depletes its own food supply, so that it, too, nearly disappears. The few pests remaining may require several years to reach damaging numbers again. When the pest is again abundant, the few parasites that have survived may also require several years to reach a population that can again bring the pest near extinction. The result is a cycle of pest outbreaks. The grape mealy bug is an example of a pest whose numbers fluctuate over a period of many years, declining or flourishing according to the abundance of its parasites. Before the chlorinated organic insecticides, such as DDT and the like, a similar cyclic course was recognized in the grape leaf hopper. Extensive research is being devoted to the evaluation of this interaction between the pests, their parasites, and the chemical insecticides used in pest control. Known as "integrated control" studies, such research may involve examination of vineyard ecology, population densities of pests and parasites, and the use of nontoxic controls such as microbial insecticides (Flaherty *et al.*, 1969).

Cultivation practices may help control some insects. For example, early spring cultivation reduces the breeding places of the grass thrips by turning under grasses, weeds, and cover crops. Similarly, cultivation may destroy many of the pupae of insects (rose chafer, grape root borer) that pupate near the surface of the soil, or it may bury the cocoons of others (grapeberry moth) that overwinter on the surface of the ground. Irrigation in most areas of California has markedly reduced the damage of the western grape rootworm. Even at their best, however, cultivation practices do not give complete control in all seasons. Supplemental chemical control is necessary for some insects in some years and for the more serious insects in all years.

The following discussions are based in part on "Grape Pests in California," by Smith and Stafford (1955). The various insects are grouped by the parts of the vine where they inflict major damage. Such grouping is convenient—but it is arbitrary, since some insects feed on more than one part of the vine. Descriptions and life histories are given where these are important in identifying or controlling the pests. Information on pests and their control in humid regions is given by Lafon *et al.* (1961).

INSECTS THAT ATTACK LEAVES

GRAPE LEAF HOPPER

The grape leaf hopper, *Erythroneura elegantula* Osborn, is the most widely distributed of the grape insects in California. A closely related species, the variegated leaf hopper, *Erythroneura variabilis* Beamer, feeds on grapes in southern California. It is not found north of the Tehachapi Mountains.

The leaf hopper and the variegated leaf hopper are similar in appearance and behavior. The adults are about one eighth of an inch in length and are slender. The leaf hopper is pale yellow, with reddish and brown markings; the variegated species is usually darker, with larger areas of brown on the forewings. The markings of the overwintering forms are somewhat darker than those of the summer generations. The variegated form also has a yellow spot on the forewings, usually absent on the wings of the leaf hopper. Both species vary considerably in coloring.

The adults overwinter, and during warm weather they feed on any green vegetation in and around the vineyard. During wet or cold weather they take refuge among leaves, vegetation, and trash close to the ground. Prolonged periods of cold weather reduce the numbers that survive. As soon as vine growth starts in spring, the hoppers move to the grapevines and feed exclusively on them until the leaves drop in the autumn. Egg laying starts about two weeks after the hoppers move to the vines; it may continue for several weeks if the weather is cool. Eggs are deposited singly in the epidermal tissue of the leaf. They appear as minute, capsule-shaped blisters beneath the epidermis. A female lays 75 to 100 eggs. The eggs hatch in seventeen to 20 days in the spring, and in a shorter period in hot weather. The nymphs (immature form) of the first generation appear in late May and June. They are semitransparent and have red eyes. They pass through five nymphal stages or molts, each resembling the other except for size and developing wings. The nymphs of the second generation appear in July and August, and those of the third generation in late August or September, depending on the temperature. There is much overlapping in the second and third generations. The sequence of reproduction and development for the entire season is shown in figure 130.

The nymphs feed almost exclusively on the lower surface of the leaves. When disturbed, they often run with a crablike sideways movement. In three weeks or less the nymphs attain maturity, and in another three weeks they mate and begin laying eggs. At higher temperatures the periods of development are shorter; at lower temperatures, longer. When the season at Fresno is above normal in heat summation, there is a fourth generation.

Damage.—Feeding is done by inserting the mouth parts into the leaves and sucking out the liquid contents. Leaf hopper damage first appears as a scattering of small white spots; with continued feeding, the spots become more and more numerous until a pale-yellow or whitish-yellow blotching results from removal of the chlorophyll. The leaves may dry up and fall prematurely. The damage is in direct proportion to the numbers present. Unless the overwintering adults are exceedingly abundant, the injury they produce is unimportant; but their offspring may cause defoliation. The defoliation, which increases as the season advances, frequently exposes the developing grapes to sunburn injury, causing heavy losses. Defoliation also

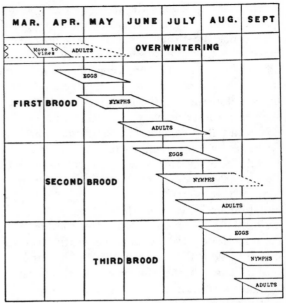

FIGURE 130: Diagram representing the life history of the grape leafhopper for a season in a hot region. (*Courtesy of Prof. E. M. Stafford*)

retards sugar accumulation in the grapes, thereby delaying ripening and lowering the quality. Leaf hopper excrement on grapes is objectionable. According to the most authoritative estimates, the tonnage of raisin and table grapes was reduced 25 to 30 per cent in the early 1930's as a direct result of injury from leaf hoppers. This estimate does not include losses from lowered fruit quality and decreased capacity of the vines, which may be intensified by long periods of high temperature and inadequate soil moisture.

If numerous at harvest, the leaf hoppers may be a nuisance to the pickers. Swarms of leaf hoppers emerge from the vines when they are disturbed, flying into the eyes, ears, and nostrils of the pickers. They may increase discomfort by attempting to feed on the workers.

Control.—The two kinds of leaf hoppers are similar in appearance and habit. Control measures are also similar. Some of the modern insecticides have shown marked effectiveness in control, but the leaf hoppers have soon developed immunity or resistance—so that every few years a new insecticide has been necessary. It therefore seems useless to list control material (see footnote on p. 440). DDT, Malathion and Sevin were effective for several years after they were first used. These chemicals now are either prohibited for use in vineyards or are carefully regulated by local authorities. Jensen, *et al.* (1961) have shown that combinations of insecticides are more effective at present. Controls are most effective if applied against the overwintering adults when they have moved into the vineyard and before they have laid eggs, or against the first brood while they are still nymphs.

Low leafhopper populations do not need treatment. A periodic survey of the number of nymphs present on those leaves with most evident feeding should be made. As long as the population stays below 10 nymphs per leaf insecticide application should be delayed.

Recent research in California by Jensen, *et al.* (1969) has shown that if the parasitic wasp, *Anagrus epos*, is found to be active on the eggs of the first brood, the early treatments for leafhopper control may be withheld. The parasite activity is indicated by leafhopper eggs that have turned red. They encouraged growers to establish refuge plantings of wild blackberries (*Rubus* spp.) which would help sustain an over-wintering population of the parasitic wasp.

Should chemical insecticides be necessary, the following are suggested: endosulfan 50 per cent W, carbophenothion 4F, carberyl 50 per cent W, or ethion 25 per cent W.

GRAPE LEAF FOLDER (GRAPE LEAF ROLLER)

The grape leaf folder, *Desmia funeralis* Hübner, is a serious vineyard pest in the central-southern San Joaquin Valley. It requires treatment in some vineyards every year. In year of heavy infestation, up to one-third of the acreage in this district may require treatment. The adult moths of this insect are dark-brown to black, with a wingspread of about 1 inch. The forewings have two oval white spots; the back wings of the males have one white spot, whereas those of the females have two such spots.

The first moths of the season emerge from pupae that overwinter in old leaves and trash or under shreds of bark on the vine. Emergence is from early April to late May, depending on the temperature. Eggs from which the first generation arises are laid almost as soon as the moths appear. The eggs are placed on the underside of the leaves, between the large veins, and on the shoots. Incubation requires ten to fifteen days, depending on the temperature. The young larvae feed in groups, between webbed-together leaves, devouring the leaves except for the upper epidermal layer and the veins. Later they disperse and make leaf rolls and feed on the edge of the leaf that has been rolled inside (fig. 131). The rolls, which are about pencil size, are made by spinning strands of silk from the edge of the leaf to points nearer the center. As the strands dry, they roll the edge of the leaf inward. Other strands are then placed to complete the formation of the roll. The feeding larvae are bright green, with a dark brown head and a brown spot on each side of the first two segments. They are about 1 inch

A

B

FIGURE 131: A, larvae of the leaf folder; B, roll of leaf formed by the larva. Note the silk strands used to form the roll. (*Courtesy of E. M. Stafford*)

long. When disturbed, they wiggle vigorously and fall to the ground. They mature in three to four weeks and pupate in a fold near the edge of the leaf.

Adult moths emerge from the pupae in ten to fifteen days. These moths lay the eggs for the second generation. There are, normally, three generation annually in California.

Damage.—The rolls made by the larvae restrict exposed leaf surfaces, and their feeding reduces leaf area. When infestation is heavy, the vines are practically defoliated. Individual vines or local areas of the vineyard are usually affected most seriously. Late in the season the larvae of heavy infestations materially reduce the quality of tables grapes by running over the clusters, thereby removing the bloom, or by actually feeding in the clusters. The breaks they make in the skin of the berries in feeding serve as courts of entry for rot organisms.

Control.—Parasites often tend to keep the leaf folder population from building up or spreading. The grower should not overlook this possible aid in control. That is, he should make sure that chemical control is necessary before he uses it.

When chemical control becomes necessary, as it has in most years of late in the San Joaquin Valley, the best results are obtained by directing it against the first-generation larvae. A persistent pesticide should be applied against the larvae before they forms rolls, in mid-May.

The use of chemical control for this pest has complicated other management practices. For example, use of Carbaryl has effectively controlled the leaf folder, but resulted in serious increases in mite populations. An older agricultural chemical, standard lead arsenate, is effective against leaf folder; however, it cannot be applied after bloom. Recent research in vineyards by Jensen (1966) and Jensen and AliNiazee (1972) with microbial insecticides show promise for a feasible solution to this dilemma brought on by the wide use of chemical insecticides. The development of high potency strains of the bacteria, *Bacillus thuringiensis*, give promise of highly effective control. Used either as a spray or dust, with thorough coverage, effective kills of leaf folders have been obtained and the material has a residual effect for several weeks.

OMNIVOROUS LEAF ROLLER

The omnivorous leaf roller, *Platynota stultana* Walsingham, was only recently found to be infesting California vineyards. It has become a serious pest of grapes in the San Joaquin Valley. First reported on grapes in 1963, the omnivorous leaf roller seriously damaged the crop in 1970; in some valley vineyards up to 50 per cent of the crop was lost.

The pest overwinters as 3rd, 4th, and 5th instars. These overwintering insects occupy nests in unpicked clusters on the vines, in decayed bunched on the ground, in dried grapes "mummies" and in dried grape leaves under the vines. In early spring, as temperatures rise, the overwintering larvae pupate inside their webbed nests. Depending upon the temperature, the first moth flight may occur from early to late March. These adults deposit overlapping eggs in masses on newly emerged grape leaves and shoots or on surrounding weeds to give rise to overlapping generations. The eggs hatch in about seven days and the young, yellowish-white or creamy larvae move vigorously or hang from the foliage by a silken thread. During this period they are spread easily by wind to other vines. Young larvae move to protected places, such as the rolls made by the grape leaf folder or where two leaves are touching to make their nests by webbing and folding the leaves. Later in the season, many larvae make nests inside the clusters. The life cycle of the insect, under San Joaquin Valley temperatures, is completed in 30 to 45 days. The biology of this insect and its damage on grapes is thoroughly discussed by AliNiazee and Stafford (1972).

Damage.—The leaf-tying, folding, webbing and feeding of larvae can cause much injury to grape foliage. Newly hatched larvae often feed on new growth and terminal shoots to retard shoot elongation. Significant damage to berries does not occur until mid-summer. Fruit damage is two-fold. Early-season feeding causes cavities and scars on the berries. Later season feeding by larvae breaks the skin of the berry and allows yeast and fungi to initiate bunch rot. The rot then spreads through the cluster, often

FIGURE 132: The omniverous leaf roller. Note damage to berries in upper part of cluster. (*Courtesy of F. Swanson*)

resulting in its entire destruction. Later infestations can cause defoliation followed by sunburn injury to fruit.

Control.—In the early years of the development of this insect in California vineyards, sprays of Cryolite or standard lead arsenate were used for control. Today growers are urged to employ the microbial insecticide, *Bacillus thuringiensis.* Effective control is obtained by this means when careful applications are made to obtain complete coverage.

ORANGE TORTRIX

Although the Orange Tortrix, *Argyrotaenia citrana* Fernald, has been known to be present in California since 1885, economic damage to grapes was not reported until 1968. At that time it was found in young vineyard plantings in a newly developing area in the Salinas Valley in Monterey County (Kido *et al.*, 1971). Morphologically it is identical to the Apple Skinworm, a pest of deciduous fruits, ornamentals, and weeds in several coastal counties of both northern and southern California. It is not an economic pest in the warm, dry interior valleys of the state.

The Orange Tortrix moth can be recognized by the brownish or buff color with a "saddle" of a darker shade across the folded wings. When at rest, the folded wings flare out at the tip like a bill. The female, somewhat larger and more robust than the male, is about three-eighths inch long. The eggs of the Orange Tortrix are laid on the smooth surfaces of the vines' leaves, shoots, or berries. The oval flat cream-colored eggs are deposited in masses, overlapping like shingles. A single female may lay up to 200 eggs, usually deposited in several egg masses. When full grown a larvae is about one-half inch long, usually straw-colored but may be greenish, dark grey or smoky-colored.

In the Salinas Valley the insect can be found in various stages of development in the vineyards throughout the year. Larvae may be found on any part of the vine, but tend to congregate in certain areas on the vine accordingly; in early spring they may be found in or on swollen buds; as shoots develop they feed on the developing leaves and tips; then, on the leaves which they web together; and, still later, the larvae are found in the clusters where they web berries together to form nests deep within the cluster.

During the dormant season larvae may be found in cracks of the bark on canes and arms. They also may overwinter on grasses or weeds in the vineyard or in the mummified clusters left on the vines.

There are usually from five to seven generations per year. In the Salinas Valley about 59 days are required from egg to adult.

Damage.—In addition to contaminating the clusters, the Orange Tortrix larvae feed on the berries and stems within the cluster (fig. 133). Secondary infections by spoilage micro-organisms then cause decay of the fruit. Feeding on the framework of the cluster causes berry drop, and in some cases, when the rachis is cut or girdled causing portions of the cluster to dry up.

Control.—The Orange Tortrix in the Salinas Valley vineyards was found by Kido *et al.* (1971) to be parasitized by an ichneumonid wasp, a braconid wasp, and a tachinid fly. Green lacewing larvae also feed on the larvae and eggs. Although the ultimate effects of the predators on the Orange Tortrix populations in the vineyard has not, as yet, been determined, serious considerations are being given to their biology in designing control programs for this pest.

Chemical control, using the usual stomach or contact insecticides, such as standard lead arsenate, Cryolite or carbaryl, is effective, but the best control programs for growers in the Salinas Valley is still under intensive study.

FIGURE 133: Showing the damage of orange tortrix on a cluster of grapes. (*Courtesy of H. Kido*)

PACIFIC MITE

There are two spider mites that attack vines in California. These are small organisms, barely visible to the naked eye. The more destructive one is the Pacific mite, *Tetranychus pacificus* McG.

The Pacific mite can usually be recognized by its yellow-amber body and the two, four, or six black spots on its back. This is in contrast to the pale, yellow body and the row of inconspicuous black dots along each side of the Willamette, the other mite that attacks grapevines rather regularly.

The adult females of the Pacific mite overwinter under the loose bark of the vines. Preferred places for hibernation are the ripples in the bark on the underside of the arms at the point where the arms join the trunk. The number of mites in these favored areas is usually an indication of the probable seriousness of the spring infestation. During hibernation their body color changes to orange, and the black spots disappear. They emerge in spring as soon as growth starts. All are out of hibernation by the time the new shoots have 4 to 6 leaves. They feed on the lower leaf surface, usually in small groups. As soon as feeding begins, they turn amber again, and the black spots reappear. Egg laying starts a few days after the adults emerge in spring. A generation is completed in ten to twelve days in warm weather; hence the mites multiply very rapidly under favorable conditions, and many generations may occur in a single year. The summer forms are pale yellow to pale greenish-yellow. Adult females are about one fiftieth of an inch in length. A light web is formed when the mites are numerous. Natural enemies, when abundant, destroy many of the mites, but often not enough to prevent vine injury.

Damage.—The mites feed mainly on the underside of the leaves, sucking the juices from epidermal cells. In the red and black grape varieties, the leaves begin to turn red, usually between the primary veins, sometime in the early part or middle of the summer. As the season advances, the color develops progressively in the leaf tissues until the entire leaf may become red or bronze-red except for large primary (and occasionally secondary) veins, which for the most part remain green and are frequently bordered by narrow margins of green tissue. Parts of the leaf may dry and turn brown. With some seasonal variation, the leaves usually begin to drop a few weeks after the red color appears, and the veins may become mostly or entirely defoliated. After early defoliation a growth of new leaves develops toward the ends of the canes and on short laterals. The fruit of mildly affected vines often fails to mature properly, or, after the leaves in the center of the vine begin to drop, many of the clusters directly exposed to the sun may burn badly on the exposed sides. On severely affected vines the clusters wither from the tips; the berries progressively shrivel and dry up. Often this condition develops before the vines become defoliated. The leaves of white grape varieties turn yellow instead of red, and areas on the leaf may dry out and turn brown. Leaves drop, as with the red and black varieties, and the fruit is affected similarly. The conditions described may involve only localized areas or entire vineyards.

Control.—Treatment for Pacific mite should not be undertaken until an average of eight or more leaves per vine show yellow spotting. Experience has shown that if predaceous mites are present treatments may not be required. Even a greater amount of yellow spotting can be tolerated when the activity of the predators appears to be increasing. If chemicals are used, sprays are preferred over dusts for control; however, sprays should not be used on table grapes. Suggested materials are Zolone and tedion.

WILLAMETTE MITE

Very soon after the vines leaf out in spring the Willamette mite, *Tetranychus willametti* McG, may appear on the basal leaves of the young shoots. It is a serious pest in the San Joaquin Valley from Fresno southward. Smith and Stafford (1955) described a strain, resistant to dusting sulfur that has developed in that area. It also occurs in other vineyards throughout California, but does little damage. In all areas except the southern San Joaquin Valley its population is restricted by the sulfur dust used to prevent powdery mildew.

For differences from Pacific mite see the discussion above. The Willamette mite differs further from the Pacific mite in that it overwinters in large numbers and thus can do serious damage in spring almost before shoot growth is started. Except in the area from Fresno southward, fortunately the first sulfuring for mildew prevention will control this outbreak. In late summer, when the sulfur dust has mostly disappeared from the vines, there may be a marked build-up in population. This mite is very agile, so that the predators, which usually also increase late in the season, have a difficult time containing it. Escape from predators accounts for the large populations that sometimes overwinter.

Damage.—Even as the buds start to open in spring, the overwintering mites feed on the leaves. Under their attack the lower leaf may turn black and die before it reaches half the normal size. Then they move on to the second and other leaves. These too may be destroyed when the population is very great. More often, however, the lower leaves are misshapen and mottled, with a bronze-glazed appearance. In vineyards other than those south of Fresno the misshapen, mottled, and glazed condition is the typical damage, since the first sulfuring to prevent mildew restricts the population. South of Fresno, in contrast, the mites continue to feed and move up the shoots. There the damage may be very severe if it goes uncontrolled.

The mites then feed on the undersides of the leaves throughout the summer, and the leaves develop the bronze-glazed appearance.

Control.—Except for the area south of Fresno, where the Willamette mite is sulfur resistant, the sulfur applied to prevent powdery mildew will control the population. Where the sulfur-resistant strain occurs, control measures for the Pacific mite will also control this mite.

GRAPE RUST MITE

The feeding of the grape rust mite, *Calepitremeris vitis* Can., on the surface of the leaves causes the leaves of white grape varieties to turn yellow and those of colored varieties to become a brilliant red.

These mites are light amber in color and even smaller than the Pacific mite. Seen under magnification, they are elongated, with some broadening near the head. They overwinter in the buds and lay eggs as soon as growth starts in spring. The young feed on both sides of the leaves. On the upper surface they tend to cluster along the larger veins.

Natural enemies usually prevent this slow-moving mite from attaining damaging numbers. The sulfur dust used to prevent powdery mildew helps restrict it.

FIGURE 134: Galls formed by the erineum mite (erinose). Left, felted masses on lower surface of leaf; right, bulging of upper leaf surface. (*Courtesy of Profs. Smith and Stafford*)

ERINOSE (ERINEUM MITE)

The work of the erineum mite, *Eriophyes vitis* Pgst., appears as swellings or galls on the upper surface of the leaf, with a corresponding concave area beneath, densely lined with a felty mass of curled hairs. The felty patches are called erinea.

The mites are very small, about one seventieth of an inch in length, slender, and not visible until magnified 20 to 50 times. They have short forelegs. The adults emerge with the start of growth in the spring. They feed on the young expanding leaves. Eggs are laid among the felted hairs in the erinea, and the young usually feed and mature there. Full-grown leaves are seldom attacked. In late summer the adult mites migrate to the base of the petiole of the leaf and crawl under the bud scales, where they hibernate.

Damage.—Although erinose often causes the grape grower some concern in spring, very little damage is done to the vines. The felty mass on the underside of the leaf is at first white and gradually turns yellow, then rust colored, and finally dark brown (fig. 134). The upper surface of the leaf remains nearly a normal green until late in the season. The pockets are generally isolated and few in number, but in severe cases they run together.

Control.—The erinose mite is easily controlled by dusting with sulfur. The sulfur applied in commercial vineyards to control powdery mildew likewise controls erinose. In fact, the presence of erinose indicates that sulfuring for mildew control has been inadequate.

WESTERN GRAPELEAF SKELETONIZER

The western grapeleaf skeletonizer, *Harrisina brillians* B. and McD., described by Lange (1944), is native to Mexico and the states of Arizona, New Mexico and Texas. It was first found in California in 1941, in San Diego County. It overwinters in the pupal stage in cocoons in fallen leaves and trash. The moths emerge in late May.

The adult is a metallic-looking bluish-black or greenish-black moth with a wing expanse of about 1 inch. Its eggs, in clusters or masses of a few or as many as a hundred, are usually deposited on the lower surface of the leaves. The larvae are yellow, with two transverse purplish bands and several narrow black bands; they feed on wild and cultivated grapes and Virginia creeper, much the same as does the Eastern species, *Harrisina americana* Meréville. Each body segment has four tufts of black spines. The spines are poisonous and, if touched, produce welts similar to those produced by nettles. The mature larvae are about a half inch in length. They spin a silken cocoon in which to pupate. After emerging from the cocoon, the moths mate, and eggs are laid.

Damage.—The young larvae, starting from the mass of eggs from which they hatch, feed side-by-side, soldier-like, retreating as they feed by eating out the parenchyma, or soft leaf tissue. The skeleton framework (veins) and upper epidermis of the leaf are left intact by the young larvae, but the full-grown larvae consume all of the leaf tissue except the larger veins. It has been observed that the larvae from a single egg mass are capable of defoliating an entire vine. Detection is not easy until damage to the vine may be serious.

Control.—Chemical insecticides such as carbaryl are quite effective against this pest. However, timing applications as broods emerge is essential. Control applications against the first-brood larvae should be done in mid-June. If necessary, dusting is repeated in mid-July to control the second-brood larvae. The time indicated for dusting is for western San Diego County, the area where this pest was first encountered in California. In 1961 it was found in the Kerman area of Fresno County. There it has been eradicated. Sporadic outbreaks have been reported elsewhere, these too, have been or are being eradicated.

FALSE CHINCH BUG

When grasslands adjacent to a vineyard dry up in the spring, the nymphs of the false chinch bug, Nysius ericae Shilling, may migrate into the vineyard in countless numbers and crawl up the trunk to feed on the shoots and leaves, which may be wilted in a few hours and killed within a day. Seldom are more than the two or three rows of vines adjacent to the grasslands affected.

The nymphs are wingless and small, about one eighth of an inch in length; pale gray, with reddish-brown abdomens, they match the color of dry grass and soil to a remarkable degree. The adults are about the same length, but colored light or dark gray. This species normally breeds and feeds in the native grasslands. In the spring (May and June) and again in the fall (September and October), the nymphs swarm from the grasslands into adjoining cultivated areas and feed on nearly all green and growing plants. After the spring swarming the nymphs soon mature into adults, and eggs are laid in cracks in the soil or on grasses or weeds. There are four to seven broods a year. The winter may be passed in egg, nymph, or adult stages, but in the West the nymph stage predominates. Damage is most serious in warm and dry regions where crops, including grapes, are grown with irrigation. The bug has a wide distribution throughout North America.

Control.—When possible, the dry grass from which the bugs are migrating should be burned. Since the bugs migrate mainly in one direction, and since the wilted vines along the edge of the vineyard clearly show the line along which they are entering the vineyard, it is possible to lay down a chemical barrier across the line of march. A band of chlordane or benzene hexachloride dust, 20 to 30 feet wide, will usually be effective. The land should be dusted until the ground appears white, usually at a rate of about 100 pounds per acre. The dust should be applied to the soil just ahead of the spread of the bugs. Infested vines in the border rows should be dusted with a lindane dust. (CAUTION: Do not apply this dust to vines after bloom.)

Several species of sphinx or hawk moth larvae feed on grapes, as well as on many other plants. Most common in California are the achemon sphinx, *Pholus achemon* Drury, and the white-lined sphinx, *Celerio lineata* Fabr. These two are sometimes seen on vines in the eastern states, as are also the pandora sphinx, *Pholus pandorus* Hübn.; the grapevine hog caterpillar, *Ampelophaga myron* Cram.; and Abbot's sphinx, *Sphecodina abbotii* Swain. Other species are occasional pests in other parts of the world.

The larvae are large, 2 to 4 inches long, and smooth-bodied, and have on the next-to-last body segments a strong horn that has given to them the common name of hornworms. In many species, including the achemon sphinx, the horn is present in only the first one or two stages, disappearing with the next molt and being replaced by a bright eye-spot. They eat ravenously; one or two caterpillars alone will sometimes strip the leaves from a young vine. When numerous, they defoliate large vines in a few days. The color of the larvae usually changes, more or less, as they grow. The achemon sphinx larvae when young are light green with a long reddish-brown to black horn; when mature, they vary in color from yellowish-green to reddish-brown, marked with yellow, and have no horn. The white-lined sphinx larvae vary in color from yellowish-green, with black markings, to nearly black, with yellow markings.

The adult achemon sphinx moth is marbled brownish-gray, with maroon patches on the forewings and on the body at the base of the wings. The hind wings are a rich, rosy pink, with a brown border. The wingspread is 3 to 4 inches. The white-lined sphinx moth is dull brown, with white lines on the head, forepart of the body and forewings. The hind wings are dark brown, with a wide rose-colored band across the middle. The wingspread is 2.25 to 3.5 inches.

The life history is about the same in the various species, except that the number of generations a year in the northern regions is only one for some species, two for others; most species probably have two generations in the warmer areas. They hibernate over winter in the soil as large, dark-brown pupae; the moths emerge in the spring—May in California. Most are night fliers. Eggs are laid on the foliage and are hatched in a few days. When two generations occur, the second generation of larvae appears in late July.

Control.—In most cases the control practices used for the grape leaf hopper controls the larvae of these moths. On occasions special insecticide applications may be required to prevent vine defoliation. To prevent migration of larvae into the vineyard from wild host plants, insecticide should be applied to the bottom of a trench across the path of migration. The ditch should be about 15 inches wide with the steep side towards the vineyard. The insecticide should be renewed as required.

WHITE FLY

The grape white fly, *Trialeurodes vittatus* Quaintance, is a mothlike insect that in the larvae stage sits immobile on the leaves, usually on the upper surface. During this stage the larvae closely resemble a scale insect. They have a lemon-yellow body surrounded by a narrow border of white wax. As the larvae approach maturity, their bodies become brown. When mature, they emerge as adults, leaving their discarded shells attached to the leaf. The adults have immaculate white wings. The life cycle requires about a month, and there are several generations a year.

Damage.—A liquid, sugary honeydew is excreted, in which grows a black, sooty mold. The honeydew and the accompanying mold spoil the appearance and value of the grape clusters.

Control.—Dusts or sprays applied for leaf hopper control will also control the white fly.

GRASSHOPPERS

Several species of grasshoppers damage grapes in California. The green valley grasshopper, *Schistocerca shoshone* Thomas, is found from Bakersfield northward. The vagrant grasshopper, *Schistocerca vaga* Scudder, is found from Fresno southward. A third species is the devastating grasshopper, *Melanoplus devastator* Scudder, which occurs primarily in low foothills over the entire length of the state.

There is one generation per year. The species of *Schistocerca* hibernate in the adult stage; the devasting grasshopper overwinters as eggs.

Damage.—The green valley and vagrant grasshoppers become active in spring, when they may enter vineyards in large numbers. Damage may be severe within a short time. The eggs of the devastating grasshoppers hatch from May to July; hence they enter the vineyard later in the summer, usually when the vegetation in the foothills is drying up. They feed on the leaves and young shoots.

Control.—All grasshoppers may be controlled by application of stomach poisons. When large numbers of wingless hoppers are observed in rangeland adjacent to vineyards, it may be feasible to control them there with poison bait applied outside the vineyard. Dry baits, prepared by mixing wheat bran with a poison, are recommended in the dry foothill areas. The bait is then spread uniformly over the area, especially in the path of migration of the insects.

INSECTS THAT ATTACK FLOWERS AND FRUIT

HOPLIA BEETLES

The grapevine hoplia, *Hoplia* (*oregona*) *collipyge* LeConte, emerges from the ground in the spring and attacks many kinds of plants, including grapes. Hoplia beetles devour the blossoms, young leaves, and young fruit.

The beetles are one quarter to one third of an inch in length and rather broad, with the backs mottled grayish or reddish-brown and the heads darker; the underside is silvery and shiny. There is, however, variation in both size and color. Eggs are laid in grassy areas, and the larvae require two years to develop, pupating during the second winter. When disturbed, the feeding adults feign death and drop to the ground.

Damage.—Since the beetles often move and feed in groups, severe damage may be localized on individual vines or groups of vines. They may appear and feed on the flower clusters and leaves about the time that the shoots are 10 to 15 inches long. Clusters not completely devoured may be badly misshapen because parts were eaten. After one to two weeks of feeding, the beetles do little further damage; they move from the vineyard to lay eggs.

Control.—Dusting with Parathion as soon as feeding is observed should be effective.

GRAPE MEALY BUG

The grape mealy bug can quickly destroy the marketability of a cluster of grapes by turning it into a sticky, sooty mess. This insect, *Pseudococcus maritinus* Ehrhorn, also feeds on many other plants. Mealy bugs may feed on leaves, stems, and bunches, or under the shedding bark.

Mature mealy bugs are three sixteenths of an inch in length, oval, and covered uniformly with fine, white, waxy powder. Fine filaments of wax protrude from the margins of their flat bodies. There are longer filaments at the front and rear ends.

The grape mealy bugs overwinter as eggs or as young on the trunk and arms of the vine. By June these forms have matured. Their eggs are laid in a loose, cottony wax sac usually deposited on the rough bark. The second generation lays its eggs during the fall. The young arising at this time overwinter.

Damage.—Where it feeds, the mealy bug excretes a honeydew that collects in drops. This may be found on the leaves, on the bark, or on the clusters. When it collects in quantity, it may run or drip. Wherever it collects, it supports the growth of a black fungus that imparts a sooty appearance to the leaves and clusters. Sooty, sticky grape clusters with whitish mealy bugs and their cottony wax masses are valueless on the basis of appearance alone.

Control.—Natural enemies and hot weather help control the mealy bug. When parasites and predators ordinarily present in large numbers are driven away by ants, poison baits to control ants will permit their enemies to control the mealy bugs. Insecticides should be used sparingly, to avoid unnecessary reduction of the population of predators.

The waxy secretions prevent many insecticides that might otherwise be effective from reaching the mealy bugs. This has not been the case with a spray of liquid lime-sulfur and either dormant emulsifiable oil or dormant oil emulsion in water. This spray is effective when applied just before the buds swell. Good control may also be obtained with a dormant spray of emulsifiable Parathion. Thorough coverage is necessary with either spray. In applying the Parathion spray, Smith and Stafford (1955) stress that the object should be to obtain a heavy, uniform deposit. This is achieved by using a moderate pressure and a large disk opening in the spray gun. The Parathion spray may be combined with sodium arsenite to control mealy bugs and black measles at the same time.

THRIPS

Several species of thrips attack grapes. The European grape or vine thrip, *Drepanothrips reuteri* Uzel, was first reported in California in 1926. Bailey (1942) reported that it is now present in most areas of the central San Joaquin Valley. There are about six generations each year, the first group of larvae appearing in early April; thereafter there is a generation every twenty to twenty-five days. The adults overwinter in the soil, surviving only in small numbers. The flower or grass thrips, *Frankliniella* sp., are more widely distributed. They often come into vineyards in the spring in large numbers, as grasses and weeds in the area become dry, and largely disappear again from the vines by the time the berries are one-third grown. They have five to seven generations a year and overwinter as larvae or adults on weeds and ornamentals. The bean thrips, *Hercothrips fasciatus* Perg., sometimes damage vines like the flower thrips, particularly in unirrigated areas. Occasionally the citrus thrips, *Scirtothrips citri* Moultin, which are pale yellow or orange, also attack grapes, but only in hot, dry areas where citrus trees are growing near the vineyard. It is sometimes very difficult to distinguish between these and the grape thrips, which, however, are usually more brownish-yellow in color.

All of these thrips are small, one fiftieth to one twenty-fifth of an inch in length, elongated, narrow bodied, and active. They have two pairs of fringed wings, carried lengthwise over the back when not in use. Besides flying and running rapidly, many adults can hop.

Damage.—The damage is done by feeding, with the insects sucking the juices from the tissues. Some scraping or rasping is done, however, to puncture the epidermal cells and start the flow of the plant juices. The effect is a silvering, bleaching, or russetting of the surfaces of berries, stems, and leaves (fig. 135). Eggs deposited in the young berries produce a characteristic type of injury called "halo spot." This is a serious defect in table grapes. Once injured, growing tissue rapidly becomes deformed or dried-up, often cracking later. Flowers that are injured may fail to set; berries injured when young are deformed, scarred, and often cracked when mature.

In the past few years another type of scarring has shown up on berries of Thompson Seedless table grapes (*see* fig. 136). Its cause was studied by Luvisi and Kasimatis (1972) and by Luvisi and Jensen (1972). They attribute the scarring to the rasping of the berry skin cells in feeding by flower thrips under persistent calyptras (caps). Without sticking caps there

FIGURE 135: Scarring of berries caused by thrips. (*Courtesy of Prof. Bailey*)

was no damage. Adult flower thrips are attracted to the clusters when blooming begins and lay eggs. The nymphs appear near the 50 per cent bloom stage and reach a population peak around shatter. The injury follows the pattern of the sticking caps and sometimes resembles a starfish in shape.

The bloom time spray with gibberellin, to berry thin, accentuates the scarring by stimulating the development of the rasped cells and by producing larger berries. The shatter time spray, to enlarge the berries, also accentuates the scarring, but less; thus, some growers omit the former spray, but they must use the latter in order to have marketable fruit.

Thrips attacking the growing point will stunt or dwarf the growing shoots. Young leaves that are attacked remain small, become cupped, and often are severely burned at the margins and between the veins.

To check further for the presence of thrips, one may jolt or slap the cluster or shoot tip in the palm of the hand. When thrips are present, they will fall on the open hand.

Control.—The grape thrip is usually controlled by the treatment used in controlling the grape leaf hopper. The grass thrips often do their damage before the dust or sprays for the control of leaf hoppers are applied. If these build up to damaging proportions early, a control should be applied. This might well be in combination with dusting sulfur which also serves

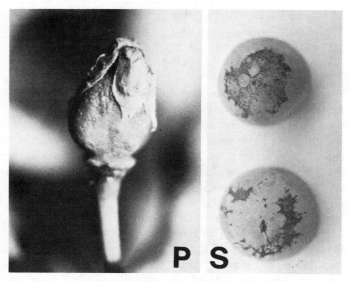

FIGURE 136: Stylar scarring of Thompson Seedless berries. P, persistent calyptra; S, scarring resulting from the feeding of thrips larva under persistent calyptra. (*Courtesy of Fred Jensen*)

as the first dusting to prevent powdery mildew. The scarring by flower thrips nymphs under the sticking caps was reduced to a non-damage level by one or two sprays of dimethoate (Cygon).

CONSPERSE STINKBUG

In late summer and fall the consperse stinkbug, *Euchistus conspersus* Uhler, may move from surrounding areas into vineyards. It feeds on the vine leaves and petioles by sucking out sap. More serious, however, is the damage from punctures they make in feeding on the ripening and ripe berries.

The stinkbugs are large, about three eights of an inch in length and a quarter inch or more in breadth. They are shield-shaped, brown above, pale green underneath, with amber-colored legs on which there are small black spots. The body is hard. They can fly considerable distances.

The adults overwinter under trash and emerge early in April. They feed on many annual plants and lay their eggs on them. It is only when these sources of food are removed, as in the cutting of alfalfa or the drying-up of grassland, that they move to vineyards. The young bugs mature during July, August, and September. They, in turn, lay eggs that develop into adults in September and October. Overwintering is primarily by adults that develop late in the year.

Damage.—In feeding, the consperse stinkbug inserts its sucking mouthparts into the ripening berries. After the stinkbug is through feeding, juice of the berry exudes from the puncture to form a brown, sticky, and unsightly mess. The puncture injury, described by Smith and Stafford (1955), causes a rapid internal breakdown of the berry, which then shrivels and drys up or becomes rotten.

Control.—Since this pest invades the vineyards at or shortly before harvest, chemical control is not possible. Application of poisons at this time would leave intolerable residues on the harvested fruit. Chemical control must be in adjacent fields or pastures before the migration to the vineyard. A drenching spray containing Parathion or lindane will kill these bugs. Whether these materials may be applied in adjacent fields will be determined by the nature and intended use of the crop.

ROSE CHAFER (Not present in California)

About the time that the grapes are in bloom in the central United States, swarms of the common rose chafers or rose bugs, *Macrodactylus subspinosus* Fabr., may suddenly appear, first feeding on the blossoms and later attacking the young fruit and foiliage. Quaintance and Shear (1926) state that the chief damage is destruction of blossoms and newly set fruit. In extreme cases leaves may also be eaten, except the larger veins. The beetles feed on many plants, including practically all deciduous fruits and many ornamentals, such as Spiraea, Deutzia, and roses.

This pest is widely distributed east of the Rocky Mountains and extends westward to Colorado. It is particularly destructive in the middle western states when the vineyard adjoins areas of uncultivated light sandy soil occupied by grasses and weeds whose roots the larvae feed on.

The beetle is about one third of an inch in length, light-brownish, and covered with numerous lighter hairs; it has long, spiny legs. It is very clumsy in its movements. After feeding for three or four weeks, it moves to grass cover and lays eggs singly beneath the surface of the soil. The eggs hatch in two or three weeks, and the larvae feed on the roots of grasses and other vegetation. By fall the larvae are nearly full grown; they then go deeper into the soil, below the frost line, to hibernate. In the spring they come near the surface and pupate in April or early May, depending on the latitude. Pupation lasts ten to thirty days, depending on the temperature. There is one brood a year.

The western rose chafer, *Macrodactylus uniformis* Horn, occurring in Arizona and New Mexico, has similar habits.

Control.—Eliminate grasses and other perennial weeds in and adjacent to the vineyard, especially on sandy soils, by spring and summer cultivation. A spray application of standard lead arsenate and blackstrap molasses just before bloom is effective against this insect. The sprays recommended for berry moth will probably hold the rose chafer under control too.

GRAPE-BLOSSOM MIDGE (Not present in California)
Eggs of the grape-blossom midge, *Contarinia johnsoni* Sling, laid in the flower clusters of the grape in late May and early June, hatch in a few days into whitish larvae (maggots) that feed on the flower parts, especially the pistil. The flowers are destroyed and are dropped from the cluster. After feeding for about two weeks, the larvae drop to the ground and continue their development. At the time of leaving the clusters they will have changed to an orange or reddish color and be about one twelfth of an inch in length. In the soil they form an earthen cocoon, in which they pass the winter; they probably pupate the next spring. The adult midges or flies emerge in May. They mate very soon, and the female deposits her eggs in the flower clusters. They live only a few days.

The insects are found rather generally over grape-growing areas along the south shore of Lake Erie; they have not been reported as a serious pest elsewhere. Early-blooming varieties of grapes, such as Moore Early and Worden, are believed to be more subject to attack than late-blooming varieties, such as Concord and Niagara. In most seasons this midge is only a minor pest, probably held under control by natural enemies.

GRAPE-BERRY MOTH (Not present in California)
The larvae of the grape-berry moth, *Polychrosis viteana* Clem., according to McGrew and Still (1972), are the most common cause of wormy grapes

throughout the New England, Middle Atlantic, and middle western states. The pest occurs from Canada to the Gulf and westward to the Great Plains states.

The moths appear in the spring soon after the buds break, continuing to emerge for several weeks. The adult is a small, inconspicuous, purplish-brown moth with wings expanding to about a half-inch. Eggs are laid on the developing flower clusters by the early-emerging moths and on cluster stems, and young grapes by the later ones. The very small, flat, scalelike eggs, stuck to the surfaces of stems, flower buds, or young berries, appear as glistening whitish or pearl-like spots. The eggs hatch in a few days, and the larvae mature in about three weeks. The mature larva is about three eights of an inch in length, dark greenish to dark purplish in color, with a light-brown head and black thoracic shield. It moves from the cluster to a leaf, where it cuts out a piece of the leaf on three sides, folds it over, and fastens down the free edge with a web. A cocoon is formed inside the protecting leaf fold, in which the larva changes to a light greenish-brown pupa, from which the moth emerges twelve to fourteen days later. The larvae of the second generation that mature before mid-August will pupate and give rise to a third generation. The winter is passed in the cocoon, which falls out of the leaf fold onto the ground or drops to the ground with the leaf.

Damage.—The larvae of the first generation feed on flower buds, blossoms, and small berries, tying together with a web the parts of the cluster in which they work. The blossoms or berries attacked are destroyed and dropped. Damage at this stage might be even greater than that done by later generations if the larvae were as numerous. The eggs of the second brood are laid on the berries, and the larvae bore into the green and ripening fruit, feeding on the pulp and immature seeds. At the point of entry a purplish spot forms that, except for the hole, resembles injury by the black rot disease. The damage berries decay in moist weather and may dry up in warm, dry weather.

Control.—Results are best from a combination of methods. Cultivation should be discontinued in August to leave the cocoons on top of the ground, where many or most will be killed by natural agencies. Spring cultivation should be such as to bury the cocoons beneath 2 or 3 inches of soil and leave them undisturbed until two weeks after blooming is over. A comparatively shallow covering of soil prevents emergence of the moths. After the time of moth emergence is past (two weeks after blooming), the soil can be cultivated away from the vines.

In combination with the cultivation treatment just described, spraying or dusting with a contact insecticide such as carbaryl is effective.

GRAPE CURCULIO (Not present in California)
The larvae of the grape curculio, *Graponius inaequalis* Say, feed on the pulp and immature seeds of the berries, causing wormy grapes such as those caused by the berry moth. The curculio larvae are white, footless grubs, about one third of an inch long when full grown, whereas those of the berry moth are greenish, have well-developed legs, and are quite active. The adult curculio is a small, stout beetle, brown, about one tenth of an inch long and nearly as broad. It is common from Arkansas to Minnesota and east to New York and North Carolina.

The beetles hibernate over winter in or near the vineyards, especially along the edge of woodlands. In June and July their eggs are laid in small cavities cut into the berries. The eggs hatch in four to six days. The larvae mature in twelve to fifteen days; then they eat their way out of the berry, drop to the ground, and pupate. Pupation requires eighteen or twenty days. The adult beetles feed until fall, when they go into hibernation under trash of various kinds. Eggs are laid by the new beetles, but few of them develop.

Damage.—The beetles appear about the time that the grapes bloom; they feed on the grape foliage until the berries are about one-fourth grown. The characteristic feeding marks occur on the upper surface of the leaves as short, somewhat curved lines, usually in groups. Presence of this insect in vineyards can best be detected early by the feeding marks on the leaves.

Control.—Sprays or dust as recommended for the berry moth will control this insect perfectly.

COCHYLIS (EINBINDIGER TRAUBENWICKLER) (Not present in United States)
In Europe the cochylis, *Clysia ambiguella* Hübner, damages the flower clusters and green berries in a manner similar to that done by the berry moth of the eastern United States. It is more difficult to control because the larvae pupate underneath the bark of the vines or in cracks in the stakes, instead of the leaves that fall to the ground in the autumn. It is a very old and very destructive pest, probably flourishing in the Middle Ages and positively known as early as 1740. Although it occurs in nearly every vineyard region of Europe, it is not equally serious in all.

The moths begin to emerge in spring soon after the buds break. Emergence continues for two or three weeks. Eggs, laid in the flower clusters, hatch in ten to fourteen days. The larvae mature in four or five weeks and pupate under the bark or in crevices. The moths of this brood emerge in July. The moth has a wingspread of a half to two thirds of an inch and is light gray, with yellow forewings marked with a brownish-black or dark-gray trapezoidal bar across the middle. The eggs of the second brood are laid on the berries. In August, before the grapes are ripe, the larvae leave the berries and pupate as in the first generation. The pupae of this second generation overwinter and emerge as moths the next spring.

Damage.—The larvae are reddish-brown, with a black head. They feed on unopened flowers, flowers, and young berries, destroying them. The parts of the cluster in which the larvae feed are bound together in a web. Most of the flowers on the cluster may be destroyed, the crop being reduced accordingly. Damage is greatest when cool weather prolongs the blooming period, and least when clear, warm weather causes a short bloom.

The larvae of the second generation feed in the berries, causing them to dry up in clear weather and to rot in wet weather. As the larva moves from one berry to another, the berries, like the blossoms earlier in the season, are tied together with a web. Whole clusters may be destroyed—if not by the larvae directly, then by decay organisms that pass from the worm-damaged berries to sound adjacent berries.

EUDÉMIS (BEKREUTZER TRAUBENWICKLER) (Not present in United States)
Worms in ripe grapes in the warm regions of Europe are most often the larvae of the eudémis moth, *Polychrosis botrana* Schiff., described by Stellwaag (1929), which is a close relative of the berry moth of North America. They are a dull yellowish-green, with olive-brown heads. The forewings of the adults are yellowish and marbled with reddish-brown. Its life history is similar to that described for the berry moth, except that the eudémis moths begin to emerge a few days earlier in the spring and their cocoons, for pupation, are located under the rough bark on the vines and in cracks and crevices of the stakes, as with the cochylis, instead of in folds on the leaves that fall to the ground, as described for the berry moth. The first two generations practically coincide with the two generations of the cochylis. In cool regions the second-generation pupae overwinter, as do those of the cochylis, but in warm regions three generations are normal; in occasional very warm seasons a partial fourth generation may appear in October. In Europe the cochylis and the eudémis together are usually considered to be, next to phylloxera, the most serious insect pests of the grape. The insects, the nature of the damage, and the control measures are similar. In the cool regions the cochylis is likely to predominate; in the warm regions—e.g., in southern France and Italy—the eudémis is more important because of the additional (third) generation.

PYRALE (SPRINGWURM) (Not present in United States)
Immature larvae of *Sparganothis pilleriana* Schiff. hibernate over winter in cocoon-like cells underneath loose bark. About the time of bud break in the spring, the larvae leave their winter quarters and move onto the expanding shoots. When mature (in July) the caterpillars are about 1 to 1.25 inches

long. They pupate in cocoons in webbed-together leaves, emerging in ten to fourteen days as moths. The moth is light brown, with darker brown bands across the forewings, and has a wing span of three quarters of an inch to 1 inch. Eggs are laid in masses on the upper surface of the leaves. These hatch into larvae, which, when mature, crawl underneath the loose bark, spin themselves a cocoon-like cell, and hibernate until the following spring. This pest is present over most of Europe, North Africa, and Asia Minor.

Damage.—The larvae feed on the young leaves and tie them together in a web. Feeding continues for about five weeks. If the worms are disturbed, they flee nimbly, by flipping the body (hence the German name, *Springwurm*) or by dropping on a silken thread to the ground. When numerous enough, the larvae may almost defoliate the vines.

Control.—Natural enemies, among which are many parasitic insects, destroy many eggs and larvae, often causing the Pyrale to almost disappear for a period of years. When necessary, the Pyrale may be controlled by spraying or dusting with Parathion or other compounds as recommended for the area where control is to be carried out.

MEDITERRANEAN FRUIT FLY (Not present in United States)
Although grapes are rarely infested with larvae of the Mediterranean fruit fly, *Caratitis capitata* Wied, Perold (1927) reports that in 1915 a high percentage of the crop of Almeria on a pergola at the Paarl Viticultural Experiment Station was destroyed by it. He used poison bait as a spray on the leaves to control it in following years. Poison bait is no longer permissible on vines with ripening fruit. Recently Myburgh (1961) found that an organic phosphate offered possibilities for the control of this pest.

CALENDRA (Not present in United States)
Adult beetles of *Phlyctinus callosus* Bohem. emerge from the soil in the spring and eat all green parts of the vine and a number of other plants. Greatest damage is to the clusters. Stems may be damaged to the extent that parts of clusters or whole clusters dry up. Berries injured early in the season drop; those attacked later are scarred. There is but one brood a year. The winter is passed in the larval and pupal stages in the soil. The insect, described by Lounsbery (1910), is indigenous to South Africa.

Control.—Spray the vines before bloom with lead arsenate and a suitable spreader.

DROSOPHILA
Drosophila is also called "fruit fly" and "vinegar fly"; its scientific name is *Drosophila melanogaster* Meig. The fruit fly feeds and reproduces in any fermenting fruits, pomace piles, fruit dumps, cull fruits, and vegetables left in field, orchard, or vineyard. It is in these that the build-up in population

occurs. As a result, there is always a large population present to attack grapes when the bulk of the crop matures in September and October (Berg, 1959).

In grapes the flies feed on the berries wherever there are cracks in the skin. Rapid berry enlargement during ripening causes some berries to crack. An irrigation in early-maturing grapes, especially when the stress for moisture has been acute, will cause the berries of some varieties to crack. Tight clusters also cause splitting of berries within the clusters. These fresh cracks are ideal places for the adult flies to lay their eggs.

The fruit fly multiplies very rapidly. In summer in the interior valleys of California the complete life cycle from egg to egg requires only six to eight days. In winter it may require sixty to eighty days. Under favorable conditions the flies live four to five weeks and a female lays 500 to 1,000 eggs. Temperatures around 100° F. are injurious to the flies, yet they survive by finding shelter in dense parts of vines and remaining inactive.

At the peak in populations there seems to be a general movement of flies over considerable distances. Tagged flies have been checked in movements of two to five miles in a day. As a rule, they move upwind.

Damage.—It is not only the laying of eggs in the cracked berries and the feeding of the maggots that damages the fruit. Stombler (1960) indicated that this fly is known to be a carrier of plant diseases. Among others, it carries Rhizopus, a fungus that commonly causes cluster rot in grapes (Yerington *et al.*, 1960). Then, too, as the flies feed, the berries leak juice, which runs over parts of the infested cluster as well as over other clusters beneath. This provides favorable conditions for the development of other types of cluster rot.

The presence of flies, eggs, or maggots or any part of these on the grapes constitutes contamination according to the Food and Drug Administration. Similarly, wine made from such grapes may be deemed to have been produced under unsanitary conditions. The fruit fly is, therefore, a problem of both the grower and the processor. This fly is likewise a major pest in winery operation.

Control.—Under any conditions, control is difficult because of the fruit fly's habit of breeding, feeding, and migration. In vineyards the control problem is complicated by the protection the heavy foliage provides the flies. Coverage would have to be very thorough, and the task is made more difficult by the problem of residues on the grapes.

In a single test on Carignane grapes Stafford (1959) showed that a high degree of control was obtained with two materials: dibrom and dimethoate. The materials were used as dusts. Two dustings were applied, a week apart. The trials were on an acre basis. Careful consideration must be given to the timing of any chemical application, however, to avoid contamination of fruit at harvest.

Successful control must include destruction of places where the fly breeds: cull fruits and vegetables, fruit dumps, pomace piles, and the like. In view of this, control becomes a regional, county, or state-wide problem. Without such an approach, an attempt at control can be wiped out overnight by a mass movement of flies.

INSECTS THAT ATTACK BUDS AND YOUNG SHOOTS

CUTWORMS

The larvae of several species of night-flying gray-brown moths climb vines in the spring and eat out the inside of buds that are just starting to grow or cut off new shoots at the base. During daylight the worms take refuge in the soil at the base of the vines or under trash. They can often be found, if the soil is loose, by digging one to two inches deep a few inches round the vine. The full-grown worms are 1 to 1.5 inches long, soft, smooth-bodied, and variously colored according to the species. At night they climb the vines and attack the breaking buds or the new shoots. They also feed on many other plants.

Some of the common species are: the greasy cutworm, *Agrotis ypsilon* Rottemburg; the variegate cutworm, *Peridroma margaritosa* Haworth; and the brassy cutworm, *Orthodes rufula* Groti. After the worms are full grown, they pupate in the soil in late spring. The moths emerge and lay eggs in midsummer. The young larvae feed on roots and crowns of grasses and other low-growing vegetation until the next spring.

Control.—Natural enemies are very important. Countless numbers are destroyed by parasitic tachinid flies, hymenopterous parasites, and predaceous ground beetles. When the natural controls fail, an effective control can be obtained by applying a banded treatment around the vine trunks using a carbaryl-apple pomace bait.

GRAPE BUD BEETLE

The beetles of *Glyptoscelis squamulata* Crotch, a quarter inch in length and light gray, with a hard shell, emerge from the ground in early spring and feed on the opening grape buds. Ebling (1939) stated that, usually, only a few beetles feed at a time; the majority remain hidden. A grower observing only a few should not be misled into believing he has only a few. In California the pest is very destructive in the Coachella and Imperial valleys and in parts of Fresno County. Elsewhere it is not serious. The beetles feed mostly at night and spend the day in seclusion in the trash or soil at the base of the vine. Eggs are laid in the bark, and the larvae, on hatching, drop to the ground and feed on the roots of the vines. There is one generation a year.

Damage.—The buds the beetles feed on may be entirely destroyed, or only the primary growing point may be destroyed. If one or both of the side growing points should grow, the shoots may be unfruitful, especially on Thompson Seedless. Hence the crop may be markedly reduced. Once the shoots are 1 to 2 inches long, the injured buds are conspicuous because of lack of growth.

Control.—Baiting around the vine trunks with a carbaryl-apple pomace mixture has been effective.

FLEA BEETLES

When grape buds are swollen or just breaking in the spring, they are often eaten into or entirely destroyed by the adult of *Haltica torquata* LeConte. Essig (1959) described this insect as a small, metallic-looking blue or purple beetle, one eighth to one fifth of an inch in length, robust, and able to jump a considerable distance when disturbed. After feeding for a few days, the female beetles lay small light-brown eggs in cracks in the bark or at the base of the buds, or in a cavity eaten out of the bud. The eggs hatch when the new leaves are expanding. The larvae feed on the upper surface of the leaf for three to four weeks, eating out irregular holes in the leaf tissue. The full-grown larvae are about one third of an inch in length and yellowish brown, with black markings. The mature larvae drops to the ground and pupates in the soil. A week or two later the beetles emerge and feed sparingly; no damage is done. There is only one generation each year.

Damage.—Flea beetles often appear in countless numbers in southern California, Arizona, and New Mexico, and may destroy all of the buds on the vines. Usually, however, they attack only part of a vineyard.

The flea beetle first described by Hartzell (1910) on grapes in the eastern United States, *Haltica chalybea* Illiger, is occasionally a most destructive pest. In Europe the species *Altica ampelophyaga* Guér., a native of Spain, may be injurious, particularly in the warm Mediterranean region.

Control.—The carbaryl bait control described for the grape bud beetle is suggested.

CLICK BEETLES

Click beetles are adult wireworms. The adult beetle of the Pacific Coast wireworm, *Limonius canus* LeConte, frequently feeds on grape buds in spring, while the wireworms are a serious pest of truck crops. Despite its name, it usually appears only in the vineyards of the interior valleys.

The adults are three eighths to one half of an inch in length. The female is the larger; she has reddish-brown wing covers and a dull-brown head and thorax; the male lacks the distinctive reddish tinge in the wing covers and is dull grayish-brown. They reach the buds by flying rather than by walking up the vine trunk as the cutworm and bud beetle do. When an adult beetle is held between the thumb and finger, it will arch its body backward, then straighten out with an audible snap or click.

Damage.—The adults overwinter in rubbish on the ground and emerge to feed when the vines start growth. They eat out the grape buds, the injury being very similar to that of the bud beetle and cutworms. Unlike these pests, the click beetles feed in the daytime.

Control.—The carbaryl bait control used for the grape bud beetle is suggested.

GRAPE BUD MITE

In many of the grape-producing areas of California there has been observed a strain of erinose mite, *Colomerus vitis* Pgst., that inhabits the grape buds. As described by Smith and Stafford (1948), it is indistinguishable from the erinose mite, except that it lives in the buds and therefore does not produce the characteristic leaf galls with felty pads on the underside. The mites overwinter in the buds. When the shoots elongate in spring, both mites and newly laid eggs are carried up on the shoot. As new buds are formed in the axils of the leaves, the mites move into them. Nevertheless, the population is highest in the buds on the basal portion of the shoot.

Damage.—By feeding on the tissues in the dormant buds and on the expanding shoots as the buds break, the bud mites produce a dwarfing and stunting of new shoots by causing a shortening of the first five or six internodes (fig. 137). Sometimes the terminal bud or growing point of the new shoot is killed, so that five or six lateral buds, in the leaf axils of the new shoot, will push out together, causing a "witches' broom" condition. Such affected shoots are zigzag in growth and produce no fruit. In severe cases many of the dormant buds on the spurs or fruit canes are killed during winter and early spring, with the result that the vine produces, mostly, nothing but water sprouts from latent buds. Several consecutive years of such severe damage could kill the vine but fortunately the same vines are seldom severely injured in consecutive years. The mites live in the buds and produce many generations a year. Outbreaks are sporadic and localized, but they are very damaging to the crop and the shape of the vines when they occur.

Control.—Although much research has been done on this pest, no chemical control has been found successful. Chemicals that penetrate the bud and kill the mites also damage the growing points in the buds. Sulfur dust, which effectively controls erinose, is of no value for bud mite control.

APHIDS

At least four European and two American species of aphids attack grapes, but they seldom cause serious damage. The brown grape aphid, *Macrosiphum illinoisensis* Shimer, occasionally causes some coneern on home

FIGURE 137: Bud mite damage. The short internodes of growth and the death of the shoot tip are typical. Normally the mites overwinter in the dormant buds, and the damage occurs at the base of the shoot. Here it is just above the point of inoculation. (*Courtesy of Prof. Stafford*)

vines east of the Mississippi River. It infests the shoot tips, the leaves, and sometimes the clusters. Its dark brown color and large size make it conspicuous. The winter is passed in the egg stage on twigs of the black haw, *Viburnum* sp. In spring the aphids move to grapes and may go through a dozen or more generations before fall, when a migrant generation is produced that returns to the haw. Natural enemies usually hold it in check. The mealy plum aphid, *Hyalopterus pruni* Fabr., is occasionally a minor pest in European vineyards.

Control.—If control measures are required, a spray consisting of nicotine sulfate with soap as a spreader, is effective.

INSECTS THAT ATTACK PERMANENT PARTS OF THE VINE

BRANCH AND TWIG BORER

At times this beetle, *Polycaon confertus* LeConte, has increased in numbers in some areas and has done appreciable damage to grapevines.

The beetles are brown or black, cylindrical, and one third to one half of an inch in length. As they eat their way through the wood, they plug the burrows behind them with frass (eaten wood) and chewed wood. The eggs, which are laid singly in crevices in dead or dying wood or bark, produce white, wood-boring grubs that bore into the trunk and arms of vines. The larvae usually enter through dead or drying areas; once inside, however, they readily invade the living wood. The beetles are always most numerous in the vicinity of piles of orchard and shade-tree prunings and firewood made from pruning brush or vine trunks held over from the previous year; the drying prunings furnish an ideal breeding place for the borer. It occurs throughout California and Oregon.

Damage.—When the shoots are 6 to 10 inches long in the spring, the adult beetles bore holes into the spurs at the base of the young shoots. The burrow, which begins in the crotch formed by the shoot and the spur, undermines the base of the shoot and causes it to wilt, to break off suddenly, or to droop and die. Close examination should reveal the beetles feeding in the burrows. In severe attacks the loss may amount to half or more of the shoots; occasionally whole vines are killed.

The adult beetles of the western twig borer, *Amphicerus cornutus* Pallas, sometimes cause very similar injury by boring into spurs at the base of the shoots, but the beetles of the species are usually not numerous enough to cause serious damage. Their range covers parts of Mexico, Texas, New Mexico, Arizona, and southern California.

Control.—Prune off all dead and very weak arms and remove the dead vines. Burn all pruning brush from orchards, vineyards, and shade trees before the vines start growth each spring. If firewood in made from the prunings, store it in a screened shed to prevent access for egg laying. Piles of drying pruning-brush and stumps, and firewood made from them, furnish the main breeding places for the insects. If these are eliminated, other control measures are usually not needed. Direct application of insecticides is of little value.

GRAPE CANE BORER (APPLE-TWIG BORER) (Not present in California)

The adult grape cane borer, *Amphicerus bicaudatus* Say, by boring into the spurs and canes at the base of the shoots causes an injury very similar to that described for the branch and twig borer by Quaintance and Shear (1926). The larvae, however, do not feed in the live wood of vigorous vines.

This beetle occurs east of the Rocky Mountains. It has been most destructive in states bordering the Mississippi River, from Iowa southward. Life history and control are the same as for the branch and twig borer.

The lead-cable borer, *Scobicia declivis* LeConte, which derives its name from its habit of boring holes in the lead sheathing of telephone cables, also burrows into living fruit trees and dry wood of all kinds, including wine casks.

The adult is a black, cylindrical beetle, about one quarter inch in length, with a tan or reddish spot on each side of its body. It is a strong flyer. This beetle breeds almost exclusively in oak trees—the live oak and black oak. It prefers sound oak wood that has been cut or broken and has been drying for several weeks. The eggs are laid just beneath the bark. There is only one generation per year.

Damage.—The adult beetles are attracted to barrels and casks, and their greatest damage to the industry is done by boring small holes in wine casks, especially oak ones. The wood probably attracts more than does the contents, for new, unused oak barrels are attractive to the beetles. Redwood casks are attractive, but less so.

Control.—Control is largely a matter of sanitation in the surrounding area. If no piles of freshly cut wood are permited to accumulate near by, there will be no place for breeding.

Infested casks can be cleared of beetle activity by filling them with water and bringing it nearly to boiling. This will kill the beetles or drive them out. To protect against infestation or reinfestation, apply a hot saturated solution of alum to the outside of the wine casks and, when dry, paint with raw linseed oil. Individual insects can usually be destroyed by pushing a small wire into the burrow.

These beetles rarely appear in sufficient numbers in vineyards to do more than minor damage.

At least thirteen species of scale insects attack grapes, including the grape scale, *Dispidiotus uvae* Comst.; the brown apricot scale, *Lecanium corni* Bouché; and the cottony maple scale, *Pulvinaria vitis* Linn. der Kulturländer.

These scale insects belong to two groups—those that feed on more than one part of the vine and those that remain in place once they start feeding. The first group is further characterized by its sugary liquid excrement. When mature, the scales of this group are about one fifth of an inch in length. The brown apricot scale and the cottony maple scale belong to this group. An example of the group that feeds only in one spot is the grape scale. It is about one tenth of an inch in diameter.

The adults of the brown apricot scale are brown, one eighth to three sixteenths of an inch in length, and nearly hemispheric in shape. They may be found on any part of the vine, but most will be on one- to three-year-old wood. They occasionally occur on the shoots. There is one generation. These scales produce copious amounts of honeydew, making the grapes a sticky, sooty mass.

The white, cottony masses or eggs sacs that the cottony maple scale produces in May are rarely seen on grapes in California. The mature females that overwinter are about one seventh to one sixth of an inch in length, brown, flat, and oval. By the time they attain full size, in May, their length is one fifth of an inch. They usually feed on one-year-old wood. The sugary excrement damages the grapes much the same as does that of the brown apricot scale.

The grape scale belongs to the second group. When present in large numbers, they give the vine a dirty-white appearance. They usually feed on the two-year-old wood, but may also settle on the old vine parts. They are small in comparison to other scale insects that infest grapes. Once they settle down to feed, they do not move.

Control.—In California, scales seldom occur in sufficient numbers on vines to warrant special control measures, except in home vineyards. In the eastern states and in Europe, however, they sometimes become a serious pest. There they are also more injurious in home vineyards. When abundant, the scales check growth materially. Rate of spread from vine to vine, and especially from row to row, is generally slow. Pruning removes many of the insects, and rapid exfoliation of the bark pushes most of the remainder away from their food. When chemical control is necessary, treatment consists in spraying in midwinter with a dormant oil emulsion. All parts of the vine should be wet thoroughly, especially the arms. Removal of loose bark before spraying makes the treatment more effective, but is usually not necessary.

DARKLING GROUND BEETLE

The adults of the darkling ground beetle (species of *Blapstinus*) feed on wounds on the trunk of young vines (tissue exposed by pruning cuts of cultivation injuries) or the callus forming around such wounds. By their feeding they extend the wounds, which in severe attacks may even girdle the vines. When such girdles are wide, which they may well be, the vines die. The adults vary from black to bluish-black, often with reddish legs.

Control may be achieved by use of the banded bait control suggested for cutworms and bud beetles.

TERMITES

Grape growers generally recognize the damage that termites do to stakes and trellis posts, but they may fail to realize that these same pests damage vines. The species that feeds on vines is the subterranean termit, *Reticulitermes hasperus* Banks.

The adult sexual forms are black, with two pairs of long slender wings. They are often mistaken for ants, although they have a broad waist and ants have a slender, threadlike waist. The termites swarm and mate after the first fall rains. Each pair establishes a new colony. They usually do this in the ground, raising a brood of wingless workers that seek wood on which to feed as soon as they are able. Wounds, beetle holes, or decaying saw cuts serve as courts of entry.

Damage.—Termites eat heartwood and avoid the living sapwood. The entire center portion of the vine may be honeycombed, leaving only a shell of sapwood intact. The vine may show no visible damage, but its structural strength is so reduced that the least unusual strain causes breakage. Termites are most damaging in old vines. As a rule, such vines have both more and larger wounds, exposing more of the acceptable heartwood to termite invasion.

Control.—Termites are controlled by preventing their becoming established. Large pruning cuts and tillage wounds are to be avoided. Primary means of preventing termites are careful training, so as not to have any wounds on the trunk of the newly established vine, and careful cultivation, so as not to produce wounds. Wounds 12 inches or more above the ground are, probably, rarely entered by termites unless the firm structure of the heartwood has been reduced by twig borers or wood-rot fungi.

Stakes or posts of nonresistant wood should be treated with chemicals to protect them against termites. For such treatment see p. 268.

CICADAS

The adult female cicada, *Platypedia minor* Uhler, occasionally damages grapes by drilling holes in the shoots and inserting its eggs. The eggs hatch and the young drop to the ground. From two to three years are spent below the ground before the young are fully grown. The larvae are known to feed on the roots of orchard trees, but whether they feed on grape roots is not known. The adults are about three quarters of an inch in length, with black or bronze-black bodies and two pairs of large, colorless, transparent wings. The produce a noise similar to that made by rolling two marbles together. When approached, they move around the shoot and keep always on the side away from the observer.

Damage to grapes is minor, and control measures are seldom required. Where needed, control is achieved by cultivation. When nearly grown,

the young cicadas make their way up to within an inch or two of the surface of the soil. Disking the soil in late April crushes many of them.

INSECTS THAT ATTACK ROOTS

PHYLLOXERA

Dactylasphaera vitifoliae Shimer, formerly *Phylloxera vitifoliae* Fitch or
Phylloxera vastatrix Planchon, is the most widely known of the aphids
because of its destruction of grapes the world over. It is native to the
United States east of the Rocky Mountains. It has not established itself
on the native vines of California (*V. californica* and *V. girdiana*) in the
wild state. In Arizona it occurs on wild grapes, but it is largely confined
to the leaves and is not yet a pest of commercial plantings.

Phylloxera reached France about 1860, but the insect was not identified
until 1868. Somewhat earlier, American vines had been taken to France
in connection with powdery mildew control studies or as museum specimens. With these plants, unknown to the importers, came phylloxera.
In France the environment was as favorable to this organism as its native
habitat—or more so—and it ran rampant in the vineyards. About 75 per
cent of the vines of France were destroyed within thirty years.

Phylloxera was identified in California in 1873. The question has often
been raised as to whether the original infestation was brought from the
eastern United States or from France. It could have come from either
source, since vines were being imported from both areas. More vines by
far were being brought from France, which might lend support to those
who credit France as a source. On the other hand, the merits of certain
American grapes, such as Catawba, were being extolled in the *California
Farmer*, a farm newspaper, in the middle 1850's, and the phylloxera is as
likely to have been brought in from the eastern United States. Where it
came from, however, makes little difference; the tragedy is that it was
introduced to our vineyards and is still being carried to other new grape
areas. The early introduction and spread of this organism in California,
as in France, was unsuspected.

Life cycle of phylloxera in California.—The life cycle of phylloxera in
California differs from that in the eastern United States in that all of the
insects are oviparious parthenogenic females. The adults are oval to ovoid
in shape, one twenty-fifth of an inch in length and half as much in width,
and varying from yellow-green in summer to yellow-brown in autumn; they
occur on the roots and are known as root forms (C of fig. 138). The eggs
are lemon yellow. The late autumn eggs hatch into larvae which hibernate
on the roots during the winter. When conditions become favorable, 50° F.
(10° C.) or warmer, the hibernating larvae develop to maturity and produce the first generation of the year. There are usually three to five gen-

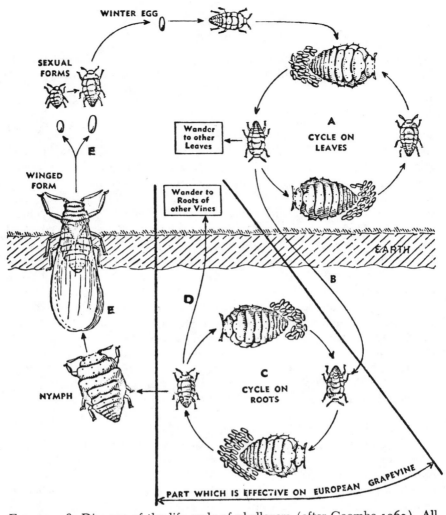

FIGURE 138: Diagram of the life cycle of phylloxera (after Coombe 1963). All stages are to scale except that eggs are too small; the eggs should be just smaller than the insects hatched from them.

A. Cycle of 4 to 7 generations which form galls on the leaves of American vines during summer; showing eggs, larvae and adults

B. In late summer an increasing proportion of the insects in the galls on the leaves migrate to the roots.

C. Cycle of 4 to 7 or more generations of the root forms which feed on the roots of both American and European vines: its effects kill the latter.

D. In late summer an increasing number of the root forms wander to the surface of the soil and through cracks in the soil in search of new roots to be attacked.

E. A winged form develops on American vines during autumn, flies, and lays eggs which hatch into sexual forms. After mating a winter egg is laid. This part of the cycle never takes place in California, and is always abortive on *vinifera* vines.

erations, but there may be as many as eight from April to November. Many of the young root forms of each generation leave the roots of the infested vines through soil cracks or go up the trunk in search of new vines; thus they are called wanderers (D of fig. 138). Some of the organisms appearing from midsummer to the end of October are winged migrants (E of fig. 138). These winged migrants lay male and female eggs that give rise to the sexual forms, but these forms do not mature in California. In consequence, the gall form is absent. That is, the above ground forms of the life cycle (E and A of fig. 138) do not occur in California.

In contrast to the above, the life cycle of phylloxera in its native habitat and in other humid regions includes the winged sexed females, which deposit the winter egg (E of fig. 138). The stem mother, or fundatrix, hatches in spring from the winter egg and gives rise to the gall forms on the leaves (A of fig. 138). This form has been observed in California on only two occasions. Aside from supposedly regenerating the organism, these phases are the primary multiplication and colonization forms.

Spread.—As indicated by the life cycles of figure 138, there is a marked difference in the mode of spread of this insect in humid areas and in California. In humid areas there are three natural means of spread: by the winged insect, by newly hatched wanderers crawling on the soil surface and and in cracks in the soil, and by the gall forms. Only the spread by wanderers occurs in California. Therefore the natural spread is slow.

Other than natural agencies of spread are cultivating implements, vine supports and picking boxes, vine stumps, man and animals, flood or irrigation water, and rooted vines. It has been demonstrated time and again that this organism may be carried from infested to clean areas by each of these agencies. Common sense and some care will stop spread by all of these agencies except rooted vines. Control of the insect on rooted vines is more difficult, since land may be thought to be clean, because never planted to vines, yet be infested; clean vines may be heeled-in in soil that is thought to be free of the insect yet is not; or the vines may be disinfected and, through carelessness, become reinfested. Even so, this means of spread has been greatly reduced by control procedures.

Damage.—Phylloxera feed by sucking. On a new rootlet a characteristic hook-shaped gall forms at the puncture, and the root usually stops growing. In about a month the gall dies and decays. Feeding on older roots usually causes small, half-spherical swellings that give the root surface a roughened or even a warty appearance. These also decay within one or two months, and the phylloxera then move to another place on the root and produce more galls. It is believed that the decaying galls and a poisonous saliva injected into the vine by the phylloxera are responsible for the stunting and decline of the vines. Destruction of actively growing and feeding roots is, of course, partly responsible for lack of growth.

Control.—Vineyards planted in very sandy soil are relatively immune to phylloxera attack. Soils containing clay expand in volume on wetting and contract on drying. The contraction on drying forms cracks and pulls soil away from the roots. The insects are thus enabled to move about over the roots and to the surface along the roots and trunk or through the cracks, and thence to adjacent vines. Sandy soils that contain but little clay do not crack or pull away from the roots on drying; therefore in such soils the wandering forms are restricted in their movements. Once on the roots, they will, in time, infest the entire root system of a vine and will move to adjacent vines whose roots touch the infected vine. Insects that reach the surface and gall forms that attempt to migrate to the roots cannot penetrate soils that are so sandy that they do not crack or form crusts upon drying after being thoroughly wetted.

In the San Joaquin and Sacramento valleys the heavy-textured soils of the Madera, San Joaquin, and similar series are favorable to infestation by phylloxera. The sandy loams of the Hanford and Foster series are less favorable, and the Madera and Oakley sands and the Fresno sand and sand loams are practically free of phylloxera.

The control of phylloxera is basically a matter of prevention. Nursery stock can be completely freed from phylloxera and made safe for planting in uninfested soil by first washing all soil from the vines and roots and then treating by either of the following methods: (*a*) fumigation with methyl bromide (CH_3Br) in an airtight chamber, at the rate of 2 pounds of methyl bromide per 1,000 cubic feet of space, with the temperature above 65° F. and air circulation from a fan or blower; or (*b*) nicotine and oil disinfection. The latter is done by submerging the vines for not less than five minutes in a solution of the following formula: 1.5 gallons of medium summer oil of viscosity 72 to 80 and unsulphonated residue test of 90 or above, 1 pint of 40 per cent nicotine sulfate, 1 pint of sulfated alcohol liquid-spreader, and 100 gallons of water. The solution must be renewed at regular intervals. After treatment the vines should be packed or heeled-in in clean sand, shavings, moss, or other material that will prevent drying and reinfection.

No direct methods of control are fully effective. Submerging the land with water for prolonged periods kills many of the insects. Submersion for 6 weeks is necessary in midwinter. According to Davidson and Nougaret (1921), one larva under observation survived immersion from October 16 to November 20. Several others lived under water for three to fourteen days. Treating the soil with carbon disulfide kills many of the insects, but this treatment, as indicated by Simmons, *et al.* (1951), is overly expensive and must be repeated frequently.

Once phylloxera is established in the soil, the only effective control is rootstocks that resist it. Resistance is high in numerous selections of American species and hybrids of American species or hybrids of American species and *vinifera* varieties. *Vinifera* varieties grafted on stocks that are well adapted to both the variety and the soil produce very satisfactorily. Resistant rootstocks for California vineyards are discussed in chapter 24.

ROOT-KNOT NEMATODE

Injury to vines from the feeding of nematodes was first identified in California about 1930. The importance of this pest grows as knowledge of its capacity for destruction increases and the causes of vine decline are diagnosed more accurately—particularly of decline occurring in the lighter soils of the warm interior valleys. The most widely distributed nematode pest of grapes is the root-knot nematode, *Meloidogyne incognita* var. *acrita* Chitwood.

Development.—In its young stage this nematode is microscopic in size and worm-shaped. The mature female is pearly white, pear- or gourd-shaped, and slightly thicker than a pinhole. The males are smaller and worm-shaped. Mating is not necessary for reproduction. Eggs are deposited in a mass, which may be entirely or only partly inside the root tissue. The eggs hatch into free-living, active larvae; these may work their way to a new location in the same root, or they may move to other roots—going into and through the soil by way of the film of water that surrounds the soil particles. The individual eggs and larvae cannot ordinarily be seen by the naked eye unless they are present in large numbers. Since the larvae feed only in living plant tissues, they do not develop while free in the soil; yet they may survive for months without food if conditions are favorable. The larvae usually enter the rootlets near the growing tip and, once established, give up all activity except feeding and reproducing. Most of the larvae that develop in vigorous roots are females, which grow rapidly and begin laying eggs. A single female may lay 500 to 1,000 eggs, and in warm climates there may be five to ten generations in a year.

The rate of development of nematodes varies with temperatures between 55° and 85° F. In cool weather they are less active and fewer of them are able to penerate the roots. Damage is thus less severe in cool regions than in warm.

Although destroyed by desiccation, nematodes will survive in a soil that is apparently dry. Favorable moisture conditions make for greater activity and damage. Water, however, cannot be withheld to check them without also injuring the vines.

Spread.—The root-knot nematodes are most frequently spread into new areas by the movement of infested plants, such as infested rootings. Plants of all sorts, when grown in nematode-infested soil, are common carriers. The infestations can spread from infested to uninfested vineyards by the movement of infested soil—as, on cultivation implements, or in flood water or poorly tended irrigation water.

Damage.—In the roots where they feed, root-knot nematodes cause abnormal cell growth that results in characteristic swellings, especially when the nematodes are present in large numbers. The swellings or galls may sometimes be confused with those caused by phylloxera. On young rootlets, however, phylloxera galls have the swelling mostly on one side of the root and make a hook-shaped knot, whereas the nematode galls appear as an enlargement of the whole root. A series of knots somewhat resembling a string of beads is often caused by nematodes on a root, or the swellings may be so close together as to cause a continuous rough thickening of the rootlet for a distance of an inch or more (fig. 139). In severe cases most or all of the small roots are irregularly thickened, sometimes to more than four times their normal diameter. The size and number of swellings will depend largely on the number of nematodes according to Tyler (1933), but will also vary with the kind of grape.

Whether or not the nematode secretes a toxic substance, it causes an irritation that stimulates abnormal growth and distorts the sap-conducting vessels. The gall is characterized by a knot of these gnarled and broken vessels, surrounded by fleshy tissue that may be discolored and furrowed; it is the first part of the root to die, and the large galls are usually more or less decayed. Root functions are disrupted, and the vines grow poorly,

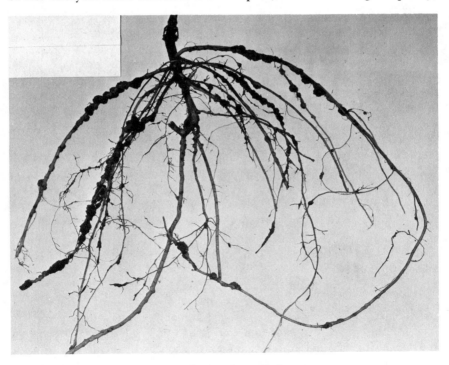

FIGURE 139: Roots showing root-knot nematode damage.

are unproductive, and in extreme cases will die. Young vines, having shallow roots, will suffer more severe injury than old, deep-rooted vines that became established before the nematode population built up to a damaging extent.

The aboveground symptoms of vines damaged by nematodes are not definite. Infested vines are usually stunted, but beyond this there are no constant differences from stunted sound vines. In fact, there is no means of separating the shoot and leaf symptoms of vines infested with nematodes from those of vines infested with phylloxera. Not only does the stunting look alike in both conditions—the spread of the areas is also similar. The infested area spreads in all directions, with the degree of injury decreasing from the center outward. This pattern is not always so definite with nematodes as with phylloxera.

Control.—Vines are severely damaged by root-knot nematodes only when growing in porous sandy or sandy loam soils. The more open and porous the soil, the more serious is the damage. Such soils seem to be favorable for both the multiplication and the spread of the organisms. The effect of heavy soils is to make travel by the larvae difficult, and fewer larvae become established in roots. Once a larva enters a root, the soil texture seems to have little effect on its further development and reproduction.

Raski, *et al.* (1965) have outlined the diagnostic procedures needed to assay nematode injury in vineyards and the recommendations for soil fumigation practices. The light sandy soils lend themselves readily to fumigation as the most direct control for nematodes. For effective fumigation the soil must be well prepared by deep cultivation and the removal of as many as possible of the live roots. Immediately after the treatment, the surface should be rolled, to seal it. Fumigation with at least 60 gallons per acre of DD or 45 gallons per acre of Telone has provided new plantings with favorable conditions for becoming established, according to Raski and Lider (1959). No control measure, however, has yet eradicated nematodes on a field scale; the population always builds up again.

Fumigation of established vineyards has been tested on a rather extensive scale in recent years. Dibromochloro-propane, an effective nematocide, has been used safely around grapes at rates up to 10 gallons of active ingredients per acre. Response has been irregular. Remarkable increases of vine growth and production resulted in some tests, but in most experiments no difference could be detected.

In areas where the increase in nematode population is rapid—e.g., in very open, porous soils—the best control, if vines are to be planted, is the use of nematode-resistant rootstocks. Such rootstocks are discussed in chapter 24.

Lear and Lider (1959) reported that nematodes on nursery stock can be effectively destroyed by submerging the thoroughly washed rootings in water for five minutes at 125° F. Or the time and temperature may vary: 118° F. for thirty minutes; 120° F. for ten minutes; 127° F. for three minutes; and 130° F. for two minutes. The treated vines must be cooled quickly and must be planted immediately or else be stored in a moist, cool, nematode-free medium (sand, sawdust, or wood shavings).

ROOT-LESION NEMATODE

The root-lesion nematode, *Pratylenchus vulnus* Allen & Jensen, causes poor growth of vines and reduced yields. In contrast to the root-knot nematode, it does not produce galls on the roots. This organism functions as a migratory parasite, moving in and out of the root tissue.

These nematodes penetrate the roots; when the population is high, the smaller roots are destroyed. As a result, growth is retarded by the limitation of the root system. Soil fumigation is promising as an aid in establishing new plantings, though its effectiveness over long periods must still be determined. Information on resistant rootstocks is lacking.

DAGGER NEMATODE

Several species of dagger nematodes occur on grapes in the United States and abroad. Two are widely distributed in California and have similar effects on vines. One species, *Xiphinema index*, is important because of its role as the vector of fanleaf, yellow mosaic, and several other viruses (see p. 471). This nematode is responsible for the reinfection with these viruses of new grape plantings on old-grape land. Even though several years may have elapsed following the removal of old virus-infected vines, live pieces of roots remain as sources of the virus. *Xiphinema index* is most commonly found in the coastal valleys but has been also reported on vines in parts of the San Joaquin Valley. The other dagger nematode in California is *Xiphinema americanum*. It has not been definitely identified as a vector of grape virus diseases, but is known to do considerable damage to vine roots. It occurs more commonly in the interior valleys.

Xiphinema italiae, *X. diversicaudatum*, and *X. vittenezii* are found in Europe. Of these *italiae* is a vector of yellow mosaic, *diversicaudatum* probably of Arabis mosaic, and *vittenezii* of Hungarian chrome mosaic.

Control.—The recommended control for *Xiphinema* nematodes is to apply a deeply placed soil fumigant. The old vine must be removed as completely as possible. The soil is then ripped to a depth of 36 inches in two or three directions and the surface cultivated to seedbed condition. Treatment with the fumigant is made in summer or fall when the soil is dry and warm. A double injection is recommended, placing a majority of the fumigant 30 to 36 inches deep with shanks 24 inches apart and the remainder 8 to 10 inches below the surface with shanks 12 inches apart.

The fumigant is then sealed in by compacting the surface with a ring roller.

Recent interest has been shown in the possibilities of resistance in *Vitis* species to *Xiphinema index*. Kunde *et al.* (1968) reported that several species did in fact carry some tolerance to this pest. Also, the rootstock, Couderc 1613, was to some degree resistant. A hybridization and selection program is now underway at the University of California to find usable rootstocks resistant to this pest.

WESTERN GRAPE ROOTWORM

The larvae of the western grape rootworm, *Adoxus obscurus* Linn., was reported by Quayle (1908) to feed on the roots of grapes and other plants. The larvae overwinter in the soil at a depth of 2 feet or more; in the spring they come within a few inches of the surface and pupae. In May the adult beetles emerge and work their way to the surface of the soil. Not many succeed in getting through a tight, hard crust. They are dark-brown or black, about one fifth of an inch in length and one eighth of an inch in breadth, and covered with a pubescence of short gray hairs. After feeding for about two weeks, the beetles lay eggs in clusters on the old wood in crevices underneath the loose bark. The eggs hatch in eight to twelve days, and the young larvae make their way to the ground and enter the soil to feed on the roots for the rest of the season.

Damage.—Small roots may be eaten off entirely. On large roots the larvae eat out pits or long channels, one tenth to one fifth of an inch wide, through the bark and outer wood. The channels may extend in almost any direction; on small- and medium-sized roots they are usually parallel to the axis of the root, but they may be transverse or crudely spiral. Roots, even large ones, are sometimes girdled and killed. The frass (eaten bark) is left behind in the furrows by the larvae and is characteristic of their work. The full-grown larvae have a length of about one fourth of an inch in their naturally curved position and about one third of an inch when straightened out. They are white, with yellowish-brown head, brown or black mouth part, and three pairs of legs near the head. When the larvae are numerous, the vines are severely weakened and may even be killed in two or three seasons. Several acres or whole vineyards may be affected, with a serious reduction in crop. Attacks usually, however, are not so damaging, and the rootworm is not regarded as a major pest in California, though it does occasionally require control. The adult beetles feed on the upper surfaces of the leaves, where they eat out linear or slitlike holes about one twentieth of an inch wide and one eighth to one-half inch long. Sometimes the leaves are so badly eaten that they look like lace. This damage may be severe enough to injure young vines, but it is usually not important on mature vines. The beetle also gouges out strips of the bark of tender shoots, leaf petioles, and cluster stems and may eat channels in the berries themselves. Affected berries become misshapen and cracked. When disturbed, the feeding adult beetles feign death and fall to the ground.

In Europe and North Africa similar species, *Adoxus vitis* Four., *Bromius obscurus* L., causes similar injury.

The grape rootworm of the eastern United States is a related species, *Fidia viticida* Walsh. The damage it does is almost the same as that of the western species, and its life history is similar, except that the eggs are laid on the shoots instead of the old wood and the larvae drop to the ground on hatching. It is a major vineyard pest in many areas, but it is most destructive in neglected vineyards on sandy or gravelly soils.

Control.—Since the beetles feed on the leaves for two to three weeks before laying eggs, they can be killed with cryolite or standard lead arsenate. The rootworm rarely requires chemical control in irrigated vineyards.

GROUND PEARLS

The ground pearl, *Margarodes vitis* Phillipi, is a scale insect found attacking and causing severe injury to the roots of grapevines in some areas of Chile, Argentina and Uruguay. According to Gonzales *et al.* (1969) the insect is indemic on several species of native shrubs in the central valleys of Chile. The pre-adult female is a round cyst found attached to roots. It attains a diameter of approximately $\frac{3}{16}$ to $\frac{1}{4}$ inch and is covered with a hard, waxy covering of a pearly, yellowish color—hence the name ground pearl.

No known source of resistance to this pest is known within the genus *Vitis*; however, field trials with phylloxera resistant stocks and species of *Vitis* are being conducted in Chile. Gonzales *et al.* (1969) describe extensive trials with soil fumigants and other attempts at chemical control; however, none of these have been commerically successful. Barnes *et al.* (1954) described a related species, *Margarodes meridionalis* Morr. which is found on roots of grapevines in the Imperial Valley of California. It is also widespread on the roots of bermudagrass in that area, especially along irrigation canals where it is subject to spread to new areas. High populations of this insect have been found on roots of grapevines planted in sandy soils but not on vines in heavy clay soils. Damage to vine roots has not been of economical importance.

Other species of *Margarodes* have been reported as pests of grapes in Brazil and in South Africa.

RAISIN INSECTS

Insect infestation is the most common type of raisin deterioration, though discoloration and microbiological deterioration are also important. Insects and insect eggs can be killed by fumigation, but it is highly desirable to do everything possible to minimize infestation on the vine, in drying, and in storage. Vineyard and dry-yard sanitation are extremely important. The finished raisins should be handled in thoroughly washed boxes. It is desirable to fumigate raisins when they are placed in storage—even in temporary storage in the vineyard.

The insects that do the greater part of the damage to raisins are the raisin moth, *Cadra figulilella* Greg.; the Indian-meal moth, *Plodia interpunctella* Hln.; the dried-fruit beetle, *Carpophilus hemipterus* Linn.; and the saw-toothed grain beetle, *Oryzaephilus surinamemsis* Linn.

RAISIN MOTH

The raisin moth is known to feed on ripening grapes on the vine, but it is of primary concern in raisins because it lays eggs on the almost-dry grapes. The infestation increases in the stacked or rolled trays and during storage in the vineyard. The larvae feed on the ridges in the surface of the raisins and may bore into the flesh. The mass of excreta and webbing they leave behind is damaging to quality.

The adult moth is about three eighths of an inch in length and has a wingspread of five eights of an inch. The forewings are drab gray, the hind wings whitish and without distinct markings. When the larva is full grown, it leaves raisin storage to find a suitable place to pupate. A dry, dark place, such as under boards, behind paper, or in the soil, is acceptable. Here the larva spins a silken cocoon, in which it may pass the winter. The overwintering pupae appear as moths in late spring or early summer. The moths are active in the evening for three to four hours, beginning a half hour after sunset. The adults live about two weeks; there are three overlapping generations per year.

The moths that emerge in late spring and summer do not lay their eggs on stored raisins; instead, they fly about, looking for new drying fruit. Mulberries that have dropped to the ground are usually the first suitable fruit to become available. These are followed by cull figs and fallen apricots, peaches, and other fruits, so that by the time a new crop of raisins is nearly dry the population of raisin moths is high.

Control.—Sanitation is of the greatest importance. Fallen mulberries, apricots, peaches, figs, and the like should be disked into the soil, to bury them; or they may be raked out into the sun, so that the eggs layed on them in the evening will be destroyed the next day by the heat of direct sunlight. Similarly, when raisins are enclosed in "biscuit" rolls, the rolling should be done in late afternoon, after the hot sun has killed the eggs laid the previous evening; thus the raisins are free of eggs when rolled, and the biscuit roll itself retards reinfestation. Raisins on stacked wooden trays or in "cigarette" rolls are exposed to attack by the raisin moth. Furthermore, the shading effect of the wooden trays may also give some protection to the eggs.

Running the raisins from the trays over a cleaner-screen at the time they are boxed will remove both sand and a high percentage of the raisin moth larvae and eggs. After boxing, the raisins are normally held several weeks for curing or sweating. Prompt delivery to the processors after curing is desirable, since infestation increases in the farmyard during favorable weather, whereas reinfestation is negligible in storage in packing houses. If boxed raisins are to be held for a time, covering them with mothproof and gastight cover prevents new infestation. The gastight cover also facilitates fumigation to destroy infestations already present.

INDIAN-MEAL MOTH

The Indian-meal moth is a serious pest in stored raisins. Unlike the raisin moth, it lays its eggs in the cracks of sweatboxes, picks, and bin walls. The young larvae may then crawl to the raisins inside the containers. The Indian-meal moth is often found in pantries, where it lays its eggs on packages of dried fruit on the shelves. As with the raisin moth, losses are owing largely to the lowering of quality, expense of recleaning, and possible rejection by the purchaser. Infested raisins are also subject to seizure under the Food and Drug Act. Infested raisins, besides having living larvae, are increasingly polluted by excrement, dead larvae, webbing, and cocoons.

The Indian-meal moth is about the same size as the raisin moth. The inner third of the forewings is cream-colored, while the outer two thirds are a dark coppery brown. This coloring of the forewings distinguishes the Indian-meal moth from the raisin moth. The winter is passed in the larval stage, either in the cocoon or lying quiescent in the raisin storage. The moths arising from the overwintering larvae appear from March to May. There are usually five generations per year.

Control.—This moth is primarily a storage pest. Its control is fostered by strict sanitation. Infested raisins are fumigated with methyl bromide or some other acceptable fumigant.

In processing, raisins undergo stemming, sorting, and cleaning, all of which reduce or remove infestations that may be present. Raisins that have been fed on, being lighter, are blown out. To protect clean packaged raisins for a reasonable period a liquid fumigant, such as ethyl formate, is run into the full package before it is sealed. This sterilizes the package and its contents. Reinfestation may result from defects in the machine-sealed packages. If raisins are to be kept in the home for any period they should be held in sealed containers.

DRIED FRUIT BEETLE

This beetle is often found in mushy, rotting cull fruit and melons. It will infest raisins whenever conditions are favorable. Especially susceptible to attack are raisins that have become moist enough for fermentation to start or raisins that were never dried completely. Little infestation occurs in the vineyard when raisins are produced only from sound grapes.

The adult beetles are about one eighth of an inch in length, oval, and robust. They are brown, with light-brown or amber areas on the wing covers. The wing covers are short, leaving the tip of the abdomen exposed. Antennae and legs are reddish or amber. The antennae have knobs at their tips. The developing larvae are about one fourth of an inch in length and of creamy white color, becoming brownish at both ends. During warm weather there may be a generation every three weeks. This short period, together with the large number of eggs laid by each female, makes possible very rapid increases in population. The mature larvae enter the soil in the fall and may not emerge as adults until spring.

The damage of this insect results from direct feeding on the flesh of the raisins, together with the excreta and cast skins, which make a mess that materially reduces the quality of the raisins.

Feeding does not occur below 40° F. Other control measures are the same as those indicated for control of the Indian-meal moth.

SAW-TOOTHED GRAIN BEETLE

This insect feeds on all dried fruits and on cereals, flour, starch, copra, dried meats, and the like. Raisins are one of its favorite foods.

The adult is an active, slender, flattish, brown beetle about one tenth of an inch in length. On either side of its thorax are sharp projections resembling saw teeth. The larvae are pale yellow, with a dark band on each segment and a covering of long hair. The head is yellowish-brown. The larvae are about one tenth of an inch in length. In warm weather there is a generation every forty days. In autumn the adults that are outdoors normally hibernate; in a warm building, however, the usual activities of life continue throughout the year.

This beetle attacks all parts of the raisin, feeding in the folds as much as on the ridges. There is no web formation. The excreta of this pest are yellowish, and the pellets are more elongated as well as smaller than those of the Indian-meal and raisin moth larvae.

Control measures are the same as those used against the Indian-meal moth.

RODENT PESTS AND DEER

Rabbits.—Jack rabbits and other rodent species are often destructive in newly planted and young vineyards. They come back to the same spot night after night, eating the leaves and eventually killing the vines or weakening them severely. The most effective control is to fence the young vineyard with rabbitproof wire netting extending 2.5 feet above the ground and a few inches into the ground. If the rabbits are not very numerous and if only occasional vines are attacked, these vines may be protected by placing individual pieces of wire netting around them. They may also be sprayed with a deer repellent, which will usually cause the rabbits to avoid them.

Gophers.—Gophers may girdle young or old vines just below the surface of the ground. These pests may be trapped, or they may be poisoned by conventional methods. Strychnine or strychnine alkaloid 1080, applied on carrot bait or other root vegetables, gives effective control. Compound 1080 is superior to strychnine. Thrust a probe repeatedly into the ground near fresh gopher mounds until it hits a tunnel. A sudden drop in the pressure required to push the probe indicates that a tunnel or runway has been hit. Enlarge the probe hole somewhat and drop in two pieces of bait. Then close the probe hole with a clod or press it shut with the heel.

Pieces of raw carrot of pencil thickness and about 1.5 inches long make a bait of convenient size. Place two bait pieces per probe and at two or three locations in each burrow system. The bait pieces per burrow should carry about 20 mg. of compound 1080 or 50 milligrams of strychnine. Treat the bait pieces by dusting them with the poison, adding a little at a time, and then shaking or rolling them in a jar or mixing drum. Repeat until all the poison is added. The repeated additions with shaking or rolling are necessary for uniform distribution.

When the gophers are numerous, they should be poisoned with a mechanical gopher-bait applicator. This implement makes an artificial burrow between the vine rows and seeds it at intervals with strychnine alkaloid (3 per cent) or 2 ounces of compound 1080 (0.125 per cent) per 100 pounds of grain—either clean wheat, hulled barley, or lightly rolled oat groats. This and the above method of poisoning must be supervised by the County Agricultural Commissioner's staff. Either type of bait is very toxic and must be handled with great care (Kepner *et al.*, 1958).

Deer.—The only effective control for deer is fencing. Several types of fences are described by Longhurst *et al.* (1962): an eight foot vertical fence; a four foot vertical fence with a four foot horizontal mesh addition projecting outward from its top; and an incline mesh fence rising from the ground outward at an angle of 45° to a height of 4 to 5 feet. Whatever type is used it must be deer tight. Deer repellents have not proven effective.

BIRDS

For years birds have been pests in isolated vineyards largely surrounded by brush or forest. They are now causing damage in areas planted largely to vines and well removed from forests. Their depredation is definitely increasing. The damage is in direct loss of fruit from feeding, rot that develops where the berries have been pecked, the spilling of juice on berries not pecked, and, in table fruit, the added cost of trimming. At present Linnets and starlings are doing the most damage. However, the damage by other species is increasing in California.

Various control measures have been tried such as flashing metal disks, shooting, noise-making devices (firecrackers, acetylene bombs set to explode at given time intervals), poisoning, and covering with open mesh cloth. In Europe these additional methods have been used to prevent depredation by starlings: driving them from their roosting places with smoke, helicopters, and rockets; scaring them from the vineyards by broadcasting the danger (warning) cry of the starling, through loud-speakers; suspending—from balloons—models of the birds that prey on the starling; and keeping them out of the vines with covers of strips of synthetic material.

Boudreau (1972), of Almaden Vineyards, had fairly effective control of finches by inducing them to feed on bait treated with strychnine. (This treatment must be cleared through the Agricultural Commissioners.) He also had fair success using trapping and natural alarm sounds for both starlings and finches. The alarms were from both fixed or mobile equipment, along with occasional gunfire as required.

BIBLIOGRAPHY

AliNiazee, M. T., and E. M. Stafford. 1972. Notes on the biology, ecology, and damage of *Platynota stultana* on grapes. Jour. Econ. Ento., 65:1042–1044.

———, ———. 1972. Virgin female traps aid in control of omnivorous leaf roller. Calif. Agric., 26(1):5–6.

Bailey, S. F. 1942. The grape or vine thrips, *Drepandothrips reuteri*. Jour. Econ. Ento., 35:382–386.

Barnes, M. M., C. R. Ash, and A. S. Deal. 1954. Ground pearls on grape roots. California Agr., 8:5, 10.

Berg, H. W. 1959. Investigation of defects in grapes delivered to California wineries. Amer. Jour. Enol. Vitic., 10:61–68.

Boudreau, G. W. 1972. Factors related to bird depredations in vineyards. Amer. Jour. Enol. Vitic., 23:50–53.

Coombe, B. G. 1963. Phylloxera and its relation to South Australian viticulture. Dept. Agric., South Australia, Tech. Bull. No. 31.

Davidson, W. M., and R. L. Nougaret. 1921. The grape phylloxera in California. United States Dept. Agr. Bull., 903:1–128.

Ebling, W. 1939. The grape bud beetle, *Glyptoscelis squamulata*, Crotch. California State Dept. Agr. Bull., 28:459–465.

Essig, E. O. 1959. Insects and mites of western North America. New York, Macmillan. (See pp. 445, 476.)

Flaherty, D. L., C. D. Lynn, F. L. Jensen, and D. A. Luvisi. 1969. Ecology and integrated control of spider mites in San Joaquin Valley. California Agric., 23(4):11.

Gonzalez R. R. H., H. Kido, A. Marin, and P. Hughes. 1969. Biología y esayos preliminares de control del margarodes des de la vid, *Margarodes vitis* Philippi. Agricultura Tecnica, 29:93–122.

Hartzell, F. K. 1910. A preliminary report on grape insects. New York Agr. Exp. Sta. Bull., 331:494–514.

Jensen, F. L. 1966. Grape leafhopper control with Bacillus Thuringiensis. California Agric., 20(7):2–3.

———. 1969. Microbal insecticides for control of grape leaf folder. California Agric., 23(4):5–6.

———, and M. T. AliNiazee. 1972. Microbal insecticides for grape leaf folder control. California Agric., 26(7):5.

———, D. L. Flaherty and L. Chiarappa. 1969. Population densities and economic injury levels of grape leafhopper. California Agric., 23(4):9–10.

———, E. M. Stafford, H. Kido, and C. D. Lynn. 1961. Field tests for control of grape leafhoppers resistant to insecticides. California Agric., 15(7):13–14.

Kepner, R. A., W. E. Howard, M. W. Cummings, and E. M. Brock. 1958. U.C. mechanical gopher-bait applicator, construction and use. Univ. of Calif., Agric. Ext. Ser. Pub. AXT 32:1–11.

Kido, H., E. M. Stafford, and N. F. McCalley. 1971. Orange tortrix on grapes in Salinas Valley. California Agric., 25(7):10–11.

Kunde, R. M., L. A. Lider, and R. V. Schmitt. 1968. A test of *Vitis* resistance to *Xiphinema index*. Amer. Jour. Enol. Vitic., 19:30–36.

Lafon, J., P. Couillaud, and R. Hude. 1961. Maladies et parasites de la vigne. II. Insects et accidents. Paris, Baillière et fils, pp. 288.

Lange, W. J. 1944. The western grape skeletonizer *Harrisima brillians* in California. California State Dept. Agr. Bull., 33(2):98–104.

Lear, B., and L. A. Lider. 1959. Eradication of root-knot nematodes from grapevine rootings by hot water. Plant Disease Reptr., 43(3):314–317.

Longhurst, W. M., M. B. Jones, R. R. Parks, L. W. Neubam, and M. W. Cummings. 1962. Fences for controlling deer damage. Calif. Agr. Exp. Sta. Circ., 514:1–19.

Lounsbury, C. P. 1910. The calandra of the vine. Agr. Jour. Cape of Good Hope, 37:448–450.

Luvisi, D. A., and F. L. Jensen. 1972. Thompson Seedless scarring trials. Mimeo. Kearney Field Station.

———, and A. N. Kasimatis. 1972. Scarring of Thompson Seedless table grapes. California Agric., 26(8):3–5.

McGrew, J. R., and G. W. Still. 1972. Control of grape diseases and insects in the Eastern United States. U.S. Dept. Agric. Farmers' Bull. 1893.

Myburgh, A. C. 1961. A new approach to the fruit fly problem. The Deciduous Fruit Gr., 11:161–165.

Perold, A. I. 1927. A treatise on viticulture. London, Macmillan. (See p. 497.)

Quaintance, A. L., and C. L. Shear. 1926. Insect and fungus enemies of the grape. United States Dept. Agr. Farmers' Bull., 1220:1–54.

Quayle, H. J. 1908. The California grape rootworm. California Agr. Exp. Sta. Bull., 195:1–28.

Raski, D. J., W. H. Hart, and A. N. Kasimatis. 1965. Nematodes and their control in vineyards. Calif. Agr. Exp. Sta. Circ., 533:1–22.

———, and L. A. Lider. 1959. Nematodes in grape production. California Agric., 13:13–15.

Simmons, P., D. F. Barnes, and E. Snyder. 1951. Control of grape phylloxera. Wines and Vines, 32(12):22–23.

Smith, L. M., and E. M. Stafford. 1948. The bud mite and the erineum mite of grapes. Hilgardia, 18:317–334.

———, ———. 1955. Grape pests in California. Calif. Agr. Exp. Sta. Circ., 445:1–61.

Stafford, E. M. 1959. The Drosophila problem in the vineyard. Wines and Vines, 40(3):27.

Stellwaag, F. 1929. Die Weinbauinsekten der Kulturländer. Berlin, Paul Parey.

Stombler, V. 1960. Drosophila problems as related to peaches and tomatoes. California Fig Inst. 14th Ann. Conf., 39–41.

Tyler, Jocelyn. 1933. The root-knot nematode. California Agr. Exp. Sta. Circ., 330:1–30.

Yerinton, A. P., E. M. Stafford, and H. Kido. 1960. Experiments in chemical control of drosophila in fig orchards and vineyards. California Fig Inst. 14th Ann. Conf., 33–35.

20

Harvesting and Packing
Table Grapes

Most of California's table grapes are marketed 2,000 or more miles from the vineyards in which they are grown. The successful marketing of grapes at such distances and at prices that encourage consumption has required special methods of handling. The general methods have become rather highly standardized, but improvements in detail are constantly being made. The methods, along with the important changes, are discussed in this chapter.

STANDARDS FOR MATURITY

Since table grapes are grown primarily to be eaten, a first consideration in harvesting should be consumer acceptance. If the season's first grapes of a particular variety or from a particular area do not please the consumer, they are rejected, and, unfortunately, buyer resistance usually affects, for some time, all succeeding lots from the same area.

The importance of this reaction was recognized soon after California table grapes began to move in volume to markets in the eastern United States. Practically no information was available then on the relation of stage of maturity of table grapes to palatability. Since however, degree Brix * had proved its usefulness as a measure of maturity for wine pro-

* Degree Brix is synonymous with the term Degree Balling. Both are measures of the total soluble solids in a solution, as gms. per 100 ml. In this text the term Degree Brix (° Brix) is used throughout this book.

duction, the table grape industry decided to use it. It was found to be closely correlated with palatability. Its use as a measure of the maturity of table grapes was given legal recognition in the first California Fruit, Nut and Vegetable Standardization Act, in 1915. The industry was awakening to the fact that a minimum standard of maturity was a most important guard against disappointing the consumer and that it thereby benefited the producer as well.

Although degree Brix (or a similar density indicator) has long been used to determine the maturity of grapes, both here and abroad, and Winkler (1932) indicated its high correlation with palatability (fig. 140), it has not been entirely adequate. The reason is that no single constituent of the maturing or mature grape controls eating quality. This follows from the definition that a grape is mature when the changes in the several constituents (color, sugar, acid, pH, tannin, etc.) of the fruit have proceeded to a point where their combined effect on palatability is the nearest approach to the ideal for the variety in the use to which it will be put. In the range of maturity of most interest to table grape producers, most interference has been from high (and to a much lesser extent lower) levels of acidity.

Winkler's investigations of interference of acidity with the reliability of degree Brix alone as a measure of palatability showed that acidity at a

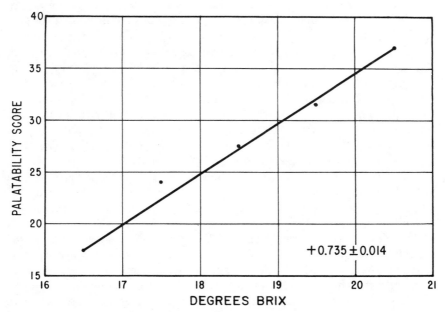

FIGURE 140: The relation of degree Brix to the palatability of grapes.

given degree Brix is markedly influenced by the level of temperature during the period while the grapes are ripening. Grapes of a single variety at the same degree Brix differ in palatability according to whether they were grown under hot or cool conditions. Further, temperature averages in a single area of California during the ripening period may differ enough from year to year to affect the level of acidity drastically, even at the same degree Brix, thereby affecting palatability. For example, Thompson Seedless in the same vineyard of Fresno County and in the ripening stage of 17° to 19° Brix had an acidity of 0.67 per cent in a year when the temperature was high during the ripening period, with 85 per cent of the samples of fruit tasting "good," whereas the fruit had an acidity of 1.03 per cent in a year that was cool during the ripening period, with only 11 per cent of the samples tasting "good."

The accuracy of degree Brix as a measure of palatability is probably also affected by abnormally low acid contents. Taste studies by Nelson *et al.* (1963) showed poor acceptability when both sugar and acid were low even at a high Brix-acid ratio. This condition may be intensified by overcropping, which delays attainment of the desired degree Brix, by permitting the fruit to become overripe in hot seasons, or when the vines are attacked by insects or infected with leafroll. The influence of low acidity is not so marked as that of high acidity, but its effects deserve attention.

The differences in acidity between regions and seasons, though marked only in certain years, make it clear that degree Brix alone cannot be expected to be an entirely satisfactory measure of palatability. With a cool ripening period, the grape will be sour at the minimum degree Brix requirement; with a very hot ripening period, the taste may actually tend to flatness. This variation from the degree Brix standard is substantiated by five years of analytical and sensory evaluation data on the table grapes— Thompson Seedless, Malaga, Ribier, Emperor, Tokay, and Red Malaga— in their ripening range of maturity. The minimum degree Brix standard of 1959 permitted from 8 to 24 per cent of the fruit scoring poor to pass, while excluding 0.0 to 3.6 per cent of fruit scoring fair or better. The elimination of fruit scoring poor was less effective in the years that were cool during ripening. One may ask why the consumer should not be displeased with the percentage of fruit scoring poor that is admitted. Yet, raising the degree Brix requirement to eliminate more poor fruit would exclude too much fruit of acceptable palatability.

The above investigations suggested that a minimum standard be based on the Brix-acid ratio. This ratio has a sounder basis for a maturity standard, in that it combines both the sugars (sweet) and the acids (sour)— primary tastes that are predominant factors in the eating quality of grapes. Using the same five years' data, as above, with a Brix-acid ratio standard it was found that only 1.4 to 3.5 per cent of fruit scoring poor was passed and only 0.0 to 1.1 per cent of fruit scoring fair or better was excluded. Thus, the separation of poor and good fruit using the Brix-acid ratio was much more efficient than that by degree Brix alone. In applying the Brix-acid ratio as a standard, the use of a minimum degree Brix would be desirable. This would materially reduce the number of acidity determinations required and, of greater importance, would discourage overcropping to the point of delaying maturity.

The industry has adopted alternate standards to the minimum degree Brix based on the minimum Brix-acid ratios for a number of varieties. There is no doubt that the industry could greatly strengthen its position by thinking in terms of the Brix-acid ratio as the citrus industry has done, rather than only in terms of degree Brix. Most of the older European grape-producing countries have done a great deal of research on maturity standards, and in every case their conclusions point to a ratio. The nature and extent of the earlier work was summarized by Dalmasso and Venezia (1937), who indicated Brix-acid ratios for more than thirty varieties. These range from about 20:1 to 35:1. Progress toward using ratios in France has been reported by Hugues and Bouffard (1937). They state very pointedly that an increase of 100 per cent in the sale of table grapes in France between 1930 and 1935 was a result of improvement in the quality and palatability of the fruit offered. They recommended a Brix-acid ratio of at least 25:1 for the Chasselas doré, the leading table grape of France. Similarly, the export of Chaouch and Dattier from Bulgaria increased from 1.8 per cent of world exports of table grapes in 1930 to 24.6 per cent in 1935. According to Nedelchev and Kondarev (1934), this increase was the result of government control of the quality and maturity of grapes offered for export. The standard Brix-acid ratio was 25:1 for the Chaouch and 22:1 for the Dattier.

In view of the extensive use of Brix-acid ratio as a minimum standard of maturity for table grapes abroad and the reluctance of the California industry to put it to full use led Nelson *et al.* (1963) to make a further study of the chemical and sensory variabilities in table grapes. A number of refinements were made in the former procedure. The clusters of Perlette, Cardinal, Thompson Seedless, Ribier, and Tokay to be analyzed were picked with the aid of hand refractometers to represent fruit of 1° Brix below the minimum degree Brix standard, at the standard, and 1° or 2° Brix above the standard. The picked fruit was cooled immediately in a mobile refrigerator. In preparing the fruit for analyses the individual berries were cut from the clusters, then separated into the desired single degree Brix lots by floatation in sugar solutions. One part of each lot of fruit was used for chemical analyses and the other for sensory scoring. For scoring, the fruit was at 70° F. (20° C.), and each sample was scored by 25 or more individuals of the taste panel of 56 members. The results of this study support the superiority of the Brix-acid ratio over degree Brix alone as a method of indicating palatability of table grapes.

On "Grape Day" at Davis in 1961, 325 growers and allied industry people scored Thompson Seedless of the same lots scored by the University panel. The graph of their scores of acceptability paralleled that of the University panel's scores. Last season, Nelson *et al.* (1972) had 375 customers of a supermarket in Chicago score Perlette grapes that had been harvested in the same degree Brix range and prepared for tasting in the same manner as the grapes placed before the University panel. Acceptability increased markedly with increase in degree Brix. Using Thompson Seedless grapes prepared as above, Nelson *et al.* (1973) reports the finding of 1,374 tasters in six Safeway Supermarkets. This study further substantiates the ratio as the best index of eating quality. With the indications of these and earlier tastings it seems that industry, even if it does not want a Brix-acid ratio standard, should be considering consumer acceptability when harvesting table grapes rather than thinking only of meeting a minimum Brix requirement.

HARVESTING

In determining the best time or stage of development for picking table grapes, the chief considerations are that the grapes should (a) be attractive in appearance and eating quality, (b) have good shipping and keeping qualities, and (c) reach the market when prices are favorable.

Time to harvest.—It is not often possible to pick grapes in California when all three of the above factors are at their best. A compromise is usually necessary. Very early in the season prices are high, and therefore many of the very early table grapes are picked as soon as they reach the minimum degree of maturity permitted by law. This early fruit usually sells for very high prices. If immature, however—and it often is—it has a depressing effect on the market. Grapes that ripen in midseason are usually allowed to reach prime appearance, palatability, and shipping qualities, but prices are lower because of the more abundant supply. Late in the season prices are again high. In sections of the state where harvest is naturally late, or with late maturing varieties, the fruit is permitted to attain full maturity and then harvested for shipment or to be placed in cold storage.

Ripening, as it interests the grower and consumer, consists in an increase in sugars (degree Brix), a decrease in acidity, and the development of color, texture, and flavor characteristic of the variety. These changes are continuous so long as the grapes remain on the vine, but they stop as soon as the grapes are harvested. Under normal conditions, and level of crop, such changes result in a gradual improvement until the optimum stage is reached, followed by a gradual deterioration. The optimum stage, the proper time to pick, represents a compromise of the three considerations. The first-mentioned consideration—satisfaction to the consumer—should usually be the deciding factor. The second is involved in the first, for the fruit must be good not only when it is removed from the vines, but also when it reaches the consumer. Always important in determining price is the condition of the general market at the time the grapes are sold—a week or so after they are shipped. Firm-ripe grapes ship and store better than either under-ripe or over-ripe. With the rapid release of information on daily shipments and selling prices, it is possible to predict rather closely what the supply in the major markets will be and what effect this will have on the selling price.

Selection of clusters.—Only when vines carry a very light crop will all of the clusters, even on a single vine, reach picking stage at the same time. With the usual level of cropping, two pickings, and sometimes three, are necessary to ensure harvested clusters that are uniform in appearance and palatability. The characters generally used to determine which clusters should be picked are as follows:

1. *Appearance of the berries.*—As grapes mature, they develop a color characteristic of the variety in the given environment. The color of red and black grapes becomes more intense and brilliant as ripening progresses. The green color of white varieties becomes more nearly white or yellow. The hue and brilliance of the color are also influenced by climate and, possibly, by soil. Just as "ripe grapes" of a given variety are not always the same color, neither is a well-colored grape necessarily a ripe one. Nevertheless, on a given vine in a given vineyard the grape of the most desirable color is usually of the best quality. (For factors affecting color development see p. 158.) Because of the influence of temperature and light on color development, it is well to correlate color roughly with refractometer readings at the beginning of picking. By doing this with the pickers, the grower can help them determine which clusters to pick, thereby facilitating harvest and improving quality.

2. *Color and condition of cluster stems.*—As the berries mature, the cluster stems also mature. A wood, straw, or yellow color of the stem, depending on the variety, indicates that the berries, too, are mature. It also indicates that the fruit on the cluster is likely to be of good quality for the variety. Not all varieties, however, develop a characteristic stem color that is usable as a guide in picking. The oft-repeated saying that the stems of certain varieties, such as Emperor or Malaga, must be "sealed" before the fruit is mature for storage refers solely to maturation of the bark of the stems. As the stem bark changes from green to brown there is a reduction in stem diameter, though the vessels inside the stem are not affected. The brown stem, nevertheless, is a good indicator of fruit maturity. Here the

extent of stem coloring can be correlated with the refractometer as a further guide in picking. This stem color is not to be confused with the "brown stem" that results from delayed or inadequate precooling after harvest.

3. *Taste.*—The greenest grapes on a cluster are practically always those near the tip. If these are good to eat, the entire cluster is ripe for picking. The sense of taste, however, is quickly dulled, and a picker who tastes berries frequently will soon lose the ability to tell whether the grapes are ripe or not. Thus, the picker should correlate taste with berry or stem color and condition, so that he can judge by these, making only an occasional check by taste.

In harvesting table grapes it should be remembered that the removal of clusters (in harvest or thinning) improves conditions for development of the retained clusters: they mature more uniformly. This is simply a thinning effect (Winkler, 1934). The effectiveness of thinning on the overall development of the fruit is greatest when it is done early (see p. 341). At any time, however, removing excess clusters and unmarketable fruit improves the remaining fruit (Benvegnin, 1954). It is generally recognized by table grape growers that a picking tends to accelerate the ripening of the remaining fruit. Some growers in the early areas therefore make a final adjustment in their crop by removing clusters a relatively short time before the first picking. Doing this earlier would increase the effects (advance ripening and improve berry size and uniformity of color), but sometimes only uniformity of coloring needs improvement, and this can be achieved by the late thinning. Thinning may also be delayed to guard against losses such as that from sunburn.

Picking and trimming.—The cluster should be handled only by the stem. The berries are covered with a waxy substance, the cuticle, usually called the bloom. To rub the bloom even lightly changes its structure and impairs the natural appearance of the grapes. Also, some varieties tend to discolor if they are rubbed hard. Further care in handling is necessary to avoid breaking the skin around the point of attachment of the berry to the pedicel (cap stem). Where breaking occurs, deterioration may ensue and give decay-causing organisms a port of entry.

The picker should grasp the cluster by the stem (peduncle) and remove it from the vine by cutting the stem with picking or trimming shears near its attachment to the cane. Then, still holding the cluster by the stem, he should carefully remove all broken, decayed, or otherwise defective berries by cutting the pedicels or the small branches of the cluster with trimming shears. Green or poorly colored, small, or misshapen berries and straggly parts of the cluster may also be removed. The extent to which this is profitable is determined by the cost of labor and the value of the grapes. Sometimes picking and trimming are done by different workers.

The manner of doing these operations properly, however, remains the same.

PACKING

The word "pack" as used by growers, packers, and shippers may refer to the places of packing, the type of container, and the arrangement of the clusters in the container. The grape packs that are commonly used in California may be classified as follows:

By place of packing:

Vineyard $\left\{\begin{array}{l}\text{Packs completed along vine rows}\\ \text{Packs made in avenue}\end{array}\right.$

House or shed

By containers used:

Lug boxes (usually 23 pounds) $\left.\right\}$ $\begin{array}{l}\text{Made of light wood}\\ \text{or}\\ \text{Corrigated fiberboard}\end{array}$

Chests for sawdust packaging

Climax basket—only for American type grapes

By arrangement in the container:

Stems-up pack

Chest (sawdust) pack

Consumer-unit packs—rarely used, except at terminal market.

Wrapped packs

Place of packing.—Table grapes should be packed at a place that makes possible minimum but careful handling, thorough fruit trimming, limited exposure to high temperatures, and a uniform pack of attractive fruit. Another factor may be economy. Much has been said about the relative merits and faults of row and avenue packing in the vineyard—vineyard field packing—and of packing in a specially equipped building—house packing. Both places are suitable, but each is best suited to a different set of circumstances.

In *row packing* the grapes are placed directly from the vine into marketing container in which they will be sold. The picker does the trimming as well as the packing (fig. 141). There is no rehandling of the fruit. This type of packing requires that each picker be an expert packer. Adequate supervision is difficult and expensive, and the packs often lack uniformity.

Field packing involves the least investment in equipment, which sometimes may be only the shears that the workmen use in picking and trimming the clusters. In other cases, stands support the boxes at a tilt and height convenient for packing. When stands are not available, the box being packed is placed crosswise in an empty box to hold it at the tilt for

FIGURE 141: Packing grapes along the vine row (vineyard packing).

convenient packing. In many instances, packing stands are equipped with scales to ensure a given weight per pack.

Row packing may be considered when the clusters are good and require but little trimming, when varieties (such as Rish Baba or Olivette blanche) do not stand rehandling well, and when enough skilled pickers are available.

Avenue packing (a form of vineyard packing) is done along the avenues or roadways of the vineyards. In this system one or a number of skilled workers do the packing. It is done on a light bench with or without scales but with facilities for supporting the full boxes (field lugs) and a rack to hold the lug or lugs in position while they are being packed. When a number of packers work together, the packing bench has several or more packing positions, is usually mobile, and is pulled by tractor or pickup truck. The larger mobile packing lines bring more of the advantage of the house pack to the vineyard—good scales, better facilities for handling the lugs, better shade, and supervision. Some even pack two grades of fruit. The packers usually stand on the ground or there may be a place for them to stand on the packing rig. The packed lugs are lidded with snap on lids and set off to be picked up shortly, loaded on pallets on the truck and hauled to the precooler.

The grape pickers use light-weight boxes or sometimes regular shipping lugs. They pick and trim the fruit, place it in the field boxes, then carry or haul the full boxes to the avenue on light weight carriers with large pneumatic tires that hold a number of boxes.

When operating in small units, one man packs the fruit brought to him by 4 to 6 pickers (fig. 142). This size unit is often composed of a family. They may leapfrog other similar units down the avenue as they finish the 2–4 rows they work on at a time. With several or more packers working together, the picking and trimming crews will appropriately be larger.

This system of vineyard packing makes somewhat greater use of skilled packers. The completed packs are more uniform, and adequate supervision

FIGURE 142: A bench for avenue packing, showing the incline for the full field lugs at left, two incline supports for holding shipping lug during packing (these have scales), and in back roller conveyor for receiving full field boxes. (*Courtesy of K. E. Nelson*)

is easier. The time between vine and precooling is about minimal. At present it is the most widely used system of harvesting and packing used in California.

House packing, properly organized, can get grapes under refrigeration with but little more delay than is usual in row or avenue packing.

The pickers remove selected clusters from the vines, and place them carefully, stems up, one layer deep, in field lugs. The full lugs may be carried to the avenue but more often they are left under the vines. They are collected and palletized on flat bed trucks. Some vineyardists use mechanical elevators to lift the lugs to the handlers on the trucks. The full pallets are then hauled to the packing house without delay. In the house the packing crew trims and packs the fruit into the container in which it will be sent to market. The packers are skilled workers, usually women. The work is highly centralized, supervision is easy and efficient, and working conditions are good, or at least better than in the vineyard.

Modern packing houses are equipped with packing benches, double packing racks, and scales that enable the packer to fill the boxes to a predetermined weight (figs. 143, 144). The packer usually handles two grades of fruit, the better or top grade and the lesser one, segregating clusters to maintain the uniformity of the grades, particularly the top one. Most of the houses are well equipped with labor-saving conveyers. The new houses are air-conditioned.

FIGURE 143: Packing grapes in a packing house. Note the completed packs and the two lugs in front of each worker for packing. One of these is usually filled with the best fruit, while the other receives that of lesser quality.

Harvesting and Packing Table Grapes

FIGURE 144: View of facilities in a large packing house. The inclined bench by each packer has room for two lugs to permit packing two grades of fruit at the same time.

House packing is of value for the packing of fruit that requires much trimming. It is not well adapted for grape varieties that are especially subject to mechanical injury in rehandling. House packing is usually somewhat more expensive than field or avenue packing, owing to the greater capital investment.

CONTAINERS

The types and inside dimensions of standard containers for grapes are set forth in the Agricultural Code of the California State Department of Agriculture (1967).

The *lug* is the container most generally used; over 95 per cent of the grape harvest moves to the market in lugs. The widely used lugs are 16⅛ inches long, 13½ inches wide, and 3¾ to 5¾ inches deep. Although lugs are generally packed to contain 23 pounds in the San Joaquin Valley, 22 pounds in the desert region and 32 pounds in chests, the net weight of fruit must be stamped on the container. There are other variations in weight, but they are minor and are indicated in the discussion of such packs. The depth of the lug is varied to facilitate the packing of different varieties and to meet the wishes of the grower or shipper. It is usually constructed of light pine wood and vented for easy cooling and fumigation of the fruit packed in it. In use the lug has a bottom pad of shredded paper or excelsior with side and end guards and a light pad or curtain on top. Recently, considerable interest has developed in substitute material. Corrigated fibreboard lugs of several designs, of about the same dimensions as the wooden lug, have found a limited place in some segments of the industry.

The *sawdust chest*—18⅝ inches long, 14¹⁵⁄₁₆ inches wide, and 7¾ inches deep—has been the principal container used for packing grapes for export to Europe, South America, and the Far East. When packed, it contains 32 to 34 pounds of grapes and 9 to 11 pounds of sawdust. It is an expensive pack. With the combining of conventional fumigation with the two-stage sulfur dioxide generator the standard lug is rapidly displacing the chest (sawdust pack) for export (see p. 603).

Consumer units, or similar containers for small quantities of grapes, are rarely used (see p. 570), except at terminal markets.

The *climax basket* is the principal container used for marketing American grapes. It measures 14 by 6½ inches at the top and 12 by 4½ inches at the bottom and is 4¹¹⁄₁₆ inches deep. It is seldom, if ever, used for *vinifera* grapes.

There are other standard containers that are rarely used. Those who are interested may refer to the Agricultural Code of the California State Department of Agriculture (1967), which gives the dimensions of these containers and the conditions under which they may be used as standard containers.

ARRANGEMENT IN THE CONTAINER

Up to the early 1920's, practically all table grapes were house packed, mostly in crates as faced packs. The manipulation of the clusters for such packs required that the grapes be somewhat wilted, which meant that they might stand in field lugs for twenty-four to forty-eight hours before being packed. The resulting deterioration in the fruit caused some packers and shippers to question the practice. Some compared packs of fresh and wilted grapes on their premises. The results pointed up the better appearance and quality of fruit that was packed immediately. The comparisons also indicated the need for a different container for packing fresh grapes. This need was met, at least in part, by shifting from the four-basket crate to the lug being used for other fruits. The faced pack continued in use, though it was not satisfactory for freshly harvested grapes. Then, in 1922, the most important single development in the history of grape marketing in California was made by George F. Johnson, a desert grower and shipper, when he introduced the *stems-up pack*. It met the needs for handling fresh grapes so well that today more than 95 per cent of all table grapes shipped out of California are packed with the stems up. The development of this pack also made field packing practical. Today all table grapes in lugs, regardless of the place of packing, are packed with the stems up, except for some specialized packs.

Stems-up pack.—For making this pack, the lug is tilted endwise at an angle of 25 to 30 degrees on the packing stand. To begin the packing, clusters are laid horizontally on the bottom at the low end of the lug, forming a row across the container. Then clusters are placed next to and atop these, on end, with the stems up and the basal part of the cluster from about a half inch to 1 inch above the edges of the lug—not more. The tilt in the box helps to keep the upright clusters in place. As required, other clusters are laid in a horizontal position to fill the spaces between the tapering upright clusters and to support the main bulk of the contents at the proper height. When the packing is finished, the bases of the upright clusters should all be at the same height, with the stems above. When well made, this pack is attractive, even though cluster stems are in full view. Fresh grapes can be packed in this manner with very little handling injury. Likewise, the clusters can be removed from the lug without breaking them to pieces. For unpacking, the box should be tilted in the same manner as for packing, and the grapes removed in reverse order. The boxes are always packed from the end with the label; therefore this end should also be down in unpacking.

Stems-up pack for near markets.—There is a growing trend in California toward handling grapes for markets within the state in field lugs or similar unlidded containers. The reason is greater economy. Regular field lugs are returned for reuse. There is, also, interest in a nonreturnable container with dimensions similar to those of the field lug. It would have the distinct advantages of being new and clean, and of eliminating the holding and returning of containers, which can be a costly chore in large markets. It would likely create a disposal problem.

The packing of the lugs and comparable containers is identical with the stems-up pack just described. The fruit is picked, thoroughly trimmed, and then placed one or two layers deep in the container. The upper level of the fruit is just below the top of the lug. The containers are not lidded. Full lugs are loaded directly onto the truck that will take them to the market. Precooling and treatment with sulfur dioxide are omitted. The purpose of this pack is to get the grapes to market in fresh condition with the least possible handling and at minimum cost.

Chest pack.—The packing of the 32- to 34-pound "sawdust chest" proceeds exactly as does the packing of lugs, except that an excelsior pad which has paper wings long enough to extend over the pack is placed in the chests. In the completed pack the clusters do not project above the top of the container. Sawdust to fill the spaces around and between the grapes is not added until just before shipment. To be effective, sulfur dioxide treatment and precooling must be carried out before the sawdust is added. Similarly, if the fruit is to be held in cold storage, it is held without sawdust, so that it can be retreated with sulfur dioxide at regular intervals. In storage, racks or dunnage strips are placed between the unlidded chest to facilitate sulfuring and cooling (see fig. 154).

When the chests are to be prepared for shipment, they are filled with "moisturized" sawdust, especially prepared. The sawdust as it comes from the mills is bolted, fanned, and graded to remove fine material and splinters. Then it is kiln-dried to set gums and resins that might otherwise impart odors and flavors to the grapes. Since the sawdust is almost devoid of moisture when it reaches the packing house, its moisture content must be brought back to about 12 per cent, so that it will not absorb undue moisture from the grapes. It should be precooled before being run into the packed chests.

Faced pack.—Besides the stems-up pack, a few specialty packs are occasionally used. The four-basket crate is used to a limited extent to provide a faced pack. The fruit in the space above the baskets is faced; that is, the bases and tips of the clusters are tucked under, so that none of the framework of the clusters shows. This pack requires great skill, and it is not suitable for freshly harvested grapes. When well made, it is attractive, but the grapes cannot take the manipulation required without injury.

Another specialty pack used from time to time is the *star*, or *cluster*, *pack*. In this, the baskets of the crate are packed without special arrangement. Then four large, attractive clusters are placed on top with their stem ends near the center of the pack and their tips at the four corners. Small clusters may be placed between the four large ones. Their tips, too, must point outward. The center, where the stems of the radiating clusters meet, is covered with colored paper ribbons or similar material. Rarely used at present.

Consumer-unit pack.—Some 15 years ago there was widespread interest, especially among retailers, in packages of a size ready for sale to the consumer. The favored package was a 1½–2 pound pasteboard box or film over-wrapped plastic basket, a dozen of which would fit into a shipping tray. A single cluster usually was not large or heavy enough to fill the basket, and even if it was, its shape would not fit into its rectangular shape and depth. A considerable amount of cutting of clusters was necessary which gave the appearance of having been made of trimmings. Then, too, if something went wrong in the basket after it left the packer it could not be reconditioned nor could it be stored successfully. This pack has all but disappeared at the point of production.

Most grapes in the East are consumer packaged in paper pulp (or plastic shallow trays overwrapped with heat sealed film). In other locations the grapes may be placed in clear plastic bags. This is done in the back of the supermarket or at the distributional center of a chain of stores. This has been successful since it is done when the grapes are in or, at most, one day from, the retail market. The packages, ranging in weight from 1 to 3 pounds (or fractions thereof) or usually machine stamped indicating the variety, weight, prices per pound and the price of the unit.

Wrapped packs.—Two wrapped packs are used to a limited extent in California. In one, chimney wrap, individual clusters are wrapped in tissue paper and packed stems up in standard lugs. The wrap does not cover the upper end of the cluster in the lug; the stem end of the cluster is visible when the lid of the lug is removed. Since wrapped clusters do not fit together so closely as unwrapped clusters, these packs contain 18 to 22 pounds of fruit.

Cooling and sulfur dioxide penetration are slowed down by the wraps. Under the low humidity of some storage houses or in prolonged storage, however, these disadvantages seem to be compensated by a slower loss of moisture by the grapes and a longer retention of good stem condition.

In the other wrapped pack, the individual clusters are wrapped completely in tissue paper. The wrapped clusters are then placed in a single layer on a pad of wood wool (excelsior). Wood wool is also placed between the clusters to prevent movement. Another pad of wood wool is placed over the fruit. This pack (not used in California) is most generally employed in the transportation of South African and South American table grapes to markets in the Northern Hemisphere. The container for this wrapped pack is 22⅛ inches long, 15 inches wide, and 4⅞ inches deep. The wrapping and the wood-wool filler materially slow cooling and sulfur dioxide penetration, but they also slow loss of moisture, thus preserving stem condition. Because of the generous use of wood wool, this pack usually contains only 10 pounds of grapes. The pack offers excellent protection against rough handling on the docks.

MAINTAINING THE QUALITY OF HARVESTED GRAPES

Grapes do not ripen after harvest. In grapes there is no reserve, such as starch, that might by hydrolyzed to increase the sugar content after picking and thereby improve the flavor or balance of the fruit. Thus, the grape is at its best when it is cut from the vine. If it is not mature and of high quality at that time, it never will be. All changes after harvest are deteriorative. The rate of deterioration, however, can be slowed appreciably by proper post-harvest handling of the fruit.

Trimming.—Whether the trimming is done in the vineyard or in a packing house, it must be thorough. The removal of injured, undesirable, and diseased berries not only improves the initial appearance of the clusters, but also materially reduces the likelihood of infection later, which would be particularly damaging to appearance.

Careful handling.—The trimmed clusters must be handled with care. If not, additional injuries will be inflicted on both berries and stems. Damage to the berries will provide new courts of infection by organisms, and injuries to the stems will accelerate deterioration. For instance, the clusters of one of two identical lots of grapes were handled so that the laterals and pedicels were bent freely—similar to the manner in which many packers roll the cluster in one hand while they remove undesirable berries with the other—and the clusters of the other lot were subjected to minimum handling. After six days in cold storage Nelson (1955) found that the roughly handled clusters had three times as many dry stems and soft berries, five times as many brown stems, and a slightly greater weight loss than the clusters that were handled carefully. Careless handling also removes bloom, reducing attractive appearance.

Stem browning.—Grapes are one of the few fresh fruits whose stems are an important factor of quality. The stems are essential for handling and trimming, and their condition is an indicator of the treatment the fruit has received. They are the first part of the cluster to deteriorate. Nelson found that a greater percentage of the stems of Tokay turned brown in two hours at 100° than in eight hours at 70° F. The rates of stem browning he found at different temperatures in different areas of California during harvesting were 1.6 per cent per hour at 70°, 2.9 per cent at 80°, 4.4 per cent at 90°, and 7.3 per cent at 100° F.

Water loss.—A cluster of grapes, being composed of numerous berries, has an extensive surface area—the skins—enclosing a comparatively small volume. This high ratio of surface exposure to drying explains, in large part, why harvested grapes deteriorate so rapidly at high temperatures when relative humidity is low. For example, Nelson (1955) found that berry softness of Tokay increased at the rate of 6 per cent per hour at 100° F. Similarly, the loss in weight at 100° F. was six times as fast as at 70° F. The effect of temperature on weight loss is further emphasized by the observation that grapes lose less weight in six weeks under good storage conditions than in six hours at 100° F. Storage was at 31° F. and 95 per cent relative humidity, so humidity was also a factor in slower weight loss. Even a small water loss causes the berries to become soft and unattractive to both eye and palate—quality has been irretrievably reduced. This loss of quality as well as that caused by the browning of the stems points up the importance of rapid movement from the vine to precooling.

Equipment.—Oversize trucks can be a severe hindrance in the maintenance of quality in grapes. There is always a temptation to wait for a full load, which may seriously lengthen the time between picking and precooling.

Bruising.—Beside damage from careless handling in packing, a surface injury referred to as "bruising" may occur in hauling and in transit to market. It is usually confined to berries that rub against the sides or are pressed against the bottom of the rough wood of the containers. Some varieties, such as Rish Baba and Italia, are especially subject to bruising. In the markets the bruised areas of these varieties turn brown, and the container bruises of all varieties tend to bleach when the fruit is fumigated with sulfur dioxide. Bruises, either brown or bleached, render the fruit unattractive (Nelson *et al.*, 1970).

Bruising is further increased in *slack packs* which allow undue movement of the berries during transit and rough handling. This adds to the polishing, spread of juice, breaking of stems, and stem detachment; all of which give the grapes a poor sales impression.

Bruising is reduced by adequate pads on the bottom of the container, smooth liners to prevent the fruit from rubbing the wooden sides and ends, and a smooth lid or a curtain under the lid.

Though not yet in commercial use, K. E. Nelson *et al.* (unpublished data) have shown that *tight fill*, settling in lieu of conventional packing, will reduce some of these problems. This is really a regulated jumble pack which is then vibrated to settle the fruit to a density that all but eliminates movement within the pack.

The above account of the deterioration of table grapes after harvest emphasizes the importance of the following:

Pick when the fruit is as cool as possible, and keep it cool

Trim thoroughly and handle the fruit carefully

Keep the time from the vines to precooling to a minimum

Make sure that the fruit is fumigated and thoroughly precooled before it is shipped

BIBLIOGRAPHY

Benvegnin, L. 1954. De l'influence de prélèvement de raisin de table sur la qualité du most. Rev. Romande Agric. Vitic. et Arboricult., 8(3):24; 10(3):23–25.

California State Department of Agriculture, Bureau of Fruit and Vegetable Standardization. 1959 and 1967. Extracts from the Agricultural Code.

Standards of maturity and type and dimension of containers, Secs. 802–802.6, 828–828.15, 828.45, 828.53 and 829.15. Sacramento, State Printing Office.

Dalmasso, G., and M. Venezia. 1937. Il controllo del grado di maturita delle uve da tavola e l'applicazione del rifrattometro. R. Staz. Sper. di Vitic. e di Enol., Conegliano, Ann., 7:339–396.

Hugues, E., and E. Bouffard. 1937. Sur le degré de maturité des raisins de table. Anns. Fals. et Franc., 30:91–94.

Nedelchev, N., and M. Kondarev. 1934. Maturity standards for the Chaouch and Dattier de Beyruth grapes. [Trans. title.] Ann. Univ. Sofía, Faculty Agron. et Sylvic., 12:487–504.

Nelson, K. E. 1955. High picking temperatures and rough handling can reduce consumer acceptability of California fresh table grapes. Blue Anchor, 32: 6–10.

———, M. Ahmendullah, and F. G. Mitchell. 1970. Effect of container and packing on injury and transportation of table grapes. Amer. J. Enol. Vitic., 21:101–108.

———, J. W. Allen, and H. G. Schultz. 1972. Effect of grape maturity, sample order, and sex of the taster on the flavor response of supermarket customers. Amer. J. Enol. Vitic., 23:86–95.

———, G. A. Baker, A. J. Winkler, M. A. Amerine, H. B. Richardson, and F. R. Jones. 1963. Chemical and sensory variability in table grapes. Hilgardia, 34:1–42.

———, H. G. Schutz, M. Ahmendullah, and J. McPherson. 1973. Flavor preference of supermarket customers for Thompson Seedless grapes. Amer. J. Enol. Vitic., 24:31–40.

Winkler, A. J. 1930. Berry thinning of grapes. California Agr. Exp. Sta. Bull., 492:1–22.

———. 1932. Maturity tests for table grapes. California Agr. Exp. Sta. Bull., 529:1–35.

———. 1934. Pruning *vinifera* grapevines. Calif. Agric. Ext. Ser. Cir., 89:1–68.

21

Harvesting Wine Grapes

Wine grapes in California are harvested at a single picking. Maturity must therefore be determined accurately; its correctness largely determines the quality of the product—within the limits or possibilities of the variety or varieties concerned. The finer the variety, the more important its proper maturity. A wine grape is ripe when it reaches a chemical and physical composition that is the optimum of the variety and environment for the particular wine type for which it is intended.

Vines in the same vineyard vary in maturity—and the difference may be marked in different parts of the same vineyard because of variations in soil type, depth, fertility, and water penetration. Even vines of the same age and vigor that have been pruned differently will vary in date of maturity because of different crop levels. Beyond these differences, there are effects of regional and seasonal temperature conditions that may greatly alter the compositional balance of the fruit at a given stage of maturity; grapes maturing in hot climates or hot seasons have more sugar and less acid than those maturing in cooler weather. Moreover, they have less acid at the same degree Brix, and the malic acid is lower. How these and other conditions affect the compositional balance of the fruit at maturity may be summarized as follows for California grapes:

1. The ratio of tartrate to malate at maturity for a given variety in a given region is relatively constant. This will be true if there are no unusual climatic conditions during harvesting. Amerine and Winkler (1942) found few exceptions.
2. Amerine (1951) and Robinson *et al.* (1959) found that the cooler the

region, the greater is the per cent malate and per cent titratable acidity owing to malates.

3. The late- and early-ripening varieties should be lowest in malic acid —the late-ripening varieties because they hang on the vines so long, and the early ripening varieties because they ripen during the warmest weather. Exceptions occur when (*a*) there is no very hot period during ripening in a warm region, or (*b*) there is a very hot period during ripening in a cool region.

4. Both the total acidity and malic acid content of the fruit will be low on overcropped vines because the fruit must hang on the vines beyond the normal ripening date to attain the desired degree Brix (table 33) and in cool areas the fruit will not mature (Decker, 1961; Galley *et al.*, 1960).

VINEYARD SAMPLING

Because the causes of variability in the composition of fruit are so various, it is obvious that maturity must be tested in all parts of the vineyard. Various sampling procedures have been tested. André *et al.* (1950) reported that a fair indication of maturity was obtained from samples of 20 clusters taken at random from various sides of vines within the vineyard. Benvegnin and Capt (1935) compared berry sampling and cluster sampling for small numbers of samples and preferred the berry sampling. Huglin and Julliard (1959) reported that mean values for Brix were similar, whether obtained from 50 to 100 berries or the same number of clusters. Amerine and Roessler (1958a, 1958b) and Roessler and Amerine, (1958), working with a number of varieties in five different locations, compared three sampling systems: 100 to 200 berries taken at random from a large number of vines, 10 to 20 clusters from fewer vines, and all of the fruit from a single vine. Their data indicate that berry sampling is simplest and most accurate in assessing maturity. It is also the most economical of time and of fruit.

For practical purposes, under field conditions in California each variety must be sampled separately. If a variety is planted in more than one field, it will need to be sampled in each field. Sampling should start two or three weeks before the probable date of harvest. The berry samples should be collected at random from vines in all parts of the field. End vines and vines near trees should not be sampled. Brix, titratable acidity, and pH should be determined. Limiting values should be established for each of these, and for the Brix-acid ratio. When the minimum degree Brix is reached, then the other values should be carefully checked. This will ensure that the grapes have enough sugar to provide the necessary alcohol content when they are fermented and, at the same time, will prevent allowing them to remain on the vines until titratable acidity is too low or pH or Brix-acid ratio too high for producing the desired quality of wine. Each winery should determine the optimum Brix, acidity, pH, and Brix-acid ratio for its own conditions and varieties.

CRITERIA FOR HARVESTING

As has been indicated, the most significant criteria of wine grape maturity are sugar, acidity, pH, and Brix-acid ratio of the freshly pressed juice. The criterion most commonly employed for determining when to harvest is sugar content. What is usually determined is the total soluble solids content by Brix or some other hydrometer. While this test is not so specific as might be desired, it is capable of giving consistent results if the hydrometer is properly calibrated; if the temperature is measured, and if the juice is clear and is placed in a large cylinder. Hydrometers with degrees calibrated to 0.1° are obviously preferable to those calibrated to 0.5°. The hydrometer must be kept clean. Hydrometers with enclosed thermometers facilitate the measurement of temperature correction. The juice must be clear. Floating skins or debris will keep the hydrometer from coming to the correct equilibrium.

More satisfactory than the hydrometer is the Abbé refractometer. The newer laboratory models are very convenient to use and not too expensive for wineries that maintain control laboratories. Where maturity is being measured in the laboratory, they are to be preferred.

The hand refractometer is an efficient aid in harvesting individual clusters of table grapes, but it is not intended for use in determining the proper maturity of a vineyard of wine grapes.

Although total soluble solids are generally emphasized in determining when to harvest, acidity should also receive consideration. Under California conditions, where there is usually an excess of heat, the level of acidity at harvest becomes very important. A compromise between the desirable level of total soluble solids and the level of total acidity may be necessary at times to prevent the acid from falling too low, especially if the weather is very hot during the ripening period. Maximum wine quality can be secured only if the level of total acidity is followed during maturity as a guide for setting the harvest date.

To a limited extent pH has been used as the sole basis for determining when wine grapes should be harvested. It is true that pH is important to taste and color in table grapes, but wines are made to be drunk—not simply to be looked at. Aroma and alcohol content are also critical factors in determining quality. Then, too, the development of flavor is more or less parallel with that of sugar, and no wine grape attains its full, distinctive, characteristic flavor until it reaches 20° Brix or more. The practice of harvesting certain white varieties at 16° to 18° Brix for certain wines in the interior valleys is a mistake. It is uneconomical, and no variety harvested at that degree Brix has its full flavor. Neither will such wines develop much bouquet. There may be slight variations from 20° Brix, but that measure immediately sets a minimum sugar content. Under conditions where grapes often do not ripen and where excess acidity is a regular problem, sugar content remains the only important or necessary criterion for harvesting. This is not true, however, of California and a number of other regions where too low an acidity must be avoided.

The Brix-acid ratio has been found to be a more sound basis than sugar content alone for determining the time to harvest. For that matter, it is better than any criterion based on a single constituent of the grape. The reason is that the ratio embodies two of the primary taste factors of the grape—sweet and sour—besides being based on the two compositional constituents present in largest amount. It has the further value of indicating the relation of sugar to acid as the fruit advances in maturity.

In contrast to table grapes, grapes for wine are normally harvested in the maturity range of 20° to 25° Brix. Many of these grapes must attain this degree of maturity if their wines are to possess the characteristic varietal aroma, flavor, and balance. With this advanced maturity, especially in warm regions and as a result of prolonged hot periods during ripening, acid content may drop so low that the quality of the fruit suffers. A similar effect results from overcropping, which delays maturation. In view of these factors and the attendant danger of imbalance of the principal constituents, the higher Brix-acid ratio, the better (with a favorable acidity) the wine quality.

The value of the Brix-acid ratio was pointed up by Amerine and Winkler (1940) for California conditions in experiments showing that grape varieties could be classified into primarily table-wine and dessert-wine types according to their maximum Brix-acid ratio at 20°, 22°, and 24°. Berg (1960) showed that the Brix-acid ratio with degree Brix, besides serving as an accurate indication of maturity, can be used to predict the potential wine quality of grapes. The interpretation of potential wine quality was achieved by establishing a series of quality grades for a given variety of a viticultural region, based on a given acidity at each degree Brix. Grade 1 represents the best 25 per cent of the average crops of the fruit for a number of years, grade 2 the next 25 per cent, grade 3 the next 25 per cent, and grade 4 the poorest 25 per cent. The limits of the grades are based on the Brix-acid ratio of thousands of loads of grapes at the time of delivery to wineries in all the principal producing areas of California. Wineries that have used this system report most favorably on it, stating that its use has markedly improved the quality of their wines.

TABLE 33

RELATION OF LEVEL OF CROP TO TIME OF MATURING, ACID CONTENT,
AND QUALITY GRADE OF CERTAIN WINE GRAPE VARIETIES
IN CALIFORNIA

Variety	Crop in tons	Date of harvest	Degrees Balling	Per cent acidity	Grade
Muscat	6	Sept. 11	20.0	0.58	2
	9	Sept. 30	21.0	0.52	4
	12	Oct. 13	20.2	0.46	6
Mission	7	Sept. 22	23.5	0.62	1
	9	Sept. 30	23.0	0.57	1
	10	Oct. 7	23.0	0.35	6
Zinfandel	6	Sept. 9	21.5	1.13	1
	8	Sept. 28	22.2	0.83	1
	10	Oct. 12	21.7	0.71	4

SOURCE OF DATA: Winkler (1954).

PROPER MATURITY

To be judged ready for harvesting, wine grapes should have reached the stage of development where the relation of the different components of the fruit—sugar, acid, pH, and, especially, Brix-acid ratio—is optimal for production of a quality wine of the desired type.

The fruit must also be sound and have the carrying quality necessary to reach the winery in good condition. This consideration is related to readiness for harvest, in that the fruit that has reached proper maturity in the vineyard must still be acceptable when it reaches the winery. Another important consideration is care in handling. Grapes become more subject to handling injuries as they approach full maturity; the degree, of course, differs among varieties, but overripe grapes of all varieties are very susceptible to mechanical injuries. The length of the haul to the winery is also to be considered. Grapes can be harvested at a more mature stage for short hauls than for long hauls.

CARE IN HARVESTING AND HANDLING

Harvest procedure is an important factor in keeping wines sound. In removing the clusters, the berries should be injured no more than is absolutely necessary. This requires that the stems be cut individually and that the clusters not be tossed into the buckets used for gathering. Throwing the clusters, as is sometimes done, cracks many of the berries, creating conditions that favor decay-causing organisms, certain of which, under subsequent lax conditions, greatly hinder the making of sound wines of quality.

As soon as the delivery containers are full, they should be moved to the winery. The relation of the temperature of the picked grapes to the development of decay is overlooked or neglected by some producers. Although excellent facilities are wisely provided by the winery owners to keep fermentation temperatures down, they often give little thought to the seriousness of high (80° and 90° F.) temperatures of cracked and partially crushed grapes when the grapes are not protected from undesirable micro-organisms. Allowing decay-causing organisms to get a sufficient start in the grapes will make the wine maker's task more difficult and his product less good.

In well-managed wineries in California the grapes are crushed and in the fermentation tanks within a reasonable period after their removal from the vine. The table grape growers, realizing the advantages of rapid handling, have maintained the quality of their product to a very marked degree on its arrival in Eastern markets. Wine men should likewise maintain the potential of the mature grapes by keeping short the interval between vine and fermentation tank. The shorter this interval, the less is the chance that objectionable organisms may get a start.

Truck size should be in proportion to the size of the picking crew. The truckmen should continuously keep up with the pickers, so as to get the grapes to the crusher at the winery as soon as possible after they are picked. An overlarge truck carries with it an irresistible temptation to wait until the load is full, despite the fact that delivery is delayed and, under most conditions, the grapes are permitted to take up additional heat. Admittedly, the large truck, especially the 10-ton gondola, is the most economical means of delivering grapes; but grapes so delivered, other things being equal, also arrive in the poorest condition. Sampling patterns for taking representative fruit of large gondola loads have been indicated by Berg and Marsh (1954) (fig. 145).

Long hauls should be avoided. The futility of attempting to make first-quality wines from grapes that have been hauled hundreds of miles in open gondolas holding 10 or more tons, in a temperature around 100° F., must be obvious to all who have even the slightest understanding of sanitation, the structure of grapes, and the fact that many kinds of spoilage organisms are always present on mature grapes. The best efforts of the wine maker cannot produce a clean, sound product when the grapes contain rot and volatile acid and are fermenting before he receives them. The industry is hardly ready to restrict the length of hauls; however, limiting hauls to the viticultural region in which the grapes are produced would:

Make it possible to deliver grapes to the wineries in more nearly sound condition than is usual with long hauls;

Make it obligatory to ferment the grapes in the region of production;

Place a more nearly equitable value on the grapes and the wines of the different regions.

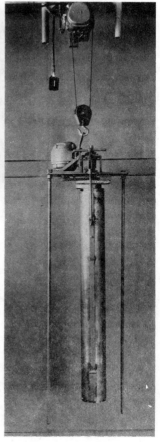

FIGURE 145: Above, sample being taken from a gondola load of wine grapes. At right, an 8-inch oscillating-types grape sampler. A pawl at the bottom of the sampler holds the sample until released. (*Valley Foundry and Machine Work, Fresno, California*)

If necessary, wines could be moved between regions. The likelihood of deterioration of wines in transit is small, as compared with mature, harvested grapes that have suffered a certain degree of injury in harvesting and loading into a gondola. This becomes even more critical with machine harvesting in which a greater degree of injury occurs.

HARVESTING PROCEDURE

The harvest of grapes for wine has been undergoing one change after another since World War II. Numerous devices for mechanization have been developed, and some of these have handled the grapes quite economically—yet very roughly. The currently accepted methods generally employ one or another of the following old or new devices: the 50-pound field box;

the 1-ton tank; the 2-ton detachable tank; and the 3- to 5-ton mounted tank with hand harvesting.

The field box.—The 50-pound field box is the traditional container for carrying wine grapes from the vines to the crusher. It is 21 inches long, 14 inches wide, and 9 inches deep. Although rarely used in California today, boxes are still the simplest and best containers. The grapes are handled but once—from the vines directly into the boxes—and, if carefully picked, can be delivered in sound condition. Another advantage of the box is its small size. It takes but a short time to fill, and, used with small trucks that do not have to wait long for a full load, it can deliver the grapes at the crusher a short time after they are picked.

When vine spacing does not permit trucks between the rows, the full boxes must be carried to the avenue. This added labor and the cost of box upkeep have all but eliminated its use, except in some small vineyards of the central coastal region. The boxes, being made of wood, must be cleaned frequently to be kept sanitary.

The 1-ton tank.—The 1-ton tank measures about 4 feet by 4 feet, with a depth of about 3.5 feet (fig. 146). It is made of sheet metal, welded securely, and is treated inside with a high-grade lacquer to protect it against corrosion. Two sills are attached to the bottom for raising it so the prongs of the fork lift can slide under.

This tank has been in rather general use in some coastal areas where the spacing in vineyards is too close for a tank truck to pass between the rows. In such situations the tanks are spotted along the side of the avenue at spacings convenient for receiving the grapes from the vines of eight or twelve half-rows. The grapes of the other half of these rows move to tanks spotted at the other end of the block. The grapes are picked into large buckets or field boxes and are carried in these to the tank and emptied into them.

A fork lift picks up the full tanks and, when the winery is near by, hauls them directly to it. When the winery is farther away, the full tanks are put on a truck and hauled there. In either case the tanks are weighed before they are dumped into the crusher. Weighing provides both a record of crop and an accurate basis for paying the pickers. The tanks are dumped into the crusher by a fork lift, being lifted onto a rack which can be tilted to spill the grapes.

The 2-ton detachable tank.—Made of moderately heavy sheet-steel, the 2-ton detachable tank is coated inside with a high-grade lacquer for protection against corrosion. It is about 8 feet long, 4 feet wide, and 3.5 feet deep. Loops are provided above the top at the middle of each side for the hooks of hoists.

For filling, these tanks are set on a narrow, two-wheeled trailer which can be pulled between the vine rows by a small tractor. Two rows of un-

FIGURE 146: Harvesting wine grapes into a 1-ton tank placed in the avenue of a closely planted vineyard. The tanks are handled by forklift.

trellised vines on each side of the middle through which the tank is being pulled are picked into it as it moves along. Only one row of trellised vines on either side of the tank is usually harvested at once. The grapes are picked into buckets and are dumped from these into the tank. Usually, five or six pickers work together. When the tank is full, the tractor moves on, and another tractor and empty tank take up the same position.

The full tank is hauled to the vineyard side, where it is weighed and transferred to a large truck by a tractor-mounted hoist. The weight provides a record of crop and a basis for paying the pickers. An empty tank is put in its place on the trailer for return to the vineyard. The large truck usually carries five tanks. When the haul is long, a truck trailer may move additional tanks to the winery. There are special devices for holding the tanks in place on the large truck or trailer and while they are being dumped at the crusher. The tanks are dumped in the usual manner by a mechanical hoist. Producers who have used both 2-ton tanks and 10-ton gondolas have stated that the cost per ton is essentially the same for either, with the same scale of operations. The fruit, however, should be in much better condition when it is delivered in the tanks, since delivery by the large gondola requires an additional handling—usually that of turning the harvested grapes onto a belt conveyer, which elevates and dumps them into the gondola in the field.

The 3- to 5-ton mounted tank.—Also called gondolas, these tanks are of heavy steel and are permanently mounted on a four-wheel trailer or, more rarely, on two wheels for use as a semitrailer. The trailer is pulled by a small tractor in the vineyard and by a small truck on the highway; the semitrailer requires a special tractor, which is used both between the vine rows and on the highway. The tanks are 42 to 84 inches wide and constructed with the wheels beneath the corners so that they can pass between rows 8 feet to 12 feet apart without damaging the vines. The tank is mounted to permit dumping at the crusher by means of a hoist; one side rests on the wall of the crusher bin and the other is lifted by the mechanical hoist.

In the vineyard the tanks, or gondolas, as pulled between the vineyard rows as the grapes are picked from three or more adjacent rows of untrellised vines on both sides. Where vines are trellised, only the two adjacent rows are picked. The grapes are picked into buckets and dumped into the tank. Six to eight pickers may work along one tank or gondola. With such a large crew, it is usually necessary to keep a record of the number of buckets, weight of the filled buckets, and condition of the fruit handled by each picker. The number of buckets or the tons picked may be the basis for paying the pickers.

The filled tank or gondola moves on, and an empty one takes its place. The full tanks are taken directly to the winery for unloading (fig. 147). When the distance from vineyard to winery is less than ten miles, the time

FIGURE 147: A five-ton gondola load of grapes being unloaded into crusher bin. The gondola may be tipped over for emptying. (*Courtesy of H. B. Richardson*)

from picking to crushing should not exceed one to two hours. With sound grapes at picking and this lapse of time, the grapes delivered to the winery are fresh. There has been no time for post-harvest spoilage to develop.

Tanks mounted on two-wheel trailers and of 1- and 2-ton capacity are also used extensively in many vineyards. These are pulled along by light tractors and filled in much the same way as the others. When the tank is full, it is moved to the vineyard side, and an empty one takes its place. At the vineyard side the fruit is transferred from the small tank to a large gondola, which hauls it to the winery. The small tanks are hoisted up bodily and their contents dumped into the gondola, or the fruit is dumped onto a belt conveyer that elevates it into the gondola. In either case, the fruit is handled very roughly and many berries are broken or detached from the stems. This treatment does not favor delivery of sound grapes. Methods that would eliminate the second handling should be sought.

As new devices are developed, it must be remembered that wine grapes will not stand rough handling and that the time from the vine to the crusher must be short. The very large gondola is unsatisfactory in both respects, and ways must be found to eliminate it except, possibly, in mechanical harvesting, when it can be filled in a reasonably short time and without rehandling of the grapes.

MACHINE HARVESTING WINE GRAPES

Mechanical harvesting of grapes has received attention in a number of grape producing countries—Australia, France, Germany, Italy, Russia, the United States, and others. Each has advanced ideas, such as the cutter bar, rotary cutters, suction, impactors, and vibrators. Supports to better position the fruit for the machines are also being developed (see p. 264).

Mechanical harvesters are being accepted. Not because everyone is satisfied with their present performance, but because of the need for greater efficiency. Approximately 15 per cent of the fruit crush in California in 1972 was harvested by machine.

There are a number of machines available. Their action is similar. Three methods of action are now in use to remove the grapes from the vines. Namely, the "slapper," "horizontal impactor," and the "vertical impactor." These are the action units in the machine that straddle the vine row. The slapper and horizontal impactor action units are interchangeable in the same chassis of some makes of machine.

The slapper action unit is adapted for vertical trellises. As the machine moves along astride the vine row, three foot fiberglass rods or paddles slap or beat the vines by horizontal pivotal action (fig. 148). This method works effectively on varieties of medium vigor; heavy shoot growth and dense foliage create a problem.

The horizontal impactor unit is also adapted for vertical trellises. As the

FIGURE 148: Harvesting wine grapes with a slapper type action unit machine. The fiberglass rods (visible in middle, astride the row) beat the vines by pivotal action to detach the fruit, which falls on the conveyors below. These convey it to cross conveyors in the back from where the fruit is elevated by conveyors on either side of the harvester (the heads of these are visible) to a cross conveyor that conveys it across the adjacent row to a gondola. (*Up-Right Harvesters, Berkeley, Calif.*)

machine moves along astride the vine row, polyurethane fingers, about an inch in diameter and one foot long, move in and out of the vines, knocking the clusters off in their entirety, as parts of clusters, or as single berries (fig. 149). To compensate for the machine's forward movement, the fingers oscillate in an elliptical path; thus there is little or no raking action, which reduces the injury to the permanent parts of the vine.

The vertical impactor unit requires a wide-top-trellis with 2 wires at a fixed distance apart, usually 3 to 4 feet. The crossarms supporting the wires must be semi-flexible or the wire must be placed in a 3 to 4 inch vertical, wire slot at the ends of the rigid crossarm. This permits the trellis wire to move up and down when hit by the impact of the impactor rods. This support is similar to the "Genvea double curtain" used in the Eastern States. This impaction, as the machine moves along the vine row, literally

FIGURE 149: A horizontal impactor action unit. The two sets of fingers oscillate at 200 to 300 strokes per minute. The fruit falls onto the two conveyors which move it to cross conveyors at the back of the machine.

causes the clusters to break off or shatters them owing to the jolting and vibration of the wire. Some clusters are hit directly as the baton comes up (fig. 150).

Both the slapper and horizontal impactor action units can be adjusted for height and width of the band of fruit along the row, and the vertical impactor for height of the trellis wires. Proper adjustment cuts down on unnecessary vine damage and improves efficiency of harvesting. The speed of the action units is adjustable in each type of harvester; usual operation would be about 250 strokes per minute.

FIGURE 150: Showing the impactor rods (see arrows) of a vertical impactor unit of a grape harvester. The rods retract and then strikes the trellis wire from below as they come out and up. A like action unit operates on the opposite side of the row. (*Courtesy of Upright Harvesters*)

In all methods the harvested fruit falls on the catching conveyors (see fig. 149). The synthetic flaps in the center of this figure hug the vine trunks and reduce fruit loss. These flaps are replaced on newer harvesters with flexible wings. The leaves and cane parts that fall with the fruit are blown out on the cross conveyor at the back of the machine. With this improvement, according to Olmo (1971), the amount of leaves and cane pieces delivered to the crusher is usually less than that in hand harvested fruit.

The variety has a marked influence on the effectiveness of machine harvesting. Olmo (1971) reports that the varieties with soft, juicy textured berries and firm stem attachment, like Burger, are especially difficult if not impossible to harvest by machine. His appraisal of the harvesting of a cross section of representative varieties is as follows: The premium quality variety—Chardonnay—can be harvested, but the clusters are mostly broken into clumps of berries or single berries that are smashed. The loss of juice with the present conveyors is considerable. The same is true of Zinfandel and Ruby Cabernet, which have very tough stems and strong berry attachment. The clusters of Cabernet-Sauvignon, with their firmer berries, too, are broken into pieces, but the loss of juice is small. Most of the cluster stems and branches remain on the vine. Muscat blanc and Barbera are harvested efficiently; so are Tokay, Malaga, and Thompson Seedless; a high percentage of all three of these varieties is now crushed.

As the above indicates, most varieties can be harvested, but the conveying of the harvested fruit from the vine to the gondola or crusher must be improved to reduce losses, especially of juice. A cane-lifting device that would pass the canes up and over the slapper or horizontal action units as the machine moves along the row would preserve leaves and make the fruit more accessible to the machine.

Delivery and protection of the harvested fruit to the winery is of great importance. Ough and Berg (1971), working with five varieties of white grapes that had undergone treatment simulating mechanical harvesting and gondola transport, found the following: "For the best quality of product of white grapes from Regions IV and V, the sooner the juice is separated from the skins, treated with sulfur dioxide, and inoculated with yeast, the better will be the quality of the wine. There is a flow of some chemicals

FIGURE 151: Mechanical grape harvester equipped with a crusher and conveyor to move the crushed fruit across the adjacent row into a mounted must tank that may be sealed. In the case of white grapes the juice may be separated from the marc. Other machines may be equipped with a built on tank to hold crushed stemmed grapes or must. One bank of fingers of this horizontal impactor machine is just visible in the front middle. (*Up-Right Harvesters, Berkeley, Calif.*)

from the cellular tissue by the juice which is accelerated by increased temperature and agitation. Sulfur dioxide between 75 and 100 ppm holds browning of the must to a minimum up to 8 hours. Carbon dioxide appears to have little influence on quality, though it does reduce the level of browning slightly in the skin-contact must."

The loss of quality in machine-harvested white grapes in regions I, II, and III is somewhat slower than in regions IV and V, owing to the more moderate temperatures. However, with the higher quality potential of the varieties grown, the treatment from the vines to the fermentation tank is of even greater importance. Field crushing, separation of the juice, treatment wth sulfur dioxide, and inoculation with yeast in closed tanks are mandatory (fig. 151). In no case should the time to the start of the fermentation of these grapes exceed 8 hours. To cover the juice in the closed tanks with CO_2 may prove to be beneficial with these varieties.

Ough *et al.* (1971), working with red varieties, found that the most favorable handling of the harvested grapes was field crushing, stemming, and treatment of the must with 150 ppm of sulfur dioxide. Time, too, is important but not as critical as with white grapes. It should be kept to a minimum, never exceeding 12 hours.

Benedict *et al.* (1971), using mechanically harvested Concord grapes in Arkansas, showed that there was ample time for moving the fruit from the vineyard to the processing plant (winery) without critical loss of quality when it was tightly sealed in plastic bags.

At this early stage in the introduction of machine harvesting, and in view of continuing changes, it is difficult to make an economic evaluation. This, however, should receive consideration by those using machines or contemplating their use. Daily *et al.* (1971), have done this using the closed system of harvesting Concord grapes in Washington State. They found that the "break-even" point in a 7-ton vineyard, with custom harvesting at $18 per ton, would require harvesting 171 acres or 1197 tons.

Harvesting for out-of-state shipment.—Wine grapes that are shipped to distant markets must be handled in much the same way as table grapes; uniformity of fruit and symmetry of clusters are of less importance, however. The entire crop of wine grapes is harvested at a single picking. Clusters not good enough to be packed are discarded if there are only a few, or they are kept separate for local crushing. Since wine grape varieties are usually softer than table grapes, and the skin is broken more easily, the handling must be as careful as that given table grapes, so as to avoid injuries that encourage spoiling. In trimming, however, only decayed, wet, and broken berries are removed; minor defects in appearance are ignored.

Wine grapes are always field packed. Usually there is no definite arrangement of the clusters in the lug box. They are simply filled in with care, and an effort is made to have the corners of the lug firmly filled. This is generally referred to as the "jumble pack." The standard lug for wine grapes holds 34 pounds.

Careful, but speedy, handling from vines to iced car is necessary. Once the car is loaded, the wine grapes are fumigated with sulfur dioxide, as in the initial fumigation of table grapes (see chap. 22). Packed wine grapes are not, as a rule, stored, but they should by all means be precooled.

BIBLIOGRAPHY

Amerine, M. A. 1951. The acids of California grapes and wines; II. Malic acid. Food Tech., 5:13–16.

————, and E. B. Roessler. 1958a. Methods of determining field maturity of grapes. Amer. Jour. Enol., 9:37–40.

————, ————. 1958b. Field testing of grape maturity. Hilgardia, 28:93–114.

————, and A. J. Winkler. 1940. Maturity studies with California grapes; I. The Balling-acid ratio of wine grapes. Proc. Amer. Soc. Hort. Sci., 38:379–387.

————, ————. 1942. Maturity studies of California grapes; II. The titratable acidity, pH, and organic acid content. Proc. Amer. Soc. Hort. Sci., 40:313–324.

André, C., M. Lemineur, R. Orizet, and Vedel. 1950. Contribution a l'étude de la maturation du raisin. Bul. inst. natl. appl. orig. Vins et eaux-de vie, 32:52–81. See also Prog. Agr. et Vitic., 136:99–103, 115–126, 141–152.

Benedict, R. H., J. W. Fleming, and J. R. Morris. 1971. Post-harvest changes in quality of mechanically harvested Concord grapes. Arkansas Farm Res., 20:10. See also 17 (2 and 6).

Benvegnin, L., and E. Capt. 1935. La maturation du raisin eu 1934. Ann. Agr. de la Suisse, 41(4):492–497.

Berg, H. W. 1960. Grade classification by total soluble solids and total acidity (revised). San Francisco, Wine Institute. (Mineo., 53 p.)

————, and G. L. Marsh. 1954. Sampling deliveries of grapes on a representative basis. Food Tech., 8:104–108.

Dailey, R. T., R. J. Folwell, and R. C. Bevan. 1971. The economics of owning and operating mechanical grape harvesters in Washington. Wash. Agric. Exp. Sta. Cir., 540:1–14.

Decker, K. 1961. Die optimale Augenzahl oder Belastung des Weinstockes. Deut. Weinbau, 16:858–859.

Galley, R., H. Leyvarz, and J. L. Simon. 1960. Influence de la charge de raisins sur la qualité de la vendage. Rev. Rom., 16(5):48.

Huglin, P., and B. Julliard. 1959. Le controle de la maturation du raisin par le prélèvement basis. Progr. Agr. et Vitic., 152:11–16, 37–41.

Olmo, H. P. 1971. The year machine harvesting came of age. Wines and Vines, 52(2):30–31.

Ough, C. S., and H. W. Berg. 1971. Simulated mechanical harvest and gondola transport. II. Effect of temperature, atmosphere, and skin contact on chemical and sensory qualities of white wines. Amer. Jour. Enol. Vitic., 22:194–198.

——, ——, R. J. Coffelt, and G. M. Cooke. 1971. The effect on wine quality of simulated mechanical harvest and gondola transport of grapes. Amer. Jour. Enol. Vitic., 22:65–70.

Robinson, W. B., N. Shaulis, G. C. Smith, and D. F. Tallman. 1959. Changes in the malic and tartaric acid contents of Concord grapes. Food Res., 24:176–180.

Roessler, E. B., and M. A. Amerine. 1958. Studies on grape sampling. Amer. Jour. Enol., 9:139–145.

Winkler, A. J. 1954. Effects of overcropping. Amer. Jour. Enol., 5:4–12.

22

Precooling, Fumigation, and Storage of Table Grapes

Early in the season, all grapes are sold as soon as they are mature enough to harvest. Later, as the supply of mature fruit equals or exceeds demand and the prices decline, market congestion may be relieved by keeping grapes longer on the vines or diverting some to cold storage. Grapes, unlike many other fruits, ripen slowly. In favorable weather, table grapes may remain on the vines for 15 to 30 days after they first become palatable. It is indeed difficult to determine, within a week, just when table grapes are "ripe," except with regard to the legal minimum standard. Two pickings of table grapes are usually made from the same vines over several weeks. The rainless summers of California are, of course, exceedingly favorable to this practice. The decision to allow the fruit to hang longer on the vines will be influenced by variety, stage of maturity, availabilty of labor, storage space, and the time in the harvest season. When late-maturing varieties that are especially suitable for storage are well mature, most of the fruit goes directly into cold storage.

Grapes that are sold in California, immediately after harvest, are usually moved to market in covered trucks, and precooling is omitted. If more than one or two days elapse before the fruit reaches the consumer, its holding quality will be improved by precooling and fumigation with sulfur dioxide. All grapes that are in transit more than one or two days, as well as all grapes destined for cold storage, should be precooled and fumigated as soon as possible after removal from the vines.

PRECOOLING

The usual harvest temperatures of table grapes in California are favorable for rapid transpiration and for the development of decay-causing fungi; water loss is the more damaging to quality (see p. 572). The benefits of precooling are indicated in the general rule that, within the limits at which fresh grapes are usually handled, a reduction in temperature of 15° F. halves the rate of respiration and doubles the keeping period. A fruit temperature below 40° F. greatly retards the development of all fungi and prohibits the growth of some. The best means of maintaining the initial quality of the fruit is prompt removal of the field heat of the grapes after packing. In addition to its benefits just indicated, Nelson (1955) has shown that it checks stem desiccation, browning, berry softening, and shatter.

Development of precooling.—Precooling was initiated by Stubenrauch and Dennis (1910), but, because precooling took time and added costs, it was not until after 1930 that it became a factor in grape transportation and storage. In 1932 the railroads altered tariffs permitting grapes to be shipped with modified (reduced) icing in transit. This tended to remove the economic barrier to precooling, and, as a result, numerous refrigeration systems and methods of handling air for cooling sprang into being. The number has now been reduced to only a few that are economically feasible and technically practical. Of these, "forced-air cooling," in which the cold air is forced crosswise through the packed lugs, and "parallel flow" in which the cold air flows along the sides of the containers of grapes is now commonly used. The former is used almost exclusively in the desert areas, while "parallel flow" is widely used in the San Joaquin Valley.

Forced-air precooling.—The need for the rapid movement of the air in precooling has been indicated. Yet even when extra fans are used in precooling rooms to circulate the air, warm air in the lugs of grapes seems to defy replacement with cold air. Then, too, air is, at best, a slow heat-transfer medium. To make it work more effectively in cooling, it must be forced through the lugs and around the grapes.

The first real progress toward forced air cooling was the development of the tunnel cooler. This cooler was effective, but it was uneconomical. Guillou (1960) recently designed a cooler that forces the cold air through the packed lugs by creating a pressure differential of 0.1 to 1 inch of water pressure. The principle is shown in figure 152. With the load of fruit as shown in the figure, grapes can be cooled to 40° F. ± in two hours, whereas the minimum time for conventional precooling is approximately 18 to 24 hours (fig. 153). In commercial practice the stack of fruit has been increased to three tiers of lugs, the usual pallet load, thereby slowing the cooling somewhat. Still, with appropriate stacking of the lugs, at right angle to the air flow, the rate is several times faster than that of any other

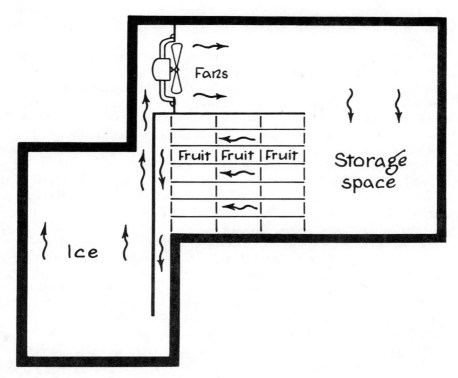

FIGURE 152: Principle of forced-air cooling. (*From Calif. Agr. Exp. Bull. 773,* *1960*)

common method of precooling (Mitchell *et al.*, 1972). Solid liners in the lug or wrappers around the clusters will slow the cooling in the same proportion as in the other methods of precooling.

Room precooling.—Most of the table grape cold-storage plants have a number of rooms of small size—holding one thousand to several thousand packed lugs. These rooms have more refrigeration capacity and greater air movement than the regular storage rooms. The small size is desirable in order that the rooms may be filled rapidly and that the extra refrigeration and air volume may speed the cooling. As soon as grapes are moved into one of these rooms, the cooling machinery is turned on and kept going until the center lug of the last pallot of grapes to be moved in is precooled to the desired temperature (40° F.). The cooling capacity of each of these rooms should be sufficient to remove 40° F. of heat from a full load in twenty-four hours. This requires blowers capable of moving 6,000 to 8,000 cubic feet of air per minute per 1,000 lugs of grapes. The flow of air to all parts of the room must be uniform to ensure even cooling. This is "parallel flow" cooling. Cooling by this arrangement is appreciably faster than that obtained in a conventional cold room, but not as fast as in well equipped forced air precooling rooms.

The phasing out of re-icing by the railroads together with the general use of mechanical refrigeration in railroad cars (reefers), trucks, and piggy-back trailer vans has made the precooling in these transportation units impossible. When loaded with cold fruit the mechanical units in these cars, trucks, etc., have the capacity to hold the temperature of the load, but not to precool it. The grapes must be, and generally are, precooled prior to loading.

Rate of precooling.—The rate of cooling the fruit depends primarily on three factors: the accessibility of the fruit to the cooling medium (air in the cooling of grapes); the difference in temperature between the fruit and the cooling medium; and the velocity of movement of the cooling medium.

Accessibility of the grapes to the cooling medium is influenced by the type of container and any liners, wraps, or filler material and the arrangement of the containers in the cooling chamber. For example, Pentzer *et al.* (1945) found that, in circulating cold air in precooling, a cellophane curtain over the face of a pack made its cooling much slower than that of packs without curtains. Similarly, the slower cooling of wrapped packs resulted from the reduced accessibility of the cooling medium.

The greater the difference in temperature between the grapes and the cooling medium, the more rapid is the cooling. The temperature, of course, must not be low enough to freeze the grapes. Richardson *et al.* (1973) found, when packed lugs were "parallel flow" cooled, the downstream fruit cooled approximately 35 per cent faster with cross channels, and 45 per cent faster when the layers were separated by spacers. They also showed that forced air cooling reduced half-cooling time (time required to reduce the temperature difference of the grapes and that of the cooling media by one half) about 90 per cent as compared to room cooling, other things being the same (see fig. 153).

High velocity of the cooling medium is necessary for rapid as well as effective and economical cooling. Offhand, it might seem that high velocity of the air would remove excessive moisture from the grapes, but such is not the case. The more rapidly the temperature of the grapes can be lowered to the temperature of the cooling medium, the less moisture will be lost. When air is at a temperature of 31° F., the vapor pressures (inches of mercury) at 94.3 per cent relative humidity and 79.5 per cent relative humidity are respectively 0.164 and 0.136, and the difference is insignificant, compared to the vapor pressure of grapes at higher temperatures—for example, about 0.99 at 80° F. This principle was illustrated by Dewey's

Precooling, Fumigation, and Storage of Table Grapes

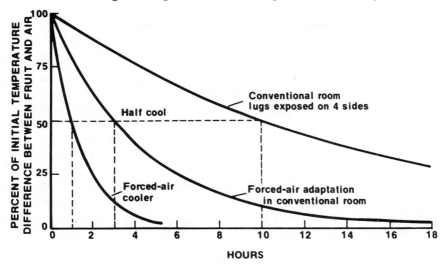

FIGURE 153: Comparative rates of cooling grapes by different methods, average fruit pulp temperature in lidded lugs. (*From Calif. Agr. Exp. Bull. 773, 1960*)

(1950) study of moisture loss from cherries and grapes. Using an air blast, he found that grapes in small lots were completely cooled in less than an hour, whereas more than seven hours were required for cooling in still air. The loss of moisture by the grapes in the air blast was not significantly different from that in still air. The same was true of water loss from grape stems.

Refrigeration required.—In English-speaking countries heat quantities are usually expressed in B.T.U. (British thermal units). One B.T.U. is the quantity of heat required to raise the temperature of 1 pound of water by 1° F. To cool 1 pound of grapes by 1° F. the removal of 0.83 B.T.U. is required. Thus the heat that must be removed in cooling 1,000 23-pound lugs of grapes may be computed by first subtracting the desired temperature after cooling from the original temperature of the fruit, multiplying the difference thus obtained by 0.83 (the B.T.U. per pound of grapes), and finally multiplying this product by 23,000 (the total pounds of fruit in the 1,000 lugs). If the original temperature is 85° F. and the desired temperature is 40° F., the equation will be:

$$45° \times 0.83 \times 23{,}000 = 847{,}900 \text{ B.T.U.}$$

To cool the containers, which weigh 4 pounds each and require the removal of 0.33 B.T.U. for cooling 1° F., the equation will be:

$$45° \times 0.33 \times 4{,}000 = 59{,}400 \text{ B.T.U.}$$

Since each pound of ice in melting absorbs 144 B.T.U., the total ice required to cool 1,000 lugs, with their grapes, would be 7,264 pounds (3.62 tons).

If the cooilng extends over a considerable period, additional heat will be produced by the respiration of the grapes. Acording to the findings of Wright *et al.* (1954) and Lutz and Hardenburg (1968), 1 ton of Tokay grapes at 62.5° F. releases about 2,800 B.T.U. per twenty-four hours. Since 62.5° F. would be the average temperature during precooling, the vital heat would amount to 2,800 × 11.5 (tons of grapes in 1,000 lugs) = 32,200 B.T.U., and its removal would require 230 pounds of ice or its equivalent in mechanical refrigeration. Other varieties do not have the same rate of respiration as Tokay, but the release of vital heat would be only slightly different. In terms of refrigeration need, the differences are small, though they may be significant as a factor in storage life. The refrigeration need will also be affected by motors, electric lights, and air leakage into or from the precooling room.

FUMIGATION WITH SULFUR DIOXIDE

Investigations at the California Agricultural Experiment Station by Winkler and Jacob (1925) and Jacob (1929) showed the effectiveness of sulfur dioxide in retarding the activity of decay-causing organisms in fresh grapes. The process was applied in commercial practice in 1924; by 1928, according to Harvey (1960), from 10,000 to 15,000 carloads of fresh grapes were being treated annually. In the early 1930's Pentzer and others (1933 and 1934a) at the Federal Horticultural Field Station, Fresno, made important findings on the use of sulfur dioxide in the storage and transport of table grapes.

The principal benefit of fumigation with sulfur dioxide is suppression of the fungi that attack grapes at storage and transportation temperatures. Its greatest value lies in its control of gray-mold rot in storage. Gray mold, *Botrytis cinerea,* is capable of causing severe destruction of grapes even at low storage temperatures. The first fumigation destroys all micro-organisms and spores on the surface of the grapes and completely sterilizes the wounds made during packing. However, as shown by Harvey (1955) and Nelson (1958), this initial fumigation is ineffective against field infections within the berries. The prevention of spread from these infected berries requires properly timed refumigation. Its effect on most other decay causing organisms, which occasionally occur on grapes at low temperatures, is similar to that indicated for gray mold.

Winkler and Jacob (1925) first showed that fumigation with sulfur dioxide reduces the rate of respiration of grapes. Pentzer *et al.* (1934)

found that the respiration rate of Emperor grapes containing only 22 ppm of sulfur dioxide was reduced to 82 per cent of normal at 32° F. With 87 ppm in the grapes, the respiration was reduced to 8 per cent of normal, but high concentration severely damaged the fruit. Thus, even though the respiration rate rises again between fumigations, Marias (1952) found the loss of sugars from the grapes to be reduced, and storage life lengthened.

Winkler and Jacob (1925) found that next in importance to the control of decay-causing organisms is the effect of sulfur dioxide on the color and condition of the stems. The original color and condition will be retained for months, whereas the stems of untreated grapes soon turn brown or black. The retained stem condition, according to Lutz (1938) and Reyneke and du Plessis (1943), tends to reduce shatter.

Winkler and Jacob (1925) found that berries injured in handling or otherwise will absorb sulfur dioxide more rapidly than sound fruit; hence a barrier is set up where, without the fumigation, the decay-causing organisms would have a port of entry.

Properties of sulfur dioxide.—Sulfur dioxide is produced by burning elemental sulfur, which is a gas at ordinary temperatures and atmospheric pressure and is 2.2 times as heavy as air. It is colorless, has an extremely pungent odor, and is very irritating to the eyes, nose, and mouth. It is highly toxic to fungi and bacteria. According to Cuey and Uota (1961), when *Botrytis cinerea* is treated with sulfur dioxide, the subsequent reduction in spore germination is quantitatively proportional to the sulfur dioxide concentration and the exposure time. The toxicity increases with the per cent relative humidity. At a R. H. of 96 per cent it is more than 20 times as effective as at 75 per cent R. H. It has been used extensively for many years in the food industries for the control of fungi and other organisms and as a bleaching agent in dried-fruit production.

Fumigation.—The initial fumigation is preferably carried out in special small rooms or precooling rooms, holding a 1,000 lugs, where the forced air fans drive the sulfur dioxide (0.5 per cent) laden air through the packed lugs at ordinary air temperature. Fumigating in these rooms saves one handling of the fruit. After the fumigation the precooling is turned on and continued until all the fruit in the room is cooled to the desired temperature. In practice the fumigation is usually done at the end of the day, so that it will not interfere with other operations—packing, loading, and the like. Even in the best-controlled procedure some of the sulfur dioxide will occasionally escape—which can be very annoying to the packers and other employees.

In the initial fumigation, under favorable conditions, a concentration of 0.5 per cent of sulfur dioxide for a period of 20 minutes is adequate. To accomplish this the absorptive capacity of the lugs and fruit as well as the space they occupy must be taken into account. Nelson and Baker (1963) found the sulfur dioxide may be determined with the following formula:

$$A = \frac{B \times C}{D} + (E \times F)$$

when

- A = the pounds of sulfur dioxide required.
- B = the per cent concentration of sulfur dioxide desired.
- C = the cubic feet of free space of the room (total cubic feet of the room minus 0.5 cubic foot for each lug of fruit).
- D = the volume occupied by one pound of sulfur dioxide gas (5.5 cu. ft. at 32° F. and 6 cu. ft. at room temperature).
- E = the pounds of sulfur dioxide absorbed by each carload unit of packed lugs of grapes (each carload unit consisting of 1,000 lugs, each lug containing 22–26 pounds of fruit).
- F = the number of carload units of fruit.

When the fruit is sound, the room relatively gas-tight, and the air velocity past both sides of the lugs is 50 fpm or more (75–100 fpm when the clusters are wrapped or when curtains are used), one pound per car for factor E is adequate. On the contrary, a higer value of 1.5 to 2 pounds per car may be required when the conditions are less favorable, such as rain damaged fruit.

For uniform treatment it is necessary that the sulfur dioxide be thoroughly mixed with the air and distributed quickly and evenly to all parts of the room. There should be a gas outlet in front of each room fan. Proper container alignment and adequate fan capacity are necessary for uniform fumigation both at the initial treatment and during refumigations. The lugs should be oriented parallel to the air flow with channels ¾ to 1½ inches on each side and extending unobstruced completely through the stack of fruit.

The fumigant is usually released into the room from a steel cylinder containing the calculated amount of gas in liquid form or it is weighed as released from a large container. When liquid sulfur dioxide is injected directly into the treating chamber, the fans should be operating to volatize and mix it with the air instantly. When the cylinder is placed in a bath of hot water, the sulfur dioxide boils off rapidly as a gas. This gas, too, must be mixed with air and then distributed in the room to facilitate uniform application.

After the 20-minute exposure of the grapes to the gas, the residual sulfur dioxide is removed from the room by blowing it out through appropriate ceiling vents, or by passing it through the water spray used as the refrigerant. If so, the water must be neutralized from time to time to prevent the build up of sulfurous acid which is very corrosive.

Refumigation.—As has been indicated, the principal value of fumigation is its destruction of decay-causing organisms. Infections within berries that occurred before the initial fumigation, however, are not destroyed; they continue to develop and in time will spread to sound berries. It is to hold down or prevent this spread that the grapes must be refumigated. The retreatment also slows respiration and helps maintain good stem condition.

In the refumigating, a 0.1 per cent concentration of sulfur dioxide is usually most effective. The dosage is calculated by the above formula, using an absorption factor of 0.67 pounds of sulfur dioxide absorbed by each carload of lugs at 0.1 pound concentration. When the grapes are unusually sound and free of infected berries, the concentration may be reduced to 0.05 per cent and the absorption factor to 0.5 pounds of sulfur dioxide per carload. On the other hand, when the fruit contains decaying berries to the extent that *no* further spread can be tolerated during storage the concentration may have to be stepped up to 0.2 per cent sulfur dioxide with the absorption factor becoming 1.0 pound of SO_2 per carload of grapes. Unfortunately, this rather high dosage will cause considerable bleaching of the berries, especially after long storage. The gas laden air is left in the room for 30 minutes. With brine spray and ice refrigeration, the heat-exchange surface must be bypassed or most of the gas will be absorbed by the brine or the water on the ice. Auxiliary fans are sometimes used to mix the gas with the air in the room. At the end of fumigation the residue of gas is removed as in precooling rooms and cars.

In practice, stored grapes are usually fumigated at approximately weekly intervals. This is supported by the studies of Nelson and Baker (1963), who found that the decay owing to *Botrytis* that developed in three months was inversely related both to the initial fumigations and the refumigations in storage. It was directly related to the interval between refumigations. Fumigation injury to the fruit, on the other hand, was directly related to the initial treatment and inversely to the interval between refumigations. Their best decay control with minimum injury to the fruit was obtained with the 7-day interval.

Continuous exposure to sulfur dioxide.—Studies in South Africa by Marias (1952) have indicated that continuous exposure to a low concentration of sulfur dioxide (30 ppm) controlled decay with less damage to the grapes than was incurred by refumigation with higher concentrations at weekly intervals. A device for automatic control of the concentration of sulfur dioxide made continuous treatment possible. Such continuous fumigation may be applicable under some conditions, such as packing in wood wool or other bulky materials. Some of these materials have enormous ab-

Precooling, Fumigation, and Storage of Table Grapes

sorptive capacity for sulfur dioxide which makes it difficult to calculate the proper dosage. Its use is very limited and its adaptability to large storage rooms—holding 40 or more carloads—remains to be demonstrated.

FUMIGATION WITH BISULFITE

The benefits of gas fumigation of grapes largely disappear after a short period. Yet it is impossible to re-treat with gas in sawdust packs and lugs packed for immediate export, and fumigation in the holds of ships is impossible because of the presence of other fruits and storage materials that would be damaged. In such cases sodium bisulfite may be used. Sulfur dioxide is released as the bisulfite reacts with the moisture in the air of the containers of grapes. When the air in the packs is only moderately moist, the release of the sulfur dioxide is quite slow; as a result, the grapes are exposed to a low concentration during a long period. If there is too much moisture, sulfur dioxide may be released so rapidly that the fruit will be injured. In the early 1930's Pentzer and Asbury (1934) indicated the possible benefits of placing bisulfite in packed lugs of grapes. With 10 grams of bisulfite sifted into the paper hay pad, there was no decay and only slight to moderate injury after 60 days storage at 32° F. The method of treatment, however, was not recommended pending the development of a method which would insure more uniform distribution of the sulfur dioxide among the grapes. A method approaching such distribution was developed by Nelson *et al.* (1969). It consisted in placing bisulfite tablets in an uniform fixed spread under the top curtain and/or on the bottom pad. Their most effective treatment was a combination lined (unvented) container with the bisulfite tablets affixed to a paper insert which could be removed when the package was opened. This was with shallow African packs of ten pounds each. With the deeper containers used in California, both bottom and top inserts were necessary to insure an effective concentration of sulfur dioxide in the center of the pack.

Fideghelli and Monastra (1969) placed 10 grams of bisulfite, dissolved in 140 cc of water, in a number of polythene sachets which were then placed on top of the grapes in a 10 kilogram pack. The sachets were made of 0.05 mm polythene. The treated pack was placed in a ventilated polythene bag of 0.1 mm thickness. This treatment doubled the storage life of the Italia grape. The rate of release of sulfur dioxide could, no doubt, be further controlled by using sachets of different wall thickness or a higher or lower concentration of the bisulfite.

Sachets of sulfite of potassium ($S_2O_5K_2$) solution were also tested by Grncarevic and Lewis (1969–1971) for the preservation of Ohanez (Almeria) grapes in cool-room storage. The sachets were polythene 0.075 mm (75 u) thick and 6 cm x 6 cm in size containing 15 ml of 1.5, 3, 6, or 12 per cent of the sulfite solution. Eight sachets of the same per cent solution were placed on top of a 4 kilogram (8.8 lbs.) pack of grapes. The pack was then wrapped in ventilated polythene of 0.35 mm thick. Check packs received no sulfite solution. After 4 weeks the stems in the checks showed rapid drying with some completely moldy berries, while packs with sachets had but one moldy berry (at 3 per cent), and the stems were green and mostly plump. Sachets with sulfite up to 6 per cent are considered safe; 12 per cent produced sulfur dioxide burns.

Continuing with earlier trials, Gentry and Nelson (1968) developed a two-stage generator of sulfur dioxide for closed (unvented) containers. For the first-stage a 7 x 15 inch sheet of polyethylene-impregnated "tea-bag" stock was heat-sealed to plain Kraft paper on a multiple packaging machine entrapping granular sodium bisulfite in 16 rectangular pouches. The second-stage generator was the same size but made of polyethylene-coated Kraft paper and heat-sealed in the same manner. The first-stage device contained 1.5 grams of sodium bisulfite, the second-stage 5.7 grams. In the trials one sheet of each was placed on the bottom pad and one of each under the curtain, with the first-stage device next to the grapes. Although effected by the moisture in the container, the first-stage generator begins releasing sulfur dioxide within several hours and reaches a maximum release by the second day. The second-stage begins generating sulfur dioxide after the fifth day, reaching a maximum in 12 to 15 days, and continuing to generate for as long as two months at storage temperatures. By varying the weight of the dose in either or both generators the release of sulfur dioxide and its time effectiveness can be altered.

Decay control and bleaching injury with the two-stage generator has been essentially the same as with the initial and refumigation with sulfur dioxide. An added benefit of the two-stage generator in unvented containers, as indicated by Nelson and Ahmedullah (1970) is the preservation of the freshness of the berries and the green color and turgidity of the stems. A further improvement in the first and second stage sulfur dioxide generators was reported by Nelson and Ahmedullah (1972). The use of polyethylene and cellulose acetate films of different thickness has provided a greater degree of control over both the rate and length of period of sulfur dioxide release.

This method of treatment with bisulfide is especially adapted for export shipment. Nelson (1970) states that it overcomes most of the objection to the sawdust chest, namely higher cost, sometimes off-odors, and unattractive appearance. A pilot shipment to London, England of unvented standard lugs and unvented fiberboard containers supplied with two-stage sulfur dioxide generators demonstrated that grapes can be placed there in essentially the same condition as in the eastern United States. The unvented containers kept the berries and stems fresher, and the sulfur dioxide

Precooling, Fumigation, and Storage of Table Grapes

generators minimized the danger of decay. The containers can be palletized and enclosed in polythene to further reduce water loss and to discourage pilfering in transit.

Recently this method of supplying sulfur dioxide was combined with the conventional method to provide the possibility of protecting grapes packed in domestic lugs in export, without the usual sawdust filler. The grapes, packed in standard vented lugs, are fumigated in the usual manner, with sulfur dioxide from an external source, and refumigated periodically as long as they are held in cold storage. Then, when the grapes are prepared for export, months later (1 to 3), a two-stage generator is inserted over the fruit and under the lid in each lug. The pallets of fruit are then

FIGURE 154: Packed chests in cold storage. Note slats between chests to facilitate cooling and refumigation until actual shipment.

entirely enclosed in a polyethylene wrapper to retain the sulfur dioxide generated by the inserts and to minimize water loss.

Some grapes may still be packed in sawdust, but with the combination of conventional and the two-stage generator the use of sawdust is diminishing. In actual practice, grapes packed in chests are stored without sawdust in order to facilitate precooling, fumigation, and refumigation (fig. 154). The sawdust is run into the chests when they are being readied for shipment. When bisulfite is added, it is mixed with the sawdust just before the latter is run into the packs or dusted on the surface of the pack. Moisturized (12 to 15 per cent) sawdust will reduce water loss from the berries, but it must not be so moist that the increase in the release of sulphur dioxide will injure the grapes.

Other promising fungicides.—Wrapping grape clusters in tissue paper impregnated with sodium o-phenyphenate, o-phenylphenyl acetate, or o-phenylphenyl butyrate, and sodium metabisulfite reduced decay in cool storage. The phenol derivatives so applied were equally effective, and their potency was 4.3 times that of sodium metabisulfite (Scott and Roberts, 1965). CAUTION: these materials definitely require further testing. They are not registered for use with grapes in the United States.

FACTORS AFFECTING ABSORPTION OF SULFUR DIOXIDE

The amount of sulfur dioxide absorbed by grapes in a given time is influenced by a number of factors, such as the variety of the grapes, maturity of the fruit, temperature of the fruit, soundness of the fruit (handling injuries), concentration of the gas, and time of exposure to the gas.

Variety.—Some varieties absorbed sulfur dioxide much more rapidly than others. For example, from the same concentration of gas, Thompson Seedless absorbed as much in thirty minutes as Gros Guillaume did in sixty minutes. The Emperor was intermediate in rate of absorption. Similarly, different varieties tolerate different amounts of sulfur dioxide without injury. Thompson Seedless showed commercial injury at 30 ppm, Malaga at 18, Emperor at 14, Muscat of Alexandria at 26, and Gros Guillaume at 65. In addition to these varietal differences in absorption and tolerance, Pentzer *et al.* (1933) found appreciable variation within a variety in different vineyards and seasons.

Maturity.—Winkler and Jacob (1925) found that immature grapes absorb sulfur dioxide more rapidly than do mature ones. For example, Muscat of Alexandria grapes of 27°, 18°, and 13° Brix, respectively, absorbed 43, 77, and 262 ppm. These results indicate that for uniform fumigation the grapes should be uniform in maturity. Very mature fruit, which is subject to more handling injuries, should possibly have a slightly higher concentration of the gas. Grapes of a low degree Brix, in contrast, are easily overfumigated.

Fruit temperature.—Warm grapes, according to Jacob (1929) and Pentzer and Asbury (1934), absorb more sulfur dioxide than cold grapes from the same concentration of the gas in a given time. Thompson Seedless absorbed twice as much sulfur dioxide at 72° as at 39° F. whereas Malaga absorbed almost three times as much at 75° as at 48° F. Temperature is of particular importance when precooled grapes and grapes directly from the field are fumigated together.

Concentration of sulfur dioxide and length of exposure.—The higher the concentration and the longer the exposure, the more sulfur dioxide is absorbed by grapes. The concentration, speed of entry into the room, fan distribution, and time of exposure are doubtless the most important factors in regular, uniform fumigation. The concentration must not only be appropriate, 0.5 per cent for the initial gassing, but must also be uniform throughout the room. Similarly, the above factors of gassing must be constant if absorption is to be uniform. That is why the length of the gassing, twenty minutes, is emphasized.

In view of the many factors that affect rate of absorption, it must be realized that much work has gone into determining the recommendations of 0.5 per cent and 0.1 per cent for initial fumigation and refumigations and twenty to thirty minutes for exposure time. Nevertheless, these are average figures for average conditions. Experienced operators may vary concentration or exposure to meet special conditions.

Even the 0.5 to 1 per cent concentration of sulfur dioxide generally used in California may or may not be used with equal success everywhere. In South Africa, for example, Reyneke and Piaget (1952) reported that 20 ppm is the upper limit grapes will tolerate without injury and that concentration was obtained when the grapes were exposed to 0.25 and 0.3 per cent concentrations of the gas for twenty minutes.

Other factors.—More recent studies by Nelson and Richardson (1961) have shown that factors and conditions within the storage room, such as air velocity, types of lugs and liners, types of packs and wraps, and the orientation and alignment of the lugs, may markedly influence the uniformity of the absorption of sulfur dioxide by grapes.

PRECAUTIONS IN FUMIGATION

The pungent odor of sulfur dioxide is readily recognized at very low concentrations. At 400 ppm the gas is extremely irritating and causes injury to the tender tissues of the nose, eyes, and mouth. At the concentration used in fumigating grapes in storage rooms it can cause respiratory spasms and death if the victim cannot escape to fresh air. If it becomes necessary to enter a room with even a very dilute concentration of sulfur dioxide, goggles and a gas mask must be worn. The mask must be effective against acid-type gases.

Sulfur Dioxide Injury.—Bleaching is the most common type of sulfur dioxide injury to grapes. This injury is always most pronounced around the pedicel. In the handling incident to packing, the skin adjacent to the pedicel is often cracked, allowing the sulfur dioxide to be absorbed more rapidly. The gas also enters this part of the berry through the vascular strands of the pedicel to cause bleaching. The tissue under the bleached area dries out and collapses, forming a depression. According to Pentzer *et al.* (1942), other bleached, sunken areas may also appear elsewhere on the surface of the berries, especially in the Tokay. These form around minute injuries to the skin. The bleached pits may pass unnoticed while the grapes are at low temperatures, but after two or more days at room temperature they become conspicuous.

Bleaching, beginning around the pedicel, progresses toward the tip of the berry. The color of red varieties becomes very pale, and the berries take on a dull, lifeless appearance. In the black varieties the change in color is from blue-black to reddish blue. In white varieties the change is initially a yellowing, followed by development of a dull, ashen, pale yellow. After one or more days at room temperature, the bleached areas begin to brown. With severe injury, browning may occur in the storage rooms. The changes in color are usually accompanied by objectionable changes in taste.

Immediately after fumigation, all grapes have a sulfurous taste. This disappears after several days unless the fruit has been badly overtreated. Grapes showing noticeable changes in color, however, retain a cooked taste and are irretrievably damaged.

Studies by Nelson (1958) indicate that most of the retarding effect of sulfur dioxide on the spread of *Botrytis* on grapes in storage was obtained during the first five to ten minutes of the refumigation period. This suggests that short fumigation periods might be used to reduce fruit injury.

Wetness.—Wetness, as used here, refers to the accumulation of droplets of juice on the surface of the berries and pedicels. Wetness is associated with sulfur dioxide injury yet not identical with it, since that injury may occur without wetness. Nelson (1958b) has shown that wetness results from leakage of juice through the lenticels or through microscopic injuries to the skin after the cells of the underlying tissue have been rendered permeable by sulfur dioxide injury. The wetness increases with the concentration of sulfur dioxide used in the initial fumigation and with the number of refumigations. As a result, it is particularly severe in weak fruit —immature or from overloaded vines—or fruit held in storage for a long time. Wetness may be increased by an active infection of *Botrytis*, which also injures the tissue beneath the skin. Wetness also seems to increase at very high relative humidity.

The droplets that collect on the surface of the berries have a sugar concentration the same as or somewhat higher than that of their expressed juice. Droplets are often found on bleached areas. While the fruit remains undisturbed, the droplets remain intact, but as soon as the fruit is handled, or is shaken in transit, they are smeared over the surface of the berries, giving the appearance of wetness.

Simulated transit testing of containers for grapes has indicated that vibration in transit, particularly if the container is not filled tightly enough to immobilize the berries, may result in mechanical injury around the pedicels. In tests, this led to sunken areas about the pedicels, leakage of juice, and wetness, closely simulating SO_2 injury.

Most of the bleached areas on the surface of the berries become associated with sulfur dioxide injury through microscopic injuries and field punctures to the skin rather than through the lenticels. These injuries, according to Nelson (1958b), may also arise from the berries' rubbing against the side of containers, the liners, or the dust coated surface of other berries. Penter *et al.* (1942) observed that a bleached and pitted condition of Tokay was most serious where the bloom had been rubbed off or where the berries had been bruised by rubbing against the side of the container.

Injury to other fruits.—The grape differs from all other fruits in its tolerance of sulfur dioxide. Concentrations of this gas regularly used with grapes cause severe injury to other fruits and vegetables. Thus it is not feasible to keep grapes in the same storage house with them. Great damage would be done if only a small amount of sulfur dioxide should leak into the rooms containing other agricultural products.

Corrosive action on equipment.—Sulfur dioxide readily dissolves in water to form sulfurous acid, which is very corrosive to most metals found in storage plants—especially iron, zinc, and aluminum. Expansion coils, brine-spray chambers, and other metal equipment will deteriorate very rapidly if not protected by acid-resistant paints.

COLD STORAGE OF GRAPES

Fruit may be cold-stored to extend the marketing period or to relieve temporary market congestion. With grapes, extending the marketing period is by far the more important object. Its importance has increased with improvements in the storage environment. Improvements have resulted from advances in the procedures of precooling, more effective use of sulfur dioxide, better temperature and humidity control, and more appropriate handling of the grapes. These advances in the cold storage of late-maturing

FIGURE 155: Palletized stacks of packed lugs of grapes in cold storage. Channels are left between rows of palletized lugs for air movement. The pallets facilitate mechanical handling.

varieties, together with the production of very early-maturing varieties, have made it possible to have fresh California grapes available each month of the year. The factors in the storage environment that affect the storage life of grapes most directly are temperature, relative humidity, air movement, and (as discussed) fumigation with sulfur dioxide.

Temperature.—The lower the storage temperature, other conditions being favorable, the longer the fruit may be held. The danger of freezing determines the lowest temperature that may be used. The fruit of most varieties, according to Carrick (1930) and Wright (1942), when well mature, will not be damaged by storage temperature as low as 25° F., while

Pentzer *et al.* (1945) reported that the stems, which are always lower in sugars, will be injured at a higher temperature. Thus, to provide a margin of safety in storage plant operation and to allow for normal temperature variation, present recommendations are 30° to 32° F. in storage rooms.

Temperature maintenance is facilitated by the manner in which the containers are arranged in the storage rooms. In most of the new storage plants the grape lugs are stacked on pallets, with the pallet loads stacked three high—to the ceiling (fig. 155). Two principles must be observed: the side of the lugs should be in the direction of the air movement, and, according to Ryall and Harvey (1959), the spacing between rows and between pallets must be uniform. Heat transfer is accomplished more readily from the thin, partially open side of the lug than through the thicker, solid ends. Uniform spacing of the rows and pallets is necessary for the even distribution of air and the maintenance of uniform temperature.

Relative humidity.—The relative humidity should be high in grape storage rooms, as close to saturation as possible. The figure for relative humidity represents the percentage of saturation of air with water vapor at a given temperature. Warm air holds more water vapor than cold air; for example, air of 80 per cent relative humidity at 75° F. contains much more water by weight than air of the same relative humidity at 35° F. As the relative humidity of the air in a storage room increases, the vapor pressure increases and water loss from the grapes decreases. That is why a relative humidity of 92 to 96 per cent (saturation) is recommended for grape storage rooms.

Humidity in a grape storage room depends on the balance between losses and gains of water. Most water loss is owing to condensation on the cooling surfaces, yet absorption of moisture by containers, pads, walls, and ceilings may be important. Moisture may be gained by loss from the grapes or by evaporation from water used to cool air in a packed cooling tower or by fog spray. Air circulation in the storage rooms should be sufficient to limit the temperature rise of humidified air. Relative humidity in precooling or storage is reduced by about 4 per cent for each 1° F. rise in air temperature. Moisture loss may sometimes be checked by using large, effective cooling surfaces operating at a close-to-air temperature. The figures in table 34 give calculated values for water condensation in a storage room with the return air at 35° F. (Mitchell *et al.*, 1972).

Cooling surfaces, in California, are usually designed to operate at about 10° F. below air temperature in normal storage and 20° F. below during precooling. Under these conditions considerable condensation of water, evaporated from the grape, will occur on the cooling surfaces, and the relative humidity in the rooms will be reduced to 70 or 80 per cent. The humidity in the rooms, however, may be kept at the desired levels by using

Precooling, Fumigation, and Storage of Table Grapes

fog sprays to offset the condensation of the water on the cooling surfaces. Adding 1 gallon of water per hour per ton of refrigeration will offset condensation under severe conditions. On the other hand, the spray-system regulation and maintenance can be eliminated if air in the storage rooms is cooled by contact with showering cold water in a packed cooling tower. Air moving upward in the tower can be brought within a degree or less of the temperature of the water supply and near 100 per cent relative humidity. An arrangement of horizontally-stretched plastic filaments is widely used in packing these cooling towers in California.

In the newer storage plants the principle of the packed tower system is used, while in the older plant the fog spray is used to maintain the desired humidity. The latter system has drawbacks: some of the added moisture collects on the refrigerator coils as ice or dilutes the brine in the brine-spray type of plant. Even so, the ice on the coils can be readily removed by defrosting, and added salt will offset dilution of the brine. The amount of water to add by fog spraying is shown in table 34.

To maintain the net additions of moisture indicated in table 34, it is necessary to allow for water absorbed by the dry lugs. Mitchell *et al.* (1972) found that wooden grape containers held in 90 per cent relative humidity in tests at Davis gained about the following amounts of their dry weight per day: 0.5 per cent initially, 0.25 per cent after twenty days, 0.125 per cent after forty days, and so on.

TABLE 34
CONDENSATION ON COOLING SURFACES

	Relative humidity of return air at 35° F.			
	95	90	80	70
	Condensation (gallons) per hour per ton of refrigeration			
T (° F.) *				
20	0.5	0.4	0.4	0.2
10	0.5	0.4	0.3	0.1
5	0.5	0.4	0	0
4	0.4	0.3	0	0
3	0.4	0.2	0	0
2	0.3	0	0	0
1	0	0	0	0

SOURCE OF DATA: Mitchell *et al.*, 1972.
* T = The temperature difference between the air returning from the storage room and the cooling surfaces over which that air will pass.

Air movement.—Air movement within a storage room should be only enough to remove vital heat and heat that leaks in through the floor, walls, ceiling and swinging doors and to prevent a temperature rise. Ample air movement in a well-insulated, tight room is 10 to 25 linear feet per minute. More than 25 FTM only adds to product shrinkage. It has been shown by Allen and Pentzer (1936) that doubling the air movement increased moisture loss by about one third and was equivalent to a drop of about 5 per cent in relative humidity. Air movement is controlled with fans or blowers and stacking patterns (Anon., 1968).

REFRIGERATION SYSTEMS

Storage plants built specifically for cold-storing table grapes are refrigerated by one of the following systems: individual rooms with air cooled by dry refrigerated surfaces; central chambers with brine sprayed over refrigerated surfaces and air ducted to individual rooms, air from individual rooms circulated upward through chilled water sprayed over stretched plastic filaments (for very high humidity); or individual-room ice bunkers. Each, when properly designed and operated, provides a satisfactory environment for storing table grapes.

Both design and the efficiency of operation fall in the province of engineering, which is outside the scope of this discussion. It might be stated, however, that for long-term storage, including fumigation with sulfur dioxide, the individual-room dry-coil bunker and water spray design systems have distinct advantages. On the other hand, the individual-room ice-bunker system is peculiarly well adapted for short-term storage.

VARIETIES FOR COLD STORAGE

Many of the most flavorsome grapes of almost every grape-growing country are too delicate for storage. Varieties that ripen early or in midseason are risks in storage, even though they possess good keeping quality, because they come into direct competition with fresh late-ripening grapes when they must be marketed. Thus the varieties for extending the marketing season for grapes by cold storage are largely those that ripen late and are grown in areas free of early frosts and early autumn rains.

In general, the varieties that keep well in cold storage have a low rate of respiration. For example, Thompson Seedless grapes, which have a maximum storage life of three months, respire more rapidly and evolve more vital heat than Emperor or Almeria (Ohanez) at 32° F. Emperor grapes of best quality can be stored successfully for four to six months. In addition to their slower rate of respiration, grapes that store well for long periods have a firm pulp and a thick and relatively tough skin. The approximate storage life of several varieties that are fairly regularly stored in California are shown here (see also Ryall and Harvey, 1959).

Variety	Storage life, months
Italia	
Tokay (Flame Tokay)	1 to 2
Thompson Seedless	
Red Malaga (Molinera)	2 to 3
Ribier (Alphonse Lavallée)	
Almeria (Ohanez)	3 to 5
Emperor	

The findings of Lutz (1938) indicate that a number of American grapes have a storage life of four to eight weeks. Concord and Worden keep in good condition for four to six weeks, and Catawba and Delaware up to two months. American grapes are not fumigated with sulfur dioxide because of their susceptibility to injury. Muscadine grapes keep even less well in storage.

Grapes to be stored should be selected for quality more rigidly than grapes sold immediately. Firmness of berry, color, toughness of skin, maturity of fruit and stems, and freedom from injury and infection are the factors of quality to be most seriously considered. With Emperor, clusters having lignified (sealed) stems are desired. The trimming should be thorough, and the packing should be carried out with care to reduce packing injuries to a minimum.

Grapes going into storage are regularly precooled and given the initial fumigation with sulfur dioxide before being placed in the cold-storage rooms.

DETERIORATION OF GRAPES IN STORAGE AND TRANSIT

Grapes, unlike many other fruits, do not ripen after harvest. There is no reserve material, such as starch, so there can be no normal increase in sugars after the grapes are removed from the vine. Nevertheless, the harvested grape is still a living entity in which normal life processes are taking place. The most important is respiration, in which the sugars are consumed very slowly, oxygen is taken up, and carbon dioxide, water, and heat are given off. Since these normal changes are retarded but not stopped in storage, the grapes deteriorate until loss in quality is perceptible.

As grapes approach the end of their storage life they take on a dull and tired-looking appearance. The white varieties gradually develop a slight amber color, which later becomes brown; the red and black varieties change to a grayish purple. The berries take on an oxidized or slightly cooked taste, and softening of the pulp is evident. Grapes must not be held until they show the first signs of these changes—by then they are lost as table fruit.

Shatter or berry drop.—There are several types of shatter or berry drop in storage and transit: that from brittle or weak stems; that in which the brush is pulled from the berry ("wet drop"); and that in which an abscission layer is formed to separate the berry from the pedicel ("dry drop").

The shatter owing to brittle stems is characteristic for a few varieties, such as Kandahar and Rish Baba. When the fruit of these varieties is packed carelessly or loosely or the packed lugs roughly handled, the stem laterals are broken and small clumps of berries are found in the lugs. The weak pedicels of Thompson Seedless and Monukka are also responsible for shatter; in this case the shatter is as individual berries. Shatter of berries, according to Nelson (1955), may and does occur to a lesser extent in other varieties, especially when the stems are permitted to dry from too long a period between harvest and precooling. Jacob (1931) and Weaver (1956) report that girdling and treatment with growth regulators to increase pedicel thickness and toughness have reduced this type of shatter. Pentzer (1941) found that naphthalene acetic acid treatment shortly before harvest has reduced drop in other fruits, but not in grapes.

The shatter in which the brush is pulled from the berries—"wet drop" —is the result of rough handling in packing and transit. This shatter, according to Nelson et al. (1970), can be reduced by producing only well-made, firm packs that are firmly braced in the railroad car or truck. According to Nelson (1955), cultural practices that strengthen the attachment of the stems to the berries, as well as careful yet rapid handling from the vine, through precooling, fumigation, and into storage, will also reduce wet drop. Wet drop results not only in loss of the berries that drop: the other fruit in the lugs is damaged by wetness. Nelson (1958a) points out that this wetness is not to be confused with that from sulfur dioxide injury.

In a few varieties, shatter results from the formation of an abscission layer at the attachment of the berries. This type of shatter was reported with Watham Cross (Dattier) in South Africa by Boyes and de Villers (1933) and with Muscat Hamburg in Israel by Lavee (1959). According to Beyers (1938, 1939a, and 1939b) this type of shatter in South Africa is increased by soil moisture stress just before harvest, hot dry weather during harvest, early harvest, and a reduced number of seeds in the fruit. Studies by Beyers (1939a) and Lavee (1959) showed that a delay in getting the fruit of both Waltham Cross and Muscat Hamburg into cold storage increased the drop very much. Although early spray trials by Pentzer (1941) with growth regulators had no effect, Lavee (1959) found that spraying four days before harvest reduced this drop appreciably.

Precooling, Fumigation, and Storage of Table Grapes

Freezing.—The temperature at which grapes will freeze is determined largely by their sugar content. The freezing point of a 17 per cent dextrose (grape sugar) solution is 28.5° F.; that of a 20 per cent solution, 27.7°; and that of a 23 per cent solution, 26.8°. Experimental tests by Carrick (1930) demonstrated that ripe grapes of similar percentages of total soluble solids, as determined by the Brix hydrometer, will not freeze until the same, or slightly lower, temperatures are encountered. When frozen berries have thawed, their color is dull and the fruit is soft and flabby, with a disagreeable cooked or oxidized taste.

Because of their lower sugar content, stems and pedicels are frozen by temperatures that do not damage berries. The frozen stems, after thawing, are at first limp and pliable, with a water-soaked appearance, but they soon become dry, brittle, and dark-colored. Stems of grapes that have been fumigated with sulfur dioxide also become dry upon freezing, but they retain their green or straw-yellow color.

Water loss.—As indicated by work of Jacob (1929) in California and of Beyers (1938) and Du Plessis and Reyneke (1939) in South Africa, the period of most critical water loss is that immediately after picking. It is emphasized that grapes should be picked in the cool of the day, be kept cool, and be precooled as soon as possible. The curbing of water loss nevertheless remains an important factor of quality maintenance as long as the grapes remain in storage. Low relative humidity and too-rapid air movement in the storage rooms or too long storage are the usual causes of water loss. As has been stated, relative humidity should be maintained between 92 and 96 per cent. Once the fruit is cooled, the air movement in the storage rooms should be only enough to maintain the desirable temperature of the grapes. Other conditions being equal, immature fruit loses water more readily than well-matured fruit. The difference was shown by De Villers (1926) to be owing to the increase in cutinization of the skin of the berries as they mature. This supports the experience of many growers that Emperor clusters should not be harvested for storage until well matured, with the branch stems yellow-green and the main stems lignified or brown. It is also in agreement with observations that fruit from overloaded vines, which never matures normally, stores poorly. The poorer keeping quality of such fruit is, in part at least, owing to its more rapid water loss.

Berry cracking.—The turgidity of fruits may increase during cooling. The berries of some of the thin-skinned varieties, such as Thompson Seedless and Tokay, according to Ryall and Harvey (1959), may actually crack soon after they are placed in storage. The circular cracks are usually limited to the tips of the berries. In a study of the critical pressure of berry splitting Considine and Kriedemann (1971) found that in the varieties prone to crack the turgor pressure required was near 15 atmospheres (90 lbs.

psi), while in resistant varieties it may be as high as 40 atmospheres. No effective means of control for cracking has yet been perfected; rigid control of irrigation just before harvest should allay the trouble.

The organisms attacking grapes in storage and transit—*Botrytis, Cladosporium*, and *Alternaria*—are discussed in chapter 18, on grape diseases.

PREDICTING DECAY IN STORAGE

With the efficient control of temperature and relative humidity in modern grape-storage houses and the effective fumigation provided by sulfur dioxide, sound grapes of the appropriate varieties can be held for long periods. Effective fumigation in the storage environment prevents new infections of the grapes in storage, but it does not control the infections that were in the fruit at harvest. These field infections are largely the gray mold, *Botrytis cinerea*. This fungus continues to grow in the individual berries in the storage environment despite refumigations.

Harvey (1955) developed a procedure for correlating the number of field infections of a given lot of grapes with its storage life. To do this he took samples of individual berries from each lot of grapes to be stored. The samples were placed in individual glass jars and fumigated with sulfur dioxide to destroy all organisms on the surface of the fruit. Then they were covered and held under sterile conditions at room temperature and high relative humidity. Under these conditions, decay that would require several months to develop in the storage environment develops in ten days. When this procedure is used, the percentage of decay that develops in the test berries indicates what may be expected of grapes of the same lot of fruit in the storage rooms. For the results obtained with the fruit held at room temperature to be of value in predicting storage life, the test berries must be representative of the lots of fruit in storage.

In the packing house, samples can be taken by clipping individual berries from the packed lugs as they go to the lidding machine. He found that this method of sampling provided a representative indication of the potential decay present in each lot of fruit going into storage. It is efficient and is applicable to both field- and house-packed fruit.

This procedure should be of special value when new lots of grapes are brought into storage; that is, grapes without storage history. Within two weeks it provides the owner or manager with information regarding the potential storage life of these grapes. This enables him to fit the lots into their proper places in the marketing schedule for the season. Similarly, when a number of different lots of grapes are to be stored for long periods, the individual lots can be marketed to best advantage when the potential storage life of each lot is known.

The accuracy of forecasts of decay in storage is illustrated by figure 156.

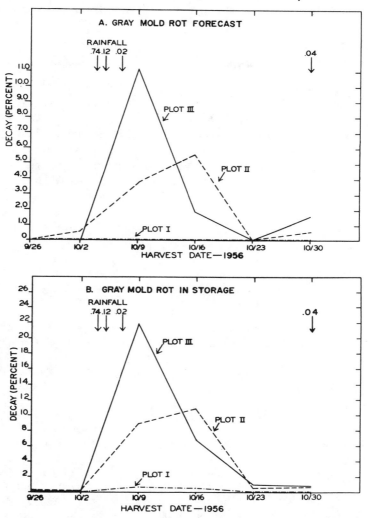

FIGURE 156: Percentage of gray mold rot in Emperor grapes harvested from three plots during the 1956 season: A, forecast of decay; B, record of decay in storage after about 3 months. (*From U.S.D.A. Marketing Ser. 392, 1960*)

The graphs show the results obtained by Harvey (1960) with grapes from three different plots. The graphs above indicate the graymold forecast; those below show the actual mold that developed in storage. The forecast of gray-mold rot indicated that the fruit from plot I for all harvesting dates could be safely stored. Grapes from plots II and III, in contrast, could be stored safely only if harvested from September 26 to October 2 (before the rains) or from October 23 to 30.

TRANSPORT

California table grapes are shipped to markets throughout the United States and Canada in refrigerated railroad cars and trucks. Grapes exported to the Far East, South America, and Europe are shipped under marine refrigeration. Local markets, including the San Francisco and Los Angeles areas, are supplied by trucks, with or without refrigeration. On these hauls the trucks move principally at night, and the grapes are delivered to the retailers the morning after they are harvested.

BIBLIOGRAPHY

Allen, F. W., and W. T. Pentzer. 1936. Studies on the effect of humidity in the cold storage of fruit. Proc. Amer. Soc. Hort. Sci., 33:215–223.

Anon. 1968. The commercial storage of fruits, vegetables, and florist and nursery stocks. USDA Agric. Handbook, No. 66, p. 1–31.

Beyers, E. 1938. Drop berry and desiccation of stalks in Waltham Cross grapes. Union of South Africa, Dept. Agr. and Forestry. Low Temp. Res. Lab. Capetown, Ann. Rept., 1936–37, pp. 91–101.

————. 1939a. Relationship between "drop" and seedlessness in Waltham Cross grapes. Union of South Africa, Dept. Agr. and Forestry. Low Temp. Lab. Capetown, Ann. Rept., 1937–38, pp. 87–90.

————. 1939b. Further investigations of factors affecting drop and desiccation of stalks of Waltham Cross in storage. Union of South Africa, Dept. Agr. and Forestry. Low Temp. Lab. Capetown, Ann. Rept., 1937–38, pp. 79–87.

Boyes, W. W., and J. R. de Villers. 1933. Effect of delayed storage on quality of table grapes. Union of South Africa, Dept. Agr. and Forestry. Low Temp. Res. Lab. Capetown, Ann. Rept., 1933, pp. 96–99.

Carrick, D. B. 1930. Some cold-storage and freezing studies on the fruit of the *vinifera* grape. Cornell Agr. Exp. Sta. Mem., 131:1–37.

Considine, J. A., and P. E. Kriedemann. 1971. Berry spliting in grapes: Definition of the critical turgor pressure. Aust. J. Agric. Res. 23:17–24.

Cuey, H. M., and U. Uota. 1961. Effects of concentration, exposure, time, temperature, and relative humidity on the toxicity of SO_2 to spores of *Botrytis cinerea*. Phytopathology, 51:815–819.

De Villers, F. J. 1926. Physiological studies of the grape. Union of South Africa, Dept. Agr. Sci. Bull., 45:1–97.

Dewey, D. H. 1950. The effects of air blast precooling on the moisture content of the stems of cherries and grapes. Proc. Amer. Soc. Hort. Sci., 56:111–115.

De Plessis, S. J., and J. Reyneke. 1939. Experiments on the control of dry stalk and wastage in export grapes. Union of South Africa, Dept. Agr. Sci. Bull., 195:2–25.

Fideghelli, C., and F. Monastra. 1969. Conservazione frigaratora dell'uva Italia secondo el metodo del "sacchetto" generatore (Cold storage of the table grape Italia by the generation Sachet method). Viv. Vitic. Enol., 21:457–464.

Gentry, J. P., and K. E. Nelson. 1968. Further studies on control of decay of table grapes by two-stage generator of sulfur dioxide within unvented containers. Amer. J. Enol. Vitic., 19(1):70–81.

Grncarevic, M., and W. Lewis, 1969–71. Storage of table grapes in plastic films with sachet of sulphite solution. Report Div. Hort. Res., C.S.I.R.O., Adelaide, pp. 48–49.

Guillou, R. 1960. Coolers for fruits and vegetables. California Agr. Exp. Sta. Bull., 773:1–65.

Harvey, J. M. 1955. A method for forecasting decay in California storage grapes. Phytopathology, 45:229–232.

———. 1960. Instructions for forecasting decay in table grapes for storage. United States Dept. Agr., Marketing Res. Rept., 393:3–12.

Jacob, H. E. 1929. The utilization of sulfur dioxide in shipping grapes. California Agr. Exp. Sta. Bull., 471:1–24.

———. 1931. Girdling grape vines. California Agr. Exp. Ser. Cir., 56:1–18.

Lavee, S. 1959. Physical aspects of post harvest berry drop in certain varieties. Vitis, 2:34–39.

Lutz, J. M. 1938. Factors influence the quality of American grapes in storage. United States Dept. Agr. Tech. Bull., 606:1–27.

———, and R. E. Hardenburg. 1968. The commercial storage of fruits, vegetables and florist and nursery stocks. U. S. Dept. Agric. Handbook No. 66:1–94, Superintendent of Documents, Washington, D.C. 20402.

Marias, P. G. 1952. Automatic control of sulfur dioxide with a photoelectric cell in the long-term storage of grapes. Union of South Africa Dept. Agr. Sci. Bull., 322:1–10.

Mitchell. F. G., Rene Guillou, and R. A. Parsons. 1972. Commercial cooling of fruits and vegetables. Calif. Agric. Exp. Sta. Ext. Ser. Manual, pp. 1–44.

Nelson, K. E. 1955. High picking temperatures and rough handling can reduce consumer acceptability of California fresh table grapes. Blue Anchor, 32(2):6–10.

———. 1958a. Some studies of the action of sulfur dioxide in control of *Botrytis* rot of Tokay grapes. Proc. Amer. Soc. Hort. Sci., 71:183–189.

———. 1958b. Some factors influencing bleaching and wetness of Emperor and Tokay grapes. Proc. Amer. Soc. Hort. Sci., 71:190–198.

———. 1970. Packing and handling trials on export grapes. Blue Anchor, 47:9–13.

———. 1973. Advances in postharvest handling of table grapes. Unpublished data, Department of Vitic. & Enol., University of California, Davis.

———, and M. Ahmedullah. 1970. Effect on Cardinal grapes of position of sulfur dioxide generators and retention of gas and water vapor in unvented containers. Amer. J. Enol. Vitic., 21:70–77.

————, ————. 1972. Effect of type of in-package sulfur dioxide generator and packaging materials on quality of stored table grapes. Amer. J. Enol. Vitic., 23:78–85.

————, ————, and F. G. Mitchell. 1970. Effect of container and packing method on injury and transportation of table grapes. Amer. J. Enol. Vitic., 21:101–108.

————, and G. A. Baker. 1963. Studies on the sulfur dioxide fumigation of table grapes. Amer. J. Enol. Vitic., 14:13–22.

————, and J. P. Gentry. 1966. Two-stage generation of SO_2 within closed containers to control decay of table grapes. Amer. J. Enol. Vitic., 17(4):290–301.

————, ————. 1968. Packaging grapes in unvented containers. Blue Anchor, 45(2):33–37.

————, L. Ginsburg, and G. H. de Swardt. 1969. The effect of method of sulfur dioxide application and packaging on waste control, gas injury, and stalk condition of grapes. Dec. Fruit. Gr., 19:313–320.

————, and H. B. Richardson. 1961. Further studies on factors affecting the concentration of sulfur dioxide in fumigation atmospheres for table grapes. Proc. Amer. Soc. Hort. Sci., 77:337–350.

Pentzer, W. T. 1941. Studies on the shatter of grapes with special reference to the use of solutions of naphthalene acetic acid to prevent it. Proc. Amer. Soc. Hort. Sci., 38:397–399.

————, and C. E. Asbury. 1934. Sulfur dioxide as an aid in the preservation of grapes in transit. Blue Anchor, 11(8):2–4, 23.

————, ————, and W. R. Barger. 1945. Precooling California grapes and their refrigeration in transit. United States Dept. Agr. Tech. Bull., 899:1–63.

————, ————, and K. C. Hamner. 1933. Effects of fumigation of different varieties of *vinifera* grapes with sulfur dioxide gas. Proc. Amer. Soc. Hort. Sci., 29:339–344.

————, ————, ————. 1934. The effect of sulfur dioxide fumigation on the respiration of Emperor grapes. Proc. Amer. Soc. Hort. Sci., 30:258–260.

————, C. O. Bratley, and W. G. Tufts. 1942. Report on sulfur dioxide injury in commercial shipments of Tokay grapes. United States Dept. Agr., Div. Fruit and Veg. Crops, unnumbered memo.

Reyneke, J., and S. J. du Plessis. 1943. The treatment of table grapes for local markets. Farming in South Africa, 18:443–445.

————, and J. E. H. Piaget. 1952. The use of bisulphites in the control of wastage in fresh grapes. Farming in South Africa, 27:477–479.

Richardson, H. B., K. E. Nelson, and D. Meredith. 1973. Cooling tests of palletized units of table grapes. Unpublished data, Dept. Vitic. Enol., University of California, Davis.

Ryall, A. L., and J. M. Harvey. 1959. The cold storage of *vinifera* grapes United States Dept. Agr., Agriculture Handbook, 159:1–46.

Scott, K. J., and E. A. Roberts. 1965. On evaluation of fumistats for purple Cornichon grapes. Aust. J. Exp. Agric. Animal Husb., 5:296–298.

Stubeurauch, A. V., and S. J. Dennis. 1910. The precooling of fruit. United States Dept. Agr., Yearbook of Agriculture, pp. 437–448.

Precooling, Fumigation, and Storage of Table Grapes

Weaver, R. J. 1956. Plant regulators in grape production. California Agr. Exp. Sta. Bull., 752:1–26.

Winkler, A. J., and H. E. Jacob. 1925. The utilization of sulfur dioxide in the marketing of grapes. Hilgardia, 1:107–131.

Wright, R. C. 1942. The freezing temperatures of some fruits, vegetables, and florists' stocks. United States Dept. Agr. Cir., 447:1–12.

———, D. H. Rose, and T. M. Whiteman. 1954. The commercial storage of fruits, vegetables, and florist and nursery stocks. United States Dept. Agr., Agriculture Handbook, 66:5–10.

23

Raisins

Raisins have been a staple food for centuries. Preserving the fruit of the grape by drying probably antedates preserving by fermentation. At present raisins are the second most important product of the vine, wine being first.

For the past thirty years, or longer, the annual world production of raisins has averaged about 730,000 tons. During the period 1968–1970, California produced about 30 per cent of this amount; Turkey, 23 per cent; Greece, 21 per cent; Australia, 10 per cent; and Iran, 6 per cent (Proton, 1968–1970). Smaller amounts were produced in Russia, Spain, South Africa, Argentina, Cyprus, Chile, Italy, and Morocco.

In recent years (1968–1970) the annual production of raisins in California has consisted, roughly of the following types and quantities:

	Tons, dried	Per cent
Natural Thompson Seedless	215,000	91.4
Bleached Thompson Seedless	14,800	6.3
Natural Muscats	1,900	0.8
Natural currants	2,800	1.3
Other	500	0.2

Source of Data: Henderson and Kitterman (1968–1970)

California's production of raisins from the Muscat of Alexandria grape has been shrinking, and production of currants is barely holding its own. There is a slight decline in total raisin production paralleling that of other dried fruit. This is a result of difficulties encountered in exports since World War II and the steady decline in per capita consumption of raisins in the United States—from 3.1 pounds in 1920–1924 to 1.2 pounds in 1967. A gradual decline has also been occurring in per capita consumption of table grapes.

RAISIN GRAPES AND TRADE NAMES

The word "raisin" is from the French *raisin sec*, meaning "dry grape." Any dried grape, therefore, has some right to be called a raisin. By usage, however, the term has become limited mainly to the dried grapes of a few varieties. Three of these—Thompson Seedless, Black Corinth, and Muscat of Alexandria—produce nearly all the raisins of international trade. The grape called Thompson Seedless in California is known as Sultana in Australia and South Africa; Oval Kishmish in Turkey, Iran, and other countries of Asia; or, sometimes in the Near East, *Sultanina*. The Black Corinth is also known as the Zante currant, currant, or simply "Zante" in English-speaking countries, and as *staphis* (meaning "raisin") in Greece; the name Panariti is used occasionally. The Muscat of Alexandria has various synonyms; perhaps the most common are Gordo Blanco (Australia), White Hanepoot (South Africa), and Zibibbo (Italy); it is a favorite in all warm grape producing countries. Other varieties are of local importance, such as the Sultana of California (the Round Kishmish of Turkey and Iran); Rosaki and Dattier in Greece and also in Turkey and elsewhere in Asia Minor; Monukka in Russia and the United States; and Cape Currant in Australia and South Africa. Certain wine and table grapes are occasionally dried; these should be called dried grapes to distinguish them from the raisins of commerce.

The trade names applied to raisins may signify, besides grape variety, the method of drying (natural, golden-bleached, sulfur-bleached, lexia); the principal place of origin (Vostizza, Patras, Pyrgos, Smyrna, Málaga, Valencia); the condition in which the raisins are offered for sale (layers, loose, seeded); the size grades (4 crown, 3 crown, 2 crown, and so on); United States Maturity grades—B or better, C, and substandard (Anon., 1968), and the quality grades (extra standard, standard, substandard; extra fancy, fancy, choice). Often the trade terms have different significance in different regions or with different kinds of raisins. For example, the crown grades are used in California to indicate only the size of Muscat raisins; when applied to the Sultana and lexia raisins of Australia, they also indicate color and quality. The Greek terms Vostizza, Patras, and Pyrgos, while primarily names of producing regions, are also suggestive or indicative of quality.

KINDS OF RAISINS AND THEIR PRODUCTION

Thompson Seedless naturals.—Raisins of the Thompson Seedless grape are dried in the natural condition, without dipping treatment, mainly in California, Iran, and Turkestan (U.S.S.R.). In California they are called "Thompson Seedless" or "naturals" to distinguish them from dipped raisins. Sometimes the trade knows them simply as "seedless". They are dark —grayish black or grayish brown—with the natural bloom largely intact; rather tough-skinned, but meaty, and of characteristic oxidized flavor; dry on the surface, with no stickiness or oiliness, and, when properly dried, with little tendency to cake in storage. For dessert purposes—eating out of hand—they are often preferred. For cooking, their dark color, tough skins, and strong flavor may not always be desirable. Other types—lighter-colored, tenderer, and less oxidized—seem to be preferred in all but the American and Scandinavian markets. In California more than 90 per cent of total raisin production is from Thompson Seedless grapes, and of these raisins more than 90 per cent are of the natural sun-dried type.

Production of naturals.—Most raisins produced in California are dried by the "natural" method, in the vineyard. Before picking begins, most growers smooth the soil between the east and west oriented vine rows, using an angle blade that fits a three-point hookup to a small tractor. The soil is pushed to the north in the middle, thus forming a smooth incline to the south. The workers pick the grapes into a pan that holds a tray load and then spread them, one cluster deep, on the tray (figs. 157, 158). Very large clusters should be cut into pieces so that drying will be uniform. The tray is placed so that it will receive a maximum of direct sunlight. After the top layer of berries has browned and shriveled—usually a week or ten days after spreading—the trays may be turned. According to Fischer (1959), turning shortens the drying time one to four days, but has no effect on quality. When the grapes are dry enough for stacking, the long sides of the tray are turned in and the trays are rolled into "biscuits" (fig. 159), or cigarette-like rolls are made without the edges being turned in. The stacked or rolled raisins remain in the vineyard for curing until they are ready for boxing. The time may range from ten days to two or more weeks. Naturally, grapes or raisins on paper trays, whether rolled or not, are very susceptible to damage in case of rain, when they may become badly sanded as well as moldy. When the raisins are so dry that juice cannot be squeezed out by pressing between the fingers, they are ready to be boxed. A desirable practice is first to pass the raisins from the trays over a shaker. This treatment eliminates a high percentage of sand, insects, and insect eggs that may be present on the new raisins. The sweat boxes, picks (small sweat box), or pallet-size containers usually remain in the vineyard in a stack for several weeks before delivery to the packing house in order

FIGURE 157: Placing the grapes on a 2x3-foot heavy paper tray for drying. This picker is using a wooden-rim frame to keep the grapes from spilling off. (*California Raisin Advisory Board, Fresno*)

to permit final curing (equalization of moisture). They are fumigated (see storage in the vineyard p. 631).

Mechanical harvesting of Thompson Seedless for making raisins.—As developed by Studer and Olmo (1971), the cutting of canes in conjunction with the use of a mechanical harvester, Thompson Seedless grapes can be detached as individual berries (fig. 160). When the fruit is mature, the canes bearing the fruiting shoots are cut near their base and left on the trellis wires for some days. During this time the cluster stems dry; the smaller divisions, the capstems (pedicles), are first to become brittle. At this stage it is possible to harvest the grapes as single berries with any type of vibratory harvester. Many capstems remain attached, while a smaller percentage are separated smoothly from the berries. Less than 2 per cent

FIGURE 158: Spreading the grapes to a uniform depth over the tray. After this, the wooden-rim frame is moved to the next tray to be loaded. (*California Raisin Advisory Board, Fresno*)

of the single berries are damaged. When the cut canes are left too long on the wire, larger cluster stems become brittle, and clumps of berries are broken off. The most appropriate time to let the cut canes dry is 4 to 8 days depending on the weather. The harvesting should proceed during the driest part of the day.

The harvested berries are conveyed into the hopper of a machine, that was developed by these same men, to spread them evenly on a continuous paper tray (fig. 161). This machine may be drawn behind the harvester or pulled by a tractor in an adjacent middle to those in which the harvester is operating. The spreader lays the continuous paper tray and meters the berries onto it (fig. 162). Studer and Olmo (1971) found that for proper drying 2 pounds of grape berries could be spread per square foot of tray.

FIGURE 159: When the raisins are nearly dry, they are rolled for further cur-ing. The biscuit roll is made by folding the long edges of the tray inward and then rolling it lengthwise. (*California Raisin Advisory Board, Fresno*)

An accurate estimate of the crop per row will enable the grower to deter-mine the width of the paper tray required. Not all vine rows carry the same amount of fruit, nor is it spread uniformly among the vines in the row. Hence, the hopper of the spreader machine must have sufficient ca-pacity to carry a fraction of the heavy load of one part of the row or vines and spread it along with the lighter load of another part of the row or vines. Only when this is done correctly is the tray used efficiently and are conditions for drying made uniform.

The single berries spread on the tray dry uniformly without turning and

FIGURE 160: Machine harvesting Thompson Seedless grapes, 4 to 8 days after the canes were cut. Most of the fruit comes off as individual berries which are conveyed to the hopper of the machine shown in figure 161. (*Courtesy of Upright Harvesters*)

in 5 to 7 days, less time than the usual clusters of hand-harvested grapes (fig. 158). When the berries are dry, they are picked up by another machine designed by the same men, fig. 163. This machine has metal fingers that run under the paper tray to guide it to revolving brushes that put the raisins onto conveyors that carry them to bins for transport to the processing plant. In this process, the paper tray is gathered up for disposal or it may in the future be rerolled for reuse the next year.

The effect of cane cutting at harvest on future vine performance is still to be determined. It is receiving attention in California as well as Australia (see p. 639).

The Thompson Seedless berries are too large to dry entirely into raisins on the cut canes without pretreatment (see Sultana production on the vine, p. 638).

FIGURE 161: Machine for catching single berries from the harvester and metering them onto the continuous paper tray which it also lays. (*Courtesy of H. E. Studer*)

FIGURE 162: A continuous paper tray loaded with freshly harvested single berries of Thompson Seedless. (*Courtesy of H. E. Studer*)

Handling Raisins After Drying

Raisins are not offered for consumption as they come from the vineyard or drying yard, but are first stored for some time for curing and are cleaned, stemmed, and sorted. This work is ordinarily done in a packing house. Even so, the success of the packing process and of the whole raisin industry is dependent on the grower's care and skill all along the way from growing the grapes until he delivers the raisins to the packing house. A grower's failure to dry his raisins sufficiently and to store them properly so long as they are in his possession may result in partial or complete loss of the product.

Proper degree of dryness.—Overdrying reduces the weight of dried products to no good purpose, but thorough drying is essential to good keeping quality. According to the best information available on the relation of moisture to keeping quality, raisins should contain from about 13 to not over 15 per cent moisture. If these limits are not exceeded, the fruit should

FIGURE 163: Machine for picking up the finished raisins, conveying them to bins on the back, and gathering the spent tray for disposal. (*Courtesy of H. E. Studer*)

over 15 per cent moisture. If these limits are not exceeded, the fruit should keep well during prolonged storage and necessary moisture can be added during processing at the packing house without risk of spoilage. The relation of moisture content to keeping quality varies with the year and the district. When the sugar content of the fruit is high, deterioration is low; when sugar content is low, spoilage is likely to increase. As a general rule, growers cannot accurately determine the moisture content in their product; they must depend on certain rather crude tests, and skill in these tests is acquired with experience. For example, it should not be possible to squeeze out any sirup from the individual raisins with the fingers. On the other hand, the fruit should not be so dry as to rattle and sound like pebbles when pushed about or shaken on the trays. When a handful is squeezed, the raisins should feel pliable, yet on release they should separate immediately and return to their original shape, not stick together to form a ball.

Curing.—During the first several weeks in the boxes, some moisture is transferred from wet to dry raisins, either by direct contact or by evaporation into the air spaces and absorption therefrom. It is from the latter type of transmission that the curing process gets the more common name of "sweating." Until this equalization of moisture is virtually complete, it is difficult to judge accurately whether moisture content is satisfactory in lots that are near the upper limit of moistness. Sweat boxes, picks, or pallet-size containers are ideal for the curing process.

Storage at the vineyard.—For the safety of the raisins, it is best that they be delivered to a packing house not less than two weeks nor more than a month after they are removed from the trays. Packing houses have better facilities and better provision for supervision and storage than are available in most vineyards. But, whether storage on the farm is short or long, conditions should be the best that can be provided. The storage space should be cool, dry, well lighted, and ventilated. Care should be taken to exclude rodents, poultry, and other animals. Extreme care should be taken to prevent insect infestation, which may ruin the raisins at the vineyard or, later, at the packing house. The building should be thoroughly cleaned before use and, if possible, either washed with a steam hose or fumigated. Farm fumigation is feasible and desirable, but the grower must take proper precautions to prevent injury to workers or farm animals. All fumigants are dangerous; otherwise they would not kill insects. For fumigation to be effective, the building must be made tight by closing all openings and sealing all cracks. Stacks of full boxes can be effectively fumigated in the vineyard. An airtight covering is required for the stacks of picks or sweat boxes. A frame of smooth 1-inch-by-4-inch laths is placed over the stack of boxes and then covered with a gas tight paper, such as sisal kraft, or with 4- or 6-mil black polyethylene. When provided with a sloping top, such a gastight covering will furnish adequate weather protection for some time. Moisture content changes little in this type of storage. Precautions must be taken to prevent the entrance of rodents.

HANDLING RAIN-DAMAGED RAISINS

During the season for raisin drying, difficulty from rain may be expected in some years. In the event of rain, the raisins on wooden trays should be stacked—before the rain starts, if possible—and empty trays should be put over the stacks. The wooden trays should be spread again as soon as possible after the weather clears. The processes of stacking and spreading must be repeated as often as the weather changes. The difficulty of handling raisins on paper trays under these circumstances is obvious, and a heavy rain, even a short one, is likely to cause serious damage, since such trays cannot be stacked. Moving the paper trays to drier soil when possible and stirring the fruit on the trays is very desirable.

When the weather is very rainy and the trays and fruit become thoroughly wet, treatments likely to be of use are (a) dusting or (b) finishing the drying in a dehydrator. Dusting with the newest fungicides on rain-soaked trays of raisins has shown little promise. Sulfuring, as was formerly done, is impossible with paper trays.

There are now in the state many dehydrators, in which part of the raisin crop is normally dried. Dehydration is the ideal way out of the rain difficulty. It should be applied as promptly and fully as possible. For natural raisins, the temperature should not exceed 140° to 160° F. The great difficulty in saving raisins or any drying crop that is caught in rain is the matter of time. The need seemingly always greatly exceeds the capacity of the facilities for doing the drying within the time that makes the difference between loss or saving.

OTHER DRYING METHODS

Though all currants, nearly all Muscats, and most Thompson Seedless grapes in California are dried by the natural method, a small part of the Thompson Seedless crop is dipped and sulfured to produce the so-called golden-bleached and sulfur bleached; the Greek process or the soda-oil-dipped, and soda dip raisins.

Golden-bleached.—In California light-colored (bleached) raisins are produced mostly by the golden-bleach process. They are brilliant lemon yellow to golden yellow, moderately tender, and sometimes a little sticky. To some persons their sulfur dioxide taste is objectionable for eating out of hand; this taste disappears entirely when they are used in baking or otherwise cooked. The sulfur dioxide is necessary during drying and storage to preserve the yellow color.

In international trade the golden-bleached raisins of California compete successfully with the Australian-type sultanas from other regions.

These raisins are produced by first sorting the Thompson Seedless grapes to remove clusters of damaged, immature, or overripe fruit. Next the fruit is dipped two to three seconds in an almost boiling solution of 0.2 to 0.3 per cent sodium hydroxide (caustic soda). Fine checks in the skins after a cold-water rinse indicate the correctness of the dip. While still moist, the grapes are exposed for two to four hours to the fumes of burning sulfur in a sulfur house. The quantity of sulfur used varies from 2 to 4 pounds per ton of grapes—the fruit should acquire a uniform light-yellow color. (If economy permits, the burning of sulfur may be replaced by an appropriate amount of liquid sulfur dioxide.) After sulfuring, the grapes are dehydrated at 140° to 160° F. The finished raisins should be a brilliant lemon yellow to golden yellow. Where dehydrator fuel is reasonable in cost, the golden-bleached raisins can be produced at fairly low cost.

Sulfur bleach.—Sulfur-bleached raisins are first dipped, rinsed, and sulfured in the same manner as golden-bleached raisins and spread on wood trays. The trays are then spread in the sun, turned after three hours to one day (the time will depend on the weather), and stacked after twice that length of time. Sometimes they are exposed to the sun for only three hours and then stacked. The fruit near the ends of the trays should be pushed toward the center to protect it from the sun, which can cause subsequent discoloration. After about ten days, the fruit is turned by placing an empty tray over a full tray and "flipping them over." Several weeks are required for drying. Final curing (moisture equalization) is done in boxes. The finished product should be of a yellowish-white, waxy color. Overexposure to the sun will produce an undesirable pink-brown or amber.

In the *Greek process* Thompson Seedless grapes are immersed in a water solution containing 4.5 per cent potassium carbonate, 0.5 per cent sodium carbonate, and 1 per cent completely emulsified olive oil. Any floating oil is skimmed off. The dip is correct when 75 to 80 per cent of the bloom is removed. Dipping time is about five minutes. The dipped grapes, after draining, are spread on trays and dried in the sun. The trays are turned after two days and stacked after four or five days. Under favorable drying conditions the finished product is light in color, not sticky, and of soft texture. The objection to the Australian and Greek procedures in California is the necessity for favorable drying weather in order to produce a light-colored product. Furthermore, California producers would probably find it costly to produce raisins requiring so much hand labor. In recent years the sulfuring of dipped grapes has been practiced in some Mediterranean countries in order to obtain good color consistently. It thus would seem that the California producers have folowed the expedient course in developing the "golden-bleach" as a light-colored raisin.

Soda-oil-dipped.—Thompson Seedless grapes for the so-called soda-oil-dipped raisins are dipped in a sodium carbonate solution having a thin film of olive oil floating on the surface. The dipped grapes are dried on trays in direct sunlight. The raisins are medium to dark brown in color, fairly tender, and slightly oily, but not sticky.

Soda-oil-dipped raisins are made in two somewhat different ways. In one, the grapes are dipped for thirty seconds to three minutes in a warm (100° F.) solution containing about 30 pounds of cooking soda (sodium bicarbonate) and 1 pound of lye in 100 gallons of water, on which a film of olive oil is floated. About 5 pounds of sodium bicarbonate and 1 quart of olive oil are consumed in dipping 1 ton of grapes. The other method involves a hot sal soda or cooking soda solution (170° F.), with a film of olive oil on the surface. In both cases the dip is correct when 75 per cent of the bloom is removed. The grapes acquire a perceptible film of oil as they leave the dip. After draining, the grapes are dried in the sun. The finished product is usually dark in color and has a slightly oily surface.

Neither the soda dip nor the soda-oil dip is now used in the commercial production of raisins in California. The soda-oil dip was used extensively in the 1920's when raisins were being produced on a broad scale in the Sacramento Valley. Both processes hold some promise should the industry wish to shift away from the natural process to dehydration. The soda-dip followed by dehydration would produce a dark raisin, preserve most of the A and B vitamins, and aid growers in their continuous effort to improve sanitary conditions in raisin production. A shift to dehydration or some process that accelerates drying would increase costs. This, however, would be offset in small part by reducing or eliminating the weather hazard during drying and in the satisfaction of having a cleaner product.

Soda dip.—Thompson Seedless are dipped two to three seconds in a 0.2 to 0.3 per cent sodium hydroxide (caustic soda) solution at 200° to 212° F. Faint checks show in the skins after the grapes are cooled by rinsing in cold water. Some growers prefer the weaker sal soda (sodium carbonate) or the still weaker cooking soda (sodium bicarbonate) solution in order to avoid the danger of overdipping. A very small quantity of olive oil may be added to the dip. When lye (caustic soda) is used and the solution kept at or near the boiling point, immersion for three seconds or less will produce the numerous very small cracks desired. The cracks or checks vary greatly with the maturity and general condition of the fruit. For uniform checking, the grapes must be of uniform maturity, since immature fruit checks much more readily than the fully mature. After being rinsed in fresh water, the grapes are spread on trays and exposed to the sun, turned after three or four days, and stacked in about a week. The finished raisins are somewhat translucent and of a distinct reddish-brown color.

Currants.—Currants (Black Corinth raisins and Zante currants) are dried, without preliminary treatment, in a manner similar to that used for natural sun-dried Thompson Seedless raisins. When the weather is hot, currants are dried on stacked trays without direct exposure to the sun. The raisins are dark and very small, with a tart taste and a characteristically mild flavor. They are highly esteemed for cooking and baking.

On-the-vine-drying.—The clusters of Black Corinth are small which makes hand harvesting expensive. Christensen *et al.* (1970) showed the way to overcome this by drying the fruit on the vines and then harvesting the currants by machines. The on-the-vine drying was initiated by cutting the fruit canes at the base when the fruit was mature and leaving them on the trellis during the drying process. The currants, when dry, were harvested by machine and delivered directly to the packing house.

Unlike the larger berried Thompson Seedless, the small Black Corinth berries dry perfectly on the vine without pretreatment. In fact, vine-dried currants are more attractive than those dried on trays. There is less berry breakage and the bloom is more nearly intact. Fruit on canes cut in mid-August dry in 3½ to 5 weeks. Either one of the several types of mechanical harvesters removes the currants effectively. There was little shatter during drying, and the harvesting loss was negligible. The vines must be cane pruned. To date it is not known what effect harvest-time cane cutting will have on future vine growth and production. In view of the work in Australia, the effect on this early maturing variety should not be too serious.

Muscat.—Natural sun-dried raisins are produced of Muscat of Alexandria grapes, principally in California and the province of Málaga in Spain. The California raisins are called "loose Muscats" if stemmed and not seeded, and "seeded Muscats" if the seeds have been removed. Unstemmed raisins, called "layers" or "clusters," were also formerly produced in California. The raisins from the Spanish province of Málaga are carefully dried on the clusters and packed without stemming and are known in world markets as Malagas. These raisins are very large; grayish black or grayish brown, with the bloom mostly intact; and very meaty, with strong Muscat-raisin flavor and rather tough skins.

Valencias, lexias.—In Spain and Australia large quantities of Muscats are dipped before drying. The Spanish raisins are dried in direct sunlight, but may be covered with muslin sheeting at night or during rain. When dry, they are stemmed and sold as "Valencias." The Australian product is rack-dried in the same way as the sultanas and is called "lexia," a term sometimes also applied to the Valencia raisins of Spain.

Grncarevic and Hawson (1971) compared the raisins of Gordos (Muscat) and Waltham Cross (Dattier) which had been produced with the hot caustic dip, the modified cold dip, and the cold dip. They found no appreciable differences in the raisins of the several treatments. However, the caustic dipped fruit was slightly more subject to attack by vinegar flies and mold in bad drying weather, while the modified and cold dip fruit could be sprayed to provide protection. The latter raisins also handled better during processing and deseeding since their skin was intact. These raisins are normally brown, but they can be darkened by spraying with a one-half strength cold dip solution while the fruit is still on the rack.

Sultanas.—In Australia, South Africa, and other British import countries the name "sultana" is applied to the light-colored, tender raisins made from the variety called Thompson Seedless in California and prepared by various processes other than natural sun-drying. Most commonly, the grapes are dipped into a solution containing potassium carbonate, with an oil emulsion. They may be dried in direct sunlight, as in Turkey, Greece, Iran, and Turkestan, or on covered wire-shelved racks, as in Australia and South Africa. The raisins vary in color from greenish-yellow to medium brown. A uniform yellow or light amber color is preferred; it is obtained most often from whitish-yellow or yellow grapes that are rapidly dried, with no exposure to dew and rain, and are shaded during the latter part of the drying period. In some regions sulfur dioxide treatment of the grapes or raisins is occasionally used to brighten the color. The raisins are tender-skinned; when used by bakers, they will slice along with the loaf instead of hanging onto the slicing knife and being dragged through, as may happen with the tougher-skinned natural Thompson Seedless. They are attractive in light-colored cakes and puddings. The surface is often slightly oily, and the flavor is characteristically nutlike. For eating out of hand, however, many persons consider them less desirable than the natural raisins.

The product from Australia and South Africa is always sold as "sultana." Similar raisins from Greece, Turkey, Iran, and Turkestan are usually referred to in English-speaking countries as sultanas or sutlana-type, but in the regions of production other names are applied. Occasionally, other raisins dried by similar processes are known as sultanas, and the term is also sometimes used loosely to include the light-colored golden-bleached and sulfur-bleached raisins of California.

In the United States the name "Sultana" is applied to a round-berried, nearly seedless grape variety—the Round Kishmish of Asia Minor—and to its natural sun-dried raisins. Although these raisins resemble the natural Thompson Seedless, they are usually considered inferior, being less meaty and more acid, with occasional semihard seeds. They are very different from the light-colored, tender-textured sultana raisins of Australia and South Africa.

Producing Sultana raisins.—Sultana type or light colored raisins have been produced in volume for many years in Turkey, Greece, Australia, Iran and other countries.

In Australia's progressive program of producing Sultanas, the pretreatment consists of an alkaline oil-in-water emulsion as a dip or spray. The emulsion contains 12.5 pound potassium carbonate, one quarter pound caustic potash, and 1.5 pints of dipping oil in 50 gallons of water. The oil must be thoroughly emulsified. The freshly prepared dip has a pH of 11. According to Radler (1964), the dip oil used is a mixture of ethyl oleate, sulphonated base oil, and oleic acid. During use the dip is tested at regular intervals with suitable pH paper and when the value falls below pH 9.5 potassium carbonate, hydroxide and dipping oil should be added in the above proportions to raise it to pH 11 again.

According to Grncarevic and Hawker (1971), the clusters (berries) must be completely wetted, since unwetted berries dry more slowly and show up as darker colored berries in the finished product. The waxy coating itself is not removed and, in fact, the effect of the dip can be reversed by washing with water (rain). Chambers and Possingham (1963) report that the dip causes a physical modification in the structure of the waxy coating to greatly increase the rate of water loss.

In practice a number of baskets of freshly harvested grapes of 23° to 26° Brix are immersed in a tank of the dip emulsion. As much as one half ton of fruit may be dipped at one time. Usually 1 to 3 minutes in the dip is required to thoroughly wet all the berries. After dipping, the grapes are drained and then spread evenly on the drying rack, see fig. 164. The shelves of the drying rack are spaced about 12 inches with a roof on top. Spraying the grapes on the drying rack with half-strength dip solution after 4 days hastens drying. A follow-up spray of half-strength dip emulsion is also done in unfavorable weather.

Studies by Grncarevic (1967–1969) have shown that the freshly harvested grapes may be spread directly on the drying racks and then sprayed with the full strength dip emulsion. Another spray at one-half to two-thirds strength is applied four days later. The finished product of rack spraying compares favorably with that which was dipped. When clean fruit is placed on the rack and rack-sprayed, the finished raisins are markedly free of grit and contamination. The rack spraying must be thorough or there will be variations in color of the raisins. This procedure is rapidly being adopted in Australia. In case of rain or foul weather the rack-sprayed fruit must also be resprayed.

The raisins are ready to be removed from the rack when the moisture content approaches 18 per cent. A shaker drops them onto a tarpaulin at the bottom of the rack. The raisins are then spread on plastic or sisalcraft sheets on the ground for finishing. In favorable weather the raisins will dry to about 13 per cent moisture in 1 to 3 days and take on the desirable

FIGURE 164: A wire rack used for the drying of Sultana Raisins in Australia. (*Amer. J. Enol. Vitic.*, 21:19–25, 1970)

light amber color. This may also be accomplished by applying heat to the raisins in an enclosed rack or in some other chamber. If the raisins are very green in color, they are sprayed with water at mid-day, when they are hot, and covered for several hours. They are then uncovered, spread out and raked from time to time to obtain a uniform color.

On-the-vine-drying of Sultanas.—May and Kerridge (1967) cut the canes bearing the fruiting shoots of Sutlana vines near their base when the fruit was mature. Subsequently, the fruit was sprayed with the standard dip emulsion. After about 4 weeks, the fruit had dried to near 15 per cent moisture content and was ready for harvesting as raisins. This was done by hand in the experiments, but it could be done by either vibratory type of mechanical harvester. Although there was some rain and a strong wind during the drying period on the vine, there was no loss of fruit. The quality of the Sultanas produced was equal to rack-dried raisins and free of grit and contamination. Handling costs were reduced.

The use of the oil emulsion spray is esesntial to this technique of on-the-vine drying. Without the spray, fruit on cut canes will seldom dry below 30 per cent moisture. Also, uniformity of the application of the spray mix is essential to obtain an evenly colored product. The research of May and Scholefield (1969–71) indicates that the first spraying can be delayed until leaves on the cut canes are wilted. This will improve coverage of the berries; a second spraying about four days later will allow the mix to penetrate more completely into the centers of the partially dried clusters.

Long-term results obtained by May and Scholefield (1972) indicate that cane cutting (harvest-pruning) will not lead to increasingly severe reduction in productivity, but that losses of up to 15 per cent could possibly occur. They suggest a wider trellis to reduce leaf damage by the spray or possibly the use of biennial cane cutting in different vineyards. In California the injurious effect may be less since no spray is involved. Delaying the cane cutting will preserve the entire leaf surface longer, and the advancing maturity should produce raisins of higher quality (see p. 646).

Natural Sultanas.—According to Grncarevic and Lewis (1969–71), there is an increasing demand for natural sun dried raisins in Australia. The most successful procedure for producing "naturals" there has been to dry the grape on trays on the ground under a clear plastic cover which protects them from occasional rains. The product is of a uniform bluish-purple color with the bloom intact.

Factors of Quality in Raisins

Any condition that affects food value or attractiveness is a factor of quality. Such conditions are the varietal flavor and the seediness or seedlessness of raisins are determined by the grape variety used. Certain color, flavor, and texture differences results from the method of drying. These factors of quality and their relation to raisin types were briefly discussed in the preceding section. Within any given type, additional factors of quality are recognized. The most important of these are (*a*) size of the raisin berries; (*b*) hue, uniformity, and brilliance of the color; (*c*) condition of the berry surfaces; (*d*) texture of the skin and pulp; (*e*) moisture content; (*f*) chemical composition; (*g*) presence of decay (rot), mold and yeast, of foreign matter; and (*h*) insect infestation, or contamination by insect remains and excreta. These factors of quality may be influenced by the maturity and the physical condition of the fresh fruit, the weather during drying, the care and skill used in harvesting, the predrying treatment (if any) and drying, the sanitation practices used in handling and caring for the fruit and equipment, and storage conditions.

Size of berry.—The size of the raisin is determined by the size of the grape berry from which it is made and by maturity of the grapes. Grape berry size, within the same variety, differs between districts (probably owing to natural conditons of climate and soils) and between vineyards in the districts (usually owing to cultural practices). Crop per vine is by far the more important factor in determining berry size.

At least a minimum crop is, of course, an economic necessity, since enough grapes must be produced, whatever their size, to show a profit. Above this minimum, increasing the berry size by restricting the crop may add to both quality and financial return. The effect of crop on the weight of berries of Thompson Seedless is illustrated by the following comparisons between vineyards in certain locations in California:

Location	Crop, tons	Berry weight grams
Davis, Yolo County	6.1	2.7
	9.3	1.8
Stanislaus County	8.1	3.2
	12.5	2.4
Fresno County	7.5	3.1
	12.5	2.6

Very heavy crops markedly lower quality by decreasing the weight (size) of berries, their attractiveness, and the degree Brix.

Degree Brix at harvest, through its effect on the drying ratio, also affects the size of the raisin berry. Grapes of high degrees Brix at harvest contain correspondingly more solids in relation to water and shrink less in drying (see table 35).

Color.—Uniformity and brilliance of color seem to be almost as important as shade or hue. Off-colored berries are always objectionable. Raisin color is uniform when maturity of the grapes and processes of pretreatment are uniform and when the fruit is properly dried under favorable conditions.

With the natural sun-drying method, uniform color within a lot is easily obtained. For the best color, only mature and sound fruit should be used. Brilliant color is obtained by preserving the natural bloom on the grapes through careful harvesting and placing on the trays and by protecting the raisins from rain during drying. Raisins are nearly always dull and unattractive if the bloom has been removed by excessive or careless handling of the grapes or if they have been wet by rain while drying.

For uniform color in golden-bleached raisins, the fruit must not be only mature, but also approximately uniform in color. Green-colored fruit produces greenish-yellow raisins, whereas the more desirable golden yellow is obtained from yellow or cream-colored fruit. The grape clusters should be color-sorted by hand before or after dipping. This procedure, which is neither costly nor laborious, should be adopted by all producers of such raisins. Practically all dipping installations are provided with a shaker that is placed just ahead of the dipping vat and is used to remove sand, leaves, loose berries, and rubbish. One sorter standing beside the shaker, or beside the conveyer belt leading to the shaker, can remove clusters that are green, sunburned, bird-pecked, rotten, overripe, or otherwise undesirable. The off-grape fruit can be dried to produce low-grade raisins or be sent to wineries for use as distilling material. Other factors contributing to brilliancy and uniformity of color are: (*a*) proper dipping to cause many small cracks and but few large ones in the skin; (*b*) rinsing to cool the fruit rapidly and remove the slightly alkaline residue of the dipping solution; (*c*) adequate sulfuring to bleach the grapes and to check enzyme activity (Hussein *et al.*, 1942); and (*d*) adequate drying (to 15 percent moisture) at moderate temperature (between 140° and 165° F.) and low humidity (Nichols and Christie, 1930).

The Australian-type Sultana raisins, processed by dripping in a solution of potassium carbonate containing emulsified oil, are frequently subject to defects in uniformity and brilliance. At best, their natural color is a somewhat dull yellow or light amber—not unattractive, but not the striking, brilliant yellow of the golden-bleached product. Sorting the fresh fruit according to maturity and color, preferably done by the picker, is essential. According to Bottrill and Hawker (1970), green-colored grapes produce raisins of an undesirable greenish yellow or greenish brown, requiring bleaching by exposure to sunlight and/or heat when nearly dry. Dark-colored or partially raisined berries remain dark. Immature fruit requires a lower concentration of potassium carbonate in the dipping solution than does full mature fruit; otherwise it suffers carbonate burn and becomes dark brown around the pedicel. Broken and bruised berries are also burned by the dip and on drying will turn to a dark brown. The best color is obtained from yellow or cream-colored grapes, mature but not overripe, free of dark-colored or partially dried or broken berries, and dipped and dried during clear, hot weather without being even slightly wetted by dews or rains. If rain falls during the drying period, the raisins must be covered; otherwise they may become dark brown or nearly black.

Condition of berry surfaces.—It is always desirable that raisins be clean and dry. Products of natural sun-drying offer few difficulties in these respects unless they have been wet by rain or unless many of the fresh berries are broken or mashed. Even unbroken berries become wet with the juice of the broken or mashed ones and may become sticky. Dust and sand collecting on the sticky surfaces may be so tightly cemented to the skin or so deeply imbedded in the pulp of the broken berries that thorough cleaning is difficult.

Stickiness in golden-bleached and sulfur-bleached raisins results from overdipping the fruit or from rough handling in filling the drying trays. Overdipping causes large cracks in the skins, through which the juice will exude. Severe overdipping may even cause some of the berries to peel, in which case the dried raisins will be very sticky, liable to cake in storage, difficult to handle, and objectionable to the consumer. A sulfur-bleached product dried in the open may, if sticky, collect dust and sand that may be difficult to remove. Since golden-bleached raisins are rapidly dried in a dust-free dehydrator, there is no explanation except carelessness when raisins of this type are dirty.

Excessive oiliness may cause Australian-type sultana or other oil-dipped raisins to collect dust and sand. The dirt is removed from them more easily than from sticky raisins, although special washing is required. The oil may sometimes become rancid, imparting a disagreeable odor and flavor.

"Sugaring" refers to crystallization of fruit sugars on the surface and in the pulp of the raisins. It occurs most often in raisins of high moisture content, particularly if they are stored under conditions of high humidity. Australian-type sultana raisins and sulfur-bleached raisins seem to be more liable to this defect than natural or golden-bleached; none can be entirely free of it.

Texture of skin and pulp.—Good raisins should always be plump, pliable, and meaty. They can be produced only from mature fruit. Raisins from immature fruit are deeply wrinkled, likely to be hard, and often tough. A good index to the texture is the weight-per-unit-volume measurement, devised by Chase and Church (1927) and still used in a modified form by one large firm to grade grower's lots upon delivery. Its usefulness is largely limited to natural sun-dried Thompson Seedless.

Tenderness of skin, a desirable characteristic in raisins for cooking or baking, is largely a function of the grape variety and the drying method. Muscat of Alexandria has a somewhat tough skin, Thompson Seedless is medium in this respect, and Black Corinth is rather tender; Australian-type sultana raisins are the tenderest. Golden-bleached, sulfur-bleached, and soda-dipped Thompson Seedless and soda-dipped Muscats (Valencias and lexias) are moderately tender. The conditions under which the grapes are grown also influence tenderness or toughness, but only slightly.

Moisture content.—As delivered to the stemming and cleaning plant, most raisins contain 10 to 15 per cent moisture. If cleaning with water, they necessarily will absorb some of it. If the total moisture rises to more than 18 per cent, the raisins may deteriorate in storage. Slightly overdried raisins may be reconditioned and brought to the desired moisture content without injury. Badly overdried raisins—of 5 per cent moisture or less—may have a caramelized or scorched taste that cannot be removed. It is to the grower's advantage to deliver raisins at the highest permissible moisture content, but it is much safer to dry them to 15 per cent moisture or slightly less. The figures reported in this chapter for various constituents of raisins are on the basis of 15 per cent moisture.

Chemical composition.—The food value of raisins lies chiefly in their sugars, fruit acids, and mineral salts (see table 35 below). In Thompson Seedless raisins the sugar content varies within rather narrow limits, depending on grape maturity and the drying method. The total acid content varies within rather wide limits and inversely with the maturity of the grapes. Some mineral salts vary slightly with grape maturity, whereas other salts remain fairly constant. Except for some deficiency in vitamin content, raisins are nearly equivalent to fresh grapes in food value. The caloric value of Thompson Seedless raisins is 268 per 100 grams (Sherman, 1952).

Presence of decay, mold, and yeast, or foreign matter. Rain during drying and the use of rotten or moldly grapes are mainly responsible for decay and mold. Very slow drying owing to unfavorable weather sometimes allows yeasts to grow in raisins, particularly in the pulp of cracked berries. The yeast growth may not be serious if it affects only a small percentage of the berries and those only around the pedicel. If, on the contrary, many of the raisins have one fourth or more of their surface affected with yeast, mold, or decay, the lot may no longer salable as raisins. The grower can hold these defects to the minimum by discarding clusters that are seriously affected with cluster rot, discolored or cracked by mildew, or damaged by birds, or by trimming off the bad parts, by preventing crushing during harvest, and by protecting the grapes from rain during drying. A grower who puts defective grapes on the trays is more often than not inviting trouble. Because rain falls so seldom in California during the drying period, most growers are not prepared to cope with it. As a result, the crop is damaged in years when appreciable rain does fall.

Over 90 per cent of the California raisin crop is dried on paper trays between the rows of vines. Inevitably, some dust and sand will accumulate. If the berries are not mashed or broken, the particles of dust and sand adhering loosely to the surfaces can be mostly removed by passing the raisins over a shaker screen (Mrak and Long, 1941) when they are boxed for storing. Nearly all the remaining dirt is removed in stemming and cleaning. When the raisins are sticky, or if they have been wet by rain, some types of dust may be cemented to the skin, making cleaning more difficult. For a method of determination of grit and contamination see p. 653.

Insect infestation.—Sanitary measures, including a thorough cleanup of all materials that might furnish food or breeding places, will aid in the control of insects. Every effort must be made to prevent infestation or to eliminate the insects at the egg or early larval stages by fumigation. Killing large larvae or adults means leaving in the raisins the remains of insects bodies and pellets of excreta, a serious defect that will be detected by a competent inspector.

The Influence of Grape Maturity on the Yield and Composition of Raisins

The main constituents of ripening grapes are water and sugar. As maturity advances, the sugar increases and the water decreases. During drying, raisins lose most of the water and retain nearly all the sugar. Obviously, therefore, the greater the percentage of sugar (soluble solids) of the harvested grapes, the greater will be the yield of raisins and the higher their quality.

Although this relationship has been observed for centuries, its magnitude, particularly with regard to its effect on quality, did not receive the attention it deserved until Jacob's (1942, 1944) monumental studies showing the relation of grape maturity to the drying ratio, sugar content, acid content, size of raisin, and especially the quality of raisins. Using grapes in the range of maturity from 17° to 29° Brix and using the methods of drying discussed above (p. 624 to 635), he amassed a most basic lot of data. The two methods most extensively used in California—"natural sun-drying" and "golden bleached"—showed the greater differences in the various constituents of the raisins; hence, the figures obtained with them are shown in table 33. The data obtained with other methods of drying are intermediate to these. The averages given in column 1 include the results of all methods used. All lots of fresh fruit that tested between 17.5° and 18.4° Brix are averaged together and presented as a group. The same is true of lots testing between 18.5° and 19.4°, between 19.5° and 20.4°, and so on. This average degree Brix was taken as the index of maturity.

Drying ratio.—The data in column 2 of table 35 indicate that the more favorable drying ratios are obtained with the golden bleach, but the differences are not statistically significant. All the methods using dehydration produced more favorable drying ratios than did those with sun-drying or rack drying; natural sun-drying was the least favorable.

The increase in yield of raisins per ton of grapes for each 1° Brix was 23 pounds for the natural sun-drying and 24 pounds for the golden bleached method.

With Muscat of Alexandria, as with Thompson Seedless, an advance in grape maturity produced an increase in the yield of raisins, but not so nearly in proportion to the Brix degree of the grapes.

Sugar.—The sugar content of Thompson Seedless raisins increases slightly with advancing maturity of the grapes up to 23° Brix; thereafter there is no appreciable change. These trends are best illustrated in column 3 of table 33, which gives the averages of sun-drying and golden bleach methods of drying. Grapes averaging 17.8° Brix dried to raisins averaging 66.6 and 69.3 per cent sugar; 23.1° Brix, 69.4 and 71.1 per cent sugar; still riper grapes, 69.3 and 71.8 per cent sugar, respectively. The small differences above 23° Brix are not significant.

Raisins

TABLE 35

THE INFLUENCE OF GRAPE MATURITY ON THE DRYING RATIO, SUGAR
CONTENT, ACID CONTENT AND WEIGHT OF RAISIN BERRIES [a]

1	2		3		4		5
	Drying ratio [b]		Sugar content		Acid content		Weight
Average grape maturity	Natural sun-dried	Golden bleached	Natural sun-dried	Golden bleached	Natural sun-dried	Golden bleached	per 100 berries
° brix			per cent	per cent	per cent	per cent	grams
17.8	4.85	4.82	66.6	69.3	3.09	3.97	26.1
19.6	4.51	4.30	68.3	71.4	2.53	3.11	31.4
21.0	4.26	4.02	68.9	70.4	2.38	2.71	35.6
22.0	3.97	3.80	69.0	70.9	2.10	2.58	38.2
23.1	3.82	3.63	69.4	71.1	1.88	2.41	39.7
24.2	3.63	3.44	69.3	72.0	1.79	2.08	39.0
24.7	3.50	3.39	70.0	71.9	—	—	42.9
26.9	3.26	3.10	69.3	71.8	1.57	1.80	47.2

SOURCE OF DATA: Jacob (1942, 1944); Miller (1963); Kasimatis and Lynn (1967).

[a] All results are calculated on the basis of 15 per cent moisture in the raisins.

[b] Drying ratio = Weight of fresh grape divided by weight of raisins produce at 15 per cent moisture.

The highest sugar content is that of the golden-bleached raisins; the lowest (about 2.0 per cent lower), that of the natural sun-dried. The raisins of the other methods of drying, not listed, had intermediate sugar contents; no differences may be assumed to exist among them. The higher sugar content of the hot-dipped and dehydrated raisins over undipped and sun-dried is owing to a more rapid death of the tissues, which shortened the period of active respiration. The tissues of hot-dipped grapes are killed within a few minutes or, at most, a few hours, and become rapidly discolored unless treated with sulfur dioxide. Undipped grapes and those treated with the Austrialian cold dip retain living tissue for several days before being placed on the trays or racks. As long as living tissue is present, energy-producing materials, such as sugars and certain acids, are used up in respiration and other life processes. Undipped dehydrated raisins should have the same sugar content as the soda-dipped dehydrated lots. The temperature of the dehydrator—140° to 160° F.—rapidly killed all grape tissues; hence, no appreciable respiration or other changes occur.

The sugar content of Muscat of Alexandria raisins averages, roughly, 4 per cent lower than that of Thompson Seedless. The general trend of the sugar content of the raisins in relation to grape maturity is essentially the same as the two varieties; it increases slowly with advancing maturity up to 23° Brix. Beyond that, it does not increase appreciably. As with Thompson

Seedless, Muscat of Alexandria raisins of soda-dipped dehydrated and soda-dipped sun-dried lots have a higher sugar content than those prepared by natural sun-drying.

Acid.—The data in column 4 of table 35 show the decrease in acid content of Thompson Seedless raisins as grape mautrity advances. The decrease is rapid with the greenest fruit, slows up in the middle part of the ripening range, and nearly ceases as the fruit becomes very ripe. The acid content of the grapes shows a similar trend, but with small differences from one stage of maturity to another.

In the early part of the ripening range, the acid content of the raisins is about equal to or slightly less than the product of the acid content of the grapes multiplied by the drying ratio for the particular maturity group. Some acid is lost during drying in the least-mature fruit. Since the loss seems to be greatest in natural sun-dried lots and least in dehydrated lots, it can be assumed that some acid, especially malic, was oxidized during the first days of exposure to the sun (Bobadillo and Navarro, 1949). At the middle of the ripening range the acid content of the raisins is about the same as the assumed acid content of the grapes multiplied by the corresponding drying ratio; but above the middle range of maturity it is greater. The acid content of Muscat of Alexandria raisins shows a similar trend.

Sulfured raisins are clearly higher in acid content than are other comparable lots. This is accounted for by the combined sulfur dioxide.

Weight of raisin berry.—The weight of individual raisins is determined by the fresh berries and the drying ratio. In column 5 of table 35 all drying methods are averaged together, and the results are expressed as the weight of 100 raisin berries. As the data clearly show, raisin weight increases as the grapes mature. The increase is rapid in the early part of the ripening period, but continus slowly until the grapes begin to shrivel.

Large size (weight) is always desirable in dessert raisins. For cooking and baking, size is less important than color and texture. Bakers prefer small sizes. In retail trade, however, the large Muscat raisins usually command a higher price than the small ones.

RELATION OF GRAPE MATURITY TO RAISIN QUALITY

In view of the very definite relation of grape maturity to the factors shown in table 35, Jacob (1944) deemed it desirable to evaluate the relation of grape maturity to raisin quality. For this purpose he submitted representative samples of natural sun-dried raisins to a judging committee representing six large commercial packers of raisins who were familiar with the concept of quality in raisins. The degree Brix of the grapes and the quality score of the raisins is shown at the left to table 36.

The figures of table 36 very definitely show the relation of grape maturity

TABLE 36

RELATION OF GRAPE MATURITY TO THE QUALITY SCORE OF
NATURAL SUN-DRIED THOMPSON SEEDLESS RAISINS

Grapes from Davis and Marysville		*Grapes from Fresno and Madera counties*	
Average degree brix	*Quality score*	*Average degree brix*	*U.S. grade*
17.4	46	16	50
21.6	52	17	61
23.3	66	18	70
25.1	71	19	77
26.8	88	20	83
28.2	96	21	87
		22	90

SOURCE OF DATA AT LEFT: Jacob (1944); Miller (1963, 1964).
SOURCE OF DATA AT RIGHT: Kasimatis and Lynn (1967).

to raisin quality. It would appear that the subjective scoring of the raisins at the left was more severe than the objective grading at the right. Nevertheless, the increase in score or grade parallels the increase in maturity of the grapes.

As convincing as Jacob's data was, it had relatively little influence on production practices or on those working in industry. It was reasoned, though falsely, that since his work was done with grapes grown at Davis and near Marysville it would not apply to raisin production in the mid-San Joaquin Valley. Baranek *et al.* (1970) carried out a similar study in Fresno and Madera Counties. The figures on the relation of grape maturity to raisin grade shown at the right of table 36, by Kasimatis and Lynn (1967), were obtained in that study. Miller (1963) shows a straight line correlation between degree Brix and drying ratio of grapes of that study, which parallels similar readings taken from Jacob's work. His graph showing the relation of grape maturity to weight of raisin berry also parallels that based on Jacob's figures. While Baranek *et al.* (1970) do not include data which make possible a direct comparison with Jacob's, their results show a very high degree of correlation (0.868) between grape maturity and U. S. raisin grades as determined by the airstream sorter. The sorter was adjusted to separate the raisins into lots comparable to U.S. grades.

These studies have proved beyond a doubt that well matured Thompson Seedless grapes have the potential for producing raisins of high quality wherever grown. Similarly, poorly matured grapes regardless of cause—overcropping, inadequate pest control, poor cultural practices, or place of growth—will only produce raisins of poor quality.

OTHER CONSTITUENTS OF RAISINS

Water-insoluble solids.—Jacob (1944) regarded as water-insoluble solids of raisins all the substances that failed to dissolve after six hours' leaching with warm water. In Thompson Seedless most of the insoluble material consisted of fiber from the skins and pulp; in Muscat of Alexandria about half of it consisted of seeds. In Thompson Seedless the insoluble solids in the raisins decreased with advancing maturity of the grapes. The actual percentages of insoluble material ranged from 7.97 per cent in the natural sun-dried raisins made from grapes averaging 17.8° Brix downward to 4.86 per cent in those made from grapes of 29.7° Brix. Golden-bleached raisins made from grapes of the same degrees Brix had respective insoluble solids of 6.6 and 4.4 per cent.

The percentage of water-insoluble materials in Muscat of Alexandria raisins is, roughly, double that in comparable lots of Thompson Seedless: 11.7 per cent in dehydrated raisins made of grapes of 17.1° Brix and 9.9 per cent in raisins made of grapes of 25.1° Brix. The insoluble-solids content fluctuates more in Muscat than in Thompson Seedless raisins. This is owing mainly to variability in the number and size of seeds.

Mineral constituents.—Jacob (1944) provided substantial data for four of the principal minerals in raisins. Lesser amounts of data are available in source books for these and other minerals. Recent work by M. W. Miller (unpublished data, Department of Food Technology, University of California, Davis) has supplied additional information. Table 37 shows the content of the important minerals found in Thompson Seedless and Muscat raisins.

Jacob found that the levels of potassium, calcium, and magnesium remained fairly constant in Thompson Seedless raisins during the entire range of maturity, from 17.8 to 29.7 degrees Balling. The phosphorus level decreased slightly. This would mean that the increase in potassium, calcium, and magnesium paralleled the increase in sugar during ripening, and that the increase in phosphorus was slightly slower.

The figures for iron in table 37 are in keeping with the normal amounts found in grapes grown on soils of varying iron content when allowance is made for the concentration that occurs during drying (see table 5).

In addition to the above constituents and vitamins that follow, raisins contain approximately 77 per cent total carbohydrates, 2.5 per cent proteins, 0.5 per cent fat, 0.97 per cent crude fiber, and 2.0 per cent ash (M. W. Miller, unpublished data).

Vitamins.—Natural sun-dried raisins contain no Vitamin A. Dehydrated grapes and golden-bleached raisins retain this factor in full (Morgan *et al.* 1935). Vitamin C is largely lost in all the current processes of raisin production (Morgan 1935).

TABLE 37
Mineral Content of Raisins
(In grams per 100 grams)

Raisins and minerals	Range, grams per 100 grams	Sources of data
Thompson Seedless:		
Potassium	0.708–0.95	1, 2, 3, 4
Calcium	0.05–0.078	1, 2, 4, 5
Magnesium	0.02–0.041	1, 2, 3, 4
Phosphorus	0.094–0.129	1, 2, 4, 5
Iron	0.0015–0.0033	1, 3, 4, 5
Sodium	0.013–0.087	1, 3, 4
Copper	0.00022	1
Zinc	0.00023	1
Muscat of Alexandria:		
Potassium	0.67–0.777	
Calcium	0.065–0.075	2
Magnesium	0.019–0.031	
Phosphorus	0.083–0.099	

sources of data: 1, Miller (Unpublished data, Dept. of Food Technology, University of California, Davis); 2, Jacob (1944); 3, McCance and Widdowson (1946); 4, Sherman (1952); 5, United States Department of Agriculture (1950).

The amounts of the B-complex vitamins found in natural sun-dried and golden-bleached Thompson Seedless raisins are shown in table 38.

The figures of table 38 indicate that the losses of pyridoxine, nicotinic acid, riboflavin, and, possibly, pantothenic acid are greater in sun drying than in golden bleaching. The greatest loss is in riboflavin. The golden-bleached raisins retained 90 per cent or more of the pyridoxine and nicotinic acid of fresh grapes, but less than 60 per cent of the riboflavin.

There is no significant difference in the biotin level of the raisins processed by the two methods. Some 60 per cent of the biotin of the fresh grapes is present in the raisins.

The greatest difference in the two methods of processing is shown in the loss of thiamine in the golden-bleached raisins. Morgan and Hall (1953) report that golden bleached have only 10 per cent of the amount in natural raisins. This is to be expected because of the sulfuring.

Folic acid in raisins made by natural sun-drying is one third that in fresh grapes; in raisins made by the golden-bleach process it is one half.

According to Morgan (1935), raisins should not be sulfured, but should be lye-dipped and dehydrated to preserve their good content of vitamins A and B, and should not be counted on for vitamin C.

TABLE 38

B-COMPLEX VITAMIN CONTENT OF THOMPSON SEEDLESS RAISINS

Drying method and vitamins	Micrograms per 100 grams	Sources of data
Natural sun-drying:		
Thiamine	100–120	1, 2
Riboflavin	25–30	1, 2
Nicotinic acid	620	1, 2
Pantothenic acid	55–60	1, 2
Pyridoxine	230–240	1, 2
Biotin	4.5–4.48	1, 2
Folic acid	10	3
Golden bleach:		
Thiamine	10	
Riboflavin	70	
Nicotinic acid	940	
Pantothenic acid	140	2
Pyridoxine	370	
Biotin	4.13	
Folic acid	20	

SOURCES OF DATA: 1, Miller (Unpublished data, Dept. of Food Technology, University of California, Davis); 2, Morgan and Hall (1953); 3, Morgan, Brinner, and Hall (1954).

Work on the phlobatannin (vitamin P) fraction of natural sun-dried Thompson Seedless raisins (United States Department of Agriculture, 1953) has shown that these physiologically active compounds in fresh grapes are partly preserved during drying.

WHEN TO HARVEST

Tables 35 and 36 show the high positive correlation between the maturity of the grapes and the composition and quality of raisins. In the Thompson Seedless, the drying ratio (or yield) is a straight-line function of the degree Brix of the grapes. The yield is directly proportional to the degree Brix; each advance of 1° in maturity increases raisin yield per ton of fresh grapes —about 22 pounds for natural sun-dried raisins and 24 pounds for golden-bleached raisins.

A yield of 8 tons of Thompson Seedless grapes per acre at 18° Brix will, when properly dried, produce 433 pounds of raisins for each ton, whereas a ton at 22° Brix will produce 524 pounds of raisins; 91 pounds more per ton, or 728 pounds per acre. At $300 per ton this would amount to $109.20 per acre. In view of this benefit, it should be perfectly clear that grapes for raisins should not be harvested until they are fully mature. Not only is there an increase in yield, but the quality of the raisins—the meatiness and plumpness—is markedly improved.

Certain aspects of climate have a direct bearing on vine functioning in the production and drying of raisins. Those typical of California are shown in table 39. The blooming dates, taken from phenological records, closely fit the date when the normal mean daily temperature reaches 68° F., or about May 19 at Fresno. The ripening dates for Thompson Seedless for raisins should be about 2,500 degree-days after full bloom. With this summation of heat, the fruit of vines carrying a normal crop will be 22° to 23° Brix. The fruit of overloaded vines will require additional degree-days of heat, according to the extent of the over-crop.

The first rain likely to damage raisins is interpreted as the first one after September 1 that drops 0.1 inch or more of water. Rains in August, or light showers of short duration preceded and followed by clear weather, are not likely to do any damage.

In a period of fifty-eight years (1913 to 1971), no damaging rain occurred in the San Joaquin Valley south of Merced before September 17. The area of the valley northward of Merced, however, had rains in fourteen of these years by October 1 and in twenty-two of the years by October 10. At Modesto and Davis the earliest damaging rain fell on September 3. In this more northerly area, conditions for sun-drying become less favorable rather rapidly after the middle of September.

The mean temperature averages about 10° F. lower in October than in September, and the relative humidity is 8 per cent higher. Both temperature and humidity materially affect the drying rate. Thompson Seedless

TABLE 39

CLIMATIC CONDITIONS RELATIVE TO RAISIN DRYING IN THE
CENTRAL SAN JOAQUIN VALLEY, FRESNO, CALIFORNIA
(averages for 58 years—1913 to 1971)

	Normal rainfall	Relative humidity (4 PM)	Mean temperature
August	.01	21%	80° F.
September	.15	26%	74° F.
October	.54	34%	64° F.

Rain sufficient to damage drying raisins (0.1 inch or more)

Years of rain by September 20	7
Years of rain by October 1	10
Years of rain by October 10	21

SOURCE OF DATA: California Section, Climatological Data, U.S. Weather Bureau.

with medium-sized berries will dry to *natural* raisins in about twelve days at 80° F. (daily mean temperature), twenty days at 70° F., and forty days at 60° F.; and small berries will dry more quickly than large ones. The precise effect of humidity changes on the rate of drying has not been determined.

The rate of drying is largely governed by physical factors. Very important among these is the surface area of the berries. The Muscat of Alexander grapes used in Jacob's investigations of 1942 and 1944 were almost exactly three times as large as the Thompson Seedless. The surface area of the berries was of a ratio of 18.3 to 12.7. The dehydrator took sixty hours to dry the undipped Muscats and forty-one hours to dry the Thompson Seedless—almost exactly an inverse ratio to the respective surface areas. Table 40 gives the time required to sun-dry (without dipping) and to dehydrate (after dipping) the common varieties of raisin grapes. Since the data in the table are assembled from three different sets of experiments, minor irregularities may be present.

Martin and Scott (1957) report that of the total loss, under favorable conditions for drying 95 per cent is water, 2 per cent carbon dioxide, and 3 per cent unaccounted for. The rate of loss decreases markedly during the latter stages of drying.

The proper time to pick raisin grapes represents a compromise between two considerations: (a) larger yields and better quality from well-matured fruit, and (b) more favorable drying weather early in the season. In the middle part of the San Joaquin Valley drying weather may be expected to be excellent until about September 20. As the season advances the days become shorter, the temperature lower, and damaging rains more likely. On the basis of data of tables 33, 34, and 37 the following general rules may be formulated:

TABLE 40

DRYING TIMES OF THREE RAISIN GRAPE VARIETIES

	Method of drying	
Variety	*Natural sun-drying*	*Dehydration after dipping*
	days	hours
Black Corinth	10	—
Thompson Seedless	21	18 hours (at 145°–150° F.)
Muscat of Alexandria	30	33 hours (at 145°–150° F.)

SOURCE OF DATA: Unpublished data, Department of Viticulture and Enology, University of California, Davis.

1. Grapes of less than 20° Brix should not be dried for raisins except as a salvage operation to avoid loss.
2. Harvesting should start when the grapes reach 22° or 23° Brix or September 1, whichever comes first. If the grapes have not reached that degree Brix by September 1, it is an indication that the vines are carrying an overcrop and measures should be taken to correct the condition in future years.
3. Thompson Seedless grapes for the golden-bleach process should be allowed to approach 24° Brix or a uniform yellow color, since weather is only a minor factor in dehydrator operation.

RAISIN SORTER AND GRITOMETER

Air-stream sorting.—Many types of sorters for raisins have been proposed and tested. The purpose has been to obtain an effective and purely objective method for grading raisins. The latest type developed, by Fischer *et al.* (1961), consists of a controlled vertical air-stream into which the sample of raisins is fed at a slow, constant rate by an enclosed belt. As they drop off the feeder belt, individual raisins are caught in the air stream, and, under controlled conditions, low-quality raisins are carried upward and into a collecting container. At the same time, high-quality raisin berries descend in the air stream and are deposited in a collecting container at the base (fig. 165).

Separation is based on weight in relation to the surface of the individual raisin berries, indicating quality much as does the weight-per-unit-volume test. The separation is equal to that made by trained and experienced technicians and is free of the personal element. There are interfering factors, such as air flow, air temperature, and the moisture content of the raisins, but these have been accounted for in controls or in correction tables. The raisins of mature grapes will grade high in quality, whereas those made of immature grapes will suffer a high "blowout" because of the lack of weight in relation to surface (see table 36).

Gritometer.—Hawker and Grncarevic (1970) developed a simple and rapid device for determining the grit (sand) on raisins. Natural as well as dipped raisins sometimes collect sand or grit which imparts a "gritty taste" to the product. The threshold at which grit was detected by the taster lies between 20 and 30 milligrams per 100 grams raisins.

To separate the grit for measurement, a given quantity (200 grams) of raisins is soaked in hot water containing a detergent. The sample is then washed through a series of sieves, and grit and organic matter of more than 0.005 mm size is collected on the lower (finest mesh) sieve. The material collected on the fine sieve is then transferred to a funnel containing

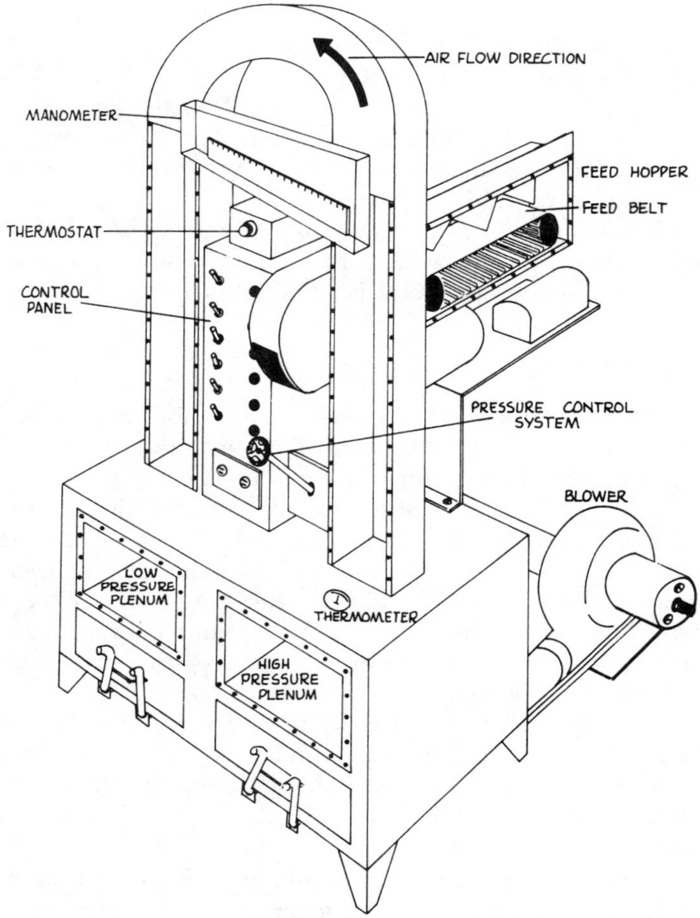

FIGURE 165: Airstream raisin sorter. The raisin sample is slowly fed into the vertical updraft airstream. Lightweight, poorly developed raisins are carried up and over with the airstream and are collected in the drawer in the low-pressure plenum. Meaty, well developed, good-quality raisins descend through the airstream into the high pressure plenum sample drawer. The rate of air flow is adjustable. (*From Baranek et al., Amer. J. Enol. and Vitic. 21:19–25, 1970*)

a saturated solution of potassium carbonate. The organic matter floats while the grit is collected in a 2 mm tube which is calibrated for weight of grit. Hence, the height of grit in the tube indicated the amount of grit in the sample of raisins.

BIBLIOGRAPHY

Anon. 1968. United States standards for grade of processed raisins. U.S.D.A. Consumer and Mktg. Serv., Washington, D.C., Fifth issue.

Baranek, P., M. W. Miller, A. N. Kasimatis, and C. D. Lynn. 1970. Influence of soluble solids in Thompson Seedless grapes on airstream grading for raisin quality. Jour. Amer. Soc. Enol. Vitic., 21:19–25.

Bobadillo, G. F. de, and E. Navarro. 1949. Vino de Jerez; Estudios de sus ácidos desde el período de madurez de la uva hasta el envejecimiento del vino. Bol. Inst. Nacl. Invest. Agron. (Madrid), 9:473–486.

Bottril, D. E., and J. S. Hawker. 1970. Chlorophylls and their derivatives during drying of Sultana grapes. J. Sci. Fd. Agric., 21:193–196.

Chambers, T. C., and J. V. Possingham. 1963. Studies of the fine structure of the wax layer of Sultana grapes. Aust. J. Biol. Sci., 16:818–825.

Chase, E. M., and C. G. Church. 1927. Tests of methods for the commercial standardization of raisins. United States Dept. Agr. Tech. Bul., 1:1–23.

Christensen, P., C. Lynn, H. P. Olmo, and H. E. Studer. 1970. Mechanical harvesting of Black Corinth raisins. Calif. Agric., 24(10):4–6.

Fischer, C. D. 1959. Experiments on possible quality influencing factors of natural sun-dried raisins. Twenty years of raisin research. Calif. Raisin Adv. Board., Fresno, p. 39–40.

————, A. P. Sidwell, and C. Golumbic. 1961. Sorting raisins by the airstream method. United States Dept. Agr., Marketing Res. Rept., 451:4–16.

Grncarevic, M. 1967–69. Spraying as an alternative treatment of Sultanas. Report, Division of Horticultural Research, C.S.I.R.O., Adelaide, Australia, p. 67.

————, and J. S. Hawker. 1971. Browning of Sultana grapes during drying. J. Sci. Fl. Agric., 22:270–272.

————, and H. Hawson. 1971. Dips for raisins. Mallee Horticulture Digest., 18(4):22–23.

————, and W. Lewis. 1969–71. Production of naturals with the help of plastic covers. Report, Division of Horticultural Research, C.S.I.R.O., Adelaide, Australia, pp. 47–48.

Hawker, J. S., and M. Grncarevic. 1970. The siro gritometer for determination of the grit content of dried vine fruit. J. Sci. Food Agric., 21:76.

Henderson, W. W., and J. M. Kitterman. 1968–1970. California fruit and nut statistics. State Dept. Agric., Sacramento.

Hussein, A. A., E. M. Mrak, and W. V. Cruess. 1942. The effect of pretreatment and subsequent drying on the activity of grape oxidase. Hilgardia, 14: 349–357.

Jacob, H. E. 1942. The relation of maturity of the grapes to the yield, composition, and quality of raisins. Hilgardia, 14:321–345.

————. 1944. Factors influencing the yield, composition, and quality of raisins. California Agr. Exp. Sta. Bull., 683:3–44.

Kasimatis, A. N., and C. Lynn. 1967. Raisin maturity. Univ. of Calif. Agric. Ext. Service, AXT-235:1–20.

Martin, R. J. L., and G. L. Scott. 1957. The physical factors involved in the drying of Sultana grapes. Austral. Jour. Agr. Res., 8:444–459.

May, P., and G. H. Kerridge. 1967. Harvest pruning of Sultana vines. Vitis, 6:390–393.

———, and P. B. Scholefield. 1969–71. Drying Sultanas on the vine. Report, Division of Horticultural Research, C.S.I.R.O., Adelaide, Australia, pp. 41–42.

———, ———. 1972. Long-term response of Sultana vines to harvest pruning. Vitis, 11:296–302.

McCance, R. A., and E. M. Widdowson. 1946. Chemical composition of foods, No. 235. London, His Majesty's Stationery Office. (See p. 81.)

Miller, M. W. 1963. Grapes to raisins. Twenty Yrs. Raisin Res. Calif. Raisin Adv. Board, Fresno, pp. 19–23. (Pub. 1969.)

———. 1964. Study of the influence of grape maturity on the quality and yield of raisins. Twenty Yrs. Raisin Res. Calif. Raisin Adv., Fresno, pp. 12–18.

Morgan, A. F. 1935. Nutritive value of dried fruits. Amer. Jour. Pub. Health, 25:328–335.

———. 1953. Vitamin analysis of California's grapes and raisins. Twenty Yrs. Raisin Res. Calif. Raisin Adv. Board, Fresno, pp. 456–458.

———, L. J. Brinner, and A. P. Hall. 1954. Progress report on vitamin assays of raisins. California Raisin Advisory Board, Ann. Rept., sec. III, Research, pp. 16–18.

———, and A. P. Hall. 1953. Summary of B vitamin assays of the 1953 crop. Thompson Seedless grapes and raisins. Twenty Yrs. Raisin Res. Calif. Raisin Adv. Board, Fresno, pp. 451–452.

———, L. Kimmel, A. Field, and P. F. Nichols. 1935. The vitamin content of Sultanina (Thompson Seedless) grapes and raisins. Jour. Nutr., 9:369–382.

Mrak, E. M., and J. D. Long. 1941. Methods and equipment for the sundrying of fruits. California Agr. Exp. Sta. Cir., 350:1–69.

Nichols, P. F., and A. W. Christie. 1930. Dehydration of California grapes. California Agr. Exp. Sta. Bull., 500:1–31.

Proton, R. 1968–1971. Situation de la Viticulture dans le Mond (Situation of viticulture in the world). Bul. Office Internat'l Vigne et du Vin, Vol. 41, 42, and 43.

Radler, F. 1964. The prevention of browning during drying by the cold dip treatment. J. Sci. Food Agric., 15:864–869.

Sherman, H. C. 1952. Chemistry of food and nutrition. New York, Macmillan. (See p. 686.)

Studer, H. E., and H. P. Olmo. 1971. The severed cane technique and its application to mechanical harvesting of raisin grapes. Trans. Amer. Soc. Agric. Engineers, 14:38–43. (*See also:* California Agric. 27(3):10–12 and 27(8):3–5.)

United States Department of Agriculture. 1950. Composition of foods, handbook No. 8.(See p. 42.)

———. 1953. Research on raisins. Twenty Yrs. Raisin Research, Calif. Raisin Adv. Board, Fresno, pp. 457–458.

24

Grape Varieties

Probably about 8,000 varieties of grapes have been named and described. About 20 per cent of them may be growing somewhere in vineyards, gardens, and variety collections; certainly not more than sixty or seventy varieties can be considered important in California.

The following paragraphs cover the purpose, importance, and adaptability of each of the varieties of raisin, table, and wine grapes and resistant rootstocks now being grown in California. A brief viticultural description is included; long, detailed ampelographic accounts are purposely avoided. Ampelographic descriptions may be found in Viala and Vermorel (1909) in French; Constantinescu *et al.* (1960) in Romanian; Frolov-Bagreev (1946–1958) in Russian; and, for American grapes, in the work of Hedrick (1907).

A number of the leading varieties of American origin, French hybrids, and Muscadine grapes grown in the United States are included.

The names given first are the one most appropriate in California. The names in parentheses are those commonly used here or elsewhere in the world.

Varieties not named in the text are to be regarded as not recommended for planting in California at present. The varieties in the tables are of only limited interest, or new, or insufficiently tested to permit a definite recommendation. Discussions of the raisin and table grape varieties are based on personal observations, those of wine grape varieties on the studies of Amerine and Winkler (1944 and 1962), and those of rootstock varieties as indicated in the introductory note to that section.

The 1972 estimated California acreage of each variety is shown in parentheses at the end of the discussions (Anon., 1972).

The Variety Situation

Production of raisin and table grapes in California has developed continuously and is now based on a few well-proven varieties. For many years only three varieties have been grown on a commercial scale for raisin production. Thompson Seedless accounts for almost 95 per cent of the raisin production. Of the table grapes shipped to out-of-state markets, Cardinal, Emperor, Perlette, Ribier, Thompson Seedless, and Tokay account for about 95 per cent. There have been other varieties, which have declined in importance, and new ones will appear, especially if and when varieties are produced that combine distinct flavor and eye appeal with good shipping and keeping quality.

Orderly development of the wine-producing phase of the grape industry was interrupted by Prohibition during the years 1918 to 1933. In that period the wineries deteriorated to the point where recovery was almost impossible, most of the experienced employees were lost to other occupations, and the good wine varieties were grafted to or replaced by plantings of varieties that could be shipped to the eastern United States and were, mostly, capable of producing only common wines. In the East these grapes were usually mixed with poor table grapes and made into wine with improvised facilities.

It now seems that a taste was developed for those wines, which were all that could be had at the time, and that appreciation of the requirements of varieties for the production of quality wines was all but lost. When repeal of Prohibition came, and even for years thereafter, many growers and wine producers failed to understand the difference in the value of good wine varieties as contrasted with table or raisin varieties for wine production. As a result, grapes of all but a few varieties were purchased on a sugar-point (degree Brix) basis. It is not surprising that under such unrealistic conditions the situation did not improve with regard to grape varieties for wine.

Because there was no meaningful difference in prices, many growers planted table (two-way) and raisin (three-way) grapes because they thought thereby to ensure security of outlet for their crops. When all three outlets (table, raisin, and wine) were fully supplied, security disappeared. Yet varieties such as Tokay and Thompson Seedless, because of their very high productivity, have continued to occupy prominent places in the new and replanted acreage. And, without price differences to offset their high tonnages, why not plant them? The Thompson Seedless is a most economical producer. Cane pruning enables it to develop, early in the season, a very large leaf area that can nourish and mature very large crops year after year. With its fruiting habit, which requires fruit canes, thinning the crop for crushing or for raisins is rarely necessary. The Tokay, of an entirely different fruiting habit, requiring spur pruning, is also a heavy producer. These varieties are acceptable for the production of grape spirits and beverage brandy, but it is generally ageed that they should not be used as wine stocks except for sherry or formula wines.

Since about 1946 public interest in table wines in the United States has grown steadily. The affluence of the American society and the increasing awareness of European wines and foods has stimulated consumption of dinner wines. The acreage of the premium quality varieties, the basis for these wine types, has expanded as a result. This trend accelerated in the past five years, resulting at the end of 1972 in about 100,000 acres of non-bearing wine grapes in California.

Dessert wine varieties have not followed this trend. There have been some plantings, but the increase in acreage is very moderate.

Thus, after many years of confusion or indifference as to varieties, the still young but very much wiser wine-producing segment of the industry is growing up. The importance of variety is being recognized generally, and more and more of the good varieties are being planted. It is evident, however, that some varieties not properly to be regarded as wine grapes will be crushed for years to come. Meanwhile, the traditionally recognized varieties will constitute an increasing share of the new plantings, and new varieties, with somewhat different aromas and tastes, will find a place.

RAISIN GRAPE VARIETIES

Thompson Seedless (Sultanina).—More than half the world's raisins and about 95 per cent of California's raisins are made of Thompson Seedless, which originated in Asia Minor and was first grown in California by William Thompson near Yuba City. It is also called Oval Kishmish, in the eastern Mediterranean regions, and Sultana, in Australia and South Africa.

In California more than 40 per cent of the total grape acreage is Thompson Seedless. Besides being the principal raisin variety, it is the leading table grape. Also made from it are large quantities of white dessert wines and much distilling material to furnish alcohol for arresting the fermentation of other dessert wines and for beverage brandy.

The clusters are large; heavily shouldered, long cylindrical; well filled. The berries are uniform; medium-sized; ellipsoidal elongated; greenish-white to light golden; always seedless; firm and tender in texture; neutral in flavor; very sweet when fully ripened; moderately tender-skinned. Since the pedicels are somewhat weak, the berries shatter in transit unless the vines are girdled or the clusters are sprayed with a growth regulator. The fruit ripens early in the season. The grapes dry easily into raisins of soft texture and excellent quality. The vines are very vigorous and productive. Cane-pruning is required.

The Thompson Seedless is well adapted to all parts of the San Joaquin Valley where grapes are grown and to the warmer parts of the Sacramento Valley. In the hot desert it has been used as an early shipping table variety; however, the earlier maturing seedless variety, Perlette, is taking its place. It is unsuited to the cooler regions. (232,000 acres.)

A pink variation—Sultanina rose—is of interest for home use. Except for its pink or rose color, it is almost identical with the Thompson Seedless. It is somewhat less productive.

Muscat of Alexandria.—The Muscat of Alexandria is a very old variety, of North African origin, from which are made the raisins of Spain—the cluster Malagas and the stemmed Valencias or Muscatels. Muscat of Alexandria accounts for less that 1 per cent of California production of raisins, but it is a more important raisin variety in Australia.

As a table grape it is highly esteemed for home gardens and local markets. Its pronounced flavor, large size, and juicy but not watery pulp make it a favorite with nearly all who are familiar with it. It has only fair shipping quality; the bloom is easily rubbed off in handling, exposing its dull-green ground color. It lacks the attractive appearance that stimulates sales of a fresh fruit and is therefore relatively unimportant among table grape shipments to the Eastern markets.

As a wine grape the Muscat of Alexandria is extensively used for muscatel, a dessert wine. When the vines are not overcropped and the grapes are allowed to mature fully, it produces a wine of very good quality, particularly in regions where the fruit does not sunburn. Dry wines made from it are of only standard quality, but it is very pleasant as a light, sweet muscat flavored table wine. With a residual sugar of 1.5 to 2.0 per cent, it retains its rich, flowery muscat flavor.

The clusters are medium-sized; shouldered, conical; loose, often straggly. The berries are large; obovoid; dull green; normally seeded; pulpy, strongly aromatic (muscat) in flavor. The thin, moderately tough skin is covered with a gray bloom easily rubbed off. The ripening period is late midseason, and the grapes dry easily into large raisins of soft texture and excellent quality. The vines are medium in vigor and very productive; they are head- or cordon-trained and spur-pruned. In some regions and in many soils the flowers set poorly; the results are straggly clusters, many shot berries, and, frequently, poor crops. The setting of the flowers can often be improved by daubing the fresh pruning wounds with zinc sulfate, as recommended for "little leaf," or by longer pruning and flower-cluster thinning.

The Muscat of Alexandria is adapted only to hot regions. It thrives in most of the grape-growing areas of the San Joaquin Valley, the warm parts of the Sacramento Valley, and the warm valleys of the south coast region. It is not suited, however, to the hot desert, because of its tendency to sunburn in extreme heat. (12,500 acres.)

A pink variation—Flame Muscat—unimportant in California, is grown in South Africa under the name Red Hannepoot.

Black Corinth (*Zante currant*).—For centuries Zante currant raisins have been made in Greece, where the variety probably originated and where much of the world's supply is produced.

The clusters are small to medium in size; winged, uniformly cylindrical; well filled to compact when vines are girdled, straggly on ungirdled vines. All the commercial plantings in California are now sprayed with growth regulators to obtain full crops. The berries are very small; spherical to oblate; reddish black; mostly seedless, with an occasional seeded berry of medium size; very juicy; neutral to spicy in flavor; very thin and tender of skin. They ripen early and dry readily into very small raisins of soft texture with a pleasing tart taste.

The vines are vigorous and are productive if girdled or treated with a growth regulator. They may be head-trained and cane- or long spur-pruned. If they are cordon-pruned, long spurs are required.

The Black Corinth is well suited to the central and lower parts of the San Joaquin Valley. It has also done very well in experimental plantings at Davis. (1,700 acres.)

Seedless Sultana (*Round Seedless*).—This grape resembles the Thompson Seedless, but differs in having smaller, oblate to round berries—a few containing partly hardened seeds. It has been largely displaced by the Thompson Seedless. The crop of the acreage still in bearing is diverted to winery use. (1,000 acres.)

Monukka (*Black Monukka*).—The Monukka has not been grown extensively. Its raisins are somewhat larger than those of Thompson Seedless; have a mild, nutlike flavor; and are prone to becoming sticky in storage. In some years the seeds of some berries develop sufficiently to be objectionable in the raisins. The Monukka is a very vigorous grower and performs well with cordon-training and spur-pruning.

The clusters are large, very long; conical irregular; loose to well filled. Berries are medium; oval; pink to reddish-black; mostly seedless or with soft tasteless seed coats which impart a pleasant nutty character to the raisins.

TABLE GRAPE VARIETIES

Almeria (*Ohanez*).—Spain produces and exports large quantities of Almeria, a late-ripening table grape, packed in granulated cork. It is also one of the important late export table grapes in Western Australia and Chile. The variety is not of great importance in California, because of its susceptibility to Ohanez spot, seemingly a form of heat injury, and its requirement for a large framework of permanent wood for successful fruiting.

The clusters are medium or large medium; short conical; well filled to compact. The berries are large medium; cylindroidal; greenish white; normally seeded; firm; neutral in flavor; with thick, tough skins. The stems are tough, with the berries firmly attached. Shipping and keeping qualities are excellent. The vines are vigorous and are usually productive when they are cane-pruned. The variety does best when trained on arbors. The fruit ripens late.

The Almeria has been successful only in local areas in Tulare and Kern counties, on the east side of the San Joaquin Valley. (1,150 acres.)

Calmeria.—The Calmeria is an open pollinated seedling selection of Almeria. It originated at the United States Horticultural Field Station, Fresno, California. Introduced in 1950, it was soon found to be a shipping and storage grape of merit. Some plantings of this variety were disappointing because much of the early planting stock was infested with fan-leaf virus. The recent availability of new virus free clones has stimulated new plantings in California, and it now exceeds the Almeria in acreage.

The clusters are large; long, conical; well filled. The berries are large and cylindrical; with thick and rather tough skins and firm pulp. The flowers have upright stamens. The general appearance of the vine resembles that of Almeria. (3,500 acres.)

Cardinal.—The Cardinal, introduced in 1946, is a cross of Tokay x Ribier made by Snyder and Harmon (1952) at the United States Horticultural Field Station, Fresno, California. The vines are very vigorous and productive, with enough foliage to protect the fruit from sunburn. It is successful with cordon-training and spur-pruning; flower-cluster or cluster thinning is used, depending on the soil type.

The clusters are large medium in size; conical; loose to compact. The berries are very large; cherry red, becoming reddish black with advancing maturity; round to short oval; depressed at the apex, frequently with one or more shallow sutures; with a slight formic acid flavor when well matured. This is the earliest red table grape now grown in California. Like the Ribier, one of its parents, it is adapted to hot areas. It has performed well in the desert and in the San Joaquin Valley south of Fresno. (2,650 acres.)

Dattier.—Dattier is an important table grape in Austrialia and South Africa, where it is called Waltham Cross. It is also a leading table grape in a number of countries—Regina in Italy, Bolgar in Bulgaria, and Afus Ali in Romania. The vines are vigorous, but production in California has been largely disappointing because of irregular berry size owing to fanleaf virus. Virus free vines should do well in our state. Results have been best with cordon-training and long-spur pruning.

The clusters are large; long conical to cylindrical; loose to well filled. The berries are mostly very large; oval elongated; greenish to whitish yellow; firm and juicy, with a pleasing characteristic flavor; ripening in midseason. A Dattier rid of virus diseases should find a place in California. Very late pruning—when upper new shoots are 3–5 inches long—is recommended in Australia.

Emperor.—The origin of the Emperor is unknown. First in popularity as a red table variety, it owes its importance to its late ripening, its attractive appearance, and its excellent shipping and storage qualities. Large quantities are held in cold storage to extend the marketing season.

The clusters are large; long conical; well filled. The berries are uniform, large; elongated obovoid or ellipsoidal; light red to reddish purple; normally seeded; moderately firm; neutral in flavor; with thick, tough skins. The stems are tough, and the berries adhere very firmly. The variety ripens late. The vines are very vigorous and productive. They are cordon-trained and spur-pruned.

The Emperor is profitable only when it attains a red color and large berry size. It most nearly attains perfection near the foothills along the east side of the San Joaquin Valley in Tulare, Fresno, and Kern counties. About 90 per cent of the Emperors are produced in this area. (22,000 acres.)

Italia.—The Italia came to us from Italy. It is one of the varieties produced by Professor Pirovano. Its vines are vigorous and, with cordon-training and spur-pruning, productive. The fruit rarely sunburns. The clusters are large medium in size; conical; well filled. The berries are very large; long oval; with heavy orange-white bloom and mild but distinct muscat flavor.

Although the skin is fairly thick, the berries bruise easily and turn brown where they rub against the wood of the shipping box. Liners and aprons are necessary for distant shipment. This defect has limited new plantings of this variety. (1,200 acres.)

Malaga.—The Malaga, once California's leading table grape variety, has been almost entirely replaced in the market by the Thompson Seedless. As a table grape the Malaga now occupies a very minor position, and most of the production is used for grape spirits or low-grade wines.

The clusters are large to very large; conical; well filled. The berries are uniform, large; ellipsoidal; whitish-green to whitish-yellow; normally seeded; firm; neutral in flavor; with thick, moderately tough skins. The stems are tough, and the berries adhere firmly. Shipping and keeping qualities are good. The vines are vigorous and very productive. Cordon-training with spur-pruning is best. The ripening time is midseason.

The Malaga is grown in various parts of the San Joaquin Valley. (3,900 acres.)

Olivette blanche.—The very large size and regular, elongated shape of the

Olivette blanche make it an attractive table grape. Because of its poor shipping quality, however, it is of only minor importance.

The clusters are very large; irregular conical; well filled. The berries are very large; uniformly oviod elongated, almost pointed; bright greenish to greenish-white, often with a pink blush; neutral in flavor; low in acid; firm and tender; thin-skinned, easily bruised, and inclined to discolor where bruised. The stems are somewhat brittle. The vines are very vigorous and productive if cane-pruned. The fruit ripens in late mid-season.

The Olivette blanche does well in all grape-growing areas of the San Joaquin and intermediate Central Valley regions. (125 acres.)

Perlette.—The Perlette, a hybrid released by Olmo (1948b), is the earliest-maturing variety now grown in California. It is vigorous and productive, and it very rarely sunburns. Its clusters are very compact along both the lower rachis and the individual branches of the cluster. This habit increases thinning costs very materially, so the variety should be considered for planting only in the areas of earliest production, where high prices for early grapes help cover the increased cost of thinning. Cordon-training with spur-pruning and extensive berry thinning have produced good crops of acceptable fruit.

The clusters are large medium in size; conical, shouldered; very compact. The berries are of medium size; round; seedless; mild aromatic in flavor; white and waxy in appearance. (4,000 acres.)

Red Malaga (Molinera).—The clusters of Red Malaga are very large; widely branched and irregular in shape; loose to well filled. The berries are large medium; spherical to short ellipsoidal; pink to reddish-purple, often faintly striated; normally seeded; very crisp and hard; neutral in flavor; low in acidity; tender-skinned. The stems are tough, with berries firmly attached. Shipping and keeping qualities are fair. The vines are very vigorous and productive when cordon-trained with long spur-pruning and when flower clusters are thinned. The grapes ripen in early mid-season, usually just before the Malaga.

The Red Malaga is well suited to most of the San Joaquin Valley, where it ripens earlier than the Tokays of the intermediate Central Valley region and can be marketed before they are ripe. After the Tokays are in the market, the demand for Red Malaga decreases. (1,200 acres.)

Ribier (Alphonse Lavallée).—This beautiful table grape, misnamed Ribier in California, is one of the finest of European hothouse varieties; the grape grown in California is the Alphonse Lavallée, not the Gros Ribier of Europe. It is the principal black table grape in the state, and in total production ranks third among table grape varieties.

The clusters are of medium size; short conical, often heavily shouldered; varying from loose to compact. The berries are very large; oblate to short ellipsoidal; depressed at the apex; jet black; normally seeded; firm; neutral in flavor, but mildly astringent; low in acid; moderately tough-skinned;

ripening in early midseason. The stems are tough, with the berries firmly attached. Shipping and storage qualities are good. The vines are moderately vigorous and very productive. They are cordon-trained and short spur-pruned. (7,300 acres.)

Rish Baba.—The very much elongated berry of the Rish Baba, a variety of Persian origin, has given it about the same importance as the Olivette blanche. Both have been indiscriminately marketed as "Lady Fingers." Both have essentially the same merits and defects.

The clusters are of small medium size; long cylindrical; very loose. The berries are large; much elongated, with one side nearly straight, the other bulged near the middle, and the ends rounded; pale greenish-white to light yellow; neutral in flavor; very low in acid; very tender; thin-skinned; easily bruised. The stems are brittle. The vigorous vines are moderately productive when cane-pruned. They ripen in early midseason.

The Rish Baba does best in the intermediate Central Valley region. (30 acres.)

Tokay (*Flame Tokay*).—The Tokay was once California's premier table grape. It is now surpassed by a number of other varieties. It owed its importance primarily to its brilliant red color, not always attained unless berry thinned, and its fair shipping and keeping qualities. With poor handling and slow movement from vine to the precooler, however, it deteriorates rapidly. The variety has been increasingly utilized in the wine industry to the detriment of its position as a table grape. In recent years, up to 90 per cent of the production has been crushed—largely for beverage brandy.

The variety is believed to have originated in Kabylia, a region in Algeria, where it is known by the Arab name of Ahmeur bou Ahmeur.

The clusters are large; shouldered, short conical; compact. The berries are large; ovoid truncate; brilliant red to dark red; normally seeded; very firm; neutral in flavor; with thick, fairly tough skins. The stems are large and tough, and the berries adhere firmly. The grapes ripen in midseason and are very sensitive to sunburn. The vines have usually been head-trained and spur-pruned, but will do equally as well or better with cordon-training.

The principal producing area is around Lodi. If grown in hotter regions, the variety fails to color well and sunburns badly, whereas in the cooler coastal sections it does not ripen well or the color is too intense. (19,800 acres.)

Thompson Seedless.—For a discussion of the Thompson Seedless variety, see the section on raisin grapes. When grown for table fruit, berry size is increased by berry thinning combined with either girdling or treatment with a growth regulator or both (see chap. 14). The treatments also improve its shipping quality.

"American" varieties in California.—Certain of these varieties having

the *labrusca,* or foxy, flavor are much desired by former residents of the midwestern and eastern states, where such grapes are common. Some can be grown fairly satisfactorily in the cooler parts of California's coastal valleys and mountain areas. Even in favored locations, however, the quality of the fruit obtained is inferior to that of the same varieties produced in good locations in the East and Middle West. Their usefulness in California is limited to home gardens and local markets, and, on a larger scale, for sweet juice, either unmixed or, more likely, blended with the juice of *vinifera* varieties.

Wherever grown, they should be trellised, generally cane pruned, and

TABLE 41
LESS WELL-KNOWN TABLE GRAPE VARIETIES

Variety	Period of maturity	Color	Size of berry	Shape of berry	Special characteristics
Barlinka	Late	Black	Large	Short oval	A prominent South African variety
Beauty Seedless	Very early	Black	Small-medium	Oval	Neutral seedless
Black Hamburg	Midseason	Black	Large-medium	Round	Standard for table grapes quality in England
Early Muscat	Very early	Yellow	Medium	Round	Strong muscat flavor
Exotic	Midseason	Black	Large	Irregular oval	Ribier-like, larger clusters; cracks easily
Gold	Early midseason	Golden sheen	Large	Oval	Mild muscat flavor
Kandahar	Midseason	White, pink tinge	Very large	Cylindroidal	Brittle stems, very difficult to pack
Muscat Hamburg	Midseason	Black	Medium	Oval	Strong muscat flavor
Pearl of Csaba	Very early	Light green	Small-medium	Round	Slight muscat flavor; will not ship
Queen	Midseason	Red	Large	Oval	Neutral flavor; good shipper

irrigated more frequently than *vinifera* varieties. Being more resistant to powdery mildew than the *vinifera* grapes, they need be sulfured only once or twice each season—often not at all. Otherwise, the cultivation and care are the same as for *vinifera* varieties.

The best for California planting are: black—Concord, Pierce, Early Niabell, and Niabell; red—Agawam, Iona, Vergennes, Delaware, and Catawba; white—Niagara and Golden Muscat.

The Early Niabell and Niabell released by Olmo and Koyama (1962) are tetraploids, with very large berries. Of the American varieties named above, only the Pierce approaches these new varieties in vigor and productivity in the interior valleys of California. Although not comparable to the Concord flavor of the eastern north-central states, they possess a distinctive, *labrusca*-type flavor. (For important American varieties outside of California, see p. 683.)

The clusters are of small medium size; short conical; well filled. The berries of Early Niabell are short oval and purplish black, whereas those of Niabell are spherical and jet black. Their fruit ripens in midseason and is suitable for table fruit, sweet juice, and semisweet wines. The vines are somewhat tolerant to powdery mildew. (125 acres.)

Table grape varieties of minor importance.—Of the many other known varieties of table grapes, those listed in table 41 possess qualities that make them suited to home gardens and local markets. Some of these are poor shippers, and others have not been tested in transit.

RED WINE GRAPE VARIETIES

Aleatico.—Aleatico has a pronounced muscat flavor. It is the variety from which *vino santo*, a natural sweet wine of Italy, is made. In Tuscany the mature clusters were formerly hung on strings in a well-ventilated room and allowed to become partly dry in order to secure a higher concentration of sugar. Now they are placed on trays. This grape has a naturally high Brix-acid ratio at maturity, but is deficient in color. The vines are moderately vigorous and will produce well under normal spur pruning. The variety is adapted to regions IV and V, and possibly III. It is used for the production of red and black muscatel and light muscat wines. Because of its low color, the variety should not be planted ahead of demand. Its wines are low in both color and acidity.

Clusters are of medium size; cylindrical; winged to double. The berries are medium large; oblate; reddish brown. (225 acres.)

Alicante Bouschet.—Alicante Bouschet is one of the few varieties grown in California—along with Grand noir, Petit Bouschet, Alicante Ganzin, and other—that have a red juice. Of these, it is the one that is grown the most extensively. Wines made from it have no character or merit. The color is intense at first, fading with age; acidity is low. In fertile soils the variety is very productive. Since the grapes have fair shipping qualities, many are sent to eastern markets for wine production.

The clusters are of medium size; shouldered, conical; well filled to compact. The berries are of medium size; spherical; brilliant black, with a blue-gray bloom; ripening in late midseason.

The Alicante Bouschet is suited best to fertile soils in the warmest parts of the coastal valleys and in the intermediate Central Valley region—region IV. Additional plantings in California are not recommended. (6,900 acres.)

Barbera.—The Barbera was brought from the Piedmont region of Italy. There it produces a well-known varietal wine. Here its wines have equal promise, yet the very high acid content of its mature fruit makes it especially valuable for blending to produce red table wines in warm regions. Used alone, its wines possess distinct character, but they age slowly unless they are drawn off the pomace early. The variety is adapted to the warmest areas of the coastal valleys, the intermediate and interior valleys, regions IV and V. It has averaged over 7 tons per acre at Davis with head-training and spur- or cane-pruning. The recent increase in interest in table wine production has lead to a major increase in planting of this variety in the interior valleys, with nearly 10,000 acres being set in the last two years.

The clusters are of medium size; conical, winged; well filled. The berries are medium-sized; ellipsoidal; black, with abundant color in the skin; of characteristic varietal flavor—astringent and high in acid content; ripening in midseason. (12,900 acres.)

Cabernet-Sauvignon.—The famous claret wines of the Médoc and Saint-Émilion regions of France derive their flavor and character from the Cabernet-Sauvignon and from related varieties. In suitable locations in California it produces a wine of pronounced varietal flavor, good acidity, good color, and excellent balance. It is one of the two most renowned red wine varieties. It has produced some of the finest red table wines in California.

The clusters are of small to medium size; irregular in shape, but usually long conical; loose to well filled. The berries are small; very seedy; nearly spherical; black, with a gray bloom. The skin is tough, the flavor pronounced and characteristic. Ripening is in late mid-season. The vines are very vigorous and productive when cane-pruned.

The variety is best adapted to regions II and III of the coastal valleys where the grapes attain their highest quality. Plantings of this variety in these districts have rapidly increased in recent years.

This variety has produced 4.2 to 4.7 tons per acre in the research vineyard at Oakville. It is highly recommended for grower-wine-producer planting. (10,600 acres.)

Carignane.—Of Spanish origin, the Carignane has been grown in the south of France since probably the twelfth century. There, and in Algeria, it is one of the most important wine varieties. It is most useful in California for the making of bulk red table wines. Carignane wines are of medium acidity and color, usually with little varietal character. This grape, being very susceptible to powdery mildew, should not be planted in locations subject to frequent summer fogs.

The clusters are medium-sized; shouldered cylindrical; well filled to compact. The berries are of medium size; ellipsoidal; black, with a heavy, blue-gray bloom; ripening in late midseason. The vines are very vigorous and very productive. The canes are large, semierect to erect in habit of growth. Head- or cordon-training with spur-pruning is recommended.

The Carignane, though grown extensively in nearly all wine-producing districts of California except the coolest, is best adapted to fertile soils in the warmer parts of the coastal valleys (region III), in the intermediate central valley (region IV), and in the cooler part of region V. The present acreage of this variety has expanded in recent years as the demand for red wines has increased. (28,500 acres.)

Carnelian.—Carnelian, one of Professor Olmo's new varieties, was derived from crossing a selection of the Carignane x Cabernet-Sauvignon with Grenache. The first cross was made in 1936 and the selection F2-7 crossed with the Grenache. The variety was released to the industry in 1972.

The variety is best adapted to the warmer areas of the Central Valley—region IV—and since 1961 has undergone trials in plots from Lodi to Bakersfield. Yields have been higher than Ruby Cabernet and slightly lower than Grenache, about 10 tons per acre in the best plots.

The vine resembles Grenache and produces clusters about 1 pound in weight which are usually compact. Carnelian is much more resistant to fruit spoilage than Grenache.

The wine is of medium body, of excellent red color and is most useful as a dry red table wine that can either be consumed early or aged to produce a wine of better quality. Rosé types of superior quality are a promising outlet. The fruit has a low pH and high acidity at harvest time, the end of September. The sugar content is fairly low, 20 to 21 Brix at full maturity.

Gamay.—Gamay is an important variety of the Beaujolais region of France. In California, it or a variety resembling it has been called Napa Gamay. It is a vigorous grower, and very productive when head-trained and spur-pruned. In regions II and III the wines of this variety, both red and rosé, have been distinctive. Because of its productivity, it has been popular with growers. Acreage is steadily increasing in the coastal valleys.

The clusters are large medium; conical; well filled. Berries are large medium; round; with thick, tough skins. Usually there are a number of small green shot berries. Ripening is in late midseason. Although the early growth is semiupright, the shoots droop late in the season, and the vines are characterized by many laterals. The leaves are medium large; almost entire; medium green; somewhat rough. (2,400 acres.)

Gamay Beaujolais.—This variety, a clone of Pinot noir, was apparently introduced into California from the Beaujolais region of France, hence its name.·It has little resemblance to the other Gamay varieties. Under California conditions it is more vigorous and more productive than the Pinot noir. At Oakville it has averaged 5 tons per acre. It may be head-trained and spur- or cane-pruned. Its adaptation is to region I and II and the cooler parts of region III. Its wines, resembling those of Pinot noir, are of excellent quality. It is being planted extensively in the coastal valleys.

The clusters are of small medium size; conical; shouldered to winged; compact. The peduncles are dark green. The berries are small medium; short oval; black. The seeds are small and light-brown. The leaves are medium; bright dark-green, with grooves at veins; glabrous above; mature leaves showing tufts of wool below.

The recommendation for planting is the same as that for the Pinot noir (see below). (2,550 acres.)

Grenache.—The Spanish variety, Grenache, is grown in California for the production of both rosé and port-type wines, for which it is well suited. It thrives in the moderately warm areas of regions II and III, as well as in the relatively hot regions IV and V. Set of fruit is heavier and more uniform from year to year in the hotter regions. This variety has ample color for rosé wines, but it will require blending for the production of full colored port-type wines. It is productive with either head- or cordon-training and spur-pruning. Cordon-training is to be preferred in the interior valleys; it spreads the fruit.

The vines are very vigorous and erect in growth habit. The clusters are large medium; short conical, sometimes shouldered or winged; loose to compact. The berries are small medium; short oval to nearly spherical; reddish purple to black; ripening in late midseason. The stems of the clusters are very thick. (16,250 acres.)

Grignolino.—This variety came from northwestern Italy. The vines are moderately vigorous and productive. It does well with head-training and spur-pruning. The adaptation is for regions II, III, and IV.

The clusters are medium in size; long conical; well filled to compact. The berries are small medium; oval; reddish brown. The seeds have a long, plump beak. The leaves are dull above, lightly tomentose below; some with shallow sinuses, but many entire. The leaves are small medium in size.

The Grignolino normally produces an orange-pink wine that is distinctly different from most rosé wines. When it is blended to produce a red table wine, it loses one of its outstanding characteristics—its color—and becomes simply another red wine. Moderate planting for the production of wine of the true Girgnolino type may be recommended. (250 acres.)

Mataro.—Like the Carignane, the Mataro is of Spanish origin and is of value in California primarily for bulk wines. Mataro wines lack varietal characteristics and have low acidity and color. In most locations the Carignane is preferred because of its greater vigor and higher productivity. The Mataro is less susceptible to powdery mildew than the Carignane, however, and also starts its buds slightly later in the spring, a characteristic that may be important in locations subject to spring frost.

The clusters are large medium in size; usually two-shouldered, conical; compact. The berries are medium-sized; spherical; black, with a heavy blue bloom; firm; pulpy; ripening in late midseason. The vines are moderately vigorous, erect in growth, and moderately productive with head-training and spur-pruning.

The Mataro has been grown extensively in the south coast region and in the foothill districts on the eastern side of the lower Sacramento Valley. It should not be planted in regions II or III. Its acreage has been steadily decreasing in recent years; further planting is not recommended. (1,800 acres.)

Merlot.—Next in importance to Cabernet-Sauvignon in the Bordeaux region of France, the Merlot is now recognized as a variety of real merit in California. It is fairly productive with head-training and either long spur- or cane-pruning and matures ahead of Cabernet. Its wines have a fine bouquet, are softer, and age more rapidly than those of Cabernet-Sauvignon with which they are usually blended.

The clusters are medium large; long conical; loose to compact with long peduncles. Berries medium size; round; and bluish-black in color. The leaves are glaberous above, tomentose below, deeply 5 lobed with petiolar sinus open.

Mission.—The Jesuit missionaries planted the first variety of *Vitis vinifera* in California at the San Diego Mission in the latter part of the eighteenth century. The variety was the Mission, which was the principal variety in California until about 1870. Since then it has been gradually displaced by other varieties in the coastal regions and is now grown mainly in regions IV and V, where it is valuable as a dessert wine grape. It has always been associated with the making of sweet white wines. It is low in acidity and too deficient in color to be used alone for red wines.

The clusters are large; conical, but heavily shouldered; stiffly loose—the stems rigid enough to cause the individual berries to stand apart. The berries are medium-sized; oblate; reddish purple to black; ripening in late midseason. The pulp is firm but juicy. The vines are very vigorous, and single vines occasionally attain enormous size. Given room to develop, the Mission bears heavily; if it is crowded or pruned too short, the crops tend to be irregular.

The present acreage seems to be ample. (6,300 acres.)

Petite Sirah.—In suitable locations this variety yields well and is valuable for red table wine. Wines made from it are of good quality, with a distinctive, recognizable flavor and moderate acidity. The skin has an abundance of color, which is stable. In hot regions or hot seasons the fruit may sunburn badly. In years of early rainfall it rots badly.

The clusters are medium-sized; winged, cylindrical; compact. The berries are of medium size; slightly ellipsoidal; black, with a dull bluish-gray bloom; ripening in early midseason. The vines are of moderate vigor and productivity. On dry hillside soils short-spur pruning is satisfactory; on fertile soils long-spur or cane-pruning may be required.

The Petite Sirah is best adapted to the valleys of regions II and III, where good dry table wines may be made from it. Today it is being planted widely in California, especially in the cooler portions of the interior valleys. It is recommended for less fertile soils, where its growth will not be too rank and its fruit will mature early. (7,400 acres.)

Pinot noir.—The Pinot noir is the variety from which are made the fine Burgundy wines of France. It is recognized as one of the outstanding red wine varieties of the world. In California it is only moderately vigorous and is of low productivity.

The clusters are small; cylindrical, winged; well filled; with grass-green peduncles. The berries are small medium; oval; black. Seeds are large; plump; light brown. The leaves are medium-sized; bright dark-green; grooved at veins; glabrous above, with a few long hairs below.

On good soils in its region of adaptation this variety should produce 3 to 4 tons per acres. Wines made from it in a favorable environment have been of excellent quality. It should be head-trained and cane-pruned. Planting should be restricted to region I and II. It ripens very early and sunburns badly in the warmer districts. It is recommended for the grower-wine-producer. (4,700 acres.)

Pinot Saint George.—This variety has no resemblance to Pinot noir in vine, fruit, or wine. It is a moderate grower and, with head-training and cane-pruning, a good producer. It is adapted to regions II and III. Its wine, at best, is only standard. It is not recommended for planting.

The clusters are medium; long conical, winged; compact; with very short peduncles (0.5 in. or less). The berries are of medium size; oval. The leaves are 3- and sometimes 5-lobed; dark-green; medium tomentose below, with some hairs above. The rapidly growing shoot tips are whitish-woolly. (540 acres.)

Refosco.—The Refosco is above average in vigor and moderately productive. Its rangy habit of growth opens the vine and makes it subject to sunburn in region V. The variety is adapted to regions II, III, and IV. Head-training and spur-pruning are appropriate. The variety ripens in late mid-season. Its fruit is resistant to early rain damage.

The clusters are medium large; conical, often winged; well filled. The peduncle is long; thin; lignified to the first branch or tendril and usually bent sharply at this junction. The berries are medium large; round; black. The rather tough pulp adheres to the seeds, which are long and have cylindrical beaks. The leaves are glabrous above, tomentose below; and with an open petiolar sinus.

An above-average standard wine is produced under favorable conditions. This variety should find an increasingly important place in the production of standard wines in California. (325 acres.)

Rubired and Royalty.—Rubired is a hybrid of Alicante Ganzin x Tinto cão, and Royalty a hybrid of Alicante Ganzin x Trousseau (Olmo and Koyama, 1962). They are promising as varieties to improve color for the production of port-type wines and for blending. Their fruit has ample color, sugar, and acidity. The vines are vigorous and productive. They may in time replace the Alicante Bouschet and Salvador in regions IV and V.

The clusters are of medium size; loose to well filled. The berries are small; ellipsoidal; very resistant to spoilage; ripening in midseason. They are moderately tolerant to powdery mildew. The juice of Royalty is a dark red, which, along with its other qualities, makes it suitable for the production of port-type wines. Its growth is semierect, with heavy foliage. In contract, the growth of Rubired is prostrate, with leaves covering the fruit. Its juice is a very intense red, which makes it suitable for the production of port-type wines or concentrates and for blending. The acreage of Royalty is limited with interest centered in winery owned vineyards of the interior valley. (2,400 acres.) The planting of the more productive Rubired has increased rapidly in recent years. (6,500 acres.)

Ruby Cabernet.—The Ruby Cabernet is a hybrid of Carignane x Cabernet-Sauvignon (Olmo, 1948). In some locations it has been very productive; in others the yield has occasionally been disappointed. Early plantings of the variety were plagued with both leafroll and fanleaf virus. This variety has much of the Cabernet aroma, but lacks the characteristic flavor. It is a valuable variety in regions III, IV, and V for improving the general quality of standard wines. It has ample, stable color, and above-average acidity. Planting in regions III, IV, and V are being expanded.

The clusters are large medium; long conical; loose to well filled; with a large and very woody peduncle. The berries are small medium; round; with a distinct flavor. The leaves are large; deeply lobed; glabrous above, slightly tomentose below with the petiolar sinus narrow to closed. The canes are somewhat upright; large; with short to medium internodes. (9,900 acres.)

Sangioveto.—This is the variety from which the Chianti wines of Italy derive their character. The vines are above average in vigor and moderately productive. The variety is adapted to regions III and IV. It lacks acidity in warmer areas. Cane- or long spur-pruning has been required for full crops. Its fruit ripens in midseason.

The clusters are of medium size; cylindrical, shouldered or winged; well filled. The berries are small medium; oval; brown to black. The seeds are very large for the size of the berry. The leaves are small and moderately lobed, with very sharp serrations. (100 acres.)

Salvador.—The Salvador is a hybrid of *Vitis rupestris* x *Vitis vinifera*. The vines, of moderate vigor, are very productive when cane-pruned. The importance of this variety stems from its very intense color, which is fairly stable in the wine. Its wine is used only in blending and, in small amounts, to improve the appearance of wines of varieties deficient in color. It is adapted to regions IV and V. The Salvador is surpassed in quality of product and in vigor and productivity by both Rubired and Royalty.

The clusters are small; cylindrical, sometimes shouldered; with a long peduncle. The berries are small medium; short oval; with gelatinous pink pulp and red juice when the fruit is well matured. The leaves are thick; pale grayish-green; of *rupestris type.* (2,400 acres.)

Souzão.—The Souzão is one of the better varieties of the port-producing regions of Portugal. It is very vigorous and productive—6.5 tons per acre at Davis—under normal spur-pruning. Its wines are deeply colored, with good acidity, and of very good quality. It is highly recommended for regions IV and V.

The clusters are of medium large size, cylindrical, and sometimes shouldered. The berries are medium; round; bluish black, with red pulp. The leaves are large; 3-lobed; thick; yellow-green; woolly on both surfaces; turning red in autumn. (260 acres.)

Tinto cão.—Although vigorous in growth, the Tinto cão is low in productivity. Its canes are fairly upright, yet the fruit is well covered. It is a producer of grapes for port-type wines of distinction. The variety is well adapted to regions IV and V. With long-spur or cane-pruning, it does well. It may be an excellent variety for the grower-wine producer despite its low production, only 4.6 tons per acre at Davis.

The clusters are of small medium size; conical, often winged; loose; with thick peduncles. The berries are small; round; black. The leaves are light yellow-green, with parallel sides; upper sinuses often have single serration at base. The vines have a yellow-green appearance.

Tinta Madeira.—Tinta Madeira has contributed much to the improvement of port-type wines in California. The vines are vigorous and productive—6.7 tons per acre at Davis. With cordon-training and spur- or cane-pruning to spread the fruit, its performance has been satisfactory. It produces excellent port-type wines. It is adapted to regions III, IV, and V, and is recommended for further planting. In recent years considerable tonnage has found its way into the standard red table wines of the interior valley where its deep color and rich flavor have improved quality.

The clusters are of medium large size; broad conical, winged; well filled to compact. The berries are medium; long oval; jet black. Some undeveloped small green berries are usually present. The 5-lobed leaves have sinuses of medium depth and are tomentose below (920 acres.)

Touriga.—The Touriga is another important variety in the port-producingin region of Portugal. It is vigorous and productive—8 tons per acre at Davis—and suited to long-spur or cane-pruning. The port-type wines of Touriga are of excellent quality. The variety is adapted to regions IV and V, where its fruit ripens in midseason. This variety is highly recommended for planting for the production of port-type wines.

The clusters are large medium; long conical, occasionally winged; well filled. The berries are medium; short oval; black. The leaves are of medium size; 5-lobed; sinuses open; moderately rough; slight cobwebby tomentum above; woolly and whitish below. The canes are moderately thick, with short internodes, turning yellow early.

Trousseau.—The Trousseau is grown extensively in both the Jura region of France and the port region of Portugal. In the latter region it is called Bastardo. The vines are vigorous, of semierect growth, and productive. Its canes are of medium size, with very short internodes and many laterals. It is adapted to regions III and IV and to cooler parts of V. It is deficient in color. There is some question whether this variety should be planted. Other varieties produce wines of very similar quality and with ample color. It is not recommended.

The clusters are small; long conical; compact; with grass-green peduncles. The berries are medium; long oval; reddish black. The leaves are medium small; light green; slightly rough; with shallow lobes.

Valdepeñas.—The Valdepeñas comes from east-central Spain. It ranks with the most vigorous and productive of grape varieties. Generally its wines from region IV grapes are low in acidity and lacking in definite character. They have been clean, standard-quality, red table wines. Nevertheless, it is probably best adapted to region IV, where it may find consideration for the production of bulk wines because of its productivity. Beyond this it cannot be recommended.

The clusters are medium-sized to large; long conical, well filled, shouldered to irregular. The berries are small medium; oblate; black; with gelatinous pulp. The leaves are large; deeply lobed; tomentose below. The canes are semiupright. (2,100 acres.)

Zinfandel.—In acreage and total production the Zinfandel is the leading wine-grape variety of California. A similar type is grown extensively in the southeastern area of Italy under the name of Primativo di Gioia. The wine, which has a characteristic varietal flavor, is of medium acidity and color. The variety is best suited to the cooler districts because of its tendency to raisin and sunburn. In irrigated vineyards it is susceptible to bunch rot.

The clusters are medium-sized; winged cylindrical; well filled to very compact. The berries are medium-sized; spherical; reddish-black to black; juicy in texture. The apical scar is irregularly shaped and slightly depressed. The grapes ripen in early midseason. The vines are moderately vigorous and very productive. Cordon-training with spur or cane-pruning is recommended.

The Zinfandel, though best adapted to regions II and III of the coastal valleys, is also grown extensively in the intermediate Central Valley in region IV. The best dry wines of this variety are made from grapes grown in the cooler regions. In region IV it is sometimes made into an excellent port-type wine.

The Zinfandel is recommended for only limited further planting owing to its defects: irregular ripening, tendency to raisin, and cluster rotting. (23,300 acres.)

Other red wine grapes.—Some of the world's important red wine grape varieties are excluded from the foregoing descriptions because they are not grown extensively in California. Very brief notes on some of them are given in table 42.

TABLE 42
RED WINE GRAPE VARIETIES NOT EXTENSIVELY PLANTED IN CALIFORNIA

Variety	Region of probable adaptation	Period of maturity	Acidity	Intensity of color	Productivity	Probable wine use and other characteristics
Aramon	IV, cooler V	Late	Medium	Low	High	Dry table, pink
Charbono	II, III	Late	High	High	Medium	Dry, table, heavy
Fresia	III	Early	High	Medium	Low	Dry, varietal
Malbec	II, III	Mid-season	Medium	Medium	Medium	Dry, varietal, Cabernet type
Nebbiolo	III, IV	Late	High	Medium	Medium	Dry, varietal
Saint-Macaire	IV, V	Mid-season	Medium	High	Medium	Dry, table, standard
Tannat	II	Early	High	High	Medium	Dry, varietal

WHITE WINE GRAPE VARIETIES

Aligoté.—The Aligoté is used for the standard white Burgundy wine of France. It is a better producer than Chardonnay and is grown on the flatland. In California its product merits a rating of above standard. The vines are of average vigor. Aligoté is adapted to region II and III and produces well with spur-pruning. In region II it has averaged 4.4 tons per acre. Although important in Eastern Europe, this variety has not made a place for itself in California.

The clusters are small medium; conical, some with wings; compact. The berries are small; round to oval; with skins that slip readily. The leaves are slightly 3-lobed to entire; dark green; thick; glabrous above, slightly tomentose below. The petioles and young shoots are reddish purple.

Burger.—Where the soil is fertile and the climate warm, the Burger produces enormous crops. In cool locations it does not ripen well, and early rains may cause bunch rot. In the warmer parts of the coastal valleys —regions II and III—it produces a light, neutral wine of fair quality. In the south coast and the intermediate Central Valley—region IV—it ripens better and yields more heavily. Its primary usefulness is for blending in bulk wines. When the vines are overcropped, the acidity at maturity is low.

The clusters are of large medium size; shouldered to winged cylindrical; compact. The berries are large medium-sized; spherical; whitish yellow; very juicy, soft; late ripening. The vines are vigorous and do well with cordon- or head-training. The present demand is not likely to increase. (2,200 acres.)

Chardonnay (Pinot Chardonnay).—The Chardonnay is the variety from which the famous white Burgundy wines of France are produced. When grown in a favorable location, it has produced excellent wines. This variety is a vigorous grower and moderate producer. The rootstock may be a factor in its production. When it grows very vigorously, the crop may be increased by girdling. It should be cane-pruned. It is adapted to regions I and II. The Chardonnay on moderately fertile soil will produce 2.5 to 5 tons per acre. It is highly recommended for grower-wine-producer planting. There has been a spectacular increase in new plantings of Chardonnay in the coastal valleys of California in the past few years. Currently, 50 per cent of the acreage is under four years of age.

The clusters are small; cylindrical, winged; loose to well filled. The berries are small; round; usually with one seed. The leaves are large; almost entire; with the basal veins often naked to the first branch. (4,150 acres.)

Chenin blanc.—The Chenin blanc is the leading variety of the middle Loire region of France, where it is used to produce dry and natural sweet table wines as well at *mousseux* (sparkling) wines. The vines are very vigorous and productive—almost 6 tons in region II and 10 tons in region IV. Chenin blanc should do well with head or cordon-training and cane-pruning, which would spread the fruit and tend to reduce bunch rot. Both its dry and natural sweet table wines are of good quality in regions II, III, and IV. It has been planted extensively in recent years; the demand continues to exceed the supply.

The clusters are large medium; long conical; compact; with a thick peduncle, medium to long. The pedicels are of medium size, with brown warts (lenticels). The berries are medium; oval; with tough skins. The canes are semierect; medium large, with medium short internodes. The leaves are of medium size; gray-green; 3- and sometimes 5-lobed; slightly hairy above and medium tomentose below; with red veins, reddish petioles, and petiolar sinus medium to closed. (12,500 acres.)

Folle blanche.—Before the phylloxera reached France, the Cognacs were produced principally of the Folle blanche. It could not, however, be successfully reestablished on resistant rootstocks in the highly calcareous soils of the Cognac region.

When grown under favorable conditions—regions II, III, and IV—this variety produces characteristic wines. Its high acidity also places a high priority on its wines for blending. There should be more acreage of it in areas where, while still retaining its characteristically high acidity, it matures before the early rains. It is used extensively for sparkling wine stock. With head-training and spur-pruning it has averaged 4.7 tons per acre at Oakville.

The clusters are of small to medium size; shouldered or winged; compact. The berries are small medium; spherical or short ellipsoidal; whitish or yellowish green; soft; neutral in flavor; high in acid. The leaves have 5 lobes; medium-deep sinuses; dull green color; with a few long hairs above and cobwebby tomentum below. The fruit ripens in midseason. (250 acres.)

French Colombard.—A combination of high productivity of the vines and high acid content of the grapes gives the French Colombard a place in the moderately warm areas—regions III, IV, and V—for producing standard-quality dry wines. It has averaged about 6 tons per acre in region II and up to 10 tons in region IV. Before Prohibition the French Colombard was rather widely grown under the name of West's White Prolific. There is demand for more fruit of this variety. Extensive plantings have been made during the past three years throughout the interior valley of California with nearly 13,000 non-bearing acres in the state as of 1972. Its wine is also used for sparkling wine stock. For this purpose the berries should not be permitted to become overripe. It does well with cordon or head-training and spur- or cane-pruning depending on the location.

The clusters are of medium size; long conical; well filled. The berries are medium; ellipsoidal; yellowish green, sometimes with a pink tinge; neutral in flavor and high in acid. The canes are semierect; large; with internodes of short to medum length. The leaves are yellow-green; glabrous above, medium tomentose below; with green veins, shallow sinuses, and the petiolar sinus V-shaped. (22,700 acres.)

Gewürztraminer.—The Gewürztraminer has been grown in Germany for several centuries. As the name indicates, its wines possess a pronounced, spicy, aromatic flavor. The vines are only moderate growers, but they produce well with cane-pruning. It has averaged about 6 tons per acre at Oakville. This variety is adapted to region I. In warmer regions its acid is too low to produce fine wines. It is highly recommended for grower-wine-producers. Plantings have increased in the past few years.

The clusters are small; cylindrical; compact. The berries are small; oval; pink to bluish-brown; with firm pulp, characteristic spicy flavor, and tough skins. The leaves are medium small; dull green; rough. The canes are small, with short internodes. (1,000 acres.)

Gray Riesling.—Gray Riesling bears the name but is lacking in the genuine aromatic qualities of the Riesling. It is grown in Europe principally in the Arbois region of France. Its product has a mild spicy flavor, but little more. Its vine and fruit characters, except for less fruit color, bear a fairly close resemblance to the Trousseau. The variety is a strong, vigorous grower. It produces well with head-training and spur- or cane-pruning. Adaptation is for region II and cooler parts of region III.

The clusters are small to medium in size; slightly conical; compact. The berries are medium; long oval; dull reddish-tan. The leaves are small; rough; only slightly lobed. The canes are semierect, with short internodes. (1,000 acres.)

Muscat blanc (Muscat Canelli, Muscat Frontignan).—Muscat blanc would seem to be the appropriate name for this variety. It is descriptive, has been used for many years, and is the most generally used. There are numerous local names, such as those given above, but these have limited geographic application. Two well-known wines of this variety are Muscat Frontignan (still), in southern France, an *Asti spumanti* (sparkling), in northern Italy.

This variety has consistently produced the best muscatel wine, wherever it has been grown. Its flavor is pronounced, yet delicate for muscat. The vines are moderate in vigor and productivity. The open character and semierect growth of the vines expose the fruit to sunburn in region V. The variety is recommended for planting. Cordon-training with spur-pruning has been the usual practice, yet short cane-pruning may be appropriate for machine harvesting.

The clusters are of medium size; conical; well filled to compact; oil-soaked in appearance when mature. The berries are of medium size; round; with a pronounced muscat flavor. The leaves are of medium size; slightly lobed; with sharp serrations. (400 acres.)

Orange Muscat.—Orange Muscat is the *Muscato fior d'arancio* of Italy.

Grape Varieties

The vines are of only average vigor and are moderately productive—about 7 tons per acre in region IV. Its wines are rich in muscat aroma, but not so delicate and rich an aroma as those of Muscat blanc. In flavorable locations its wines surpass those of Muscat of Alexandria. The variety is adapted to regions IV and V. Head-training with spur-pruning is satisfactory. The Orange Muscat should find a place for itself in region IV— where Muscat blanc will sunburn in certain years and Muscat of Alexandria will fail to mature properly.

The clusters are of medium size; short conical; compact. The berries are medium; oblate to round; firm; orange in color. The leaves are dark green, with rounded serrations and depressed veins; the petiolar sinus is only a slit or is closed.

Palomino.—In some parts of California the Palomino is erroneously called Golden Chasselas. It is the principal sherry grape of Jerez (Spain). Widely adaptable to various soils and climates, it thrives in nearly all the warm grape-producing areas of California. The vines are very vigorous and productive. It is adapted to regions IV and V, where, if cropped and vinified properly, it will produce an excellent sherry. It makes an inferior dry wine. At Davis its crops have averaged 8 tons.

The clusters are of large medium size; shouldered and widely branched; stiffly loose to well filled. The berries are medium; oblate; greenish yellow, with a heavy white bloom; firm to somewhat tough. They ripen in late midseason. The vines are very vigorous and very productive. The leaves are dull, dark bluish-green, rough on the upper surface, with a heavily felted pubescence on the lower surface; 5-lobed, with moderately deep sinuses. Cordon-training with spur-pruning is the most satisfactory. (6,300 acres.)

Pinot blanc.—The Pinot blanc is grown rather extensively in France. Its wines are distinct in aroma and flavor, smooth, and of good balance, though prone to darken. The vines are below average in vigor and moderately productive. The variety fruits well with head-training and cane-pruning. It is adapted to regions II and III. It will produce 4 to 5 tons per acre. It should be planted as a grower-wine-producer variety only.

The clusters are small to small-medium in size; long conical, sometimes winged; compact. The berries are small; round. The leaves are large; entire; rough; dark green. (800 acres.)

Saint Emilion (Ugni blanc, Trebbiano).—This variety is grown as Saint Emilion in the Cognac region, as Ugni blanc in the south of France, and as Trebbiano in central Italy. It is now the principal variety grown in the Cognac region. With head-training and spur-pruning, the vines are moderately vigorous and very productive. The variety seems to have little future in California except for brandy production. If grown, its acidity will be very low unless it is grown in regions II and III, or possibly in cooler areas, so long as it can mature.

The clusters are large and long; shouldered, cylindrical; often branched at the tip. The berries are medium; round to oblate; white to pink. The leaves are very large; yellow-green; rough; deeply lobed. (1,050 acres.)

Sauvignon blanc.—The grape from which the white Graves wines derive their character and next to the Sémillon, it is the most important variety of the sauterne wines. Used alone, it makes a fine wine of pronounced character. In the proper blend with Sémillon it is considered to be superior to the wine of either variety used alone.

The clusters are small; conical; loose. The berries are small; spherical; whitish yellow; ripening in early midseason. The vines are very vigorous and require cane-pruning.

The Sauvignon blanc is best suited to regions II and III of the coastal areas. At Oakville it has averaged 6 tons per acre. It is highly recommended for grower-wine-producer planting. (1,600 acres.)

Sauvignon vert.—The origin and true name of the variety grown in California under the name of Sauvignon vert is obscure. Its wine has moderate varietal flavor and aroma, but is low in acid, is harsh, and does not keep well. The fruit is highly subject to attack by bees and molds, and, in years of early rainfall, it rots badly.

The clusters are small to medium in size; cylindrical; loose to compact. The berries are small medium; short ellipsoidal; greenish yellow; soft in texture; juicy; thin-skinned; ripening in early midseason. The vines are vigorous, semiupright in growth habit; very productive.

Sauvignon vert is best suited to the valleys of the coast—regions II and III. Further planting of this variety is not recommended. (850 acres.)

Sémillon.—The world-famous sauternes of France derive their character from the Sémillon grape. This variety, one of the truly fine wine grapes of the world, does very well in certain parts of California. However, owing to the dry climate, the "noble rot" (*Botrytis cinerea*) does not grow on the grapes as they ripen; hence, the finished wines differ from the French sauternes in flavor and aroma. For machine harvesting it will be head-trained and cane-pruned.

The clusters are of medium size; short conical; well filled. The berries are of medium size; spherical; golden yellow; soft of pulp; with a characteristic figlike flavor. They ripen in early midseason. The leaves are large; round; convex; tomentose. The vines are vigorous and moderately productive.

The Sémillon is best suited to region III. Because of the excellent quality of its sweet wines, it can be recommended for further planting. (2,300 acres.)

Sylvaner (Franken Riesling).—The Sylvaner is best known as the source of the Stein wines of Franconia, Germany. It endures more heat than the White Riesling. Its wines, when grown in regions II and III, possess a

Grape Varieties

TABLE 43

WHITE WINE GRAPE VARIETIES NOT EXTENSIVELY PLANTED
IN CALIFORNIA

Variety	Region of probable adaptation	Period of maturity	Acidity	Productivity	Probable wine use and other characteristics
Chasselas doré	I, II	Early	Low	Medium	Dry, table; weak grower
Emerald Riesling	II, III	Late	High	High	Dry, table
Feher Szagos	V	Midseason	Low	High	Dessert, sherry; fruit cracks and rots
Flora	I, II, III	Early	High	Medium	Dry, varietal
Grillo	IV, V	Midseason	Medium	Medium	Sherry
Helena	II	Midseason	Medium	Medium	Dry, varietal
Inzolia	IV, V	Late	Low	High	Dessert
Malvasia bianca	IV, V	Midseason	Low	Medium	Dry or dessert, Muscat
Mantuo pilas	V	Midseason	Low	High	Dessert; not equal to Palomino
Peverella	III, IV	Midseason	Medium	Medium	Dry, table
Red Veltliner	II	Late	Medium	Medium	Dry, table

delicate and distinct character. The vines are of medium vigor, and moderately productive, but very subject to powdery mildew.

The clusters are small; cylindrical, winged; compact. The berries are medium; round; bluish to yellow-green. The leaves are of medium size; almost entire; round in outline; yellow-green. (1,250 acres.)

White Riesling (Riesling, Johannisberger Riesling).—The wines of the Rhine and Moselle valleys of Germany are made from the White Riesling. Its wines possess a strong varietal flavor and bouquet, and the other constituents harmonize to produce a superb product.

This variety is suited only to cool areas of the coast regions, such as region I and II and the cooler parts of region III. On moderately fertile soils it has produced 4 to 4.5 tons per acre. It is highly recommended for grower-wine producer planting.

The clusters are small; cylindrical; well filled. The berries are small medium; spherical; greenish-yellow, speckled with russet dots; sprightly, somewhat aromatic in flavor; juicy. They ripen in early midseason. The vines are vigorous and moderately productive with cane-pruning. (2,600 acres.)

Other white wine grapes.—New varieties and certain additional varieties of white wine grapes, important in other countries but not extensively grown in California, are listed in table 43.

GRAPE VARIETIES OF AMERICAN ORIGIN (Shaulis and Jordan, 1960)

Concord.—The Concord is the leading commercial grape variety in North America, outside of California. It is by far the most widely grown grape on the continent. As well, it makes up over 80 per cent of the plantings in the states of Washington, Michigan, Ohio, and New York. Concord is adapted to a wide range of soils and climatic conditions. It is a vigorous vine, yet relatively winter hardy. It is the only important variety for sweet juice, jelly, and preserves. Its pronounced aromatic, "foxy" flavor makes it a good dessert grape. In the states where it is grown, it is also used in quantity for wine production.

Concord produces an attractive, round blue-black berry on medium sized clusters. It has a tough skin that separates readily from the pulpy flesh. It matures rather late in the season. In cool localities with heavy crop maturity can be a problem. It is quite susceptible to dead-arm disease.

Catawba.—Catawba is a late ripening red variety, hence adapted only to carefully chosen sites with long growing seasons. It is grown principally in the Finger Lakes District of New York State where it produces a very high quality white wine which is in great demand for champagne blends. In that district it comprises about 10 per cent of the fruit processed annually. The vine is vigorous and winter hardy. It, however, is considered to be relatively sensitive to fungus diseases, which may have caused it to fail in southern Ohio after the era of Longworth.

Delaware.—The standard of quality among American grapes wherever grown. Highly prized for champagne production, white still wines of character and as table fruit. It produces small compact clusters of medium sized red berries. The fruit has a distinctive, spicy, aromatic character. Although a slip-skin variety, the berries are delicately tender and may crack under conditions of high relative humidity or fall rains. The fruit ripens 10 to 14 days earlier than Concord.

This variety does best on deep, fertile, well drained soils. Its crops may approach those of Concord. It is relatively sensitive to fungus diseases, particularly on the foliage.

Isabella.—This is a very old, black variety. It is the most widely grown American variety in other parts of the world, but in North America it has been largely replaced by other varieties—especially Concord. The vine is only moderately winter hardy and matures its fruit quite late. Isabella is produced commercially in tropical and sub-tropical regions such as parts of

Colombia, Brazil and India. It is a favorite for home gardens in many other parts of the world.

Niagara.—Niagara is the leading white variety among American grapes. It is an old variety, not as winter hardy as Concord, but still fruits dependably in all of the eastern grape districts. Its acreage in New York is limited mainly to the Niagara County district, where it makes up about 20 per cent of the production. It is used for white wine production and for table use. The berries are large, with moderately acid, medium degree Brix, and a strong, "foxy" flavor. Niagara is moderately subject to the principal grape diseases.

FRENCH HYBRIDS FOR AMERICAN VINEYARDS

In recent years considerable interest has developed in the use of a group of varieties known as "French Hybrids" for wine production in the eastern portion of North America. These varieties have been derived from crosses between *vinifera* varieties with certain *Vitis* species native to America. It was the goal of the European hybridizers to produce varieties which would resist the attack of phylloxera, be more tolerant to fungus diseases, and still produce wine of acceptable quality. These varieties are of interest to the American grape growers because they produce a fairly neutrally flavored table wine, possess a fair degree of winter hardiness, and are somewhat resistant to cryptogamic diseases. Following are brief notes on those varieties of current commercial interest.

Aurora (Seibel 5279).—This is the most widely planted of the French hybrids in America. It is a very early white variety with large, loose to compact clusters. It produces a delicate neutral flavored white table wine. The vine is vigorous, a dependable producer, and adapted to most vineyard soils.

Baco noir (Baco No. 1).—Baco noir is an extremely vigorous, disease-resistant hybrid capable of producing an intensely colored astringent red wine. It buds out very early and thus is often subjected to spring frosts. It is only moderately cold hardy.

Marechal Foch (Kuhlmann 188-2).—Foch is a very early, small clustered, black variety capable of producing a well colored, neutral flavored, red wine. The vine is only moderately vigorous and productive and performs best on fertile sites. It also does better when grafted onto vigorous stocks. It is winter hardy but susceptible to powdery mildew.

Rosette (Seibel 1000).—This is an old hybrid and one of the first to be grown in New York State. It is a midseason to late black variety with medium to small clusters. It lacks the intense color of most black hybrids and is frequently used for rosé wines. It is a vigorous grower and good producer that is winter hardy; it is highly susceptible to powdery mildew; further planting should be questioned.

Grape Varieties

Seyval (*Seyve-Villard* 5-276).—This is a midseason ripening white variety with large, compact clusters. It is capable of producing a superior quality neutral but fruity flavored wine. It is only moderately vigorous and should be planted on deep fertile, well-drained soils. The variety is only moderately tolerant to cold.

MUSCADINE GRAPES

Muscadine grapes are native to and grown commercially in the southeastern quadrant of the United States. They have distinctive aromas and flavors; the wines are a specialty product. The fresh fruit is generally sold locally, owing to the rapid deterioration in aroma and flavor under the usual methods of handling.

These grapes are used extensively for home planting because they are seldom affected by diseases or pests—control measures are rarely necessary. The clusters are short with usually 5 to 20 berries; sometimes there are more, especially on the perfect-flowered varieties. Berries are round to short oval, usually large and vary in color from green to black. The fruit for commercial use is usually harvested by jarring the vines; the berries being caught on tarps.

Propagation is by layering or by soft wood cuttings. Dormant cuttings seldom root. For rooting soft wood cuttings, see p. 202.

There are many varieties; most of the best with only pistilate flowers, while others, those of more recent origin, have perfect flowers. Scuppernong is the oldest variety—it was found in North Carolina. There are many selections of it. A few of the more popular varieties are:

With pistillate flowers.

Hunt.—The preferred all-purpose black sort. Berries and cluster large, maturing early and uniformly. Good vine vigor and dependable productivity.

Scuppernong.—Clusters small, shatter badly owing to uneven maturing. Berries medium large, bronze in color; distinctive flavor. Yields variable, vines vigorous. It is the oldest cultivated North American grape.

Thomas.—Another old standard. Berries red-black, medium small; very fine, crisp flavor. Prized for sweet juice. Vines very vigorous and productive.

Topsail.—Preferred by many because of high maturity. Berries medium large, green-to-bronze, skin smooth. Vines vigorous, but cropping somewhat irregular.

With perfect flowers.

Burgaw.—A selection of Thomas. Fruit reddish-black, fair quality. Berries medium sized.

Dearing.—Berries medium in size and better quality than other light colored perfect-flowered varieties. Vine fairly vigorous and productive.

Tarheel.—Berries very small, borne in large loose, clusters. Characteristic varietal flavor. Vine very vigorous and productive.

Willard.—Berries medium size, greenish-bronze. Clusters large, loose.

According to Anon. (1961), these perfect-flowered varieties are used primarily as pollinizers for the above and other pistillate sorts. Their pollen is of high germinability, and in addition they produce good crops of fair quality fruit. Otherwise, they are more subject to diseases and pests than the pistillate sorts.

PHYLLOXERA-RESISTANT ROOTSTOCK VARIETIES

When phylloxera was introduced into California in the late 1850's it soon revealed its great potential for destruction of vineyards on the shallow unirrigated soils of the coastal valleys. This led to investigations for eradication or control. As in Europe, eradication was found to be infeasible, so work with rootstocks of various *Vitis* species was expanded. The early orientation work was followed by the investigations of Bioletti *et al.* (1921), Husmann *et al.* (1939), and Jacob (1942), and, more recently, of Snyder and Harmon (1948), Harmon (1949), and Lider (1957, 1958). In the earlier studies the primary contribution was the elimination of unworkable stocks and those of insufficient resistance. In the later work the adaptation of stock and scion to environment, the rooting and grafting ease of the stock, and the quantity and quality of the fruit of the scion were considered. The discussion of resistant rootstock varieties that follows is based on the results of these studies.

In the deep, fertile soils of irrigated vineyards of the interior valleys of California, phylloxera has been much less important. On such soils in areas where climate is very favorable for vine growth, vines have grown and produced in spite of phylloxera. Their extensive and deeply penetrating root systems along with the occasional irrigation, no doubt, contributed to their survival. This situation prevailed in a number of locations, such as Lodi, for the duration of the initial plantings. As need has arisen for replanting of the vineyards, the phylloxera problem has become more serious, so resistant rootstocks are now necessary in some of these areas. With time, the need for resistant stock is likely to expand to other regions now considered to be largely free of this pest. The spread of this organism, however, if past experience is a guide, will be slow. Nougaret and Lapham (1928) have stated that the sandy soils of the San Joaquin Valley and the desert areas should remain free.

Rupestris St.-George.—St.-George is one of the most meritorious rootstocks. Without question, it has been planted more extensively than any other resistant rootstock. In many of the other grape-producing countries it is known as Rupestris du Lot.

In California, St.-George has been the standard phylloxera-resistant stock for wine grape varieties on the unirrigated soils of the coastal valleys. Except on deep, fertile soils with ample moisture, it is the recommended stock. It is vigorous, roots well from cuttings, grafts well, and is highly resistant to phylloxera and to drought.

The chief deficiencies of St.-George are the tendencies of scion varieties on it to produce straggly clusters and, under some conditions, to set many shot berries. It still has its place—on shallow unirrigated soils that are often low in moisture in the late summer. In such locations its resistance to phylloxera may be the prime criterion in its choice as a stock. Longer pruning of the scion varieties and more elaborate trellising should be used to balance the fruiting of vines on this stock with the vigor they display. This will in large part compensate for the poorer clusters. St.-George also produces rootstock suckers. This defect can be overcome by thorough disbudding of cuttings, except for the top bud, before planting in the nursery.

The shoots of St.-George are mostly upright; glabrous; with medium internodes and red tips. The leaves are entire; gray-green; thick; leathery; broader than long; with the petiolar sinus very wide. It produces only staminate flowers.

Ganzin 1 (*Aramon* x *Rupestris Ganzin* #1).—The "A x R #1," an old stock, has been widely tested both here and abroad. It is a vigorous grower, roots its cuttings very easily, and grafts easily. That its resistance to phylloxera is not high has been demonstrated in other countries. In very dry, shallow soils, or where phylloxera can be very serious, it may do poorly or even fail. Viala and Ravaz (1903) have shown that it has little or no tolerance to lime. In extensive trials reported on by Lider (1957, 1958) on soils of low lime content in California, this stock has done remarkably well. The varieties grafted on it have been consistently high producers. For California conditions it would seem to be the nearest approach to an all-purpose rootstock in the coastal counties. On more fertile soils adequately supplied with moisture—that is, on the valley floors of such counties—it is at present the best choice. This is a case where the choice of a stock cannot be based entirely on its resistance to phylloxera.

Leaves are of medium size; glabrous; medium green; leathery, with wide, V-shaped petiolar sinus. Petioles and tendrils are bright purple. There is profuse development of staminate flowers.

Mourvedre x *rupestris* 1202.—The "1202," another *rupestris* x *vinifera* hybrid, is slightly more resistant to phylloxera, as well as more tolerant to lime, than A x R #1. As a result it has performed well in the trials conducted by Lider (1957, 1958) on shallower and drier soils. In general, however, the A x R #1 has been more vigorous and more productive than 1202 on deeper soils of the coastal valleys.

The leaves are of medium size; glabrous; medium green; leathery, with narrow, U-shaped petiolar sinus. Petioles and tendrils are dull purple. A moderate crop of very seedy, worthless blue grapes is produced.

Couderc 3306 and Couderc 3309 (Riparia x Rupestris 3306 and 3309). —These are among the oldest hybrids used today. They have been thoroughly tested both here and abroad. They are quite resistant to phylloxera; their cuttings root with ease and graft readily. Both have produced satisfactorily in California, but Lider (1958) found neither outstanding in field trials. In both vigor and production they are surpassed by one or more of the other rootstocks. The vigor of 3309 is slightly greater than that of 3306, and its yields are somewhat larger. From trials and observations of performance in California vineyards for many years, they cannot be recommended for further planting. The two rootstocks are easily distinguished, since the petioles and young shoots of 3309 are almost glabrous, whereas those of 3306 are densely coated with short, erect hairs.

Richter 99, R 110, R 57, and R 44 (Berlandieri x rupestris 99-R, 110-R, 57-R, and 44-R).—These four rootstocks are very resistant to phylloxera, root their cuttings readily, and, according to Jacob (1942), graft with ease except with a few varieties of little importance in California.

The rootstock R 99 has been consistently the best stock of the four in all field trials. In some instances it even outproduced St.-George in dry, unirrigated soils. Its scion varieties do not display as much vigor or develop as rapidly as those on other stocks; however, when the vines on R 99 do reach maturity they have yielded good crops of very good fruit. By far the best of the four rootstocks, it merits further testing in California. It will have to be grown beside St.-George for some years on shallow unirrigated soils of the coastal valleys before a choice can be made between them. St.-George, of course, is already widely known.

The leaves of R 99 are small; brilliant medium-green above, lighter green below; glabrous; broader than long; with small, blunt serrations. Petioles and shoots are reddish-purple; glabrous except for the tip of the shoot. No fruit is borne.

There is considerably less information on rootstocks for the interior valleys. The reason is that the spread of phylloxera to these areas is more recent and has had, generally, milder consequences on the deep, fertile, irrigated soil. There are also extensive areas of sandy soil, on which this organism is not a problem.

On the basis of present knowledge, St.-George and A x R #1 are the best available phylloxera-resistant rootstocks in the interior valleys. Each will produce vigorous, productive grafted vines. Performance has been most consistently good by A x R #1. Although St.-George has been very satisfactory with both raisin and wine grapes, it has not been entirely satisfactory with red table grapes. For Emperor and Tokay the color was hardly acceptable on St.-George. The defects in color are pointed up by the fact that many vineyards on their own roots are phylloxera-free and are producing fruit of the most accepted color. It is the comparison of the color of this fruit with that of the grafted vines that tends to discredit the rootstocks. If all the vines were on rootstocks, the color of both varieties would be more acceptable.

Oppenheim 4 (Selection Oppenheim No. 4, SO 4).—The phylloxera rootstock, SO 4, is one of the seedlings arising from crosses by Teleki between V. *berlandieri* and V. *riparia*. In some respects it is similar to the other Teleki hybrids, such as Teleki 5-A, 5-BB, etc. One principal difference, however, is its somewhat lower vigor. This underlies its popularity with growers in Northern Europe. It is quite tolerant to lime, is highly resistant to phylloxera, and roots fairly readily and grafts with ease.

SO 4 has only recently been placed in field trials in California vineyards. The moderate vigor of its scions indicates that it may not be suitable on high stress sites. For example, in a non-irrigated trial in Napa Valley, it has developed slowly, producing relatively small vines during the first few years. On the other hand, it may be quite satisfactory on irrigated, more fertile sites. This new stock to California deserves a thorough and intensive study in phylloxerated districts.

NEMATODE-RESISTANT ROOTSTOCK VARIETIES

Nematodes were recognized as serious vineyard pests about 1930. Experience gained in combating phylloxera, another root pest, has assisted progress in the control of nematodes. Snyder (1936) reported that all *Vitis vinifera* varieties were susceptible to injury by the nematodes, but that a few species, such as *Vitis solonis*, V. *champini*, and V. *doaniana*, showed moderate to high resistance. The following discussion of nematode-resistant varieties is based largely on the trials of Harmon and Snyder (1956) and Lider (1960).

Couderc 1613 (Solonis x Othello 1613).—At present the most useful nematode-resistant stock for grapes in California is the hybrid Solonis X Othello 1613. It is well adapted to fertile sandy and sandy-loam soils. Its moderate resistance to phylloxera, combined with its resistance to nematodes, is of great advantage where both pests occur—as, in the central San Joaquin Valley.

Table grape varieties grafted on 1613 grow with moderate vigor, and the fruit characteristics are generally good. The clusters tend to be medium-sized, well formed, and loose; the berries are large and firm. The color of red table grapes has not been so brilliant as on own-rooted vines.

Rootstock cuttings of 1613 root easily in the nursery and graft readily to nearly all fruiting varieties.

In unirrigated or very sandy soils of low fertility, 1613 has insufficient vigor, and vines grafted on it are weak and low in productivity. In comparative tests under these soil conditions, the more vigorous Dog Ridge and Salt Creek rootstocks grow and produce much better than does 1613.

Some instances of late maturity, low acidity, and poor coloring have been reported with 1613. Most of these cases, however, can be traced directly to virus disease carried over from the mother vines. With the supply of certified disease-free planting stock now available, this should no longer be a problem.

Despite its defects, this rootstock will continue to be widely used in California until a better stock is found. It is a generally useful stock, especially useful for table grapes on highly fertile soils infested with rootknot nematodes.

The 1613 has large gray-green leaves, with few long hairs above and felty tomentum below; large veins noticeably set down; petiolar sinus wide and V-shaped; serrations large and sharp. Some seedy fruit is produced.

Dog Ridge.—This stock, a seedling from the wild grape species *Vitis champini*, is recommended for use with heavy-producing wine and raisin varieties on light sandy soils, where nematode infestations may be heavy. It produces the most vigorous grafted vines of all rootstocks so far tested.

Although this great vigor can be a problem, vines grafted on Dog Ridge have made large but manageable growth and have produced fruit of good quality in sandy, nematode-infested soils. Fruit set can be improved by training vines grafted to Dog Ridge to a large head or long cordon and by retaining more buds at pruning during the early life of the vineyards. As a result, leaves are abundant early in the season, and the vigorous growth tends to be checked early. Once vines grafted on this stock are curbed, so that they set satisfactorily, very heavy crops are produced.

On some soils the extreme vigor of Dog Ridge is a drawback because it accents zinc deficiency and can induce shy-bearing tendencies in its scions. In addition, clusters are often small and straggly, with many shot berries. Zinc deficiency ("little leaf") can be overcome by putting zinc on fresh pruning wounds. Excessive vine growth in late summer is controlled by less-frequent or shallow irrigations.

Both Emperor and Tokay on Dog Ridge tend toward a purple-red berry rather than the desired bright red.

Cuttings of Dog Ridge root with great difficulty. Once rooted, however, they graft readily.

This rootstock probably should be the choice for replanting those parts of the vineyard that have demonstrated the inability of vines on their own roots, or vines on other rootstocks, to produce profitably. It is doubtful that high-quality table grapes can be produced regularly on this stock, yet it seems suitable for the heavy-producing raisin and wine varieties.

Leaves are medium large; bright green above, gray-green below; glabrous except for a few hairs on ventral veins. Shoots, petioles, and tendrils are green, with long hairs; tendrils are medium long, bifid, and reddish pink; the shoot tip is white, with a pink tinge.

Ramsey (*Vitis champini*).—Known as Salt Creek to California growers, the true identity of this old stock was described by Loomis and Lider (1971). The true Salt Creek variety, a seedling of *Vitis doaniana*, is not used commercially. Therefore, in common useage the name "Salt Creek" will no doubt continue to be applied to this *Vitis champini* selection. In fertile sandy loam soils, vines grafted on Salt Creek rootstocks are extremely vigorous. As with Dog Ridge, this vigorous growth is often accompanied by "little leaf" symptoms of zinc deficiency, poor fruit set, and lowered fruit quality, but the excessive growth is controlled more easily than that of Dog Ridge.

Cuttings from this stock are difficult to propagate. Special care is needed in the nursery to ensure a good nursery take. Vines grafted on this stock occasionally start slowly, but they develop rapidly after they are established.

When excessive growth of this stock has been controlled, its performance with wine and raisin varieties has been quite satisfactory. It can be recommended for use with these varieties on the lighter, less fertile soils.

Leaves are medium large; 3-lobed; bright gray-green; with wide, blunt serrations. There is a tufted tomentum on the ventral veins. Hairs on the shoots, petioles, and tendrils are long; tendrils are long, bifid, and purple; growing tips are grayish white.

Harmony.—This relatively new nematode rootstock is an open-pollinated seedling from a parent combining the varieties Dog Ridge and Couderc 1613. It was selected by Weinberger and Harmon (1966) at Fresno, California. Harmony is quite resistant to root-knot nematodes, *Meloidogyne* species. It roots and grafts very readily and produces scions of moderate vigor. In field trials it has performed well with table grape varieties, providing a balance of vegetative development and high fruit quality. In sites of severe nematode infestation and low soil fertility it tends towards producing scions of excessively low vigor.

Couderc 1616 (*Solonis* x *riparia 1616*).—This rootstock is mildly resistant to nematodes. In California tests—which have been few—it has performed well. In sandy loam soils it has produced scions of moderate vigor that yield good crops of high-quality fruit. In very sandy soils yields have been low and undependable. It has shown promise with Zinfandel in the Lodi area. It must be tested more extensively before a general evaluation can be made.

The leaves are medium large; glabrous above, with many short hairs below; medium green; leathery; slightly 3-lobed; with long sharp serrations. Shoots and petioles are reddish purple, with numerous short hairs on the petioles. No fruit is borne.

Teleki 5-A (Berlandieri x riparia 5-A).—The "5-A" is a hybrid that shows a moderate degree of resistance to nematodes and is noted for resistance to phylloxera. The stock has shown good vigor and has produced scions that are both strong and productive. Its tolerance to nematodes seem sufficient to allow the stock to grow in infested sandy soils. It is worthy of further testing, but cannot yet be recommended as a nematode-resistant rootstock.

The leaves are large; glossy dark green above, bright medium green below; glabrous; with sides parallel and serration short and blunt. There are some long hairs on the reddish-purple petioles and shoots. No fruit is borne.

BIBLIOGRAPHY

Amerine, M. A., and A. J. Winkler. 1944. Composition and quality of musts and wines of California grapes, I. Hilgardia, 15:493–673.

———, ———. 1962. Composition and quality of musts and wines of California grapes, II. California Agr. Exp. Sta. Bull. 794:1–83.

Anon. 1961. Muscadine grapes, a fruit for the south. U.S. Dept Agric., Farmer's Bull. No. 2157:1–16.

———. 1972. California grape acreage. Calif. Crop and Livestock Reporting Serv., Calif. Dept. Agric., Sacramento, California.

Bioletti, F. T., F. C. H. Flossfeder, and A. E. Way. 1921. Phylloxera resistant stocks. Cal. Agr. Exp. Sta. Bull., 331:1–139.

Constantinescu, G. E. Negreanu, V. Lăzărescu, I. Poenaru, O. Alexei, and C. Bourneau. 1960. Ampelografia. 3 vols. Bucharest, Editura Acad. Republicii Populare.

Frolov-Bagreev, A. M. 1946–58. Russian ampelography. 6 vols. Moscow, G. Pishcheromizdat.

Harmon, F. N. 1949. Comparative value of thirteen rootstocks for ten *vinifera* grape varieties in the Napa Valley in California. Proc. Amer. Soc. Hort. Sci., 54:157–162.

———, and E. Snyder. 1956. Comparative value of three rootstocks for Sultanina grape in rootknot nematode-infected soil. Proc. Amer. Soc. Hort. Sci., 67:308–311.

Hedrick, U. P. 1907. The grapes of New York. Parts II of New York Agr. Exp. Sta. Rept. Albany, J. B. Lyon Co.

Husmann, G. C., E. Snyder, and F. L. Hysmann. 1939. Testing *vinfera* grape varieties grafted on phylloxera-resistant rootstock in California. United States Dept. Agr., Tech. Bull., 697:1–63.

Jacob, H. E. 1942. Examples of incompatibility between grape varieties and rootstocks. Proc. Amer. Soc. Hort. Sci., 41:201–203.

———. 1944. Vineyard planting stock. California Agr. Exp. Sta. Cir., 360:1–12.

Lider, L. A. 1957. Phylloxera-resistant rootstock trials in the coastal valleys of California. Amer. Jour. Enol., 8:58–67.

———. 1958. Phylloxera-resistant grape rootstocks for the coastal valleys of California. Hilgardia, 27:287–318.

———. 1960. Vineyard trials in California with nematode-resistant grape rootstocks. Hilgardia, 30:123–152.

Loomis, N. H., and L. A. Lider. 1971. Nomenclature of the "Salt Creek" grape. Fruit Var. Hort., Digest, 25(2):41–43.

Nougaret, R. L., and M. H. Lapham. 1928. A study of phylloxera infestation in California as related to type of soils. United States Dept. Agr., Tech. Bull., 20:13–18.

Olmo, H. P. 1948a. Ruby Cabernet and Emerald Riesling. California Agr. Exp. Sta. Bull., 704:1–9.

———. 1948b. Perlette and Delight; two new early maturing seedless table grape varieties. California Agr. Exp. Sta. Bull., 705:3–8.

———, and A. Koyama. 1962a. Niabell and Early Niabell. Calif. Agr. Exp. Sta. Bull., 790:3–10.

———, ———. 1962b. Rubired and Royalty. Calif. Agr. Exp. Sta. Bull., 789:3–13.

Shaulis, N. J., and T. D. Jordan. 1960. Cultural practices for New York vineyards. New York Sta. Col. of Agric. Ext. Bull., 805:3–35.

Snyder, E. 1936. Susceptibility of grape rootstocks to rootknot nematode. United States Dept. Agr. Cir., 405:1–15.

———, and F. N. Harmon. 1948. Comparative value of nine rootstocks for ten *vinifera* grape varieties. Proc. Amer. Soc. Hort. Sic., 51:287–294.

———, ———. 1952. Grape breeding summary 1923–1956. Proc. Amer. Soc. Hort. Sci., 60:243–246.

Viala, P., and L. Ravaz. 1903. American vines. Trans. by R. Dubois and E. H. Twight. San Francisco, Freygang-Leary Co.

———, and V. Vermorel. 1909. Ampélographie. 7 vols. Paris, Masson et Cie.

Weinberger, J. H., and F. N. Harmon. 1966. Harmony, a new nematode and phylloxera resistant rootstock for *vinifera* grapes. Fruit Var. Hort. Digest, 20:63–65.

Index